Contemporary Security Studies

Edited by Alan Collins

OXFORD
UNIVERSITY PRESS

OXFORD
UNIVERSITY PRESS

Great Clarendon Street, Oxford OX2 6DP

Oxford University Press is a department of the University of Oxford.
It furthers the University's objective of excellence in research, scholarship,
and education by publishing worldwide in

Oxford New York

Auckland Cape Town Dar es Salaam Hong Kong Karachi
Kuala Lumpur Madrid Melbourne Mexico City Nairobi
New Delhi Shanghai Taipei Toronto

With offices in

Argentina Austria Brazil Chile Czech Republic France Greece
Guatemala Hungary Italy Japan Poland Portugal Singapore
South Korea Switzerland Thailand Turkey Ukraine Vietnam

Published in the United States
by Oxford University Press Inc., New York

First published 2007

British Library Cataloguing in Publication Data
Data available

Library of Congress Cataloging in Publication Data

Contemporary security studies / edited by Alan Collins.
p. cm.
ISBN 978–0–19–928469–6
1. Security, International. I. Collins, Alan, 1967–
JZ5588.C675 2006
355′.033—dc22 2006034950

Typeset by Newgen Imaging Systems (P) Ltd., Chennai, India
Printed in Great Britain
on acid-free paper by
Ashford Colour Press Ltd, Gosport, Hants.

ISBN 978–0–19–928469–6

10 9 8 7 6 5 4

Acknowledgements

With all projects there are many people to thank and this is no exception, for without their support this book could not have been produced. First and foremost thanks must be given to the contributors for both agreeing to write their chapters and then diligently submitting them on schedule, complete with pedagogic features. Thanks must also be given to those anonymous reviewers who commented in detail on the synopsis; the book has benefited from, and been adjusted in light of, their useful thoughts. Special thanks also go to Kerrie Bramhall, who was responsible for preparing and producing the resource centre that supports the book. I am also grateful to Professor John Baylis for originally encouraging me to take on this task, and finally, thanks also go to Sue Dempsey and especially Ruth Anderson at OUP for her professionalism and assistance during the preparation of this book.

Brief Contents

Detailed Contents

Part 3 Traditional and Non-Traditional Security 223

Notes on Contributors

Jonathon Barnett. Australian Research Council Fellow in the School of Anthropology, Geography and Environmental Studies at the University of Melbourne, Australia. He is the author of *The Meaning of Environmental Security: Ecological Politics and Policy in the New Security Era* (London: Zed Books, 2001).

Helen Brocklehurst. Lecturer in International Relations in the Department of Politics and International Relations at the University of Wales Swansea, UK. She is the author of *Who's Afraid of Children? Children, Conflict and International Relations* (Aldershot: Ashgate, 2006).

Barry Buzan. Professor of International Relations at the London School of Economics, UK. His latest books include *From International to World Society? English School Theory and the Social Structure of Globalisation* (Cambridge: Cambridge University Press, 2004) and *The United States and the Great Powers: World Politics in the Twenty-First Century* (Oxford: Polity, 2004).

Alan Collins. Senior Lecturer in International Relations in the Department of Politics and International Relations at the University of Wales Swansea, UK. He is the author of *Security Dilemmas of Southeast Asia* (London: Macmillan, 2000) and *Security and Southeast Asia: Domestic, Regional and Global Issues* (Boulder, CO: Lynne Rienner, 2003).

Neil Cooper. Lecturer in International Relations and Security in the Department of Peace Studies at the University of Bradford, UK. He is the author of *The Business of Death: Britain's Arms Trade at Home and Abroad* (London: I.B. Tauris, 1997) and co-author of *War Economies in Their Regional Context: The Challenges of Transformation* (Boulder, CO: Lynne Rienner, 2004).

Christopher M. Dent. Senior Lecturer in the East Asian Economy at the University of Leeds, UK. His latest books include *The Foreign Economic Policies of Singapore, South Korea and Taiwan* (Cheltenham: Edward Elgar, 2002) and *New Free Trade Agreements in the Asia-Pacific* (Basingstoke: Palgrave, 2006).

Stefan Elbe. Senior Lecturer in International Relations in the Department of International Relations and Politics at the University of Sussex, UK. He is the author of *Europe: A Nietzschean Perspective* (London: Routledge, 2003) and *Strategic Implications of HIV/AIDS*, Adelphi Paper 357, International Institute for Strategic Studies (Oxford: Oxford University Press, 2003).

Ralf Emmers. Assistant Professor and Deputy Head of Studies in the Institute of Defence and Strategic Studies (IDSS) at the Nanyang Technological University, Singapore. He is the author of *Cooperative Security and the Balance of Power in ASEAN and the ARF* (London: RoutledgeCurzon, 2003) and *Non-Traditional Security in the Asia-Pacific: The Dynamics of Securitisation* (Singapore: Eastern University Press, 2004).

Jeanne Giraldo. Director of the Programme for Drug Control Strategy and Policy, Centre for Homeland Security and Defence at the Naval Postgraduate School, Monterey, USA. She is co-editor of *Terrorism Finance and State Responses: A Comparative Perspective* (Palo Alto, CA: Stanford University Press, 2006).

Eric Herring. Senior Lecturer in the Department of Politics, University of Bristol, UK. He is co-author with Glen Rangwala of *Iraq in Fragments: The Occupation and its Legacy* (London: Hurst and Cornell University Press, 2006) and co-author with Barry Buzan of *The Arms Dynamic in World Politics* (Boulder, CO: Lynne Rienner Publishers, 1998).

Richard Jackson. Senior Lecturer in the Centre for International Politics at the University of Manchester, UK. He is the author of *Writing the War on Terrorism: Language, Politics and Counterterrorism* (Manchester: Manchester University Press, 2005). He is presently writing a new book entitled *What Causes Intrastate War? Towards an Understanding of Organised Civil Violence* (Manchester: Manchester University Press, forthcoming).

Peter Viggo Jakobsen. Associate Professor in the Department of Political Science, University of Coperhagen, Denmark. He is the author of *Western Use of Coercive Diplomacy After the Cold War: A Challenge for Theory and Practice* (Basingstoke: Macmillan Press, 1998) and *Nordic Approaches to Peace Operations: A New Model in the Making?* (London: Routledge 2006).

Caroline Kennedy-Pipe. Professor of International Relations in the Department of Politics at the University of Sheffield, UK. Her publications include *Russia and the World* (London: Edward Arnold, 2000), 'Women and the Military' in *Journal of Strategic Studies* Vol. 23. No. 4. December 2000, 32–50 and 'Whose Security? State-Building and the "Emancipation" of Women in Central Asia' in *International Relations* Vol. 18. No. 1 March 2004, 91–109.

Pauline Kerr. Director of Studies in the Asia-Pacific College of Diplomacy (APCD) at the Australian National University, Australia. She is the co-author of *Presumptive Engagement: Australia's Asia Pacific Security Policy in the 1990s* (St Leonards: Allen & Unwin, 1996).

Brenda Lutz. Research Associate, Decision Sciences and Theory Institute, Indiana University-Purdue University at Fort Wayne, USA. She is the co-author of *Global Terrorism* (London: Routledge, 2004) and *Terrorism: Origins and Evolution* (New York: Palgrave, 2005).

James Lutz. Professor in the Department of Political Science at the Indiana University-Purdue University at Fort Wayne, USA. He is the co-author of *Global Terrorism* (London: Routledge, 2004) and *Terrorism: Origins and Evolution* (New York: Palgrave, 2005).

Patrick Morgan. Professor of Political Science and holds the Thomas and Elizabeth Tierney chair in Global Peace and Conflict Studies at the University of California, Irvine, USA. He is the author of *Deterrence Now* (Cambridge University Press, 2003) and *International Security: Problems and Solutions* (CQ Press, 2006).

David Mutimer. Associate Professor in the Department of Political Science at York University, Canada, and Principal Research Fellow in the Department of Peace Studies in the University of Bradford, UK. He is the author of *The Weapon State: Proliferation and the Framing of Security* (Boulder, CO: Lynne Rienner Publishers, 2000).

Paul Roe. Associate Professor in the Department of International Relations and European Studies at the Central European University, Budapest, Hungary. He is the author of *Ethnic Violence and the Societal Security Dilemma* (London: Routledge, 2005).

Paul Rogers. Professor of Peace Studies in the Department of Peace Studies at the University of Bradford, UK. He is the author of *Losing Control: Global Security in the 21st Century* (London: Pluto Press, 2nd edn, 2002) and *A War Too Far: Iraq, Iran and the New American Century* (London: Pluto Press, 2006).

Joanna Spear. Director of the US Foreign Policy Institute, The Elliott School of International Affairs, George Washington University, USA. She is the author of *Carter and Arms Sales: Implementing the Carter Administration's Arms Transfer Restraint Policy* (London: Macmillan, 1995).

Stan A. Taylor. Emeritus Professor of Political Science and Research Fellow at the David M. Kennedy Center for International Studies at Brigham Young University, Utah, USA. He is the co-author of *America the Vincible: U.S. Foreign Policy for the 21st Century* (New York: Prentice-Hall, 3rd edn, 2005).

Harold Trinkunas. Associate Professor in the Department of National Security Affairs at the Naval Postgraduate School, Monterey, USA. He is the author of *Crafting Civilian Control of the Military in Venezuela: A Comparative Perspective* (Chapel Hill, NC: University of North Carolina Press, 2005).

Ole Wæver. Professor of International Relations in the Department of Political Science at the University of Copenhagen, Denmark. He is the co-author of *Regions and Powers: The Structure of International Security* (Cambridge: Cambridge University Press 2003, with Barry Buzan) and *Security: A New Framework for Analysis* (Boulder, CO: Lynne Rienner, 2nd edn, 2007, with Barry Buzan and Jaap de Wilde).

James Wirtz. Professor in the Department of National Security Affairs at the Naval Postgraduate School, Monterey, USA. He is the author of *The Tet Offensive: Intelligence Failure in War* (Cornell University Press, 1991, 1994) and co-editor of *Balance of Power: Theory and Practice in the 21st Century* (Stanford: Stanford University Press, 2004).

List of Figures

List of Tables

List of Boxes

KEY IDEAS

THINK POINTS

BACKGROUNDS

CASE STUDIES

KEY QUOTES

Guided Tour of Learning Features

This text is enriched with a range of learning tools to help you navigate the text material and reinforce your knowledge of Security Studies. This guided tour shows you how to get the most out of your textbook package and do better in your studies.

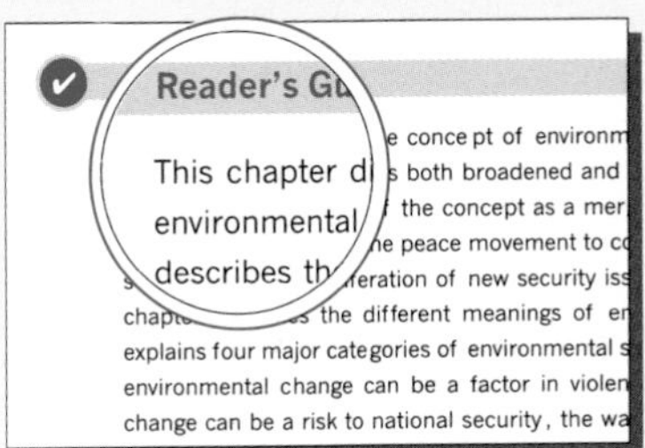

Reader's Guides

Reader's Guides at the beginning of every chapter set the scene for upcoming themes and issues to be discussed, and indicate the scope of coverage within each chapter topic.

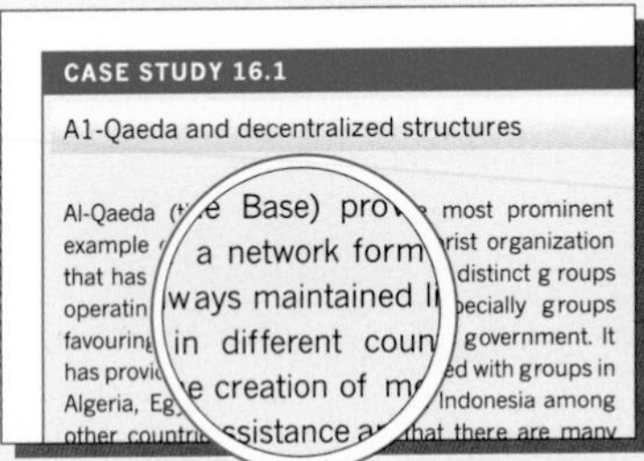

Boxes

A number of topics benefit from further explanation or exploration in a manner that does not disrupt the flow of the main text. Throughout the book, boxes provide you with extra information on particular topics that complement your understanding of the main chapter text.

There are five types of box:

'Key Ideas' boxes outline the thoughts of key political thinkers relevant to the chapter's argument.

'Think Point' boxes will expand your understanding of the subject area.

'Background' boxes will enable you to understand the context within which events take place and subjects develop.

'Case Study' boxes demonstrate how political ideas, concepts and issues manifest in the real world.

'Key Quotes' boxes include memorable quotes from politics past and present and help bring ideas and concepts to life.

Glossary Terms

Key terms are bold-faced in the text and defined in a glossary at the end of the text, to aid you in exam revision.

Key Points

Each main chapter section ends with a set of Key Points that summarise the most important arguments developed within each chapter topic.

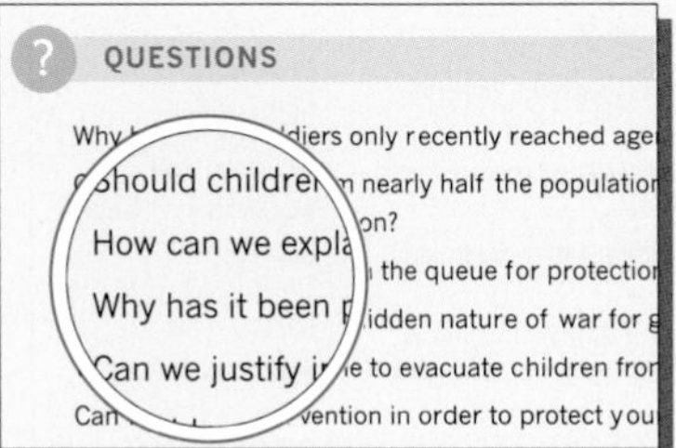

Questions

A set of carefully devised questions has been provided to help you assess your comprehension of core themes, and may also be used as the basis of seminar discussion and coursework.

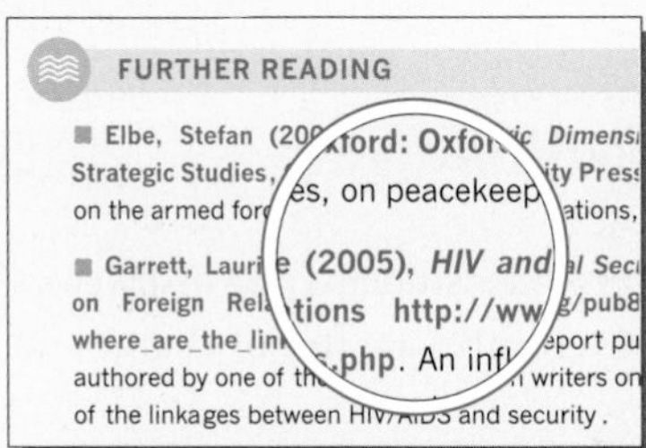

Further Reading

To take your learning further, reading lists have been provided as a guide to find out more about the issues raised within each chapter topic and to help you locate the key academic literature in the field.

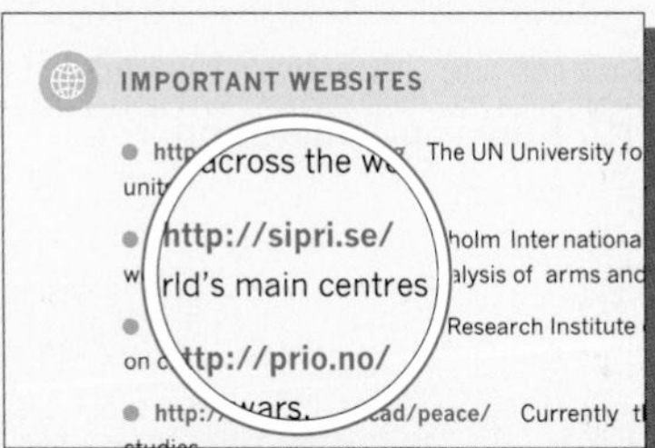

Important Websites

At the end of every chapter you will find an annotated summary of useful websites that are central to Security Studies and that will be instrumental in further research.

Guided Tour of the Online Resource Centre

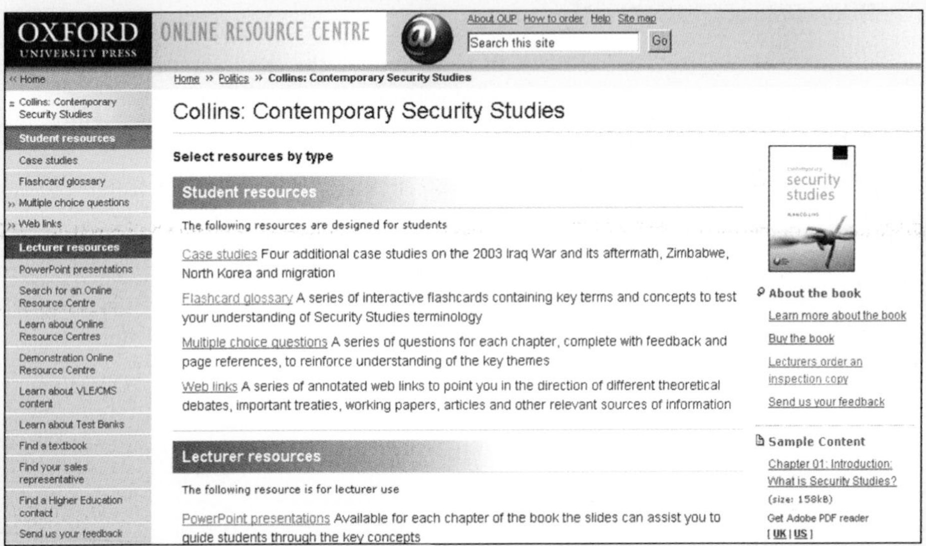

 **www.oxfordtextbooks.co.uk/orc/collins/**

The Online Resource Centre that accompanies this book provides students and instructors with ready-to-use teaching and learning materials. These resources are free of charge and designed to maximise the learning experience.

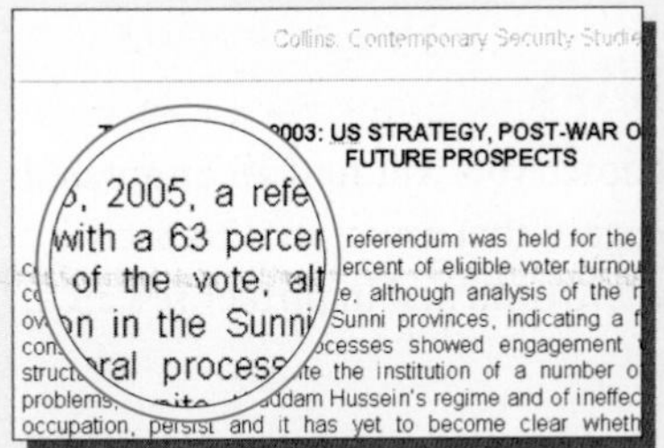

Case studies

Four additional case studies on the 2003 Iraq War and its aftermath, Zimbabwe, North Korea and migration.

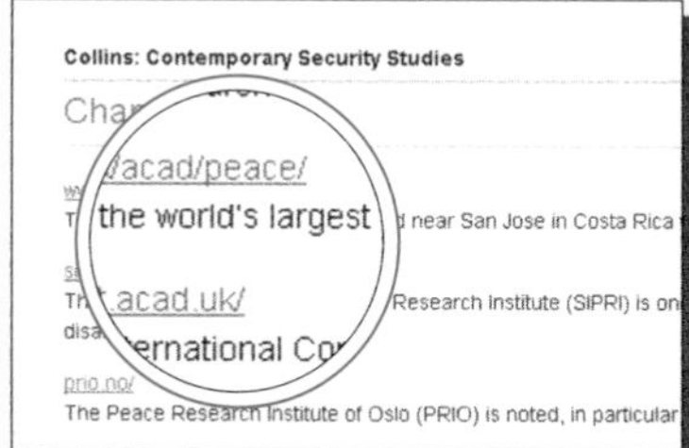

Web links

A series of annotated web links have been provided to point you in the direction of different theoretical debates, important treaties, working papers, articles and other relevant sources of information.

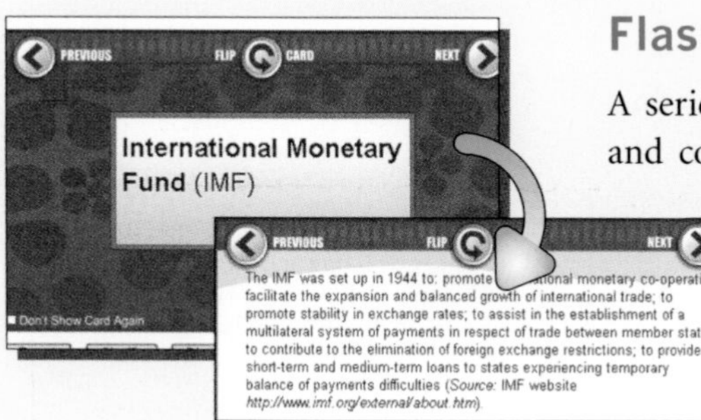

Flashcard glossary

A series of interactive flashcards containing key terms and concepts have been provided to test your understanding of Security Studies terminology.

Multiple choice questions

The best way to reinforce your understanding of Security Studies is through frequent and cumulative revision. As such, a bank of self-marking multiple-choice questions have been provided for each chapter of the text, and include instant feedback on your answers and cross-references back to the main textbook.

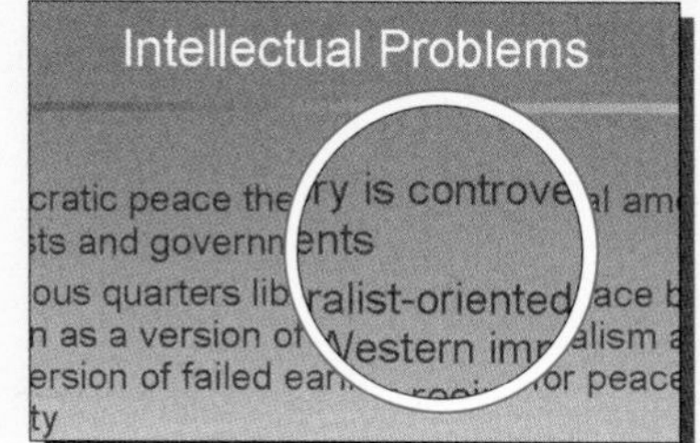

PowerPoint slides (instructors only)

These complement each chapter of the book and are a useful resource for preparing lectures and handouts. They allow lecturers to guide students through the key concepts and can be fully customized to meet the needs of the course.

1

Introduction: What is Security Studies?

ALAN COLLINS

Chapter Contents

Introduction

Welcome to Security Studies: *the* sub-discipline of International Relations. It is the study of security that lies at the heart of International Relations. It was the carnage of the First World War, and the desire to avoid its horrors again, that gave birth to the discipline of International Relations in 1919 at Aberystwyth, United Kingdom. This concern with the origins of war and its conduct enabled International Relations to 'distinguish itself from related disciplines such as history, economics, geography, and international law' (Sheehan 2005: 1). It is the survival of agents, which for much of the discipline has meant sovereign states, that has become accepted as the dominant explanatory tool for understanding their behaviour. Security is a matter of high politics; central to government debates and pivotal to the priorities they establish. Quite simply, 'no other concept in international relations packs the metaphysical punch, nor commands the disciplinary power of "security" ' (Der Derian 1995: 24–25).

Definition of security

Welcome, then, to a subject of great importance and, since you are about to embark upon the study of this subject, no doubt you would like to start with a definition of security. Or, what it means to be secure? You will see in Key Quotes 1.1 (Definitions of security) that many scholars have done so. The good news is that a consensus has emerged on what security studies entails—it is to do with threats to survival—and the even better news is that hidden within that simple definition lies the complexity that you are about to delve into. What is most striking about the definitions in Key Quotes 1.1 is that while war and the threat to use force is part of the security equation it is not exclusively so. The absence of threats is sufficiently far-reaching that Security Studies encompasses dangers that range from pandemics, such as HIV/AIDS, and environmental degradation through to the more readily associated security concerns of direct violence, such as terrorism and inter-state armed conflict. The latter, which so dominated the discipline that during the Cold War it became synonymous with Security Studies, is actually a sub-field of Security Studies and is known as Strategic Studies. Oxford University Press publishes a textbook that is concerned with Strategic Studies: it is called *Strategy in the Contemporary World*.

With the Cold War over, Security Studies has re-emerged and core assumptions about what is to be secured, and how, have come to occupy our thoughts. Traditionally the state has been the thing to be secured, what is known as the referent object, and it has sought security through military might. In the chapters that follow you will find alternative approaches to security; approaches that offer different referent objects, different means of achieving security and which indicate that past practice, far from enhancing security, has been the cause of insecurity. You are, then, about to study a subject that is undergoing great change as it questions its past assumptions, deepens its understanding of what should be secured and broadens its remit to encompass a diverse range of threats and dangers. Of course, this broadening of the subject matter creates a blurring in the distinction between Security Studies and the study of International Relations more generally. In this sense the broadening of Security Studies mirrors the wider blurring between International Relations and Political Science. The process of globalization has led to internal issues

KEY QUOTES 1.1

Definitions of security

'Security itself is a relative freedom from war, coupled with a relatively high expectation that defeat will not be a consequence of any war that should occur.'

Ian Bellamy, 'Towards a theory of international security', *Political Studies*, **29/1 (1981), p. 102.**

'A nation is secure to the extent to which it is not in danger of having to sacrifice core values it if wishes to avoid war, and is able, if challenged, to maintain them by victory in such a war.'

Walter Lippman, cited in Barry Buzan, *People, States and Fear* **(Hemel Hempstead: Harvester Wheatsheaf, 1991), p. 16.**

'National security may be defined as the ability to withstand aggression from abroad.'

Giacomo Luciani, 'The economic content of security', *Journal of Public Policy*, **8/2 (1989), p. 151.**

'A threat to national security is an action or sequence of events that (1) threatens drastically and over a relatively brief span of time to degrade the quality of life for the inhabitants of a state, or (2) threatens significantly to narrow the range of policy choices available to the government of a state or to private, nongovernmental entities (persons, groups, corporations) within the state.'

Richard H. Ullman, 'Redefining security', *International Security*, **8/1 (1983), p. 133.**

'Security, in any objective sense, measures the absence of threats to acquired values, in a subjective sense, the absence of fear that such values will be attacked.'

Arnold Wolfers, *Discord and Collaboration* **(Baltimore: Johns Hopkins University Press, 1962), p. 150.**

'Security-insecurity is defined in relation to vulnerabilities—*both internal and external*—that threaten or have the potential to bring down or weaken state structures, both territorial and institutional, and governing regimes (emphasis in original).'

Mohammed Ayoob, *The Third World Security Predicament* **(Boulder: Lynne Rienner, 1995), p. 9.**

'Emancipation is the freeing of people (as individuals and groups) from the physical and human constraints which stop them carrying out what they would freely choose to do . . . Security and emancipation are two sides of the same coin. Emancipation, not power or order, produces true security. Emancipation, theoretically, is security.'

Ken Booth. 'Security and emancipation', *Review of International Studies*, **17/4 (October 1991), p. 319.**

'If people, be they government ministers or private individuals, perceive an issue to threaten their lives in some way and respond politically to this, then that issue should be deemed to be a *security* issue (emphasis in original).'

Peter Hough, *Understanding Global Security* **(London: Routledge, 2004), p. 9.**

'Security . . . implies both coercive means to check an aggressor and all manner of persuasion, bolstered by the prospect of mutually shared benefits, to transform hostility into cooperation.'

Edward A. Kolodziej, *Security and International Relations* **(Cambridge: Cambridge University Press, 2005), p. 25**

becoming externalized and external issues internalized. The role of domestic agents and policy concerns appear prominently on global agendas, whether it is the future political structure of Iraq or deforestation in the Amazon. This blurring of the demarcation between International Relations, Political Science and Security Studies can be seen in the breadth of topics covered in this book and the centrality of security in theories of international relations (for more on this see Chapter 21). This is to be welcomed. I know it can appear confusing and it would be much easier to categorize topics neatly, but this is to misunderstand the nature of the social sciences. These disciplines are sub-disciplines precisely because they overlap and have 'something to say' about the same topics. Instead of looking for different subject matters it is better to think about different approaches. Despite the contested nature of security you know that ultimately we are interested in how referent objects are threatened and what they can do to survive. With that thought in mind, examining this diverse range of topics might seem rather less daunting.

Structure

The book is not designed to be read from start (Chapter 1) to finish (Chapter 21) because this is not the way to read an academic text. If this seems a peculiar thing to write then let me explain. You are not reading a novel in which the aim is to keep you in suspense until the final pages where you discover who committed the crime or whether the lovers live happily ever after. You want to know the questions and the answers as soon as possible and then, because, as important as the answers are, they are not the most important thing, you should want to know why these are the answers and how they were reached. Think of it as a complicated maths question in which the mathematician has scribbled furiously on the blackboard (or more likely whiteboard today) a series of, to a layperson, unintelligible equations that eventually lead to an answer. It is the bit in between the question and the answer (the bit in between are those impenetrable equations) that reveal why the answer was found and found in that particular way. It is like this with your studies too. You should want to know, and your tutor certainly will, why you believe in the answers you have found: to know your thought processes. Knowing why you think about a subject the way that you do, so these thought processes can be convincingly articulated in oral and written form, is what reading for a degree is all about.

Therefore in this book when reading the chapters it is perfectly fine to read the introduction and then the conclusion, but you then have to read the bits in between to know why the answers found in the conclusion were reached. To understand the author's thought processes will help you develop yours. So, having read what this book contains, which you will find in this chapter, then read the conclusion. Chapter 21 will present you with the state of Security Studies, and the theorizing that has taken place in the discipline. It provides you with the context of why we, students and tutors (scholars of the subject), think about the subject the way that we do. In particular the chapter reveals the differences between American and European approaches to theorizing about security as it traces past, present and possible future trends in how security is studied by today's scholars. For those new to Security Studies and/or International Relations it will be a testing read, but stick with it because it will be a chapter that you will want to read more than once as you increase your knowledge of this subject; in each read you will discover something new. Once Chapters 1 and 21 have been read the book becomes a pick 'n' mix, so if you want to start with weapons of mass destruction (Chapter 15) or terrorism (Chapter 16) then go right ahead. That is not to say that the structure has no meaning and I would strongly advise that you at least begin with the approaches section and especially Chapter 2 in order to appreciate the primary role that states and power have had in the study of security. By beginning with the approaches section you will be able to appreciate just how hugely important different approaches are in establishing what constitutes security; a point that will be evident once you read Chapter 21.

The book is divided into three sections: differing approaches to the study of security; the broadening and deepening of security; and finally, a range of traditional and non-traditional issues that have emerged on the security agenda. The authors come from a range of countries and their examples are global in scope. Nevertheless the field of Security Studies, as with International Relations more generally, is dominated by Western thought and approaches. One of the refreshing changes in post-Cold War Security Studies is that the security problems of the developing world are no longer either ignored or seen through the prism of the East–West conflict. We are therefore examining these security problems and, perhaps, in doing so we will witness the emergence of specifically African or Asian approaches to the study of security that will force us to rethink core assumptions and gain a greater understanding of the Security Studies field.

In the meantime the field, while global in scope, remains dominated by Western thought.

Approaches

In the book's first substantive chapter, Chapter 2, Patrick Morgan provides an accessible explanation of why states have been the core concern for Security Studies. In this chapter you are introduced to the two traditionally dominant explanations of why and how states have sought security: Realism and Liberalism. We can think of these as traditional approaches because they underpinned security studies for much of our thinking during the previous century; they remain, though, hugely influential and just because they are labelled traditional does not mean they have been replaced by more recent thinking. New thinking about security has emerged, especially in the post-Cold War period, and such approaches are explained and examined in the other chapters in the Approaches section. You should think of these new approaches as challenging the dominance of the traditional insights offered by Realism and Liberalism. It may be that you find the traditional explanations of how security can be conceived of and achieved convincing; which is fine so long as you reach that conclusion with an understanding of the other approaches. In other words, to find an approach to understanding security convincing, not based on ignorance of other approaches but with a full understanding of them.

An alternative approach and one that also has a long tradition is Peace Studies, although as a formal field of study its origins are found in the post-1945 period. Here the approach to security is distinctively broad based, both in the nature of threats that the field covers and also its approaches to finding solutions. Thus although initially concerned with the arrival of nuclear weapons, peace studies, long before the post-Cold War era, was noting the security implications of environmental degradation and poverty. With a wide agenda it is not perhaps surprising to learn that academics working in Peace Studies come not just from politics and international relations but other disciplines in the Social Sciences, notably anthropologists and sociologists and the Natural Sciences, such as physics and mathematics; it is a truly interdisciplinary field. In Chapter 3 a leading authority, Paul Rogers, provides a historical account of how Peace Studies developed, highlighting its characteristics and revealing its continued relevancy to contemporary security studies.

The next chapter captures the reflections that took place by some scholars studying security in the immediate post-Cold War period. These reflections predate the end of the Cold War but they have flourished since the removal of the nuclear sword of Damocles that hung over the study of security. Labelled Critical Security Studies (CSS), David Mutimer provides an explanation of the different approaches that have developed since CSS first arrived on the scene in 1994. For those new to critical thinking it is a demanding read but thoroughly worthwhile because, amongst many of the things it will give you pause to ponder, it unashamedly forces you to think through your assumptions and it reconnects security with its normative origins.

A criticism aimed not just at security studies but the wider field of international relations is the failure to appreciate the important insights that gender provides. Caroline Kennedy-Pipe reveals two elements that gender can provide in our understanding of security: a practical appreciation of the role women have been ascribed in the security field and a discursive element that reveals the implicit link between militarism and masculinity. The latter highlights how the notions of honour, nobleness and valour are associated with masculinity and war, implicitly therefore leaving femininity devoid of such positive attributes. The former notes how women, if they are mentioned at all, are portrayed in a secondary, supporting role to men, whereas the reality is that in many ways (rape, prostitution, breeders) women are victims and their plight has remained a silence in the study of security.

One of the new 'buzz words' in the security literature is Human Security. It shares much in common with critical approaches to security; the most notable being it is a critique of the state-centrism of the traditional approach. As the name suggests, the referent for security are humans, but as Pauline Kerr explains in Chapter 6, while this change of referent object reveals the close connection between development and security, it also brings many challenges to maintaining analytical rigour. By dividing human security proponents into narrow and broad schools it is possible for you to appreciate the vast arrays of threats that exist to humans and their livelihoods and thus enables you to make your own judgement about what constitutes security. The chapter also compares the state-centrism of realism with human security to reveal both of their strengths and weaknesses.

The final chapter in the approaches section, Chapter 7, examines a process known as 'securitization' that was introduced to the literature by scholars working at the Conflict and Peace Research Institute (COPRI) in Copenhagen. Known collectively as the Copenhagen School, these scholars place primary importance on determining how an issue becomes a security issue, by how it is articulated. That is, we think of something as a security issue because the elite, such as political leaders, have convinced us that it represents a threat to our very survival. They are therefore interested in the 'speech acts' that the elite use in order to convince an audience that in order to counter a threat they require emergency powers. It is then a subjective approach to determining what constitutes security. A threat exists because an audience has been convinced it exists by the elite and they have granted the elite the authority to use emergency powers to counter the threat. The threat therefore is not something that simply exists; it has to be articulated as a threat for it to become a matter of security. Ralf Emmers explains this process, notes limitations with the concept of securitization and uses case studies ranging from Australian reaction to undocumented migration to the invasion of Iraq in 2003.

Deepening and broadening

The middle section of the book examines the deepening and broadening that has taken place in Security Studies. As will have become evident from the Approaches section, the theoretical approach you take towards examining security will determine the type of subject matter that you consider constitutes security. This part of the book contains five sectors of security; these are the recognizable sectors that you will find in the Security Studies literature. The exception is Regime Security, which I have included instead of political security because firstly, political security has a tendency to become a miscellaneous section in which security issues that cannot fit in the other sectors end up, and secondly, while political security is concerned with external threats (concern with recognition) its greater utility lies in internal threats (concern with legitimacy) to the regime. Labelling the chapter Regime therefore clarifies what the referent object is and also highlights the internal dimension of this security sector. Whether these sectors do constitute security is contentious, so, as with all your reading, adopt a critical, enquiring mind, and see if you are persuaded.

We begin with military security because it is the home, or turf as Eric Herring, the author of Chapter 8, writes, of our traditional understanding of what constitutes security. The purpose here is to show that the approach you adopt in studying military security, and here securitization and constructivism are used, determines what constitutes military security. Traditionally, the agenda for military security has been synonymous with strategy as a tool of statecraft and this remains a powerful interpretation of military security today. This, though, is a constructed interpretation of military security, not a natural or innate one. Adopting a constructivist approach allows us to ask questions about what constitutes the threat and how it is perceived. Using a variety of cases, including the Cuban Missile Crisis and Columbia, this chapter reveals (i) the broad agenda of issues to be examined in the military sector and (ii) the narratives, or discourse, which frame our understanding of threats in this sector.

Turning our attention to the security concerns within states enables us to appreciate that life in the developed world is far from indicative of that lived by most of the planet's inhabitants. The majority of people living in the developing world face a vast range of insecurities, from half a million people dying each year from the use of light weapons to

40,000 dying each day from hunger. There is, as Richard Jackson writes in Chapter 9 on regime security, 'a profound disjuncture between the kinds of security enjoyed by a small group of developed nations and the kind of security environment inhabited by the majority of the world's population'. In this chapter you will have the opportunity to understand the underlying causes of the developing world's inherent insecurity and why it is that, far from being the provider of security, governing regimes become the main source of their peoples' insecurity. It is a bleak picture that is portrayed but after reading the chapter you will appreciate the complexities that make bringing security to these millions of people both urgent and yet extremely difficult. The notion of an insecurity dilemma not only captures the spiralling nature of the violence but also how problematic finding a solution is.

The broadening of security so that it means more than a preoccupation with the state and military defence should by now have become appreciated. In Chapter 10 on societal security an alternative to the state, and indeed the individual, is posited. In this instance you will be introduced to the notion of a collective of people becoming the thing to be secured. In recent times the term 'ethnic' has become a popular label for describing conflict between groups within states. In this chapter Paul Roe introduces you to a means of examining the dynamics behind those ethnic conflicts where identity lies at the conflict's core. Importantly he does so by focusing on non-military issues that can give rise to insecurity and thereby shows how ambiguity in such seemingly non-threatening issues, such as education, can indeed become matters of great concern. If you have an interest in the nexus between security and identity, this is a must-read chapter.

Although it predates the end of the Cold War it was in the 1990s, and especially concern over ozone depletion and global warming, that environmental change began to be thought of as a "new" security threat. In Chapter 11, while you will be exposed to the vast array of environmental degradation that is occurring in today's world, the question of interest is what makes environmental change a matter of security? Jon Barnett provides an explanation of why the environment emerged on the security agenda before providing six interpretations of environmental security. You will therefore have the opportunity to consider whether the environment really is a security issue and whether labelling it as a matter of security helps or hinders attempts to reverse environmental degradation. For those with a normative interest in studying international security, this is an important chapter to read.

The final chapter of the deepening and broadening part of the book, Chapter 12, looks at a sector that will seem less problematic in terms of its connection to security; the economy. A state's economy and its access to resources are essential components in determining a state's ability to protect itself in an anarchical self-help environment. This, though, is only part of the equation and actually tells us little of what economic security is. In this chapter Christopher Dent uses the term economic-security nexus to describe the above and thereby distinguish it from economic security. The chapter will use a specific definition of economic security to highlight that what is being secured is not just the economy but also its ability to provide prosperity in the future. In this sense economic security concerns promoting activities that enhance a state's, or region's, economic growth. You will be introduced to eight types, or typologies, of economic security, including accessing markets and finance; transborder economic cooperation; the ideologies that underpin economic activity. In so doing you will be able to note the role institutions such as the International Monetary Fund and World Trade Organisation play as well as appreciate the economic security issues raised by such crises as the East Asian Financial crisis of 1997–98.

Traditional and non-traditional

The final section of the book highlights a series of traditional and non-traditional security issues that have emerged on the Security Studies agenda. The section begins with traditional security concerns and then moves to the non-traditional issues that have emerged as the subject area has expanded. We begin by addressing the traditional security concern of the threat and use of force. This is examined by looking at how Western strategy has evolved post-Cold War away from deterrence to compellence and in particular the use of coercive diplomacy. This captures the logic behind Western, and in particular US, strategic thinking.

The Bush administration's willingness to talk of 'pre-emptive' use of force, and indeed to implement it, has revealed a significant change in strategic thinking in the West. It is no longer simply enough to deter an opponent from taking action, it is now necessary to persuade, coerce and, on occasion, force them to change their behaviour. This, as Peter Viggo Jakobsen writes, has led to the post-Cold War era witnessing the pursuit of coercive diplomacy. Coercive diplomacy is the threat, and if necessary the limited use of force, designed to make an opponent comply with the coercer's wishes. It is action short of brutal force and thus an attempt to achieve a political objective as cheaply as possible. It has been used to respond to acts of aggression, halt WMD programmes and stop terrorism. Chapter 13 provides you with the criteria for what constitutes coercive diplomacy and the obstacles to its success, and concludes that Western efforts have largely failed. If you want to understand the strategy that underpins Western, and specially US, policy on the use of force since the end of the Cold War, this is a chapter for you.

The role of intelligence in determining security concerns and outcomes has never been more prominent than in today's security environment. Chapter 14 explains the different types of intelligence agencies that exist and how they collect information. Stan Taylor explains the intelligence cycle so that you can appreciate what a lengthy process it is, and more importantly how errors can occur. Covert action is examined and, with reference to the 2003 invasion of Iraq, intelligence failure, or what might more properly be called policy failure, is examined. This chapter ties in closely with coercive diplomacy since the threat to use force in order to successfully compel an opponent requires knowledge about their goals. In a world of pre-emption good intelligence is a necessary condition for success.

Since the tragic events of 9/11 the acronym WMD has been catapulted into everyday usage. Weapons of Mass Destruction, and the fear that rogue states or terrorists will target the USA or Europe with such weapons, has become a central concern for Western states. The belief that Iraq had an undisclosed arsenal of WMD provided the justification for the USA's decision to remove Saddam Hussein's regime, and it is the nuclear programmes of both North Korea and Iran (the former a declared weapons programme; the latter a potential and feared possibility) that earned them membership of Bush's 'Axis of Evil'. What, though, are WMD, why are they considered so different from conventional weapons, how easy are they to use and what has been their impact on international relations? These are the questions that James Wirtz addresses in Chapter 15.

Terrorism, perhaps even more so than WMD, has come to occupy a top spot on the security agendas of states. In Chapter 16 Brenda and Jim Lutz provide a definition of terrorism and explain the various types (religious, ethnic, ideological) and causes of terrorism. Using a typology that sees terrorism as either a form of war, or crime, or disease, they are able to explain why certain countermeasures are adopted by states and their implications for civil liberties. The chapter will provide you with details of terrorists ranging from the Ku Klux Klan to Al-Qaeda and reveal the incidence of terrorism that has occurred throughout the world in recent times.

Chapter 17 examines the last of the traditional security issues in this book: the arms trade, or what Joanna Spear and Neil Cooper call the defence trade. In this chapter they examine the reasons why states procure weapon systems, ranging from the action-reaction model to technological determinism, before providing details of trends in defence expenditure, the state of the market and the different types of goods and services that constitute today's defence trade.

AIDS is a pandemic; it is estimated that 40 million people are living with HIV and on average almost three times as many people die from

AIDS-related illnesses *every day*, than died during the terrorist attacks on 11 September 2001. In Chapter 18 Stefan Elbe introduces you to an illness that may well claim more victims than the Spanish influenza epidemic of 1918–19, which is estimated to have killed between 25 and 40 million people and in all likelihood will exceed the numbers killed by the bubonic plague, estimated to have killed 137 million in three major epidemics in the 6th, 14th, and 17th centuries. Examining human, national and international security, this chapter shows how AIDS/HIV can be thought of as a security issue, including how peacekeeping operations can be responsible for spreading AIDS/HIV. While it is clearly an exacerbating factor for national security it is in itself a direct threat when individuals are the referent object.

In 1999 Thailand identified the narcotics trade as the country's number one threat to national security. Drug-trafficking, along with, among others, human-trafficking and money laundering across national frontiers, are all forms of transnational crime and as the Thai experience reveals, this non-traditional security issue has risen rapidly up the national security agendas of states in the post-Cold War era. In Chapter 19 Jeanne Giraldo and Harold Trinkunas reveal the multiple ways in which transnational crime impacts directly, and indirectly, on human and national security. They explain why it has become more prevalent since the 1990s, the links between organized crime and terrorism, and the various responses that states have taken to curb its operation. If you want to appreciate a 'dark side' of globalization and how transnational criminal activity has impacted on international security, this is a must-read chapter.

The examination of what non-traditional issues constitute security studies today concludes by examining the role of children in war. Children have increasingly become important actors in our understanding of combat, whether that be their role in guerrilla warfare or the legal implications child soldiers create for humanitarian intervention, and they have become more important to our thinking more generally about security in pre- and post-conflict torn societies. They are an undertheorized and underutilized political agent and in this chapter Helen Brocklehurst brings to the fore their role and the implications this has for our thinking about war and security.

Conclusion

You are, as I am sure you appreciate having read the above, about to embark upon a whirlwind tour of a fascinating subject: a subject that has undergone, and continues to undergo, a thorough introspection of its core assumptions. It is a wonderful time to be a scholar of the discipline—and by scholar I mean students and tutors—because there is so much new and innovative thinking taking place that it is impossible for it not to open your mind. Listen to the ideas contained in the chapters that follow and if, by the end of it, you are more confused than you are now, then it has been a worthwhile enterprise. A caveat should, though, be added: that your confusion is a reflection not of ignorance but an appreciation of how complicating and complex the subject is and how challenging it is to therefore be a scholar of security studies. The chapter began with the question: What is Security Studies? It is all the above and more. Happy reading.

Visit the Online Resource Centre that accompanies this book for lots of interesting additional material: www.oxfordtextbooks.co.uk/orc/collins/

PART 1

Approaches to Security

2 Security in International Politics: Traditional Approaches

PATRICK MORGAN

Chapter Contents

Reader's Guide

The most influential explanations of international politics, realist and liberalist, are reviewed in this chapter to give readers an understanding of how they treat security matters and as a basis for comparing them with the other conceptions of security discussed in this book. Topics include the conception and importance of the state, the international system and its structure, power, cooperation, and community-building in creating and shaping responses to security problems.

Introduction: states as central actors

As we will see, a state is a territorially based entity with a government to rule over its territory and recognized as a state by other states. Approaches to security focused on states have long dominated international relations thinking, in two senses. First, states have been the central actors in international affairs. Second, security has been considered their most important concern. As a result international relations theory and analysis has long sought to explain the core elements of *security* relations *among states*.

Focusing on states makes sense because states: (1) developed through the fierce pressures of international politics—more than other political institutions they were shaped by international politics, particularly its security-related features; (2) are unique concentrations of power; (3) remain the ultimate focal points of most people's loyalty and sense of identity; and (4) have created or embody the largest, most powerful, and most effective human communties. Therefore, states remain central to international politics militarily, economically, politically, and psychologically.

State security is complex and normally Janus-faced (it faces two ways). A state must sustain security against external threats, such as other states and other international actors such as terrorists. It must also maintain security against *internal* threats to its character, rule, or territorial and demographic integrity. The security *behaviour* of states is similarly two-sided. On the one hand, states are defensively oriented. When threatened—presently or potentially—they react. Simultaneously, they often pose aggressive threats to each other, and to people in their own societies. They are threatened and threatening, fearful while being armed and dangerous.

A state's security strongly affects the security its citizens feel they enjoy; one way they judge whether they are secure is whether their government and state seem safe. In turn, interstate security relations shape assessments of international systems as secure (stable, orderly, safe) or insecure. After 1953, for example, the major players in the Cold War never fought with each other but their intense political conflicts generated widespread feelings that the international system was quite insecure. (Hence the term 'Cold War'.)

State security contains four basic elements: physical safety, autonomy, development, and rule. Safety from attack is obvious. Governments can go to extraordinary lengths to eliminate possible threats of military harm. More often they settle for trying to deter, or limit and defeat, a military attack. They treat state survival from attack, in particular, as enormously important.

However, autonomy is frequently taken to be even more important by governments and citizens. Autonomy is freedom from having to take orders from and be controlled by others, and politics at every level involves struggles over the autonomy individuals and groups enjoy. States have the most elaborate political autonomy in the world. To retain it rulers and governments will often knowingly risk state survival. Indeed, leaders and regimes often describe survival in terms of autonomy; without the latter their state would cease to exist. North Korea is a good recent example. It goes to some lengths to compel others to give it what it needs to survive, such as seeking to develop and claiming to possess nuclear weapons, rather than asking for help and having to accept the conditions under which it is offered because that would mean losing too much autonomy.

For individuals and groups, autonomy by having *their own state* has been a compelling objective in domestic and international politics for which people have readily risked their lives and other important possessions. The collapse of colonialism provided numerous examples of peoples willing to accept slower development as long as they could have their own state. Autonomy is often considered more important than rule; when a government loses autonomy it may easily lose power and authority too, through outsider interference and declining legitimacy in the eyes of its citizens. Much of the impetus behind the revolution that destroyed the Chinese empire in 1911 was popular disgust with the government's loss of autonomy to colonial powers.

National development—economic, social, educational, political improvements—is a central component of state security. A typical (though not universal) preoccupation of states and rulers is gaining more resources, which are then used for many purposes: enrichment of the rulers, strengthening the state militarily, raising living standards, boosting state prestige, etc. Modern governments have typically felt that the more arms, population, wealth, technological advancement, and the like their societies accumulated—absolutely and comparatively—the better. Gaining resources is often important for the *domestic* survival of a dynasty, regime, party, or ruler as well. In the past development often involved seizing wealth, territory, etc. from others. Now it comes primarily through expanded internal capabilities and foreign interactions.

The final component of state security, rule, is the capability to run one's domain—having the power, reach, and legitimacy to gain obedience and quell disobedience. Even states secure from outside threats, enjoying autonomy and rising resources, can nonetheless feel insecure at home. A good example was China in 1989 in the national demonstrations for democracy that focused on Beijing's Tiananmen Square. The government ordered that they be militarily suppressed, knowing the political repercussions at home and abroad would be substantial but fearing any lesser response would jeopardize survival of the communist party-ruled political system.

The most influential theoretical and prescriptive approaches on security in international politics have been the *Realist, Liberal*, and *Marxist* (Doyle 1997). The labels are not literally accurate but are too deeply entrenched to be discarded. This chapter discusses the first two, with liberal converted to *liberalist* to distinguish it from 'liberal' in domestic politics and analysis, which has different meanings. The Marxist view is now somewhat in eclipse but may make a comeback in the future. Classical Marxism has important similarities with liberalist thinking on international politics, while Marxist-oriented governments (Soviet Union, North Korea) have usually behaved in ways fitting the realist tradition. Thus elements of the Marxist approach are captured in discussing realist and liberalist conceptions. (See Key Ideas 2.1)

KEY POINTS

- Traditional theoretical perspectives on security focus on security relations among states, the most powerful international actors.
- States work to sustain security against external and internal threats.
- Components of state security include safety, autonomy, development, and rule.
- States and citizens are strongly interested in sustaining state autonomy.
- The most influential theoretical perspectives on security have been the Realist, Liberalist, and Marxist.

KEY IDEAS 2.1

The Marxist approach

Marxist analyses have always stressed that international politics is ultimately an offshoot of the continuing development of the international capitalist system. In that system the dominant actors are classes and their representative economic entities, which in turn dominate states and utilize state power to pursue their own interests. Under capitalism, development proceeds via exploitation—in international politics it proceeds by capitalist penetration of less developed societies to exploit them as markets, sources of valuable resources, and supplies of inexpensive labour. The world is increasingly being knitted together in a process that transforms the underdeveloped societies. International politics is dominated by the division between largely exploitative developed countries and the rest, by the penetration of the latter by the former, by the struggles between the developed countries over their competing economic interests, and by the struggles between the developed countries and less developed countries over the exploitation.

The Marxist approach has shared with realists an emphasis on competition and rivalry among states, including the importance of military power and an expectation that frequent wars are likely. Marxist governments have therefore often behaved much like a realist analysis would expect—preoccupied with survival and national autonomy, tough in the pursuit of national interests, ready to use force to secure themselves and their interests, uneasy about the virtue of cooperation with others. The two perspectives also share the depiction of international politics, under capitalism, as inherently conflict-ridden, insecure, and violent.

The Marxist approach shares with liberalists the idea that the behaviour of governments depends on which elements in society control them, not the international system per se—the Marxist counterpart to democratic peace theory is that building truly socialist societies and governments leads to peace among them. They also share the idea that international politics is evolving, developing over time, with rising interactions and interdependence leading eventually to a change in its basic character.

Various elements could contribute to resurgence of the Marxist approach. One is the penetration of many societies by the forces of globalization since that produces transitions to more capitalist patterns of organization that display many elements which are or seem exploitative and which generate or reinforce international inequalities among societies. Another is the resentment at Western domination and the pursuit of a liberalist agenda, since this can find appealing the Marxist insistence that this is the selfish interests of Western elites at work, not the promotion of truly universal values.

The realist perspective

The realist view has a long pedigree in political theory, with analysts from ancient China or Greece to Hobbes, Machiavelli, and Rousseau regularly cited. Of the four components of security mentioned above realists: (1) see states preoccupied with physical safety; (2) assume state preoccupation with autonomy; (3) treat national development mainly as a means, helping sustain and strengthen state autonomy and safety; and (4) regard rule as primarily important instrumentally—rule must be competent enough to meet foreign challenges to the state's autonomy and safety.

This makes development and rule generally less important than security and autonomy, but realists in power can be flexible on this. While some states care little about development, this can be a grave mistake for others by eroding their relative national power. As for rule, very hard-headed, power-oriented leaders sometimes put rule ahead of safety and even autonomy. In the treaty that took Russia out of the First World War, the Bolsheviks accepted German control over a significant part of the former Tsarist empire territory in Europe, and accepted serious vulnerability to a future German attack, so they could concentrate on consolidating their rule. China's Chiang Kai-shek downplayed fighting the Japanese occupation of his nation during the Second World War, then accepted Soviet intrusions into Chinese territory and autonomy, so as to focus instead on later (unsuccessfully) fighting the communists in a civil war over rule. Under a realist approach, therefore, one might find little concern for development and rule or a total preoccupation with them or anything in between, depending on the circumstances.

The realist view has always found international politics distinctive because of anarchy, the absence of any ultimate power and authority over states. In international politics there is little rule. Realists claim that absence of rule makes *power*, *autonomy*, the international political *system*, and its *structure* different from domestic politics. Anarchy makes international security relations significantly system-driven. The nature of the system, and its pressures and constraints, are the major factors determining the security goals and relations of national governments. In this regard they are more important factors than their domestic character, the qualities of their leaders and political systems, their ideological preoccupations, or their decision-making processes. Foreign policy is largely a more or less rational response to external necessities.

This means a state exists *somewhat apart from society*, having its own identity and interests vis-à-vis international politics. Thus it can be thought of, to simplify analysis, as a unitary, self-interested actor pursuing a strategy for dealing with other states. This is why realists expect considerable continuity over time in a government's foreign policy, particularly in basic objectives such as security. Leaders and governments come and go, their tactics and preoccupations fluctuate, but not the basic thrust of the foreign policy.

Power, autonomy, system, and system structure take on a distinctive character because there is only a limited *community*. Governments lack a strong sense they are part of a larger (political, economic, social, cultural) entity in international politics with overarching interests, goals, perspectives, and values they all share. Associations among states form but they are normally limited in scope, episodic, uneven in importance, and fleeting. Why so little community? Classical realists often stressed that without rule people readily behave in selfish, criminal, violent ways, citing the analysis of this by philosopher Thomas Hobbes, and said this is what happens in international politics. Instead of community there is a "Hobbesian" world of cut-throat competition and violence. Modern realists emphasize, instead, the need, under anarchy, for states to act in a self-reliant, self-centred fashion. Each looks out for itself and this restricts community because it limits interactions and cooperation. There is also some preference for autonomy over community among states since autonomy offers an appealing freedom for states and their citizens.

The limited development of community leads to distinctive forms of autonomy, political power, and structure. In domestic systems autonomy is a sphere of limited freedom and control within a higher structure of power and authority—like regional autonomy within a state. In international politics that higher structure is very limited and exists by states' *limiting themselves* via treaties they can still abandon or creating international institutions they can pull out of. Politically, therefore, state autonomy is unique in scope. And it has typically included governing without outside interference and using force when it thinks this is necessary in domestic and international affairs, rights almost never accorded other political actors. Several centuries ago this was embodied in the legal concept and status of sovereignty—the state and its rule are sovereign, unlike all other political entities. Ultimately a state is sovereign by being officially recognized by others as in control of a territory and its residents. With this, states turned a basic aspect of their situation into a distinctive status with a unique identity that remains highly attractive today.

With no higher structure of power and authority, i.e. government, to provide protection, states are said to be structurally insecure—their existence suffused with risk. Each must arrange for protection itself. This makes military strength to cope with possible attacks the most vital kind of power. Therefore states are natural competitors for *relative*

THINK POINT 2.1

Security dilemmas

The essence of a security dilemma is that in taking action to keep safe a government (or other actor) produces reactions that detract from its security. When the term is used in the field of international politics it almost always refers to the way in which a government may arm itself solely in order to be safer from possible attacks but in doing so scares other governments into arming as well, so that everyone's security is not improved and may even be diminished. The analysis is often extended into suggesting that such an action–reaction dynamic can feed suspicions, arouse fears and hostility, contribute to misperceptions, and, in the end, help provoke a rivalry and even a war.

In fact the concept has several other applications. It is now applied by some analysts to internal conflicts, such as those among different ethnic groups. For instance, if a state becomes weak and unstable the ethnic groups in the country might begin to be uneasy about the future—what if ethnic conflict springs up and the state is too weak to repress it? This can lead an ethnic group to take steps to prepare for possible trouble—acquiring some arms, maybe organizing a militia to provide defence against an attack, maybe checkpoints set up to limit access to the group's main residential areas. But such steps, and the political rhetoric that helps lead the group to take them, can incite other ethnic groups to develop similar fears, take similar steps, and set off a similar action-reaction sequence.

Another application has to do with the pursuit of security at different levels. When a government is facing a crisis or war it is very likely to become much more authoritarian vis-à-vis its population—repressing dissent, arresting suspicious people, censoring media, and the like to a greater extent than normal. This is done to increase the security of the state and, it will be said, of the people, but for a good many people it means that their personal security declines. A number of governments and societies currently concerned about terrorism have found themselves in this situation, in which steps taken to enhance security of one sort have the simultaneous effect of encroaching on security of another sort. This is clearly a security dilemma as well.

In the same way, multilateral efforts to pursue security in the international system by preventing nuclear proliferation require putting a sharp limit on the autonomy of a number of states—they are told they are not entitled to develop nuclear weapons, that sovereignty and national autonomy do not extend that far. But often the states that want to develop nuclear weapons feel they face a serious security threat and need the weapons to help cope with it. Thus pursuit of security for the international system as a whole can lead some members to feel that their security is being sacrificed or at least made more tenuous. Once again, steps taken to promote security at one level lead to a reduction in perceived security for someone at another level.

military power, and accordingly competitors for things that build military power—wealth, natural resources, strategically valuable positions, technology, population.

Competition is enhanced by the fact that when one state expands its power so as to be safer, the fears of others naturally rise. This produces the '**security dilemma**': because additional military power for defence might also enhance one's capacity to attack, states' individual efforts to become safer collectively sustain, even enlarge, their insecurity (see Think Point 2.1). Competition is further exacerbated by the relative nature of military power and the scarcity of its components. There cannot be enough of power or its components to satisfy every state; each is almost always eager for more.

Furthermore, competition encourages some governments to enlarge their relative power. They can do this via expanding their military might, then using force or other means to expand their territories, wealth, populations, etc. They can then use that additional power to gain still more. Such 'expansionist' governments seek to alter the international system in their favour so as to get more of what they want. Perhaps every government would love to do this. Of special concern, however, are ones determined to do this, by force if necessary, making them particularly threatening.

Why such regimes appear is debated. One view is that the inherent competition and insecurity in international politics breeds an urge to be as secure as possible by becoming as strong as possible. Another is that states and governments periodically detect the appearance of unusual opportunities to become much more powerful—finding a new source of great wealth, spotting serious weaknesses in rival states, or some other favourable development. They then attempt to exploit this situation, and greater power brings expanded ambitions. Another argument is that states are typically ruled by people strongly interested in, even addicted to, power; for them, seeking more comes naturally. Regardless of the explanation, realists have long depicted security as endangered by aggressive, revisionist, or revolutionary states.

Hence the essence of international politics is competition for power, with power consisting ultimately of coercive capabilities. The core component of political power is military strength, unlike in a typical domestic system. International politics is distinctive in that states relate to each other primarily in terms of relative power, with each restricted in using its power primarily by the opposing power of others. In any historical period, the distribution of power among the small number that are the strongest states provides the international system's fundamental pattern of political decision and action—the power distribution drives states' behaviour. As a result it is the key political structure in the system (Waltz 1979). It takes the place of a constitution, legislative and executive institutions, a legal system, and other elements of a domestic political structure in determining how decisions are made and who can do what.

Understanding this, governments work hard to accurately assess the distribution of power and grasp its implications for their behaviour (although they are often mistaken in doing so). This then leads them to be preoccupied with generating and maintaining a 'proper' or 'appropriate' power distribution, as vital for being secure (see Think Point 2.2). The proper distribution is one that results in order and stability by curbing warfare and containing conflicts, providing meaningful security for the system and its members. The problem, of course, is that states disagree, sometimes strongly, about the proper distribution—particularly about the relative power each should have. What some find satisfactory for security others consider inadequate.

It is debatable whether the international system is ever managed or just has tendencies toward equilibrium generated by member efforts to improve their individual situations. In any case, what management there is has to do primarily with emergence, deliberately or inadvertently, of a suitable power distribution among major states, that is, one they will all tolerate for the time being, and having it not be unduly disturbed. Within such a stable system rivalries will be contained and competition restricted. When this power distribution cannot be sustained—breaks down, is challenged by strong states—trouble readily emerges. Altering the key element of the entire system, by shifting smoothly from one distribution of power among major actors to another or sharply altering who has what scale of power within an existing distribution, is a formidable challenge. It is so formidable, in fact, that analysts suggest it seldom occurs peacefully—a major war or period of warfare is needed to create a new power structure. This brings severe insecurity for those involved in fighting and for others in the system.

Since international politics is basically rivalry, conflict, and insecurity, realists insist that true *cooperation*, especially among major states, is rare, particularly on security-related matters. Therefore cooperation cannot be sufficiently effective in generating a highly secure system and only occasionally alleviates members' insecurity. First, governments (and often citizens) value autonomy and sovereignty too much for the cooperation needed to create a transnational government, effective international law on sensitive topics, and permanently binding treaties on major security matters. For instance, governments reject tough limitations on or elimination of weapons they consider vital. They cooperate to create alliances but alliance treaties have escape clauses and states often abandon alliance commitments when trouble arises. Other major treaties usually have provisions for easy withdrawal. If there are no loopholes in agreements that they find too confining, governments invent some.

THINK POINT 2.2

The 'balance' of power

One of the enduring concepts in the study of international politics is the balance of power. It is sometimes used to describe what frequently happens as a result of the competition among states; they compete and the result is that over time a rough balance of power among the competitors emerges, constraining all the actors. This is because the major states always try to gain ground relative to each other, and thus react competitively to success by any rival, often imitating whatever is producing that success. Next, the term is used to describe a deliberate policy that states may employ. They fear the emergence of a dominant state so they deliberately attempt to construct and maintain a balance of power instead. A third way the term is used is simply to refer to the distribution of power in an international system—regardless of what that distribution looks like. There are frequent suggestions that China's development is sharply altering the balance of power in East Asia, which means that China's development is changing the relative power of the major actors in East Asian international politics so that the dominant states, the US and Japan, will be less dominant. In effect, the balance of power is becoming more balanced!

I refer instead to states seeking or settling for an appropriate or suitable distribution of power. This does a better job of capturing what takes place. Governments have only a limited influence on what the distribution of power is or will be; they have limited resources for seeking changes in it and many of the relevant factors shaping it are beyond their control. Governments typically prefer a distribution of power heavily in their favour. However, they will often settle for a distribution of power in which they, alone or in combination with their friends, are the equal of any states they are concerned about. They often settle for a distribution of power in which they are weaker than other states that might be threats, but powerful 'enough' to try to protect their interests, even if only by making it costly to ignore or attack them.

Thus a suitable or acceptable distribution of power for a specific government, and what governments consider a suitable distribution for an international system, will vary a great deal and may not look at all 'balanced'. What the term really refers to, therefore, is what distribution of power, from the point of a particular observer, seems best for meeting that observer's perceived needs. And any strategy of pursuing security via the distribution of power is one of trying to get close to the distribution that seems best, in competition with other actors' pursuit of the distribution that would be best for them.

Second, cooperation that occurs is likely to be inadequate because governments often cheat, defecting from it to get a better payoff. They do this not just for their benefit but because they assume others will cheat and they must keep up with them. Third, any cooperative arrangement benefits some states more than others. Since governments cannot afford to fall behind others, they may reject signing or upholding even cooperative deals that benefit everyone if others benefit more than they will. Finally, since a cooperative arrangement is unlikely to last, governments often avoid the most important step in cooperation: to accept agreements not very beneficial (or even harmful) for themselves now because eventually the cooperation will pay off handsomely. They often insist agreements pay off for them now—waiting to benefit over the long run is too big a gamble. That makes agreements harder to obtain and less effective.

Thus realists expect cooperation, especially on security, to occur only among limited groups of states, as in alliances, or on relatively uncontroversial matters, and even then it will be hard to sustain. Even when it occurs, individual governments will be tempted to free ride—to get the benefits while evading the costs (like when citizens enjoy government services but cheat on paying taxes). Free riding limits the benefits and durability of cooperation. It means too little of what the cooperation is supposed to provide is actually provided. And free riding flourishes with no higher authority around to punish it.

Security for the system as a whole, therefore, is some semblance of order maintained in uneven, often haphazard ways. Analysts have identified several power structures as typical; they offer some order and stability, but with limitations. In one, the distribution of power among the most powerful members is multipolar. Here, at least three and maybe several more governments have a great deal more power than any others, and are roughly equal in power among themselves. Under multipolarity, general order and stability are maintained because centralization of power in the hands of one state or group of states will be opposed by others—will be 'balanced' by their efforts to prevent this, efforts that might extend to fighting to cut the rising power or powers down to size. (This is the most appropriate use of the frequently misused term balance of power.) As a deliberate policy or simply a by-product of their strenuous competition, therefore, states keep each other contained. They do this by enlarging their military strength, alliances, or undercutting the most powerful state in other ways. With no dominant power state autonomy and survival are maximized. The same thing happens in rivalries among lesser states or groups of states—deliberately or via competition they offset the power of rivals.

The result is not a high level of security, it is the beneficial impact of living with low level insecurity—states work hard to keep safe because they are always somewhat unsafe. Competition is constant so insecurity is pervasive, but it is the insecurity of competition, not the insecurity from loss of autonomy or a state's existence.

In a bipolar power distribution, two states or tight collections of states have far more power than any others. The Cold War was always characterized as bipolar—two superpowers and their blocs dominated the system. The two dominant states have more autonomy than others because they are so powerful. But they compete with and therefore balance each other so they are far from fully free or safe—they compete for allies, economic and technical advantages, breakthroughs in military power, control of strategic areas. This can generate intense feelings of insecurity. Bipolar competition in the past sometimes brought repeated wars or a gigantic war to settle it. But analysts have argued that with only two leaders or blocs it is easier than under multipolarity to agree on cooperation to create at least some additional order in the system and reduce insecurity. For example the US and USSR eventually cooperated somewhat to limit nuclear proliferation during the Cold War.

With a unipolar distribution a single state, or cluster of states, is far more powerful than any others. This state or coalition is termed a hegemon. This situation could make all other states terribly insecure—they might be destroyed and eliminated by the hegemon or at least forced to be highly subservient. However, analysts are intrigued by cases in which the hegemon is not expansionist or is too powerful to be militarily challenged but not so powerful that it does anything it wants. The hegemon can then use its power for management of the system. After all, it benefits most if everyone behaves—what fun is dominance if it involves a constant struggle to keep order? With hegemonic management, other states can be less fearful, allowing more cooperation than normal to occur. The hegemon can encourage and help enforce that cooperation, further expanding order and security. Some analysts see periods of hegemony as the most stable and secure in international political history, giving rise to hegemonic stability theory as an explanation of why and how this is the case.

Still, unipolarity poses obvious problems. There are bound to be governments scheming to become number one or to change unipolarity into bipolarity or multipolarity. Staying on top is therefore tough and has never been permanent. If the hegemon makes international politics less competitive, violent, and insecure, it follows that once it begins weakening, rivals to it spring up, rivalries among other states emerge, and cooperation declines. Insecurity rises steeply and, say some analysts, the result is always major warfare to determine the new distribution of power—hegemonic or otherwise.

In thinking about change in the system, a striking feature of the realist perspective is that almost any change, especially in the power distribution, is—from someone's realist viewpoint—dangerous. Hence this perspective is fundamentally pessimistic about security. It detects threats even in peaceful relationships and encourages what is known as worst-case analysis in national security decision-making, even in periods of peace and stability. Worst-case analysis involves always emphasizing what could go wrong, using a pessimistic analysis of what others are up to, how developments will turn out, which leads to readily detecting potential threats.

KEY POINTS

In the realist perspective:

- Anarchy shapes a distinct politics among states and their governments that makes international politics a realm of insecurity.
- The pressures and constraints of the international system are the major determinants of states' security goals and relations.
- International or transnational community is limited in favour of sovereignty and national community, restricting cooperation and the management of security.
- States as unitary, self-interested actors are inherently insecure, competing for power as the key to security. That competition creates security dilemmas.
- The structure of the international system is the distribution of power among the leading states.
- States seek to develop and maintain suitable distributions of power for maintaining security—disagreeing about what a suitable distribution (multipolar, bipolar, or unipolar) is and how much power each state needs.

Realist disputes

There are cleavages within realism. One of note is the distinction between 'offensive' and 'defensive' realists (Mearsheimer 2001). Defensive realists believe governments are so caught up in the burdens of international politics that they typically focus on survival and pursue only incremental gains on other security matters. They are concerned with deterring or defending against possible attacks, while preserving their relative position in the system—not with taking major and risky steps to sharply improve it. Such cautious, status-quo oriented actors compete in only a limited fashion. Offensive realists feel the international system makes governments, particularly great powers, always hungry. Each wants to be the most powerful in the system, or its regional system, or its neighbourhood. They are always looking to expand their power, not just for protection from attack. To offensive realists, therefore, security is hard to come by and international politics is dangerous. For defensive realists most states are usually secure and are less constrained, such as when pursuing cooperation, by fears of the worst.

Another disagreement is over how often, and how long, the system can be dominated by a hegemon. The traditional view is that hegemony is rare and fleeting—other states fear it too much and work strenuously to prevent or undermine it (Layne 2004). But some analysts see hegemony as fairly common and sometimes durable (Gilpin 1981). This is of special interest now, producing contrasting views of how hard others will work to undermine American hegemony, and how successful they will be in accomplishing this. Defensively realist governments could find a suitably operated American hegemony congenial and might bandwagon more than balance, aligning themselves with, not against, the US.

A third disagreement concerns domestic systems. 'Neoclassical' realists assert that while the international system shapes how states behave, its specific impact is frequently determined by domestic factors. Systemic influences are filtered through leaders' ideological views and other perspectives, domestic and bureaucratic politics, and the like. Thus governments do not react similarly to similar external circumstances and pressures—to understand their behaviour we must trace how the system's impact interacts with domestic factors in each country.

For instance, there is evidence that a serious revolution inside a country alters threat perceptions there and in neighbouring countries because of shifts in *perceptions*, not just adjustments in relative power (Walt 1996). Many realist-oriented analysts believe leaders vary in being risk-avoidant or risk-acceptant, so that coercive threats work better against the former than the latter. (Revolutionary leaders, for instance, might be highly risk-acceptant.) This could be important in practising deterrence or explaining governments' differing reactions to the distribution of power. A very appealing conception is that a government reacts not to another government's power but to whether it looks like it is a *threat*, which is a different matter, a perception or judgment about that government (Walt 1987). Another suggestion is that in choosing whether to pursue cooperation or undertake an arms buildup to keep safe, leaders are influenced by their assessment of who usually has an advantage in their era—attackers (offence) or defenders. If, for instance, military technology seems to favour attackers, a status-quo oriented government will see cooperation, such as in disarmament, as dangerous because if a rival cheats to get into position to attack, the rival will have acquired a decisive advantage because technology favors the offence. Alternatively, if technology favours the defence, then a potential attacker would need to gain a much larger advantage by cheating to be a real threat and consequently the cheating if more likely to be discovered and offset by the status-quo state, making cooperation less risky. Whether offence or defence is perceived as providing the greatest advantage is therefore important.

Of course, this adds considerable complexity to analysis while the appeal of realism has always been that it simplifies. The dominant realist thinking during the Cold War, neorealism or structural realism, emphasized having a simplifying theory: domestic factors are relevant but what mainly drives international politics are the systemic pressures. Analysts too focused on domestic factors were called 'reductionist'. The neorealists' main target was classical realists. Now neoclassical realists assert that neorealism is so simplifying it is simplistic.

One other disagreement concerns what gives the system its character. Traditionally, realists stress anarchy, the autonomy and sovereignty of states, and the distribution of military power as determining the nature of the world states confront. An alternative view cites, as well, the capacity for transactions/interactions among states and societies. The level of technology and development of societies, the scale of information flows, and other factors sharply expand transactions and other interactions, and in turn raise the necessity for and ability to develop cooperative arrangements, management capabilities, and other elements of order. This view partly crosses the border into liberalist thought (Buzan, Jones and Little 1993).

KEY POINTS

- There is a cleavage between offensive and defensive realist perspectives.
- Realists currently disagree about the durability of unipolarity (hegemony).
- Neoclassical realists believe that the impact of systemic factors on state behaviour is mediated by domestic factors.
- One revision of realism treats the scale and capacity of interstate and intersociety interactions, which vary over time, as a component of any international system.

Difficulties with realist analysis

We close discussion on realism by noting some major problems that call its relevance into question. First, the collapse of the Cold War toppled a bipolar system that neorealists insisted was intrinsically more stable and durable than other configurations. Next, according to most observers, the Cold War collapsed due to *internal* developments in communist states. Instead of collapse due to a great war or other systemic pressures, or a sharp decline in communist governments' relative military power, it was because of a *failure of rule* and of their attempts at cooperation among themselves. Communist regimes were unable to govern well enough to retain legitimacy and support. And their effort to build a community to ease security and other burdens lost its appeal in comparison with the West's similar effort. From a realist perspective they should not have just given up in the Cold War—they should have feared being attacked by the other side in the aftermath. But they didn't fear this, and for good reason; they were in danger from domestic unrest far more than any Western attack. *Internal* factors outweighed systemic pressures in shifting their behaviour. These societies and their new governments soon moved toward becoming Western-style political and economic systems and joined Western community institutions, turning to cooperation or at least bandwagoning for their security.

Next, realists see states as constantly worried about their survival. Yet with myriads of small weak governments around, the durability of states is very high. None has disappeared since the Second World War due to military conquest. The real threat to many comes from inside—as in Yugoslavia, the Soviet Union, currently Iraq. (Most worried now about being invaded to death is Taiwan because its claim to statehood is so tenuous.) Analysts suggest that a strong norm against eliminating a state militarily has emerged and sustains the survival of even the most dubious ones. If so, such a norm—reflecting the existence of a community of states—does not fit a realist view very well.

Many realists expected the end of the Cold War to result in some version of multipolarity. Instead it brought American hegemony, which has yet to provoke the responses realism would expect. The US has yet to pick out a potential rival and try to suppress it—it continues to facilitate the continuing development, for example, of the European Union, Japan, and China. And other states are not working hard to develop a balance to the military power of the US. China continues military modernization and raising its defence spending but other major states are not, and China's defence spending increase has been exceeded by that of the US. There are no anti-US alliances—closest is Russia–China cooperation, which both governments insist is not an alliance. Opposition to the US by other great powers has been intermittent, depending on the issue, and expressed largely by voting in the UN Security Council to oppose American policies. The chief goal has been to have the US use force only with prior Security Council approval, not a particularly realist sort of approach. This opposition has led analysts to refer to 'soft balancing' to capture, for instance, French, Russian, and Chinese positions on the Iraq war, but that is an amorphous concept. Serious balancing involves tough steps to limit someone's power; soft balancing seems like disagreement about policies. On the other hand, it is not bandwagoning either.

Another serious problem is persistently greater cooperation than a realist might expect. A premier example is the deepening and enlargement of European integration. Some realists contended that integration flourished mainly because of the Soviet threat and was bound to dissolve when that threat disappeared. Efforts at cooperation remain elaborate on other matters like preventing nuclear proliferation, environmental issues, human rights concerns, promoting expanded trade and foreign investment, and terrorism.

The best realist replies are as follows. One is time: over time realist expectations will be borne out as American hegemony declines, great-power rivalries intensify, conflicts become more violent (as in US–China relations), while integration turns the EU into a rival superpower. Insecurity will flourish. Realists argue they have history on their side, not an easy argument to dismiss. A second is that several regional international systems operate in a realist pattern, as do some domestic conflicts (realist thinking, such as the concept of the security dilemma, has been successfully applied to some civil wars). Many analysts today view the East Asia situation in the following realist terms: a rising rivalry between the US/Japan and China is leading to US steps to contain China (like overtures to India, Vietnam, Indonesia) and Chinese steps to isolate the US in the region (via expanded ties with Southeast Asia, Russia, South Korea). If this is correct the likelihood of a fundamental conflict in East Asian system is high.

KEY POINTS

- Various aspects of the collapse of the Cold War are difficult to handle from a realist perspective.
- Currently, state survival seems threatened mainly from internal, not international, factors.
- Post-Cold War international politics displays features—unipolarity, the responses to it, levels of cooperation—difficult to explain from a realist perspective.

The liberalist perspective

The liberalist perspective has a shorter history but wasn't born yesterday. From roots in the 18th century enlightenment, it reached prominence early in the 20th century, particularly after the First World War, and has been important ever since. Like the realist view it treats states as primary actors in an international politics characterized by elements of anarchy. However, it recognizes the presence of significant other actors, and sees anarchy as less pernicious. Liberalists agree that international politics can be highly realist in character; they depart from realists on whether it *must* be.

Liberalists tend to treat the state as less important *in itself*—governments are major actors but typically this is in their capacity as agents for domestic groups. While states have their own interests and concerns, the main determinant of governmental policies is who rules—which elite(s), leader(s), or party(ies), runs(run) the government. There is constant struggle over who controls the government and further conflicts between officials and agencies representing the state's interests and those pressing the views and interests of domestic political groups. Thus states are not unitary actors. Since they are instruments of domestic forces, values, interests, and perspectives those elements are also significant factors in international politics.

If state security must fit what influential domestic elements think is good for *their* concerns and interests, this has implications for the four components of security: safety, autonomy, development, and rule. Quite a gap may exist between the views of officials about safety for the state and the policies that appeal to important domestic groups. Business sectors may see their incomes as more important than do officials who want to maintain strict controls over trade and investment with a potential enemy. Leaders often justify highly authoritarian rule as necessary for state security (as was the case in South Korea for years) while domestic groups worry most instead about the threat to domestic security posed by that government. Leaders have frequently put staying in power or pursuing their foreign ambitions above state safety and national development—Kim Jong Il and Saddam Hussein come to mind here.

The liberalist perspective puts considerable emphasis on state survival, less on autonomy. Its adherents expect the emergence of and usually support arrangements that curtail state autonomy but enhance development, including international interactions that promote development even if they erode sovereignty. This includes strong support for multilateral agreements and institutions which involve trading some autonomy for better management of international affairs. Liberalists have typically had a strong interest in development for its payoffs to citizens, not just for making the state and the society safer. This perspective has also increasingly emphasized, over time, that rule by governments should be limited, legitimate in the eyes of the citizens, and effective. When a government is not restrained, legitimate, and effective, harmful consequences ensue at home and, potentially, abroad, causing trouble for other governments and even turning it into a threat. Such a government can be sanctioned, perhaps even removed. In this perspective, rule is not strictly a domestic matter, shielded by sovereignty from interference in every instance.

This puts liberalists at odds with realists on the nature of anarchy, international politics, and power. Concerning anarchy, the liberalist perspective has a spectrum of interpretations. On one end is the conclusion that anarchy is not necessarily detrimental to relations among states, does not inherently force them into competition and rivalry that undermine security. An example is the long liberalist commitment (with fair success) to promoting free trade and as a result making international economic affairs more anarchical and more competitive, by cutting governments' interference with their societies' economic interactions. More free trade requires that governments agree to exchange some freedom of action for the promise of a broad, though uneven, improvement in everyone's welfare. This is possible only if anarchy does not prevent cooperation among governments on a large scale in important matters. Claims that it does are incorrect. Typically this is because powerful domestic interests develop a large stake in free trade and pressure their governments accordingly.

At the other end are liberalists who believe anarchy does have pernicious consequences, making cooperation difficult. However, they feel that in reaction governments often install successful international management arrangements—the UN, the International Atomic Energy Agency, arms control and environmental regimes, the World Bank and International Monetary Fund. Hence the harmful effects of anarchy are not self-reinforcing; they can be deliberately and cooperatively set aside. Thus neoliberal institutionalists argue that governments often tire of life in a highly competitive environment and can appreciate cooperation—on trade, arms races, nuclear proliferation, terrorism, etc. International organizations, treaties, explicit rules, and general working understandings are widely used to make the international environment more transparent, more predictable, less risky and dangerous. Those arrangements help solve coordination problems, making cooperation easier. International politics entails much more, and much more significant, cooperation than realists expect, cooperation that is durable when it meets important needs and interests.

In between these two poles is the rich liberalist tradition of promoting multilateral institutions, plus related arrangements such as networks of rules, patterns of accepted behaviour, and coordinated expectations which provide some order and are referred to as **international regimes** (or just regimes). Many liberalists believe that multilateral institutions and regimes not only facilitate simple cooperation, they can help alter governments' behaviour. This occurs through adjustments they help promote in conceptions of the national interest held by official and major domestic actors (elites, interest groups, publics), making them less self-centred and selfish.

A central conclusion of liberalists, in theory and practice, is that the security dilemma is not inherent in international politics. States can, and many do, reach such a satisfactory level of agreement and cooperation that being heavily armed, even with weapons of mass destruction, does not lead them to regard each other as intrinsically threatening. A widely cited form of this benign interaction is a pluralistic security community, pluralistic in that members are sovereign and a security community in that they do not fear each other (Adler and Burnett 1998).

For building such a community liberalists champion expanded international interchanges of almost all sorts, including intergovernmental ones. Rewarding interactions are believed to contribute significantly to a reduction in conflict and rivalry, a rise in cooperation, the growth of international management, and therefore improvements in security for states, societies, and the system. Involved are not only trade and investment flows, but flows of information, technology, entertainment and the arts, students, tourists, and so on. They help limit misunderstandings and misperceptions, facilitate cooperation, build a healthy interdependence and an appreciation of common interests, all of which reduce chances of conflict and war. Closed societies and tightly controlling governments should therefore be viewed with suspicion and sometimes hostility, not just because of their specific policies but because their behaviour in general clashes with what makes a better, safer, more peaceful world.

Ultimately, this invites thinking of international politics as the gradual construction and further evolution of effective international community, global or regional. People and governments come to accept that security is interdependent—seeking security unilaterally is ultimately futile. They come to appreciate that economic interactions and interdependence produce more welfare than competitive mercantilism under which economic interactions are structured to provide greater gains for your country than the other side. They take a global view on the environment, terrorism, epidemics, disasters—not a narrowly national one—as the only practical basis for coping with those problems. Developing community is certainly not easy but it is a familiar challenge; community building has long been difficult inside states, too, but not impossible.

The liberalist image of an ideal international politics expects significant additional, voluntary reductions in anarchy and state autonomy over time, and forcible intrusions on the autonomy of certain troublesome states. States and societies will retain significant autonomy and sovereignty, but numerous non-state actors (international organizations, multinational corporations, international humanitarian outfits) would flourish, contributing to a steady rise in general well being. Some analysts see this kind of world as emerging out of continued economic development plus phenomena like globalization and the information revolution. Thus international politics is evolving away from the realist image of a Hobbesian world.

Another powerful component of the liberalist perspective is the assertion that since states reflect preferences of influential domestic political elements, the nature of international politics is deeply affected by the *domestic character of states, their political systems, and their societies*. The nature of a government politically, and the nature of its society, do much to shape its external behaviour, and by extension, the nature of the actors in an international system shape its character. International politics among autonomous states therefore varies depending on the character of the members.

Regarding security this assertion has multiple origins. By early in the 20th century increased emphasis was being placed on the alleged impact of capitalist economies and their rising interdependence. Supposedly, business and other domestic interests in such societies, especially those heavily involved in trade and foreign investment, would oppose warfare as disruptive, expensive, and destructive in terms of their interests. War was bad for business, and capitalist expansion was demonstrating that war was no longer necessary for national development. In one form or another, this idea remains influential. For instance, promoting economic interdependence as an important contribution to peace was a major rationale for European integration.

There are contemporary variants of this. One is the argument that when national elites rise to power in the members of a regional international system that are commited to export-led growth for rapid national development, they see that a peaceful regional environment is crucial (war is bad for business). As a result they try to resolve or downplay their nations' conflicts, promote relaxation in tensions, cut military spending, and expand regional cooperation in things like arms control. The result is a sharp decline in warfare and rising national and regional security (Solingen 1998). An example often cited is the East Asian international system over the past four decades.

Another way to depict the nature of the domestic system as crucial is to emphasize democracy. Beginning with the German philosopher Immanuel Kant, there has been speculation that democracies can behave differently than non-democracies in international affairs. This idea was influential in the American Revolution; its leaders felt their democracy could opt out of the autocracies' frequent warfare. It was a central tenet of Wilsonian internationalism, and Woodrow Wilson's desire to build a League of democratic states. One justification was that wars often result from rulers pursuing personal agendas or states pursuing only state interests; if they had a say, citizens who bear the costs and harm of warfare would be more reluctant to practise it. Democracies would therefore be more peaceful.

Today the emphasis is on democratic peace theory, the notion that democracies are naturally peaceful *among themselves*. Descending from Kant as well, this contention was largely ignored until well into the twentieth century. It was revived inductively via the slowly spreading observation that modern liberal democracies (some analysts say all democratic governments) never go to war with each other. Equally impressive, though given less prominence, is that while democratic governments readily go to war with undemocratic ones and have long been among the most powerfully armed, they don't appear to even plan seriously for possible wars with each other. They just don't see each other as threatening—they constitute a very large pluralistic security community. This would mean international politics is different—certainly on security—among democracies.

Democratic peace theory offers various explanations—here is a sample. Some analysts believe that combining democracy and an open economy and society is what produces this result—it isn't just democracy but the combination that does the trick. Others argue that democracies are more transparent in policies and policy making than non-democracies, and more open to foreign influence in shaping their decisions, which makes for less suspicion, rivalry, and conflict among them. Another view is that democratic politics assumes compromise and the peaceful resolution of disputes through discussion. This carries over into dealings with other democracies, and rarely carries over well in dealing with non-democracies.

Not surprisingly, a liberalist perspective sees power differently too. As noted above, the liberalist view sees economic actors and economic power as important. In emphasizing international community building and open societies, this perspective also highlights the role of international institutions and private international groups in community development. Their efforts include promoting democracy and human rights, protecting the environment, expanding global health and welfare, attacking corruption (governmental or corporate), spreading private enterprise principles and practices, and encouraging arms control, disarmament, and the peaceful settlement of conflicts. In recent years these activities have been seen as signs of an emerging international civil society. This envisions expanding webs of activities by private citizens and organizations, like those that energize domestic democratic political systems, wielding rising influence over the foreign policies of governments.

From there it is just a short step to seeing soft power in international politics as important, supplementing or substituting for hard military power (Nye 1990). Soft power consists of prestige, moral authority and other elements of leadership, the ability to build coalitions and promote cooperation among states and other international actors, and the leverage for using pressure and persuasion to uphold international community standards. Coercive power is often of limited influence in domestic politics and, it is said, the same is increasingly true in international politics. Many kinds of power are now relevant because many kinds of actors and situations cannot be effectively dealt with by coercion.

Clearly, adherents of the liberalist perspective see international politics as changing over time in a positive direction—it is basically an optimistic conception. Democracy has slowly spread. Capitalism has gradually come to dominate international and national economic activities. Interactions and interdependence have grown and at a rising rate. Classic realist thinking is therefore of steadily declining relevance, as are many lessons often drawn from the history of international politics.

KEY POINTS

- The liberalist perspective is flexible about the impact of anarchy on governments' behaviour.
- It emphasizes the existence of internal cleavages over control of the state and its policies—states are not unitary actors.
- States and societies can accept and achieve significant cooperation, interdependence, community, and security management, through voluntary reductions in anarchy and state autonomy.
- The classic security dilemma is not inherent in international politics; states can develop a community with a high level of security even when members are well armed.
- The behaviour of states in international politics is shaped by the character of states, their political systems, and their societies; this includes the avoidance of wars among democratic political systems and societies.
- Power comes in various forms, is not necessarily coercive; actors are of many sorts, not just states.
- The liberalist approach is more optimistic about security than the realist approach, anticipating that the spread of democracy, capitalism, national development, and penetrating interactions will modify the system, its members, their interdependence, their perceived interests, and their ability to interact peacefully.

A liberalist age?

The liberalist approach is currently the dominant perspective in the *practice* of international politics. While governments are not all that enamoured of democratic peace theory's explanations, they are ready to go on the evidence and not worry about how to explain it. Thus the world's most powerful and influential states—the US, European Union members, Japan—and their closest associates are strongly committed to expanding democracy and capitalism, and to the development of international community and management. They believe in open societies, increased interdependence, greater progress in enlarging human rights. Usually they believe in the value of multilateral institutions. While they see all these things as beneficial for themselves, they also fully expect these developments to produce a more peaceful world and a higher level of national security for any government. This view is also widely reflected or endorsed by many other observers.

Its dominance is displayed in the organized pressure against states seeking to develop nuclear weapons, including threats of coercion and, in the case of Iraq, a military invasion. It is also demonstrated in pressure and direct interventions into states and societies considered extremely deficient in terms of democracy, human rights, economic management and development, and provision of decent living standards. States and societies wracked by internal conflict and humanitarian disasters are now candidates for being declared 'threats to international peace and security' and subject to interventions on behalf of the 'international community'. Such an intervention typically includes efforts at 'peacebuilding' or societal recovery and development, including steps to promote and install democratic institutions and practices, legal reform and the rule of law, effective police and military forces under civilian control, respect for human rights, decent education, health, and welfare services, free enterprise economic activities, and an open economy liked to the international economic system. This is precisely the liberalist prescription for a better world.

KEY POINTS

- The liberalist perspective currently dominates international politics, being employed by many of the most powerful and influential governments.
- This leads to considerable pressure on, even intervention into, states and societies that are considered—from a liberalist view—as threats to peace and security.

Liberalist issues

There are significant issues within the liberalist view. There are recurring tensions in theory and practice over priorities. The standard argument over expanding Western relations with China concerns whether the West should promote rapid economic growth to make China evolve faster into a peaceful democracy, or use pressure and sanctions to weaken the grip of its autocratic government first. For peace and security, is it vital to cooperate with autocratic governments in arms control and disarmament agreements, or to sanction and isolate them because they lack democracy? (A typical problem in relations with Russia.) Is the best approach to a difficult government like North Korea an honest and sincere engagement—including economic assistance, normal relations—or a sustained effort to undermine that regime? Which should come first in priorities in peacebuilding—a stable, effective, reasonably democratic government or installing better economic policies and practices (a good tax system, cuts in bloated government spending). Putting democracy first may cancel the economic improvements—why would desperately poor citizens vote for better tax collections and cuts in government jobs? Should it be democracy first or decent human rights improvements (like equal treatment for women)? Why should citizens approve greater rights to women if that is disparaged in their religion and culture? On the other hand, how will economic, human rights, and other reforms take hold without a reasonably strong democracy to make them legitimate?

The oldest such conflict is the tension between self-determination and the need for viable states. As Woodrow Wilson discovered, creating a state for a disaffected minority often alarms the other minorities that lie within its boundaries. Their fears of being mistreated are often well founded. The problem has arisen repeatedly recently in connection with new states carved out of the old Soviet Union, and is now evident in Iraq. The liberalist perspective offers no ready way to resolve all these disputes in theory or in helping governments make the relevant decisions.

There is also great difficulty sorting out when to use force. It comes in two forms. In one, governments disagree about when force is justified or how to determine the will of the international community, i.e. how to 'legitimize' using force. This was the problem between the US and others over the invasion of Iraq in 2003. Should action always be suspended when there is serious disagreement? The other is when there is unhappiness with a particular situation and a willingness to see force used to deal with it but widespread reluctance to bear the costs—typical on serious security problems in Africa. The moral and analytical justifications for force often conflict with the political, financial and other considerations involved.

KEY POINTS

- The liberalist view offers little guidance on the relative importance of various goals that can be in conflict.
- It is of limited assistance on specifically when the use of force is justified, necessary, and legitimate, as well as on who should bear the burdens involved.

Intellectual problems

There are also serious intellectual problems this perspective must confront. Some analysts remain suspicious of democratic peace theory, believing the correlation between democracy and the absence of war is spurious, that some third factor is responsible for the absence of war among democracies. For example, critics have argued that modern democracies simply share common interests and similar basic perspectives and values. Hence their disagreements are not serious enough to fight about and they make natural allies. This, not democracy, is the key variable. Analysts have also pointed out that newly formed democracies often display prickly and expansive nationalist passions that can lead to wars—spreading democracy to promote peace might sometimes backfire.

Another problem is raised by analysts and observers who feel that modern peacebuilding is the latest variant of Western political, economic, and social imperialism, one more effort to impose Western ways on other peoples, societies, and cultures (Paris). This charge is made forcefully by governments too, like China and Russia who feel threatened by the rise in power of liberalist-oriented governments and their ideas.

In general, liberalists put less emphasis on states to give more attention to other actors, international and domestic, seeing nationalism as being eroded by forces like globalization and interdependence. The difficulty is that there is plenty of evidence that nationalism and states remain powerfully attractive. They continue to be vehicles for evoking and conveying the most intense human feelings now in play in international politics. Maybe, as with Mark Twain, the reports of their demise are greatly exaggerated.

Also disturbing is that the leading states in the North Atlantic-European region actively promoted democracy, capitalism, an open international economy, and rising interdependence seveval times in the past. After the first such era, the military savagery of the First World War ensued.

The second era occurred after the First World War highlighted by Wilsonian internationalism, and did not prevent the Second World War. The third effort was mounted in the first decades of the Cold War, helping shape Western efforts to woo the developing countries by offering them rapid progress toward modernization. Broadly speaking, that effort failed, despite the immense efforts and resources employed. Things went much better when governments worked out for themselves why and how to introduce Western values and methods. What if elements of the Western world cannot be readily transferred but must be absorbed by others only at their own pace?

Finally, the current liberalist emphasis in international politics may merely reflect Western dominance. And what if, as many analysts suspect, Western dominance is coming finally to an end, with the rapid development of non-western states and societies that encompass well over half the world's population? If the sun sets on the West's preeminence, will it also set on the liberalist perspective? If so, the implications might include a clash of regions or civilizations, perhaps the return of a very realist world.

KEY POINTS

- Democratic peace theory is controversial among analysts and governments.
- In various quarters liberalist-oriented peacebuilding is seen as a version of Western imperialism and a new version of failed earlier recipes for peace and security.
- The liberalist approach could fade in impact as Western dominance of international politics recedes in the future.

Conclusion

There is nothing daunting or unduly complex about the basic elements of the realist and liberalist perspectives that should discourage students. And elements of these perspectives at work can readily be detected in official statements, analyses, commentaries, and scholarly works about international politics, where they are treated in everything from sophisticated to simplistic sways. It is important to keep in mind that in practice the two perspectives overlap and elements of each are often blended in discussions about international affairs and what should be done. In fact, security-related policies of governments are normally a combination of the two, reflecting intellectual and political compromises typical in foreign policy decision making.

Keep in mind that the chapter describes general tendencies, not tightly knit bodies of thought. While the basic elements are straightforward, sorting out the detailed variations of each perspective is complicated and at times confusing. Thus neither offers a precise guide to policy or a tightly knit, intellectually powerful theory. This has given rise to considerable frustration with them and concerted efforts to come up with alternative approaches, as much of this book indicates. This has not kept them from being enormously influential and a good understanding of both is therefore important.

QUESTIONS

What are the major components of security for states?

In the realist perspective, how does anarchy shape the incidence and nature of conflict and cooperation among states?

What are the alternative structures for an international system and how do they affect security for the members of that system?

In what ways have the collapse of the Cold War and the character of the Post-Cold War international system called into question the appeal and relevance of the realist approach?

Explain how and why the liberalist approach is more optimistic than the realist perspective on the prospects for security in international politics?

How do the realist and liberalist perspectives differ on the nature of power and its role in international politics?

From a liberalist perspective why are states not unitary actors and how do the characteristics of states, political systems, and societies influence state behaviour in international politics?

How is the contemporary dominance of the liberalist perspective displayed in international politics?

What is the classic security dilemma and how is it treated in the realist and liberalist perspectives?

Which perspective is more optimistic about cooperation in international politics, and why?

FURTHER READING

- **Morgenthau, Hans J. (1967), *Politics Among Nations*, 4th edn, New York: Knopf.** The classic analysis of international politics from a realist perspective in the twentieth century and enormously influential for many years.

- **Mearsheimer, John (2001), *The Tragedy of Great Power Politics*, New York: Norton.** The leading contender for title of classic analysis from a realist perspective in the twenty-first century, utilizing an offensive realist perspective very aggressively.

- **Paul, T.V., Wirtz, J., and Fortmann, M. (2004) (eds.), *Balance of Power: Theory and Practice in the 21st Century,* Stanford: Stanford University Press.** A valuable collection of efforts to revise or dismiss realist theory in view of the developments beginning with the collapse of the Cold War, including a discussion of 'soft balancing'.

- **Vasquez, J. and Elman, C. (2003) (eds.), *Realism and the Balancing of Power: A New Debate*, Upper Saddle River, NJ: 2003.** Another important collection on the contemporary status of the realist approach.

- **Waltz, Kenneth N. (1979), *Theory of International Politics*, New York: Random House.** A presentation of the dominant form of realist analysis in the second half of the Cold War, which incited elaborate efforts to build on that analysis and powerful critiques from other perspectives.

- **Bull, Hedley (1977), *The Anarchical Society: A Study of Order in World Politics*, New York: Columbia University Press.** A very influential work that suggests ways the realist and liberalist traditions can overlap and the most important work in the modern elaboration of the 'British school' of analysis of international politics.

■ **Organski, A.F.K. and Kugler, J. (1980), *The War Ledger*, Chicago: University of Chicago Press.** A good example of works asserting that power is often quite imbalanced in international politics, that this is usually good for order and stability, and that a closing of power gaps generally sets off greater rivalries and a much higher likelihood of war.

■ **Gilpin, Robert (1981), *War and Change in World Politics,* Cambridge: Cambridge University Press.** One of the key works in the development of the hegemonic stability theory.

■ **Keohane, Robert O. (1984), *After Hegemony,* Princeton, NJ: Princeton University Press.** The most elaborate theoretical discussion of the neoliberalist approach which blends realist and liberalist analyses.

■ **Doyle, Michael W. (1997), *Ways of War and Peace: Realism, Liberalism, and Socialism*, New York: W.W. Norton.** An excellent analysis of the roots in classical political thought of the realist, liberalist, and Marxist approaches to IR theory and a comparative evaluation of those approaches.

■ **Adler, Emanual and Barnett, Michael (1998), *Security Communities*, Cambridge: Cambridge University Press.** An exploration of the development of, among other things, pluralistic security communities.

■ **Ikenberry, G. John (2000), *After Victory*, Princeton, NJ: Princeton University Press.** An extensive account of how the United States led the way in the construction of a Western community of nations along liberalist lines after the Second World War.

IMPORTANT WEBSITES

- **www.geocities.com/virtualwarcollege/ir_realism.htm** This provides an introduction to the Realist tradition in international relations.
- **http://www.geocities.com/virtualwarcollege/ir_liberal.htm** This provides an introduction to the Liberalist tradition in international relations.

Visit the Online Resource Centre that accompanies this book for lots of interesting additional material: www.oxfordtextbooks.co.uk/orc/collins/

3 Peace Studies

PAUL ROGERS

Chapter Contents

- Introduction
- Origins and early years
- Evolution amidst controversy
- What is peace studies now?
- Responding to the new security challenges
- Conclusion

Reader's Guide

This chapter examines the origins and development of the field of peace studies after the Second World War, especially in relation to the East–West confrontation and the nuclear arms race. It analyses how peace studies responded to the issues of socio-economic disparities and environmental constraints as they became apparent in the 1970s, and explores its development as an interdisciplinary and problem-oriented field of study, often in the midst of controversy. The chapter then assesses the state of peace studies now, before concluding by examining how it is relevant to the new security challenges now facing the world, especially in the post 9/11 environment.

Introduction

Peace studies is a field of study that developed after the Second World War, largely because of the failure of a range of social and internationalist movements to prevent the outbreak of two world wars within 25 years. Its early development in the 1950s was hugely conditioned by the East–West nuclear arms race and the very real threat of a catastrophic nuclear war but peace studies was also quick to embrace major issues of the North–South wealth/poverty divide and the potential effects of global environmental constraints. It is a field that has had more than its share of controversies—peace studies was frequently labelled 'appeasement studies' at the height of the Cold War, but has survived and thrived, especially in recent years, with a marked increase in interest in issues of peacekeeping, conflict resolution and post-conflict peace-building. There has been a particular interest in many parts of Latin America, Africa, the Middle East and much of Asia, and the concern of the peace studies community to rise above the Western ethnocentric attitudes that still dominate much of international relations has been greatly aided by this global context.

Origins and early years

Peace studies only became established as a formal field of study, with its own institutions and journals, in the post-1945 period, but its origins go back much further, not least to the work of pioneers of interdependence theory such as Norman Angell and Francis Delaisi in the early years of the twentieth century. The more general development of international relations in the 1920s had been, in part, a reaction to the carnage of the First World War. While that had been primarily a 'soldier's war' rather than a war of civilians, the loss of some 11 million young men within four years, very largely from European countries, had had a particularly marked effect on intellectuals. Moreover, the post-war pandemic of influenza was to kill at least three times as many people as the recent war, a pandemic made worse by the privations that were a legacy of the war.

In addition to the developing field of international relations, during the inter-war years a small number of pioneering researchers sought to draw on empirical evidence in order to more fully understand the causes of war and even to seek predictive models. These could be described as early peace researchers and among them were Pitrim Sorokin, Quincy Wright and the British meteorologist, Lewis Fry Richardson, although Richardson's work only became widely known in the 1950s (Sorokin 1937; Wright 1942; Richardson 1960).

A more sustained interest in peace studies developed after the Second World War (Galtung 1969). The failure of the League of Nations at the end of the 1930s, coupled with the much greater violence of the war and the onset of the Cold War, was to lead to a renewed interest in peace studies and the establishment of a number of centres and journals in the 1950s. The war itself was a far more global war than the First World War, which was largely limited to Europe. Between 1937 and 1945, the European and Pacific/East Asian wars largely overlapped into rapidly moving conflicts in which aerial bombardment, mass movements of refugees, and more mechanized forms of warfare contrived to kill at least 40 million people and to wound and maim many tens of millions more.

Furthermore, the end of the war saw the start of the nuclear age, with the destruction of the Japanese cities of Hiroshima and Nagasaki, killing close to 200,000 people. Although these were, in one sense, extensions of the mass conventional bombings of cities such as Dresden, Hamburg and Tokyo, and were seen by strategists in this way, they clearly represented a new level of warfare that, to the general public, meant a degree of potential destruction that was far in excess of anything that had gone before.

The nuclear arms race, the Cold War and the need to research peace

Any hope that the sheer carnage of the Second World War might lead to a powerful intergovernmental movement away from interstate conflict was dashed by the end of the 1940s. While the United Nations was established as a hopefully more effective replacement for the old League of Nations, early attempts to bring the new atom bombs under control through the Baruch and Gromyko plans failed. By the end of the decade the United States had already produced an arsenal of over 200 nuclear bombs, the Soviet Union had tested its first nuclear device and Britain was well on the way to being the world's third nuclear weapons state.

Furthermore, by the early 1950s, the Cold War was in full swing both in Europe and in East Asia. The Berlin Airlift of 1948/49 had accelerated the division of Europe, NATO had been formed in 1949 and much of Eastern Europe had come under Soviet influence if not overt control. In East Asia, the communist revolution in China had been completed in October 1949 and was followed the next year by the start of the devastating three-year Korean War, killing well over a million people, most of them civilians.

By the early 1950s, too, a series of wars of decolonization or liberation were under way. India may have been partitioned in the violent upheavals of 1947, and some other countries such as Indonesia had achieved their independence, but elsewhere there were bitter wars between a number of European powers and anti-colonial insurgents. One of the most bitter was the eight-year Indo-China War between the French and the Viet Minh, culminating in the fall of the French garrison at Dien Bien Phu in May 1954 and the subsequent and rapid French withdrawal from the region. Elsewhere, the British were fighting insurgencies in Malaya and Kenya and facing increasing unrest in Cyprus, and the French were having difficulties controlling Algeria.

The combination of the early years of the nuclear arms race, the proxy wars of the Cold War era such as Korea, and the violence in a number of colonies, all contributed to a perception of a world of profound instability, even more shocking given that this was barely a decade after the world's worst ever conflict. It was in this pessimistic environment that the origins of peace studies are to be found.

The universities get involved

In these early years, peace studies developed primarily in North America and Western Europe, with some of the developments even preceding the tense years of the 1950s. Theodore Lenz's Peace Research Laboratory was founded in St Louis in 1945 and in Europe the Institut Français Polémologie was established in the same year. One of the main European contributors to the new field of peace research was the Dutch jurist, Bert Rolling. He had been a judge at the Japanese war crimes tribunal and went on to establish peace studies, or polemology, in the Netherlands.

Another key feature of peace studies was established in the early post-war era—the entry into the field of mathematicians and natural scientists into what was otherwise a social sciences area of study. This was later prominent both in the contribution of the Pugwash movement and in the publication of the *Bulletin of the Atomic Scientists*. It has been an enduring feature of peace studies over the past fifty years that its interdisciplinary nature stretches well beyond the range of social science disciplines to embrace the physical and natural sciences and mathematics.

One of the earliest initiatives in the United States was the publication in the *American Psychologist* in April 1951 of a letter from two social scientists, Kelman and Gladstone, arguing for a serious and systematic study of pacifist approaches to foreign policy. Coming at a time of heightened tensions, and with anti-communism rampant in the United States, this was a courageous suggestion and it resulted in the establishment of the *Bulletin of the Research Exchange on the Prevention of War* the following year.

The middle 1950s were to see major developments on both sides of the Atlantic. In the United States a key research group came together at Stanford University's Center for Advanced Studies in the Behavioral Sciences. As well as Herb Kelman, this included Kenneth and Elise Boulding and Anatol Rapoport. Joining them was Stephen Richardson, the son of Lewis Fry Richardson, who brought with him his father's copious but largely unpublished material on microfilm. This combination produced a highly active and innovative group that was to develop the *Bulletin* into the *Journal of Conflict Resolution*, based at the newly established Center for Conflict Resolution at the University of Michigan. In the first issue of the *Journal* the editors gave two reasons for establishing it, and these give the flavour of those early years:

> “The first is that by far the most important practical problem facing the human race today is that of international relations—more specifically the prevention of global war. The second is that if intellectual progress is to be made in this area, the study of international relations must be made an interdisciplinary enterprise, drawing its discourse from all the social sciences, and even further.”

(*Journal of Conflict Resolution*, Vol 1, No 1, p. 3, 1957)

In parallel with these developments in the United States, peace studies developed apace in Europe and Japan, with the establishment of more departments, research centres and journals (see Background 3.1: Peace Centres and Journals). In addition to the markedly interdisciplinary nature of this new field, two particular features of peace studies centres are worth noting. Some, including SIPRI, were essentially started at the instigation of governments and obtained most of their money from central government sources, continuing to do so successfully over many

BACKGROUND 3.1

Peace centres and journals

Away from the United States, the Norwegian peace researcher, Johan Galtung, founded the forerunner of what became the Peace Research Institute of Oslo (PRIO) in 1959 and Bert Rolling founded the Polemological Institute at the University of Groningen in the Netherlands. PRIO had initially formed part of the Norwegian Institute of Social Research. It became independent in 1966, having started publication of the *Journal of Peace Research* two years earlier.

Two of the largest peace studies centres were to be established in Sweden and the United Kingdom. To celebrate 150 years of peace, the Stockholm International Peace Research Institute (SIPRI) was set up in 1966 and went on to establish a worldwide reputation for its work on arms races and arms control. Its yearbook, *Arms and Disarmament*, has long been seen as an essential source of data. Seven years after the founding of SIPRI, members of the Society of Friends (Quakers) in Britain sought to establish a British equivalent and were able to aid the University of Bradford in setting up a Department of Peace Studies in 1973. Thirty years later, the Bradford department had grown to be the world's largest university peace studies centre, with a thriving undergraduate programme, 200 postgraduate students from over 40 countries and five associated research institutes.

Elsewhere, the Japanese Peace Research group was founded in 1964, the Canadian Peace Research and Education Association was established two years later and the Tampere Peace Research Institute was founded in Finland. One of the other key journals, *Peace and Change*, was started by the US Conference on Peace Research and History which had itself been formed in 1963. Given the global spread of this new field, the final development was the formation of the International Peace Research Association, which holds biennial conferences.

years. As such, they had a degree of financial support that was welcome, but such centres could also be subject to sudden political change. The Peace Research Centre at the Australian National University in Canberra failed to survive a change of government, and the Copenhagen Peace Research Institute was to lose its independence in a centrally directed amalgamation of institutes.

The other feature was the frequency with which centres in Western Europe and North America were supported and sometimes established at the behest of 'peace churches' such as the Quakers and Menonites. Furthermore, some of the Quaker charitable trusts provided essential support for the more ground-breaking research. In Britain, for example, an innovative multi-year study of non-nuclear defence options, the Alternative Defence Commission, was supported by some of the Rowntree and Cadbury trusts in the early 1980s at a time when the political climate dictated that such research would not remotely have been funded from conventional sources.

KEY POINTS

- Peace studies developed as a response to the carnage of the First and Second World Wars.
- The Cold War and the risk of nuclear disaster provided a further impetus in the 1950s.
- Most early work on peace studies was carried out in North America and Scandinavia.
- By 1970 there were established centres and journals.

Evolution amidst controversy

Meanwhile, in the early 1960s, there were sharp divides between the outlooks of peace researchers and those of the 'realist' school in international relations. Realist IR scholars saw the failure of the League of Nations and the intensity of the ideological division between western liberal democracies and the totalitarian systems of the Soviet bloc as providing an urgent need to undertake research that would essentially favour the survival of the former. The standpoint was very much that of an Atlanticist outlook.

Many peace researchers, on the other hand, saw this as a narrow Western ethnocentric outlook that failed properly to analyse what they saw as the reality of two competing systems locked into a single dynamic of military confrontation and escalation. They had much in common with 'idealist' outlooks in international relations, and their work attracted particular attention at a time when the nuclear arms race was accelerating.

There was, in particular, widespread concern over the repeated atmospheric testing of nuclear weapons leading to world-wide atmospheric contamination with radioactive materials such as Strontium-90. The Soviet launch of the world's first artificial satellite and the first experimental intercontinental ballistic missile in the late 1950s had resulted in a perception of a 'missile gap' in the United States and a considerable increase in spending on nuclear weapons and their delivery systems.

In late 1962, the United States and the Soviet Union came very close to an all-out nuclear confrontation over the latter's plans to deploy medium-range nuclear missiles in Cuba, less than 150 km from the United States. The crisis was resolved, with difficulty, after days of profound international tension and foreboding and one consequence was a new-found determination by the United States and the Soviet Union to seek progress in arms control. The 'Kennedy Experiment' of 1963 involved unilateral offers by President John F Kennedy which were indirectly reciprocated by the Soviet leadership and one early result was the Limited Test Ban Treaty, agreed within a year of the Cuba missile crisis.

Within five years, other significant multilateral treaties had been agreed, including the Outer Space Treaty, the Latin American Nuclear-Free Zone Treaty and, most significant of all, the Non-Proliferation Treaty. There was even some progress being made by the end of the decade towards a bilateral US/USSR agreement on limiting strategic nuclear weapons—the Strategic Arms Limitation Treaty, or SALT I.

The new agenda of the 1970s—environment and poverty

Given that peace studies had developed partly in response to Cold War tensions and the risk of global nuclear war, it might have been expected that it would have gone into decline in the wake of these improvements in East–West relations. In practice this did not happen, as other major international issues were coming to the fore that were to become central to the developing field.

By the end of the 1960s three international trends were becoming clear that were to have a substantial impact within peace studies. One was the widely held view that former colonies had successfully achieved political independence in the 1950s and 1960s but had certainly not achieved economic independence—the much-vaunted Development Decade of the 1960s has simply not seen the anticipated progress. The United Nations had established the UN Conference on Trade and Development in 1964 with the express aim of linking the need to achieve fair trading relations with enhancing development. UNCTAD met in Geneva in 1964, New Delhi in 1968 and Santiago, Chile, in 1972, but failed to have much impact on North–South trading relations. This was partly because of disunity on behalf of the Southern bloc of less developed countries, the Group of 77, but much more because key northern industrialized countries such as Britain, France, Germany the United States and Japan were simply not prepared to forgo their trading advantages. Commodity agreements, tariff preferences, compensatory finance initiatives and other vehicles for fair trade were simply not allowed much space on the international agenda.

Such a view, common in the newly developing field of development studies as well as within peace research, was regarded as a radical analysis by most mainstream economists. As far as the discipline of international relations was concerned, North–South relations were simply not important and received scant attention from most scholars, an aspect that to this day tends to differentiate peace researchers from most of the international relations community.

A second issue, surfacing initially in the late 1960s, was the state of the global environment, which came to the fore mainly as a result of ecological and toxicological studies on the impact of industrial societies on their immediate natural environments. Earlier concerns over pesticides developed into much wider critiques of the impact of unbridled economic growth through atmospheric and water pollution, land dereliction and resource depletion. Much of this concern was criticized on the grounds that it essentially focused on the parochial problems of industrialized states, with minimal concern for the much wider issues of global underdevelopment.

The first UN Conference on the Human Environment, in Stockholm in May 1972, met such objections by embracing the concerns of southern states and by placing emphasis on the possible limits to economic growth if the global ecosystem was to prove to be unable to cope with rapidly increasing human impacts. This suggested that such growth alone could not meet the needs of the majority of humankind in the South. Environmental security therefore had to be linked to development aspirations, and prospects for international development were necessarily linked to the asymmetric environmental impact of industrialized states. Otherwise, a world beset with deep socio-economic divisions that also had finite limits on its economic growth potential set by environmental constraints, would be a world of much potential violence, fragility and insecurity. This debate of thirty years ago is now being revisited with even greater urgency as the impact of climate change becomes rapidly more apparent, and the Persian Gulf, with its massive fossil fuel resources, becomes a locus not just of economic competition but for open warfare (see Case Study 3.1 Conflicts to come I—energy wars).

CASE STUDY 3.1

Conflicts to come I—energy wars

Whether or not the termination of the Saddam Hussein regime in Iraq had much to do with the control of Iraq's oil reserves, it is certainly the case that the United States acquired influence over oil reserves that are about four times as large as total US domestic reserves, including those of Alaska. Moreover, even though Iraq's reserves are substantial, they are just one part of a regional concentration that is quite remarkable. Just five Gulf states, Saudi Arabia, Iran, Iraq, Kuwait and the United Arab Emirates, together control well over 60% of known oil reserves, and there is believed to be considerable potential for further discoveries, specially in western Iraq.

During the latter part of the Cold War, the United States became particularly concerned about a possible Soviet threat to Gulf oil resources, and this resulted in the establishment of the Rapid Deployment Force at the end of the 1970s. Following the 1979–80 Iranian Revolution and the start of the 1980–88 Iran–Iraq War, the Rapid Deployment Force was elevated into a full unified military command, Central Command (CENTCOM), and it was this organization that fought the 1991 Iraq War and has been responsible for operations in Afghanistan and Iraq since 2001.

The key reason for potential conflict in the region is that all the world's major industrial regions, including Western Europe, the United States and East Asia, are becoming increasingly dependent on Gulf oil reserves as their own production decreases and demand rises. China, in particular, has been assiduous in cultivating links with Gulf producers, and has signed very large long-term agreements with Iran in recent years.

Meanwhile, the al-Qaida movement is quick to characterize the occupation of Iraq as a neo-Christian attempt to control an historic Islamic state. However realistic this portrayal is, it carries plenty of weight in the region, and has resulted in increased support for the movement. One of the key issues for the next two decades is whether there can be sustained international cooperation of the utilization of Gulf oil reserves, or whether the region will be a focus for conflict. This is, in any case, part of a wider problem of whether the global community can continue to rely on fossil fuels or whether the security implications of climate change will make that mode of living redundant (see Case Study 3.2 on Climate change).

Vietnam and the 'maximalist' agenda

Finally, one specific conflict, the Vietnam War, was to cause deep controversy as some radical peace researchers argued that the injustices were such that there could be occasions when violence could be justified in the pursuit of justice. That brief controversy was in the context of the development of a 'maximalist' agenda emerging in European peace research, especially with Johan Galtung's conception of structural violence (1969). This proposed that the condition of peace required not just the absence of overt violence but also of structural violence—the persistence of economic and social exploitation in societies that might otherwise be said to be at peace. In similar vein, Herman Schmid (1968) argued that much of peace research was not critically engaged with defining peaceful societies as entities in which justice genuinely prevailed. An absence of war could obscure deep injustices that made a mockery of notions of peace. Others engaged in peace research saw this as a constant expansion of the peace research agenda 'acquiring the qualities of an intellectual black hole wherein something vital, a praxeological edge or purpose, is lost' (Lawlor 1995).

This dispute, sometimes described as between maximalists and minimalists, has never been fully resolved but most peace researchers came to accept that, in addition to the original aim of seeking to prevent nuclear war, other themes were of legitimate concern for those working in the field. The primary issues were initially those of global North–South disparities and the risk of an environmental crisis but, significantly, a concern for gender inequalities also came to prominence rather earlier than in the fields of development studies or international relations.

New goals—equality, justice and dignity

By 1973, and as a result of such changes, the editors of the *Journal of Conflict Resolution* sought to broaden its original remit beyond its previous concentration on interstate conflict and the nuclear issue:

> " The threat of nuclear holocaust remains with us and may well continue to do so for centuries, but other problems are competing with deterrence and disarmament studies for our attention. This journal must also attend to international conflict over justice, equality, and human dignity; problems of conflict resolution for ecological balance and control are within our proper scope and especially suited for interdisciplinary attention. "
>
> **(*Journal of Conflict Resolution,* Vol 1, No 1, p. 5, 1983)**

By the end of the 1970s, this much broader focus was embedded in peace studies but was then overtaken by the development of the final and perhaps most dangerous phase of the Cold War. The Soviet invasion of Afghanistan, the Iranian Revolution and hostage crisis, the election of the Reagan and Thatcher governments and the deployment of new generations of strategic nuclear weapons all combined to give a renewed urgency to those very issues that peace researchers had largely eschewed. For the best part of a decade, many researchers returned to issues of deterrence and disarmament, contrasting their analysis markedly with that of international relations realists and, on occasions, earning the enmity of their own governments.

Even so, issues of environment and development continued to be addressed, and there was a substantial increase in research on techniques of mediation and other forms of conflict resolution, on peacekeeping and post-conflict peace-building (see Think Point 3.2). Partly because of this a number of peace studies centres not only survived the sudden ending of the Cold War in 1989–90 but were able to adjust to the post-Cold War world much easier than many of the international relations centres that were, to an extent, floundering in the face of such unexpected change.

KEY POINTS

- Peace studies sought to provide a non-state-centric and more global view of major issues of conflict.
- By the 1970s it was responding to issues of socio-economic divisions and environmental constraints.
- In the 1980s, in the final period of the Cold War, there was bitter opposition to what was sometimes seen as 'appeasement studies'.
- Within peace studies, one of the later developments was a major interest in conflict prevention, conflict resolution and peacekeeping.

What is peace studies now?

Peace studies in the early twenty-first century is an established and thriving field with a range of journals, a number of research institutes such as the Peace Research Institute of Oslo (PRIO) and the Stockholm International Peace Research Institute (SIPRI), many centres in universities and colleges, and an international body, the International Peace Research Association (IPRA). The UN University for Peace has been revitalized and now works from its campus in Costa Rica and in centres across the world, putting particular emphasis on aiding under-resourced universities in poorer countries to develop their own courses. Indeed, it is in countries of the South that there has been a real increase in interest in peace studies in the past ten years, with a particular concern with what peace studies can offer in countering violence and open conflict. Furthermore, since the effects of wars can be so much more long-lasting in poorer regions, there is an added impetus to work towards war termination, conflict resolution and peace-building.

What are the main characteristics of peace studies? Ramsbotham suggests a number of features that mark it out as a defined field of study (Rogers and Ramsbotham 1999).

1. *Underlying causes.* A concern to address the root causes of direct violence and to explore ways of overcoming structural inequalities and of promoting equitable and cooperative relations between and within human communities. This means that peace studies goes well beyond the absence of war to work towards societies that are intrinsically more peaceful. This means addressing a wide range of inequalities whether rooted in class, race or gender divisions, with these analysed at a range of levels from the individual and community through to the international.

2. *Interdiscipinary approaches.* A realization that an interdisciplinary response is essential, given the multi-faceted nature of violent conflict. The larger peace studies centres will have among their staff people drawn from political science, international relations, psychology, anthropology, economics, history, sociology and other disciplines. They may well have people trained originally in mathematics, physics or the biological sciences. This both leads to conceptual enrichment, but can also cause disputes about appropriate methodologies and theoretical frameworks.

3. *Non-violent transformations.* A search for peaceful ways to settle disputes and for non-violent transformation of potentially or actually violent situations. This does not mean endorsing the status quo, since unjust and oppressive systems are seen as some of the chief causes of violence and war. It does mean the comparative study of peaceful and non-peaceful processes of social and political change; and of ways to prevent the outbreak of violence, or, if it does break out, ways to mitigate it, bring it to an end and prevent its recurrence thereafter. Within these parameters there is continuing debate about the efficacy and legitimacy of the use of force in certain circumstances. This is especially true in the case of humanitarian intervention in internal conflicts.

4. *Multi-level analysis.* The embracing of a multi-level analysis at individual, group, state and inter-state levels in an attempt to overcome the institutionalized dichotomy between studies of 'internal' and 'external' dimensions that are seen to be inadequate for the prevailing patterns of conflict. This is seen as particularly significant given the relative decline of interstate conflict and the rise of sub-state conflict. It is also seen as relevant in analysing the tendency towards 'trans-state' conflict. This may include detention without trial, across state borders, of individuals who have status neither as conventional criminals nor as prisoners of war under the terms of the Geneva Conventions. This has become a feature of the global war on terror, as has the 'rendition' of individuals—their transfer to countries likely to use torture in extracting information.

5. *Global outlook.* The adoption of a global and multicultural approach, which would locate sources of violence globally and regionally as well as locally, and draw on conceptions of peace and non-violent social transformations from all cultures. Such an approach has become even more relevant as peace studies centres have increased in number in East and South Asia, Africa and Latin America.

6. *Analytical and normative.* An understanding that peace studies is both an analytic and a normative enterprise. While there has been a tendency to ground peace studies in quantitative research and comparative empirical study, the reality is that most scholars have been drawn to the field by ethical concerns and commitments. Deterministic ideas have been largely rejected, whether in realist or Marxist guises, with large-scale violence and war seen not as inevitable features of the international system, but as consequences of human actions and choices.

With ethical commitments among the core motivations of peace researchers, it can be argued that such an environment can result in the sloppy pursuit of causes with little concern for academic rigour. This was a particular issue in several countries in the 1980s (see Think Point 3.1: The war on peace studies), but the level of critical analysis of peace studies programmes actually helped ensure that unusually high standards had to be, and were, set.

7. *Theory and practice.* Linked to this is the close relationship between theory and practice in peace studies. While a clear distinction is persistently made between peace studies and peace activism, peace researchers very frequently engage systematically with non-government organizations, government departments and intergovernmental agencies. They frequently see this as part of a process of empirical testing of theoretical insights, regarding it also as a two-way process.

Many people working in the field regard the policy implications of their work as more significant than its reception among fellow academics. Given the modern era of 'research assessment' in some Western countries that is primarily geared to academic output in the conventional literature, this can be a disadvantage for the discipline. Furthermore, this 'engagement' with the policy process does not fit in with the prevailing academic culture in most Western countries, even if it is more commonly found in academic centres in the majority world.

THINK POINT 3.1

The war on peace studies

In the early years of the 1980s, Cold War tensions were particularly high. President Ronald Reagan had taken office in the United States in 1981, both the US and the Soviet Union were developing highly accurate 'first strike' intercontinental ballistic missiles and the UK government under Margaret Thatcher had decided to purchase the Trident submarine-launched ballistic missile. Britain was also to be the site of a new and highly accurate US system, the ground-launched cruise missile. Ninety-six of these were to be based at Greenham Common near Reading and another sixty-four at Molesworth near Huntingdon but, at times of crisis, they would be dispersed on mobile launchers.

There was a strong perception of renewed danger, with a palpable risk of all-out nuclear war, and this fed into a burgeoning anti-nuclear movement across Western Europe, together with a renewed interest in peace studies, especially in schools but also in universities. In Britain, political polarization was particularly evident and conservative opponents of peace studies viewed it as unpatriotic appeasement studies, one noble lord describing the Peace Studies Department at Bradford University as a 'rest home for urban guerrillas'. Books and pamphlets were written about the subversive threat stemming from the study of peace, amidst claims that peace researchers were intrinsically pro-Soviet.

The opposition was focused very largely on politicians and rarely stretched to the armed forces—indeed the defence colleges were keen to debate the issues openly and frequently asked peace researchers to lecture to their students. The 'war on peace studies' lasted from around 1981 to 1987, but died away as the Cold War came to an end. Indeed, Peace Studies attracted much greater attention over the following few years as much of the many other areas of peace research, such as the theory and practice of peace-keeping and issues of environmental security, came to the fore.

Some of the academics involved in peace research at that time now reflect that the 'war on peace studies' was very good for the emerging discipline. As well as attracting some particularly able students into the area, the constant critical scrutiny of research output, especially on areas such as armaments and arms control, meant that standards of work had to be particularly high. Peace researchers became subject to far tougher scrutiny of their work than most other scholars in international relations and many of them now think that they became better academics as a result.

KEY POINTS

- Core elements of modern peace studies include a concern with underlying causes of conflict and the search for non-violent approaches to conflict transformation.
- It remains an interdisciplinary field that embraces multi-level analysis from the individual to the international.
- It is both analytical and normative, frequently involving ethical motivations on the part of students and researchers.
- Peace studies engages persistently with opinion formers and policy makers.

Responding to the new security challenges

Given these characteristics, how relevant is the peace studies agenda today and how valuable might it be in responding to the major issues of conflict and insecurity that might face us in the coming decades? To answer these questions we need to analyse the main security challenges likely to face us and then look at the main attributes of peace studies in terms of its possible contribution.

Global security during the forty-five years of the Cold War was dominated by the East–West confrontation but was also a period of major conflicts in many parts of the world with over 100 wars leading directly to more than 20 million deaths and well over 50 million injuries, as well as much more suffering in post-war environments especially in impoverished communities. The ending of the Cold War, while leading to the settlement of some long-standing disputes, also increased instability, not least in the Caucasus and the Balkans, and there were also continuing tensions in the Israeli/Palestinian confrontation, the 1991 Iraq War and the devastating conflicts of the Great Lakes region of Central Africa.

By the end of the 1990s, a number of these conflicts had been transformed into an uneasy peace, and others such as Northern Ireland and Sri Lanka also showed some prospects of settlement (see Think Point 3.2—A more peaceful world?). Against this, the attacks in New York and Washington in September 2001 were to herald a vigorous military reaction from the United States, leading to the termination of regimes in Afghanistan and Iraq and the beginnings of potentially long-drawn-out conflicts in both countries.

While these were immediate issues of conflict in the early twenty-first century, they were evolving in an international context in which two much broader issues are becoming salient. The first is the deep and enduring inequalities in the global distribution of wealth and economic power, likely to ensure that, within thirty years, one seventh of the world's population will control three-quarters of the wealth, largely but not entirely on a geographical basis. While there have been immense efforts at development, almost entirely from within the poorer countries themselves, the global picture is one of enduring disempowerment and increasing socio-economic polarization. This is not just the case at the global level but is particularly marked in countries, such as China, that may be experiencing rapid economic growth but with most of the increases in wealth being concentrated among a minority of the population.

Furthermore, environmental constraints are likely to exacerbate the effects of human activity on the global ecosystem, making it increasingly difficult for human well-being to be improved by conventional economic growth. The combination of wealth–poverty disparities and limits to growth is likely to lead to a crisis of unsatisfied expectations within an increasingly informed global majority of the disempowered.

THINK POINT 3.2

A more peaceful world?

In the years since the 9/11 attacks, most people in Western countries would probably say that the world has become distinctly more dangerous. It is not just the memory of the planes crashing into the World Trade Center followed by the collapse of the towers, but it is also the impact of the subsequent wars in Afghanistan and Iraq. With 30,000 civilian deaths and the United States forces mired in a violent insurgency in Iraq, as well as numerous paramilitary attacks in Madrid, Bali, London, Istanbul and many other cities there is a presumption of an unstable and fragile world in which sudden violence can break out when least expected.

This may actually be an illusion, as some research suggests that the world has actually become more peaceful since the end of the Cold War. The *2005 Human Security Report*, for example, cites a 40% decrease in armed conflicts overall since the early 1990s and an 80% decrease in major conflicts. The study was undertaken at the Liu Institute for Global Issues at the University of British Columbia in Vancouver, and the resulting report is a powerful antidote to many common assumptions.

As well as an overall decrease in conflicts, the report points to a decline in the number of autocratic regimes, with their penchant for human rights abuses, and also claims that an expansion in UN peacekeeping operations, as well as a much greater emphasis on conflict prevention, have combined to good effect. The results may seem surprising but are supported by a number of similar studies from the Center for International Development and Conflict Management at the University of Maryland.

In addition to the impact of conflict prevention and peacekeeping operations, other factors may be at work. The Cold War era was characterized by numerous 'proxy wars' fought on an East–West axis but rarely involving the two superpowers in direct conflict. These included Korea, Vietnam, Afghanistan and the Horn of Africa. Furthermore, the early part of the Cold War period coincided with numerous wars of decolonization, including French Indo-China, Malaya, Kenya, Cyrus and Algeria. Almost all the colonial conflicts had ended by the 1970s.

There were also particular conflicts associated with the ending of the Cold War, especially in the Caucasus, as well as the break-up of Yugoslavia. These had reduced if not ended by the turn of the century, and even the enduring conflicts in Northern Ireland, Sri Lanka and the Basque region of Spain seemed to be winding down. When all these factors are put together, it is more easy to understand the results from the *Human Security Report*. The question remains as to whether this is a long-term trend or a welcome but potentially short-lived period of relative calm before new conflicts kick in, especially over issues such as energy resources and climate change.

On the basis of these issues, three broad conflict trends are probable. The first arises from a greater likelihood of increased human migration through economic, social and environmental motives. Focusing on regions of relative wealth, this is already leading to shifts in the political spectrum in recipient regions, including increased nationalist tendencies and cultural conflict, not least in Western Europe and Australasia. Such tendencies are often most pronounced in the most vulnerable and disempowered populations within the recipient regions. If, as seems probable, climate changes induce a partial 'drying out' of the tropical land masses (see Case Study 3.2: Conflicts to come II—climate change) then the migratory pressures will be greatly accelerated.

Secondly, it is probable that environmental and resource conflict will escalate. This may be local or regional, on issues such as food, land, fresh water or marine resources, and global on issues such as fossil fuel and mineral resources. The Persian Gulf, as the repository of most of the world's remaining reserves of fossil fuels, is likely to be a particular focus for competition and conflict (see Case Study 3.1).

CASE STUDY 3.2

Conflicts to come II—climate change

Although climate change (previously termed global warming) was seen as an important issue by the early 1990s, it was expected that the major effects would be felt by the richer countries of the North and South in temperate latitudes. Countries such as Britain might experience warmer, wetter and windier weather, Spain, Portugal, Southern France, Italy and Greece might get warmer and drier, but at least they would have the wealth to make the adaptations necessary to counter such effects.

There was also a fear that sea level rise might affect coastal cities, including tropical cities such as Mumbai, Kolkata and Manila, and that tropical storms might become more violent. These were serious matters and formed powerful arguments for moving away form excessive dependence on fossil fuels, but they were not necessarily world-shattering in their potential effects.

By the mid-1990s, though, some of the climate modelling was showing a disturbing picture of much greater effects on tropical climates than had previously been thought likely. In particular, there was a growing likelihood that climate change would have a major impact on rainfall distribution across the tropics and sub-tropics, the main effect being a tendency for rainfall to decrease substantially over these land masses and increase over the world's oceans and over the polar regions (Hind 1995).

If this does happen, and the timescale is over perhaps 3–5 decades, then the effects will be profound. The majority of the world's population, well over four billion people, live in the tropical and sub-tropical land masses, with almost all of them dependent on locally grown food. If the tropical regions 'dry out', then there will be a substantial decrease in the 'ecological carrying-capacity' of some of the world's richest croplands. If this happens, then the effects will be massive, not just in terms of increases in famine and malnutrition, but in increased migratory pressures as many millions of people seek to move to countries where they can survive. The phenomenon of climate change and the tropical land masses may become one of the key security issues of the mid-twenty-first century. Countering such effects over the next decade or so, and moving more insistently towards sustainable economies, could be one of the greatest single contributions to ensuring a more peaceful and stable world.

Finally, and probably most important, competitive and violent responses of the disempowered should be expected within and between states and also in the form of transnational movements. The Zapatista revolt in Southern Mexico, the earlier Shining Path guerrilla movement in Peru, the recent neo-Maoist rebellion in Nepal and disempowerment responses in North Africa, the Middle East and South Asia may all be early examples of a developing trend, not infrequently exacerbated by political, religious and nationalist fundamentalisms. This is linked to underlying historically conditioned weaknesses in many post-colonial states, struggling as they are to accommodate twin pressures of globalization and fragmentation, and a prey to sectarian and factional exploitation. Increased internal political tensions, particularly secessionist movements, in populous states such as China, India and Indonesia, would have very wide repercussions.

The key development that links with socio-economic divisions and environmental constraints is the marked improvement in education, literacy and communications across much of the majority world in the past forty years. Achieved largely through indigenous efforts, primary-level education is now much more prevalent than at the end of the colonial period, and this has been accompanied by substantial improvements in levels of literacy. While male literacy levels increased first, levels of female literacy are now starting to catch up.

Coupled with these changes, there has been an explosion of technological change in relation to radio, television and the print media. For much of the world's 'data-poor' majority, the impact of the web, e-mail and even DVDs is still to come, but the changes that have already taken place mean that there is a much greater awareness of world developments. The implications of this are fundamental, in that there is a much greater recognition among the disempowered majority of the world's population of that very disempowerment. The end result is not so much a revolution of rising expectations, a feature of consumerism in the 1970s, as a revolution of frustrated expectations as the levels of exclusion become more readily apparent.

Moreover, the development of non-Western satellite news channels such as al-Jazeera means that reporting of events in Iraq and other countries of the Middle East is no longer under the influence of local elites and therefore subject to censorship. Nor is it more widely dominated by transnational broadcasting organizations that may provide minimal coverage to their international audiences except in instances of major violence (see Case Study 3.3: War, peace and the media—the al-Jazeera effect).

Consequences of the effects of marginalization are legion, from the high levels of urban crime in many Southern cities, the need for heavily protected gated communities for the elite rich, the outbreak of violence in France in late 2005, through to some of the radical and extreme social movements in Nepal and elsewhere. Although the al-Qaida movement may be rooted in South-West Asia and specific to extreme interpretations of one religious tradition, its evolution into a transnational phenomenon owes much to the persistent publicising of the human consequences of the war on terror, not least in Iraq.

A choice of responses

Responses to socio-economic divisions and environmental constraints might best take the form of consistent cooperation for sustainable development, including debt relief, trade reform and development assistance at a level much higher than that

CASE STUDY 3.3

War, peace and the media—the al-Jazeera effect

Although the world wide web, e-mail, DVDs and mobile phones have all had a major effect on communicating issues of conflict and peace to wider audiences, one of the other notable developments has been the rise of independent satellite TV news channels such as al-Jazeera, based in Qatar, and al-Arabiya, based in Dubai.

Al-Jazeera, in particular, has had a transforming effect in reporting regional conflicts, especially in Israel/Palestine and Iraq, but it is also notable for having free-flowing debates on major political and social issues that many of the region's ruling elites find distinctly uncomfortable.

At the start of the current Iraq War, in March and April 2003, many of the Western media outlets had the opportunity to 'embed' reporters and camera crews with US military units, accompanying them as they raced towards Baghdad and recording the remarkable results of their firepower. There was also occasional coverage of collateral damage and civilian casualties, although much of this was self-censored because of the horror of the images. Al-Jazeera, on the other hand, was persistent in its coverage of such effects, especially in Baghdad, and earned the enmity of the coalition authorities because of its insistence on screening images of the dead and injured.

Across the Middle East it now has tens of millions of viewers, runs Arabic and English websites that are regular sources of information across the world and, as of late 2005, plans an English TV News channel to supplement its existing Arabic service. Such has been its impact that the BBC World Service plans a competing Arabic service, cutting some of its European output to allow the funding of the new venture—one of the most significant indications of the growing importance of the Middle East in general and the Persian Gulf in particular.

of recent years, coupled with a multiplicity of programmes for conflict prevention and resolution as embodied in the UN Agenda for Peace.

They might, on the other hand, take the form of a vigorous programme of maintaining the status quo, ensuring that the wealthy sectors of humankind maintain their privileged position by appropriate trading and financial measures, backed up by military force where necessary. Described as 'liddism', or keeping the lid on a potentially fractured international system, this would appear to be the current trend, not least in terms of the US-led response to the 9/11 attacks. The consequence of this might well be Brooks's fear, expressed thirty years ago, of 'a crowded glowering planet of massive inequalities of wealth buttressed by stark force and endlessly threatened by desperate people in the global ghettoes . . . ' (Brooks 1974).

By late 2005, some four years after the 9/11 attacks, the prevailing security paradigm was dominated very much by the United States and buttressed by stark force. Two regimes had been terminated, over 30,000 civilians had been killed in the process, 15,000 people were detained without trial and torture had become accepted as an instrument of Western security policy. Even so, the al-Qaida movement remained highly active, with associates capable of mounting attacks across the world at a level substantially higher than in the four years preceding 9/11, and US forces were deeply mired in insurgencies in Iraq and Afghanistan.

Whether this paradigm will collapse under the weight of its own inadequacies or whether it will survive and prosper will depend on the further evolution of the '**global war on terror**' but may also depend on the degree of critical analysis of its underlying assumptions, coupled with the promotion of viable alternatives that might be undertaken by a vigorous academic community.

This is a challenge for the international relations community as a whole, and the peace studies community in particular. The short-term responses include the principal *Agenda for Peace* peace support elements, themselves in part drawn from peace research terminology, such as crisis prevention, peace-keeping, peace-making and the shorter-term elements in post-settlement peace-building. This also involves ethically based intervention and regional and global arms control and demilitarization. They are required of an international community of states that shows little evidence of wisdom or leadership and consequently places most responsibility on an under-resourced UN system. While improvements in efficiency and capability must come from within the UN, the NGO role is substantial, especially in the more powerful states of the UN, with improved links between NGOs and the academic community an essential part of the process.

There are longer-term processes involved in conflict resolution and conflict transformation (see Think Point 3.3: Conflict resolution). This is a wide agenda, but now quite well understood and reasonably clearly focused, involving contextual, structural, relational and cultural elements in the analysis of protracted social conflict with, beyond this, an increasing need for fundamental responses at the global level.

KEY POINTS

- Major issues for the future centre on the effects of a combination of socio-economic divisions and environmental constraints.
- The 9/11 attacks and the subsequent war on terror have yet to address the underlying reasons for current perceptions of insecurity.
- Responding to a potentially fragile and insecure international system will require sustained analysis combined with persistent efforts to suggest viable alternatives to the current security paradigm.

THINK POINT 3.3

Conflict resolution

The area of study and practice usually grouped under the term 'conflict resolution' has been one of the fastest growing aspects of peace studies in the past two decades, but has not been without its controversies. Involving such processes as mediation, conflict transformation and post-conflict peace-building, it has been an active field of academic study as well as burgeoning into an 'industry' involving non-government organizations and international agencies.

Two problems have emerged, one theoretical and one practical. At the theoretical level, some critical theorists have argued that conflict resolution is palliative rather than transformative—being concerned with a 'sticking plaster' approach that may appear to promote peace but does not address underlying reasons for conflict. In a sense this is a replay of the 'maximalist' controversy of the 1970s.

At the practical level, many of the organizations attempting to resolve conflicts, at whatever level, need to demonstrate success, not least to ensure their continuing sources of funding. There can therefore be a tendency to overdo their claims of progress. In practice, the best forms of mediatory intervention are those with very modest expectations of success and an ability to remain unpublicized. Some of the 'peace churches' such as the Quakers have a good record in this respect.

As to the wider criticism, many peace researchers would argue that conflict resolution should properly be seen as a specific and integral part of the peace studies tradition. As Ramsbotham, Woodhouse and Miall (2005) argue: 'We suggest that peace and conflict research is part of an emancipatory discourse and practice which is making a valuable and defining contribution to emerging norms of democratic, just and equitable systems of global governance. We argue that conflict resolution has a role to play in the radical negotiation of these norms, so that international conflict management is grounded in the needs of those who are the victims of conflict and who are frequently marginalized from conventional power structures.'

Conclusion

If the analysis offered in this chapter of a polarized, constrained and potentially fragile and unstable world is correct, then the issue of rich–poor confrontation is likely to acquire a far greater saliency in future. This will demand a comprehensive rethinking of concepts of security, incorporating unprecedented cooperation for sustainable international economic development and environmental management. This needs to be paralleled by progressive demilitarization linked to the establishment of regional and global conflict prevention processes. For peace researchers there is now an even greater imperative for them to deepen their understanding of the interconnected problems of international economic relations, the possibilities of sustainable development and their relationship to security. Peace studies has developed over the past half century and has seen the rigidities and dangers of the Cold War evolve into a more uncertain and unpredictable world. In its own development it has embraced a strong interdisciplinary outlook, a consciously global orientation and a determined linkage between theory and practice. While it has sought to respond to the problems of conflict in the past fifty years, in all probability, its greatest challenges are yet to come.

QUESTIONS

What was the impetus for the development of peace studies in the 1950s?

Why did peace studies develop beyond its Cold War focus and how did it come to put an emphasis an wider issues such as socio-economic divisions and environmental constraints?

Why was there such bitter opposition to peace studies in the 1980s and how did it affect the subsequent development of peace studies?

Is it possible for peace studies to be both analytical and normative or does this produce irresolvable tensions?

Should students of peace studies engage with policy makers or should they concentrate on academic discourse?

Should peace studies explore underlying causes of conflict or should its main emphasis be on more immediate responses to specific conflict situations?

Is the post 9/11 security paradigm of rigorous control of threats an adequate response?

Is climate change a threat to security?

How are 24-hour news reporting and the evolution of the internet affecting the coverage of conflict?

To what extent have the conflicts in the Persian Gulf since 1980 been about the control of oil?

FURTHER READING

- **Black, Jeremy (1998), *Why Wars Happen*, London: Reaktion Books.** A deeply informed book covering five centuries and using a remarkable range of resources.
- **Booth, Ken and Dunne, Tim (eds.) (2002), *Worlds in Collision: Terror and the Future of Global Order*, London: Palgrave.** Responses of a wide range of scholars and analysts to the 9/11 attacks.
- **Curtis, Mark (2003), *Web of Deceit: Britain's Real Role in the World*, London: Vintage.** One of the best examples of careful empirical research combined with critical analysis.
- **Graham, G. (1997), *Ethics and International Relations*, Oxford: Blackwell.** A stimulating text raising many issues significant in peace studies.
- **Jeong, Ho-Won (2000), *Peace and Conflict Studies: An Introduction*, London: Ashgate.** A good introductory text.
- **Kegley, Charles and Wittkopf, Eugene (2006), *World Politics: Trend and Transformation*, 10th edn, New York: St Martin's Press.** One of the few international relations textbooks that avoids an excessively Western ethnocentric style.
- **Liu Institute for Global Issues (2005), *The Human Security Report 2005*, Oxford: Oxford University Press.** The first of a series of annual reports on international security trends.
- **Myrdal, Alva (1980), *The Game of Disarmament: how the United States and Russia run the arms race*, Nottingham: Spokesman Books.** A definitive and well-informed account of the Cold War arms race and of processes of international militarization.
- **Ramsbotham, Oliver, Woodhouse, Tom and Miall, Hugh (2005), *Contemporary Conflict Resolution*, Cambridge and Malden: Polity Press.** The second edition of what has rapidly become the standard work on conflict resolution.

IMPORTANT WEBSITES

- **http://www.upeace.org** The UN University for Peace, centred near San Jose in Costa Rica with units across the world.
- **http://sipri.se/** The Stockholm International Peace Research Institute (SIPRI) is one of the world's main centres for the analysis of arms and disarmament.
- **http://prio.no/** The Peace Research Institute of Oslo (PRIO) is noted, in particular, for its work on civil wars.
- **http://brad.ac.uk/acad/peace/** Currently the world's largest university centre for peace studies.
- **http://incore.ulst.acad.uk/** INCORE (International Conflict research) is a joint project of the University of Ulster and the UN University.
- **http://humansecurityreport.info/** The site for the new series of Human Security reports from the Liu Centre for Global Issues at the University of British Columbia, Vancouver, Canada.
- **http://opendemocracy.net** One of the liveliest open source sites, especially on international issues.
- **http://fpif.org** Foreign Policy in Focus is a US site providing wide-ranging analysis on international security and foreign policy themes.

Visit the Online Resource Centre that accompanies this book for lots of interesting additional material: www.oxfordtextbooks.co.uk/orc/collins/

4 Critical Security Studies: A Schismatic History

DAVID MUTIMER

Chapter Contents

Reader's Guide

This chapter provides a partial history of a label. It is partial both in that it is not, and cannot be, complete, and in that I am both the author of, and participant in, the history. It is therefore partial in the way all other history is partial. The label is 'Critical Security Studies'. The chapter tells a story of the origin of the label and the way it has developed and fragmented in the past ten years. It sets out the primary claims of the major divisions that have emerged within the literatures to which the label has been applied: constructivism, Critical Theory, and post-structuralism. Ultimately, the chapter suggests that Critical Security Studies needs to foster an 'ethos of critique' in the study of security, and that the chapter is an instance of that ethos directed at Critical Security Studies itself.

Introduction: 'Follow the sign of the gourd'

Very soon after being identified as the Messiah in *Monty Python's Life of Brian*, Brian is chased by a growing crowd of would-be followers. In his haste to get away, Brian drops the gourd he has just bought and loses one of his sandals. Several of the followers remove one of their shoes and hop about on one foot, convinced this is what their newly found Messiah has told them to do. One follower picks up the shoe and shouts: follow the sign of the shoe. Another picks up the gourd, shouting: follow the sign of the gourd. Perhaps predictably, within seconds, those hopping are fighting those who are following the shoe who are fighting those who are following the gourd. Brian's 'ministry' has splintered into sects before it has even had the chance to establish itself as a ministry. The Python gang were, of course, satirizing the tendency of religious movements to fragment, as they had at the outset of the film satirized the similar tendency of political movements: 'Are you the Judean People's Front?' 'Fuck off! We're the People's Front of Judea . . . Judean People's Front . . . SPLITTERS!'

Sadly, perhaps, this all too human tendency to fragment into ever-smaller and more exclusive and exclusionary clubs affects academic movements every bit as much as it does religious and political. Any society of ideas is, in addition, a potential source and expression of power. It provides the intellectual resources around which to mobilize people and resources of other kinds: whether these are tithes /alms, ballots/arms, or even tenure/articles. None of this should be in any way surprising to those who work within the area covered by this chapter. While the chapter will show the divisions into which critical security studies has rapidly fallen, one of the shared commitments of the work it will discuss is to the political potency of ideas. The social world is produced in and through the ideas that make it meaningful, which are themselves necessarily social. A consequence of this observation is that study of the social world is inextricably bound up with the world it studies; it is part of the productive set of ideas that make the world.

This chapter provides a partial history of a label. It is partial both in that it is not, and cannot be, complete, and, in that I am both the author of, and a participant in, the history. It is therefore partial in the way all other history is partial. The label is 'Critical Security Studies'.[1] It is a label that has (one of) its origins in a conference held at York University in Canada in 1994. As a label, it has been fought over rather more than it has been applied. It does not denote a coherent set of views, an 'approach' to security, rather it indicates a desire. It is a desire to move beyond the strictures of security as it was studied and practised in the Cold War, and in particular a desire to make that move in terms of some form of critique. It is a desire articulated in the first line of the first book bearing the title 'Critical Security Studies': 'This book emerged out of a desire to contribute to the development of a selfconsciously critical perspective within security studies' (Williams and Krause 1997: vii).

The form of security studies against which Critical Security Studies was directed has been neatly captured by one of the proponents of the traditional approach:

> "Security studies may be defined as the study of the threat, use, and control of military force. It explores the conditions that make the use of force more likely, the ways that the use of force affects individuals, states, and societies, and the specific policies that states adopt in order to prepare for, prevent, or engage in war."
>
> **(Walt 1991: 212)**

[1]When I refer to the label or to the 'field' of inquiry that is increasingly gathered under that label, I will capitalize Critical Security Studies. Otherwise, I leave the terms in the lower case.

KEY QUOTES 4.1

Definitions: Critical Security Studies

Critical Security Studies has proven reasonably resistant to clear definition. This has been largely intentional, as the provision of a definition is limiting in a way that those behind the *Critical Security Studies* text wished to avoid. Nevertheless, there are some definitions in the literature:

Williams and Krause (1997)

'Our appending of the term *critical* to *security studies* is meant to imply more an orientation toward the discipline than a precise theoretical label, and we adopt a small-c definition of *critical*. . . . Perhaps the most straightforward way to convey our sense of how *critical* should be understood in this volume is Robert Cox's distinction between problem-solving and critical theory: the former takes "prevailing social and power relationships and the institutions into which they are organised . . . as the given framework for action", while the latter "calls them into question by concerning itself with their origins and how they might be in the process of changing". Our approach to security studies . . . thus begins from an analysis of the claims that make the discipline possible—not just its claims about the world but also its underlying epistemology and ontology, which prescribe what it means to *make* sensible claims about the world.'

Buzan, Wæver and de Wilde (1998)

'An emerging school of "critical security studies" (CSS) wants to challenge conventional security studies by applying postpositivist perspectives, such as critical theory and postructuralism. Much of this work . . . deals with the social construction of security, but CSS mostly has the intent (known from poststructuralism as well as from constructivism in international relations) of showing that change is possible because things are socially constituted.'

Erikkson (1999)

'Critical security studies deal with the social construction of security. The rhetorical nature of "threat discourses" is examined and criticized. . . . Critical security studies consider not only threats as a construction, but the objects of security as well. . . . Critical security studies . . . have an emancipatory goal.'

Booth (2005)

'Critical security studies is an issue-area study, developed within the academic discipline of international politics, concerned with the pursuit of critical knowledge about security in world politics. Security is conceived comprehensively, embracing theories and practices at multiple levels of society, from the individual to the whole human species. "Critical" implies a perspective that seeks to stand outside prevailing structures, processes, ideologies, and orthodoxies while recognizing that all conceptualizations of security derive from particular political/theoretical positions; critical perspectives do not make a claim to objective truth but rather seek to provide deeper understandings of prevailing attitudes and behavior with a view to developing more promising ideas by which to overcome structural human wrongs.'

The focus on the threat, use and control of military force imposed a series of important strictures on the study of security in this period. Military forces are generally the preserve of states, and what is more, there is a normative assumption that they *should* be the preserve of states, even when they are not. Indeed, our common definition of the state is that institution which has a monopoly on the legitimate means of violence. Therefore, by studying the threat, use and control of military force, security studies privileges the position of the state. Furthermore, such an approach implies that the state is the primary object which is to be secured—that is, the state is the referent object of security. Finally, and most obviously, thinking of security as the threat, use and control of military force reduces security to *military* security, and renders other forms of security as something else.

The various scholars who followed the desire toward a critical security study were troubled by all three of these major assumptions underlying the conventional study of security. They wondered, first of all, whether our concern needed to be only on the state and its security. What of the security of people living within states? The standard assumption of security studies is that the people are secure if the state is secure, but those drawn towards Critical Security Studies wondered about those times when this was not the case: when states ignored the security of some of their people, when they actively oppressed some of their people, or when the state lacked the capacity to provide security for its people. They were therefore led to wonder whether we should be thinking about referent objects other than the state.

Questioning the referent object of security leads inexorably to questioning the exclusive focus on the threat, use and control of military force. Large, powerful, stable states such as those in which 'security studies' tended to be practiced—the United States, the United Kingdom or Canada—may only be seriously threatened by war. On the other hand, other potential referent objects, particularly people and their collectives, can be threatened in all sorts of ways. Therefore, once you question the referent object of security, you must also question the *nature and scope* of security, and thus of security studies.

Not everyone who questioned the referent object and the nature and scope of security would be drawn to the desire for a critical security study, however. That desire was driven by a recognition of the power of ideas, and thus a discomfort with the way traditional security studies focused on the state. The concern was not that there were other objects to be secured in other ways, but rather that the *effect* of studying security as the threat, use and control of military force tended *in and of itself* to support and legitimate the power of the state. While other scholars sought to broaden and deepen security studies to consider other referents and other threats, those whose desire ran to a 'self-consciously critical perspective' were centrally concerned with the politics of knowledge. Security studies as it had been practised provided intellectual and, ultimately, moral support to the most powerful institution in contemporary politics: the state. Those drawn to a critical security study sought a different security politics as well as a different security scholarship.

The remainder of the chapter traces what happened as scholars acted on this desire for a self-consciously critical security study. In doing so, it sets out the major fault lines that have emerged among those initially animated by this shared desire. The signs that have driven these fault lines are not simply Monty Python's signs of the shoe and the gourd, but rather represent disagreements about the nature of critique and thus of different forms of critical security study. Thus, while the chapter outlines the sects into which critical desire has fractured, it also sets out a range of answers to the question of what critical security studies might be.

My history of these splits begins in 1994.

Toronto desire: *Critical Security Studies*

In May 1994, a small conference was held at York University in Toronto entitled *Strategies in Conflict: Critical Approaches to Security Studies*. It brought together from around the world a variety of scholars, both junior and senior, with interests in security and with a concern about the direction of security studies in the early post-Cold War era. It was in the course of the discussions at and around that conference that the label 'Critical Security Studies' started to be applied to the intellectual project that drew the participants to the conference, and it was used as the title of the book, edited by Keith Krause and Michael C. Williams, that the conference produced: *Critical Security Studies: Concepts and Cases*.

The conference and book were an expression of the desire for self-consciously critical perspectives on security, but they both worked extremely hard to avoid articulating a single perspective in response to that desire: 'Our appending of the term *critical* to *security studies* is meant to imply more an orientation toward the discipline than a precise theoretical label . . . ' (Williams and Krause 1997: x-xi). The book therefore served to launch the label Critical Security Studies, but not to fill it with a precise content (see Key Quotes 4.1 for some of the ways in which Critical Security Studies *has* come to be defined). Metaphorically, it threw open the doors of the church of critical security and tried to welcome the followers of the shoe *and* the gourd, and even those hopping around on one foot.

In their contribution to that volume, Krause and Williams aimed to set out the scope of a critical security study, and it has served as a touchstone in the further development of Critical Security Studies. They began their case for Critical Security Studies from the concerns with the traditional conception of security I recounted above. In particular, Krause and Williams began by questioning the referent object of security: who or what is to be secured. The traditional answer to this question is that the referent object is the state: security refers to protecting the state from external threats, and the people living within the territory of the state are considered secure to the degree that the state is secure. As Krause and Williams put it, such a view largely reduces security for the individual to citizenship: 'Yet, while to be a people without a state often remains one of the most insecure conditions of modern life (witness the Kurds or the Palestinians), this move obscures the ways in which citizenship is also at the heart of many structures of insecurity and how security in the contemporary world may be threatened by dynamics far beyond these parameters' (Krause and Williams 1997b: 43). If the focus on state as a referent object is insufficient, what if we adjust our focus to the individual human being, or perhaps to the community in which humans live? What, indeed, if we ask about the security of humanity as a whole, beyond rather than within the states in which most of us now find ourselves? These are the questions Krause and Williams pose as the foundation of Critical Security Studies. They argue that posing such questions opens a broad and complex agenda for security studies, an agenda that is largely hidden by the traditional focus on the state and the military. Suddenly we can ask about the ways states pose threats to their own people, as well as asking about the responsibility for providing security when the state does not. This question of the responsibility of an international community for the security of those inside a state cannot be seriously posed within traditional security studies, and yet only a few years after the Toronto conference, an International Commission on Intervention and State Sovereignty proclaimed a 'responsibility to protect' those subject to radical insecurity within their own states (see Background 4.1).

While the broadening of the security agenda was an important feature of the foundations that Krause and Williams were attempting to lay, rather more significant was the epistemological implications they drew from the challenges to the traditional conception of security. They argue that by looking at individuals, and particularly the communities in which they live, a critical security study has to take seriously the ideas, norms and values which constitute the communities which are to be secured. Traditional security studies treats its referent object as just that: an object. The state is a 'thing' that is found, out there in the world, and subject to objective study by security analysts. By contrast, Krause and Williams argue that thinking of the varied communities in which people live requires an interpretive shift, a recognition that ideas (at least in part) constitute communities and that therefore the ideas of analysts are not entirely separable from the objects studied.

Having opened the doors of what they hoped would be a broad church, Krause and Williams set out the agenda of what would attract scholars to the service. Critical Security Studies would:

- question the referent object of security: while states were clearly important, human beings were both secured and rendered insecure in ways other than by states and military force. Critical Security

BACKGROUND 4.1

The responsibility to protect

In 1999 and 2000 the UN Secretary General challenged the members of the UN to address the questions raised by recent incidents of genocide and ethnic cleansing: Somalia, Rwanda, Bosnia and Kosovo. In particular, in a world of sovereign states, what could and should the international community do when those inside the state were subject to extreme abuses of their human rights? In response, funded largely by the Government of Canada, the International Commission on Intervention and State Sovereignty (ICISS) was formed, and in 2001 the Commission released its report, *The Responsibility to Protect*.

Synopsis of *The Responsibility to Protect*

Basic principles

A. ***State sovereignty implies responsibility***, and the primary responsibility for the protection of its people lies with the state itself.

B. Where a population is suffering serious harm, as a result of internal war, insurgency, repression or state failure, and the state in question is unwilling or unable to halt or avert it, the principle of non-intervention yields to the international responsibility to protect.

Elements

The responsibility to protect embraces three specific responsibilities:

A. ***The responsibility to prevent***: to address both the root causes and direct causes of internal conflict and other man-made crises putting populations at risk.

B. ***The responsibility to react***: to respond to situations of compelling human need with appropriate measures, which may include coercive measures like sanctions and international prosecution, and in extreme cases military intervention.

C. ***The responsibility to rebuild***: to provide, particularly after a military intervention, full assistance with recovery, reconstruction and reconciliation, addressing the causes of the harm the intervention was designed to halt or avert.

(International Commission on Intervention and State Sovereignty 2001: XI)

Studies would engage in research that recognized this observation and explored its implications;

- consider security as more than just military security: once the referent object was opened up, so too were the questions of what rendered referents insecure, and how security was to be achieved, both for the state and for any other referent objects; and
- change the way security was studied, as the objectivity assumed by traditional approaches to security is untenable. Indeed, once you consider the way human communities are constituted by ideas, norms and values, it becomes clear that this applies even to the state, and so critical security studies becomes a post-positivist form of scholarship.

With the *Critical Security Studies* text, a range of scholars responded to this invitation in a variety of different ways, laying the foundations for the variation in Critical Security Studies we continue to see.

When students and scholars discuss the breadth of the initial desire of *Critical Security Studies*, they will often make almost immediate reference to Mohammed Ayoob's contribution: 'Defining Security: A subaltern realist perspective' (Ayoob 1997: 121–46). Ayoob focuses on the first of Krause and Williams' challenges, and questions the assumed nature of the state in traditional security studies. He argues that the state in traditional security studies is the state of the advanced, industrial north. He seeks to expand that notion of security to account for the security concerns of the majority of the world's states, concerns that 'mirror the major security concerns evinced by most Western European state makers during the sixteenth to the nineteenth centuries' (Ayoob 1997: 121–22). Thus, while Ayoob questions the nature of the referent object of traditional security studies, he does not introduce alternative possibilities nor does he inquire very far into other means of providing security and certainly does not contest the epistemological nature of security study.

RBJ Walker's contribution to the volume is exemplary of a much more radical break with the traditions of security studies understood as the threat, use and control of military force. Walker seeks to understand the conditions which make possible certain ways of thinking and speaking about security, and in doing so explores the intimate connections between security and the history of the modern state. Ultimately, he argues that to think seriously about security in the present is to think about the reformulation of politics broadly: 'If the subject of security is the *subject* of security, it is necessary to ask, first and foremost, how the modern subject is being reconstituted and then to ask what security could possibly mean in relation to it' (Walker 1997: 78). This is a profound challenge, but one that has been taken up by a range of scholars who assemble around the label of Critical Security Studies, as we shall see below.

In between the avowed realism of Mohammed Ayoob and the radical political philosophy of RBJ Walker, the Critical Security Studies text showcased a number of responses to Krause and Williams' challenges (see Key Ideas 4.1 for one of the more intriguing), which drew on a range of theoretical traditions and explored concrete problems of contemporary security. Several chapters drew on the Constructivism that was making an important mark more broadly in International Relations. Others were more inclined to draw theoretical inspiration from the heterogeneous products of 20th century continental philosophy that are often lumped together as 'post-structuralism'. In addition, Ken Booth and Peter Vale, in considering critical security in the southern African context, began a journey that would lead ultimately to the post-Marxist, Frankfurt School. (See below, the section 'Aberystwyth exclusions'.)

Krause and Williams expressed the desire that led first to Toronto and then to the *Critical Security Studies* volume as seeking a 'critical perspective' on security. They worked hard to ensure that this critical perspective was not monopolized by a single theoretical approach, and so opened the conference and the volume to a range of theoretical positions. Nevertheless, the desire for a (single) perspective somehow remained as scholars responded to the challenges they laid down in creating their foundation for critical security studies. Thus, despite their claims to catholicism, Krause and Williams create the conditions for schism . . . the schism I continue to trace. In doing so, one of the key questions I consider is: if Critical Security Studies is not a perspective, not a position, what is it? The first answer is given by those of the so-called Copenhagen School.

KEY IDEAS 4.1

Security and Ken Booth

One of the most interesting and unusual contributions to *Critical Security Studies* is Ken Booth's chapter 'Security and Self: Reflections of a fallen realist' (Booth 1997). Booth came to critical security studies as a well-established practitioner of traditional strategic studies—in his own words, a realist. That tradition trains you to keep yourself out of your research and writing, because its epistemology instructs the strict separation between the object of analysis and the analyst. Critical Security Studies emerged from a tradition that rejected that separation, and in 'Security and Self' Booth explores the consequences of that change through what he describes as 'an experiment in autosociology'. He examines the way in which the field has functioned as a discipline, to produce students and teachers of a particular type and to create a field of questions and limit the types of answer that can be given to those questions. The conclusion he reaches is 'that there is a critical relationship between the me/I as a theorist of security and what it means to study security. The argument has been that the meaning of studying security is not simply or necessarily created by the changes out there in the world, but by the changes—or lack of them—in here (who we think we are, and what we think we are doing)'.

KEY POINTS

- The Critical Security Studies label emerges from a 1994 conference in Toronto, and is then used as the title for the book that conference produced.
- The initial agenda of Critical Security Studies was set by a series of challenges to the traditional conception of security: the state was not a sufficient referent object for security; thinking more broadly about referent objects required thinking more broadly about the sources of both insecurity and security; these forms of rethinking required an epistemological move beyond the empiricist, positivist traditions or security studies.
- *Critical Security Studies* tried to create a broad church for the critical study of security, seeing 'critical' as an orientation rather than a unique theoretical perspective.
- The desire for a critical security study initially drew scholars from a range of theoretical perspectives, including constructivism, post-structuralism, and post-Marxism.

Copenhagen distinctions

The year after *Critical Security Studies* appeared, Barry Buzan, Ole Waever and Jaap de Wilde published *Security: A new framework for analysis.* The book was intended to serve as a relatively comprehensive statement of a distinctive perspective on the study of security, a perspective that has come to be known as The Copenhagen School.[2] The Copenhagen approach has had an important part to play in the development of Critical Security Studies, despite—indeed, in part, because—its exponents work hard to distinguish their perspective from Critical Security Studies.

Security: A new framework for analysis is built around two important conceptual developments in the study of security: Barry Buzan's notion of sectoral analysis of security and Ole Waever's concept of 'securitization'. (Securitization as an approach to security, encompassing both elements of the Copenhagen School, is treated extensively in Chapter 7.) Both of these ideas have helped to inform the broad church of Critical Security Studies. Buzan had introduced his notion of security sectors during the 1980s, most notably in *People, States and Fear.* He suggested that, rather than security being concerned solely with the military (that is, security as the threat, use and control of military force), military security was one of five sectors, joined by environmental, economic, societal and political security (Buzan 1991a). This idea of sectors of security provided a handy organizational scheme to anyone who sought to broaden the study of security beyond the threat, use and control of military force. As I noted above, Critical Security Studies began from one such claim to a broader notion of security, as developed by Krause and Williams. While most of those whose desire led them to Critical Security Studies did not follow the full theoretical argument of *People, States and Fear*, Buzan's set of five sectors provided a widely known shorthand for the scope of security.

Of more theoretical significance to the development of the various forms of Critical Security Studies was Ole Wæver's work on securitization. 'Securitization' is perhaps the most significant conceptual development that has emerged specifically within security studies in response to the epistemological challenge Krause and Williams note. Essentially, Wæver suggests that we treat security as a speech-act: that is, a concrete action that is

[2] Bill McSweeny is generally credited with coining the label 'Copenhagen School' to refer to the work of Buzan, Wæver and a series of collaborators (McSweeny 1996).

performed by virtue of its being said. Our tendency is to think of words as referring to objects or actions outside themselves, naming what it is we see, and so to talk about security is just that: to talk *about* security. By contrast, speech-acts are actions that are performed entirely by being spoken, and so do not refer to things outside themselves. Ironically, one important example of a speech-act is naming: parents name a child, for example, by saying 'I name you Susan'. Promising and marrying are other noted examples of common speech acts: I perform the action of making a promise by saying 'I promise . . . ', and while there is generally some significant ceremony surrounding these words, marriage is created by an approved authority saying something comparable to: 'I pronounce you man and wife . . . '.

Ole Wæver suggested that we can think of security as another in this series of speech-acts. He argued that an issue was an issue of security because, and only because, it had been 'securitized', brought into the realm of security: ' "Security" is thus a self-referential practice, because it is in this practice that the issue becomes a security issue—not necessarily because a real existential threat exists but because the issue is presented as such a threat' (Buzan, Wæver, and de Wilde 1998: 24). 'Securitization' raises a number of very interesting questions that have informed critical security study since Waever introduced the concept. Among the most important are:

- Who is able to securitize an issue successfully? As with marriage, not everyone is able to perform security, and certainly not to the same degree. My saying, for example, that global endemic poverty is a security issue is likely to be rather less successful than George W. Bush saying that global terrorism is one, despite poverty producing significantly more deaths than terrorism over any period one cares to examine.
- What are the conditions for successful securitization? If it is true that simply saying that something is a security issue is not enough to make it one—that is, saying so is a necessary but not sufficient condition for securitization—under what conditions can such a claim be successful?
- What are the consequences of securitization? People do not attempt to securitize issues on a whim. To say that something is an issue of security is to say that it poses the most serious imaginable threat—an existential threat—and should that claim be accepted, there will be significant political consequences. The successful securitization of global terrorism by the US Administration following September 11, for example, has, among other things, produced the most significant reorganization of the US state since the Second World War, and is propping up a defence budget of almost unimaginable size.

These are questions that recognize the deeply political nature of security, as well as its contingency. 'Securitization' leads us to ask about how security issues, policies and practices have come to be as they are, and therefore what the politics is of that production. These are very much the kinds of question that many who have been gathered under the label of Critical Security Studies seek to ask.

Interestingly, despite this influence on Critical Security Studies, the Copenhagen School has sought to distance itself from Critical Security Studies. In part this is a function of an incoherence inherent in the approach between the sectoral analysis of security and the concept of securitization. While securitization opens the possibility of the radical openness of social life, the sectoral approach as it had developed before merging into the Copenhagen School, draws on a largely objectivist epistemology. In other words, the epistemological underpinnings of the concept of securitization do not cohere with those of the sectoral analysis of security. It is the epistemology of securitization, however, that does cohere with that called for by the desire to a critical security study.

The division between the Copenhagen approach and Critical Security Studies is explicitly developed in *Security: A new framework for analysis*. The authors argue that Critical Security Studies is informed by post-structuralism and constructivism, and thus is open to the possibility of social change. By contrast, they suggest that the

Copenhagen approach recognizes the social construction of social life, but that that construction in the security realm is sufficiently stable over the long run that it can be *treated as* objective. In other words, they resolve the incoherence I raised by assuming a long-term stability and so enabling a largely positivist epistemology (Buzan, Waever and de Wilde 1998: 34–35).

The explicit separation of the Copenhagen School from Critical Security Studies in *Security: A new framework for analysis* does more than simply announce that Copenhagen is *sui generis*. One function of the text and of the prominence of its authors is to serve to create 'Critical Security Studies' as something more concrete and less heterogenous than the original desire. The Copenhagen authors talk of Critical Security Studies an 'an emerging school', and they shorten it to CSS. What is more, they ascribe to this emerging school two specific theoretical positions, post-structuralism and constructivism. This text, then, marks an important moment in the creation of Critical Security Studies as something other than an orientation toward the discipline, and also effects conceptual exclusions which are the subject of contestation, not least by scholars focused on the University of Wales, Aberystwyth, who have considerable institutional claim to the Critical Security Studies label.

KEY POINTS

- *Security: A new framework for analysis* sets out a distinctive position on security studies, often known as 'the Copenhagen School'.
- The sectoral approach to security analysis was developed in the 1980s by Barry Buzan. It divides security into five sectors: military, environmental, economic, societal, and political.
- The Copenhagen concept 'securitization' has been important in rethinking security. It treats security as a speech-act, rather than a reflection of an existing existential threat.
- There is an epistemological incoherence at the heart of the Copenhagen School between the epistemology of sectoral analysis and that of securitization.
- The Copenhagen School resolves its incoherence by arguing that the social production of security is sufficiently stable to be treated objectively.
- *Security: A new framework for, analysis* seeks to distinguish between its approach and Critical Security Studies, and in doing so tends to produce Critical Security Studies as an emerging 'school'.

Aberystwyth exclusions

Rather ironically, the most aggressive attempt to produce a coherent approach for Critical Security Studies—to marshal all adherents to the sign of the shoe or the gourd, but not both—has been made from a position largely excluded by the Copenhagen School's characterization of Critical Security Studies as being informed by constructivism and poststructuralism. The attempt has been focused around scholars based in Aberystwyth (indeed, Steve Smith (2005) calls it the Welsh School), and has found its most complete expression to date in *Critical Security Studies and World Politics*. In this text, Ken Booth makes an explicit attempt to link Critical Security Studies to a specific theoretical tradition: post-Marxist Critical Theory.

Booth is clear and explicit on two important points. The first point is that not all those who would see themselves working within critical international theory, and particularly Critical Security Studies, would accept such a notion of Critical Theory as their starting point. In other words, he is making a clear case for restrictive understanding of critical security theory—he is saying to us, follow the sign of the shoe, and means it. That is the second point; Booth's intervention is an unapologetic desire for fragmentation. As he says: 'There are times when definite lines have to be drawn' (Booth 2005: 260). He distances himself sharply from Krause and Williams of *Critical Security Studies*, rejecting the broad church in favour of a single tradition aimed at giving rise to a coherent critical theory of security.

In developing his critical theory of security, Booth follows his Aberystwyth colleague, Richard Wyn Jones, who had drawn on the Frankfurt School tradition to think about security theory in his 1999 book, *Security, Strategy and Critical Theory*. Both see the Frankfurt School tradition as centrally important to the development of a critical theory for security studies, although Booth throws his net slightly wider than Frankfurt in identifying the tradition, adding Gramscian, Marxist and Critical International Relations to the Frankfurt School. In other words, Booth is drawing on the range of post-Marxist social theory, particularly as it has been drawn into International Relations, with pride of place to the work of the Frankfurt School in general and Jürgen Habermas in particular.

What would such a critical security theory look like? Booth argues that there are eight themes that can be drawn from the collection of post-Marxist theory useful to a critical security theory. (The eight are summarized in Key Ideas 4.2.) He begins with the central claim of the Frankfurt School, that all knowledge is a social process, that is, knowledge is not simply 'there', but rather is produced socially, and thus politically, and there are 'interests of knowledge'. Knowledge benefits some and disadvantages others; it is, in the noted words of Robert Cox in International Relations, 'always for someone and for some purpose'. A critical security theory, therefore, must reveal the politics behind seeming neutral knowledge. Such a conception of knowledge implies a critique of traditional theory, including traditional security theory which, by not recognizing its political origins and content, tends to a naturalism, assuming the ability to maintain a rigid division between the analyst and the social world she is analysing. If Critical Theory, therefore, reveals the false naturalism of traditional theory and the political content of all knowledge, it provides the basis for social change—indeed for progress. This third theme, of the possibility of progress, leads to a fourth: that the test of a social theory is its capacity for fostering emancipation. Change is possible, and progressive change is emancipatory.

The first four themes Booth derives from the broad Critical Theory tradition in social theory. To these four he adds four gathered from the specific, emergent critical tradition in International Relations. The first is that human society is its own invention. Indeed, this is a necessary condition for the operation of his earlier themes, for only if society is a social invention can knowledge serve as the basis for social change and open the possibility of emancipation. The second theme which Booth derives from critical IR is a particular claim about contemporary world politics: that regressive theories have dominated the field. If all knowledge is *for* someone and *for* some purpose, regressive theories are the ones that are *for* those presently in power

KEY IDEAS 4.2

Themes of post-Marxist Critical Theory

1. All knowledge is a social process.
2. Traditional theory promotes the flaws of naturalism and reductionism.
3. Critical theory offers a basis for political and social progress.
4. The test of theory is emancipation.
5. Human society is its own invention.
6. Regressive theories have dominated politics among nations.
7. The state and other institutions must be denaturalized.
8. Progressive world order values should inform the means and ends of an international politics committed to enhancing world security.

(Booth 2005b: 268)

with the purpose of maintaining their dominance. Critical IR theory has shown how the mainstream theories, including security studies, serve just such a purpose. If this is true, then, the final two themes Booth develops are aimed at overcoming the regressive nature of world politics. The first is that the state and other international institutions must be *denaturalized*, so as to open the possibility of change, and finally that, in effecting that change to global (security) practices, politics must be governed by emancipatory values.

These themes enable Booth to argue that a critical security theory can serve as the basis for answering three sets of crucial questions in relation to security:

- First, what is real? If we reject naturalism, which assumes that the social world can be treated as objective in the same fashion as the natural world, then we cannot assume that the social world we investigate is 'real' in the same sense as the physical. Critical Theory's focus on knowledge provides a way into understanding social ontology, and thus the creation of social facts.
- Second, Critical Theory of this kind provides a means of thinking about knowledge, or the epistemology of social life. It directs our attention to the interests that underlie knowledge claims, and leads us to ask: whom particular forms of knowledge are for, and what function they serve in supporting the interests of those people or groups.
- Finally, it suggests asking the old Leninist question, what is to be done? Critical Theory is a theory of praxis, a step in a process of political engagement designed to transform the world. As Marx put it: the point is not to understand the world; the point is to change it.

These reflections provide the basis for a specific critical theory of security (see Key Quotes 4.2 for Booth's definition of this theory). It draws on a relatively coherent body of social theory and its application to International Relations, and aims to inform scholarship and political practice in the future. While developed largely in parallel to the critical tradition in International Relations, Booth's critical security theory is quite clearly designed to

KEY QUOTES 4.3

Critical security theory

In his recent work, Ken Booth has argued for the development of a distinctive critical theory of security, and proposed the following definition of such a theory, beginning from the Frankfurt School of Critical Theory:

'Critical security theory is both a theoretical commitment and a political orientation. As a theoretical commitment it embraces a set of ideas engaging in a critical and permanent exploration of the ontology, epistemology, and praxis of security, community, and emancipation in world politics. As a political orientation it is informed by the aim of enhancing security through emancipatory politics and networks of community at all levels, including the potential community of communities—common humanity.'

(Booth 2005b: 268)

provide a specific theory of security within critical IR. What this means is that Booth and his colleagues in the Welsh School have provided a clear answer to the question I posed at the end of the discussion of *Critical Security Studies*: critical security study *should* be guided by a single, specific theory, and that theory should be informed by Critical Theory, both with capital letters.

In order to make the case for exclusion as forcefully as possible, once he has set out the elements of a critical security theory, Booth distinguishes it from other possible sources of critical security study. He explains, in other words, what is wrong with following the sign of the gourd or with taking off our shoes and hopping around on one foot. In particular he distinguishes critical security theory from four pretenders: feminism, Copenhagen School, constructivism and post-structuralism.

The exclusion of feminism is the most troubling to Booth's position in some ways, but in others the easiest to achieve. As most feminist writing will freely admit, there are various feminisms which draw in their turn from a wide variety of social theory traditions in developing analyses of gender. These traditions include the Critical Theory tradition from which Booth proceeds. Therefore, gender analysis can be considered already to be within Critical Theory, and thus within a critical security theory; however, other forms of feminist theorising are as antithetical to critical security theory as their theoretical traditions are to Critical Theory more broadly. The Cophenhagen School is similarly dismissed with relative ease. The near-naturalism of the Copenhagen approach to society—so stable it can be treated as objective—leaves it 'only marginally "critical" ', and in Booth's eyes suffers the same forms of incoherence I noted above (Booth 2005b: 271).

There remain two challengers to the critical security theory Booth champions, the same two that the Copenhagen School identified in *Security: A new framework for analysis*. The first is constructivism, which Booth argues is not a theory at all, but rather an orientation to world politics that serves as a basis on which to reject traditional theories. While Booth's argument may be true, it ignores the possibility, which I will explore below, that there are within that orientation various constructivist theories which do have something to say about security—just as other orientations, including Booth's, contain a number of specific theories within them. For Booth that leaves only post-structuralism, which is just too dangerous with its toxic mix of 'obscurantism, relativism, and faux radicalism' (Booth 2005b: 270). In other words, Booth argues, post-structuralism provides no basis for political action.

As might be imagined, and as Booth freely admits, the dismissal of constructivism and post-structuralism as elements of Critical Security Studies is not shared by all. These two theoretical positions represent, in fact, the conceptual underpinning of most of what might be drawn under the label, understood as the broad church. But even among them the sign of the shoe is defended against those hopping around on one foot.

KEY POINTS

- Ken Booth, Richard Wyn Jones and their Welsh School colleagues argue for a specific critical security theory.
- The tradition within which they develop this theory is the post-Marxist tradition identified with Gramscian and other Marxist International Relations and, particularly, with Frankfurt School Critical Theory.
- The elaboration of the Critical Theory tradition gives rise to eight themes and a definition of critical security theory.
- Critical security theory provides the possibility of answering three key questions: what is real, what is knowledge and what is to be done?
- Critical Security Studies should be organized around this critical security theory, and should not include feminism, the Copenhagen School, constructivism and particularly post-structuralism.

Constructing security

If we exclude the Copenhagen School and feminist writings on security,[3] and further if we watch those committed to a critical theory of security build a hard and fast line between themselves and the rest of what might be considered Critical Security Studies, what are we left with? Keith Krause provided an

[3] The exclusion of feminism in the production of the Critical Security Studies label is a truly fascinating issue, worthy of complete treatment on its own. As we have seen, Ken Booth effects this exclusion through arguing that feminism is a broad church in its own right and that certain feminist analyses of gender form an important element of Critical Theory. Keith Krause effects a similar exclusion in his review of the scholarship of Critical Security Studies: 'I have not treated the principal themes of feminist or gender scholarship on security as a separate category. These are dealt with in detail by [others]' (Krause 1998: 324, note 4). Lene Hansen has reflected on this same exclusion in the case of the Copenhagen School (Hansen 2000).

answer in a review of the research programme of Critical Security Studies in 1998, and it is the same answer to which Ken Booth came: constructivism and post-structuralism. Indeed, as with *Critical Security Studies*, Krause's 1998 review largely elides any difference between these two positions—the church is still broad, and so you can follow the sign of the shoe or take off your shoe and hop around on one foot if you like.

In an attempt to impose some order on the studies that compose Critical Security Studies, without resorting to the definitional strictures employed by both Booth and the Copenhagen School, Krause organises a range of literature into a broad research programme. The effect of this move is to provide a characterization of Critical Security Studies, which while still inclusive, clearly privileges constructivism. He organizes the scholarship of Critical Security Studies under three headings: the construction of threats and responses; the construction of the objects of security and possibilities for transforming the security dilemma. Krause explicitly does not intend these headings to capture the full range of critical security scholarship, nor does he suggest that scholars will tend to treat these issues separately. Nevertheless, the effect, particularly appearing at a time in which the Critical Security Studies label was being established, and coming from one of the editors of the *Critical Security Studies* volume, was to mark the character of Critical Security Studies as concerned with 'the social construction of security' (Eriksson 1999: 318).

Krause suggests that the first set of questions guiding the Critical Security Studies research programme probes the ways in which threats and the responses to threat are constructed socially. Traditional security studies takes both threats and responses as given, the precondition for security analysis: there are threats, which are military in nature, and the responses are similarly military responses. It is at this point that security studies becomes possible as the study of the threat, use and control of military force, either to pose a threat or to respond to threats you find 'out there'. Krause shows that a range of early Critical Security Studies scholarship was concerned with probing the assumption of threats and responses as given, and asking how it is that the threats of concern to traditional security studies were produced in the first place: for example, the construction of the Soviet threat, a threat from North Korea, or the threat of weapons proliferation. Similarly, the military responses to security threats are not considered to be natural or inevitable, and Critical Security Studies posed questions about the construction of those responses as well: arms control policy, nuclear brinkmanship, or deterrence. All these elements of conventional security, and others, were subjected to different forms of analysis asking questions about the ways in which they were produced, socially constructed in a contingent fashion rather than occurring naturally in a world separate from that of the analyst.

Traditional security studies not only takes threat and response as given, but also the referent object of security, the national state. Krause argues that a second theme that runs through Critical Security Studies is an exploration of the construction of the referent object, as well as other (potential) referents for security practice. In reviewing this body of work, Krause explicitly draws together a range of scholarship that draws on a number of not necessarily compatible intellectual traditions. He includes work which explores the production of women in relation to security practice among a number of feminist scholars, the construction of national interests from an avowedly modernist constructivist starting point, and post-structural analyses of foreign policy and military strategy.

The theoretical and methodological pluralism of Krause's approach is even more evident in his third category, studies exploring the possibilities for transforming the security dilemma. He begins with work that aims to build cooperative security or pluralistic security communities, and includes research that has explored the discursive foundations of the Cold War. Here the broad church over-reaches its own pluralistic grasp, as it is difficult to see how much of the work on cooperative security or security communities would reach even the minimum criteria Krause has set for critical theory as being in conscious opposition to problem-solving theory.

There are two important features of Krause's review in the story of the creation of the Critical Security Studies label. The first is that it demonstrates the impressive array of research that is being conducted and published to which this label could be attached, countering, as Krause notes 'the oft-heard charge that critical scholarship is inevitably sloppy or unsystematic' (Krause 1998: 316). Secondly, he is able to derive from the review a characterization of Critical Security Studies which is far more specific than that provided by *Critical Security Studies*, and is clearly distinct from Booth's critical security theory. Krause suggests that there are six claims that tie Critical (Security) Studies together:

1. Principal actors (states and others) are social constructs.
2. These actors are constituted through political practices.
3. The structures of world politics are neither unchanging nor determining because they too are socially constructed.
4. Knowledge of the social world is not objective, as there is no divide between the social world and knowledge of that world.
5. Natural science methodology is not appropriate for social science, which requires an interpretive method.
6. The purpose of theory is not explanation in terms of generalizable causal claims, but contextual understanding and practical knowledge.

The focus on the social construction of agents and structures, together with a commitment to interpretive method and contextual understanding and practical knowledge marks Krause's account of Critical Security Studies as largely rooted within the tradition of constructivism in International Relations. It clearly shares homologies with both post-Marxist Critical Theory and with post-structuralism, but it is not the same as either. Those following the sign of the gourd are welcome, as are those hopping around on one foot, but they may feel that they are then expected to join in following the sign of the shoe.

KEY POINTS

- Social constructivism forms an important strand within Critical Security Studies.
- Constructivism takes agents and structures as constituted in and through political practices.
- Constructivism denies the division between the social world and the analyst, and thus seeks an interpretive rather than naturalist methodology.
- While attempting to maintain the broad church, the constructive account of Critical Security Studies privileges social constructivism.

Everyone's other: post-structuralism and security

Ken Booth's antipathy to post-structural approaches to International Relations in general and security studies in particular reflects a common, and commonly virulent, reaction. In addition to obscurantist, relativist and faux radical, approaches labelled post-structural have been called prolix and self-indulgent (Walt 1991), and accused of having no research programme (Keohane 1988). The virulence of the rejection of post-structural work reflects, I would suggest, its radical promise. It shares with the rest of the work discussed in this chapter a pair of key commitments: a rejection of positivist epistemology and hence methodology, and a commitment to social critique. However, unlike any of the other forms of critical scholarship I have thus far discussed, it does not stop short of the radical implications of these commitments. Indeed, a crucial commitment

THINK POINT 4.1

Traditional subjects in a post-structural gaze

Post-structural writing can take on subjects that on the surface appear to be the same as those found in traditional security studies. What the post-structural traditions provide, however, is often a radically different way of asking questions and providing answers. Here are two examples, the first 'about' nuclear weapons and the second, Canadian policy towards missile defence.

Hugh Gusterson: *Nuclear Rites*

Gusterson is a social anthropologist, whose discipline privileges a particular kind of field work leading to ethnographic writing. Traditionally such ethnographies are written about others' cultures, often the cultures of indigenous populations which have been (largely) untouched by European expansion. (Fortunately for the anthropologists, such cultures are often found on South Pacific islands!) Gusterson is part of a movement in anthropology turning the ethnographic gaze on his own society. In *Nuclear Rites* he engages in an ethnographic study of the scientists at one of the United States' nuclear weapons laboratories. Making use of both ethnographic method and Foucault's notions of discipline, he investigates the ways in which the labs function to create the conditions of possibility for the building, testing, and deployment of nuclear weapons. As the title suggests, some of what he finds is that the design, building, testing and deployment of nuclear weapons have evolved into a ritualized culture among the scientists that has little or nothing to do with the stories we tell ourselves about the needs of deterrence and defence.

Marshall Beier: Postcards from the outskirts of security

In his study, Beier reflects on a study trip he took with a number of other Canadian scholars to visit the North American Aerospace Defense (NORAD) Headquarters. NORAD is located in the middle of a mountain, usually identified as being on the outskirts of Colorado Springs. It is actually closer to the small town of 'Security' Colorado, and Beier uses this observation as the starting point for a reflection on the ways in which semiotic markers can affect group dynamics and contribute to the disciplining of dissent. He examines the ways in which opposition to missile defence was silenced within the tour, and considers the implications for the decision the Canadian government had to take on whether and how to participate in the US missile defence programme.

shared by post-structural scholarship but not by other forms of critical theory is a rejection of overarching grand narratives, and thus an acceptance that knowledge claims are always unstable and contingent. As a fairly sympathetic critic has put it: 'it is for this reason that most social constructivists and critical security studies writers are at such pains to establish the difference between their work and that of poststructuralists. Put simply, poststructuralists deny the form of foundations for knowledge claims that dominate the security studies debate. As can be imagined, this has led to much hostility toward poststructuralism . . . ' (Smith 2005: 49).

The work that is generally labelled post-structural—and, as with the other labels we are discussing, it is more commonly applied by others than by a scholar to her own work—draws on a series of intellectual traditions largely having their roots in French philosophy (as opposed to the German philosophy that animates the Welsh School, for example). While the work draws on an eclectic collection of writing, the most common points of departure are the work of Jacques Derrida and Michel Foucault. The rejection of grand narratives—such as those of 'progress' and 'emancipation' that inform the Welsh School—together with the varied and eclectic theoretical inspirations for post-structural work, means that there are no simple summaries or sets of bullet points that can be adduced, as with the other approaches. Ultimately, to borrow an expression, the only way in is through, and many of the texts called post-structural demand close and careful reading.[4] Therefore, rather than providing such a summary, I will consider a number of important authors and texts which are routinely cited, and thus form an important part of the story of the production of the Critical Security Studies label—even though few, if any, of these authors would slap the label on their own work.

One of the first of these works is Bradley Klein's 1994 book, *Strategic Studies and World Order*. In terms of the history of Critical Security Studies, the importance of the text is that it took on one of the central problems that motivate the later development of the label: what are the political consequences of traditional security studies, that is strategic studies. Klein considered strategic studies as a discourse constitutive of the global state and military system it purports to study. His approach to that discourse is informed by Foucault's work, which Foucault discusses as a history of the present, or a genealogy. Genealogical work seeks to reveal the historical trajectory that gave meaning to particular discourses and how they then function in the present. Famously, Foucault provided such genealogies, for example, of criminal punishment and Western sexuality. Klein turns this form of investigation on strategic studies, and in the process makes a compelling case for one of the founding assumptions of Critical Security Studies: that theories about the world constitute that world, and thus that theory, including security theory, has political effects. What Klein shows is that strategic studies is productive of the very system that makes contemporary global violence possible.

Perhaps the most widely cited of the scholars working within these traditions is David Campbell, and for good reason. As Steve Smith notes, 'David Campbell has written some of the best empirical work in poststructuralist security studies' (Smith 2005: 50). The first of these works is *Writing Security*, in which Campbell explores the manner in which the United States has been produced in and through discourses of danger. He asks of United States' Foreign Policy some of the same questions, inspired by Foucault, that Klein used to think about strategic studies. In the book, he shows how Foreign Policy discourse is inseparable from what he terms foreign policy (the capitalization is the key), that is the production of an American self and a (dangerous) other, or a (secure) domestic and a (threatening) foreign. As with Klein's work, the contribution to Critical Security Studies thinking is clear. In the case of Campbell's work, both what Critical Security Studies will call the *referent object* and the *agent* of security (the state in both instances) is shown to be produced in its own practices.

The principal objection Ken Booth raised to post-structuralism as part of a broad Critical Security Studies church was its supposed inability to inspire a politics, and in particular its inability to ' "shape up" to the test of fascism as a serious political challenge' (Booth 2005b: 270). This is, of course, a serious criticism of any form of critical theory that sees itself in any sense part of a politics of change, as it is difficult to imagine a politics more in need of change than fascism. It is also an argument repeatedly raised by critics of post-structural scholarship, regardless of how many times it is answered. In Campbell's case, his most extended answer came in his 1998 book, *National Deconstruction: Violence, Identity, and Justice in Bosnia*. The Yugoslav wars of the 1990s posed exactly the sort of challenge alluded to by Booth, as it appeared to mark the return to Europe of the kind of violent fascism to which all had said 'never again' in 1945. In a sophisticated and compelling text,

[4] One of the concerns with much of the criticism directed at post-structural work in IR generally is that it is not always founded on such a reading of the texts it purports to criticize. As David Campbell notes: 'What is most interesting about the conventional critics of "postmodernism" is the unvarnished vehemence that adorns their attacks. Accused of "selfrighteousness", lambasted as "evil", castigated for being "bad IR" and "meta-babble", and considered congenitally irrational, "postmodernists" are regarded as little better than unwelcome asylum seekers from a distant war zone. Of course, had the critics reached their conclusions via a considered reading of what is now a considerable literature in international relations, one would repay the thought with a careful engagement of their own arguments. Sadly there is not much thought to repay' (Campbell 1998a: 210).

Campbell shows not only how various Western discourses (including security studies) created the conditions which made the genocidal violence in Bosnia possible, but engaged directly with the question Booth demands to be answered: what is to be done?

Campbell's answer to the question of politics demands to be read, and read closely, but centres on fostering the ethos of democracy: 'Democracy is not a substance, a fixed set of values, a particular kind of community, or a strict institutional form . . . [W]hat makes democracy democratic, and what marks democracy as a singular political form, is a particular attitude or spirit, an ethos, that constantly has to be fostered' (Campbell 1998b: 196). This is not an answer that many find comfortable, because it provides no simple blueprint, no single strategy. Fostering the ethos of democracy does not mean that when you hold a competitive election and anoint a 'democratic' government your work is done, and so the politics that is demanded by Campbell's accounts of responsibility and democracy are profoundly more difficult and challenging than those found in most areas of security studies, even Critical Security Studies. The difficulty has led, in fact, to a concerted effort among a number of scholars working in a poststructural tradition to consider issues of ethics and responsibility in relation to 'the worst'. Much of their work draws its philosophical inspiration, in part, from the work of Emmanuel Levinas, as did Campbell in developing his arguments about a politics in response to Bosnia.

The idea of fostering an ethos is also central to the notion of critique in much of the writing labelled post-structural. Both Welsh School critical security theory and constructivist Critical Security Studies provide an answer to one of the questions I posed at the outset: what is meant by 'critical'. For the Welsh School, it involves revealing the interests behind knowledge-claims, with a goal of social change. Similarly for the constructivists, it is reaching contextual and practical understanding to know whom knowledge-claims serve.

Both of these are relatively static conceptions of critique: they can be done in a finite sense. Just as Campbell argues democracy is never reached, but rather is an ethos ever to be fostered, so too is critique. Post-structural writing sees its critical purposes as fostering an ethos of critique, always working to destabilize 'truths', revealing their contingency and the nature of their production. It is not a finite project, however, but rather a process in which to be constantly engaged. As with its politics, the post-structural conception of critique is difficult for many to accept, because again it is not easy. It does not allow for finite claims and finished projects, and as students of society, we are trained to provide 'findings' and test them in a settled fashion.

Neither Bradley Klein nor David Campbell—nor indeed a number of others often also included in a post-structural security studies list, such as James Der Derian, RBJ Walker, Cynthia Weber, Simon Dalby or even Michael Dillon—applies the label 'Critical Security Studies' to his work. They are surely and avowedly engaged in critical scholarship—that is the fostering of an ethos of critique—and much of their work is centrally concerned with security. Michael Dillon, for example, has written an extended political philosophy of security out of the tradition of French philosophy (Dillon 1996), and his more recent work explores Foucault's notions of biopolitics in relation to the post-9/11 security strategies of the United States and other western powers (Dillon 2006). Similarly, RBJ Walker is one of the leaders of a large research programme on 'Liberty and Security', in relation to the contemporary practices of the war on terrorism.

While most of these scholars have not entered the broad church of Critical Security Studies, their work has inspired some within it to take off a shoe and jump around on one foot. In doing so, some have hopped right back outside again, wondering what applying the label Critical Security Studies to their work adds to the project in which they are engaged. Indeed, the ethos of critique that work of this kind aims to foster demands that we turn our critical gaze on the very scholarly practices in which we are engaged. It demands that we ask about the politics of our own labelling, including the Critical Security Studies label, one of whose stories I am telling.

KEY POINTS

- 'Post-structuralism' is a marker for a diverse set of writing inspired by a number of, generally French, philosophers including Michel Fourcault and Jacques Derrida.
- A number of works in this tradition within International Relations are claimed by Critical Security Studies, most notably those of Bradley Klein, David Campbell, RBJ Walker; Simon Dalby and Michael Dillon.
- Despite criticism to the contrary, post-structural work does provide answers to questions of political action, just not the kind of comfortable answers many are seeking.
- Central to the political and critical nature of post-structural writing is the idea of fostering an ethos of democracy and an ethos of critique. These are never finite, never reached, but for which we must constantly strive.

Conclusion: Contemporary (Critical) Security Studies

This chapter has been unlike many in a textbook of this kind. I have not provided clear and unproblematic answers to questions such as: what is Critical Security Studies, what is meant by 'critical' and 'security', how do you 'do' Critical Security Studies? Rather, I have tried to turn the ethos of critique that should animate a critical study of security on the very label I was asked to discuss. I have told a story of the short history of the label and its politics, a story which attempts to reveal how Critical Security Studies came to be what it is, and what the effects are of that coming. Questions of history and politics are the questions—though by no means the only questions—that an ethos of critique leads us to ask, and the kind of story I tell here is one of the ways—though again, by no means the only way—that they can be answered.

Since the conference in 1994 with which I began this story, the issue of 'security' has taken on a greatly renewed significance. During the Cold War, the Soviet-American rivalry and the ever-present possibility of nuclear war lent an urgency to questions of security that seemed to have been lost with the fall of the Berlin Wall. Such a decline in urgency was surely to be welcomed, and led, indeed, to the possibility of an idea like Critical Security Studies to take hold. Many of the concerns which animated the conference and the book had been articulated before the end of the Cold War, but that historical context made it impossible to follow them through. Critical Security Studies was a label ripe for reception at the moment it was spoken. Now, with the events of 11 September 2001, security has regained its urgency.

In the context of a War on Terrorism, wars in Afghanistan and Iraq, annual updates of 'anti-terror' legislation, the reorganization of government to provide 'homeland security', and stories of the brutal practices of 'extraordinary rendition', security studies has never had it better. (This thought alone should give us pause, as we recognize the close connection of security studies to such extravagant violence and the abuse of people's rights and persons.) What is the state of the label Critical Security Studies in this present context? It seems the broad church is edging toward institutionalization. There are now courses taught in universities on Critical Security Studies, and departments advertise for specialists under this label. As you know from reading this chapter, textbooks include Critical Security Studies in their lists of approaches. Perhaps because of this, the followers of the sign of the gourd are still squabbling with those following the sign of the shoe and particularly with those holding their shoes and hopping around on one foot. The stakes in this contest over the label are now higher: jobs are at stake, as are authorships of chapters.

Nevertheless, in an age in which security is so important, and some of the practices of security so troubling to those committed to liberty and justice—to the ethos of democracy—security study demands an ethos of critique, even with the recognition that it does not provide a destination we can finally reach.

QUESTIONS

If you were to become a critical security scholar, which sign would you follow and why?

Why did Krause and Williams aim to create a 'broad church' of Critical Security Studies? What are the advantages and disadvantages of such a conception? Who does it favour, and who does it marginalize?

Critical Security Studies has itself been criticized for excluding feminist approaches to security and questions relating to gender more generally. Why do you think that is, and what can be done about it?

What are the various understandings of the term 'critical' that are found in the literature on Critical Security Studies? Which one do you find the most convincing?

Should the Critical Security Studies label apply to the Copenhagen School?

Do you think that the 'War on Terrorism' makes the claims of Critical Security Studies more or less convincing?

The Welsh School suggests that Critical Security Studies should be guided by Critical Theory, which is the theory developed by the Frankfurt School. This suggestion makes intuitive sense; do you agree with it?

What is the difference between 'constructivism' and 'post-structuralism' in security studies? Does it make a difference?

Do an ethos of critique and an ethos of democracy provide sufficient guidance for a progressive politics of security in the contemporary world?

How does the rendition of a 'partial history of a label' differ from other ways of presenting approaches to security studies? What difference does it make?

FURTHER READING

Constructing security

- **Krause, Keith and Williams, Michael C. (1997), *Critical Security Studies: Concepts and Cases*, Minneapolis: University of Minnesota Press.** This edited volume launched the label 'critical security studies' and continues to be a standard reference.

- **Weldes, Jutta, Laffey, Mark, Gusterson, Hugh, and Duvall, Raymond (eds.) (1999), *Cultures of Insecurity: States, Communities, and the Production of Danger*, Minneapolis: University of Minnesota Press.** While not falling entirely within the 'constructivist' paradigm, *Cultures of*

Insecurity presents the best collection of constructivist critical security studies essays, together with several from other approaches.

■ **Krause, Keith (1998), 'Critical Theory and Security Studies: The Research Programme of "Critical Security Studies"', *Cooperation and Conflict* 33/3: 298–333.** In this article, Krause provides a useful overview of the broad church of Critical Security Studies and the literature to which the label may be applied.

The Copenhagen School

■ **Buzan, Barry (1991a), *People, States and Fear: An Agenda for International Security Studies in the Post-Cold War Era,* 2nd edn, Boulder, CO: Lynne Rienner.** Buzan's work provided an important precursor to Critical Security Studies, and serves as one of the two strands which come together as the Copenhagen School.

■ **Buzan, Barry, Wæver Ole, and de Wilde, Jaap (1998), *Security: A new framework for analysis*, Boulder, CO: Lynne Rienner.** *Security* is the most elaborated statement of the Copenhagen School approach, and clearly distinguishes it from CSS.

■ **Hansen, Lene (2000), 'The Little Mermaid's Silent Security Dilemma and the Absence of Gender in the Copenhagen School', *Millennium* 29/2: 285–306.** Hansen provides a very important critique of the lack of a concern with gender in the Cophenhagen School, but which could well apply more broadly to much of Critical Security Studies.

The Welsh School

■ **Booth, Ken (ed.) (2005), *Critical Security Studies and World Politics*, Boulder, CO: Lynne Rienner.** This collection marks the most explicit statement of a Welsh School of Critical Security Studies, arguing for a specific critical security theory, rather than the broad church.

■ **Jones, Richard Wyn (1999), *Security, Strategy and Critical Theory*, Boulder, CO: Lynne Rienner.** Jones' book is the most philosophically elaborated statement of the Welsh School approach to date.

Poststructuralism and Security

■ **Klein, Bradley (1994), *Strategic Studies and World Order*, Cambridge: Cambridge University Press.** Klein's book is one of the first to draw on post-structural philosophy to think about the areas of conventional security studies, and in particular the politics of the study of security itself.

■ **Campbell, David (1998a), *Writing Security: United States foreign policy and the politics of identity* (revised edn), Minneapolis: University of Minnesota Press.** Campbell's first book is a touchstone for virtually all post-structural security studies literature. The epilogue to the second edition provides a very useful account of the distinction between post-structural IR and constructivism.

■ **Campbell, David (1998b), *National Deconstruction: Violence, identity, and justice in Bosnia*, Minneapolis: University of Minnesota Press.** In *National Deconstruction* Campbell responds to the standard criticism of post-structuralism that it cannot stand up to fascism.

■ **Gusterson, Hugh (1998), *Nuclear Rites: A weapons laboratory at the end of the Cold War*, Berkeley: University of California Press.** Gusterson's book provides a very accessible example of the application of Foucauldian arguments to issues of traditional concern to security studies.

IMPORTANT WEBSITES

- The Responsibility to Protect: the report of the International Commission on Intervention and State Sovereignty introduced the notion of the 'responsibility to protect'. The Human Security Policy Division of the Canadian Department of Foreign Affairs maintains a site dedicated to the promotion of this notion. **http://www.iciss.ca/menu-en.asp**
- Virtual-Security.net is a portal for new research which recognizes that the study of security, war, media, peace and politics has to be redesigned to meet the challenges posed by our twenty-first-century global techno-scientific civilization. **http://www.virtual-security.net**
- The Liberty & Security Project: a site at the focus of a wide-ranging project looking at the intersection of security and liberty in a world characterized by a global war on terror. **http://www.libertysecurity.org**
- The Information Technology, War and Peace Project: an online portal for a project exploring the relations among information technology, contemporary media and global security. **http://www.watsoninstitute.org/infopeace/index2.cfm**

Visit the Online Resource Centre that accompanies this book for lots of interesting additional material: www.oxfordtextbooks.co.uk/orc/collins/

5 Gender and Security

CAROLINE KENNEDY-PIPE

Chapter Contents

Reader's Guide

This chapter examines issues of gender and security. It begins with an explanation of what we mean by gender and explains why and how the issue of gender is central to a fuller understanding of security. We look at how recently, International Relations specialists have begun to explore the ways in which men and women respond differently to state policy on security, conflict and war. The chapter demonstrates that through understanding and placing notions of gender at the centre of debates on security issues we can unleash a series of interlocking understandings of the way people of either sex relate to fear, insecurity, violence and the institutions of war and peace.

Introduction

Gender and security are both concepts that invite endless political controversy. Juxtaposing them, therefore, inevitably multiplies this feature. The juxtaposition is not an arbitrary one, however, and the complexity that results is an inevitable feature of trying to understand their relations, as this chapter will seek to show. Security has been conceived in many different ways, of course (Buzan, De Wilde and Wæver 1998; Krause and Williams 1997a), and much of this difference can be understood and illuminated in terms of gender. But gender too has no fixed meaning, as its different deployment within the contemporary academy, in many fields, amply indicates (Tickner 1992).

This chapter aims to outline the significance for both of considering gender and security together by considering two angles of vision in their joint conceptualization. Despite the obvious fact that understanding gender or security will require both angles of vision, it is useful to distinguish between what I will here call 'practical' and 'discursive' aspects of the relationship of gender and security. Practical aspects are exemplified by the concrete role of women in armed forces, or as victims, bystanders or helpers of military conflict or of militarization in general. Discursive aspects are exemplified by the relationships between militarism and masculinity, or nurturing and femininity.

This distinction should be wedded to two further developments that each reinforces, though in complex and unpredictable ways, the mutual relationship of gender and security. The first involves the promotion of a broader concept of security than has been traditional. A number of terms have been used to describe this process: 'human security' or 'soft security' being perhaps the most common. This has involved a relative downgrading of the traditional focus on military matters within security, with implications both from and for the practical and the discursive aspects of the gender–security relationship. The second process is in the deployment and operation of militaries, to the extent indeed that it became plausible by 2001 to comment on the 'feminization' of military tasks (Kennedy-Pipe and Welch 2001) and which trends include the continued intensification of the technology of combat supposedly producing greater precision, remote control and Virtual War.

The chapter concludes by examining the extent to which the period since the terrorist attacks of 9/11 has introduced changes that affect the relationship between gender and security. As yet it remains difficult to identify the specificity of the new conditions (indeed the extent of their novelty is somewhat contested), and thus difficult to read off from them the implications for gender–security. But consistent with the main argument of this chapter, it will be suggested that attention to this relationship continues to be illuminating and to expose the contextuality and complexity of the nexus between man, the state, women, and violence.

Discursive representations

Perhaps one of the most general trends in recent international relations theory in general has been the growing recognition of the role of what loosely we might call 'ideas' or, perhaps better, discursive contexts in international political life (Onuf 1989; Kratochwil 1991; Walker 1993; Rengger 1999; Wendt 1999).

Perhaps the most celebrated image of the international system—that states perceive themselves as inhabiting a zero sum and therefore dangerous international environment of self-help—is taken as evidence of that; in Alexander Wendt's famous phrase 'anarchy is what states make of it' (Wendt 1992). Traditionally and certainly according to Realist accounts of international relations, states have ranked their national security or the national interest (itself always an ambiguous concept) as a priority, perhaps the very highest priority. In the interests of 'national security', large defence budgets, nuclear weapons, the military conscription of the male population (sometimes but not usually the female population), foreign invasion and intervention and the curtailment of domestic civil liberties have all been justified, at various times. The security of the state is perceived as a fundamental duty of the government and as a task that must be supported by most if not all citizens. The events of 7/7 for example, when four British suicide bombers killed 52 citizens and injured over 700 in an attack on London's public transport system, demonstrated quite clearly that certainly in the United Kingdom not all citizens shared similar conceptions of duty to the state. However, loyalty to the state has been apparent in periods of war and in times of national emergency. The provision of national security in most states has been and continues to be the almost exclusive province of the male. While many women support and underwrite what are considered to be legitimate calls for state military action, the primary task of defining and defending the security of the state has been seen as the work of men. Yet this male province has rested in many ways on the work, the co-option or the exploitation of that group known as women.

Of course, historically, war and combat in war have represented the highest aspirations of the male members of political, social and cultural elites, across time and culture. In the modern period, military service for one's country has long been regarded as a badge of honour. The power of the critical poetry of the First World War is made so by the widespread acceptance of the values that it was criticizing; it *was* widely thought that 'Dulce et decorum est, pro patria mori' (It is sweet and proper to die for one's country) (Owen 1995). War was and, many would argue, still is associated with masculine values such as physical strength, honour and courage. In ancient Greece, some form of military training was regarded as a prerequisite to manhood (Dawson 1996). Shakespeare famously has Henry V declare to his troops before Agincourt that 'Gentleman in England now abed will think themselves accursed to be not here'. In more contemporary times, Doctor Johnson is often quoted as believing that 'Every man thinks meanly of himself for not having been a soldier or not having been at sea' (Keegan 1998). Even more recently Theodore Zeldin has explained that men fight to 'kill dissatisfaction with themselves more than their foe . . . but that adventure and honour have been their goals (Zeldin 1998).

In certain societies, those men that would not or could not fight might be classified as 'women': some have even been made to don dresses as a sign of their weakness (Davie 1929). Military training was always (and is still) designed to reinforce certain notions of masculinity. The use of boot camps, a degree of violence and bullying associated with basic training are all designed to cultivate and construct certain notions of what it is to be a man (Steans 1998). Misogyny can be a useful component: males can be goaded into grinding down whatever might be regarded as womanly or feminine and thus an attribute unfit for a soldier. Norman Dixon, for example, has argued that various British military conventions were in certain periods designed to subordinate female characteristics: hence piano playing was denounced and 'defensive' assignments such as convoy duty were regarded as rather shameful tasks (Dixon 1976). To sacrifice one's life for one's country in war has been regarded as the highest form of patriotism, but a failure to fight is the act of a coward or evidence of some physical or mental weakness that renders the male less than he should be. Equally, to deny loyalty to the state or to inflict hurt on the state as the British suicide bombers did in the summer of 2005 is to question the very essence of what we consider to be the duty of a citizen.

Women, in contrast to men, have long been regarded as the carers and the nurturers of the young. In many narratives of war, women have inhabited only the private sphere tasked with the defence of that ubiquitous feature of national life—the home front, implying that women, even in war, never really left the home. (Sherry 1995). This polarization between the sexes has been described in the following terms: 'Women are excluded from war talk and men excluded from baby talk' (Elsthain 1987). Yet women, although depicted historically as 'carers' such as the nurse figure embodied in Florence Nightingale, also have had other connections with war. Frequently they have been represented as the 'spoils of war'. This perception of women as 'spoils of war' was consistent historically with the legal status of women: they were regarded as the property of the male. Rape was perceived as an injury to the male estate, and not to the women herself (Brownmiller 1975).

From the raping of the Sabine women in Greek mythology to the accounts of the sexual abuse and mutilation of women in the Balkan wars of the 1990s, the act of rape has been a common feature in both the representation and the realities of war. It was, though, not until the late 1990s that feminist scholars drew attention to female experiences of war: an area that hitherto had not been discussed nor indeed considered central to any discussion of International Relations. The rape of women during and after war is now well documented (Nicarchos 1995), as are the examples when rape appears to have been used as a 'tactic' of war to humiliate or demoralize the enemy. We now know, thanks to the work of scholars such as Anthony Beevor, of the routine use of rape by soldiers of the Red Army as it advanced on and occupied German cities in the spring of 1945. Members of the NKVD encouraged the use of rape not just as a tool of revenge but as a way of undermining the male population left in the city. Scholars have recently examined the use of rape as a supposed tactic of war by Serbian and Croatian soldiers during the conflict in Kosovo (Beevor 2002; Aydelott 1993). More recently we have become used to tales of sexual humiliation perpetrated by American soldiers on Iraqi prisoners of war. Interestingly we have also been made aware of female service personnel engaging in such behaviour and challenging notions of what it is to be female and highlighting the brutality assumed by women in positions of relative power.

Some male scholars, perhaps intent on controversy, have depicted women as the cause of war and point to the cases in which women have urged their men on to battle. The somewhat hazy representation of girls pressing white feathers into the hands of those young men reluctant to volunteer for service in the First World War is juxtaposed with the semi-mythical creatures who according to Martin Van Crevald bared their breasts to urge warriors on (Van Crevald 2001). When women do appear in the literature of war, the Amazons, Boudicca and Mrs Thatcher are all used to exemplify the war in which some women ape maleness to assert political leadership. Despite these latter characterizations, overall the female place in or rather outside war is clear. As Nietzche said in a well-known if by now somewhat tedious formulation: 'Man should be trained for war and women for the recreation of the warrior: all else is folly' (Hollingdale 1977).

These representations of women and war are important because of the connection between war, maleness and the modern state, a connection many actors in the modern world are unashamed to acknowledge. Indeed, Dixon quotes General Adna Chaffe to the effect that 'Let war cease and a nation will become effeminate' (Dixon 1976). The modern state was born in war and consolidated through war: as Charles Tilly famously put it, 'war made the state and the state made war' (Tilly 1989). In some, one might say in many, cultures masculine attributes have traditionally been rewarded with social advancement or the holding of high political office. In Israeli society, as in a number of others, military service provides a standard for manhood. The essence of womenhood is still regarded as fulfilled by marrying a hero—a man who has served (Lieblich 1997). This assigns to women, even in a state as security minded as Israel, a passive role that of the hero's wife or girlfriend (Lieblich 1997).

In the contemporary literature on world politics, perhaps the most potent reflection on the interpretations of the female, the state and war is that of Jean Elshtain. In her book, *Women and War*, Elshtain claims that a distinction between 'beautiful souls' (women) and 'just warriors' (men) has been at the core of much of the theorizing about the respective role of women and men in both war and society. She also emphasizes the key role that narratives of war play in reinforcing traditional gender roles in a domestic/social context (Elshtain 1987).

Histories of states are usually constructed in terms that are highly gendered. While nowadays nations might gather in support of (all male) football, rugby or cricket teams, within many states traditionally identities coalesce around the narration or stories or celebration of wars of independence or national liberation. Victory in battles hundreds of years ago are still revered and statues of war heroes such as Nelson far less controversial than that of disabled pregnant women. The statue of the disabled and pregnant woman in Trafalgar Square sparked enormous controversy as not worthy of a place alongside national—and male—heroes (see Think Point 5.1). Many nationalist movements have utilized a variety of gendered imagery that encourages men to fight for the establishment and defence of a country and a patch of land to be protected is usually depicted in female terms. 'Mother' Russia, 'Marianne' in France or the Statue of Liberty in America are powerful symbols of the supposed spirit of a nation. National anthems are frequently war songs and national holidays might in some countries or regions be celebrated with military or paramilitary marches usually participated in by men (Edwards 1999). It is striking even in a post-conflict Northern Ireland how the annual parades through the streets of the province are predominantly male and are certainly led by those male leaders who wish to assert a certain version of what it may be to be British or Irish.

Collective histories, as we have seen in Northern Ireland, are central to the way in which individuals and communities define themselves as citizens as well as the way in which political elites generate support for foreign policy decisions, particularly those for war. It is rare, although one can think of Joan of Arc, that such collective memory contains heroines. These are, as noted earlier, predominantly celebrations of men in war. According to some types of feminist account, the association of the male with war has necessarily privileged man because of the way in which military service and certainly during the years of the Cold War, conceptions of national and nuclear security were valued in male terms. For some feminists, usually designated as liberal feminists (see Key Points below), the gendered nature of the state is significant for the inequalities of treatment for women within society generally. Equality for women can be achieved first by gaining equal opportunities in education, in social institutions and in the workplace and then through the gradual

THINK POINT 5.1

Who or that deserves national recognition?

Marc Quinn's sculpture 'Alison Lapper pregnant' shows the disabled artist naked when she was 8 months pregnant. It was placed in Trafalgar Square for 18 months as part of a series of temporary works of art. Nearby, but on a higher plinth, is the permanent statue of Britain's greatest naval hero, Viscount Horatio Nelson, who led the crucial naval victory at Trafalgar in 1805. The placement of the statue of Lapper has highlighted a number of issues associated with both gender and disability. The first is that Nelson himself was disabled—he had only one arm and one eye—but his statue has aroused no controversy. Is this because he was wounded in action serving his country? Alternatively, is it because a depiction of female, especially disabled pregnant women is too disturbing? Could it be that we accept that Nelson deserved and still deserved his place as a national hero and that we should still honour him for his victories? Perhaps, though, it is that in the twenty-first century we look to honour or reflect different types of courage—this might be the integration of disabled persons into the mainstream. Perhaps we still want to value war heroes but also in 2006 we want to reflect on different types of courage. There are after all multiple courages.

achievement of parity of representation in the central offices of the state: within government, the judiciary, and, of course, the military. The argument was and is a simple one: men have 'captured' the state, so women must reclaim it. Here, as Jill Steans has pointed out, the armed services and military institutions are regarded as especially important to those women trying to achieve high office. To paraphrase Steans, the military plays a special role in the ideological structure of patriarchy because the notion of combat plays 'such a central role in the construction of manhood and in the construction of the social order' (Steans 1998). Therefore, by obtaining equality in this sphere, women will be able to participate in the key narratives of, to use Michael Ignatieff's phrase, 'blood and belonging' (Ignatieff 1997).

KEY POINTS

- Feminist analysts and gender analysts are not united in their views about the relationship between women, men, and security.
- Liberal feminists wish to see a complete equality of opportunity between men and women. Liberal feminists wish to see an ending to the exclusion of women in public life and are keen to see equal representation of women in the high offices of state and advocate the right of women to participate in combat.
- Radical feminists would prefer to see a shift in the dynamics of the state security apparatus. This includes a rejection of masculine values and desire to feminize institutions and conflict. Some radical feminists emphasize peace as the endpoint of changing institutions and mindsets.
- Marxist feminists work on the issue of class and gender. Their work highlights not only the subordination of women in the workplace but the general overrepresentation of women in the lowest socio-economic groups across the globe. They draw our attention to the links between economic deprivation, security, and vulnerability.

Practical contexts

According to some female scholars, even in the contemporary era, experience in combat can still be a way of earning high office or, in a state such as America, a way of securing political election (Steans 1998). Just as ancient and medieval civilizations gave special respect to citizens who had proved themselves in war; it can still be a special mark of respect to be a war veteran. This is an honour which overall is denied to women. Women have traditionally been thought unfit or unsuited for the holding of high offices associated with the military or issues of national security. If women were rarely warriors, they were equally unlikely to be heads of the CIA or strategic air command. If in olden times it was men who headed armies, it is predominantly men who still act as the heads of militaries, intelligence services, and nuclear industries. Women, though, have traditionally been employed as spies, special agents and in special intelligence units (Steans 1998). There is little need to emphasize that this type of employment might fit nicely with traditional gendered views of women as perhaps devious, cunning, and able to fool men through the use of sexual favours. Not for nothing has the reputation of Mata Hari exercised such a keen fascination.

In the United States, Sheila Tobias has suggested that there are greater hurdles to those politicians, even male politicians seeking office who have not served in the military (Elshtain and Tobias

1990). Former generals are looked upon as prime presidential material and some American politicians have run for office on the basis of their war records. In this respect during the 1984 Vice Presidential debates, George Bush sought to make a virtue of his experiences as a bomber pilot (Tickner 1992). More recently, Senator John Kerry argued that his own record in Vietnam served to make him fit to lead. It may have been thought that the election of Bill Clinton, whose own record as a 'draft dodger' was somewhat controversial, had ended the linkage between military service and electoral success but it still seems to persist. President George W. Bush of course, despite his own similar and controversial decision to shy away from service in Vietnam, has recently made a virtue out of the association between strong leadership and military prowess by appearing in combat uniform and striding manfully around the deck of an aircraft carrier!

Yet, any positive view of the way in which men have been treated after serving their country in war must be contested. Veterans of the Vietnam conflict, especially those drawn from the native African community in the United States, might find it difficult to recognize their treatment as that of heroes or to find that their combat experiences advanced them socially (Sherry 1995). The recent controversies over the level of compensation for those killed and maimed in conflicts such as the First and Second Gulf Wars also do not point to a necessary glorious post-war life for those who have served, particularly those who are not drawn from the officer class. Recent reports from the war in Iraq have demonstrated that war; or rather occupation duty after war in a hostile environment, is proving extremely stressful for young soldiers and has longer-term psychological implications (Smith 2005 and Keegan 1998).

Despite the increasing evidence of the toll that soldiering exerts on the individual, to die in combat for one's country was at least in certain narratives of war regarded as an honour and was one which was revered within many cultures. Yet, death in battle or at least honourable death as a warrior was an honour for which women could not even compete (Tickner 1992). Although many women have died in times of conflict, in the service of the state, war memorials rarely carry the names of those females killed in war. In 1995 in recognition of this, the United States dedicated a memorial at Arlington National Cemetery for those women who had served in the military from the time of the US Civil War through to the conflict in the Gulf. Again, one must be careful with this equation of maleness, honour, privilege and war as one only has to think of the 326,000 unidentified corpses from the First World War to see that an unmarked grave has been the permanent resting place of many a young man serving his country.

The construction of a male security state is not accidental. As Cynthia Enloe points out, militarism has not been 'kept going by merely drawing on a type of civilian masculinity . . . rather it requires drill sergeants . . . and men's willingness to earn their manhood credentials by soldiering: it also requires women to accept particular assumptions about mothering, marriage and unskilled work as well as policies, written and unwritten, to ensure certain sorts of sexual relations (Enloe 1993). Enloe's formulation is important because arguably it helps explain why, even though women have over the last forty years been integrated into many institutions of the state, the military and the issue of combat have remained predominantly the province of the male.

It is not just at the highest levels, that of the presidents and the generals, that scholars claim that there is a linkage between man, war and the state. The relationship between the bearing of arms and citizenship has a long history in Western political thought. Judith Hicks Stiehm argues that we in the West have traditionally held militarized conceptions of citizenship and that different categories of citizenship arise from the classes of those excluded from military service. The very young, the old, the disabled, in some societies the homosexual, are barred from combat (Hicks Stiehm 1983 and 1989). This is odd in many ways, but for our purposes it has meant historically that the fittest in society were slaughtered. As Nicolai has argued:

> “Children and old men are protected by Government, but besides them the blind, deaf and dumb, idiots, hunchbacks, scrofulous and impotent persons, imbeciles, paralytics, epileptics, dwarfs and abortions—all this human riff-raff and dross need have no anxiety, for no bullets will come hissing against them, and they can stay at home and dress their ulcers while the brave, strong young men are rotting on the battle-field”
>
> **(Pick 1993)**

Within such a rubric, women are excluded along with the infirm from battle. In the United States and within other NATO countries, as the women's movement has grown, demands have escalated from the inclusion of women into the military to an insistence on the right to participate in combat. Some feminist groups have claimed that taking part in combat will further advance the position of women in a general sense. The National Organisation for Women (NOW) was established in the United States in 1966 to promote women in public life. One component of the campaign has been an advocacy of the 'right to fight'. Those pushing for the placement of women in combat have argued that apart from the issue of political rights, those males who serve in the US military enjoy a range of economic benefits, such as free medical care and cheap loans, which are denied to women. Yet there is much that is culturally and socially sensitive here. In the words of one American official, 'a woman POW is the ultimate nightmare'. Those who have opposed the lifting of restrictions on women in combat have used the possibility of a female POW to justify the case against the full inclusion of women. This reflected the fear that female POWs might in captivity indeed be subjected to sexual assault or rape. When one army specialist, Melissa Rathbun-Nathy, was captured by the Iraqis during the Gulf War, there was much media speculation about how her Iraqi captors treated her and whether she had in fact been the subject of sexual assault (Nantais and Lee 1999). It is also claimed that during her period of captivity, several of her fellow male soldiers were told by their commanders that she had indeed been raped and or found with her head cut off / arms cut off, etc. These stories are consistent for some female scholars with the military tactic of using the 'protected' to motivate male soldiers (Nantais and Lee 1999). More recently of course much was made in the American media of the capture of a young American female soldier, Jessica Lynch, taken prisoner and then subsequently rescued by male soldiers. Lynch returned to a frenzy of excitement in the US. This 'GI Jane' even has Hollywood beckoning. Yet there were some very confused messages here about women, war and international relations. Not the least of these was what exactly we were meant to learn from the stories of female soldiers. Women can actually fight? Women can actually survive captivity? Or perhaps most cynically of all that the life of one young American female soldier was perhaps worth so much more airtime than the hundreds of young American men killed. Let us just invert part of the feminist argument here and reflect on whether the reluctance to allow women into battle and the efforts to 'save' Lynch represent a prizing, not a degradation of the female. But there is yet another layer here too which is that thousands of Iraqi women have been killed, wounded or hurt by this war but little attention has been paid to their plight. This therefore may be the paradox at the heart of the modern so-called liberal way of war, that Western women are too 'prized' to be allowed into combat or the danger zones of international relations but that non-Western women are expendable in international politics.

The issue of female soldiering, though, could be a simple extension of rights and of course duties. If women are full members of society then there is a corresponding duty to fulfil the obligations asked by the state. Until women are thought fit for military service, they will continue to be excluded not just from the highest offices of the armed services but from full equality within society. It is the linkage between man, the state and war that needs to be broken down or at least recognized and the complex, contested, contestable, and contextual structure that it is acknowledged and discussed.

KEY POINTS

- The analysis of gender is a relatively new phenomenon in International Security studies.
- International relations theorists, let alone security analysts, rarely admitted that gender was an important component of thinking about the state, the international system or international security.
- Feminist analysts introduced and answered the question of where are the women in security. They also alerted us to the idea that the experiences of women in relation to the state, state militaries and conflict are often very different from that of men.

Contradictions: biology and security

For some, of course, women are seen (as they have always been seen) as the 'weaker'—sometimes termed the 'fairer'—sex, and so will continue to be second-class citizens dependent on men for protection in both the international environment and in the domestic context. In many contemporary societies the state has conscripted its young men for service in the armed forces but women have usually been excluded. The overall effect is therefore to 'arm' men and 'disarm' women. There are to the minds of some feminist scholars important consequences of the exclusion of the female from the bearing of arms: one is to render women dependent on men for their protection. To walk women 'home' in the dark is a metaphor for how the female must need a protector to survive outside the alleged security of home and hearth. Which is why feminists who recognize the threat posed to women (and indeed men) by violence in the street talk of the need to 'take back the night' rather than looking for a 'hero' to walk you home. Both culturally and in institutional terms this function of protection has been linked to masculinity.

There are, of course, some pragmatic reasons for this at a state level. After all the slaughter of women on the battlefield along with men would decimate future generations. The phrase 'women and children' is one commonly used to symbolize the place of the female within the community—note a subordinate one, linking women with 'dependants'. It is an important place because of biology and the continual demands of the state on its female and child-bearing constituencies. Women have been used by virtue of their biology to promote certain security goals. Not the least of these has been the demand to breed for empire or the national interest. Although this may seem a rather crude formulation it is central to understanding how states and societies after war reproduce their populations and survive. Not for nothing did Stalin demand after the Second World War an increase in the birth rate (see Case Study 5.1). In the Russian population women were encouraged to have a high number of children as the Soviet state sought to recover from the ravaging of its population in the years of war (Kennedy-Pipe 2004). In certain states, women were denied access to birth control or abortion to promote and achieve a certain rate of reproduction (Buckley 1989). The most intimate of human activities arguably for women were less important than the demands of male political and religious elites that women provide a functional and biological service to the state.

This role of women as breeders remains imperative for the health of many wealthy industralized societies. In 2004 such was the concern of the French authorities over future demographics that it was announced that women would be given financial incentives, paid by the state, to produce more than one child. The problem remains familiar for some nations; women must be persuaded or coerced to breed at the whim of the central authorities.

CASE STUDY 5.1

Breeding for the state? The Soviet example

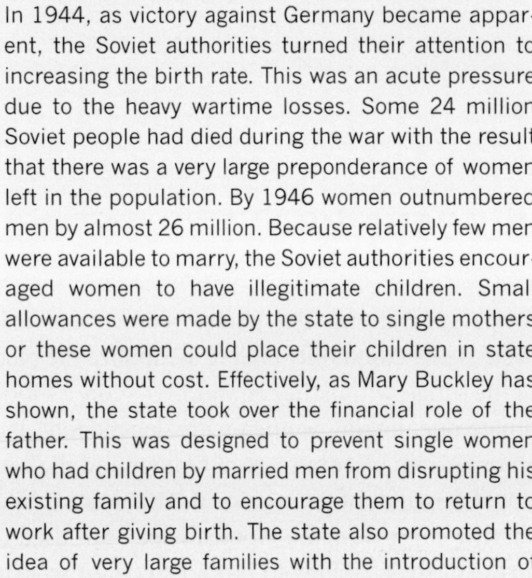

In 1944, as victory against Germany became apparent, the Soviet authorities turned their attention to increasing the birth rate. This was an acute pressure due to the heavy wartime losses. Some 24 million Soviet people had died during the war with the result that there was a very large preponderance of women left in the population. By 1946 women outnumbered men by almost 26 million. Because relatively few men were available to marry, the Soviet authorities encouraged women to have illegitimate children. Small allowances were made by the state to single mothers or these women could place their children in state homes without cost. Effectively, as Mary Buckley has shown, the state took over the financial role of the father. This was designed to prevent single women who had children by married men from disrupting his existing family and to encourage them to return to work after giving birth. The state also promoted the idea of very large families with the introduction of decorations for motherhood. Motherhood Glory went to mothers of seven, eight and nine children. After bearing ten children women became 'Heroine Mother'.

These measures were designed to address the population of surplus females and male population loss. Children were needed to address gaps in the labour market. So too were women. Despite maternity leave and some state benefits, women were also expected to return to the workplace after childbirth. The so-called women question (the emancipation of women), which had been highlighted after the Revolution by both Trotsky and Lenin, was therefore subordinated to the demands of a state recovering from war and the decimation of the male population.

Source: Mary Buckley (1989), *Women and Ideology in the Soviet Union*, London: Harvester Wheatsheaf.

Women as victims

In the age of professional armies, this reliance on women might not provide a crisis in the provision of military forces, though it might raise soft security issues of demographics, ethnic balance and age profiles. Indeed, the protection of that group—women—which can provide the future of the state or the community through their biology makes sense in certain ways. However, the protected may have had little say in the terms of how they are rendered 'safe' by either the state or by the military institutions which wage war on their behalf. In truth, recent work on how women are treated both in and after war demonstrates the somewhat ambiguous relationship that can exist between armed forces and civilian women. While women have often been the targets of violence by the enemy in conflict, it is also the case that they may suffer at the hands of their so-called 'protectors'. Recent reports from conflicts in Africa, for example, demonstrate evidence of brutal behaviour by 'peacekeeping' troops towards local women (Sorenson 1999; for more on this see Chapter 18). Again, this may actually strengthen the case for female soldiers to be engaged in certain types of peacekeeping work and to be especially employed in post-conflict situations, although the equation between female peacekeeping rests on a certain reading of female soldiering and a benign view of what experiences of war may or may not have on soldiers.

Work examining the Balkan Wars in the early 1990s and the first Gulf War has revealed a degree of violence perpetrated against women by soldiers returning home from the trauma of conflict. A claim might be made that violence against women is more prevalent both in militarized societies and within military families and that the idea that women and children are as a matter of course protected by male soldiers should be re-examined (Human Rights Watch 1999).

KEY POINTS

- Looking at women and their place in contemporary and historical conflicts helped bring about recognition that there are specific female issues relating to control of biology and reproduction.
- Women relate differently to state policy than do men.
- Women are intimately affected by state policy on contraception, abortion and marriage.
- States quite often use women to fulfil state politics in relation to demographic shortages.
- Biology is crucial to state security.

Women as peaceable

Whatever the evidence for these claims, and allegations of 'domestic' violence are difficult to substantiate, it is important therefore to be careful that we do not essentialize gender characteristics by always equating militarism with masculinity and with qualities such as strength, aggression, and violence and by suggesting that women, even female soldiers, are synonymous with the will to nourish. These stereotypical notions of men and women are to be found throughout the security studies literature. Most commonly women have been associated not with soldiering but with campaigns for peace such as that at Greenham Common during the 1980s and movements protesting against military bases such as the American base Fylingdales in North Yorkshire or in East Anglia. Female voices often lead these protests that are against the stationing of foreign troops or missiles in local areas. In the interests of national security it is not even known by those who live around such bases how many or what type of security apparatus is stationed in the local vicinity. Ironically, those protected cannot know for sure the nature or quantity of what is protecting them!

As Elshtain's discussion of 'beautiful souls' alluded to above reminds us, of course, there is a long tradition that seemingly demonstrates that women and peace are interconnected: that females as the bearers of children or the potential bearers of children are necessarily more anti-war than men. These anti-war movements have habitually treated the military apparatus of the state, especially the nuclear component, as an expression of male aggression (Alonso 1993). Within this rubric mothers are life-affirming and biology of the female kind negates male militarism. While the 'peace' women of the 1980s can justifiably claim that they did in fact influence the military debate through their actions of 'chaining themselves to fences outside nuclear bases, dancing on missile silos and jumping into convoy jeeps as they pass by', the problem was, as Christine Sylvester points out, that all of these activities can be discounted by those in power. In her words, 'Peace camps do not lead us to the edge of war. They do not stockpile weapons and hurtle us into arms races. . . . They do not matter' (Sylvester 1996). It should be noted, however, that the engagement of women with the politics of peace was actually of concern to a number of those in power. During the Cold War, the CIA monitored women's groups associated with peace campaigns with a great deal of interest. Women as a constituency with no 'natural' loyalty to their state were considered to be especially vulnerable to the propaganda campaigns of other states (Laville 1997). There is no evidence that women are more prone to the betrayal of their state than a group called man but nevertheless the engagement of women in the politics of defence seems to have aroused a great deal of state interest.

Those linkages between 'men and war' and 'women and peace' are important, even if ill founded. They imply, as the American academic Bell Hooks has argued, that women by virtue of simply being women have played little or no role in supporting and upholding the militarism of the state (Hooks 1995). Women have in this one-dimensional version of historical events been merely 'observers' of and objects in war.

Women have, however, always been engaged in the business of war. For some scholars this is important because it means that the history of war and indeed histories generally have been told in such a way that it is just that: '*his story*'. Women and their stories or narratives are therefore absent from a number of textbooks or what are regarded as the important studies of war. More recently academics have concentrated in growing numbers on the telling of female histories, and we do now have a number of works that tell some of the stories of women as victims of war—for example monographs and scholarly works that tell the stories of mass rape in war or examine the gendered effects of war (Stiglmayer 1994).

KEY POINTS

- The traditional literature on security has treated women as upholders of peace.
- Women have indeed been involved in many powerful national and international movements promoting peace and disarmament.
- We need to understand the nature of men, women, and how they relate to war and peace in specific contexts.

Women as warriors

The woman as 'victim' is, as we saw earlier, an important thread in the stories of war. Indeed, in 1990 an estimated ninety per cent of war causalities were civilians, the vast majority women and children (Silvard 1991), but contemporary scholarship has uncovered numerous examples where women have supported the role of men in war and participated in civil war and war itself. The tales of these women shed fascinating light on the work of the female in war revealing female experiences as soldiers, special agents, nurses, surgeons, laundry women, cooks and prostitutes (Isaksson 1988). They do not suggest that men and women are different in some absolute way. It may also be that such formulations ignore the contribution that many men have made to peace movements and to pacifism. Individual men have often sought to avoid combat and most conscript armies have been dogged by desertion and so-called cowardice brought about by the trauma of war. As we move into the twenty-first century, and know about the problems of trauma in war amongst even very brave and honourable people, it is difficult to see how long we can sustain the idea of war as either heroic or the natural place for a human regardless of gender.

This is not to argue that very many heroic acts do not take place in war. Contemporary warfare—as with its predecessors—is littered with not just acts of barbarism but acts of great courage and honour. Nor is it to argue that there is never any reason why war might be the least worst option. There clearly might be reasons why a war might be just or even morally required. Rather it is to say, with Michael Walzer, that even the language of the just war is for most of us (men and women alike) a 'second language' and like all second languages, we do not speak it perfectly and should recognize our imprecisions and lack of the full vocabulary (Walzer 2005).

KEY POINTS

- The act of battle and sacrifice in battle has been regarded as the key to the state.
- On the whole, citizenship, was linked to the willingness to fight for one's country.
- Recent scholarship demonstrates that war may not be heroic and that gender alone is not a determinant of bravery.

Changing roles: changing perceptions

We in the West have had the luxury of being able to acknowledge the problems of humankind and war. Indeed since the RMA there has been a gradual erosion of the state's military demands on its peoples: a trend accelerated in the Western world by the decline of Communism. By 1991, when the Soviet Union ceased to exist both the United States and Britain were relying on relatively small volunteer forces. Russia, long reliant on huge conscript armies, is moving to a voluntary system. In many democracies, the notion of the soldier as citizen has simply died. Even if we do not yet live in a post-heroic culture as Edward Luttwak has claimed, war as trial by national survival is almost certainly dead (Luttwak 1995). We, or certainly those in the Western world, live in a world where war is at a distance, our own casualties are minimized and controversial and the preferred option of democratic states at war is that of aerial bombing. Wars at a distance from our civilian engagement have changed the way in which modern militaries fight and the way in which civilian populations respond. As we saw during the Kosovo conflict of the late 1990s, liberal states were able to wage a successful war against Serbia without having to suffer a single conflict fatality. The nature of this conflict led some scholars to argue that gender made little difference to the conduct of war, as soldiers of whatever gender did not now need to be placed in harm's way. This use of 'virtual war', to use Ignatieff's term, solved the problem of men, women and war. If actual combat could be avoided then male and female soldiers could wage war on equal terms.

As the nature of war has changed after the Cold War, however, from one of war conducted by mass armies through defence by nuclear deterrence to 'virtual war', the role of both men and women in relation to conflict has changed. We in the West can engage in mass killing through technology with few apparent costs to ourselves. This might, except at the margins, mean that debates over the relative fitness of men and women for war are irrelevant. But there is a problem here and it is one that is raised in much of the security literature on women and war and development and security. The problem is, to put it bluntly, that while gender and war in the West may have been about the 'right to fight' or the right to object to state policies fought in the name of national politics, in most of the rest of the world men and women have far fewer choices. In many parts of the globe campaigns for women to be allowed to fight and die in national armies would seem bizarre. While war may be sanitized for those of us living in the West, women (and indeed men and children) in war zones such as Afghanistan, Sri Lanka, Iraq or in Latin America are victims of, witnesses, may participate in, but almost certainly seek to remove themselves from, war and violence. Conflict is rarely in these cases about the historical contract between the individual and the central authorities but a battle for individual, familial or communal survival in a local patch. Add into this the complexities of what are now known as soft security issues, Aids, illegal trading of people, economic hardship and our understanding of gender as a divide between men and women must be elaborated upon to provide a more complex picture of what it means to a man or a women in a specific time and place.

KEY POINTS

- Technology has rendered the battlefield 'gender neutral' in some respects.
- War takes many forms and for those in the third world still represents a battle for survival.

Conclusion

The traditional literature on security largely ignored the issue of gender. It was implicit in most of the literature on war and security that gender produced different roles for men and women. In short, boys would have 'toys' (weapons) and girls would have 'dolls' (children). Women as a category were ignored and on the whole regarded as unfit for either service in war or unsuited for leadership or in some cases even citizenship. While men were warriors, women were either ignored or depicted as passive in terms of security issues. Quite often even the role of women as victim was regarded as irrelevant to the business of state security. Women did, however, serve the purposes of nationalist causes with nationalism often served up in highly gendered and female terms. Female symbols of statehood were and remain a characteristic of many modern states. The figure of the women as mother to the nation is a familiar one. See Case Study 5.1.

Feminist and critical security investigations into the state, war and security allowed us in the 1980s and 1990s to go beyond the rather simple categories of men/warrior/protector and women/mother/protected. What the feminist literature did was to alert us to a series of consequences which state security policies had for women. The first was to alert us to the fact that war could have specific and gendered consequences. Not least that women were likely to be victims not only of war as indirect casualties but that war policy itself might specifically target women in terms of genocidal rape or sexual abuse. The value attached to women might, as we saw during the Balkan Wars, make them susceptible to attack and abuse. We also learnt from some feminist writings of the other sufferings inflicted on women in terms of economic and social displacement after conflict. So, for example, that women after conflict may be forced into the international sex slave trade. In a more positive fashion we also learnt that women might organize themselves to protest against state policy and certain facets of nationalism. Feminist writers and historians also alerted us to the way in which states have historically sought to control the biology of women to construct certain state policies. Women might be coerced or persuaded to produce children for the state. They might, for example, not be allowed access to abortion or contraception depending on the whim or needs of the central authorities. Perhaps more importantly, though, the feminist and gender literature allowed us to rethink notions of security which had dominated International Relations. It allowed us to ask key questions. These included the questioning of core certainties of International Relations such as the notion of state power. What does power actually mean for different men and different women, both within the state and outside? What might citizenship mean for men and women? What might war mean? Crucially, how do men and women define issues of security? Do they in fact define security differently?

Perhaps, though, the most telling feature of recent literature is that 'gender' is a way of unlocking security concerns allowing us to see that gender as a category is a social construction. That is, the way men and women act or react may be a product of sexual difference but may also be a product of circumstance. We should ask therefore how both men and women in different contexts relate to local, regional and international security apparatus. Is it the case that security policies, as some feminists have claimed, always privilege men and always discriminate against women? Or is it that we need to understand that men are not always or simply leaders, warriors or the oppressors of women?

Gender and security are terms that require, for a proper understanding of either, to be related. But, of course, this does not mean that either is reducible to the other nor that either does not have a role independent of the other. Gender—in all its forms and with all its complexities—affects many things other than security, and security—in its turn, and however it is understood—is dependent on many things other than gender. But as I hope to have shown, trying to understand either without an appreciation of the role of the other results in an impoverished understanding of both. Understanding, of course, does not necessarily lead to any change in practice, but it is an assumption that governs any reasoned (and reasonable) politics that it must be a first step.

? QUESTIONS

How do we understand the term gender?

What difference does it make to our understanding of security to ask about the place of women?

Do you think that being female makes a difference to your security?

Are women always victims in war?

Should women be excluded from combat?

What are the consequences of state policies on contraception/abortion for the security of women?

Why does rape seem to accompany every war?

Are men natural warriors?

Should citizenship be linked to militarism?

Can women be heroes?

FURTHER READING

- **Enloe, Cynthia (1989), *Bananas, Bases and Beaches: Making Feminist Sense of International Politics*, London: Pinter.** This is in many ways one of the most important readings of feminist international relations. Enloe was amongst the first to pose and answer the question 'Where are the women in international politics?' Enloe alerted us to the fact that women occupy multiple roles in security, diplomacy, trade and local and regional politics.

- **Enloe, Cynthia (2000), *Maneuvers*, Berkeley CA: University of California Press.** Professor Enloe continues her mission of uncovering the effects of militarization on women in a global context. She argues that women everywhere are affected by the presence and ethos of military institutions and the processes of militarization. Security of the female individual and community is compromised and undermined by the needs of the military.

- **Steans, Jill (1998), *Gender and International Relations*, Cambridge: Polity Press.** A clearly stated analysis of how women and men have related to the state, war and the international system. Links gender to nationalism, the construction of citizenship and explores in detail the various arguments over whether women are fit to fight. Also looks at women and development issues.

- **Tickner, Ann (1992), *Gender in International Relations*, New York: Columbia University Press.** A feminist analysis of the existing major theories of International Relations. Includes interesting and clear analysis of feminist thinking on subjects such as ecology. Especially useful on security.

- **Van Crevald, Martin (2001), *Men, Women and War*, London: Cassell and Co.** A provocative and lively account which argues against women as suited for the tasks of war. The author argues that women should not be engaged in the business of national security and war.

IMPORTANT WEBSITES

- **www.uswc.org** Connects US women working for rights and empowerment and links them with the global women's movement.

- **www.womenwarpeace.org** The United Nations Security Council in its October 2000 resolution on Women, Peace and Security noted the 'need to consolidate data on the impact of armed conflict on women and girls'. This website is the response to this. It is a portal that provides data on the impact of armed conflict on women and girls.

- **www.womenwagingpeace.net** This website provides details of the Initiative for Inclusive Security, a network established in 1999 that enables women from around the world to connect with one another and have an impact on decision makers.

- **www.dcaf.ch/women** Women in an Insecure World is part of the Geneva Centre for the Democratic Control of Armed Forces and has as its main objective the empowerment of women as security sector actors.

Visit the Online Resource Centre that accompanies this book for lots of interesting additional material: www.oxfordtextbooks.co.uk/orc/collins/

6 Human Security

PAULINE KERR

Chapter Contents

Reader's Guide

This chapter examines the concept of human security and its role within both security studies and the policy community. It argues the concept is a recent development of earlier human-centric arguments, which propose that people ought to be secure in their daily lives. The label 'human security' came into currency in the mid-1990s and now serves several useful purposes, the most important being to highlight some critical issues, especially intra-state political violence, that are not included in the state-centric paradigm that presently dominates discourse. The concept of human security does not challenge the relevance of state-centric arguments in so far as these concern the protection of the state from external military violence of a realpolitik nature. However, the human security concept does show that state-centric realism is not a sufficient security argument in that it does not adequately address the security of people inside states from political violence. It therefore does not deserve to be the dominant understanding of security. In the contemporary context the concept of security should encompass properly functioning states and their people. But so far attempts at conceptually reconciling or converging arguments about the security of the state and people are underdeveloped and vulnerable to criticism. From a practical perspective the concept of human security receives mixed responses from the policy community: some practitioners adopt both state and human-centric approaches, others reject the human security approach, and others misuse it to justify policies that have other motives. The chapter concludes with a summary of the concept's likely future in the conceptualization and practice of security.

Introduction: intellectual and empirical purpose

The idea that people ought to be secure in the conduct of their daily lives is neither new nor surprising. A human-centric focus continues to drive the very old political philosophy of liberalism, which places people and the individual at its epicentre and prescribes some necessary conditions, such as freedom and equality, for people to be secure. Likewise, the tradition of liberalism within the discipline of international relations focuses on broad normative visions that aim to ensure that people will be secure, such as through the adoption of universal human rights. International relations' sub-discipline, security studies, and its critical security school, often place the security of people at the centre of its critique of state-centric and military security. Indeed, these arguments by critical security scholars for deepening and broadening the idea of security are driven to a large extent by a vision of the conditions that ought to pertain for people to be secure.

This long philosophical and political human-centric tradition has only recently included a concept labelled 'human security'. The term apparently had its origins in policy statements emanating from the United Nations in the mid-1990s and in particular the 1994 United Nations Development Program (UNDP) Report (1994). In this document 'human security' is described as a condition where people are given relief from the traumas that besiege human development. Human security means 'first, safety from such chronic threats as hunger, disease and repression. And second, it means protection from sudden and hurtful disruptions in the patterns of daily life—whether in homes, in jobs or in communities' (1994: 23). Ensuring human security requires a seven-pronged approach to address economic, food, health, environment, personal, community, and political security. This particular understanding of human security is categorized as one of the broad definitions and is the basis for division about the meaning of human security, which we will explore in the next section.

In the meantime it is useful to ask why the concept has come into centre stage at this time and what purposes it serves within the discipline and empirically. The point to remember about concepts is that, like theories, they are developed to serve a purpose, or several purposes, and some do so more usefully than others. So, what purposes does the concept of human security serve and are they useful? Going back to the recent origins of the term, the UNDP coinage can be seen as a post-Cold War attempt to focus attention on the issue of development, or more precisely human development, so as to move human and financial resources towards poverty relief and away from simple GDP economic indicators of development and the all-consuming Cold War military and traditional security agenda. If this was the purpose then it is ironic that today there is even more attention on political violence, albeit within the state and in the context of development, with the result that more resources are being directed towards the crisis side of conflict management and less towards preventing the root causes, such as poverty. The most recent manifestation of this is the focus on managing international terrorism through military means at the expense of preventing global poverty as a problem independent from, albeit sometimes related to, terrorism.

The focus that the concept of human security puts on the nexus between conflict and development is nonetheless very useful and important. Empirical observations and several data-collection studies reveal the significance of that nexus. Conflict since the mid-1990s overwhelmingly takes place within the borders of developing states, not between states. These borders frequently surround what is often called disrupted states where governance is failing often because there is conflict among armed groups—sometimes between the government and rebels, and sometimes between competing rebel or social groups. Caught in between the warring parties are countless civilians, many of whom are women and children. Disturbingly, the main perpetrator of violence against civilians is frequently the ruling regime and state actors such as the police and military. The significance of the nexus between development and conflict is not just that it raises ethical issues about human suffering but that its frequent outcome, so called state failure, has dire local, regional and global effects (see Think Point 6.1 on the nexus between conflict and development in Africa).

The development of the human security concept also highlights the view that the threats to humans, as well as to state entities, are changing and increasing. These changes have spurred the debate about the meaning of security and the arguments for its broadening and deepening. Apart from violence within the state, there are non-military threats of environmental degradation and the effects of global warming, pandemics such as HIV/AIDS, SARS, and avian flu, and people movements (refugees and internally displaced peoples). Like internal violence, these transnational issues have serious local, regional and global effects.

From a normative perspective the concept serves to highlight the importance of good global norms. Human security is a motivation for the Universal Declaration of Human Rights, the UN Charter, the Geneva Conventions, the Ottawa Treaty, and the International Criminal Court. Human security often serves as an umbrella norm for various treaties and conventions which aim to protect vulnerable people from persecuting actors, notably the state. Developing good global norms is not only important for moral and ethical reasons but also because, as most democratic countries illustrate, they serve to enhance state and international security.

The concept of human security even serves to support some realpolitik interests. Sukhre suggests that Canada and Norway were strong advocates of human security not least because the concept could assist their lobbying efforts during the early 1990s to gain a seat as the non-permanent members of the UN Security Council (2004: 365). The concept can serve other types of realpolitik interests, as we will see later in the chapter.

Notwithstanding the point that human security can serve some realpolitik issues it is apparent from Chapter 2 that human security is quite different from state-centric security. State-centric security is focused on protecting the state from external military threats via the threat (deterrence) and use of

THINK POINT 6.1

The nexus beteen conflict and development in Africa

- Today most wars are fought in poor countries.
- By the start of the 21st century more people were being killed in Africa's wars than in the rest of the world combined.
- Most of the world's armed conflicts now take place in sub-Saharan Africa.
- Armed conflicts in sub-Saharan Africa are particularly difficult to avoid, contain or end. Prospects for peace have been harmed by a combination of pervasive poverty, declining GDP per capita, reduced aid, poor infrastructure, weak administration, external intervention, an abundance of cheap weapons and a bitter legacy of past wars.
- Moreover, violent conflicts in Africa exacerbate the very conditions that gave rise to them in the first place, creating a classic 'conflict trap' from which escape is extraordinarily difficult. Sustaining peace settlements is a major challenge in many African post-conflict countries.

Source: Human Security Centre (2005), *Human Security Report* 2005. Oxford: Oxford University Press and online at www.humansecurityreport.info

military force. Infringements of the principle of sovereignty are a central justification for the use of force. It is usually said that in state-centric arguments the state is the referent object of security whereas in human-centric arguments people are the referent object.

KEY POINTS

- The human-centric tradition, which emphasizes the desirable human conditions for people to be secure, now includes the concept of 'human security'.
- Concepts are tools and human security is no exception. The label of human security developed in the mid-1990s serves to highlight several issues in world politics: for example, concerns about human development, the nexus between development and conflict, the increasing number of transnational threats, the growing normative humanitarian agenda and even realpolitik interests.
- The main purpose that the concept serves is to focus attention on the fact that most of these issues have serious local, regional and global effects and are not included in the state-centric position—the dominant argument about security.

Is human security a valuable analytical and policy framework?

The proposition in the above discussion is that the concept of human security raises issues about the security of people that are not part of the dominant state-centric argument of security. However, even if this is the case, does the concept provide an analytical and policy framework that can challenge state-centric positions and should it be the dominant argument? Answering these questions requires an examination of the concept: its meaning according to the different schools of human security and the analytical relationship between these schools. It also requires an examination of the state-centric schools of thought and a comparison of human and state-centric arguments.

This section makes three arguments: first, that there are major differences between the schools of human security which raise questions about its prospects as a framework for challenging the dominant argument; second, that it is possible nonetheless to reconcile these differences and develop an analytical framework; third, that this framework has the potential to challenge the realist state-centric school by showing that it is a necessary but not sufficient security argument. However, that said, the human security is itself a necessary but not sufficient argument.

Tensions between the schools of human security

Human security, according to its advocates, challenges the traditional state-centric view that the state is and should be the primary object, or referent, of security. For the advocates, human security is the end and state-centric security is the means to that objective. But what does human security actually mean? Putting aside differences between state-centric and human-centric positions for the moment, the meaning of human security is contested by the different schools of human security. While all the advocates agree that people are the referent object they are divided over the type of threat that should be prioritized, or securitized. The dispute over prioritizing threats has divided advocates into the narrow and the broad schools.

The narrow school

Mack, a proponent of the narrow school, argues that the threat of political violence to people, by the state or any other organized political actor, is the proper focus for the concept of human security. The definition that Mack and his institution, the Human Security Centre at the University of British Columbia, support is that human security is 'the protection of individuals and communities from war and other forms of violence' (Human Security Centre: 2005). Mack acknowledges there are many other threats to people apart from systematic violence. However, his emphasis on conceptual clarity and analytical rigour involves treating many of these other threats as correlates of violence; for example violence correlates with poverty and poor governance (2004: 367). For Mack, there is advocacy value in expanding the security agenda to include the broad agenda below but that doing so has analytical costs. This narrow definition has been simplified as 'freedom from fear' of the threat or use of political violence and is distinguished from the broad definition below which is labelled 'freedom from want'.

The broad schools

The broad schools argue that human security means more than a concern with the threat of violence. Human security is not only freedom from fear but also freedom from want, which is the focus of human development in the UNDP Report mentioned earlier. Moreover, according to some, human security goes beyond freedom from want in underdevelopment and involves other human freedoms and values. For example, Thakur and his institution, the United Nations University in Tokyo, hold that 'human security is concerned with the protection of people from critical life-threatening dangers, regardless of whether the threat are rooted in anthropogenic activities or natural events, whether they lie within or outside states, and whether they are direct or structural' (2004: 347). Human security is '"human centred" in that its principal focus is on people both as individuals and as communal groups. It is "security orientated" in that the focus is on freedom from fear, danger and threat' (2004: 347). Thakur attempts to install some limitations to the broad school by referring to life-threatening situations which have become crises and by putting those which are not crises onto the broader development agenda. An example of the even broader definition of human security is one proposed by Alkiri. Alkiri, who was a member of the 2003 Commission on Human Security, co-chaired by Amartya Sen and Sadako Ogata, argues that the objective of human security is 'to protect the vital core of all human lives in ways that advance human freedoms and human fulfilment' (2004: 360). Thakur defends these broad conceptualizations on the grounds that although analytical rigour may be lost there is value in having inclusive definitions.

The broad definitions of human security certainly receive the most criticism and often provide the grounds for critics to dismiss the entire concept. Paris, for example, claims human security 'encompasses everything from substance abuse to genocide'. From this perspective, the problem is that the number of causal hypotheses for human insecurity are so vast that frameworks for research and policy are difficult to formulate. Paris dismisses the whole concept as being 'inscrutable' (2004: 371), a strong condemnation considering that, in the Oxford Concise Dictionary, the word means 'impossible to understand or interpret' (2004: 371).

Differences over means

Debate about the types of threats which should be included in the definition has of course implications for the means for enhancing human security. The means for the broad school are the same as those proposed in various UNDP reports, for example the 2005 UNDP Human Development Report (2005). However, because the broad school also includes definitions that go beyond the development agenda to include threats to 'vital core of all human lives' and since these can be quite subjective and variable, the means are equally variable. The broad school comprising threats to human development and particularly the very broad threats to 'vital core of all human lives', appears to have no common factor that connects all the different threats, except that each is perceived as a threat to people. Thus the means for the broad school will depend on whatever the threat is perceived to be and are therefore limitless. However, because the narrow school is connected by the common focus on the threat of political violence to people the means are directed at managing that threat. A wide variety of economic, social, and political proposals are found in the literature on managing internal conflict and transnational violence.

The means issue is further complicated by arguments over the role of the state and the appropriate agents of human security. In many situations the state is the perpetrator of violence and of other threats to its people's security and is therefore the problem, or a major part of the problem. Such behaviour by the state is often taken to be synonymous with the state-centric position on security. From this perspective, human security is hard, even impossible, to achieve if the state remains the major actor in world politics.

This perspective raises important issues about the role of the state as a means to human security. It is certainly the case that some states are at the heart of human insecurity. But there are several other issues to consider. First, because some states wilfully behave badly does not mean that all states should be dismissed as actors and that all state-centric positions work against human security; second, pragmatically, states continue to have the main material assets for logistically delivering human security; third, in reality state-building towards better states continues to be the objective of the major global institutions including the UN, and many NGOs and **civil society** groups; fourth, realistically, comprehensive normative change does not occur quickly and thus adopting a hands-off states and policy approach is not helpful in the short term when there are many current crises in which people need immediate relief from atrocities. Hence it is necessary to deal with the immediate situation while still pursuing long-term change. For that reason it is necessary to engage in a direct way in a policy agenda for human security. It is also necessary to involve a variety of actors—institutions of global governance, **non-state actors**, civil society and states—in addressing the narrow and broad agendas. Nonetheless, scepticism about the state's capacity to deliver and reform remains and hence the division over means continues to be a divisive issue.

Another major difference over the means to human security concerns the place of **humanitarian intervention** using military means in situations where systematic violence within a state is the cause of human insecurity. This is a debate that takes place between state-centric advocates and the schools of human security as well as between the schools. Realists warn human security advocates that intervention for humanitarian purposes runs the risk of prolonging warfare and therefore the long-term suffering of large sections of the population, particularly refugees. Realists also warn that, from their perspective, the principle of sovereignty has helped to prevent inter-state war and indiscriminately overriding it through intervention using force has costs for international security.

From the human security perspective humanitarian intervention also raises questions about the principle of sovereignty, the state, and international stability. Although realists may be correct that adherence to the principle of sovereignty may help to explain recent international stability it is also the case that in an increasingly inter-connected world, international stability and order will depend on human security inside states. As Hampson and others have argued, states cannot be secure if their citizens are not (2004: 350). At the international level, widespread human insecurity inside states has spill-over effects on states and people in neighbouring and distant regions. For example, in the sub-Saharan African region internal conflict has dire local, regional and global consequences. In these cases humanitarian intervention with the objective of establishing states with human security values is a source of international stability. Indeed, this connection between international peace and stability and establishing human security is one of the major justifications for the UN's support for intervention.

However, if intervention is justified on the grounds of promoting or restoring international stability then it may prioritize conflicts that are seen to have strategic implications and not those that may be more deadly and violent. Hence, the positive connection between human security and international order is not necessarily a satisfactory criterion for assessing whether or not humanitarian intervention is justified. If the priority is to establish human security then humanitarian intervention using force should be a logical choice regardless of the international dimension. This raises more questions about the proper criteria for assessing why and when intervention using force is justified. Perhaps the best guidance is offered in the 2001 report of the International Commission on Intervention and State Sovereignty (ICISS) *The Responsibility to Protect* (2001). It argues that state sovereignty implies that the primary responsibility for the protection of people from serious violent harm lies with the state itself. If the state is not willing or is unable to do so then 'the principle of non-intervention yields to the international responsibility to protect' (2001: xi). The report establishes six criteria for military intervention (see Background 6.1) and emphasizes the role of the United Nations and regional organizations as the key actors. The norm of responsibility is mentioned in an increasing number of policy documents. However, regardless of the guidelines offered in the report, the external use of force for protecting human security of others remains a contested ethical issue.

BACKGROUND 6.1

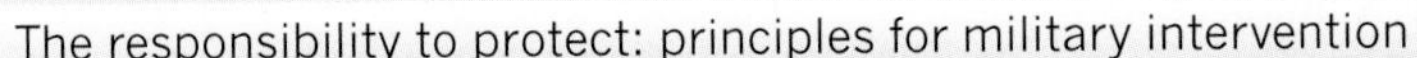

The responsibility to protect: principles for military intervention

(1) THE JUST CAUSE THRESHOLD

Military intervention for human protection purposes is an exceptional and extraordinary measure. To be warranted, there must be serious and irreparable harm occurring to human beings, or immediately likely to occur, of the following kind:

A. large-scale loss of life, actual or apprehended, with genocidal intent or not, which is the product of either deliberate state action, or state neglect or inability to act, or a failed state situation; or

B. large-scale 'ethnic cleansing', actual or apprehended, whether it is carried out by killing, forced expulsion, acts of terror or rape.

(2) THE PRECAUTIONARY PRINCIPLES

A. Right intention: the primary purpose of the intervention, whatever other motives intervening states may have, must be to halt or avert human suffering. Right intention is better assured with multiple operations, clearly supported by regional opinion and the victims concerned.

B. Last resort: military intervention can only be justified when every non-military option for the prevention or peaceful resolution of the crisis has been explored, with reasonable grounds for believing lesser measures would not have succeeded.

C. Proportional means: the scale, duration and intensity of the planned military intervention should be the minimum necessary to secure the defined human protection objective.

D. Reasonable prospects: there must be reasonable chance of success in halting or averting the suffering which has justified the intervention, with the consequences of action not likely to be worse that the consequences of inaction.

International Commission on Intervention and State Sovereignty (2001). *The Responsibility to Protect.* Report of the International Commission on Intervention and State Sovereignty. Ottawa: International Development Research Centre: XII. (Note that principles (3) and (4), which are not listed here, concern the Right Authority and Operational Principles respectively.)

Furthermore, even if the principles in the ICISS report are logically sound, it appears to be of decreasing practical guidance of late, if the lack of action taken in 2004–05 Darfur crisis is any indication (Williams and Bellamy 2005). In addition, politically, the responsibility to protect is not widely accepted by developing countries as determining operational policy, notwithstanding the agreement in the *Draft Outcome Document* produced at the 2005 World Summit by the General Assembly to accept it as nevertheless valuable (2005: 27–28). For most G77 states human security requires implementing the development agenda by the state, with help from international donors and organizations, and the continuation of unconditional sovereignty. Making sovereignty conditional is seen as yet another example of powerful Western states setting the rules of world politics and justifying an excuse for intervening in the internal affairs of recently decolonized states. Hence, the focus of the narrow school of human security on internal violence and intervention on those grounds is often not acceptable to developing states, beyond rhetorical endorsement.

In conclusion, the means for addressing human insecurity as violence will involve a range of measures and actors and their roles will continue to be contested. Regardless of critics' concerns about the role of states, properly functioning states will be indispensable actors, not least because the intervening military and police force, albeit in blue berets, will have the assets and human resources to provide immediate security from violence. The key actors for reconstruction, once security is assured, will be global institutions, local and international NGOs and civil society groups.

KEY POINTS

- There are tensions between the different schools of human security about the meaning of, threats to and the means to human security.
- The narrow school focuses on threats of violence, often called freedom from fear; the broad school focuses on threats arising from underdevelopment, often called freedom from want; and the very broad school focuses on threats to other human freedoms.
- The means to human security are also contentious, with divisions over the role the state and the justifications for humanitarian intervention using force.

Reconciling tensions

In principle the above discussion illustrating the divisions between the different schools of human security raises questions about the concept's capacity to challenge the dominant state-centric argument about security. However, this section argues that it is possible to develop analytical and policy frameworks based on both the narrow and broad schools which show that there are important connections between them.

The framework focuses upon (i) human insecurity as political violence and (ii) the causes of human insecurity as political violence. To use social science language, human insecurity as political violence (the narrow school) is the **dependent variable**. The many causes of human insecurity as political violence include the problems of underdevelopment (the broad school) and these are the **independent variables** (see Figure 6.1).

There are several analytical advantages to this formulation. First, the connections between the two schools are quite clear. Second, the causal links can be multifactorial and inter-connected: for example,

Figure 6.1 Conceptual framework

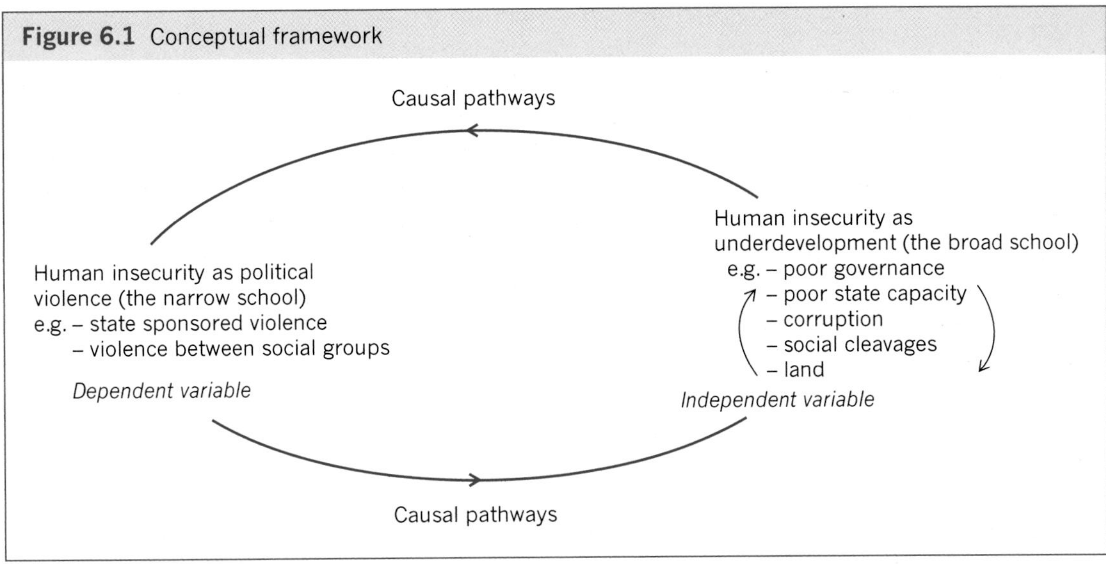

threats of poverty and disease and poor governance are two interconnected causes of political violence (see Figure 6.1). Third, causality can be a circular dynamic: for example, not only can poverty and poor governance cause political violence, it can work the other way as well, that is, political violence can cause poverty and bad governance (see Figure 6.1). Fourth, because this conceptual framework identifies the problem of violence and its causes it provides a sound basis for policy (see Figure 6.2). Importantly, it shows that crisis management of violence requires both immediate action in terms of diplomacy and, failing that, intervention. Plus at the same time it requires crisis prevention measures from the broad development agenda. Proper management requires policies that address the narrow school's focus on violence and the broad school's focus on development. Each type of policy is equally important.

This framework helps to overcome many of the tensions between the schools and it may satisfy some of the critics. It will not, however, please those human security advocates who want to include the very broad agenda of protecting the 'vital core of human lives' as human security. And it will frustrate those who want to include non-violent issues, such as horizontal inequality or people movements, as the dependent variable unrelated to violence. Finally, there is still the question of whether or not it is a framework that can challenge the dominant state-centric security argument.

KEY POINTS

- One way of reconciling the different schools and developing a framework is to focus on the nexus between the narrow school's focus on violence and broad school's focus on human development.
- Taking the narrow school's focus on political violence as the dependent variable and the broad school's focus on human development as the independent variable provides a policy framework for understanding causality and policies for crisis management and prevention.
- But, is this a framework that can challenge the state-centric argument of security?

Figure 6.2 Policy framework

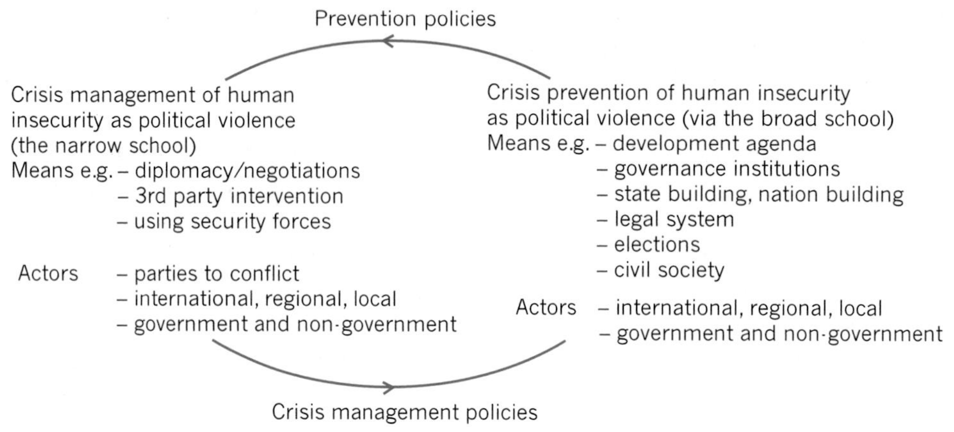

Human security and state-centric security

Having explored the debates showing the tensions with the human security argument and the possibility of reconciling the narrow and broad schools it is now possible to compare this human security framework with the state-centric arguments and question the respective value each has for our understanding of security. The argument in this section is that the state-centric concept of realism and the human-security concept are necessary but not sufficient security concepts. If this is the case then it appears both arguments are needed for understanding security.

Different threats

Realism is a necessary security argument. It provides several theories that address an important set of threats to the survival of the state and territory. These theories assume that the state and territory are the key referent objects and that external threats of a military nature are the most important. Empirically realism is certainly relevant in situations such as South Asia and the Middle East where there are military threats to states. Realists argue that this type of situation is a constant possibility for every state in the world and that history proves this is a valid concern. Arguably realism also implies that, even if the referent object is the state, protecting the state from military threats has the effect of protecting its people.

Although necessary, realism is not a sufficient security argument. It acknowledges the threat of outside military violence but ignores internal violence (along with other broader threats). Realism's focus just on the external threats to the state has failed to deliver security to many people inside states, a situation which is normatively objectionable to most people and makes the state, the referent object of realism, vulnerable to both external and internal threats. Moreover, internal threats are more common today than external military threats and contribute to the problem of state-failure which undermines international security, a key concern for realism. If realism is an argument for concentrating on state-centric security then it needs to canvass a wider range of threats to states' survival and international peace and stability.

Human security is also a necessary but not sufficient argument. Although it focuses on threats to people—95% of all battle deaths are caused by internal conflict—it ignores external military threats. While only 5% of battle deaths are the result of inter-state war if weapons of mass destruction are ever used the consequences will be horrific. Ironically, the focus of human security on internal and transnational violence and malfunctioning states is more likely than realism to lead to better governance of states and hence to enhanced international stability. That said, the primary objective of human security is not to enhance state-centric security per se but rather to ensure that people do not suffer from those versions of state-centric security that ignore internal violence and its causes.

Different views about sovereignty

Realism is also not sufficient because it ignores the centrality of internal violence and the contractual nature of sovereignty which is evident in Hobbes' version of state-centric security. Although realists claim the Hobbesian political tradition as their own they avoid some key tenets. The first is that Hobbes' state-centric position was based on the argument that security is concerned with protecting the state from threats of violence and 'warre' from within. The second is that Hobbes' state-centric position is also opposed to malfunctioning states and to leaders/sovereigns who are violent to their citizens. Hobbes' view of legitimate state-building rests on the sovereign's contract with the people to provide them with security from internal threats, in exchange for their cooperation and acknowledgement that the sovereign/state is the legitimate arbiter of the use of force. Third and most important, Hobbes suggests that people may resist if their sovereign threatens their lives and if the sovereign does not protect them (1914: xxi). Hence sovereignty is conditional on the provision of protection for the people. In ignoring the contractual nature of sovereignty which Hobbes supports, realism leaves the impression that it has reified the state at the expense of its people.

By contrast many human security advocates, although not drawing on Hobbes, endorse a contractual arrangement, that sovereignty is conditional on providing protection. Already discussed is the 2001 report by the ICISS which points out that sovereignty is not an unconditional right and that states have a responsibility to protect their citizens. This argument is frequently made in statements issued by the United Nations, most recently in the *High Level Panel Report* (United Nations 2004) and the Secretary General's response, *In Larger Freedom* (United Nations 2005) and most significantly, the *Draft Outcome Document* from the 2005 World Summit (United Nations 2005: 27–28).

This comparison between the state-centric and human security arguments suggests that both have positive and negative attributes. Realism is one version of the state-centric position, and is relevant for understanding some important threats to the state but not all of them. Realism's state-centric focus, unlike Hobbes' state-centric position, fails to acknowledge that security concerns internal violence and malfunctioning states and that sovereignty is conditional. Moreover realism fails to explicitly address if its focus on the state is at the expense of the people within. Human security, on the other hand, does address these issues. However, it fails to address the threats that realism elevates and some schools fail to accept that some state-centric positions have positive effects for human security. Overall, the conclusion is that realism is relevant but flawed and hence does not deserve its dominant position. The question that now arises from this discussion is, if both state-centric and human security arguments are necessary but not sufficient, does an understanding of security require both?

In the contemporary context both are needed

The contemporary context is one in which many many people are vulnerable to a wide range of threats. Perhaps the most vulnerable are those in situations where governance is failing and the state is either unwilling or unable to provide protection. This situation, of vulnerable people and failing states, has serious local, regional and global effects. In an interdependent and globalized world everyone is a stake-holder in human security. It is also a world in which overall the least vulnerable people live in states which act responsibly to their citizens. This suggests that some states are performing reasonably well, albeit not perfectly, and that for the present the state, in principle, can play a role in protecting its people. It is also a world in which other actors—global institutions, NGOs and civil society—do not have the capacity to perform important tasks currently conducted by properly functioning states; for example, creating and distributing wealth. Moreover, many of these organizations are themselves open to criticisms: for example, for their lack of representation, accountability and questionable implementation of measures that support human security. Finally, it is a world in which many states are vulnerable to other states' conventional military forces and weapons of mass destruction. If the current context is one in which people and states are vulnerable then it follows that, depending on the situation, security entails both human security and state-centric security. However, state-centric security is the means to human security, not an end in itself.

Conceptually, in the case of properly functioning states, the proposition has already been made that state-centric and human-centric arguments of security are both necessary but not sufficient. Lodgaard helpfully draws out the conceptual dimensions of this proposition. His starting point is that both arguments provide the 'concepts that security policies will be organised around' in the future (2000: 1–2). He proposes a reconceptualization of security as a 'dual concept of state security and human security'—the former involving defence of territory and freedom to determine one's own form of government and the latter involving people being free of physical violence (2000: 1–6). Lodgaard's approach can be elaborated into a fuller proposition in which there are not only dual referent objects (people and state), but also internal and external threats to both, and in which the means to security in each case involves a variety of measures, both the use of force and non-military measures (Kerr 2003). Nonetheless, these attempts at conceptualizing security in terms of both arguments are embryonic and abstract and there is much more work to be done to make it a clear and convincing argument. But it is a step in the right direction.

KEY POINTS

- Realism is one school in the state-centric argument and it plays an important role in highlighting an important set of historic threats to the state.
- Human security belongs to the human-centric tradition and it plays an important role in highlighting a wide variety of threats to people's security.
- Realism ignores a variety of threats that can undermine the state (its unit of analysis) and the conditionality of sovereignty. It is also unclear about its ultimate purpose regarding the protection of people. This casts doubt, not on the relevance of realism as a security concept, but on its position as the dominant concept.
- Human security addresses some of the gaps in realism and adds an important normative dimension, but is itself a necessary but not sufficient security argument given the contemporary context.
- Although in principle this suggests that both state-centric and human security are needed for an understanding of security there is much to be done to consolidate the conceptual foundations of this proposition.

Utility for practitioners

Up to this point the discussion has explored the conceptual dimensions of human security and its role within security studies. In doing so, reference has been made to the concept's capacity for policy guidance and the argument being made up to this point is that, despite the critic's claims that the concept is not useful for policy guidance, it is possible to develop a framework that is. However, the question now raised is does it offer guidance and in what way is it valuable?

Once again scholars disagree in their answers about the utility of the concept. Hubert argues that empirically it was the foreign policies of some particular states that led academics to develop and elevate the concept (2004: 351). Canadian and Norwegian foreign policies starting in the 1990s are cited as evidence for this view. That is, the concept was a response to existing practice and moreover its mandate continues to guide many states, for example those belonging to the Human Security Network. The 2003 report *Human Security Now* compiled by the Commission for Human Security offers additional guidance and encouragement to states to adopt policies of human security. From this perspective human security is operationalized, providing sound guidance and being implemented. However, Suhrke makes some different observations, arguing that there is a decline in interest in the concept as a foreign policy theme in the policies of the original promoters, Canada and Norway, and other supporters (2004: 365). Furthermore, the Commission on Human Security had little impact and the Human Security Network has a membership of just 13 states (Suhrke 2004: 365) and none of them are major players in world politics.

Several case studies on the utility of human security for policy makers, undertaken by Kerr, Tow and Hanson, suggests that the practitioners in these cases adopted the narrow human security agenda when a crisis of human insecurity in another state was perceived to be a threat to their own state's national interests (2003: 102). For example, Australia's intervention in the Solomon Islands in 2003 took place when Australian policy makers perceived that violence there had reached a crisis point and threatened Australia's national security interests. The Howard government, while not referring to the concept of human security, nonetheless adopted much of its humanitarian law and order agenda as the basis for intervention with the aim of making Australia more secure.

Another case study, on the US invasion of Iraq, demonstrates that, although the US intentions for invasion were always vague, when the post-invasion period descended into chaos the US elevated the human security agenda as a justification for the war in Iraq, arguing that the US aim was to rescue the people of Iraq from the human insecurities caused by Saddam Hussein. However, tellingly, even then the US did little to restore law and order through implementing policing and justice measures—key elements of the narrow school's policy agendas. This suggests that the rhetoric, but not the implementation, of human security was used by US policy makers when a crisis of human insecurity was perceived to undermine their state-centric interests.

From the perspective of practitioners in many developing countries, human security is a quite subversive concept. As already mentioned, the narrow version is often seen as an attempt to interfere in the internal affairs of de-colonized states and impose Western values and changing ideas about sovereignty. In the Asia-Pacific region several states champion the broad school's understanding in development terms and the broader non-military transnational threats of environmental degradation and diseases such as HIV/AIDS and SARS. However, there is little support for the narrow school's emphasis on violence inside the state and human rights. At the non-state level in the Asia-Pacific, however, there is growing advocacy for the narrow school's focus on violence.

Finally, the human security framework is a useful diplomatic framing tool for practitioners in the UN. The connections between conflict and human development are central statements in many UN policies: for example, the *2005 Human Development Report* (2005) and the 2005 Secretary General's, *In Larger Freedom* (2005), which was his response to the High Level Panel Report, and the *Draft Outcome Document* from the 2005 World Summit (2005). Among the positive outcomes of these policy objectives is the decline in internal violence since the mid 1990s which is largely explained by UN and international activism in peace operations (see Think Points 6.2 and 6.3).

THINK POINT 6.2

The decline in global political violence

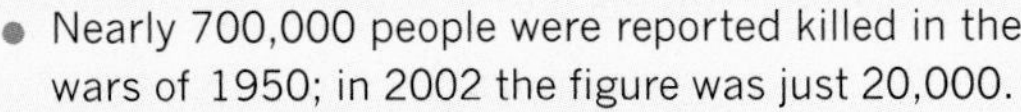

- Nearly 700,000 people were reported killed in the wars of 1950; in 2002 the figure was just 20,000.
- International wars now make up a tiny fraction of all conflicts. They started to decline in the 1970s as increasing numbers of anti-colonial struggles came to an end.
- The number of military coups and attempted coups per year has been dropping for more than 40 years. In 1963, there were 25 coups or attempted coups, the most since the Second World War. In 2004, there were only 10 coups. All of them failed.
- The number of genocides and other mass slaughters of civilians plummeted 80% between their 1988 high point and 2001, despite the horrors of Rwanda and Srebrenica.
- The 1990s also saw a dramatic drop in the number of international crises, often the harbingers of war. International arms transfers, defence budgets and armed forces personnel also dropped, while refugee numbers declined along with armed conflicts.
- Wars are not only less frequent today, they are also far less deadly. The average number of battle-deaths per conflict per year has been falling unevenly since the 1950s. In 1950, the typical armed conflict killed 38,000 people; in 2002, only 600—a 98% decrease.
- Between 1994 and 2003 reported human rights violations declined modestly in five out of six regions of the world. The real decline may well have been greater.

Source: Human Security Centre (2005), *Human Security Report 2005*, Oxford: Oxford University Press and online at www.humansecurityreport.info

KEY POINTS

- There is disagreement about the extent to which the human security concept is adopted by practitioners.
- On the one hand it appears that despite the rhetoric there is limited implementation of the human security agenda by states but on the other hand the UN's active involvement in peace operations aimed at addressing freedom from fear and want is one of the reasons why there is a decrease in internal conflict.
- In general, state practitioners appear to refer to or implement the human security agenda when it serves their material interests.

THINK POINT 6.3

Explaining the decline in political violence

- In the early 1990s, with the Security Council no longer paralysed by Cold War politics, the UN spearheaded an explosion of conflict prevention, peacemaking and post-conflict peacebuilding activities . . . [This] unprecedented surge in international activism . . . included:
  - A six-fold increase in the number of preventive diplomacy missions (which seek to stop wars from starting) mounted by the UN between 1990 and 2002.
  - A four-fold increase in peacemaking missions (those that seek to stop ongoing conflicts) over the same period.
  - A seven-fold increase in the number of 'Friends of the Secretary-General', 'Contact Groups' and other government-initiated mechanisms to support peacemaking and peacebuilding missions between 1990 and 2003.
  - An eleven-fold increase in the number of regimes subjected to economic sanctions between 1989 and 2001. (Sanctions can be used to pressure warring parties to negotiate and help stem the flow of war resources.)
  - A four-fold increase in the number of UN peace operations between 1988 and 2004.
- Peace operations in the 1990s were not only more numerous than previously, they were also far larger and more complex that those of the Cold War era.
- And they made a real difference. A recent RAND Corporation study found that two-thirds of UN peacebuilding missions were successful—a better success rate than that of the US. They were also cost-effective. The UN's 17 peace operations cost less to run for a whole year than the US spends on Iraq in a month.
- The single most compelling explanation remains the upsurge of international activism which followed the end of the Cold War.

Source: Human Security Centre (2005), *Human Security Report 2005*, Oxford: Oxford University Press and online at www.humansecurityreport.info

Conclusion

The final question to be asked concerns the future prospects of the human security concept in security studies and in the policy community. The argument in this chapter is that the concept contributes to understandings of security by showing that realism, the dominant state-centric security argument, is necessary but not sufficient, and should not be the dominant understanding of security. Because human security makes people the referent object it puts the onus on realism to explain why the state is the referent object if it is not a means to people's security. Unless the ultimate purpose of state-centric security is the security of people then the relevance of the state is questionable, and likewise state-centric security arguments. In this way the human security concept will continue to usefully highlight the point that the relationship between the people and the state and the role of sovereignty is at the centre of understandings about security.

This suggests that in the future the human security concept will continue to flourish in academic circles and in the teaching curriculum. At this level, the relationship between the state, people and sovereignty remains a robust debate and there is a normative impetus to improve the conditions for people. If this continues to be part of the job description of academics and students then the future of the concept is assured. There is a great deal of research to be done on human security: for example, on the cross-disciplinary triangular relationship between security, governance and development; and on the connections between the schools of human security. As Thomas points out, 'the ultimate test of the utility of the concept lies in the extent to which policy makers and scholars can draw out the interconnections between these two streams of concern' (2004: 354). Continuing and expanding the quantitative and qualitative databases on human security are other important areas of research. Regular editions of the *Human Security Report* published by Oxford University Press are essential to sustain. There are many text books yet to be written that will provide teachers and students with much needed curriculum guides and materials.

However, at the level of practice, despite agreement that we live in an interdependent world shared by billions of stakeholders in human security, the future of the concept is less rosy. In the first place the key actor in world politics, the US, is preoccupied with terrorism. US leadership under the present George Bush administration is failing to inspire confidence in many quarters of the world that others' security matters to the US and that security is indeed interdependent. US leadership is not setting adequate human security standards at home or abroad and that augurs badly for the human security agenda.

In developing countries the main perpetrators of human insecurity will continue to resist changes that will enhance human security because the short-term gains from holding political and economic power are too seductive. Appeals to recalcitrants will have to continue through the argument that short-term benefits are fatal for long-term survival of governing elites and the state. Diplomacy using the human security framework and hard data showing that human security and a moral conscience is in their interests should be the primary approach. Failing that, intervention following the ICISS and the UN's World Summit principles may be necessary, even though the recent record for proper intervention in Darfur is not encouraging.

It remains up to the United Nations to continue to provide leadership on human security. Despite the urgency for reform of the UN, the institution has nonetheless been instrumental in helping to reduce the incidence and scope of internal violence through peace operations. Data shows that since the mid 1990s there is a dramatic global decline in the scope and incidence of battle-related deaths from internal conflict. (See Think Point 6.2 on the decline in global political violence and Think Point 6.3 on the explanations for the decline.) Also important in reducing conflict is the continuing role of regional organizations, such as the African Union, despite many problems. NGOs and civil society groups continue to be essential actors in the decline of violence, despite the need for better accountability. Finally, the role of properly functioning states will continue to be central to improving human security.

The most significant imperative for continuing to elevate the concept of human security is that ordinary people living in the midst of political violence naturally enough want security. In public opinion polls conducted by the Asia Foundation in 2004 and published in a 2005 RAND Corporation report, two-thirds of the Afghan population believed security is the biggest problem facing the country. Some 37% of the population perceived the biggest security problem as violence. A further 29% saw poverty, the economy and jobs as the next biggest problem. Of less importance were other issues such as education, electricity, roads, and buildings (from 6% to 9% of the population rated these as security problems (2005: 94). In the same publication the results of a series of polls conducted in Iraq during 2004 provided further confirmation that 'security remained the main concern of Iraqi citizens' (2005: 165). Other research on people living in violence and who are also poor shows that their strongest wish is to be secure from violence. Everyday people everywhere want human security. States and other actors have the responsibility to provide it for ethical reasons and for the common good of us all.

QUESTIONS

What is security? Is human security important and if so why?

Can human security and state-centric security be reconciled conceptually and in practice, if so how?

Should humanitarian intervention using force for the protection of people from large-scale atrocities be conducted if it endangers international stability? Should the international community intervene in Chechnya? If not, why not?

Should the international community intervene in situations such as Darfur in 2005? If not, why not?

Is human security a concept that guides state's policies? If not, why not?

Is human security measured by the number of battle-related deaths?

What are the problems with the framework proposed in this chapter?

What is the relationship between governance, security and development?

What are the local, regional and global effects of human insecurity?

What are the advantages and disadvantages of the concept of human security?

FURTHER READING

- **Collier, P. (2003), *Breaking the Conflict Trap. Civil War and Development Policy*, Oxford: Oxford University Press**. Provides an economic view of the causes of civil war and proposals for an agenda of global action.

- **Hampson, F.O. *et al.* (2002), *Madness in the Multitude*, Toronto: Oxford University Press**. Presents a strong argument for understanding human security as a global good.

- **Human Security Centre (2005), *Human Security Report*, Oxford: Oxford University Press**. The most important quantitative and qualitative contribution to the analysis of global trends in human security.

- ***Security Dialogue* (2004) 35/3**. A special edition of the journal which provides a very good overview of the debate about human security from many of the main participants.

- **Thakur, R. and Newman, E. (eds.) (2004), *Broadening Asia's Security and Discourse Agenda*, Tokyo: United Nations University Press**. A critique of the state-centric paradigm from the perspective of a very broad understanding of human security.

- **Thomas, C. (2000), *Global Governance, Development and Human Security*, London: Pluto Press**. Focuses on the issues of governance and development that are central to human security.

- **United Nations Development Programme (2005), *UNDP Human Development Report 2005*, Oxford: Oxford University Press**. Analyses of the problems of human development around the world.

IMPORTANT WEBSITES

- The Human Security Report at **www.humansecurityreport.info** will be produced annually by the Human Security Centre at the Liu Institute for Global Issues at the University of British Columbia and Oxford University Press. It is an invaluable source.
- Human Security News, is an excellent daily report at **www.hsc.list@ubc.ca** also produced by the Human Security Centre.
- Center for International Development and Conflict Management (CIDCM) **http:// www.cidcm.umd.edu/** CIDCM regularly publishes a very good source, *Peace and Conflict*, which canvasses the interplay between conflict and development.
- International Crisis Group (ICG) at **http://www.crisisgroup.org/home/index.cfm?l=1&id=3624** regularly publishes *Crisis Watch*, a report on crises around the world.

Visit the Online Resource Centre that accompanies this book for lots of interesting additional material: www.oxfordtextbooks.co.uk/orc/collins/

7 Securitization

RALF EMMERS

Chapter Contents

Reader's Guide

The chapter introduces, assesses, and applies the Copenhagen School and its securitization model. The School widens the definition of security by encompassing five different sectors—military, political, societal, economic and environmental security. It examines how a specific matter becomes securitized, that is, its removal from the political process to the security agenda. The chapter analyses the act of securitization by identifying the role of the securitizing actor and the importance of the 'speech act' in convincing a specific audience of the existential nature of a threat. It argues that the Copenhagen School allows for non-military matters to be included in security studies while still offering a coherent understanding of the concept of security. Yet the chapter also stresses the dangers and the negative connotations of securitizing an issue as well as some shortcomings of the model. While the chapter is conceptually driven, it relies on a series of illustrations to apply the securitization model. These include the securitization of undocumented migration under the John Howard government in Australia, the securitization of the illicit trafficking and abuse of drugs in the United States and Thailand as well as the failure by US President George W. Bush and British Prime Minister Tony Blair to persuade world opinion of the existential threat posed by Saddam Hussein and his regime in Iraq.

Introduction

The Copenhagen School emerged at the Conflict and Peace Research Institute (COPRI) of Copenhagen and is represented by the writings of Barry Buzan, Ole Wæver, Jaap de Wilde, and others (Wæver 1995; Buzan, Wæver, de Wilde 1998; Buzan, Wæver 2003). The Copenhagen School has developed a substantial body of concepts to rethink security, most notably through its notions of securitization and desecuritization. The School has played an important role in broadening the conception of security and in providing a framework to analyse how an issue becomes securitized or desecuritized. It is part of a broader attempt to re-conceptualize the notion of security and to redefine the agenda of security studies in light of the end of the Cold War.

The Copenhagen School has developed its approach to security in numerous writings, most notably in *Security: A New Framework for Analysis* (1998). In this volume, Buzan, Wæver, and de Wilde start by defining international security in a traditional military context. 'Security', according to them, 'is about survival. It is when an issue is presented as posing an existential threat to a designated referent object (traditionally, but not necessarily, the state, incorporating government, territory, and society)' (Buzan, Waever, de Wilde 1998: 21). With this point in mind, the Copenhagen School identifies five general categories of security: military security as well as environmental, economic, societal and political security. The security-survival logic is therefore maintained as well as extended beyond military security to four other categories.

The dynamics of each category of security are determined by securitizing actors and referent objects. The former are defined as 'actors who securitize issues by declaring something, a referent object, existentially threatened' (Buzan, Wæver, de Wilde 1998: 36) and can be expected to be 'political leaders, bureaucracies, governments, lobbyists, and pressure groups' (Buzan, Wæver, de Wilde 1998: 40). Referent objects are 'things that are seen to be existentially threatened and that have a legitimate claim to survival' (Buzan, Wæver, de Wilde 1998: 36). Evidently, the referent objects and the kind of existential threats that they face vary across security sectors. Referent objects can be the state (military security); national sovereignty, or an ideology (political security); national economies (economic security); collective identities (societal security); species, or habitats (environmental security) (Buzan, Wæver, de Wilde 1998).

The Copenhagen School adopts a multi-sectoral approach to security that represents a move away from traditional security studies and its focus on the military sector. Four of the five components account for non-military threats to security. In addition to widening the definition of security beyond military issues, the Copenhagen School deepens security studies by including non-state actors. A crucial question though is whether the concept of security can be broadened to such an extent without losing its coherence. There is a risk of over-stretching the definition of security with the result that everything, and therefore nothing in particular, ends up being a security problem. A loose and broad conceptualization of security can lead to vagueness and a lack of conceptual and analytical coherence. In other words, the redefinition and broadening of the concept of security need to be matched by the development of new conceptual tools. This is where the Copenhagen School with its securitization and desecuritization model has sought to contribute to the debates by developing an analytical framework to study security. The Copenhagen School raises the possibility for a systematic, comparative, and coherent analysis of security.

KEY POINTS

- A narrow interpretation of security concentrates on the state and its defence from external military attacks. In response to this narrow definition of security, other approaches to security studies have called for a widening and deepening of security to include non-military threats.
- The Copenhagen School stresses that security is about survival. A security concern must be articulated as an existential threat. The School maintains the security-survival logic found in a traditional understanding of security.
- Yet the Copenhagen School broadens the conception of security. It identifies five general categories of security: military, environmental, economic, societal and political security. The School thus broadens the concept of security beyond the state by including new referent objects like societies and the environment.
- The dynamics of each security category are determined by securitizing actors and referent objects.
- It is important, however, to preserve the conceptual precision of the term security. This is where the Copenhagen School contributes to the security studies literature. It provides a framework to define security and determine how a specific matter becomes securitized or desecuritized.

Securitization model

Two-stage process of securitization

The Copenhagen School provides a spectrum along which issues can be plotted. It claims that any specific matter can be non-politicized, politicized or securitized. An issue is non-politicized when it is not a matter for state action and is not included in public debate. An issue becomes politicized when it is managed within the standard political system. A politicized issue is 'part of public policy, requiring government decision and resource allocations or, more rarely, some other form of communal governance' (Buzan, Wæver, de Wilde 1998: 23). Finally, an issue is plotted at the securitized end of the spectrum when it requires emergency actions beyond the state's standard political procedures.

The Copenhagen School argues that a concern can be securitized—framed as a security issue and moved from the politicized to the securitized end of the spectrum—through an act of securitization. A securitizing actor (e.g. government, political elite, military, civil society) articulates an already politicized issue as an existential threat to a referent object (e.g. state, groups, national sovereignty, ideology, and economy). In response to the existential nature of the threat, the securitizing actor asserts that it has to adopt extraordinary means that go beyond the ordinary norms of the political domain. Buzan, Wæver, and de Wilde argue therefore that securitization 'is the move that takes politics beyond the established rules of the game and frames the issue either as a special kind of politics or as above politics. Securitization can thus be seen as a more extreme version of politicization' (Buzan, Wæver, de Wilde 1998: 23). The Copenhagen School notes that desecuritization refers to the reverse process. It involves the 'shifting of issues out of emergency mode and into the normal bargaining processes of the political sphere' (Buzan, Wæver, de Wilde 1998: 4). For example, the end of the Apartheid regime in South Africa represents an illustration of the desecuritization of the race question in South African society and of its re-introduction into the political domain.

An act of securitization refers to the accepted classification of certain and not other phenomena,

Figure 7.1 Securitization spectrum

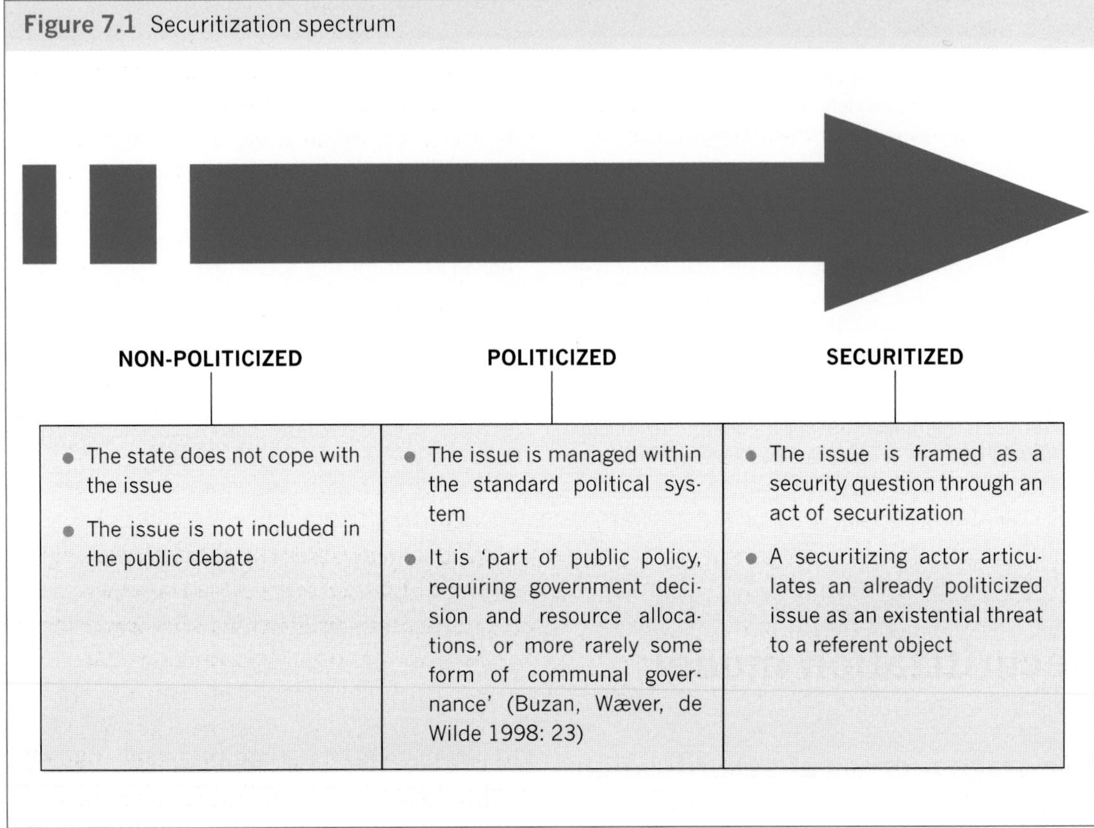

NON-POLITICIZED	POLITICIZED	SECURITIZED
• The state does not cope with the issue • The issue is not included in the public debate	• The issue is managed within the standard political system • It is 'part of public policy, requiring government decision and resource allocations, or more rarely some form of communal governance' (Buzan, Wæver, de Wilde 1998: 23)	• The issue is framed as a security question through an act of securitization • A securitizing actor articulates an already politicized issue as an existential threat to a referent object

persons or entities as existential threats requiring emergency measures. The Copenhagen School relies on a two-stage process of securitization to explain how and when an issue is to be perceived and acted upon as an existential threat to security. The first stage concerns the portrayal of certain issues, persons, or entities as existential threats to referent objects. The initial move of securitization can be initiated by states but also by non-state actors like trade unions or popular movements for instance. Non-state actors are thus regarded as important players in the securitization model. Yet securitization tends to be a process dominated by powerful actors that benefit from privileged positions. Indeed, the move of securitization depends on and reveals the power and influence of the securitizing actor, which as a result often happens to be the state and its elites (Collins 2005).

The usage of a language of security does not mean, however, that the issue is automatically transformed into a security question. Instead, the consensual establishment of threat needs to be of sufficient salience as to produce substantial political effects. The second and crucial stage of securitization is only completed successfully once the securitizing actor succeeds in convincing a relevant audience (public opinion, politicians, military officers, or other elites) that a referent object is existentially threatened. Only then can extraordinary measures be imposed. Due to the urgency of the accepted existential threat to security, constituencies tolerate the use of counteractions outside of the normal bounds of political procedures.

Central to the two-stage process of securitization is the importance of the 'speech act'. The latter is defined as the discursive representation of a certain issue as an existential threat to security. The Copenhagen School considers the speech act to be the starting point of the process of securitization.

An issue can become a security question through the speech act alone irrespective of whether the concern represents an existential threat in material terms. A securitizing actor uses language to articulate a problem in security terms and to persuade a relevant audience of its immediate danger. The articulation in security terms conditions the audience and provides securitizing actors with the right to mobilize state power and move beyond traditional rules. As discussed above, the security concern must be articulated as an existential threat (Buzan, Wæver, de Wilde 1998). This significant criterion enables the Copenhagen School to link a broadly defined security concept to the question of survival and thus to the reasoning found within a traditional approach to security studies. This avoids a broad and loose conceptualization of security that could too easily become meaningless.

KEY POINTS

- The referent objects can be individuals and groups (refugees, victims of human rights abuses, etc.) as well as issue areas (national sovereignty, environment, economy, etc.) that possess a legitimate claim to survival and whose existence is ostensibly threatened.
- The securitizing actors can be the government, political elite, military, and civil society. They securitize an issue by articulating the existence of threat(s) to the survival of specific referent objects.
- The desecuritizing actors reconstitute an issue as no longer an existential threat, thereby moving it from the securitized realm into the ordinary public arena.
- Securitizing actors use the language of security (speech act) to convince a specific audience of the existential nature of the threat.

Successful act of securitization

Governments and political elites have a certain advantage over other actors in seeking to influence audiences and calling for the implementation of extraordinary measures (Collins 2005). In a democratic system, a government benefits from the legitimacy of having been elected by the electorate. This gives it a significant advantage when seeking to convince an audience of the need for emergency actions in response to an existential threat. In democratic societies, the audience still has the right, however, to reject the speech act, namely the representation of a certain issue as an existential threat.

An important question to examine is whether an act of securitization is more likely to succeed in authoritarian states where the military plays a central role in national politics (Anthony, Emmers, Acharya 2006). The formulation of threat perceptions and the decision-making process are often dominated in undemocratic societies by the military as well as by bureaucratic and political elites. The influence of social pressure and aspirations on the securitization or desecuritization of political matters remains limited. Yet this is not to say that an audience is not part of the securitization move or that it is not expected to authorize the adoption of emergency measures. But rather that the audience excludes the wider population and consists solely of political elites and some state institutions such as the military. In such a context, political elites can abuse extreme forms of politicization to achieve specific political objectives and consolidate their grip on power. While the wider population may reject the speech act and consider the emergency measures adopted as a result to be illegitimate, the securitization act is nevertheless successful having convinced a more restrictive audience on the existential nature of the threat (Collins 2005).

It should be clear by now that the Copenhagen School regards security as a socially constructed concept. In that sense, the School is primarily constructivist in its approach. What constitutes an existential threat is regarded as a subjective matter. It very much depends on a shared understanding of what constitutes a danger to security. A person in authority first needs to speak the language of security and demand the adoption of emergency measures. The discourse of the securitizing actor has to be articulated in a fashion that convinces an audience. In other words, a collective has to accept a specific issue as an existential threat to a referent object. Consequently, every act of securitization involves a political decision and results from a political and social act (Anthony, Emmers, Acharya 2006). Only in a successful case will standard political procedures no longer be viewed as adequate to counter the threat.

In contrast to a realist approach to security studies that focuses on the material nature of the threat, the Copenhagen School predicts that an act of securitization can either succeed or fail depending on whether a separate audience accepts the discourse. As a result, it naturally asks why some acts tend to fail while others succeed. The Copenhagen School also examines why some questions are securitized in the first place while others are not. It argues that this will not just depend on material factors.

KEY POINTS

- The act of securitization is only successful once the relevant audience is convinced of the existential threat to the referent object.
- Governments and elites have an advantage over other actors when seeking to influence an audience.
- What constitutes security is a subjective matter.
- Every process of securitization involves a political and security act.
- An act of securitization can either fail or succeed depending on the persuasiveness of the discourse.

Extraordinary measures and motives for securitization

The Copenhagen School asserts that a successful act of securitization provides securitizing actors with the special right to use exceptional means. It indicates, however, that the success of the process does not depend on the adoption of such actions. It is natural to ask what is meant by 'extraordinary measures'. The latter go beyond rules ordinarily abided by and are therefore located outside the usual bounds of political procedures and practices. Extraordinary measures are expected to respond to a specific issue that is posing an existential threat to a referent object. The adoption and implementation of extraordinary measures involve the identification and classification of some issue as an enemy that needs to be tackled urgently. The types of measures to be adopted in response will obviously depend on the circumstances and the context of the threat. An existential threat to the environment, a sector of the economy, or a state ideology will demand different emergency responses (Collins 2005).

Some shortcomings of the Copenhagen School's interpretation of extraordinary measures should be mentioned. One can rather easily anticipate the types of emergency measures to be introduced by a state. Yet it is less clear what would form an extraordinary measure for a non-state actor after it has successfully convinced an audience of the existential nature of a threat. In other words, what would for instance constitute an extraordinary measure that goes beyond standard political procedures for non-governmental organizations like Greenpeace and Christian Aid? Moreover, one may question the significance of a securitization process when it does not go hand in hand with actions and policies to address the ostensible threat. According to the securitization model, transforming an issue into a security question only requires the audience's acknowledgment that it is indeed a threat. The adoption of extraordinary means is not a requirement. Buzan, Wæver, and de Wilde specifically indicate that 'We do not push the demand so high as to say that an emergency measure has to be adopted' (Buzan, Wæver, de Wilde 1998: 25). This means that a securititizing actor can make successful speech acts while still deciding to address the existential threat through standard political procedures rather than extraordinary measures (Collins 2005). Yet it can be argued that a complete act of securitization really consists of and demands both discursive (speech act and shared understanding) and non-discursive (policy implementation) dimensions (Emmers 2004; Collins 2005). In this case, a security act would therefore depend on successful speech acts (discursive dimension) that persuade a relevant audience of the existential nature of the threat as well as the adoption by the securitizing actor of emergency powers (non-discursive dimension) to address the so-defined threat.

A series of motives and intentions can help us explain a securitizing act and the subsequent implementation of extraordinary measures (Anthony, Emmers, Acharya 2006). Securitizing injects urgency into an issue and leads to a sustained mobilization of political support and deployment of resources. It also creates the kind of political momentum necessary for the adoption of additional and emergency measures. The securitization of an issue can thus provide some tangible benefits including a more efficient handling of complex problems, a mobilizing of popular support for policies in specific areas by calling them security-relevant, the allocation of more resources, and so forth. These achievements might not be obtained if the same problems were only regarded as political matters.

Yet it is crucial to highlight the danger of securitization. The process can be abused to legitimize and empower the role of the military or special security forces in civilian activities. This is particularly relevant in emerging democracies or countries where the division between the military and civilian authority is blurred. With the growing articulation of issues as threats in a post-9/11 context, an act of securitization can lead to the further legitimization of the armed forces in politics as well as to the curbing of civil liberties in the name of security in well-established democratic societies. Elites can use a securitizing act to curtail civil liberties, impose martial law, detain political opponents or suspected terrorists without trail, restrict the influence of certain domestic political institutions, or increase military budgets (Anthony, Emmers, Acharya 2006). Few checks and balances are normally imposed on implemented emergency measures opening the door for possible abuse. In undemocratic societies, the greater public is not invited to speak out and thus unable to prevent the dangers associated with an act of securitization. To highlight the potential danger linked to an act of securitization, Kyle Grayson uses a Frankenstein's Monster analogy (Grayson 2003). This metaphor for securitization helps us understand how powerful the securitizing actor can become as a result of the process as well as the loss of control that arises from a strategy that opens the door to extraordinary security actions.

Keeping Grayson's monster metaphor in mind, it is not surprising that the Copenhagen School does not regard an act of securitization as a positive value or as a required development to tackle specific issues (Williams 2003). It argues instead that societies should, as much as possible, operate within the realm of normal politics where issues can be debated and addressed within the standard boundaries of politicization. Consequently, a process of desecuritization is described by Buzan and Wæver as particularly important to re-introduce a matter into a standard politicized level. Risks to society and abuse of authority can be prevented by desecuritizing an issue and re-including it into the normal political domain.

KEY POINTS

- A successful act of securitization provides securitizing actors with the right to use exceptional means.
- What constitutes an extraordinary measure is not always well defined.
- A series of motives and intentions can explain an act of securitization.
- An act of securitization can lead to excesses and abuse of power. It can easily be abused by authoritarian regimes and/or in the name of the defence of civil liberties.
- Desecuritization can be beneficial as it re-introduces an issue into a politicized sphere.

Limitations of the securitization model

The Copenhagen School provides a framework to determine how, as well as by whom, a specific matter becomes securitized or desecuritized. Yet despite the School's prominence in the security studies literature, the dynamics of securitization and desecuritization remain insufficiently understood empirically (Anthony, Emmers, Acharya 2006). The Copenhagen School has so far primarily concentrated on framing a theoretical approach to security studies while paying insufficient attention to empirical research. Questions that need to be explored empirically include why some moves of securitization succeed in convincing an audience while others fail to do so. It is also necessary to analyse why some issues are articulated and treated as existential security threats while others are not. In other words, empirical studies on the path that leads to the securitization of public issues might lead to a better understanding of the transition from the politicized to the securitized end of the spectrum and vice versa. Finally, the Copenhagen School has not given much attention to assessing the policy effectiveness of extraordinary measures nor to the unintended consequences that they might provoke (Anthony, Emmers, Acharya 2006). It is, however, important to determine empirically whether acts of securitization contribute to an effective handling of specific issues. Securitizing an issue may in fact not contribute to a solution as desecuritization might instead be a more fruitful approach.

The Copenhagen School is also criticized for being Euro-centric (Anthony, Emmers, Acharya 2006). This Euro-centricism is less obvious though in the case of *Security: A New Framework for Analysis*, which seeks to provide a broad theoretical approach to security studies. Still, the notion of societal security, for example, which is at the core of the Copenhagen School and emphasizes society rather than the state as the primary referent object (Tow 2001), very much derives from a European experience. It refers to borderless societies that are said to exist in Europe as a result of political and economic integration. Societal security, which is examined in Chapter 10, is linked to the construction of a collective European identity and should be dissociated from state security, which relates to the preservation of national sovereignty and territorial integrity. The existence of a similar sense of community in many other regions or parts of the world is disputable.

Furthermore, it is open to debate whether the securitization model contributes to the study of international security in parts of the world that can easily be analysed through a realist mode. Northeast Asia is still very much defined, for example, by a strategic structure determined by realist characteristics. Concerns of a traditional mould continue to trouble the Northeast Asian region, including the protracted Korean peninsula problem and the risk of the proliferation of weapons of mass destruction, cross-straits tensions between China and Taiwan, and ongoing diplomatic furores between Japan on the one hand and China and South Korea on the other over the historical legacy of the Pacific War and disputed islets. The fragility of bilateral ties between China and Japan is a key concern for peace and stability in the entire region. From a US and Japanese perspective, China and its rising power also continue to present the most powerful long-term challenge to the East Asian regional order. In such a context, security is still regarded as being essentially about geo-politics, deterrence, power balancing, and military strategy. The state and its defence from external military attacks remain the primary focus of security policies. Hence, although the securitization model can indicate the various 'speech acts' as well as responses from specific audiences and the possible implementation of extraordinary measures, it may in such strategic environments not be able to reveal much more than rational theories, such as Realism.

Another shortcoming touches on the blurred distinction between the political and security realms (Anthony, Emmers, Acharya 2006). The Copenhagen School needs to further define and clarify the boundaries between politics and security. The School defines securitization as an extreme version of politicization, which contributes to the possible confusion and overlap along the spectrum of de-politicized, politicized and securitized issues. As it stands, the model may not be able to sufficiently dissociate an act of securitization from a case of severe politicization. The distinction that may exist between these processes can be blurred depending on the political context and existing circumstances (Anthony, Emmers, Acharya 2006). For instance, the separation between the political and security domains traditionally remains indistinct in undemocratic societies. Moreover, matters that are articulated in security terms even by democratically elected governments may continue to be located within the political domain and addressed through standard political procedures. Despite the use of speech acts, solutions for the resolution of non-military challenges are frequently found in the realm of politics. Furthermore, and as will be discussed in the next section, more needs to be said about the political motives to securitize an issue. Politicians can use the language of security toward public matters in order to boost their popularity and enhance their chances of re-election. Taking a tough stance on sensitive questions such as undocumented migration or drug trafficking can help them win support among the electorate. Such examples of securitization could be regarded therefore as illustrations of politicization.

Finally, the securitization model raises some important questions about the role of academia. Are academics and analysts meant to be and act solely as observers or as advocates—securitizing or desecuritizing actors in their own right—when studying a securitizing move? The Copenhagen School expects analysts to distinguish themselves from a securitization act and the role of the securitizing actor. Yet the distinction may be obscured by a variety of factors. For example, ever since the terror attacks in the United States on 11 September 2001, terrorist experts have been widely present in the media and sometimes even in contact with intelligence agencies. It can be argued therefore that such repeated interventions blur the separation between academic analysis and politics and transform the analyst into a separate and influential securitizing actor that is part of the securitizing move.

KEY POINTS

- The securitization model is still relatively new. More empirical research is required to better understand the dynamics of securitization.
- The Copenhagen School is often viewed as Euro-centric, reflecting European security concerns and questions.
- The boundaries between securitization and politicization are sometimes blurred.
- The securitization model raises questions about the role of scholars and analysts.

Cases of securitization

Securitization of undocumented migration

The securitization of undocumented migration has become a recurrent event. Migration is a complex social phenomenon that is influenced by economic, political, socio-cultural, historical, and geographical factors. Economic determinants, especially poverty and economic disparities, are the prime motivation for migrants to leave their countries of origin. They are in pursuit of better opportunities to earn an income and improve their quality of life.

KEY QUOTES 7.1

Migration

Immigration Minister Philip Ruddock said 'whole (Middle East) villages are packing up' to come to Australia and the nation was facing 'a national emergency'. (Associated Press. 23 Feb 2002) http://global.factiva.com.ezlibproxy1.ntu.edu.sg/en/eSrch/ss_hl.asp

Discussing strip searches of children, Australian PM Howard said: 'It sounds stark and authoritarian, but if you are dealing with situations where people are using children in an exploitive way—which sometimes occurs—then I think that kind of thing is justified,' Howard told Melbourne radio station 3AW. (Associated Press. 6 April 2001). http:// global.factiva.com.ezlibproxy1.ntu.edu.sg/en/eSrch/ss_hl.asp

'And we have lost control of our asylum and immigration system. At a time when Britain faces an unprecedented terrorist threat, we appear to have little idea who is coming into or leaving our country.' (Text of Conservative leader Michael Howard's speech on asylum and immigration on 22 September 2004) http://news.bbc.co.uk/1/hi/uk_politics/3679618.stm

Besides the phenomenon of economic migration, political circumstances also explain the movement of populations. Inter-state wars, domestic conflicts of ethno-nationalist origin, and authoritarian regimes with appalling human rights records create waves of political refugees leaving their countries of origin in the hope of escaping persecution and violence. Migrants face restrictive immigration policies and reduced legal immigration opportunities. This leads to a growing reliance on illegal methods to either enter or remain in a specific country, including overstaying the expiry of a valid tourist visa or work permit. Over the last ten years, the issue of undocumented migration has also been increasingly linked to organized criminal groups that now largely control the smuggling and trafficking of people. It is estimated by the United States State Department that as many as 900,000 people might be trafficked annually across international borders.

Undocumented migration can be articulated by politicians and perceived by specific audiences as representing a threat to the political, societal, economic as well as cultural security of a state and its society (Graham 2000). Undocumented migration is said to undermine the security of national borders and thus to be a threat to the national sovereignty of a state (political security). It can also have a negative effect on the fabric of a society and its economic welfare by affecting social order and increasing unrest and crime rates (societal security). Moreover, migrants are often portrayed as a threat to the lifestyle and culture of the receiving country. In addition to being blamed for contributing to a rise in crime and other social problems, undocumented migrants are sometimes described as economic migrants who are claiming asylum to take advantage of national social benefits or take away jobs from the local population (economic security). Hiring undocumented workers tends to be much cheaper for local employers, as the latter do not have to cover their welfare or medical costs. Viewed as cheap labour, undocumented migrants are regarded as threatening employment opportunities. In reality, they mostly end up doing low-skilled jobs that nationals refuse to do. Finally, the arrival of immigrants from a common ethnic or religious group can be perceived as causing a shift in the racial composition of a country and diluting its cultural identity.

The handling of the undocumented migration issue by the John Howard government in 2001 represents an interesting case of securitization (Emmers 2004). Undocumented migration had started to have a significant political impact in Australia since the late 1990s. Pauline Hanson and her political party, the One Nation Party, transformed the immigration issue into a popular political rallying point. Hanson had proclaimed her extreme views on immigration, the Aborigines, and asylum seekers. She won a seat in the Australian federal parliament as an independent candidate in 1996 and created the One Nation Party in 1997. The John Howard government first adopted a hard line on undocumented migration in the summer of 2001 over the Tampa incident. The Tampa, a Norwegian freighter, had rescued 460 Afghans on their way to Australia to claim asylum. Approaching its territorial waters, the Australian government refused the right of entry to the Tampa and ordered the ship to turn away. After the ship had failed to obey, Howard ordered units of the Special Air Service (SAS) to take control of the ship and prevent it from reaching Christmas Island or mainland Australia. A military operation had thus been undertaken to avoid asylum seekers from coming to Australia.

The Australian Prime Minister, John Howard, used, together with the issue of terrorism in a post-9/11 environment, the migration theme in his re-election campaign in November 2001. The prime minister explained that he did not want undocumented migrants who had been smuggled into Australia to jump ahead of other people recognized as genuine asylum seekers by the Australian authorities. The smuggling of undocumented migrants into Australia was also described as a threat to the national sovereignty and territorial integrity of the state. The government indicated that it could not give the impression that it was losing control over its borders, control that is so essential to national sovereignty. Finally, after the terrorist attacks of 11 September 2001, the Australian authorities were concerned that terrorists might be among the migrants smuggled into Australia. The questions of terrorism and undocumented migration were therefore to some extent intertwined in public discussions.

The referent objects in this case of securitization were the national sovereignty and territorial integrity of Australia (military and political security), the fabric of society (societal security), and economic welfare (economic security). The securitizing actor was the John Howard government. The audience consisted of the Australian public opinion (Emmers 2004). Despite a lot of domestic debates and fierce criticism, the audience generally accepted the interpretation of events set forward by the securitizing actor and acknowledged the need to implement extraordinary measures to respond to the threat. Opinion polls suggested that a majority of Australians supported Howard's hard line on undocumented migration. While migration was certainly not the sole reason for success, his conservative coalition was re-elected for a third term in office in November 2001. In other words, the securitizing actor used a discourse of security that convinced an audience of the threat posed by the smuggling of undocumented migration into Australia.

Beyond the use of rhetoric, the Howard government adopted and implemented a series of extraordinary measures to reduce the number of asylum-seekers reaching Australia (Emmers 2004). Such measures included the automatic detention of asylum seekers in camps while waiting for their applications to be processed and the interception of ships carrying asylum seekers off the coast of Australia and their diversion to Pacific Islands for processing. The Australian government built immigration detention centres both on its territory and abroad. Asylum seekers were interned on the Australian territory of Christmas Island, a remote island in the Indian Ocean located at about 1,800 kilometres from Western Australia. Offshore refuge centres were also built on Mauru and on Manus Island, in Papua New Guinea, to detain asylum seekers until their applications were processed. Finally, the Australian Federal Police (AFP) and the Australian Defence Force (ADF) increased their capabilities to ensure border and domestic security against people smuggling, terrorism, and other threats.

Securitization of drug trafficking

Besides undocumented migration, another issue that has recurrently been securitized is the illicit trafficking and abuse of drugs. Drug trafficking is a

KEY POINTS

- Undocumented migration is one phenomenon that is increasingly being securitized today.
- Undocumented migrants are often said to represent a threat to political, societal, economic, and environmental security.
- For example, the John Howard government securitized the smuggling of undocumented migrants into Australia in 2001.
- The use of the speech act was generally accepted by the wider Australian public (audience).
- The completed securitization act led to the implementation of extraordinary measures.

transnational criminal activity and most likely the largest international crime problem in the world. The global trade of illicit drugs is believed to be worth as much as US$400 billion a year. Drug trafficking is connected to other categories of transnational crime. It is the prime generator of money laundering and is linked to arms smuggling (drug dealers often outgun police forces), organized crime, corruption, illegal migration, and in some cases terrorism. Drug trafficking is viewed as a threat to societal security by increasing drug consumption and addiction, raising the level of violent crime, affecting the health of the consumers, spreading HIV/AIDS due to intravenous drug use, and undermining family structures. In addition to its social consequences, drug trafficking has significant economic and political effects. It creates shadow economies, distorts financial institutions, undermines national economies, and fuels the problem of money laundering. It also erodes the rule of law, promotes corruption, and undermines border security. This is examined in detail in Chapter 19.

The so-called 'war on drugs' waged by Thailand in 2003 is an example of a securitizing act (Emmers 2004). The consumption of illicit drugs in the country is a dramatic problem that primarily involves young adults. The most serious trend in Thailand has been the rapid increase in the use of synthetic drugs. Besides the health and social consequences of illicit drug consumption, many in Thailand view the drug trafficking activities coming from Burma as a significant national security issue. In response, the Thai Prime Minister, Thaksin Shinawatra, declared war on drugs in February 2003 vowing to the Thai population to eliminate the narcotics problem within three months. The prime minister stated at an anti-drugs event in late March 2003: 'The drugs problem is a threat to national security. Thus my government has declared war on drugs and placed drugs eradication as the nation's most urgent agenda' (BBC News 2003).

In this case of securitization, the referent objects were the national sovereignty and territorial integrity of Thailand (military and political security), the integrity and stability of the political system (political security), the Thai population (societal security), and the economic development and prosperity of the country (economic security). The securitizing actor was the Thai Prime Minister Thaksin Shinawatra and his government. Finally, the audience consisted of the Thai public opinion (Emmers 2004).

Opinion polls indicated that the audience generally accepted the articulation of drug trafficking as a threat to Thailand's national security and its society and the need for it to be addressed through extraordinary measures. Repeated pollsters indicated strong public approval of the anti-drugs campaign. The audience therefore accepted the interpretation of events set forward by the securitizing actor and acknowledged the need for emergency action. According to the Copenhagen School, this indicates a successful act of securitization—the securitizing actor had used a discourse of security and an audience had been convinced by the existential threat posed by drug trafficking to the referent objects.

The war on drugs led to the implementation of extreme measures as well as to a series of abuses (Emmers 2004). The interior ministry, the police,

KEY QUOTES 7.2

Thaksin and the War on Drugs

'I am serious about taking action against drug traffickers. Government officials, police in particular, must take action too as these traffickers destroy youths' lives, ruin the economy and damage the country.' (The Nation, 5 Oct 2004) http://global.factiva. com. ezlibproxy1.ntu.edu.sg/en/eSrch/ss_hl.asp

'We must go after all traders and producers. They are not suitable to be part of our society. They deserve to be put in jail. Drug traders who fight back must be dealt with decisively.' (Bangkok Post. 23 March 2003) http://global.factiva.com.ezlibproxy1.ntu.edu.sg/en/eSrch/ss_hl.asp

'Although we have destroyed most of the drug networks it does not mean that the drug problem is totally wiped out. They are like germs: they'll resurrect themselves when our body is weak.' (Agence France Presse. 2 Dec 2003) http://global.factiva.com.ezlibproxy1.ntu.edu.sg/en/eSrch/ss_hl.asp

'But increasingly problems such as terrorism, in all kinds of form, the trafficking of narcotic drugs, or even the SARS epidemic have equally threatened our security, especially our national economic security. The latter represents the kind of non-traditional threats to security that could strike at the very heart of any nation. Because what these threats often aim at is to destroy the economic confidence of a nation. Confidence, being the most important component of a successful economy, once destroyed or even seriously impaired, could drive the whole economy to total collapse.'

(Keynote Address by His Excellency Dr. Thaksin Shinawatra. 10 June 2003. The Willard Hotel, Washington, DC, http://www.us-asean.org/Thailand/thaksinvisit03/speech.asp)

and local authorities published blacklists of suspected drug producers, traffickers, and dealers. The blacklists were widely criticized in the media and by non-governmental organizations due to their lack of accuracy. This led to concern that the police might accuse innocent people of being drug producers or traffickers. It was also reported that more than 2,500 people had been killed primarily between February and April 2003. The Thai government blamed inter-gang warfare for most of the killings. Thaksin announced: 'It is bandits killing bandits' (Cochrane 2003: 35). Most of the killings were not investigated, nor did they lead to arrests. Human rights groups argued that a 'shoot-to-kill policy' had been put in place. They suspected the police of taking matters in their own hands and executing traffickers as part of the war on drugs campaign. Despite domestic and international criticism of the extra-judicial killings, repeated polls indicated that Thai public opinion generally supported the implementation of extraordinary measures.

KEY POINTS

- The illicit trafficking and abuse of drugs has recurrently been securitized.
- Narcotics are viewed as a threat to political, societal, economic, and health security.
- Thailand declared war on drugs in 2003. The Thai population (audience) generally accepted the articulation of drug trafficking as a threat to Thailand and its society.
- The implementation of extraordinary measures led to abuses.

The war in Iraq and the failure of securitization

We have so far noted two cases of completed acts of securitization. This is not to say, however, that all moves of securitization succeed in convincing a specific audience on the existential nature of a threat. In fact, as mentioned above, the Copenhagen

KEY QUOTES 7.3

Bush and the Iraq War

'Iraq is the latest battlefield in this war. Many terrorists who kill innocent men, women, and children on the streets of Baghdad are followers of the same murderous ideology that took the lives of our citizens in New York, in Washington, and Pennsylvania. There is only one course of action against them: to defeat them abroad before they attack us at home.'

(President Addresses Nation, Discusses Iraq, War on Terror, Fort Bragg, North Carolina. 28 June 2005) http://www.whitehouse.gov/news/releases/2005/06/20050628-7.html

'The threat comes from Iraq. It arises directly from the Iraqi regime's own actions—its history of aggression, and its drive toward an arsenal of terror. Eleven years ago, as a condition for ending the Persian Gulf War, the Iraqi regime was required to destroy its weapons of mass destruction, to cease all development of such weapons, and to stop all support for terrorist groups. The Iraqi regime has violated all of those obligations. It possesses and produces chemical and biological weapons. It is seeking nuclear weapons. It has given shelter and support to terrorism, and practices terror against its own people. The entire world has witnessed Iraq's eleven-year history of defiance, deception and bad faith.'

(President Bush Outlines Iraqi Threat Remarks by the President on Iraq Cincinnati Museum Center–Cincinnati Union Terminal. Cincinnati, Ohio. 7 October 2002). http://www.whitehouse.gov/news/releases/ 2002/10/20021007-8.html

'While there are many dangers in the world, the threat from Iraq stands alone—because it gathers the most serious dangers of our age in one place. Iraq's weapons of mass destruction are controlled by a murderous tyrant who has already used chemical weapons to kill thousands of people. This same tyrant has tried to dominate the Middle East, has invaded and brutally occupied a small neighbor, has struck other nations without warning, and holds an unrelenting hostility toward the United States.'

(President Bush Outlines Iraqi Threat Remarks by the President on Iraq Cincinnati Museum Center–Cincinnati Union Terminal. Cincinnati, Ohio. 7 October 2002). http:// www.whitehouse.gov/news/releases/2002/10/20021007-8.html

School anticipates that some speech acts will fail to do so. A relevant example is the failure by US President George W. Bush and British Prime Minister Tony Blair to convince the international community on the existential threat posed by Saddam Hussein and his regime in Iraq. In his State of the Union address on 29 January 2002, President Bush had already characterized Iraq together with North Korea and Iran as an 'axis of evil'. The US administration later sought to justify the removal of Saddam Hussein through military force by linking the issue of international terrorism to the threat of the proliferation of Weapons of Mass Destruction (WMD). The language of security was therefore utilized to justify the need for the implementation of emergency and extraordinary measures (the immediate use of military force to dispose of a foreign regime). In the meantime, critics of the American position questioned Iraq's WMD capabilities and the accuracy of its immediate threat to international peace and stability. The WMD capabilities of Iraq were also said to be less than those of Libya, North Korea, or Iran.

Opponents to the use of military force called for a diplomatic resolution to the crisis through efforts at the United Nations (UN). The UN Security Council adopted in November 2002 a new resolution that allowed UN inspectors to go back to Iraq and search for WMD after a four-year absence. In early 2003, Mr Hans Blix, head of the UN weapons inspectors, pointed out that Iraq had failed to cooperate proactively. Yet he also announced that in the two months of inspections in Iraq, his team had not found any WMDs, or in the parlance of the time, a 'smoking gun'. In the meantime, the military build-up continued in the Gulf, with the US and British military sending more and more troops and equipment.

The opposition to the war was not limited to a diplomatic level but was characterized instead by a broad popular movement. In the United Kingdom, although a key member of the US coalition, the wider population did not accept the government's speech act describing Saddam Hussein's regime as an existential threat to international peace (Collins 2005). This was indicated by opinion polls as well as by massive and repeated demonstrations against the war. Aware that they would not be able to get a UN mandate to attack Iraq, the United States and the United Kingdom launched Operation Iraqi Freedom on 20 March 2003. The opposition to the war remained particularly strong in most parts of the world. Even after the start of the hostilities, the US administration and the British government failed to convince the wider international community of the necessity and legitimacy of the conflict. The continuing demonstrations against the war reflect these elites' lack of legitimacy and perceived abuse of power. The process of securitization therefore failed to move beyond its first stage.

KEY POINTS

- Moves of securitization can fail. This results from the audience rejecting the speech act articulated by the securitizing actor.
- US President George Bush and British Prime Minister Tony Blair generally failed to convince the international community of the existential threat posed by Iraqi President Saddam Hussein.
- Members of the coalition sought to justify the military removal of Saddam Hussein linking the issues of international terrorism and the proliferation of WMD.
- The linkage was not accepted by most other members of the UN Security Council and by the wider international community.

Conclusion

The Copenhagen School, and its securitization model, is a framework for security studies that encapsulates both state security and non-traditional security concerns. It allows for non-military matters to be included in security studies while offering a coherent understanding of the concept of security. It provides a framework to determine how, why, and by whom a specific matter becomes securitized and thus succeeds in distinguishing security and non-security threats. The securitization and desecuritization model makes it possible to adopt a broader conceptualization of security without losing the central coherence of the term. In that respect, the Copenhagen School greatly contributes to the security studies literature.

The Copenhagen School structures its securitization model around a series of salient questions and steps. First, it asks who the securitizing actors might be—those who initiate a move of securitization through the speech act. These can be policymakers, bureaucracies, but also transnational actors (international institutions, non-state actors, civil society), and even individuals. Second, who or what is to be protected? States and governments are no longer the sole referent objects of security as individuals, communities, economies, eco-systems, and others are all alternative referents for security. Third, from what kinds of threats are the referent objects to be protected? The security concern must be articulated as an existential threat—thus linking the concept of security to the question of survival. Fourth, who decides on what is a security issue? The act of securitization is only completed once a relevant audience (public opinion, politicians, military officers or other elites) is convinced that the so-called security issue represents an existential threat to the referent object. Finally, what means are to be used to tackle the existential threat? Once the act of securitization is completed, extraordinary measures can be imposed that go beyond rules ordinarily abided by. The emergency measures are thus located outside the normal bounds of political procedures.

Nonetheless, the chapter has also stressed the dangers of securitization particularly in an undemocratic political system where the wider population is unable to reject an illegitimate speech act and the emergency measures adopted as a result. Even in democratic societies, there is the risk of an act of securitization leading to the curbing of well-established civil liberties in the name of security. This is especially relevant in a post-9/11 context and the growing articulation of issues as existential threats. The pejorative and possibly negative connotations of securitizing an issue have been stressed through several illustrations as well as the preference for a desecuritizing approach. Finally, the chapter has highlighted some of the shortcomings of the Copenhagen School and its securitization model. These include the Euro-centric nature of the Copenhagen School, the sometimes blurred distinction between securitization and politicization as well as the need for a deeper understanding of the dynamics of securitization through more empirical research.

QUESTIONS

Why are some issues considered as security questions while others are not?

How is a process of securitization completed?

Is an act of securitization generally dominated by powerful actors?

Is securitization more likely to succeed in authoritarian states?

What are the benefits of securitizing or desecuritizing an issue?

Assess the dangers of securitization?

What are some of the shortcomings of the securitization model?

Should undocumented migration be regarded and treated as a security question?

Is drug trafficking a national security problem?

Did the process of securitization fail in the case of Iraq?

FURTHER READING

■ **Deudney, D. (1990), 'The Case Against Linking Environmental Degradation and National Security', *Millennium: Journal of International Studies*, 19/3: 461–76**. The article casts doubts upon the tendency to link environmental degradation and national security.

■ **Doty, R.L. (1999), 'Immigration and the Politics of Security', *Security Studies*, 8, 2/3: 71–93**. The article offers 'lenses' for understanding security, arguing that a one-dimensional understanding of security is inadequate for both scholars and policy makers.

■ **Hansen, L. (2000), 'The Little Mermaid's Silent Security Dilemma and the Absence of Gender in the Copenhagen School', *Millennium: Journal of International Studies*, 29/2: 285–306**. The article offers a critique of the Copenhagen School by raising gender issues and other blind spots of securitization.

■ **Kenney, M. (2003), 'From Pablo to Osama: Counter-Terrorism Lessons from the War on Drugs', *Survival*, 45/3: 187–206**. The article looks at lessons from the war on drugs and suggests the need for policymakers to address the 'demand side' of terrorism in the war on terror.

■ **Matthews, J.T. (1989), 'Redefining Security', *Foreign Affairs*, LXVIII/2: 162–177**. This essay argues for a redefinition of national security that incorporates resource, environmental and demographic issues.

IMPORTANT WEBSITES

- **http://www.ciaonet.org/wps/sites/copri.html** This website includes the Working Papers produced at the Copenhagen Peace Research Institute (COPRI). The Institute was established in 1985 and ceased to exist in January 2005 when it was merged into the Danish Institute for International Studies (DIIS).
- **http://www.idss-nts.org/** This website contains information about the Institute of Defence and Strategic Studies (IDSS) Project on Non-Traditional Security in Asia, funded by the Ford Foundation. The website is an information hub for policymakers and academics working on Non-Traditional Security and offers analytical tools by analysing the dynamics of securitization and desecuritization.
- **http://www.midas.bham.ac.uk/theproject.htm** The Migration, Democracy and Security (MIDAS) is a research project undertaken at the University of Birmingham. It examines the securitization of the free movement of people following the terror attacks on 11 September 2001.

Visit the Online Resource Centre that accompanies this book for lots of interesting additional material: www.oxfordtextbooks.co.uk/orc/collins/

PART 2

Deepening and Broadening Security

8 Military Security

ERIC HERRING

Chapter Contents

- Introduction: the scope of the military security agenda
- Military strategy and military security: traditional security studies
- Securitization
- Constructivism
- Debating Colombia
- Conclusion: military security, self and world politics

Reader's Guide

This chapter begins with a discussion of the scope of the military security agenda, in order to communicate an awareness of some of its salient characteristics. It then examines the evolution of the traditional approach to military security, with its emphasis on the use of organized political violence by states and a new consideration of the dangers of war caused by the arrival of nuclear weapons and missile delivery systems. After that, the securitization perspective is outlined in order to put military security in the context of other sectors of security and to consider how issues get put on and are removed from the military security agenda. Such questions are very much the focus of a variety of constructivist approaches considered in the next section of the chapter. The chapter moves on to a more extended examination of the current armed conflict in Colombia in order to bring together some of the main themes which have been considered in the earlier sections. It concludes with a discussion of what is at stake when one decides how to go about studying military security.

Introduction: the scope of the military security agenda

The most frequently used conception of military security is perceived or actual freedom from the threat or use of organized violence for political purposes. It is worth going through the various elements of this definition. It is possible to believe oneself or one's state to be secure from military threat but actually to be in great danger. In 1941, Stalin assumed that Hitler would not invade the Soviet Union and that assumption proved to be false, at huge cost to the Soviet Union. Similarly, as Yugoslavia began to fall apart in the early 1990s, the United Nations at first based itself in Sarajevo in the belief that, of all the parts of the country, this ethnically diverse and integrated city would be unlikely to be involved in the escalating war. Instead, it was the location of a long and bloody siege. It is also possible to perceive a military threat where there is none or less of a threat. Such perceptions cannot be resolved unambiguously, as it is always possible that the threat was there even if no attack was threatened or launched (the classic study, and still a key resource, is Jervis 1976). Using military threats, avoiding being perceived as a military threat and interpreting the nature of possible military threats are all very challenging and enormously consequential. Not surprisingly, these issues are the subject of a great deal of controversy, and aspects of that controversy are surveyed in this chapter. Military security focuses on organized violence as opposed to the violence of individuals and it usually excludes violence for purposes which are not explicitly political (for a broader analysis of collective violence see Tilly 2003). Hence criminal violence—violence for private purposes such as personal hostility or material gain through robbery—is left out. Large numbers of people are shot dead each year in such acts. Also omitted are domestic violence (that is, within families or relationships), industrial death and injury, and road traffic casualties. Avoidable deaths and suffering caused by poverty, hunger, disease or economic sanctions are also excluded: some within the field of peace studies have sought to draw attention to such deaths and suffering by referring to this as 'structural' violence (see Chapter 3). Perhaps the exclusion of these forms of physical insecurity from the category of military security is one that we might choose to endorse, but it is not natural or inevitable. It has its roots in the privileging of concern with the armed threats to and by states, which have the resources to make that privileging appear natural and appropriate. Military security actors can be states or aspirants or challengers to state power such as **insurgent** groups, and a wide range of actors such as the Campaign Against the Arms Trade, Oxfam and the United Nations attempt to influence military security policy. In order to emphasize legitimacy, there is a tendency to use the words 'force' or 'coercion' rather than violence for the physical destruction inflicted by states rather than non-state actors such as rebels, usually to imply that their actions are more legitimate. Alternatively, force and coercion are sometimes used as euphemisms, to make violence sound less horrible and more acceptable.

Another basic choice to be made in deciding the scope of military security relates to means and ends. The darkest cell of Figure 8.1 is most clearly within the scope of military security, where military means are used for military goals. More ambiguous are the two lighter shaded cells, where military means are used for non-military goals, or non-military means are used for military goals. The unshaded cell—non-military means for non-military goals—logically

Figure 8.1 The scope of the military security agenda

Military means, military goals e.g. use of missiles to destroy tanks, or threat of such use to deter attack	Military means, non-military goals e.g. use of military personnel to deliver humanitarian aid
Non-military means, military goals e.g. use of economic sanctions to weaken an opponent's military capabilities	Non-military means, non-military goals e.g. use of economic sanctions to force the target to make debt repayments

falls outside the scope of the military security agenda.

Military security as defined at the beginning of this chapter has been associated with a whole raft of concepts, theories and debates, generally linked to the efforts of states and empires to protect and extend their control of territory, resources, populations and ideological adherents. There are debates about whether it is better to rely on offence or on defence, and whether these can even be distinguished. Military security has been pursued in myriad ways—through deterrence (making military threats to prevent an action), defence (developing the ability to successfully fight off an armed attack), offence (initiating armed conflict), balancing (internal mobilization of resources or making alliances to offset the power of an opponent), bandwagoning (actively supporting a dominant actor), promotion of particular norms and ideologies and social systems (such as anti-militarism, liberal democracy, socialism and capitalism), creation of positive peace (conflict resolution), treaties, imperial and neo-imperial dominance and even ethnic cleansing and genocide. These concepts and debates are associated with widely differing framings of the military security agenda. In discussing any subject, one must decide what to include and exclude, how to organize the material one includes, and whether or how to justify those decisions. This is what is meant in this chapter by framing. Such decisions are unavoidably pervaded by normative factors (a sense of right and wrong) and power relations (the success with which one can get that agenda accepted or even seen to be the only reasonable one). Who frames the military security agenda? Who should frame it? How is it framed? How should it be framed? These four questions underlie the content of this chapter. Traditional security studies sees military security as its home turf and so it represents a good challenge for those seeking to offer alternative approaches.

KEY POINTS

- Military security usually refers to perceived or actual freedom from the threat or use of organized violence for political purposes.
- Some advocate broadening the definition so that increased attention is given to other forms of violence.
- The topic of military security is associated with an extremely wide-ranging set of concepts and debates which are themselves framed within wider understandings of the nature of world politics.
- As the positions one takes on these issues have a powerful effect on one's analysis, it makes the position that the facts can speak for themselves very difficult to sustain.

Military strategy and military security: traditional security studies

As noted above, the traditional approach to military security starts from a commonsensical approach in which the perspective adopted is presented as objective, normal and natural. It is objectivist in the sense that it assumes that one can know what the real threats are to identifiable real interests and how best to deal with them. It is most strongly associated with realism and to a lesser extent also liberalism. War has shaped the evolution of states and states have shaped the evolution of war (Tilly 1990; Barkawi 2005; Shaw 2005). Traditional security studies developed in the service of the state. Its origins lay in the study of military strategy and the conduct of war by the military rather than civilians. The horrors of World War One—vast number of soldiers' lives thrown away in seemingly futile offensives as men struggled unprotected across muddy ground through barbed wire and in the face of a hail of machine gun bullets and artillery shells—contributed to an urge to think through how to avoid wars rather than how to fight them. It was in large part a war of attrition, in which winning would come about primarily by chewing through the men and resources of the other side to bring the other side to the brink of collapse first. Revulsion at this process fed into the early beginnings of the study of military security by civilians and academics in particular. However, the culture of militarist nationalism—in which war and military things are glorified as good and noble in themselves in the life of a nation—was by no means exhausted (for more on war as good and noble see Chapter 5). This militarist nationalism was central to the origins of the Second World War. Thinking about war and strategy remained at a premium and thinking about security remained at the margin.

The trend towards thinking about security in terms of avoiding wars as well as fighting them and civilians playing a role in thinking about both of those things was reinforced strongly by the advent of the atomic bomb in 1945 (Kaplan 1991). However, this was a trend which tended to be concentrated in the more industrialized capitalist states and especially the United States. This thinking was funded mainly by the state in order to serve the interests of the state. Prominent amongst the bodies which sprung up to institutionalize this thinking was the Research and Development (RAND) Corporation funded by the US Air Force in Santa Monica, California, where civilians mingled with the military and sometimes came to see themselves as understanding better than the military the new situation facing the United States and its allies. The perceived need to find ways of ensuring that the Cold War between the United States and Soviet Union did not become a hot war (i.e. one involving direct armed combat), due to the potential for catastrophic nuclear escalation, was underlined by the development of the hydrogen bomb and intercontinental ballistic missiles as reliable means of delivering them in the 1950s and 1960s. The hot war aspects of their competition were conducted via regional allies such as North and South Vietnam. The power of atomic bombs is generally equivalent to thousands of tons of the conventional explosive TNT (kilotons). Hydrogen bombs tend to have the power of millions of tons of TNT (megatons). For the first time ever the United States faced the potential for it to suffer enormous damage without losing a conventional war first: it could be destroyed without being defeated.

Within traditional security thinking, there have always been two divergent responses to the advent of nuclear vulnerability. The first has been to conventionalize them, that is, to treat them as if they were simply bigger bombs which could be used to fight and win wars, or the use of which by an opponent could be survived in the way that conventional bombs could. After all, more people died in the firebombing of Tokyo by the United States in 1945 than by the dropping of the atomic bomb on Hiroshima or Nagasaki. Once the United States became involved in the Korean War in 1950, Mao Zedong, leader of the new Communist government of mainland China, decided that China was going to have to enter the war on the side of North Korea. He also concluded that the Chinese state could survive US atomic bomb attack on its major cities and would not be deterred by this possible outcome because he saw a US armed presence in Korea as intolerably dangerous. As it turned out, China entered the war, the United States did not use its atomic bombs on China, and China was able to live with a divided Korea and with US forces in South Korea. During the Cold War, nuclear weapons were deployed into all branches of the US and Soviet armed forces and integrated into war planning. There was a profusion of nuclear weapons in the arsenals of the two superpowers eventually totalling around 50,000 missile warheads, artillery shells, demolition munitions and even depth charges. Much effort went into reducing the explosive power of nuclear weapons in order to make them more usable and bridge the gap between them and conventional weapons. Conventional thinking about nuclear weapons led to efforts to make nuclear war fightable and winnable or at least survivable. The planning of the North Atlantic Treaty Organisation (NATO)—composed during the Cold War of most of the West European states plus the United States and Canada—presumed that a major challenge for the alliance was convincing the Soviet Union and its East European client states in the Warsaw Treaty Organisation of the credibility of its threat to initiate the use of nuclear weapons should it be losing a conventional war in Europe. The United States also sometimes sought ways of convincing opponents that it might initiate the use of nuclear weapons during conventional crises and conflicts in Korea, Vietnam and the Taiwan Straits between Communist China and Taiwan. In the post Cold War world, there is still a substantial amount of conventionalized thinking about nuclear weapons, especially in the United States, in relation to war planning and miniaturization of them in the hope that they would then be more usable. From this perspective, nuclear deterrence of nuclear attack is difficult and requires constant attention.

The second strand of thinking about nuclear weapons within traditional strategic studies is that they are fundamentally different and revolutionary in their implications for military security due to their potential for escalation to catastrophic levels of destruction. This was present from the very earliest days but has usually not dominated in terms of policy. Soviet President Mikhail Gorbachev rejected the conventionalization of nuclear weapons as he believed that it was the possibility of nuclear arms competition getting out of control that was the real threat to military security rather than the risk of deliberate initiation of nuclear use. Hence he led the way in initiating dramatic reductions in nuclear warheads and in ending the Cold War, but the political forces he unleashed brought about the collapse of the Soviet Union in 1991. From this perspective, nuclear deterrence is relatively easy. Some see it as underpinned by a guaranteed ability to absorb a surprise attack and inflict unacceptable damage in retaliation (when shared by both sides, this situation is known as Mutually Assured Destruction or MAD). Others think that nuclear attack against vulnerable nuclear arsenals is very unlikely, either due to the potential for retaliation should the disarming attack fail even partially or due to the huge political costs which might result from launching an attack. Another relevant view here is that there is a nuclear taboo, that is, a strategic cultural prohibition against the use of nuclear weapons which involves the assumption that they should not be used rather than a conscious cost-benefit calculation of the consequences of their use. The fear has always been that a fanatical or irrational decision-maker or a non-state terrorist would not be restrained by the nuclear taboo, and this had fed into concern about the spread of nuclear weapons to more states. Ironically, strategic history thus far points to the United States as the state which has tried hardest to undermine the nuclear taboo and make nuclear weapons usable. Chemical and biological weapons have increasingly been categorized with nuclear weapons as weapons of mass destruction. However, thus far it has proven difficult to produce chemical and biological weapons which would need only small numbers of them to cause vast amounts of destruction in any targetable way and with high reliability, as is the case with nuclear weapons (for more on WMD see Chapter 15).

KEY POINTS

- Traditionally, thinking about military matters was primarily about strategies used especially by states of how to fight and win wars.
- The advent of nuclear weapons and long-range delivery systems produced a new strand of thinking which put much greater emphasis on how to achieve political goals while avoiding war. Nevertheless, the search to make those new capabilities usable in war continued.

Securitization

The themes discussed above—the conduct of major conventional wars, political-diplomatic crisis management, the use of threats, and their interaction with nuclear weapons—have been central to traditional security studies. Major debates have occurred about the implications for military security of two relatively recent events. The first was the end of the Cold War in the late 1980s combined with the collapse of the Soviet Union in 1991. The second was the al-Qaeda terrorist attacks on the United States on 11 September 2001 and the US announcement of its 'war on terror' (see Chapter 16). The most comprehensive and systematic is the securitization approach. This is discussed more fully in Chapter 7: the intention here is to focus on and contextualize its military aspect. Building on Barry Buzan's earlier work (1983, 1991a), Buzan, Ole Wæver and Jaap de Wilde (1998) represented security as having military, economic, environmental, societal and political sectors; and global, non-regional subsystemic, regional and local levels of analysis (see Figure 8.2).

The dark shaded left-hand column in Figure 8.2 indicates the scope of military security, indicating graphically how much is omitted by focusing on it. This column, combined with the lighter shaded columns, represents the much greater scope of a broader notion of security in securitization studies. Buzan et al conclude that military security has become primarily regional since the end of the Cold War, sometimes with positive consequences and sometimes negative ones. They also argue that weak states can produce a very local focus for military security as actors fight for control within a state's borders, usually with some form of outside involvement. This has clearly been the case in Iraq since the US-led invasion in March 2003 (Herring, Rangwala 2006). Furthermore, in addition to the threats posed by insurgents and terrorists, Iraqi citizens in the centre of the country also worry about the possibility of being killed by US airstrikes and ground offensives or by jumpy soldiers at checkpoints. Throughout the country they fear torture and arbitrary imprisonment by members of the state's 'security' forces. The third dimension of the securitization framework proposes three issue categories—security, political and non-political (illustrated by the third dimension of Figure 8.2). For Buzan et al to categorize something as a security issue, it should threaten survival and requires urgent and exceptional political action. This is a much more restrictive definition than is often the case. Less intensely, a political issue is one which is on state or other policy agendas for resource

Figure 8.2 Locating military security in securitization studies

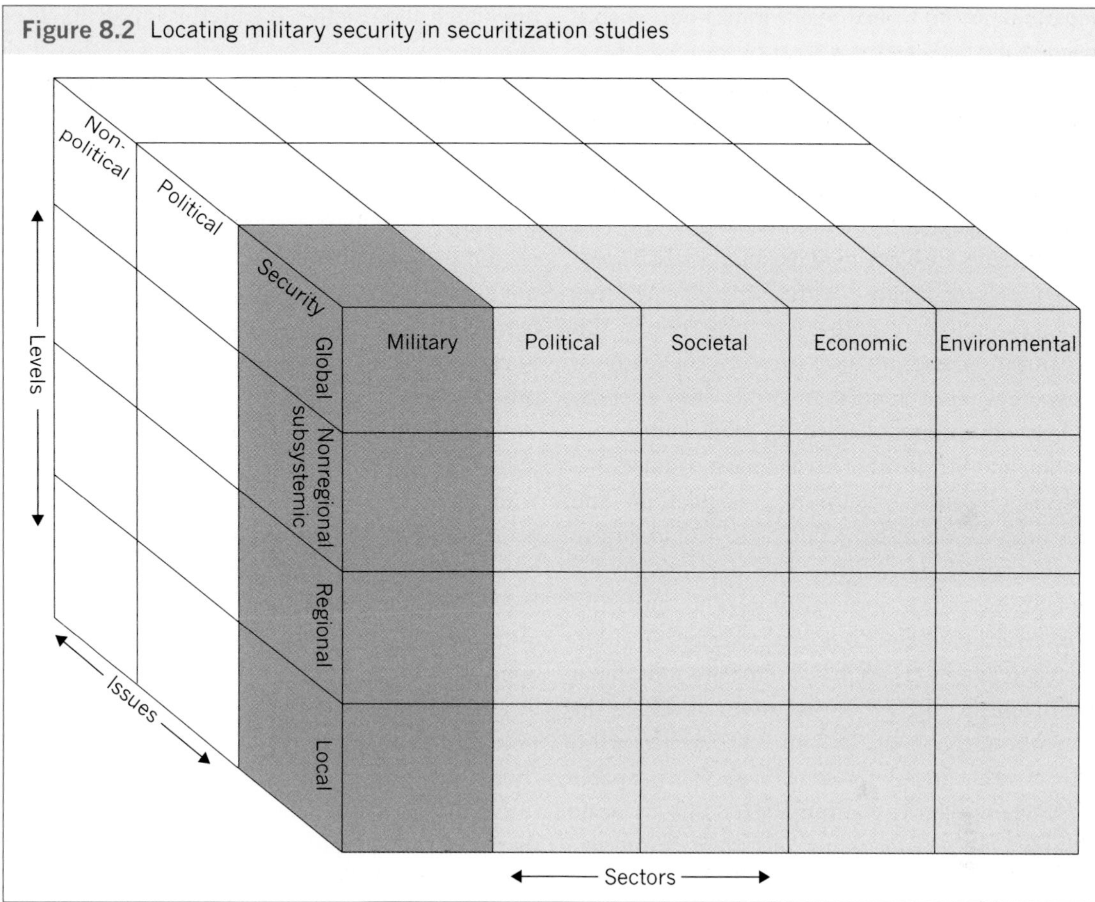

allocation, and a non-political issue is one which does not require public debate, resource allocation and action. In the view of Buzan et al, the referent object—that which is being secured—of military security is usually the state, although it can be other political actors, and the armed forces can even see themselves as the referent object and rebel against the state or launch a coup. Military issues can move up or down the security, political and non-political issue ladder.

Traditional approaches tend to focus on the security aspects of military issues. In contrast, Buzan et al argue that advanced industrial states are mostly free from threats which threaten their survival and require exceptional and urgent political action. In their framework, the use of the armed forces by such states for purposes such as peacekeeping or humanitarian intervention is a political rather than a security issue. Realists tend to worry that such an attitude will undermine the need to invest heavily in armed forces to ensure that military security threats do not arise in the first place. Such a concern is at the heart of the national security strategy of the United States published in 2002 (a document well worth reading). States are the main actors in deciding what does and does not go on the military security agenda, and have been the most successful actors at accumulating the capability for organized political violence, though there are major exceptions such as weak states. Organized violence is useful not only for destroying and threatening opponents, but also for taking and holding territory, which in traditional terms is a defining characteristic of states (along with population and political authority over that territory and population). Equally, capturing territory is not sufficient to produce desired political outcomes, as the United States found out when it invaded and occupied Iraq.

The issue of drugs is one over which there is dispute as to whether it is a political or a security issue, and whether or not it should fall within the military sector. The phrase 'war on drugs' could be read as implying both, and armed force and chemical defoliants are being used in Colombia as appropriate ways of dealing with some of the drug traffickers and their crops. For some critics, this securitization and militarization of the issue of drugs does more harm than good. They propose dealing with currently illegal drugs in the same way as alcohol (another drug but legal in most countries)—that is, through legalization, regulation and education for harm reduction. This would aim to simultaneously desecuritize and demilitarize the issue. Even issues such as non-state terrorism directed against states do not necessarily fall within the realm of military security on the grounds that it is difficult for such groups to pose a threat to the existence of that state. In contrast, state terrorism with its vastly greater resources is perfectly capable of wiping out entire communities. Some advocate dropping the 'war on terror' in favour of international policing cooperation. At the other end of the spectrum, some on the right are of the view that the issue has not been sufficiently securitized or militarized by the administration of George W. Bush. These neoconservatives, as they are known, argue for campaigns to remove the governments of Syria, Saudi Arabia and especially Iran and replace them with liberal democracies. Their reasoning is that these states are behind anti-US terrorism and can only be stopped by removing them.

According to liberal democratic peace theory, the more that states are liberal democratic, the less they threaten each other's military security (Maoz, Russett 1983: Russett, O'Neal 1991). This is seen to be due to what Zeev Maoz and Bruce Russett, among others, portray as their liberal norms of tolerance and compromise and their democratic procedures of public accountability which they argue make it more difficult for leaders to begin wars. They also portray their use of force against non-liberal states as essentially defensively orientated and reactive. If true, this is potentially of enormous significance because it suggests that, if all states were liberal democratic, there would be no more interstate war, which would be, to non-militarists, a tremendous gain. This view has been challenged in a number of ways. Some have sought to refute it directly, claiming that this positive association between liberal democracy and peace does not exist (Henderson 2002). Another approach has been to accept the underlying proposition that liberal democratic states tend not to threaten each other's military security but to provide a different explanation. Tarak Barkawi and Mark Laffey argue that liberal democratic states tend not to go to war with each other 'because they are embedded in geostrategic and political economic relations that buttress international state and capitalist power in hegemonic, i.e., non-violent ways' (1999: 419. See also Barkawi, Laffey 2001 and Barkawi 2005). In this approach, liberal democracies are not conceived of as separate states with their own territories, populations and sovereignty (that is, final political authority). Instead, they are part of a set of integrated international state practices—such as economic disciplining through the International Monetary Fund or US-led Coalition invasion and reconstruction—which are increasingly integrating them in an informal imperial hierarchy. The use of force is within this system licensed against non-liberal states in order to integrate them into a global system characterized, they argue, by extreme economic inequality.

The benefit of the securitization approach is that it offers the possibility of comparing the importance of other sectors without privileging the military one above all the others. The possible costs are that, by using the word 'security' in relation to non-military things, it could end up militarizing those other sectors, for example, by unintentionally encouraging the idea that armed threats and force should be considered in relation to dealing with actors who are causing environmental problems (for more on this see Chapter 11). Although in the securitization framework, the concepts 'military' and 'security' are independent categories, in most people's minds they are still strongly associated.

KEY POINTS

- The securitization approach offers a comprehensive framework within which to situate military security, relating it to other sectors, a variety of levels, and types of issue.
- It also offers tools for thinking about how issues become part or cease to be part of the military security agenda.
- Like any other analytical approach, it has built into it implicit and explicit normative and conceptual positions which are inevitably controversial.
- Issues such as drugs, terrorism and democratization are not necessarily part of, or separate from, the military security agenda.

Constructivism

The securitization framework of Buzan et al is significantly **constructivist** in that it looks at how social reality is produced through human interaction rather than taking the content of social reality for granted. However, the attention it gives to the social construction of military security is quite limited, and numerous versions of constructivism have been applied to this subject (e.g. Katzenstein 1996; Weldes et al 1999). A much deeper constructivism can be seen in the work of Jutta Weldes on a classic case of a crisis in military security, namely, the Cuban missile crisis of October 1962. In order to force the Soviet Union to remove nuclear-armed missiles which it had secretly deployed in Cuba, the United States went on conventional and nuclear military alert and set up a naval blockade to prevent the delivery of the remaining missiles which were on their way by ship. In the end, the Soviet Union turned its ships around and agreed to remove its missiles and nuclear weapons from Cuba, much to the fury of Cuban leader Fidel Castro. In Western scholarship, this is usually treated as a victory for rational, well-managed US coercive diplomacy (on coercive diplomacy, see Chapter 13). Some revisionist scholarship argues that the outcome was more of a compromise and that reassurance of the Soviet Union was more important in the outcome than is generally acknowledged (Lebow 1995). Others see it as one of the most dangerous incidents in human history which avoided disastrous escalation at least as much through luck as through good judgement (Sagan 1995).

Those working within the realist approach to military security argue that the national interest can be discerned for what it really is. Some of their critics use the point that realists often disagree strongly with each other in identifying the national interest to argue that the concept of the national interest is so vague and flexible as to be useless. Instead, Weldes argues that one can discern patterns in the understandings of the national interest among decision-makers, that those understandings are not objective and that analysing them in terms of the subjective psychological perception of individuals is not a very effective mode of analysis. She argues that those patterns are most usefully seen as inter-subjective, that is, they are arrived at through a process of mutual interpretation and representation of the world. To arrive at some understanding of what the interests of the state are, officials use or adapt existing cultural and linguistic resources to create an inter-subjective world of particular actors with identities and relationships attributed to them. The construction of the national interest at stake on any specific issue is very heavily conditioned by this prior inter-subjective process: there is more to the creation of meaning than the accumulation of facts. One can deduce a step-by-step constructivist analytical method with potentially wide applicability. This involves describing how a particular military security (or indeed other) issue has been characterized, specifying the cultural and linguistic resources mobilized in that characterization, mapping out how these elements have been linked to each other to create apparently but not actually natural meaning, and going through the same steps with competing inter-subjective constructions which have been marginalized. Case Study 8.1 provides an overview of the application of this method by Weldes (1999) to the Cuban missile crisis.

This kind of constructivist method might be applied to other issues and cases. It might be used to shed significant light on, for example, the current debate on the nature and implications of Iran's nuclear programme. The dominant narrative in the United States is that Iran is trying to use its civil nuclear programme to acquire nuclear weapons, and that statements such as that by Iranian President Mahmoud Ahmadinejad that 'Israel must be wiped off the map' (the usual translation of his comments—for example in al-Jazeera 2005—originally made in Persian) show that it is too risky to allow Iran to become a nuclear weapon state. This narrative also assumes that US officials have the right to make this assessment and act on it militarily and unilaterally. An alternative narrative is that Iran is hedging its power generation needs against the decline of oil reserves and is not actually pursuing nuclear weapons. Another is that Iran feels the need to become a nuclear state to provide a deterrent to and symbolic equality with US and Israeli nuclear weapons, and that Ahmadinejad's statement is rhetoric rather than an indicator of an Iranian intention to try to destroy Israel. This last point is underlined by the claim that his words in Persian—'een rezhim-e ishghalgar-e qods bayad az safheh-ye ruzgar mahv shavad'—translate more accurately as 'The Imam [former Iranian revolutionary leader Ayatollah Khomeini] said that this regime occupying Jerusalem must be erased from the page of time', supposedly indicating a desire to end a particular political situation rather than to eliminate the state of Israel. The limitation of the constructivist approach provided by Weldes and others is that it does not offer a method for choosing between or moving beyond the competing interpretations outlined. Furthermore, one might arrive at the impression that the counter-narratives set out by constructivists are the ones that they actually find more persuasive, and this reluctance to endorse particular overall narratives while still endorsing many specific narrative elements along the way is

CASE STUDY 8.1

Constructivism and the Cuban missile crisis of 1962

In their response in October 1962 to the secret Soviet deployment in Cuba of medium-range nuclear weapons capable of hitting the eastern United States, US officials saw themselves as essentially defensive, reactive and good, and the Soviet Union as aggressive, on the offensive and immoral. These constructions were taken for granted and assumed to be self-evidently true, natural, not constructed and therefore beyond question. Such constructions strongly predisposed US decision-makers to simply assume that the Soviet Union had to be forced to withdraw the missiles or that the United States would have to destroy the missiles, even at high risk of a nuclear war. The debate within the administration of President John F. Kennedy focused almost exclusively on the various options—naval blockade, bombing and invasion—to produce those outcomes.

Alternative narratives regarding the crisis—that the missile deployment was defensively motivated to stop repeated US attempts to overthrow Fidel Castro's government and as a short-cut to reducing the huge US lead in long-range nuclear weapons; that this was basically the same as the US deployment of nuclear weapons in Turkey; or that the missiles would have little strategic impact—were possible but were marginalized by the prior inter-subjective constructions among US officials about the identities of and relationships between the actors involved.

one which could be criticized by those of a more objectivist persuasion. It may be that constructivist discourse can be combined with a more social scientific approach as sub-sets of rational inquiry. Hence a discourse analysis of Iran's nuclear programme might be integrated with a discussion of Scott Sagan's (1996/97) classic essay on three models of why some states acquire nuclear weapons (for security, domestic politics and to symbolize norms such as modernity and equality) and Etel Solingen's (1994) argument that some states do not acquire nuclear weapons due to the dominance of some sectors in those states wishing to prioritize integration into the global economy.

In a more **post-structuralist** version, in which even greater emphasis is put on mapping out **discourses**, constructivism has been applied by David Campbell to understanding the nature of US foreign and security policy overall, the Iraqi invasion of Kuwait in 1990 and its aftermath, and the war in Bosnia-Herzegovina in the early 1990s (Campbell 1993, 1998a, 1998b). By taking on such substantial and contemporary military security issues, Campbell was endeavouring to show the relevance of discourse analysis on ground which more traditional military security analysts see as their usual remit. The securitization work of Buzan et al (1998: 205) argues that constructions can be so settled, depoliticized and appear so natural that they can be analysed as if they are 'inert', 'sedimented' or effectively objective. More thoroughgoing constructivists and especially post-structuralists such as Campbell challenge this head on. They argue that even those supposedly settled, depoliticized and natural constructions only appear to be so through major and, crucially, ongoing discursive practices (for an excellent review of literature on constructivism, identity and violence, see Fearon, Laitin 2000). For example, it is widely though not universally assumed that the war in Bosnia was between Serbs, Croats and Muslims, and that such identity markers were so powerful as to be settled (see, for example, Kaufman 1996). In contrast, Campbell (1998b) argues that their settled appearance was made possible only by a powerful set of discursive practices—including the murder in the name of ethnic purity of those who argued that identities are always overlapping and mixed (for an objectivist version of the argument—that 'ethnic' wars are often carried out by small groups with most of the population unwilling and fearful bystanders, see Mueller 2000). Indeed, for post-structuralists, identity is always 'transgressive' or 'transversal', that is, never neatly in separate categories with separate essential elements.

The political ethic which follows from post-structuralism in the field of military security studies is to embrace this insecurity of identity rather than seek to secure what can never exist, that is, wholly separate identity. The humanitarian military intervention debate was framed at the time as 'Should there be military intervention to protect the Muslims from the Serbs and the Croats, or are they basically all as bad as each other and so one should not pick sides?'. The post-structuralist approach might seem to suggest that the question should have been reframed to: 'Should there be military intervention to protect those who acknowledge the inescapable diversity of identity?'. The Bosnian government claimed to hold that position and objected vigorously to being labelled, as it usually was in the West, as the 'Muslim' government of Bosnia. However, for post-structuralists the problem is an even bigger one, namely, that the potential humanitarian interveners are part of the problem too in that they share the same essentialist notions of identity—be they of Britishness, American-ness—as the ethnic cleansers they would be intervening against. It is the notion of any kind of pure identity that post-structuralists maintain must be challenged. This also extends to wider discourses of the essential goodness and defensiveness of one group and essential evil and aggressiveness of another, as discussed, for example, by Weldes (1999) in relation to the Cuban missile crisis. Such debates are getting under way in relation to the invasion and occupation of Iraq in 2003 and in relation to the claim that Iraq is fundamentally divided between Kurds, Sunni Arabs and Shi'a Arabs (Feldman 2004; Davis 2005; Herring, Rangwala 2006).

KEY POINTS

- Constructivism explores how meaning in the realm of military security is constructed through discursive practices so that those meanings appear to be natural (and hence not constructed).
- According to constructivists, decisions about how to act with regard to specific military security issues (such as the potential acquisition of nuclear weapons by a particular state) are heavily conditioned or even more or less determined by the meaning that is given to those specifics through those discursive practices.

Debating Colombia

All the themes discussed in this chapter thus far could be explored in relation to the conflict in Colombia. In the last fifteen years as the Cold War drew to a close, the civil war in Colombia escalated significantly: in that period nearly three million people have been displaced and tens of thousands killed. Since 1998, the United States has backed the Colombian government through Plan Colombia and its successor the Andean Regional Initiative and there have been various peace negotiations and military offensives. In understanding the reasons for this death and suffering, competing understandings have been generated of the key actors, their relationships and the nature and meaning of the facts. The roles of the US and Colombian governments, the Revolutionary Armed Forces of Colombia (FARC) and smaller National Liberation Army (ELN) left-wing **guerrilla** groups, and the United Self-Defence Forces of Colombia (AUC) right-wing **paramilitary** group have been debated by Russell Crandall, a US academic who is an adviser to the US Department of Defence, and Doug Stokes, a British academic who is a member of the Colombia Solidarity Campaign (Stokes–Crandall correspondence 2002; Crandall 2002; Stokes 2004). The diverging perspectives of the two protagonists are summarized in Key Ideas 8.1.

Viewed from a traditional military security studies perspective, the way forward in assessing the relative validity of these positions is to gain a deeper understanding of the **empirical** aspects of the Case Study (see the 'Important Websites' in this chapter for information about the highly informative International Crisis Group, and also Green 2005). The empirical questions are certainly not trivial. If it is the case that the AUC is far more heavily involved in drug trafficking than the FARC or ELN, then it is the AUC that would need to be tackled first and foremost to carry out a war on drugs in Colombia. With regard to the US 'war on terror', until recently, the Colombian military used to be responsible for 80% of the killings in Colombia: now the AUC paramilitaries are responsible for that proportion of them. Delving further into the facts would help in working out whether this shows that reform of the Colombia military is working and so US assistance to it should be continued or increased. Alternatively, that additional information may lead one to conclude that the Colombian military is closely allied to the paramilitaries and has delegated the killings to them. In this case, US assistance to the Colombian military is doing, at best, nothing to help the Colombian people and could even intentionally be indirect support for the paramilitaries. Fundamentally, the United States is either contributing to or undermining the military security of the population of Colombia depending on whether one agrees with Crandall or Stokes, and major policy consequences flow from that assessment.

KEY IDEAS 8.1

Colombia: a war on drugs and terror or a war of terror?

Russell Crandall's perspective

The role of the United States in world politics in general and Colombia in particular is basically benign even if it makes mistakes. The end of the Cold War represented a fundamental change in world politics due to the end of the East–West rivalry. It allows the US to exercise power to promote liberal democracy and market economies without hindrance by the Soviet Union.

Under the administrations of Bill Clinton and George W. Bush, US policy towards Colombia and the Andean region more generally has been focused excessively on reducing the cultivation and export of drugs, regarding them as a threat to US national security, while not involving itself in Colombia's civil war through counter-insurgency operations against the FARC and ELN left-wing guerrillas. The United States is supporting the Colombian state to help it deal with the guerrillas, who increasingly use terrorism and traffic in drugs. With the 9/11 attacks, the United States began to label the actions of the guerrillas as terrorist and showed more interest in counter-insurgency. The United States should give counter-insurgency support to the Colombia government only if the latter has a credible political strategy for ending the civil war. The strategy should include reform of the state and pressure on the Colombian military to cut their links to the right-wing AUC paramilitaries, who are basically independent of the Colombian government. After 9/11, the United States finally declared the AUC a terrorist organisation and is right to support the Colombian government which is attempting to rebuild a Colombian army free from paramilitary influence.

Doug Stokes' perspective

Given the structural role of the US state within the global political economy, the role of the United States in world politics in general and Colombia in particular tends to be malign. There has been fundamental continuity in world politics despite the end of the Cold War because US interests continue to be the defence of the liberal international order and the preservation of US primacy. As such, global conflict is still between the United States as leader and protector of global capitalism and the global South—in other words, between those whose interests are the preservation of wealth and privilege and those who are marginalized, subordinated and policed.

The United States and the Colombian state, military and right-wing paramilitaries are all broadly cooperating with each other and share a common interest in the destruction of the insurgency and roll-back of broadly progressive social forces. They are conducting a war of terror using state-sponsored AUC narco-paramilitaries who are responsible for around 80% of the civilian deaths. The aim is to crush dissent, including democratic civil society, in order to insulate the Colombian state from reformist pressures and maintain an important source of non-Middle Eastern oil. The primary strategy of the United States is not a war on drugs. It has concentrated on trying to weaken the left-wing guerrillas who tax the drug trade (rather than participate in it directly) instead of targeting the main drug traffickers, namely, the right-wing paramilitaries.

See Stokes–Crandall correspondence 2002; Crandall 2002; Stokes 2004.

The fact that the Crandall–Stokes debate was premised on the assumption that one can prove or disprove arguments with reference to facts indicates that they share a broad commitment to objectivism. However, testing in relation to facts is made more difficult or even impossible, some would argue, without a common frame of reference. This is only partly shared by Crandall and Stokes, as the former works within the traditions of realism and liberalism whereas the latter's work has more in common with **historical materialism**. Important normative differences are related to these differing commitments. For Crandall, the United States has the right both in terms of protecting and promoting US national security interests and in terms of the universal applicability of liberalism to be deeply involved in military security issues in Colombia. For Stokes, the United States does not have this right because it is protecting and promoting only the illegitimate interests of US and Colombian elites against the interests of ordinary people in both countries. A constructivist perspective on this debate would involve unpacking how Crandall and Stokes go about presenting their portrayals of the facts, the actors and their relationships, and mapping how widely those portrayals are shared and amongst whom. Crandall paints a picture of a triangular relationship of political struggle between the Colombian government; the FARC and ELN guerrillas; and the AUC paramilitaries and their backers in the Colombian military. In contrast, Stokes argues that Colombian government and military and the AUC paramilitaries are quite closely allied against the FARC and ELN. There seems to be a two-way process here, with narratives about specific facts being used to draw conclusions about the character of the actors involved and their relationships, and the claims about the character of the actors involved and their relationships shaping the interpretation of narratives about more specific facts.

KEY POINTS

- There is fundamental dispute over which actors are causing military insecurity for the people of Colombia, and the nature of and relationships between those actors.
- One way to develop a view on such disputes is through in-depth analysis of the facts: another is to explore the fundamental assumptions which give meaning to those facts.

Conclusion: military security, self and world politics

In deciding how to study military security, major choices must be made, either explicitly or tacitly. One of the most obvious points of entry is to focus on the empirical aspects of the established military security agenda, looking for patterns and trends. The resources spent directly on the military worldwide are huge—$975 billion in 2004, only 6% lower than the high point of Cold War military spending in 1987–88 (data from SIPRI—see 'Important Websites'). This equates to $162 per person and 2.6% of world economic activity. The United States alone accounts for 47% of the world total of military spending. One could also survey the principal arms trading states (see Chapter 17). This would show that the trade is heavily dominated by a small number of supplier states—the United States, United Kingdom, Russia, France and Germany—and a larger number of purchasing states in NATO or in areas of tension and conflict (primarily the Middle East and South Asia). In contrast to the popular misconception that the end of the Cold War resulted in an increase in the number of major armed conflicts (and civil wars in particular—that is, wars primarily within individual states), there was a steadily downward trend from 32 in 1990 to 19 in 1997, a rise to 27 in 1998 followed another steadily downward trend to 19 again in 2003.

One can treat these as data to be explained in social scientific terms, or discursive constructions to be examined to see how they were arrived at and to see what they have left out. It is also possible to see the objectivist and discursive approaches as part of an overall toolkit of rational analysis to be deployed at different times or to be combined rather than seeing them as fixed and separate perspectives to which one must commit consistently. The intention of this chapter has been to introduce you to some of the central debates in the nature of data and the nature of meaning in the study of military security as well as to give an overview of some important cases. The choices you make from here will reflect your intellectual training, context, values and indeed political commitments. You cannot study military security without it shaping some aspect of your self, and the subject and you are not simply separate from world politics but are deeply implicated with it (on security and self, see Booth 1997).

KEY POINTS

- The subject of military security can be analysed in terms of major empirical patterns and trends.
- The study of military security, your identity and the practices of world politics are all mutually constitutive (i.e. they shape each other in fundamental ways).

QUESTIONS

Are civilians better at understanding military security than the military?

Why have non-nuclear states not been attacked with nuclear weapons since 1945?

Is military security best achieved through non-military means?

Is the United States conducting a war on drugs and terror or a war of terror in Colombia?

When are states a threat to the military security of their own population?

Do liberal democracies tend not to threaten each other's military security?

Is there a liberal imperial order which uses military means to protect and extend its global scope?

Can one choose between the competing narratives regarding the military security implications of Iran's nuclear programme?

To what extent is the Iraqi state militarily secure?

How have discourses of military insecurity been implicated in constructions of Iraqi identities since the invasion in 2003?

FURTHER READING

■ **Nye, Jr, Joseph S. (2005), *Understanding International Conflicts. An Introduction to Theory and History*, 5th edn, London: Pearson Longman.** Of all the further reading suggested here, this is easily the most wide-ranging of those within a **social scientific** approach and is a good, broad starting point. It explores whether there is an enduring logic of conflict in world politics and considers the origins of the First and Second World Wars and Cold War. It then surveys intervention, institutions and regional and ethnic conflicts (including a heroically brief 12-page overview of conflicts in the Middle East); globalization and interdependence; the information revolution and transnational politics. Written as a textbook, it has useful chronologies, study questions, maps, diagrams and a glossary of key terms.

■ **Barkawi, Tarak (2005), *Globalization and War*, London: Rowman & Littlefield.** Some scholars argue that globalization is producing military security and peace while others argue that it is causing military insecurity and war. In contrast to both, Barkawi suggests that war should not be seen as a separate thing caused or prevented by globalization. Instead, his view is that war is a major aspect of globalization itself (in terms of bringing about the movement of people, goods and ideas around the world) and has been so for longer than is usually thought.

- **Baylis, John, Cohen, Elliot, Gray, Colin, and Wirtz, James (eds.) (2002), *Strategy in the Contemporary World: Introduction to Strategic Studies*, Oxford: Oxford University Press.** This volume provides an excellent introduction to traditional perspectives on military security. It covers strategic theory; the history of war; the role of law; origins of war and peace; land, sea and air power; deterrence, arms control and disarmament; terrorism and irregular warfare; weapons of mass destruction; technology and war; and humanitarian intervention and peace operations.

- **Herring, Eric and Rangwala, Glen (2006), *Iraq in Fragments: The Occupation and its Legacy*, London: Hurst and Cornell University Press.** The invasion of Iraq was presented by its advocates as an important means of dealing with Iraq as a military security threat and by some of them as a means of creating a wave of reform that would usher in an unprecedented positive era of military security in the Middle East more widely. Instead, the weapons of mass destruction Iraq was supposed to have did not exist and much of Iraq has plunged into military insecurity. This study provides an in-depth assessment of events in Iraq in the three years since the US-led invasion. Military security issues are analysed in the broader context of the argument that political authority in Iraq has fragmented.

- **Buzan, Barry and Herring, Eric (1998), *The Arms Dynamic in World Politics*, Boulder, CO: Lynne Rienner Publishers.** This study aims to provide a comprehensive overview of military security from the perspective of revolutions in and the global spread of modern military technology. It explains those patterns in relation to arms racing, action-reaction and domestic structures. It considers the use of force, threats and symbolic politics and the meaning and implications of arms control, non-offensive defence and disarmament.

- **Weldes, Jutta, Laffey, Mark, Gusterson, Hugh, and Duvall, Raymond (eds.) (1999), *Cultures of Insecurity. States, Communities and the Production of Danger,* London: University of Minneapolis Press.** This challenging constructivist volume brings together scholars of sociocultural anthropology and international relations to explore discourses of insecurity among states and other communities. Although the themes are deeply theorized, the chapters also explore them in relation to diverse cases and places such as Korea, the Middle East, the genocide in Rwanda, US-Indian relations, post-Mao China and the politics of the internet. Whereas traditional security studies assumes the identities of political groups and asks how those groups can be made militarily secure, this study looks at how the construction of discourses of insecurity produce the identities of political actors and vice versa.

IMPORTANT WEBSITES

- **http://www.sipri.org/** Stockholm International Peace Research Institute. SIPRI conducts research on conflict and cooperation in order to promote understanding of how international conflicts can be resolved peacefully and how stable peace can be established. It has very extensive empirical and conceptual research programmes on many aspects of military security and especially in relation to military spending and arms transfers and attempts to control the transfer of militarily significant technologies. A massive amount of data is provided free on this site.

- **http://www.gwu.edu/~nsarchiv/** National Security Archive. Studying military security usually involves reading material like this chapter—someone's else's interpretation of someone else's interpretation of important events. The internet is a wonderful resource to allow students now to spend at least some time looking at original documents and raw data for themselves, and can trigger the desire to do original research. The National Security Archive at George Washington University in Washington D.C. uses the US Freedom of Information Act to declassify and make available vast numbers of documents on US military security policy, and selections can be accessed for free. By this indirect means, one also has access to intimate details of military security policy-making of many other countries as well.

- **http://www.crisisgroup.org/** International Crisis Group. The ICG is an NGO with over one hundred staff located worldwide. It seeks to prevent and resolve armed conflict across the world by means of field-based analysis and high-level advocacy. Its many reports on Iraq, Indonesia, Nepal, Colombia, Kosovo, Zimbabwe, Afghanistan, Darfur and other actual or potential crisis and conflict locations are free. Its in-depth yet up-to-date, locally researched reports are superb at putting military security issues into political context.

- **http://www.statecraft.org/** Michael McClintock, *Instruments of Statecraft*. This website is a free online version of McClintock's book of the same name published in 2002 and subtitled *U.S. Guerrilla Warfare, Counterinsurgency, and Counterterrorism, 1940–1990*. This valuable critical overview of this extensive military involvement worldwide can be usefully supplemented by more recent insider studies such as Nagl (2002) and Hammes (2004) and by wider understandings of the nature of contemporary war such as Kaldor (1999) and Shaw (2005).

Visit the Online Resource Centre that accompanies this book for lots of interesting additional material: www.oxfordtextbooks.co.uk/orc/collins/

9 Regime Security

RICHARD JACKSON

Chapter Contents

Reader's Guide

This chapter examines the unique security dilemma facing developing countries. It begins with an explanation of the security threats facing states with weak institutional and coercive capacity and lack of national cohesion—what are called weak states—before going on to look at the kinds of security strategies that weak state elites typically adopt to try and manage their predicament. Referred to as an 'insecurity dilemma', and in contrast to the security dilemma facing strong, developed states, weak states face a security environment in which the primary threats to security originate from internal rather than external sources. The chapter goes on to examine a number of competing theoretical explanations for how the weak state predicament arose and why it persists. It concludes with a brief discussion of international attempts to build security in weak states, and the long-term prospects of transforming weak states into strong states.

Introduction

By any measure of security, the disparity between the wealthy, developed countries of the global North and the rest of the world could not be greater. Citizens of the small group of highly developed nations face no real threat of major war and enjoy abundant food supplies, economic prosperity, comparatively low levels of crime and enduring political and social stability. Even the threat of terrorism is extremely minor compared to the everyday risks of accident or disease. Contrary to the 'culture of fear' that exists in many Western societies, at no time in history have individuals in these countries enjoyed such high levels of safety, prosperity and stability.

By contrast, the majority of people living in developing countries face profound security challenges, including perennial threats of **intrastate war** and communal violence, poverty and famine, weapons proliferation and crime, political instability, social breakdown, economic failure and, at its most extreme, complete **state collapse**. At the most basic level of physical security, between twenty and thirty million people have lost their lives in more than one hundred intrastate wars in developing regions since 1945. Around 90% of the victims were civilians, and tens of millions of people were displaced by the fighting, many of whom have remained refugees for decades after. Depending upon what measure is used, there are twenty to forty intrastate wars ongoing in any given year, all of them in developing countries. In a great many more developing nations serious internal political violence, such as military coups or rebellions, ethnic or religious violence, campaigns of terrorism or riots and disorder, is a constant threat.

In addition, half a million people are killed every year by light weapons, frequently during criminal violence and almost all in developing countries. Added to these military threats, an estimated 40,000 people die every day from hunger and tens of millions of others die annually from diseases such as influenza, HIV-AIDS, diarrhoea and tuberculosis. Tens of millions more suffer from chronic poverty, lack of employment opportunities, inadequate health, declining education standards and environmental ruin. There is, in other words, a profound disjuncture between the kinds of security enjoyed by the small group of developed nations and the kind of security environment inhabited by the majority of the world's population. From a global perspective, insecurity is actually more the norm than security is.

This situation provides us with important reasons for trying to understand the nature and consequences of insecurity in the developing world. Empirically, we need to understand why virtually all war and major political violence since 1945 continues to take place in the developing world, and why most of it originates from internal rather than external sources. Conceptually, there is an urgent need to find appropriate theories and concepts that can accommodate the unique character of the security situation in these countries. Such approaches are a necessary starting point for devising more appropriate and more effective international security policies. From a normative perspective, there are clear humanitarian imperatives to try and deal with the immense suffering caused by the lack of basic security in the world's 'zones of instability'. Finally, enlightened self-interest dictates that we make a real effort to resolve the fundamental inequality in security between the developed and developing worlds. Globalization means that insecurity in any part of the world cannot be contained within increasingly porous national borders; security is, to a large extent, interdependent. In many ways, terrorism, gun crime, illegal migration, the drugs trade and environmental damage are all spill-over effects of persistent insecurity in the developing world.

In this chapter we shall try to make sense of the profound security challenges facing developing countries and the unique security dilemma they find themselves trapped in. We shall examine the nature of the main security threats facing developing nations, the key security strategies that they have adopted to deal with these threats and the domestic and international causes of their security predicament. The argument we wish to advance in this chapter is that unlike the developed nations of the global North, the primary security threats facing weak states are potentially catastrophic and originate primarily from internal, domestic sources. They include, among others: the threat of violent transfers of power, insurgency, secession, rebellion, genocide, warlordism and ultimately, state collapse and anarchy.

Moreover, these internal threats are rooted in the fundamental conditions of statehood and governance, thereby creating an enduring 'insecurity dilemma' (Job 1992) for ruling elites: the more elites try to establish effective state rule, the more they provoke challenges to their authority from powerful groups in society. In this context, regime security—the condition where governing elites are secure from violent challenges to their rule—becomes indistinguishable from state security—the condition where the institutions, processes and structures of the state are able to continue functioning effectively, regardless of the make-up of the ruling elite. For weak states, the domestic sphere is actually far more dangerous and threatening than the international sphere.

Given this inversion of the accepted conception of the classical security dilemma (in which military threats originate primarily from other unitary states in an anarchic international system), it is not surprising that the weak state 'insecurity dilemma' has received little attention in the orthodox Security Studies literature. By focusing on a limited number of states (the great powers and developed countries), a limited set of military threats (Soviet expansionism, foreign invasion, nuclear proliferation, rogue states, international terrorism), a limited array of security strategies (national defence, deterrence, arms control, alliances), and employing a restricted conception of security (externally directed 'national security'), the security challenges facing the majority of the world's population have been largely sidelined in academic studies. Consequently, there are real limits as to what traditional or orthodox Security Studies approaches can tell us about the nature and causes of insecurity in weak states today. Widening and deepening our understanding of security therefore necessitates a new set of diagnostic tools that allow us to more fully get to grips with the security challenges facing the vast majority of the world's people and the unique kind of states they inhabit.

KEY POINTS

- There is a profound disjuncture between the security challenges facing developed and developing countries.
- There are important empirical, conceptual, normative and self-interested reasons to attend to the security of developing regions.
- Weak states face a unique set of security challenges that originate primarily from internal sources.
- Orthodox approaches to national security are severely limited in what they can tell us about the conditions of security in weak states.

The weak state insecurity dilemma

The unique insecurity dilemma facing weak states is largely a function of the structural conditions of their existence. Weak states lack the most fundamental of state attributes, namely, effective institutions, a monopoly on the instruments of violence and consensus on the idea of the state. Consequently, as incomplete or 'quasi-states' (Jackson 1990), they face numerous challenges to their authority from powerful domestic actors. In order to understand how this condition of insecurity arises in the first place, we need to examine the primary structural characteristics of weak states and the nature of the internal security threats they face.

Weak states

Assessing state strength can be a difficult and controversial exercise; scholars tend to apply different measures. Thomas (1989) associates state strength/weakness with institutional capacity and distinguishes between two forms of state power: despotic power and infrastructural power. Despotic power refers to the state's coercive abilities and the exercise of force to impose its rule on civilians. By contrast, infrastructural power refers to the effectiveness and legitimacy of the state's institutions and its ability to rule through consensus. States may be 'weak' or deficient in one or both of these capacities, but as a general rule, strong states have less need to exercise coercive power because their infrastructural power makes it unnecessary. Paradoxically, the more a weak state exercises coercive power, the more it reinforces its 'weakness' and corresponding lack of infrastructural power.

In contrast, Buzan (1991a) argues that states consist of three primary components: a physical base, institutional capacity and the 'idea of the state'. For Buzan, state strength/weakness rests primarily in the less tangible realm of the 'idea of the state' and the extent to which society forms a consensus on, and identifies with, the state. Weak states, therefore, 'either do not have, or have failed to create, a domestic political and social consensus of sufficient strength to eliminate the large-scale use of force as a major and continuing element in the domestic political life of the nation' (1983: 67).

Migdal (1988) provides a counterpoint to both these formulations. He defines state strength in terms of state capacity, or 'the ability of state leaders to use the agencies of the state to get people in the state to do what they want them to do' (1988: xvii). But then he reverses attention to how society and groups within it tolerate, permit or resist the development of the state. He argues that most developing societies end up in a state/society standoff where the state confronts powerful social forces with substantial coercive force, which in turn provokes violent resistance. In Migdal's view, weak states are less the issue than strong societies. This internal balance of power between state and society militates against the emergence of prototypical Western-style nation-states.

In summary, three dimensions of state strength appear to be important: (1) infrastructural capacity in terms of the ability of state institutions to perform essential tasks and enact policy; (2) coercive capacity in terms of the state's ability and willingness to employ force against challenges to its authority; and (3) national identity and social cohesion in terms of the degree to which the population identifies with the nation-state and accepts its legitimate role in their lives.

Empirically, it can be seen that most developing nations are weak or deficient in most if not all of these dimensions. Or, they have over-developed coercive capacities but lack infrastructural capacity and social consensus. As a consequence of these fundamental deficiencies, weak states typically display all or many of the following characteristics: institutional weakness and an inability to enact national policy or perform basic state functions such as tax collection and providing law and order; political instability, as evidenced by coups, plots, rebellions and frequent violent changes of government; the centralization of political power in a single individual or small elite who command the machinery of government to run the state in their own interest; unconsolidated or non-existent democracies; ongoing economic crisis and structural weakness; external vulnerability to international actors and forces; intense societal divisions along class, religious, regional, urban-rural and/or ethnic lines; lack of a cohesive or strong sense of national identity; and an ongoing crisis of legitimacy for both the government of the day and the institutions of state in general.

The most important characteristic of weak states is their frequent inability to establish and maintain a monopoly on the instruments of violence. Even in states with well-developed coercive power, civilian governments do not always retain the absolute loyalty of the armed forces and face a constant threat of military intervention. For most weak states, however, the armed forces are ill-equipped, poorly managed and prone to factional divisions. At the same time, a range of social actors—rival politicians with their own private armies, warlords, criminal gangs, locally organized militias, armed and organized ethnic or religious groups and private security companies or mercenaries—are powerful enough to resist the state's attempt to enforce compliance. In such a situation, even the most minimal requirement of statehood—the monopoly on the instruments of violence—is largely out of reach.

At the other end of the scale, and in complete contrast, it is suggested that *strong states* have the willingness and ability to: 'maintain social control, ensure societal compliance with official laws, act decisively, make effective policies, preserve stability and cohesion, encourage societal participation in state institutions, provide basic services, manage and control the national economy, and retain legitimacy' (Dauvergne 1998: 2). Strong states also possess high levels of socio-political cohesion that is directly correlated with consolidated participatory democracies, strong national identities, and productive and highly developed economies. Most importantly, strong states exist as a 'hegemonic idea', accepted and naturalized in the minds of ordinary citizens such that they 'consider the state as natural as the landscape around them; they cannot imagine their lives without it' (Migdal 1998: 12).

Crucially, the notion of weak and strong states is not a binary measure but rather a continuum along which states in the real world fall. Moreover, it is a dynamic condition. States can move back and forth along the continuum over time given sufficient changes to key factors: weak states can become strong by building a strong sense of national identity, for example; and strong states could potentially weaken through increased social conflict brought on by immigration, for example. Most states in developing regions fall towards the weak end of the state-strength continuum.

KEY POINTS

- The key dimensions of state strength/weakness are infrastructural capacity, coercive capacity and national identity and social cohesion.
- Weak states are typically characterized by institutional weakness, political instability, centralization of power, unconsolidated democracy, economic crisis, external vulnerability, social divisions, lack of national identity and an ongoing crisis of legitimacy.
- The most important characteristic of weak states is their lack of a monopoly on the instruments of violence.
- State strength or weakness is a dynamic continuum along which states can move; it is possible for weak states to become strong states and vice versa.

Threats to weak states

Due to their debilitating structural characteristics, weak states face a number of internal and external security challenges. *Internally*, weak states face the continual threat of violent intervention in politics by the armed forces. Such interventions can take the form of coup d'état, mutiny, rebellion or revolt over pay and conditions. There have been literally hundreds of coup attempts in Latin America, Asia-Pacific and the Middle East, and nearly two-thirds of Africa's states have experienced military rule since independence. Military rulers still govern numerous developing countries.

Weak states also face serious threats from 'strongmen', individuals or groups who exercise a degree of coercive and/or infrastructural power in their own right and who challenge the authority of the state. They may be semi-legitimate actors such as politicians or traditional and religious leaders who nonetheless command large followings and private access to weaponry. Alternately, they may be criminal gangs or warlords—charismatic individuals who command private armies and enforce a kind of absolutist rule in areas under their control, primarily for the purposes of pursuing illegal commerce. Examples of such strongmen include the drug cartels in Colombia, Myanmar and Afghanistan, and some of the rebel leaders in Africa during the 1990s, such as Charles Taylor, Foday Sankoh and Jonas Savimbi. If the state fails to accommodate or placate such groups, they may launch a violent challenge to the regime.

In other cases, weak states face challenges from various social groups such as ethnic groups, religious movements, ideological factions or local militias who organize for self-defence. Due in large part to pre-existing divisions, the inability of the state to provide adequate welfare and the tendency to employ excessive coercion, a great many ethnic groups in weak states have organized politically and militarily to protect their interests. Gurr's (2000) *Minorities at Risk* project found more than ninety ethnic minorities either actively engaged in violent conflict with the state or at medium-to-serious risk of significant political violence. Similarly, in a number of Middle Eastern and Asian countries, such as Algeria, Egypt, Saudi Arabia, Indonesia and more recently, Thailand, religious groups have launched violent challenges to the state. Ideologically driven groups also continue to threaten weak states, from the Maoist insurgency in Nepal to the Zapatistas in Chiapas, Mexico. It is a sad fact that virtually all armed groups in weak states—state armies, warlord factions and local, ethnic and religious militias—employ large numbers of child soldiers (for more on child soldiers see Chapter 20).

A final internal threat can come from the steady erosion of state institutions and processes. Increasing lawlessness and the eventual collapse of governmental institutions can create a power vacuum in which the ruling elite simply becomes one of several factions struggling to fill the void and claim the formal mantle of statehood. At various times during the conflicts in Liberia and Somalia, for example, several different factions claimed to be the legitimate government at the same time, despite lacking the necessary control of territory or governing institutions required for formal recognition. In the final analysis, any of these threats—military intervention in politics, warlords and strongmen, ethnic demands for secession or state collapse—may lead to sustained bouts of all-out intrastate war.

Due to their internal fragility, weak states also face a variety of *external* threats. Lacking the infrastructural or coercive capacity to resist outside interference, weak states are vulnerable to penetration and intervention by other states and groups. Powerful states may directly invade or may sponsor a coup or rebellion in order to overthrow a regime, such as the American invasions of Grenada, Panama, Afghanistan and Iraq and French intervention in numerous African states. Alternately, the provision of significant quantities of arms and military assistance to rebel movements, such as American support to UNITA in Angola and Soviet support for the Vietcong in Vietnam, can pose a serious threat to the ruling elite. Often, support for rebel factions or coup plotters can come from sources closer to home, such as rival neighbouring states. A great many regional rivals—such as India–Pakistan, Uganda–Sudan, Somalia–Ethiopia, Iran–Iraq—have threatened each other in this manner. In addition, very small weak states can be threatened by the tiniest of external groups: mercenary coups and invasions have been launched against The Seychelles, The Maldives, The Comoros and, more recently, Guinea-Bissau, sometimes by no more than a few dozen men. In most cases, the coups were only thwarted through assistance from powerful allies such as France or India.

A related external threat comes from the spill-over or contagion of conflict and disorder from neighbouring regions. Lacking the necessary infra-structural capacity to effectively control their borders, weak states can often do little to prevent the massive influx of refugees, fleeing rebels, arms smuggling or actual fighting. Major external shocks like this can seriously threaten the stability of the weak state. The Rwandan genocide in 1994 spilled over into Zaire, a weak and failing state; the shock eventually led to the overthrow of the Mobutu regime, invasion by several neighbouring states and large-scale factional fighting (see Case Study 9.2).

Related to this, weak states are threatened by the uncontrollable spread of small arms and light weapons. In the hands of warlords, criminals and private militias, these weapons pose a real challenge to the authority of the state and can intensify existing conflicts and seriously undermine peace efforts. Light, portable, durable and easy-to-use (even by children), small and light weapons are easily obtained through legal and illegal channels, and once in use, have a tendency to spread throughout the region. An estimated $5 billion worth of light weapons are traded illegally every year to the world's conflict zones, killing an estimated half a million people per year in criminal activity and civil violence.

KEY POINTS

- Internally, weak states are threatened by military factions, rival 'strongmen' such as warlords or criminals, rebellions from minorities, institutional collapse and disorder and ultimately, intrastate war.
- Externally, weak states are threatened by interference from powerful international actors, contagion and spill-over from neighbouring states and the small arms trade.

The weak state 'insecurity dilemma'

The combination of state weakness and internal threats creates a security challenge unique to weak states. It is distinctive because it arises from meeting *internal* threats to the regime in power, rather than *external* threats to the existence of the nation-state. The inability of the state to provide peace and order creates a contentious environment where each component of society—including the ruling elite or regime—competes to preserve and protect its own well-being. This creates a domestic situation similar to the neo-realist conception of structural anarchy where groups create insecurity in the rest of the system when they try to improve their own security. To distinguish this internally oriented condition from the classical *security dilemma*, it is helpful to think of it as an **insecurity dilemma**. This condition of insecurity is self-perpetuating because every effort by the regime to secure its own security through force provokes greater resistance and further undermines the institutional basis of the state and the security of the society as a whole.

In a sense, the weak state insecurity dilemma is caused by an initial and profound lack of 'stateness', in particular, the inability to establish a monopoly on the instruments of violence. This failure can be both normative—in the sense that the state has failed to convince the population that armed resistance is wrong or counter-productive—and practical—in that the state cannot physically disarm and control all of its rivals. Either way, the lack of a political and institutional centre with a monopoly of force creates an insecurity spiral—a semi-permanent situation of 'emergent anarchy'—where armed groups are forced to engage in self-help strategies.

Thus, within the weak state context, where ruling elites use the machinery of government primarily to secure the continuation of their rule, the concept of *national security*—the security of a whole socio-political entity, a nation-state with its own way of life and independent self-government—is wholly inapplicable. In practice, the idea of state security—the integrity and functioning of the institutions and idea of the state—and regime security—the security of the ruling elite from violent challenge—become indistinguishable. Due to the fusion of state and government, when a particular regime is overthrown, as the Syad Barre regime was overthrown in Somalia in 1991, the entire apparatus of the state collapses too. In this sense, weak state security *is* regime security.

KEY POINTS

- The weak state insecurity dilemma is primarily an internal condition based on the contradiction between societal and state power.
- It is engendered by a lack of 'stateness', most importantly, the failure to establish a monopoly on the instruments of violence.
- The weak state insecurity dilemma transforms national or state security into regime security.

Security strategies in weak states

The structural characteristics of weak states and the unique insecurity dilemma in which they are trapped, severely constrains the range of policy options open to ruling elites. Essentially, the conditions of governance create a semi-permanent condition of 'crisis politics' or 'the politics of survival' (Migdal 1988) in which short-term strategies of regime security substitute for long-term state-building policies.

Elite security strategies

Weak state elites typically employ a mix of internal and external strategies aimed at regime survival. *Internally*, elites employ a mix of carrot and stick approaches to challengers. First, lacking both infrastructural capacity and wider social legitimacy, weak state elites are often forced to rely on coercive power and state intimidation to secure continued rule. This entails creating or expanding the security forces, spending large sums of the national income on military supplies and using violence and intimidation against real and perceived opponents of the regime. This is perhaps the most common survival strategy of weak state elites, and it is reflected in the appalling human rights record seen in a great many developing countries. Typically, regimes try to suppress opposition through the widespread use of torture and imprisonment, assassination and extra-judicial killings, disappearances, the violent suppression of political expression, forced removals, destruction of food supplies and in extreme cases, genocide, mass rape and ethnic cleansing.

A key dilemma for elites is that the instruments of coercion—the armed forces—can themselves develop into a threat against the regime. For this reason, elites sometimes deliberately weaken the armed forces by creating divisions, establishing elite units such as presidential guards and fomenting rivalry between different services. Such divide and rule strategies are also used against other potential sources of opposition, such as state bureaucracies, religious groups, traditional authorities and opposition politicians. From this perspective, the deliberate undermining or hollowing out of state institutions can be a rational and effective means of preventing the rise of potential centres of opposition to the regime.

On the other side of the ledger, elites sometimes find it easier to try and create positive inducements for supporting the regime. Typically, this entails the establishment of elaborate patronage systems, whereby state elites and various social groups are joined in complex networks of mutual exchange. In this way, corruption acts as a form of redistribution and a means of integrating the state in an informal power structure. Such systems may extend to strongmen in a form of 'elite accommodation' (Reno 1998). Warlords or political leaders with private armies may be permitted control over a particular area, have state resources diverted their way or be given exclusive control over a particular commercial activity for example, in exchange for an agreement not to try and overthrow the regime or encroach on its other activities. In the settlement ending the war in Sierra Leone, the warlord leader of the rebel Revolutionary United Front (RUF), Foday Sankoh, became Minister for Mines in an attempt to buy his loyalty. Different kinds of accommodation have sometimes been found with the drug cartels in Colombia and Myanmar.

Ethnic manipulation or 'the politics of identity' is another typical strategy in weak states. In what is a form of divide and rule borrowed from colonialism, elites will sometimes deliberately foment inter-communal conflict as a means of preventing the emergence of united opposition to the regime. At other times, it is simply a method of rooting a regime's power base in what is seen to be a reliable source of support. Thus, elites will favour certain groups in the allocation of state resources, oppress minorities viewed as hostile, create minority scapegoat groups during times of unrest and appoint members of the elite's own ethnic group to positions of power. Such strategies are frequently successful, as ethnic consciousness is usually well developed and readily exploitable in many developing societies.

A final internal strategy involves the careful manipulation of democratic political processes. Due to their external vulnerability, a great many weak states have been forced by international donors—developed states and international financial institutions (IFIs) such as the IMF and World Bank—to begin the process of democratic reform. A great many weak state rulers have successfully managed the transition to multiparty democracy and retained control of the state, primarily through careful manipulation of internal opponents and external perceptions. Typically, this involved monopolizing and controlling the media, the cooption of opponents, setting up fake parties to split the vote, gerrymandering, ballot-rigging, candidate and elector disqualification and manipulating the electoral rules. Constructing the outward appearance of democracy without any substantial concessions can actually function to bolster regime security by giving it a degree of international legitimacy.

In addition to these internal strategies, weak state elites also look to form alliances with powerful *external* actors as a means of bolstering regime security. An increasingly prevalent strategy has been to employ foreign mercenaries or private military or security companies as force multipliers. There are nearly a hundred private military companies (PMCs) operating in 110 states around the world (see Case Study 9.1). Often working closely with oil and mineral companies, the industry is thought to be worth as much as $100 billion per year. Weak states employ private security contractors because they see them as being more effective and reliable than many national militaries. With superior weapons and training, these private armies have often proved to be decisive in securing weak state survival against various internal threats. In Angola and Sierra Leone, the notorious PMC Executive Outcomes turned the tide against rebel forces, re-capturing diamond mining areas in the process.

More formally, weak states seek out alliances with powerful states who can help to guarantee regime survival. During the cold war, many weak states obtained military support from one or other of the superpowers in exchange for political and strategic assistance in the East–West confrontation. In Africa, at least twenty countries entered in to defence agreements with France; subsequent military intervention by French troops was decisive in keeping several West African regimes in power, including Zaire/DRC (see Case Study 9.2), Togo and Ivory Coast. At present, the war on terror is providing weak states with another opportunity to bolster their internal security: in exchange for cooperation in fighting terrorism, the United States provides countries like Pakistan, Saudi Arabia, Indonesia and Uzbekistan (see Case Study 9.3) with vital military and economic assistance. External intervention of this kind can be crucial for keeping internal rivals at bay and ensuring regime security.

CASE STUDY 9.1

Private military companies

'Private military companies, or PMCs as the new world order's mercenaries have come to be known, allow governments to pursue policies in tough corners of the world with the distance and comfort of plausible deniability. The ICIJ investigation uncovered the existence of at least 90 private military companies that have operated in 110 countries worldwide. These corporate armies, often providing services normally carried out by a national military force, offer specialized skills in high-tech warfare, including communications and signals intelligence and aerial surveillance, as well as pilots, logistical support, battlefield planning and training. They have been hired both by governments and multinational corporations to further their policies or protect their interests.

Some African governments are little more than criminal syndicates—warlords such as Charles Taylor, the president of Liberia, or more sophisticated elites, such as the rulers of Angola. But to sell diamonds and timber and oil onto the world market requires foreign partners.

The people doing the extracting, the bribing, the arms dealing, and the deal-making are South African, Belgian, American, Israeli, French, Ukrainian, Lebanese, Canadian, British, Russian, Malaysian, and Syrian. They are a class of entrepreneur that operates beyond borders, often unaccountable to shareholders and unfettered by the regulation they would encounter in their own countries. They have become influential political players in the countries in which they operate.'

Phillip van Niekerk, 'Making a Killing: The Business of War', *The Center for Public Integrity*, 28 October 2002)

Finally, weak state elites sometimes join together with other weak states in regional defence arrangements designed primarily to prop each other up. For example, under new multilateral security agreements, both the Economic Community of West African States (ECOWAS) and the Southern African Development Community (SADC) have in recent years intervened in member states to over-turn coups or secure governments from overthrow by rebel forces. Thus, the creation of regional security architecture, including regional peacekeeping forces, can function as a strategy of mutually reinforcing regime security.

KEY POINTS

- Internal security strategies include repression and military expansion, employing mercenaries and private military companies, divide and rule strategies, deliberately undermining state institutions, patronage politics and elite accommodation, identity politics and democratic manipulation.
- External security strategies include employing private military companies and mercenaries, external defence agreements with Great Powers and joining in regional defence organizations.

Security outcomes

The perennial conundrum facing weak state elites lies in the contradiction between ensuring the short-term security of the regime and the long-term goal of state-making. Many of the security strategies described above are, in the long-run, self-defeating, as they further undermine the foundations of the state, provoke even more serious opposition from social groups and delay genuine state consolidation. For most weak state elites, however, there is no way out of this dilemma; if they neglect regime security in favour of more genuine state-building activities such as strengthening state institutions and forging a sense of national identity, they are just as likely to be overthrown in a coup or toppled by a rebellion.

CASE STUDY 9.2

Anatomy of a weak state—the Democratic Republic of Congo

The central African state of Democratic Republic of Congo (DRC) has always been a weak state. It has suffered from tremendous insecurity since its founding, and ruling elites have employed all the classic regime security strategies to avoid being toppled.

At independence in 1960, Congo was poorly prepared for full statehood, with irrational national boundaries, underdeveloped state institutions, poor infrastructure, a fragile economic base and only 100 university graduates to fill the civil service. In the first four years of independence, the country was plunged into civil war, with three main factions vying for power and the mineral-rich Shaba province attempting to secede. Order was only established with the help of a large-scale United Nations operation. In 1965, Mobutu Sese Seko took power in a military coup.

Throughout his rule, Mobutu faced numerous threats to his regime: military rebellions, dissident movements, attempts at secession, mercenary revolts, invasions and violent disputes and conflict spill-over from neighbouring states. Cobalt and copper-rich Shaba province was invaded by mercenaries and exiled dissidents on four occasions.

Following the pattern of weak state rulers, Mobutu employed a number of classic regime security strategies. He employed mercenaries to subdue the country in the first years of his rule, bribed opposition politicians to join the government, suppressed opposition movements, engaged in identity politics, hollowed out state institutions to prevent the rise of potential opponents and split the armed forces into several factions to avoid coups and rebellions. Externally, he allied with the United States, providing a conduit for getting arms to Angola's UNITA rebels. In exchange, he received massive amounts of military and economic aid, which he then used to manage internal opposition. French paratroopers and American logistical support helped Mobutu to defeat an invasion of Shaba in 1978.

In 1996, a rebel alliance led by Laurent Kabila and backed by Rwanda emerged in the east of the country in the chaos engendered by the spill-over of the 1994 Rwandan genocide. Within a few months, and despite employing a mercenary army, Mobutu's regime collapsed. The Kabila-led alliance soon fell apart, however, and full-scale civil war broke out in 1998. Rwanda and Uganda intervened on the side of different rebel factions, who control large swathes of the country, while Angola, Namibia and Zimbabwe sent troops to support the Kabila government. The war continues today, despite the presence of a United Nations peacekeeping force. The UN estimates that up to three million people have lost their lives in the conflict. DRC now exists as a semi-collapsed state, with various warlords, criminal enterprises and foreign entrepreneurs engaged in large-scale looting, trade monopolization and the exploitation of minerals.

Thus, with few genuine alternatives, elites have to persist with policies that could eventually lead to complete state disintegration and collapse.

Ultimately, of course, a key outcome of these strategies is that the weak state, or rather the regime, becomes the greatest single threat to the security of its own people. In weak states, individual citizens often face a much more serious threat from their own governments than they do from the governments of other states. Instead of ensuring individual and social security, the continual use of coercion makes the state the primary threat to security. Moreover, the threat is affected on several levels: repression and identity politics threatens their physical survival through the spread of violent conflict; and deliberately undermining state institutions and patronage politics threatens their welfare and livelihood.

KEY POINTS

- The long-term effect of elite security strategies is to reinforce insecurity for both the regime itself and the wider population.
- In extreme cases, elite security strategies can lead to complete state collapse.

CASE STUDY 9.3

Anatomy of a weak state—Uzbekistan

The Central Asian country of Uzbekistan gained its independence from the Soviet Union in 1991. From 1924 to 1991, Uzbekistan had been governed as an outlying colony in the Soviet empire. Consequently, at independence it shared many of the weaknesses of other post-colonial and post-Soviet states, such as an externally oriented, dependent economy, weak national institutions, over-developed coercive capabilities, a legitimacy crisis and a history of authoritarianism.

President Islam Karimov, a former Communist Party boss, has ruled Uzbekistan since independence. Throughout this period, the Karimov regime has been under constant threat from dissidents and anti-government campaigners, crime syndicates and drug traders, a small-scale terrorist campaign, opposition Islamic groups and spill-over from the conflicts in Afghanistan and Tadjikistan.

Karimov has clung to power using a variety of regime security strategies, most commonly, severe repression against real and potential opponents. Despite nominal constitutional protections, the government has banned public meetings and demonstrations, restricted the independent media, arrested thousands of opposition political and religious supporters and used horrific torture and murder to suppress dissent. Uzbekistan presently has the worst human rights record in the former Soviet Union. Other internal strategies used by Karimov to maintain power have included the clever manipulation of elections and referendums, re-writing the constitution to centralize all power in the president and endemic corruption among government officials.

Externally, Karimov's primary strategy was to ally the regime with the United States in the war on terror. In 2002, the two countries signed a Declaration of Strategic Partnership. In return for hundreds of millions of dollars of economic and military support, Uzbekistan provided the US with military bases from which to conduct missions in Afghanistan, coercive interrogation facilities for terrorist suspects in the controversial rendition programme and diplomatic support for US policies in the United Nations.

However, the US–Uzbek partnership has come under severe strain in recent times following the military crackdown against anti-government demonstrators in the city of Andijan in May 2005 when hundreds of unarmed civilians were killed and injured. Unable to ignore the appalling human rights situation in Uzbekistan, the US has begun to re-think its relationship with the regime. This will put pressure on Karimov to look elsewhere for regime support.

Explaining insecurity in weak states

There are different theories about the causes of weak state or regime insecurity. Taken together, they can tell us a great deal about how conditions of insecurity evolve and persist, despite international assistance. State-making theories explore the origins of the weak state insecurity dilemma in the initial state construction process. Warlord politics theories explore the impact of neo-liberal globalization and the end of the Cold War on the choices facing weak state elites. The combination of the inherited structural features of statehood and the nature and processes of the international context explain much about why weak states find it so difficult to escape from their insecurity dilemma.

State-making theories

Observing weak state insecurity, scholars like Ayoob (1995) have suggested that these conditions represent a normal stage in the long-term state-building process from which strong states will, in time, emerge. Taking a historical view, they argue that the European experience proves that state-building is a long and traumatic process, taking several centuries to complete and involving a great deal of bloodshed. Typically, it entailed sustained and bloody conflict between a centralizing state and powerful social forces before a monopoly on violence was achieved. It also took determined and sometimes violent efforts to weld disparate groups of people into a single national identity. Significantly, representative institutions emerged only gradually, after a powerful central state and a cohesive sense of national identity had been established.

The argument is that what is presently observed in developing countries is a similar process of state consolidation to that experienced by European states in past centuries, but with additional obstacles that were absent during the European experience. For example, unlike European states, today's weak states have to cope with the ongoing effects of colonial rule, which includes: the imposition of alien doctrines and institutions of statehood; irrational territorial boundaries and the lack of national identity; societies divided along class, religious and ethnic lines; stunted and dependent economies; and an entrenched culture of political violence. These factors make the state-building process even more difficult than it might have been.

The contemporary state-building process is also constrained by a shortened time-frame. Unlike European states, weak states today are expected to become effective, fully functioning, democratic states within a few decades. Moreover, they are expected to do it without the violence, corruption and human rights abuses that accompanied the European state-building process. Established international norms and rules, such as the protection of minority and human rights and the right of self-determination (which often encourages ethnic rebellion), also complicates the state-building process. A particularly problematic norm is the inviolability of statehood. Once a state achieves independence and is admitted to the United Nations, its status cannot be revoked or its territory subsumed into another state, no matter how unviable it proves to be in practice. Thus, unlike European entities such as Burgundy and Aragon which could not complete the state-building process and were absorbed into larger, more viable units, today's weak states must struggle on indefinitely.

In short, according to this approach, we can expect weak states to experience a great deal more bloodshed and violence over an extended period until stronger, more representative states emerge. Until then, they will remain 'quasi-states'—states possessing the nominal features of statehood, such as international recognition, but lacking the infrastructural capacities to create and secure a sense of genuine national identity (Jackson 1990).

KEY POINTS

- Scholars like Ayoob suggest that the conditions of insecurity in weak states are an expression of the historical state-building process.
- The European state-building process was similarly bloody and long.
- Weak states face the state-building process in an environment constrained by the experience of colonialism, a shortened time-frame and problematic international norms.

Warlord politics

During the Cold War, many weak states maintained a semblance of stability and integration through various forms of elite and social accommodation. The primary means of accommodation was the construction of a patrimonial or *redistributive state*—a system of patronage where state resources were distributed to supporters through complex social and political networks. The redistributive state was frequently maintained by direct superpower assistance, loans and development assistance from international financial institutions and periods of high commodity prices which supplied its primary national income. Temporary disruptions to the stability of the weak state redistributive system came from sudden falls in commodity prices, wider economic shocks (such as the oil shocks) and the sudden loss of superpower support (which could be compensated for by switching to the other superpower, as Somalia did in the 1970s). In many cases, these shocks resulted in serious internal violence.

The end of the Cold War signalled a period of profound transformation in the international system. A major consequence of the end of superpower conflict was the decline of military and economic support for many weak states. At the same time, international financial institutions began to demand changes in the economic and political policies of weak states—what are called 'conditionalities'—in exchange for continuing loans and assistance. In keeping with the global trend of privatization and deregulation, weak states were forced by lenders and investors to sell off and downsize government bureaucracies. These developments severely disrupted the redistributive state and forced rulers to find new ways of accommodating rival strongmen and restless social groups.

Somewhat paradoxically, elite strategies have since involved the deliberate creation of state collapse and social disorder. This entails hollowing out state institutions, fragmenting the armed forces and creating parallel informal armed groups, thereby spreading the means of violence even further into society. The logic of 'disorder as a political instrument' is that within the context of a collapsing state, elites can pursue forms of commercial activity that are not possible under normal circumstances, such as trading in illegal commodities, looting, protection rackets, coercive monopolies and the like. Thus, exploiting the shadow markets engendered by neo-liberal globalization, and in alliance with local strongmen and multinational companies, weak state elites have created a new kind of political economy, what Reno (1998) has called '*warlord politics*'. Crucial in this enterprise is the ability to employ private companies to perform state roles, especially the task of providing regime security.

As an alternative political-economic system, warlord politics provides elites with several advantages. It permits commercial activity and accumulation in the grey or shadow regions of the global economy, tapping into resources that would otherwise be unavailable to weak state elites and which are desperately needed to buy protection from rivals. In this sense, warlord politics facilitates the process of elite accommodation needed to keep regimes safe from violent overthrow. It also prevents the emergence of mass social movements because civil society finds itself trapped between a rapacious state and well-armed networks of strongmen pursuing their own illiberal agendas.

In short, warlord politics represents an innovative response to rapid global change that permits the survival of the regime under harsh new conditions. From this perspective, state collapse and widespread disorder is not a temporary aberration in the normal functioning of the state, but a new form of regime security forced on weak state elites by changes in the wider international system. Warlord political systems have been in existence for several decades now, and have become a part of the political landscape from West and Central Africa to Colombia, Haiti, Chechnya, Afghanistan, Myanmar and the Balkans—among others.

KEY POINTS

- The end of the Cold War and the adoption of conditionalities by IFIs severely disrupted the redistributive state.
- Weak state elites responded by developing new and innovative forms of political economy based on shadow and predatory commercial activities called 'warlord politics'.
- Warlord politics works to control internal threats from strongmen and mass movements.

Conclusion: prospects for the weak state

In this chapter we have examined the conditions of insecurity that affect the majority of the world's states. We have suggested that the insecurity dilemma facing developing countries is both profound and unique, and is rooted in the fundamental structures and processes of incomplete statehood. The conditions of insecurity in weak states are the result of three interrelated factors: the historical state-making process; the structures and processes of the present international system; and the security strategies employed by weak state elites. In the context of profound internal threats and constraining external conditions, national security becomes a matter of maintaining short-term regime security. The pursuit of regime security, however, is itself a profoundly contradictory process; short-term policies of regime security undermine the more important state-building project—and the security of the state and society.

From this perspective, weak state insecurity appears to be an inescapable condition. There have been very few clear-cut cases where weak states have made a successful transition to state consolidation and genuine national security. The fundamental security challenge facing weak states lies in achieving greater levels of stateness and moving towards improved levels of genuine state strength. The challenge, therefore, lies in the willingness and ability of weak state elites to substitute short-term regime security strategies for long-term state-building strategies.

Should regimes choose to take the state-building project seriously the process will undoubtedly be long and difficult, not least because a number of entrenched internal and external obstacles to effective statehood remain. These include: the continued distorting effects of colonialism; the processes of neo-liberal globalization and the imposition of external conditionalities; small arms proliferation; continuing external intervention by powerful actors; the existence of constraining international norms; and debilitating internal conditions such as poverty, social division, weak institutions, and the like. The global war on terror launched in the wake of 11 September 2001 has also had a negative effect on the state-building project, as the fight against terrorism has largely diverted international attention and resources from poverty eradication, democracy promotion and peace-building activities. Weak state elites have also been able to brand their internal enemies as terrorists, and just as during the Cold War, receive military support in exchange for cooperation in the fight against terrorism (see Case Study 9.3). In other words, the new war on terror has allowed weak state elites to re-prioritize regime security over state-building and receive vital international support for their efforts.

As during the Cold War, the problems of weak state insecurity take a low priority on international agendas compared to the interests of the Great Powers. So far, solutions to the weak state security dilemma have not moved far beyond the establishment of multiparty democracy and free markets. For neo-conservatives, it is sometimes argued that forceful 'regime change' and perhaps even a liberal or benign re-colonization such as occurred in Germany and Japan after Second World War, is the only effective long-term solution. Others stress the need for humanitarian intervention to protect the security of civilians and promote human rights. They argue that 'cosmopolitan peace-keeping' (Kaldor 1999) and so-called peace-building missions are required to transform violent domestic politics in weak states into long-term peace and stability. In practice, both approaches are based on a similar liberal perspective which envisages a minimal state devoted to protecting individual and market freedoms. The main problem is that thus far, despite decades of effort, no case of enforced neo-liberalization either through conditionalities, regime change or peace-building, has succeeded in transforming a weak state into a strong state.

Given the enormous challenges facing weak states, and recognizing the fundamental inequities of the state project itself and the failure thus far to reform illiberal weak states, some radical commentators have suggested that state-building should be abandoned in favour of alternative forms of political organization based on either smaller units—city states or ethnic groups, for example—or larger units—such as regional organizations like the European Union. The first option, sub-state political organizations, seems impractical in regions that are awash with weapons, criminal gangs and poverty; the case of Somalia, which has been without a functioning central government since 1991, is informative in this regard. The second option, regional organization, is similarly not without its limitations. While it has had a modicum of success in the European Union, in regions characterized by weak states, underdevelopment and instability such as Africa or Latin America, regional processes are severely constrained in what they can achieve.

In the end, overcoming the internal and external obstacles to state-building in the developing world will require tremendous political will and resources, and the elaboration of alternative and innovative approaches to state-building assistance. More importantly, it will require fundamental reform of international economic and political structures, including the international trade in weapons. Given the present preoccupation with international terrorism and the lack of enthusiasm by the world's developed states for debt relief, development and curbs on the small arms trade, the short-to-medium-term future of the weak state looks as bleak as it ever was (for more on the arms trade see Chapter 17).

QUESTIONS

In what ways are orthodox approaches to security limited in their explanation of the weak state insecurity dilemma?

What are the primary differences between weak and strong states?

Outline the main internal and external security threats facing weak states.

What makes the security dilemma in weak states unique?

What are the differences, if any, between national security, state security and regime security in the weak state context?

What domestic and international strategies do weak state elites adopt to try to manage their security challenges?

What are the main internal and external obstacles to state-building for weak states?

What impact has the end of the Cold War and the onset of globalization had on the weak state security predicament?

Is abandoning the state-building project in favour of alternative forms of political organization a realistic solution to the weak state security dilemma?

What role should the international community play in the state consolidation process?

FURTHER READING

■ **Ayoob, Mohammed (1995), *The Third World Security Predicament: State Making, Regional Conflict, and the International System*, Boulder, CO: Lynne Rienner**. Provides an informative analysis of the weak state security predicament in its internal, regional and international dimensions.

■ **Buzan, Barry (1991), *People, States and Fear: An Agenda for International Security Studies in the Post-Cold War Era*, Boulder, CO: Lynne Rienner (2nd edn)**. A seminal reformulation of security beyond its traditional focus to include the security predicament facing the majority of weak states in the world.

■ **Kaldor, Mary (1999), *New and Old Wars: Organised Violence in a Global Era*, Cambridge: Polity Press**. A provocative and original statement on the changing nature of warfare and the need for new approaches to peacekeeping in weak states.

■ **Holsti, Kalevi J. (1996), *The State, War, and the State of War*, Cambridge: Cambridge University Press**. An empirical analysis of contemporary warfare which demonstrates that internal war within weak states has been the primary form of international conflict since 1945.

■ **Job, Brian (ed.) (1992), *The Insecurity Dilemma: National Security of Third World States*, Boulder, CO: Lynne Rienner**. A very useful collection of essays from leading experts on some of the key dimensions of security in developing states.

■ **Musah, Abdel-Fatah and Kayode Fayemi, J. (eds.) (2000), *Mercenaries: An African Security Dilemma*, London: Pluto**. Provides a fascinating collection of essays on the security dilemma associated with the intervention of mercenaries in Africa's weak states.

■ **Reno, William (1998), *Warlord Politics and African States*, Boulder, CO: Lynne Rienner**. Provides a compelling analysis of how weak state elites have adapted governance strategies to the opportunities and constraints of neo-liberal globalization.

■ **Rich, Paul B. (ed.) (1999), *Warlords in International Relations*, London: Macmillan**. An insightful collection of essays by leading experts on the role of warlords, the small arms trade, private military contractors and other security challenges facing weak states.

■ **Thomas, Caroline (1987), *In Search of Security: The Third World in International Relations*, Boulder, CO: Lynne Rienner**. An original formulation of the weak state security predicament.

■ **Zartman, I. William (ed.) (1995), *Collapsed States: The Disintegration and Restoration of Legitimate Authority*, Boulder, CO: Lynne Rienner**. An important collection of essays on the nature, causes and consequences of weak state decay and collapse.

IMPORTANT WEBSITES

● **http://www.iansa.org/** The International Action Network on Small Arms is a global network of civil society organizations working to stop the proliferation and misuse of small arms and light weapons. The website contains resources on all aspects of small arms proliferation and international efforts to regulate the trade.

● **http://www.iss.co.za/** The Institute for Security Studies is a leading research institution on all aspects of human security in Africa. The website contains news, analysis and special reports on all aspects of security in Africa.

- **http://www.cidcm.umd.edu/inscr/** The Integrated Network for Societal Conflict Research (INSCR) programme at the Center for International Development and Conflict Management, the University of Maryland, coordinates major empirical research projects on armed conflict, genocide and politicide, minorities at risk, regime types and state failure. The website has links to all the major projects and datasets.

Visit the Online Resource Centre that accompanies this book for lots of interesting additional material: www.oxfordtextbooks.co.uk/orc/collins/

10 Societal Security

PAUL ROE

Chapter Contents

- Introduction
- A duality of state and societal security
- Society and societal identity
- Threats to societal identity
- Defending societal identity
- Societal security dilemmas
- Conclusion

Reader's Guide

This chapter explores the concept of societal security. It starts by looking at how society came to be conceived as a referent object of security in its own right. It then goes on to discuss the so-called 'Copenhagen School's' understanding of both society and societal identity, showing how societal security is tied most of all to the maintenance of ethno-national identities. In looking at threats to societal security, through examples such as the former Yugoslavia and Northern Ireland, the chapter discusses a number of those means that can prevent or hinder the reproduction of collective identity, and, in turn, at how societies may react to such perceived threats. The concept of a societal security dilemma is then introduced to show how, in the case of Hungarians and Romanians in the Romanian region of Transylvania, societal security dynamics can spiral to produce violent conflict. The chapter concludes by considering some of the main critiques of the concept as an analytical tool.

Introduction

Throughout the 1980s and early 1990s significant moves took place designed to take Security Studies beyond the confines of the dominant Realist and neo-Realist paradigms. For the most part, such moves were made possible by the winding-down and eventual end to the Cold War. The decreasing threat of nuclear war opened the way for the emergence of other, non-military conceptions of security. For example, writing at the end of the 1980s Jessica Tuchman Mathews (1989: 162–77) suggested that international security be rethought to include resource, environmental, and demographic issues. Mathews, together with a number of like-minded others (see for example, Booth 1991; Ullman 1983), came to be known as the 'wideners': those wishing to broaden the concept of security out of its military-centric confines. One such widener was Barry Buzan.

The term 'societal security' was first introduced by Buzan in *People, States and Fear* (1991a). In the book, societal security was just one of the sectors in his five-dimensional approach, alongside military, political, economic, and environmental concerns. In this context, societal security referred to the sustainable development of traditional patterns of language, culture, religious and national identities, and customs of states (1991a: 122–3). Each one of Buzan's five sectors was formulated within the confines of an essentially neo-Realist framework: all of the dimensions remained as sectors of national, that is, state, security. 'Society' was just one section through which the state might be threatened. Furthermore, threats in the military sector were seen as primary: as the priorities given to each dimension depended on their relative urgency, Buzan argued that military security was still the most expensive, politically potent and visible aspect of state behaviour (1991b: 35). Hence: 'A state and society can be, in their own terms, secure in the political, economic, societal and environmental dimensions, and yet all of these accomplishments can be undone by military failure' (1991b: 37).

Although recognizing Buzan's vital contribution to the 'broadening' of international security, a major contention was that introducing more sectors of state security was simply not enough. While security studies was indeed beginning to move away from its preoccupation with military issues, it was still very much state-centric in its focus. What was required, therefore, were other referent objects of security: that international security should be 'deepened' as well as broadened brought with it a re-focusing on what or indeed who should be secured, from the individual through to the global level. (For a fuller discussion of human versus state security, see Chapter 6.) Set against this, the concept of 'societal security' came to mark out a distinct third, and indeed middle, position; one that was reluctant to consider notions of either human or global security, but one which was also in agreement that the Realist and neo-Realist approach to international security had become just too narrow. As a result, this middle position began to talk about the security of other collectivities, or 'societies'.

A duality of state and societal security

In the 1993 book *Identity, Migration and the New Security Agenda in Europe*, Ole Waever, together with Buzan, Morten Kelstrup and Pierre Lemaitre suggested that 'societal securities' had become increasingly important vis-à-vis concerns over state sovereignty in contemporary, post-Cold War Europe.

Most crucially, the writers claimed that Buzan's previous five-dimensional approach to international security had now become untenable as context for societal security. They suggested a reconceptualization: not of five sectors relating to the state, but instead a duality of state and societal security. Although society was retained as a dimension of state security, it also became a referent object of security in its own right.

The key to this reconceptualization was the notion of *survival*. While state security is concerned with threats to its sovereignty; if a state loses its sovereignty, it will not survive as a state, societal security is concerned with threats to its identity; similarly, if a society loses its identity it will not survive as a society. States can be made insecure through threats to their societies. But state security can also be brought into question by a high level of societal cohesion. This relates to those instances where a state's programme of homogenization comes into conflict with the strong identity of one or more of its minority groups. For example, during the 1990s, the 'Romanianness' of the Romanian state was compromised as the large Hungarian minority in the Transylvania region of the country further asserted its 'Hungarianness'. (This is explored further in the chapter when going on to discuss societal security dilemmas.) In other words, the more secure in terms of identity these societies are, the less secure the states containing them may feel. For Waever (1993: 25) and his collaborators, in this way traditional security analysis had created 'an excessive concern with state stability', and thus had largely removed any sense of 'the "security" of societies in their own right'.

As a concept, societal security was conceived very much as to a reaction to events in Europe, in both the East and in the West. In the West, the process of European Union (EU) integration meant that political loyalties were increasingly being shifted, either upward to the EU level itself, or downwards to the level of the regions, thus weakening the traditional link between state and society. In the East, the collapse of some of the former socialist countries showed starkly the conflict between adherence to the state (Federal Yugoslavia) or adherence to its constituent groups (Serbs, Croats, Bosnian Muslims). As an analytical tool, the concept has therefore mainly been employed in a very much European context (see for example, Huysmans 1995; Herd & Lofgren 2001; Roe 2002). However, its applicability arguably goes much further, in particular to those 'weak states' in parts of South-East Asia and sub-Saharan Africa. And more will be said about this in the conclusion to this chapter.

KEY QUOTES 10.1

The importance of societal security

'In the West and the East, at the centre and the periphery, cultural identity and societal security have become the central theme of political attitudes and conflicts.'

(Pierre Hassner, 'Beyond Nationalism and Internationalism: Ethnicity and World Order', *Survival*, 1993, p. 58)

'With the increasing intertwining of security and identity, a new agenda has emerged, both for policy-makers struggling with the dilemmas and uncertainties of post Cold-War Europe, and for academics trying to make sense analytically and conceptually of this changed continent . . . [E]xploring the interface between security and identity can shed considerable light on the structural dynamics and underlying trends of contemporary European politics.'

(Lisbeth Aggestan and Adrian Hyde-Price, *Security and Identity in Europe*, 2000, p. 1)

KEY POINTS

- To begin with, societal security was just a sector of state security. This is where the state can be destabilized through threats to its language, culture, religion, and other customs.
- The societal security concept was (re)conceived in light of the processes of integration in Western Europe and disintegration in Eastern Europe.
- Societal security was reconceptualized as a referent object of security in its own right.
- Societal security concerns the maintenance of collective identity: if a society loses its identity it will not survive as such.
- Societal security represents a middle way between notions of individual and global security.

Society and societal identity

Put simply, society is about identity: it is about the self-conception of collectivities and individuals identifying themselves as members of that collectivity. Thus, societies are units constituted by a sense of collective identity. Waever (1993: 17) defines collective identity as simply 'what enables the word *we* to be used'. In this sense, however, a 'we' identity can vary a great deal as to the kind of group to which it applies, the intensity to which it is felt, and the reasons which create a sense of it. Moreover, societies are composed of, and support a multitude of, different identities. That is to say, societies are multiple identity units. How, then, is it possible to talk about a society's identity?

According to Anthony Giddens (in Waever 1993: 19), there are two main ways to think about society. The first one is something fixed that has boundaries marking it off from other like units. The second one is something that is constituted by social interaction; society is viewed rather as a fluid concept, referring more to a process than to an object. For Waever (1993: 19), however, defining society as a process arguably reduced it to more or less any classification of 'we': a view of society which cannot easily be employed in the analysis of international security. The interest for the so-called 'Copenhagen School', as in particular Buzan and Waever came to be known, was in 'societies operating as units in the international system'; where their reactions to threats against their identity have politically significant effects. Accordingly, Waever distinguished between society and 'social group'. Here, societal security is concerned with the security *of* society as a whole, but not the security of groups *in* society (social group).

Waever (1994: 8) notes that security action is 'always taken on behalf of, and with reference to a collectivity . . . that which you can point to and say: "it has to survive, therefore it is necessary . . . ". From this there are two main points to keep in mind. The first one is that for the collectivity there are distinctive kinds of behaviour that cannot be reduced to the individual level. Like state security, societal security must be approached as the security of societies having more than, and thus being different from, the sum of their constituent individual and social groups. Thus, society is viewed as an entity possessing a reality of its own. The second one, and following on from the first, is that societies must also be seen as having the right to survive. For example, while farmers might be considered as a distinct social group, the argument is a difficult one to make that 'farmers' also constitute a significant entity operating alongside the state in political terms. Moreover, the argument that farmers automatically have some kind of right to always be farmers is a difficult one to sustain, as farms are routinely allowed to go out of business for a number of reasons. (Although when farming, as in the case of France in particular, is tied very closely to a particular notion of collective identity—in this instance 'Frenchness'—then farmers may become part of a societal security agenda: farms in France going out of business representing a loss of what it means to be French.)

Such difficulties over defining society can be tackled further by pinning the relationship between society and societal identity to a more easily definable unit. Waever refers to Giddens' view that as 'units' modern societies are most often nation-states or based on the idea of the nation-state. Indeed, Waever (1993: 19) claims that the nation is a special case of society characterized by: attachment to territory, or at least a sense of homeland; a continuity of existence across time, from past generations to the present; and a sense of being one of the entities which makes up the social world. In this way, though, the idea of nation and state are often blurred. Waever, Buzan, and a further collaborator Jaap de Wilde recognize (1998: 121) all too well that the problem with *societal* is that the related term *society* is often used to refer to state population. Taking the example of Sudan, they emphasize that 'Sudanese society is that population contained by the Sudanese state but which is composed of many societal units (e.g. Arab and black African). This is not our use of societal; we used societal for communities with which one identifies'. Thus, while on the one hand nation can be defined in relation to 'citizenship', on the other hand it can also be defined in terms of 'ethnicity'. And this distinction is often characterized by the terms 'civic nation' and 'ethnic nation'.

Nations perform a number of roles: most prominently, the marking of borders, thereby staking claim to control a territory. For much of the time, though, the concept of nation is underpinned by common cultural (more often than not, ethnic) bonds. Nations are, in this regard, very much a response to the need for identity. Belonging to a distinct culture tells us 'who we are', and it is this process of self-identification which is key to nations.

Although nationality and ethnicity are indeed often mingled, nation and ethnic group can be distinguished in the following terms: a nation strives for a state of its own, whereas an ethnic group acts within the state as it exists. Anthony D. Smith (1993: 48–62) suggests that an ethnic group constitutes a nation when it has become 'politicized'; when not only is the group bound by a distinct culture, but when it also begins to act as a cohesive political unit. Smith's formulation is a useful one, although it must be kept in mind that politicized ethnic groups do not always strive for statehood. Nations, therefore, are often predicated on ethnicity. Shared ethnic origins provide nations with some sort of legitimacy over claims for territory and political autonomy. Thus, with regard to society, Waever duly employs the label 'ethno-national' group.

Perhaps the only rival to ethno-national identity as a political mobilizer is religion. Religion possesses the ability to reproduce its 'we' identity more or less unconsciously across generations. It is also able to generate a feeling of self-identification, which can be as intense as that of nationalism. Moreover, where religious and ethno-national identities reinforce each other (Catholic Croats, Orthodox Serbs) this can produce very defined and resilient identities.

Waever (1993: 23) concludes that the main units of analysis for societal security are 'politically significant ethno-national and religious entities', and accordingly defines societal security as 'the ability of a society to persist under changing conditions and possible and actual threats. More specifically, it is about the sustainability, within acceptable conditions for evolution, of traditional patterns of language, culture, association, and religion and national identity and custom'.

But just what 'possible and actual threats' might Waever be referring to? The next section tackles this question.

KEY POINTS

- Societies are units formed by a sense of collective identity, where collective identity is defined as what enables the word 'we' to be used.
- For security analysis, societies are different from social groups. Societies have a reality of their own, they can operate as units in the international system, and they are invariably seen as having the right to survive.
- Nations and states are sometimes difficult to distinguish. Societies may be nation-states, but do not always refer to state population.
- Society most often equates to ethno-national group, although religious groups may also be relevant units for analysis.
- Societal security can be defined as the maintenance of distinct ethno-national and religious identities.

Threats to societal identity

Objective definitions of threats to societal security are as problematic as they are for states. Indeed, perhaps more so. Given the sometimes-fluid nature of collective identities, not all changes to it will necessarily be regarded as threatening. Some change will be seen as the natural process by which groups respond to meet changing historical conditions. Nevertheless, some processes invariably carry with them the potential to harm societal security.

Threats to societal security exist when a society perceives that its 'we' identity is being brought into question, whether this is objectively the case or not. Those means that can threaten societal identity range from the suppression of its expression to interference with its ability to reproduce itself across generations. This, according to Buzan (1993: 43) may include 'forbidding the use of language, names and dress, through closure of places of education and worship, to the deportation or killing of members of the community'. Threats to the reproduction of a society can occur through the sustained application of repressive measures against the expression of identity. If the institutions that reproduce language and culture, such as schools, newspapers, museums, and so forth are shut down, then identity cannot easily be passed on from one generation to the next. Moreover, if the balance of the population changes in a given area, this can also disrupt societal reproduction.

Threats to societal security in the Yugoslav wars

Such threats to societal security were highlighted only too starkly during the wars in the former Yugoslavia. In addition to the all too well known horrors of 'ethnic cleansing', what some have termed 'cultural cleansing' was also a prevalent practice. Ethnic cleansing refers to the intentional killing, violence against (including sexual), or deportation of members of one ethno-national group by another. In terms of identity, such practices pose an enormous threat to group cohesion. By contrast, cultural cleansing is perpetrated not against members of the group as such, but against manifestations of group culture. This involved the deliberate destruction of churches, mosques, libraries, and monuments across much of Bosnia-Hercegovina and parts of Croatia, and was intended to wipe out hundreds of years of history from the former Yugoslavia. It is what some writers have described as 'culturecide', and it strikes right against the very core of societal identity.

KEY QUOTES 10.2

The effects of cultural cleansing

'You have to understand that the cultural identity of a population represents its survival in the future. When Serbs blow up the mosque of a village and destroy its graveyards and the foundations of the graveyards and mosques and then level them off . . . no one can ever tell this was a Muslim village. This is the murder of a people's cultural identity.'

(Jan Boeles, EU Monitor Mission to the Former Yugoslavia, quoted in Robert Fisk, 'Waging War on History', *The Independent*, 1990)

'In extreme circumstances, systematic discrimination threatens communal groups' most fundamental right, the right to survival. Many groups also face cultural discrimination and the risk of de-culturation or so-called cultural genocide in the form of pressures or incentives to adopt a dominant culture, or denial of cultural self-expression.'

(Ted Robert Gurr, *Minorities at Risk*, 1993, p. 6)

As a referent object of security, society can be harmed through all of Buzan's five dimensions: societal, military, political, economic, and environmental. And while some of the sectors are talked about at greater length in Chapters 8, 9, 11, and 12, it is worth describing here their specific relationship to societal identity.

The five sectors of security

Buzan, Waever, and de Wilde (1998: 121) have divided threats in the societal sector of security into three main categories: migration, horizontal competition, and vertical competition. In cases of migration, the host society is changed by the influx of those from outside; by a shift in the composition of the population. Think of recent examples in the UK where some immigrants have been characterized as bringing 'foreign' and 'strange' ways with them that are out of keeping with a sense of 'Britishness'. Horizontal competition refers to groups having to change their ways because of the overriding linguistic and cultural influences of others. For example, in the Soviet Union many of the republics were 'Russified'; Russian language and culture came to dominate over Latvian, Estonian, Ukrainian, and Kazakh identities, to name but just a few. Finally, vertical competition refers to those instances where either due to integration or disintegration, groups are pushed towards either wider or narrower identities, such as in the former Yugoslav case.

In the military sector, it is invariably the case that an external military threat will threaten the society or societies within the state. Here, threats to societal security can arguably be seen mainly in terms of depopulation: where enough members of the society are killed (or sometimes deported) to either hinder or prevent collective identity being transmitted from one generation to the next.

However, some societies within invaded states may not always view armed aggression as a threat. Some minorities may be liberated from either their own regimes or from occupation by a foreign power. Besides, while external military aggression will invariably threaten state sovereignty, it may not necessarily pose a concomitant danger to the society's identity. Take, for example, Nazi Germany's invasion of France in 1940. There was an obvious potential to threaten both the French state and French society. However, while French sovereignty was indeed violated, for the most part French society remained relatively secure: French identity was not, to any significant extent at least, intentionally suppressed. Contrast this with Hitler's prior invasion of Poland in 1939: hand in hand with the military threat to the Polish state was also a political-societal threat to Polish identity: the Poles' Slavic identity coupled with the Nazis' policy of Lebensraum. As such, except when invasion is specifically designed towards the harming of state populations, such threats are mainly directed against either the maintenance of political autonomy (puppet states) or the survival of the incumbent regime (regime change).

Military threats to societies may also come from internal aggression. Perhaps the clearest example of this is when a regime, representing one ethnic group, uses its armed forces to suppress other minorities. For more on this see Chapter 9.

In the political sector, threats to societies are most likely to come from their own government, usually in the form of the suppression of minorities. And in this way political and military threats to societal identity will be closely linked. Political threats can often be mitigated by the state itself: for example, certain legislation can be introduced in order to protect societal identity. However, when the state machinery is overwhelmingly controlled by a dominant society, then not only might the state be unwilling to provide societal security, it may itself be posing the threat.

The economic sector of security is for the most part characterized by how the capitalist system can undermine cultural distinctiveness by generating global products (televisions, computers, and computer games), attitudes (materialism and individualism), and style (English language), thereby replacing traditional identities with contemporary 'consumer' ones.

In the environmental sector, threats to societies can occur especially when identity is tied to a particular territory. This is certainly the case when culture is adapted to a way of life that is strongly conditioned by its natural surroundings. Threats to the environment may thus endanger the existence of that culture and sometimes the people themselves. For example, the loss of huge swathes of the Amazon rainforest has seriously affected many of its indigenous peoples in terms of their traditional existence as hunter-gatherer communities. In addition to deforestation, pollution, climate change, and desertification also pose similar threats to societal security.

Against perceived threats through all five dimensions of security, societies can react in two ways. First, by trying to move the threat onto the state's security agenda. And actions taken by states to defend their societies are quite common. However, second, societies can also choose, or may be forced, to defend themselves through non-state means. As Buzan (1993: 56–7) enquires: 'What happens when societies cannot look to the state for protection . . . ?' Unable to turn to the regime to guarantee their survival, societies will have to provide for their own security; they will be in a self-help situation. And just how societies help themselves is the matter of the next section.

KEY POINTS

- Objectively defining threats to societal security is difficult, especially so as some changes to group identity will be seen as a natural response to shifting historical circumstance.
- Societal identity can be threatened from the suppression of its expression through to interference with its ability to reproduce itself across generations.
- Ethnic cleansing; the deliberate killing, violence against, and deportation of members of one society by another, and cultural cleansing, the systematic destruction of institutions and symbols designed to promote and maintain group identity, are two prominent manifestations of threats to societal security, and were widely employed, for example, during the wars in the former Yugoslavia.
- Societies can be threatened through all five of Buzan's sectors of security, although the societal and military dimensions are perhaps the most important.
- States often take measures to defend their own societies. But in multi-ethnic states in particular, societies may find themselves in self-help situations where they are compelled to provide for their own security.

Defending societal identity

Perhaps most evidently, societal identity can be defended using military means. This is particularly the case if identity is linked to territory: the defence of the historic homeland. If the threat posed by one group to another is military (armed attack from a neighbouring society), then some kind of armed response is invariably required. However, in such a scenario societal security dynamics are likely to closely resemble those of armed aggression between states: defending societal identity becomes much the same as defending state sovereignty. Therefore, in order to show how societal security can be used as a distinct (from state security) analytical tool, the remainder of this section turns its attention to the intra-state level of analysis, and to multi-ethnic states where societal insecurities are most often apparent.

While some societies (as states or quasi-states) may very well have an army or at least some kind of militia that can be utilized for defence, the vast majority of intra-state groups possess no such exclusive means of protection. For them, members of the group will either make up part of the state's armed forces as a whole, or have military forces composed of the same ethnic group in a neighbouring state. Facing a threat in identity terms, such groups are therefore left with two main options: first, they can try to form their own militia/defence force as a means or protection, although this can prove to be extremely difficult; or second, they can try to defend their identity using non-military means.

Non-military means of defence

At the intra-state level, the vulnerabilities felt by many groups may often derive not so much from armed aggression as from demographic processes and political-legal means designed to deprive societies of beliefs and practices vital to the maintenance of their culture. Returning to the example of ethnic cleansing, Robert Hayden (1996: 784) highlights, how, for example, such threats to societal identity can be shaped very much by demographic considerations: 'Within areas in which the sovereign group is already an overwhelming majority, homogenization can be brought about by legal and bureaucratic means, such as denying citizenship to those not of the right group.' In more mixed areas, however, Hayden goes on, homogenization requires more drastic measures such as killing and physical expulsion. And although it is only the attempted extermination of the minority group in this regard that has widely been recognized as ethnic cleansing, 'it is important to recognize that legal and bureaucratic discrimination is aimed at bringing about the same result: the elimination of the majority'.

When the nature of the threat is non-military (legal, bureaucratic), countervailing measures are also likely to be so. In the *Identity, Migration* book, Waever et al (1993: 191) suggest that for threatened societies 'one obvious line of defensive response is to strengthen societal identity'. This can be done, Waever (1995: 68) notes succinctly, by defending culture 'with culture'. And that consequently 'culture becomes security policy'. The idea of defending culture with culture is a slightly tricky one to unpack, but John Hutchinson provides a useful starting point. Hutchinson describes the project of what he calls 'cultural nationalism'. Cultural nationalism is designed to generate a strong feeling of self-identification. It emphasizes various commonalities such as language, religion and history, and downplays other ties that might detract from its unity. In this sense, cultural nationalism celebrates what is special about *our* identity. Self-identification, as such, often takes place because societal identity has been threatened: 'Our present identity has become too weak. We

KEY QUOTES 10.3

The project of cultural nationalism

'[C]ultural nationalists establish . . . clusters of cultural societies and journals, designed to inspire spontaneous love of the community in its different members by educating them to their common heritage of splendour and suffering. They engage in naming rituals, celebrate national cultural uniqueness and reject foreign practices, in order to identify the community to itself, embed this into everyday life and differentiate this against other communities.'

(John Hutchinson, Cultural Nationalism and Moral Regeneration', in Hutchinson and Anthony D. Smith (eds.), *Nationalism*, 1994, p. 124)

therefore need to change it and make ourselves strong again.'

Defending societal identity through cultural nationalism can be seen in the case of relations between the Protestant and Catholic communities in Northern Ireland.

Protestants and Catholics in Northern Ireland

In Portadown, the Protestant Orange Order has struggled to maintain what it sees as its historic right to march down the predominantly Catholic Garvaghy Road. Likewise, many of the town's Catholic inhabitants have protested, claiming that the march is highly provocative. For the Orange Order, not to march is tantamount to surrender: 'We have been walking down this road for generations. Why should we stop now?' In this way, the right of the Orange Order to march is inextricably bound up with the maintenance of its Protestant identity: it is the right to express who *we* are, where *we* come from (and indeed, where *we* are going). It is a societal security requirement. However, for the Catholic community the march is a celebration of the Protestant victory at the 1690 Battle of the Boyne, and thus represents a serious attack on their own identity. As Michael Ignatieff (1993: 169) points out, the victory of William of Orange over the Catholic King James 'became a founding myth of ethnic superiority . . . The Ulstermen's reward, as they saw it, was permanent ascendancy over the Catholic Irish'.

In the face of what many Protestants have come to see as the erosion of their ascendant status in the province, Orange Order marches are a cultural nationalist strategy aimed at strengthening their identity; the celebration of the self.

In perhaps more concrete terms, collective identity can be strengthened when cultural nationalist strategies are manifest as 'cultural autonomy'. Cultural autonomy entails the granting of certain rights in relation to the means of cultural reproduction; the control of one's own schools, newspapers, religious institutions and so forth.

Similarly, societal groups may also employ 'ethnic' or 'political nationalism' as a means of defence. Unlike cultural nationalism, political nationalist projects have an explicit territorial element to them. Political nationalism, as manifest in 'political autonomy', often involves self-government along a wider range of issues, such as the ability to control some of its own legal and financial affairs (for example, as with the Basques in Spain). In this way, political autonomy usually equates to some kind of autonomous region within the state. In its most extreme expression, though, and if threats to societal identity are seen as particularly severe, political nationalist projects may seek outright independence outside of the existing state structure.

KEY POINTS

- Military means may often be used to defend societal identity. This is particularly the case when identity is linked to territory.
- At the intra-state level, however, many societal groups may have no such means of armed protection. Forced to provide for their own security, such groups are compelled to employ non-military countermeasures.
- Cultural nationalist strategies can be used to defend societal security. When manifest as cultural autonomy, this involves the control over those institutions that are responsible for cultural reproduction, such as schools and churches.
- Political nationalist strategies are also a means of defending collective identity. Political autonomy, however, is more territorially based and thus involves a much greater measure of self-government within the state.
- Secession is the most extreme form of defence for societal security.

Societal security dilemmas

Thus far, the chapter has noted the importance of societal security, in particular with relation to Europe's security agenda during the 1990s. It has talked about how societal identity can be threatened, and how threatened societies can respond to those dangers. In this section, the notion of a societal security dilemma is discussed. The purpose is to highlight how societal security dynamics can escalate to the point of violence and war, and importantly, to show how conflict in this way can be generated by non-military concerns.

In the *Identity, Migration* book, Buzan (1993: 46) suggests that by analogy with relations between states it may be possible to talk of '**societal security dilemmas**', and that societal security dilemmas might explain why some ethnic conflicts 'come to acquire a dynamic of their own'. But what does a societal security dilemma look like? How does it operate? How is it different, if at all, to the traditional (state) security dilemma? And what effects might it produce? Chapter 2 touches on the concept of the security dilemma. But for purposes here it is useful to briefly revisit the concept.

The (state) security dilemma

For the most part, the security dilemma describes a situation where the actions of one state, in trying to increase its security, causes a reaction in a second, which, in the end, decreases the security of the first. Consequently, a process of action and reaction is manifest whereby each side's policies are seen to threaten the other. Thus, at the core of the concept lies an escalatory dynamic. The key to this escalatory dynamic is *ambiguity* and *uncertainty*.

States usually try to increase their security by building up their arms. But most arms that can be used for defence can also be deployed for offensive purposes too. A tank, for example, can just as easily be employed to attack a neighbour's territory as it can to defend one's own. Arms, therefore, are invariably ambiguous in nature; on the one hand they are a means to protect oneself, while on the other they are a way of harming others. And it is this crucial role that arms play in being able to generate both security and insecurity that has led the vast majority of writers to conceive of the security dilemma in almost exclusively military terms.

In turn, the ambiguity of military postures creates uncertainty about the intentions of one's adversary. Faced with the indistinguishability between offence and defence, decision-makers must come to distinguish between 'status quo' states and 'revisionist' states.

Accordingly, decision-makers are forced to assume the worst. In an anarchical, self-system, it is prudent to equate capabilities with intentions: what the other can do, it will, given the opportunity. Countervailing measure are therefore taken, generating a spiral of insecurities, which, in the context of states, is often manifest as arms racing.

KEY QUOTES 10.4

The two sides of ethnicity

'On the one hand, ethnicity . . . is often perceived as backward and dangerous. On the other hand, [some] authors tend to view ethnicity as . . . the self-expression of the threatened and the marginalised. Ethnicity can be both positive and negative. Of course, the divisive nature of contemporary ethno-nationalism, its violent boundary makings, its exclusiveness, etc., must also be viewed as considerable challenges to the modern international system, as well as potentials for violence and wars. One must not forget, however, that ethnicity has also a potential for internal group solidarity and loyalty.'

(Helena Lindholm, 'Introduction: A Conceptual Discussion', in Lindholm (ed.) *Ethnicity and Nationalism*, 1993, p. 24)

The societal security dilemma

But how can this equate to societies, rather than states? While collective identity can certainly be threatened by military means, as has been pointed out, societal insecurities and responses to those insecurities may often be non-military in nature. In other words, thinking about a societal security dilemma also prompts the shift to a non-military security dilemma. In this way, a first question is what can create ambiguity if not arms?

For societal security dilemmas, ambiguity can stem from the two sides of nationalism; cultural (positive) and ethnic (negative). Many writers describe ethnic (political) nationalism in rather malign terms, often characterized in this regard with the annexation of territories and the disintegration of states. By contrast, cultural nationalism is often seen as more benign as it tends to work within existing state structures. The goal of cultural nationalists is to amend the current order and not overturn it: it is more 'status quo' than 'revisionist'.

In practice, however, clear distinctions between cultural nationalism and political nationalism are often difficult to make. Indeed, Hutchinson (1994: 125) himself notes that cultural nationalist projects may sometimes employ ethnic-nationalist strategies in order to secure their goals. That is, cultural nationalism sometimes may be compelled to change itself from a solely cultural movement into a political one in order to get its concerns onto the state agenda, or to be able to expand into a genuinely mass movement in order to realize its desires. In certain circumstances, then, cultural nationalism might be conflated with political nationalism. And ambiguity might thus be apparent in the sense that cultural-nationalist movements come to resemble a political-nationalist project: the desire for cultural autonomy becomes confused with that for political autonomy. But how might this happen?

Within the state, the desires of the group will either be communicated verbally and/or be presented in written form through official memoranda and manifestos. In such a context, such desires may not be clearly articulated to others, a problem which can be compounded if insufficient communicative channels exist within the state. Moreover, certain verbal and/or written pronouncements may contradict previous ones. Others may thus be thrown into confusion causing them to misperceive the group's intentions. Dominant actors may employ exaggerated threat perceptions. This is often with the intention of mobilizing political support in order to sustain and create national or local power bases. For each scenario, countervailing measures might then be taken, which, in turn, can result in an action reaction process and the subsequent outbreak of ethnic violence and war.

To show more clearly such dynamics, it is useful once again to turn to an empirical example.

The societal security dilemma in Transylvania

Around one-and-a-half million Hungarians currently live in the Transylvania region of Romania. Up until the end of the First World War in 1918, Transylvania was mostly ruled by Hungary. During the inter-war period, the region was incorporated back into a new 'Greater Romania', although in 1940 Transylvania was briefly wrested back by Hungary with the backing of Nazi Germany. With Germany's defeat, however, in 1945, the region was once again returned to Romania. During the following socialist era, ethnic Hungarians were widely subject to assimilatory policies: Hungarian-language education and Hungarian cultural institutions were severely curtailed, and many Hungarians were re-settled from Hungarian-majority areas of the Transylvania region. Such policies were particularly felt during the 1980s, where the country's dictator, Nicolae Ceausescu, came to assume an increasingly nationalist posture.

However, following Ceausescu's overthrow in December 1989, the mistrust, which had previously come to epitomize relations between Romania and its Hungarian minority, appeared to have receded. In January 1990, under the leadership of Ion Iliescu, the provisional government of the National Salvation Front (NSF) issued a policy plan for the country, which, among other provisions, included for the reorganization of primary, secondary, and higher education. For the leaders of the Hungarian political party in Transylvania, the Hungarian Democratic Union of Romania (HDUR), the proposed legislation seemed to include for the following: one, the reintroduction of Hungarian-language teaching into 'Romanian' schools, thereby creating mixed educational institutions; and two, the complete separation of others, thus also providing for a number of solely Hungarian ones. However, in the Transylvanian city of Cluj, ethnic Romanian pupils together with their teachers and parents took to the streets in protest after having been moved out of their school building. Matters soon became worse when a League of Romanian Students formed in opposition to the decision by Deputy Education Minister (and an ethnic Hungarian) Atilla Palfalvi to divide the city's Babes-Bolyai university along ethnic lines. In Tirgu Mures, the situation was much the same: the city's Medical University was also to be split, and there were similar protests as again Romanian students were pushed out of their schools. As a consequence, Palfalvi was dismissed for 'creating tensions between the Romanian and Magyar [Hungarian] populations in Transylvania', and under his successor, Lajos Demeney, educational reorganization was to be delayed until the next academic year.

For many Hungarians, the issue of own-language education was crucial. In the virtual eradication of separate Hungarian-language educational establishments under Ceausescu, in 1959 Cluj's Hungarian Bolyai was merged with the city's Romanian Babes equivalent, after which the number of subjects taught in Hungarian in the new university was sharply cut. The loss of Hungarian schools and universities during the Socialist period was both symbolic and pragmatic: first, it was part of the general loss of many historic Hungarian institutions in Transylvania; and second, it also represented the erosion of a distinct Hungarian identity in the region. In this way, the restoration of an independent Bolyai University together with the wider provision for Hungarian-language education symbolized the revival of Hungarian culture and history in Romania. And this was particularly felt in Tirgu Mures: up until the 1960s an overwhelmingly Hungarian city, Tirgu Mures suffered especially from Ceausescu's assimilatory policies.

But the restoration of separate Hungarian educational establishments was also seen by many Romanians as a challenge to their own collective identity. From the middle of the nineteenth century onwards, the Romanian language became a significant marker of identification for a people who, until 1918, had been scattered throughout three separate empires (Habsburg, Ottoman, Romanov). Thus, its primacy was seen as fundamental to group cohesion. Additionally, many Romanian politicians, including leading members of the NSF, were keen to stress the unitary character of Romania. The splitting of schools and universities throughout the region would, it was feared, create a separate Hungarian cultural and political elite. And such decentralization might not only lead to a nascent federalist structure, but perhaps also to the eventual outright secession of Transylvania from Romania itself.

Viewed through the concept of a societal security dilemma, what was seen in the Hungarian community as something vital to the preservation of their identity, the provision of own-language education, was subsequently viewed by many Romanians as a clear danger to theirs. As a result, Romanian opposition to school separation in Transylvania was met by ever stronger Hungarian calls for the re-implementation of education reform. And this in turn led only to greater Romanian obduracy. In other words, a clear action–reaction process had become manifest. For example, on 8 February 1990 some 5,000 Romanians attended an anti-Hungarian rally in Tirgu Mures. On the same day, 10,000 Hungarians marched in the town of Gheorghini demanding that the process of school separation continue. And two days later, on 10 February, in excess of 40,000 ethnic Hungarians once again took to the streets in Tirgu Mures, Sfintu Gheorghe, and several other Transylvanian towns.

This spiral of nationalisms became heightened the following month, when, on 15 March, celebrations were held throughout the region commemorating the anniversary of the 1848 Hungarian War of Independence. In Cluj, festivities passed off without trouble. But in Satu Mare, Oradea, and Tirgu Mures scuffles were reported between the two communities. The next day (16 March), a number of Romanians, said to have been angered by two bilingual signs hoisted in Tirgu Mures declaring 'Justice for Minorities' and 'Schools in Hungarian', set upon Hungarians in the city streets. In one incident, the Hungarian owner of a pharmacy was attacked and his shop ransacked after having written the Hungarian *gyogyszertar* next to the Romanian equivalent *farmacie* on the sign above the door.

Three days later, on 19 March, fighting broke out in Tirgu Mures. Clashes between Hungarian and Romanian mobs lasted for three days. Estimates put the joint casualty figure at six people dead and between 250 and 300 seriously injured. It was Romania's worst outbreak of ethnic violence since the Second World War, and, at the time, represented the most serious such incidence throughout the whole of post-socialist Central and Eastern Europe.

The intention here was to show how the concept might be employed as an explanatory tool. In particular, the focus was maintained on the manifestation of non-military dynamics; where the (perceived) threats to societal identity are non-military in nature, and where the responses to those threats are also devoid of military insecurities. The value in doing so lies in the fact that by concentrating specifically on questions of collective identity, the concept is able to illuminate crucial dynamics otherwise missed by its more traditional, military-centric equivalent. Educational reform may indeed not be the stuff of 'hard' security. Nonetheless, as a potential threat to societal security it does have the quality to generate outcomes (violence and war) that are certainly politically significant.

KEY POINTS

- A societal security dilemma occurs when the actions taken by one society to strengthen its identity causes a reaction in a second, which, in the end, weakens the identity of the first.
- In societal security dilemmas, actors may be uncertain as to whether the other is employing either a cultural nationalist (cultural autonomy) or political nationalist (political autonomy/ secession) strategy. Assuming the worst, this can lead to a spiral of nationalisms and, finally, violent conflict.
- In the Transylvania region of Romania, a societal security dilemma was driven by proposed educational reforms. The maintenance of Hungarian identity depended on the separation of secondary and higher educational establishments. But this in turn brought into question Romanian identity, which depended in part on the dominance of the Romanian language and culture in the region.
- As an explanation for ethnic conflict, societal security dilemmas can highlight those important non-military dynamics that traditional (state) security dilemmas miss.

Conclusion

Thus far, the chapter has shown the importance of societal security concerns and how the concept can be used profitably as an analytical tool. However, the Copenhagen School has not been without its critics. And in this concluding section some of the major contentions are considered.

The charge of reification

A first, and perhaps most fundamental, criticism concerns the Copenhagen School's view of the construction of collective identity. In a comprehensive critique of the societal security concept, Bill McSweeney (1996: 82) charges Waever, Buzan and their fellow collaborators with reification. He claims that both 'society' and 'identity' are treated as 'objective realities, out there to be discovered': seen in objectivist terms, societies and societal identities are 'things' that somehow naturally exist. McSweeney (1996: 85) takes a more constructivist view in which society is rather a fluid entity: 'Identity is not a fact of society; it is a process of negotiation . . .'. Thus, society is constantly being constructed and reconstructed, and to talk about *a* (single) societal identity as such is difficult if not near impossible. In short what is at stake here is whether societies, like states, can be seen as objects around which security dynamics can be observed.

However, as Tobias Theiler (2003: 54), in a recent review of the societal security concept, makes clear, the Copenhagen School 'manage to mount a persuasive defence'. In a direct response to McSweeney's contentions, Buzan and Waever (1997) refute the charge of objectivism, arguing that theirs is also a constructivist approach. Unlike McSweeney, though, they claim that while societal identities are indeed socially constructed (process), once constructed they can also be regarded as, at least temporarily, fixed. Theiler (2003: 254) agrees, noting that when 'beliefs and institutions become deeply sedimented' they 'change only very slowly'.

As an analytical tool, therefore, societal security is useful in accounting for specific events in specific places at specific times. An example of this is Graeme P. Herd and Joan Lofgren's (2001) study of societal security concerns between the Baltic States and their Russian minorities during much of the 1990s.

Who speaks for society?

A second major criticism concerns the separation between state and society. In particular, the question arises as to who speaks for society if not the state. For sure, where state and society coincide, in the case of relatively homogenous nation-states, societal security concerns are invariably articulated by the government or by major political parties, the very same voices who speak on behalf of the state. In such an instance, to the observer state security and societal security may very well appear as pretty much one and the same. However, while the voice may indeed often be the same, the 'grammar' may nonetheless be different: state security concerns come hand-in-hand with the language of sovereignty, while societal security concerns come hand-in-hand with the language of identity. The point here is essentially tied to the Copenhagen School's notion of securitization, which is discussed at length in Chapter 4. For purposes here, though, what is important to keep in mind is that although state and society may be coterminous, *how* the referent object is threatened gives rise to different responses.

Sometimes, though, as has already been discussed, states and societies do not coincide. And in these instances the voices of state security and societal security may be different. For minority groups, societal security concerns are not always voiced from within the government, unless minority political parties are part of the ruling coalition. Minority groups may at least have some kind of representation within the legislature. If not, though, such societies will be forced to articulate their concerns outside of the state apparatus. In this regard, cultural elites (writers, poets, academics) can try to mobilize their societies against the government (majority group).

The dangers of speaking societal security

From this second criticism comes a third, and it concerns the political implications of voicing societal security. As Michael Williams (1998) points out, although on the one hand McSweeney charges the Copenhagen School with objectivism, on the other hand he also notes how the societal security concept is dangerously subjectivist too. Politicians can use perceived threats to societal security to legitimize racists and xenophobic political agendas. For example, defending 'our' identity against 'theirs' can serve to characterize immigrant communities as dangerous others who must either be assimilated or expelled. There is certainly a risk here, but a risk that Waever (1999: 337) believes is worth taking: 'This danger [of giving rise to fascist and ant-foreigner voices] has to be offset against the necessity to use the concept of societal security to try understand what is actually happening.' This is what Jeff Huysmans (2002) has called the 'normative dilemma' of writing security.

Applying the concept elsewhere

While not really a substantive criticism of societal security, a final point worth considering is whether the concept has a potentially wider application outside of Europe. As was mentioned, the Copenhagen School's thinking about societal security was very much a response to the European Security agenda of the 1990s: to the processes of western integration and eastern disintegration. So what about elsewhere?

As an analytical tool, societal security is particularly effective for understanding the security concerns of multi-ethnic states: relations between the regime (majority group) and the country's minority groups. And this is the focus of the so-called 'Third World Security School' (see for example, Ayoob 1995; Job 1992). For many countries in the Third World, the greatest threats are often internal. During the process of nation-building, state regimes may often require minority groups to give up all, or part, of their cultural distinctiveness; where minority identities are assimilated into the majority. These ethnic differences, together with the state's inability to provide for certain sections of its people, causes the population to express its loyalty elsewhere. And it is this lack of cohesion between the state and its societies that defines the state as 'weak'. Weak states provide propitious conditions for the study of societal insecurities, and the security studies literature is beginning to utilize it (Collins 2003).

KEY QUOTES 10.5

Legitimizing racism and xenophobia

'What if [Jean-Marie] Le Pen manages to manufacture a majority consent, verified by polls or other measurement techniques, around the idea of racism and xenophobia, or if the IRA creates a "collective identity" which incorporates intense anti-British sentiment into a symbol of Irish solidarity? Such hypothetical developments are not wildly improbable, and would immediately present a serious security problem in France and Ireland.'

(Bill McSweeney, 'Identity and Security: Buzan and the Copenhagen School', *Review of International Studies*, 1996, pp. 87–88)

QUESTIONS

In what ways does societal security mark a departure from more traditional thinking about security?

Cannot Realist and neo-Realist approaches adequately capture the dynamics of nationalism and ethnic conflict?

What is the difference between society as a sector of security and society as a referent object?

How far can 'societies' be seen as rational, instrumental actors?

Is there a clear distinction to be drawn between societies and 'social groups'?

In what way might societies be said to have a right to survive?

Are societies, as the Copenhagen School claim, all about identity?

How can multi-ethnic states threaten the societal security of their minority groups? How can minorities try to counter these threats?

How differently does, for example, a map of Europe look seen through a societal security rather than state security perspective?

Is the Copenhagen School right that in saying that the European security agenda has become increasingly concerned with questions of group identity?

Why does the Copenhagen School's approach depend on a relatively fixed, and not fluid, notion of society?

FURTHER READING

■ **Aggestam, L. and Hyde-Price, A. (eds.) (2000), *Security and Identity in Europe*, London: Macmillan**. Excellent coverage of key issues facing European security; including NATO enlargement, EU integration, and the wars in the Balkans.

■ **Buzan, B. *et al.* (1990), *The European Security Order Recast: Scenarios for the Post-Cold War Era*, London: Pinter**. Precursor to the *Identity, Migration* book, the Copenhagen School's exploration of the new, emerging European security agenda through Buzan's five dimensions.

■ **Katzenstein, P.J. (ed.) (1996), *The Culture of National Security: Norms and Identity in World Politics*, New York: Columbia University Press**. Perhaps the most important edited collection concerning the impact of norms and identity on security and foreign policy and behaviour.

■ **Lapid, J. and Kratochwil, F. (eds.) (1999), *The Return of Culture and Identity in IR Theory*, Boulder, CO: Lynne Rienner**. Edited volume which covers the 'constructivist turn' in International Relations from the Copenhagen School to Postmodern and Poststructural approaches.

■ **McSweeney, B. (1999), *Security, Identity, and Interests: A Sociology of International Relations*, Cambridge: Cambridge University Press**. Provides excellent critiques of existing constructivist approaches to security and identity.

■ **Roe P. (2005), *Ethnic Violence and the Societal Security Dilemma*, London: Routledge**. One of the few books that successfully combines questions of identity with traditional security studies scholarship.

■ **Weldes, J. *et al.* (1999), *Cultures of Insecurity: States, Communities, and the Production of Dangers*, Minneapolis: University of Minnesota Press**. Introduces sociological and anthropological approaches in examining the cultural production of insecurity in local, national, and international contexts; from the Korean War, to the Cuban Missile crisis, to the conflicts in the Middle East.

USEFUL WEBSITES

- **www.ciaonet.org** Provides access to a wide range of working papers, journals, and policy briefs, including previous COPRI works.
- **http://www.cidcm.umd.edu/inscr/** Official website for the 'Integrated Network for Societal Conflict Research'. Contains working papers, reports, and databases concerning the study of societal conflicts, including Ted Robert Gurr's 'Minorities at Risk' project.
- **www.hrw.org** Excellent resource for news releases, publications, reports, and event lists concerning human- and minority rights in Europe and elsewhere.

Visit the Online Resource Centre that accompanies this book for lots of interesting additional material: www.oxfordtextbooks.co.uk/orc/collins/

11

Environmental Security

JON BARNETT

Chapter Contents

Reader's Guide

This chapter discusses the concept of environmental security. It explains the way environmental security has both broadened and deepened the issue of security. It describes the evolution of the concept as a merger of international environmental agreements, efforts by the peace movement to contest the meaning and practice of security, and the proliferation of new security issues in the post-Cold War era. The chapter examines the different meanings of environmental security, and then it explains four major categories of environmental security problems, namely: the way environmental change can be a factor in violent conflict, the way environmental change can be a risk to national security, the way war and preparation for war can damage the environment, and the way environmental change can be a risk to human security. It explains how environmental security can mean different things to different people and can apply to vastly different referent objects in ways that sometimes have very little to do with the environment.

Introduction

In its most basic sense insecurity is the risk of something bad happening to a thing that is valued. For example, people who value their jobs are concerned about the risk of unemployment, families who value having enough to eat are concerned about the regular supply of food, governments which value power are concerned about losing office, and countries which value peace are concerned about the possibility of war. So, security can apply to many different things that are valued (referent objects such as jobs, health, organizations, countries) and refer to many different kinds of risks (unemployment, lack of food, change of government, war). Given this, it is not surprising that the environment has been seen as a referent object of security, and that environmental change has been seen as a security risk. These and other connections between the environment and security fall under the heading of 'environmental security'. The purpose of this chapter is to provide a critical overview of the concept of environmental security.

Like the broader field of security studies, approaches to environmental security are diverse and reflect many theoretical perspectives. Environmental security is one of a number of 'new', non-traditional security issues that have served to deepen and broaden the concept of security. It helps to deepen security as it entails considering not just the security of states, but also the security of the 'global' environment as well as its many nested sub-systems, and various social systems. It broadens security by considering risks other than war—principally the risks posed by environmental change—to the things that people value. Further, like the concepts of human security and gender security discussed in this book (Chapters 6 and 5), environmental security is sometimes a *critical* security project in that it is used by some people to ask questions about who and what is being secured—and from what risks—by orthodox security policies (also see Chapter 4 of this book).

Like security studies more generally, environmental security has entailed much research of a more practical kind. There have been numerous attempts to assess the extent to which environmental change causes violent conflict within and between countries (this is examined in the fourth section of this chapter). There are explanations of the ways in which environmental change may undermine national security (explained in the fifth section of this chapter). There have been investigations of the ways in which war and preparations for war affect the environment (discussed in the sixth section of this chapter). Finally, there has been a growing body of research that investigates the linkages between environmental security and development issues such as poverty and human security (as explained in the seventh section of this chapter). These research endeavours have influenced policy development in some countries, notably the United States, in intergovernmental organizations such as the United Nations and NATO, and in non-governmental organizations such as the World Conservation Union and Greenpeace.

For all this research, and despite its influence on policy, there remains a debate about the usefulness of the environmental security concept. From an environmental perspective there are concerns that the concept has lead to a militarization of environmental issues. From the perspective of the dominant security paradigm there are concerns that the concept has undermined the 'hard' business of national security analysis and planning. Associated with this debate are questions about the uniqueness of environmental security given the difficulties of distinguishing between environmental problems and environmental *security* problems, and between security problems and *environmental* security problems. For most proponents of environmental security, however, its utility is the way it bridges the gap between security researchers and policymakers and those working in the environmental field, creating new fusions of theory, and new opportunities for dialogue. These issues are discussed in the last section of this chapter.

KEY POINTS

- The environment can be both an object to be secured and a source of risk.
- Environmental security means different things to different people.
- Environmental security has contributed to both a broadening and deepening of security.
- Environmental security has both critical and practical dimensions.
- There are debates about the usefulness of environmental security.

The origins of environmental security

Environmental security emerged as an important concept in security studies due to three interrelated developments beginning in the 1960s. The first of these was the growth of environmental consciousness in developed countries. A number of events stimulated and sustained the growth of the environmental movement at this time. Notable among these was the publication in 1962 of Rachel Carson's widely read book *Silent Spring* (also serialized in *The New Yorker*), which explained the impacts of pesticide DDT on animals and the food chain. Carson was among the first of many people whose use of print and electronic media create and sustain awareness of environmental issues; others include notable personalities such as David Attenborough, Jacques Cousteau, and David Suzuki.

The number of environmental non-governmental organizations—of which there now may be more than 100,000 worldwide—also seriously began to grow in the 1960s. From an international relations perspective, a notable development was the creation of large international environmental non-governmental organizations such as the World Wildlife Fund (1961), Friends of the Earth (1969), and Greenpeace (1971). Their functions have grown to include networking across countries, research, awareness raising, policy development and monitoring, capacity building, fund raising, and lobbying at local, national and international fora. Their issue-agenda is similarly broad, extending beyond conservation to include environmental justice, gender inequities, genetic engineering, indigenous rights, nuclear non-proliferation, poverty alleviation, sustainable energy technologies, and waste management. A growing number of non-governmental organizations of various scales and in various locations are incorporating environmental security issues into their work, including the African Centre for Technology Studies, the Global Environmental Change and Human Security project, the International Institute for Sustainable Development, the Stockholm Environment Institute, and the Worldwatch Institute.

The 1970s also saw the beginning of international summits on environmental issues, and a proliferation of international agreements on environmental issues. According to the United Nations Environment Program (itself established in 1972), there are 144 regional and 97 global environmental agreements relating to the environment (see Background 11.1), more than three-quarters of which were signed after 1972. The first major global environmental summit was arguably the United Nations Conference on the Human Environment (UNCHE) held in Stockholm in 1972. It initiated a number of intergovernmental investigations, meetings, and agreements on global environmental problems. These merged at times with parallel investigations into development and common security, and culminated in 1987 in the World Commission on Environment and Development's (WCED) 1987 report titled *Our Common Future*. The WCED report popularized the term 'sustainable development', and it introduced the term 'environmental security' (see key Quotes 11.1). It set the scene for the watershed United Nations Conference on Environment and Development (UNCED) held in Rio de Janeiro in 1992, and which has had follow-up conferences in 1997 and 2002.

The second major development leading to the emergence of environmental security was attempts from the 1970s onwards by a number of scholars to critique orthodox security discourse and practices by highlighting their inability to manage environmental risks to national and international security. This is the origin of the critical component of environmental security. Among the first attempts to do this were Richard Falk's *This Endangered Planet*, and Harold and Margaret Sprout's *Towards a Politics of Planet Earth* (see key Quotes 11.2). Both books argued that the international political system needs to comprehend and collectively respond to common environmental problems, as they pose threats to international stability and national well-being.

BACKGROUND 11.1

Major multilateral environmental agreements

1946	International Convention for the Regulation of Whaling
1963	Treaty Banning Nuclear Weapon Tests in the Atmosphere, in Outer Space and Under Water
1971	Convention on Wetlands of International Importance especially as Waterfowl Habitat (Ramsar)
1972	Convention on the Prevention of Marine Pollution by Dumping of Wastes and Other Matter (London Convention)
1972	Convention for the Protection of the World Cultural and Natural Heritage
1973	International Convention for the Prevention of Pollution for Ships, 1973 and Protocols (MARPOL)
1973	Convention on International Trade in Endangered Species of Wild Fauna and Flora (CITES)
1979	Convention on Long-Range Transboundary Air Pollution
1982	United Nations Convention on the Law of the Sea
1983	International Tropical Timber Agreement
1987	Montreal Protocol on Substances that Deplete the Ozone Layer
1989	Basel Convention on the Control of Transboundary Movements of Hazardous Wastes and their Disposal
1992	Convention on Biological Diversity
1992	United Nations Framework Convention on Climate Change
1996	Comprehensive Nuclear-test Ban Treaty
1997	Kyoto Protocol to the United Nations Framework Convention on Climate Change
2000	Cartegena Protocol on Biosafety to the Convention on Biological Diversity
2001	Stockholm Convention on Persistent Organic Pollutants

KEY QUOTES 11.1

'Environmental security' in Chapter 11 of *Our Common Future* (WCED 1987)

'. . . a comprehensive approach to international and national security must transcend the traditional emphasis on military power and armed competition. The real sources of insecurity also encompass unsustainable development. . . .'

'Environmental stress can thus be an important part of the web of causality associated with any conflict and can in some cases be catalytic.'

'Poverty, injustice, environmental degradation and conflict interact in complex and potent ways.'

'As unsustainable forms of development push individual countries up against environmental limits, major differences in environmental endowment among countries, or various stocks of usable land and raw materials, could precipitate and exacerbate international tension and conflict.'

'Threats to environmental security can only be dealt with by joint management and multilateral procedures and mechanisms.'

These ideas about environmental interdependence and common security have remained key themes of environmental security studies.

In 1977 Lester Brown also sought to contest the meaning and practice of national security with his Worldwatch paper titled *Redefining National Security*. Brown highlighted the inability of exclusionary national security institutions, and in particular the military, to manage common environmental problems (see Key Quotes 11.2), and suggested that disarmament and budgetary reallocations are important initiatives for resolving environmental degradation. Brown identified four 'biophysical' systems under stress, namely fisheries, grasslands, forests and croplands. He also discussed the problem of climate modification, and related this to food security. Like Falk and the Sprouts, his paper did not seriously consider the potential of environmental change to cause conflict.

It was not until 1983, when Richard Ullman published an article titled 'Redefining Security', that the idea that environmental change might cause war was seriously proposed. Ullman defined a national security threat as anything which can quickly degrade the quality of life of the inhabitants of a state, or which narrows the choices available to people and organizations within the state. He suggested that environmental degradation is 'likely to make *Third World* governments more militarily confrontational in their relations with the advanced, industrialised nations' (142). Ullman also considered the possibility of illegal immigration by environmental refugees (now a popular concern). Ullman's paper was published in a highly influential US-based security journal (*International Security*), suggesting that when environmental security is narrowly interpreted as being about national security and armed conflict, it has more purchase with the orthodox security-policy community.

Ullman's background in international relations explains his concern for the ways in which environmental degradation might cause armed conflict. However, a number of environmental scientists, notably Norman Myers and Peter Gleick, have also consistently argued that environmental degradation will induce violent conflict (see Key Quotes 11.2). In an article in 1986, Myers considered food shortages, fisheries depletion, water scarcity, climate change, and deforestation to be issues likely to induce conflict. Environmental refugees also figure prominently. Like Brown's 1977 paper, Myers also explored the costs of military security relative to the costs of environmental security. Also published in 1986, but somewhat in contrast to Myers' concern for environmentally induced warfare, was an article by Arthur Westing focusing on using environmental measures to strengthen international security (see Key Quotes 11.2).

KEY QUOTES 11.2

Early writings on environment and security

Richard Falk's *This Endangered Planet* (1971)

- 'We need to revamp our entire concept of "national security" and "economic growth" if we are to solve the problems of environmental decay' (185).
- 'A prevalent misconception persists that national efforts, if sufficient, will guard the environment. The misconception arises from the failure to appreciate the actualities of *interdependence*: what we do needs to be coordinated with what others do . . . ' (196).

Harold Sprout and Margaret Sprout's *Toward a Politics of the Planet Earth* (1971)

- 'The thrust of the evidence is simply that the goal of national security as traditionally conceived—and as still very much alive—presents problems that are becoming increasingly resistant to military solutions' (406).

Lester Brown's *Redefining National Security* (1977)

- 'Neither bloated military budgets nor highly sophisticated weapons systems can halt deforestation or solve the firewood crisis' (37).

Richard Ullman, 'Redefining National Security', *International Security* (1983)

- 'The pressure engendered by population growth in the Third World is bound to degrade the quality of life, and diminish the range of options available, to governments and persons in the rich countries' (143).
- 'Conflict over resources is likely to grow more intense' (139).

Norman Myers, 'The Environmental Dimension to Security Issues', *Environmentalist* (1986)

- 'If a nation's environmental foundations are depleted, its economy will steadily decline, its social fabric deteriorate, and its political structure become destabilized. The outcome is all too likely to be conflict, whether conflict in the form of disorder and insurrection within the nation, or tensions and hostilities with other nations' (251).

Arthur Westing, 'An Expanded Concept of International Security' (1986)

- 'It is thus inescapable that any concept of international security must in the last analysis be based on this obligate relationship of humankind with its environment' (195).

These early arguments for the connections between the environment and security were very much of peripheral concern to Western security institutions occupied with the 'hard' business of winning the Cold War. For the United States and its allies, security meant national security from the military and ideological threat of the Soviet Union and its allies, and the principal strategy to achieve this was to build and maintain military superiority. However, one notable event troubled this pure vision of security. In 1973 the Organisation of Petroleum Exporting Countries (OPEC) restricted oil exports, leading to a quadrupling of the price of oil on world markets. This created considerable anxiety for people and governments in both developed and developing economies. The oil embargo showed that the industrial capacity that underpinned the military superiority of the West was vulnerable to the dictates of the suppliers of energy. This event, and a less severe oil crisis in 1979, firmly established the idea of energy security into mainstream security planning. Beyond energy security issues, it was not until the end of the Cold War that any other alternative dimension to security gained any significant purchase on security policy.

The end of the bipolar world order created by the Cold War created something of a 'vertigo' for security policy and security studies, and for a few years old ways of thinking about security became less obviously relevant (O'Tuathail 1996). This 'vertigo', combined with the growing environmental consciousness of people in developed countries, the call for common security approaches in *Our Common Future*, and preparations for the UNCED Rio conference, created the intellectual and policy space for environmental security to enter the mainstream as one of a suite of 'new' security issues (Dalby 1992). So, from 1989 onwards there were many more publications and studies on environmental security, including in prominent security journals such as *Foreign Affairs* (Matthews 1989) and *International Security* (Homer-Dixon 1991). These were to have some influence on policy, for example environmental security issues were incorporated into the United States National Security Strategy, and they featured in the policies of the US Department of State, NATO, and the United States Department of Defense (Barnett 2001). This shift in the strategic landscape is the third reason why environmental security is now an important concept in security studies.

KEY POINTS

- Environmental security emerged as an important concept in security studies because of:
  - the development of environmentalism in developed countries after the 1960's;
  - attempts to contest the meaning and practice of security from an environmental standpoint;
  - changes in strategic circumstances, in particular the end of the Cold War.
- There are now a large number of multilateral environmental agreements.
- Both political scientists and environmental scientists have contributed to the development of the concept of environmental security.

Major interpretations of environmental security

So, since the early 1990s environmental security has been an important concept in security studies and increasingly also in environmental studies. Yet the meaning of environmental security is ambiguous, perhaps due to the vagueness of its two root words—*environment* and *security*. The basic meaning of **environment** is the external conditions that surround an entity, but it can be more accurately defined as the living organisms and the physical and chemical components of the total Earth system (Boyden et al 1990: 314). **Security** is also an all-encompassing yet vague concept, which is perhaps best defined by Soroos (1997: 236) as 'the assurance people have that they will continue to enjoy those things that are most important to their survival and well-being'. The ambiguity of these words has given rise to many different meanings of environmental security.

Six principal approaches to environmental security can be discerned from the literature (see Table 11.1). First, environmental security can be seen as being about the impacts of human activities on the environment. This interpretation of environmental security—sometimes also called 'ecological security'—emphasizes at least implicitly that it is ecosystems and ecological processes that should be secured, and the principal threat to ecological integrity is human activity (see Think Point 11.1). In this view humans are secured only in so far as they are part of the environment (Rogers 1997). This view draws on both Green philosophy and ecological theory, where systemic interdependence, complexity, flux, uncertainty, harmony and sustainability are key themes. It radically challenges security thinking in that it demands a shift in the reason for action from individual and national interest, to a concern for the overall welfare of the entire social-ecological system of the planet. This radicalism perhaps explains why this ecological security view is on the periphery of environmental security thinking.

Table 11.1 Six key interpretations of environmental security

Name	Entity to be secured	Major source of risk	Scale of concern
Ecological security	Natural environment	Human activity	Ecosystems
Common security	Nation state	Environmental change	Global/regional
Environmental violence	Nation state	War	National
National security	Nation state	Environmental change	National
Greening defence	Armed forces	Green/peace groups	Organizational
Human security	Individuals	Environmental change	Local

THINK POINT 11.1

Human impacts on . . .

Land

- In the past forty years nearly one third of existing cropland was abandoned due to erosion.
- 25% of all land is affected by some form of land degradation.

Forests

- During the 1990s 16.1 million hectares of natural forests were cleared each year.
- Between 1990 and 2000, 99.3 million hectares of forests were cleared in Africa, Latin America and the Caribbean.

Biodiversity

- 184 species of mammals, 182 species of birds, 162 species of fish, and 1,276 species of plants are critically endangered (extremely high risk of extinction).
- Approximately 27,000 species are lost every year.

Freshwater

- Eighty countries containing 40% of the world's population experienced severe water shortages in the mid-1990s.
- Approximately half of the world's wetlands were lost during the twentieth century.

Coastal and marine areas

- Approximately half of all mangrove forests were cleared in the twentieth century.
- 58% of the world's coral reefs are threatened.

The atmosphere

- Concentrations of CO_2 have increased by 30% since 1750.

Source: UNEP 2002, UNEP 2005

The second key approach to environmental security focuses on common security. The causes and impacts of some environmental problems are not confined to the borders of nation-states. Some problems such as ozone depletion and climate change are very 'global' in nature in that they are caused by cumulative emissions of gases from many countries, which in turn affect many countries. However, to say that these problems are 'global' is not to say that all countries are equally responsible for them, or that all countries are equally at risk from them (see the later discussion on climate change, and also Case Study 11.1 and Think Point 11.3). Other environmental problems, such as acid rain, smoke haze, and water scarcity and pollution are often caused by, and impact on, more than one country. This means that groups of countries with similar environmental problems cannot easily unilaterally achieve environmental security, and so their common national security interests require collective action. This is the rationale behind the many meetings and treaties discussed in the previous section. However, while many environmental problems are to some degree 'common', no two countries have exactly the same interests, and all have sovereign rights. For these reasons multilateral environmental agreements have not significantly halted environmental degradation. The four other major approaches to environmental security are each discussed in the following sections.

KEY POINTS

- Both 'environment' and 'security' are ambiguous concepts.
- Interpretations of environmental security differ according to the entity to be secured, and the source of risk to that entity.
- Most interpretations of environmental security do not require much change in security thought and practice because they are concerned with the nation state and/or the risk of armed conflict.
- The ecological security and human security approaches to environmental security challenge the security policy community to consider alternative objects of security, and alternative security risks.

Environmental change and violent conflict

The connections between environmental change and violent conflict have been a central and long-standing concern of environmental security studies. The critical questions, which have yet to be conclusively answered, are whether environmental change contributes to violent conflict, and, if so, in what ways?

Early writing on the connections between environmental change and violence borrowed heavily from realist international relations theory and focused largely on resource scarcity and conflict between states. Gleick (1991), for example, argued that there were clear connections between environmental degradation and violence, suggesting that resources could be strategic goals and strategic tools, and that resource inequalities could be a source of conflict. The early contributions from Ullman and Myers (see Key Quotes 11.2) also canvassed the possibility of interstate war caused by resource and environmental problems. The possibility of war between counties with shared water resources was often highlighted (see Think Point 11.2). However, critics of this view such as Deudney (1990), liberal theories about the ways complex interdependence and trade mitigate against resource wars, and subsequent waves of research on environmental violence have all discredited the idea that environmental change can be a cause of war between countries.

Population growth and its links to environmental degradation and subsequently violent conflict was also a theme of early writing on environmental violence (e.g. Myers 1987). Yet the linkages between both population growth and environmental change, and environmental change and violent conflict, are not overly straightforward. Poverty and technology are critical additional variables. In low-income and technology-poor societies more people means more consumption of natural resources for food, fuel, and shelter, but it can also mean more labour and this can lead to more environmentally sustainable forms of consumption. In high-income and high-technology societies people consume up to a hundred times more resources and energy than

THINK POINT 11.2

Water wars?

The idea that countries might fight over water has been widely discussed by academics, politicians, and in the media. For example, for Thomas Naff (1992: 25):

> 'the strategic reality of water is that under circumstances of scarcity, it becomes a highly symbolic, contagious, aggregated, intense, salient, complicated, zero-sum, power- and prestige-packed issue, highly prone to conflict and extremely difficult to resolve.'

Most commentators suggest that a future water war is most likely to occur in the Middle East, a region already rife with religious, ethnic and political tensions. Attention was first drawn to the problems of shared waterways and water scarcity in the region by the Egyptian Foreign Minister Boutrous Boutrous-Ghali, who later became Secretary General of the United Nations, who reportedly observed that 'the next war in our region will be over the waters of the Nile, not politics' (cited in Gleick 1991: 20).

There are 261 major river systems that are shared by two or more countries. Yet this geographical misfit between water and national boundaries does not necessarily imply that states will fight over water. Indeed, Aaron Wolf (1999) has demonstrated that despite rapid population growth and increased demand for water for agriculture, industry and cities in the twentieth century, there were only seven minor skirmishes over international water, in contrast to the signing of 149 new water-related treaties. Countries, it seems, are more likely to cooperate than fight over water. With respect to the Middle East too, detailed analyses by a number of scholars such as Allan (2002), Libiszewski (1997), and Lonergan (1997), find that there is indeed no reason to expect conflict over water in the near future.

people in developing countries; for example while India has 16.8% of the world's population it produces only 4.6% of the world's greenhouse gas emissions, whereas the United States, with 4.7% of the world's population, produces 23.2% of all greenhouse gas emissions. If anything, the linkages between environmental change and violent conflict are even more obscure than those between population growth and environmental change.

The relationship between population, environmental change, and violent conflict was most systematically explored by the Project on Environment, Population and Security at the University of Toronto. The project began in 1994, and was heavily informed by an earlier paper by its Director Thomas Homer-Dixon (1991). The Toronto Project carried out numerous case studies to investigate the links among population growth, renewable resource scarcities, migration and conflict. These studies examined cases where there had been violent conflict, and then they sought to determine the influence of environmental factors in the generation of those conflicts. At around the same time another project—the Zurich-based ENCOP (Environment and Conflict) Project directed by Guenther Baechler (1999)—also conducted case studies on the linkages between environmental degradation and violence. Both projects ended in the late 1990s.

Common findings of both projects are that: unequal consumption of scarce resources is a critical factor in violent conflicts; violent conflicts where environmental scarcity is a factor are more likely in low-income resource-dependent societies; population pressure can indirectly be a contributing factor to violent conflict; and when mechanisms that enable adaptation to environmental scarcity fail, violent conflict is a more likely outcome. Both Homer-Dixon (1999) and Baechler (1999) find that environmental change is not an immediate cause of conflict, but it can at times be an exacerbating factor. Both also find that environmental change is unlikely to be a cause of war between countries.

Since the Toronto and ENCOP projects there have been three further developments in environmental violence research. The first of these has been a series of quantitative analyses of aggregated data to test the relationships between various environmental and social variables such as resource scarcity/abundance, population growth, and income inequality. These studies have tentatively shown that 'strong states' tend to be less prone to internal conflicts whereas states undergoing significant economic and political transitions are relatively more prone to internal violent conflict (Esty et al 1999). A number of them suggest that it is the abundance of natural resources as much their scarcity that drives armed conflict (Collier 2000; de Soysa 2000). They have also shown that poverty is an important causal variable in internal wars. Because these studies are constrained by the quality of data they use, and lack detailed field-based observations, their findings are inevitably somewhat uncertain (Conca 2002).

The second new development in environmental violence research seeks to learn from peaceful responses to environmental change rather than from instances of violence. This is an important approach if the goal of research is to help prevent conflicts, because understanding what works to promote peace is as important as understanding what causes violent outcomes. Thus far the focus of this research has been on cooperation between states over shared resources such as rivers and seas (Conca and Dabelko 2002). This research endeavour serves as a useful reminder that cooperation among people and groups is also an outcome of common environmental problems.

The final new approach to environment and violence research involves detailed field-based studies of places which have experienced environmental problems and violence. These studies have stressed the importance of unequal outcomes of social and environmental changes. For example, inadequate distribution of the returns from resource extraction activities has been a factor in violence in West Kalimantan (Peluso and Harwell 2001), the Niger Delta (Watts 2001), and Bougainville island (Böge 1999). They show that a range of intervening economic, political, and cultural processes that produce and sustain power are seen as more important in causing (and preventing and resolving) violent conflict than the actual material environmental changes that take place.

KEY POINTS

- There are no strong causal relationships among population growth, environmental change, and violent conflict.
- Environmental change is not an immediate cause of conflict, but it can at times be an exacerbating factor.
- Environmental change is unlikely to be a cause of war between countries.
- Groups experiencing common environmental problems can also cooperate to address those problems.

Environmental change and national security

Most interpretations of environmental security take existing theories of national security, and then factor in environmental issues. This was certainly the approach of early theorists on environmental security, and it is one reason why there has been a lot of attention given to environmental violence. However, regardless of whether or not environmental change may cause violent conflict within or between states, in many less subtle ways it can undermine national security.

Environmental change can weaken the economic base that determines military capacity. In some developed countries, and in most developing countries, natural resources and environmental services are important to economic growth and employment. Income from and employment in primary sectors like agriculture, forestry, fishing, and mining, and from environmentally dependent services like tourism, may all be adversely affected by environmental change. It has been widely reported, for example, that China's rapid economic growth—which has funded its military modernization programme—is ecologically unsustainable due to water shortages, water pollution, and land degradation. So, in some cases, if the natural capital base of an economy erodes, then so does the long-term capacity of its armed forces. Because it exposes people to health risks, environmental change can also undermine the human development that Sen (1999) considers important for economic growth. In other words, if economic development can be ecologically unsustainable, then national security can be similarly unsustainable.

While many environmental problems countries face are principally caused by internal developments within those countries, some problems are largely beyond their control. Examples of this include the impacts of global emissions of ozone depleting substances on rates of skin cancer in southern latitudes, the legacies of nuclear weapons tests conducted during colonial times in French Polynesia and the Marshall Islands, the impacts of the Chernobyl nuclear reactor accident in 1986 on Eastern European countries, the impacts of forest fires in Indonesia on air pollution in Malaysia and Singapore, and the impacts of global emissions of greenhouse gases on low-lying countries and countries with high climatic variability (for example a 45 cm rise in sea-level will potentially result in a loss of 11% of Bangladesh's territory, forcing some 5.5 million people to relocate) (see Case Study 11.1). Transboundary flows differ from traditional external security threats in that they are uncontrolled and most often unintended, in this respect they are 'threats without enemies' (Prins 1993).

CASE STUDY 11.1

Climate change and atoll countries

Atolls are rings of coral reefs that enclose a lagoon which contain small islets with a mean height above sea-level of approximately two metres. There are five countries comprised entirely of low-lying atolls: Kiribati (population 85,000), the Maldives (population 309,000), the Marshall Islands (population 58,000), Tokelau (population 2,000), and Tuvalu (population 10,000).

Climate change is likely to cause sea levels to rise by between 9 and 88 cms by year 2100. Atoll countries are highly vulnerable to sea-level rise because of their high ratio of coastline to land area, lack of elevated land, soft coastlines, relatively high population densities, and low incomes to fund response measures. Also, climate change is likely to result in more intense rainfall events and possibly more intense droughts. The combined effect of these changes on atoll societies is likely to include coastal erosion, increases in flooding events, freshwater aquifers becoming increasingly contaminated with saline water, and decreasing food security due to reduced harvests from agriculture and fishing. The World Bank estimates that by 2050 Tarawa atoll in Kiribati could face an annual damages bill equivalent to 13–27% of current Kiribati GDP.

This combination of changes in mean conditions and extreme events driven by climate change may mean that atoll countries are unable to sustain their populations, a possibility with even a moderate amount of climate change. This danger to the sovereignty of the atoll countries is arguably greater than anything any single country could impose—indeed nuclear testing in the Marshall Islands and severe fighting in Kiribati during the Second World War had relatively minor impacts compared to the risks posed by climate change. This risk that climate change poses to national sovereignty is a very clear case of national (and human) environmental insecurity.

Source: Barnett and Adger 2003

BACKGROUND 11.2

A national security strategy for a new century—the 1998 national security strategy of the United States

The 1998 National Security Strategy was the first major national security policy statement to include environmental issues in a significant way. Here are some excerpts:

- 'The same forces that bring us closer increase our interdependence, and make us more vulnerable to forces like extreme nationalism, terrorism, crime, environmental damage and the complex flows of trade and investment that know no borders' (p. iii).
- 'We seek a cleaner global environment to protect the health and well-being of our citizens. A deteriorating environment not only threatens public health, it impedes economic growth and can generate tensions that threaten international stability. To the extent that other nations believe they must engage in non-sustainable exploitation of natural resources, our long term prosperity and security are at risk' (p. 5).
- 'Crises are averted—and US preventative diplomacy actively reinforced—through US sustainable development programs that promote voluntary family planning, basic education, environmental protection, democratic governance and the rule of law, and the economic empowerment of private citizens' (p. 8).
- 'The current international security environment presents a diverse set of threats to our enduring goals and hence to our security' . . . (including) 'terrorism, international crime, drug trafficking, illicit arms trafficking, uncontrolled refugee migrations and environmental damage' (which) 'threaten US interests, citizens and the US homeland itself' (p. 10).

However, understanding environmental problems as national security issues is not unproblematic. Daniel Deudney (1990) offers three reasons why linking environmental issues to national security is analytically misleading. First, he argues that military threats are different from environmental threats in that military threats are deliberately imposed and the cause of the threat is easily identifiable, whereas environmental threats are accidental and their causes are often uncertain. Second, Deudney argues that linking environmental issues to national security may not have the effect of mobilizing more attention and action on environmental problems, but, rather, it may serve to strengthen existing security logic and institutions. There are reasonable grounds to consider that this has been the case as Background 11.2 and the following section suggest. Deudney's third argument against environmental security is that environmental change is not likely to cause wars between countries (discussed in the previous section). So, while there is some basis for considering environmental problems as national security problems, the problem remains one of interpretation—of what constitutes national security, of who it is for, and of how it is to be achieved.

KEY POINTS

- Environmental change can put at risk the quality and quantity of resources available to a country.
- Environmental change can put at risk the economic strength of many countries.
- Environmental change poses risks to population health in many countries.
- Some environmental risks come from beyond a country's borders, and are unintentional.
- Linking environmental issues to security issues may not help solve environmental problems.

Armed forces and the environment

Linking environmental change with security inevitably means addressing the linkages between the most important of security institutions—the military—and the environment. It is when considering the role of militaries that some of the most profound contradictions with the concept of environmental security are raised. The goal of most militaries is to win wars, and so they train for and sometimes fight wars with devastating consequences for people and the environment. This contrasts considerably with the goals of the environmental movement to achieve sustainable development and peace.

Warfare almost always results in environmental degradation. The use of nuclear weapons in Japan, defoliants in Vietnam, depleted uranium ammunition in Kuwait and Kosovo, and the burning of oil wells in Kuwait, the destruction of crops in Eritrea, and the draining of marshes in south-eastern Iraq are all examples of the direct impacts of war on the natural environment. In most cases the consequences of these impacts last well beyond the end of fighting.

Warfare also has indirect—but in many ways more extensive—impacts on the environment. In many cases, spending on fighting is sustained by resource extraction, and in some cases it is resources that are the principal source of conflict. For example, timber in Cambodia and Burma, gems in Afghanistan, and diamonds in Sierra Leone have all been sources of income for armed groups. In these kinds of conflicts, control over and extraction of resources is of paramount concern and the environmental and social impacts of extraction are not considered. Violent conflict almost always involves denial of territory to opponents, sometimes with associated environmental impacts. Landmines are often used, and there are now over 100 million landmines lying in 90 countries denying access to land for productive purposes. Countries particularly affected include Angola, Afghanistan, Cambodia and Iraq.

War also affects economic development in ways that impact indirectly on the environment. Money spent on weapons, for example, is money that could have been spent on social and environmental activities. War deters foreign investment and aid, disrupts domestic markets, and often results in a decline in exports. It depletes and damages the labour force, creates a massive health burden, and destroys productive assets such as factories and communications and energy infrastructure. War often results in increased foreign debt, increased income inequality, reduced food production, and a reduction in GDP per capita. It also creates refugees and internally displaced people. There were 19.8 million people of concern to the UNHCR at the start of 2002, including 12 million official refugees. There are a further 25 million people who have been displaced but remain within their countries of origin.

These environmental, economic and social effects of war all negatively impact on people's access to the kinds of resources they need to develop themselves in ecologically sustainable ways. They also reduce the amount of economic resources available to governments and communities to implement environmental policies and programmes, restrict access to the kinds of technologies needed for sustainable economic growth, suppresses educational attainment and restrict the policy learning necessary for understanding and responding to environmental problems, damage the infrastructure needed to efficiently and equitably distribute resources such as water and electricity and food, and weaken the institutions and social cohesion necessary for a society to manage its environmental problems. So, armed forces wage war, and war is extremely bad for environmental security.

THINK POINT 11.3

The environmental impacts of armed forces

- In the 1980s the US military was the largest holder of agricultural land in the Philippines.
- The US nuclear weapons program was conducted in thirty-four states and covered 2.4 million acres of land; clean up costs are expected to be in the order of US$200–300 billion.
- Nuclear tests have been carried out at seven sites in the South Pacific, making four islands completely uninhabitable and causing above average cancer levels in residents of the Marshall Islands.
- The former Soviet Union dumped up to 17,000 containers of nuclear waste and up to 21 nuclear reactors into the Barents and Kara seas.
- The US military generates more toxins than the top five US chemical companies combined.
- In the United States there are 26 US military bases with significant toxic hazards; clean up costs are estimated to be over US$400 billion.
- Worldwide use of aluminium, copper, nickel, and platinum for military purposes exceeded the combined demand for these materials in all the developing countries.
- One quarter of all the world's jet fuel is consumed by military aircraft.
- The US military-industrial complex may be responsible for at least 10% of the United States' total CO_2 emissions, making it responsible for some 2–3% of total global emissions or more than all of Australia, Finland, Sweden and New Zealand combined.

Sources: Dycus 1996; Heininen 1994; Renner 1991; Seager 1993

As well as causing major environmental impacts in times of war, in times of peace militaries also cause environmental damage. They may indeed be the single largest institutional source of environmental degradation in the world (Think Point 11.3). This raises serious questions about the possibility of militaries having a positive role in environmental protection and recovery. Despite this, in the 1990s the United States Department of Defense (DOD) claimed it made a positive contribution to environmental security, through, for example supporting 'the military readiness of the US armed forces by ensuring continued access to the air, land and water needed for training and testing' and contributing to 'weapons systems that have improved performance, lower cost, and better environmental characteristics' (in Barnett 2001: 79). This and other responses by the United States suggests that Deudney's concern about environmental security (discussed in the previous section) has some truth: what the DOD is securing through these 'environmental security' measures is its own capacity to wage wars.

The idea that environmental change may be a cause of armed conflict also has implications for armed forces. If environmental change is likely to make for a more unstable international environment through environmentally induced wars, for example, then this suggests that armed forces are still required to help manage these negative effects. In this way arguments about the threats environmental change poses to security help to justify existing security institutions like the armed forces even though they may have significant environmental impacts.

KEY POINTS

- Armed forces have very different goals from the environmental movement.
- War causes environmental damage.
- War is harmful to sustainable development.
- Armed forces are major consumers of resources and major polluters.

Environmental change and human security

The concept of environmental security refers to a sector of security (the environment) rather than a referent object to be secured. Thus, it is possible to talk of the environmental security of the international system, of nation states, and, as explained in this section, of people (human security) (see also Chapter 6). The environment is one the seven sectors identified in the United Nations Development Program's (1994) early definition of human security (the others being economic, food, health, personal, community, and political security), and so for some time now environmental change has been identified as a human security issue.

Whereas the ways in which environmental change threatens the welfare of the international system and States are somewhat ambiguous and hypothetical, the ways in which it affects the welfare of individuals and communities is obvious. People are environmentally insecure in all sorts of ways, and for all sorts of reasons. Broadly speaking the determinants of environmental insecurity are: where people live and the nature of environmental changes in those places; how susceptible people are to damage caused by environmental changes; and people's capacity to adapt to environmental changes. For example, subsistence farmers in the mountains of East Timor rely almost exclusively on their own farm produce for food, they earn very little if any money (on average less than US$0.55 per day), their farms do not have irrigation, the soils they farm in are not very fertile and are eroding, infrastructure for storing and transporting food is not well developed, agricultural productivity is low, and rainfall is variable. So, in seasons where the rain fails, food production falls and farmers have no ability to supplement their diet with other food sources because they cannot afford to purchase food. As a result, hunger and malnutrition are widespread in East Timor in drought years, for example in 2003–4 110,000 people were in need of food aid. In this case, the environmental insecurity of Timorese farmers is a function of the physical properties of their environments—they live in steep mountainous areas with thin soils and variable rainfall, but also their dependence on farming as their only source of livelihood—if they had alternative sources of income they could afford to buy food. The capacity of East Timor's farmers to adapt to land degradation and water shortages is constrained by poverty—if they had more money they could afford to invest in irrigation systems, soil erosion control programmes, food storage systems, tractors, and fertilizers to increase production so that food would not be scarce during drought years. The causes of this environmental insecurity of Timorese farmers lie not so much in the environmental characteristics of where they live, but rather in the deep rural poverty caused by twenty-five years of occupation of East Timor by the Indonesian armed forces.

A comparison between Timorese farmers and Australian farmers underlies the ways in which human environmental insecurity is more socially created than naturally determined. Australian farmers live in similar environmental conditions (thin soils and variable climate), but they eat little if any of their own production which is instead sold to markets, irrigation is widely available, food transport and storage systems are modern and efficient, fertilizers and pesticides are easily afforded, high levels of government support are available, and there is a wide array of options for off-farm income. Therefore, when drought strikes Australia, farmers do not go hungry—at worst they lose some livestock and some income. For both Timorese and Australian farmers climate variability is likely to increase due to climate change, and while it will be difficult for Australian farmers to adapt to sustain their existing income levels, for Timorese farmers it may well be even more difficult for them to maintain enough food to keep their children healthy.

THINK POINT 11.4

Inequality and environmental insecurity

Inequalities in consumption

- The wealthiest 20% of people in the world:
  consume 45% of all meat and fish;
  consume 58% of all energy resources;
  consume 84% of all paper;
  own 87% of the world's vehicles.
- The poorest 20% of people in the world:
  consume 5% of all meat and fish;
  consume 4% of all energy resources;
  consume 1.1% of all paper;
  own less than 1% of the world's vehicles.

Inequalities in pollution

- The average person in a developed country causes as much pollution as 30 people in developing countries.
- The wealthiest 20% of people in the world produce 53% of all carbon dioxide emissions, the poorest 20% produce 3%.

Unequal insecurity

- Of the 4.4 billion people living in developing countries:
  60% do not have basic sanitation;
  30% do not have access to clean water.
- Every year poor quality water in developing countries results in 5 million deaths due to diarrhea—3 million of which are children.
- Air pollution causes:
  6,400 deaths/year in Mexico City;
  175,000 premature deaths/year in China.

Source: UNDP 1998

Environmental change therefore does not undermine human security in isolation from a broad range of social factors including poverty, the degree of support (or discrimination) communities receive from the state, the effectiveness of decision-making processes, and the extent of social cohesion within and surrounding vulnerable groups. These factors determine people and communities' capacity to adapt to environmental change so that the things that they value are not adversely affected. In terms of environmental change, for example, upstream users of water, distant atmospheric polluters, multinational logging and mining companies, regional-scale climatic processes, and a host of other distant actors and larger scale processes influence the security of individuals' use of natural resources and services. Similarly in terms of the social determinants of insecurity, larger scale processes such as warfare, corruption, trade dependency, and economic liberalization affect people's sensitivity to environmental changes and their capacity to adapt to them. Finally, past processes such as colonization and war shape present insecurities, and ongoing processes such as climate change and trade liberalization shape future insecurities.

Understanding human environmental insecurity therefore requires understanding the larger scale, past and present processes that create wealth in some places and poverty in others, and environmental change in some places and not in others. Think Point 11.4 describes some of the existing levels of inequality that generate environmental security for some people, and environmental insecurity for others. Therefore, even though the focus of human security is the individual, the processes that undermine or strengthen human security are often extra-local. Similarly, then, the solution to human environmental insecurity rests not just with local people, but also with larger scale institutions such as states, the international system, the private sector, civil society, and consumers in developed countries. In this respect, even an approach to environmental security that focuses on human security cannot avoid taking into account nation-states and their security policies.

KEY POINTS

- Environmental security is an important component of human security.
- Physical changes in the environment are only one aspect of people's environmental insecurity, other factors are the extent to which people rely on the environment for their welfare, and the ability of people to adapt to environmental changes.
- Not all people are equally environmentally insecure.
- People who are environmentally insecure are also often insecure in other ways.

Environment, or security?

Security is a power word. When a problem is identified as a security issue it can lead to state monopolization of solutions (see Chapter 7) (Waever 1995). Environmentalists have used environmental security to 'securitize' environmental problems—to make them matters of 'high' politics that warrant extraordinary responses from governments equal in magnitude and urgency to their response to more orthodox security threats. They have also used environmental security to highlight the opportunity costs of defence spending, and the environmental impacts of military activities, including war. This is the 'political rationale' of environmental security (Soroos 1994).

This securitising move has to some degree raised the profile of environmental issues among foreign and security policy makers and agencies so that there is a general recognition that environmental changes can in some sense be considered as security issues. These changes relate mostly to a broadening of the issue of security, but there has arguably been little real change in policy and action in terms of the referent object of environmental security. The focus of much of the research and writing on environmental security on environmental violence, on environmental threats to national security, and on greening the armed forces, suggests that it is the environmental security of the State that still matters most for the security policy community. Indeed, the concept of environmental security and its messages of impending danger may have helped security institutions to appropriate environmental issues in ways that help to maintain national security business as usual.

For the environmental and peace movement, therefore, environmental security has not lead to a trading off of military security for environmental security, or increased resources committed to solving environmental problems. Instead, environmental problems have been militarized; the emphasis has been placed on environmental change as cause of violent conflict rather than human insecurity; and on addressing environmental threats from other places as opposed to attending to domestic causes of environmental change. In this respect, much that is called 'environmental security' has had little to do with the environment, and much to do with security.

Arguments against involving armed forces in environmental issues also come from an orthodox national security perspective. The argument from mainstream security planners is that armed forces sacrifice operational readiness by being involved in non-traditional activities such as environmental protection.

Despite all these arguments, there are some good reasons for continuing to use the concept of environmental security. It has gained some purchase with development agencies as it helps to capture the environmental dimensions of social vulnerability. It better communicates the critical nature of environmental problems like climate change impacts on atoll countries, or the health impacts of water pollution, than standard concepts like sustainability or vulnerability. Environmental security can also serve as an integrative concept to link local (human security), national (national security) and global (international security) levels of environmental change and response. Further, in that it involves merging international relations with development studies and environmental studies, environmental security helps produce new fusions of knowledge and awareness. It offers a common language that facilitates the exchange of knowledge among people from diverse arms of government, civil society and academia across both the developed and developing worlds. Finally, environmental security still helps to contest the legitimacy of the dominant security paradigm by pointing to the contradiction between simple state-based and military approaches to national security, and the complex, multi-scale and transboundary nature of environmental flows.

KEY POINTS

- Environmental security has in some ways 'securitized' environmental problems.
- Environmental security has done little to solve environmental problems.
- Environmental security may have helped secure security.
- Environmental security helps create new coalitions of actors and interests.

Conclusion

Environmental security has been one of the key new security issues that helped to broaden the meaning of security in the post Cold-War period. It is the product of efforts by the environmental movement to raise the profile of environmental issues and contest the practices of national security, the increasing recognition that environmental problems demand common security approaches and the growth in multilateral environmental agreements, and the strategic vacuum created by the end of the Cold War. Therefore, despite some twenty years of prior thinking about the connections between the environment and security, it was not until the 1990s that the concept of environmental security came to prominence and featured regularly in academic journals, speeches by politicians and security bureaucrats, and in the work of environmental organizations.

There are many different interpretations of environmental security because there are many different approaches to security and an even broader range of approaches to environmental change. At two ends of the spectrum of views are those people who follow the orthodox national security paradigm who understand environmental security as being about the ways in which environmental change might be a cause of armed conflict between countries, and environmentalists who tend to see environmental security as being about the impacts of human activities—including military activities—on the environment. Somewhere in the middle ground are those who are concerned about the ways in which environmental change undermines human security.

The most influential interpretations of environmental security are those that fit well the orthodox security paradigm. In particular, arguments that environmental change may be a cause of violent conflict between and within countries, and suggest that environmental problems in other countries are threats to national security, have all largely been accepted by the security policy community and the armed forces—especially in the United States. So environmental security is still largely understood to be about threats to the nation-state rather than to the environment per se, to other states, or to individuals. This suggests that while environmental security may have broadened the meaning of security, it has been less successful in deepening it. This is not to say, though, that for some countries environmental change is not a major security problem, as the example of climate change and atoll countries shows.

The growing attention paid to environmental change as a human security issue does not fit so well with the Western security policy community. It does, however, have some appeal to the development policy community and to environmental groups and organizations. In the future it is likely that the concept of environmental security as human security will become more central in the fields of environmental studies and development studies, and figure more prominently in their respective policy domains. Research and policy will extend to include the impacts of environmental change on women and children, on livelihoods, and on human development. There may also be more research and policy development on institutions for cooperation on common environmental problems at a range of scales.

In the same way that environmental security did not gain much purchase with the security policy community during the Cold War, it has received far less attention since the 11 September 2001 attacks in the United States. This suggests that environmental security is a second-order security problem, which is only considered in times when more conventional dangers from armed aggression do not dominate national security concerns. The immediate future of the environment as a security issue may therefore be determined by the relevance of other security problems. However, in the longer term, environmental issues may well become paramount security concerns as the impacts of certain environmental problems seem set to increase, for example concentrations of greenhouse gases in the atmosphere are ever-increasing and so therefore will sea levels and the intensity of climatic hazards such as cyclones, floods and droughts; problems of nuclear waste have not been dealt with and the stockpile is still growing; and water demand is increasing but supply is relatively fixed. So, the relevance of environmental security will most probably increase until such time as truly common and cooperative approaches implement serious reforms to achieve forms of social organization that are ecologically sustainable. In this sense, current practices of national security are a significant barrier to achieving environmental security for all people.

QUESTIONS

Is environmental security about the impact of humans on the environment, or about the impact of environmental processes on things that people value?

What reasons explain why there has been so much effort devoted to finding connections between environmental change and violence?

What are the implications of calling environmental problems security issues?

Can armed forces enhance environmental security?

What kinds of environmental problems are national security issues? For what reasons?

What kinds of environmental problems are human security issues? For what reasons?

What causes someone to be environmentally insecure?

How is it that the securitization of environmental issues may have helped to secure security?

How could the human security and national security approaches to environmental security be reconciled?

What are the most appropriate policies to provide environmental security? Who should implement them?

FURTHER READING

- **Barnett, J. (2001), *The Meaning of Environmental Security: Ecological Politics and Policy in the New Security Era*, London: Zed Books.** A critical examination of different approaches to environmental security which promotes a human security approach.
- **Conka, K and Dabelko, G. (eds.) (2002), *Environmental Peacemaking*, Baltimore: John Hopkins University Press.** The first major book that focuses on cooperation over environmental problems.
- **Dalby, S. (2002), *Environmental Security*, Minneapolis: University of Minnesota Press.** A critical geopolitical perspective on environmental security which incorporates insights from environmental history and ecological theory.
- **Deudney, D. and Matthew, R. (eds.) (1999), *Contested Grounds: Security and Conflict in the New Environmental Politics*, Albany: State University of New York Press.** Brings together a wide range of approaches and perspectives on environmental security.
- **Diehl, P. and Gleditsch, N. (eds.) (2001), *Environmental Conflict*, Boulder, CO: Westview Press.** An extensive collection of largely quantitative studies of the causal relationships between population, environment, and conflict.
- **Elliott, L. (1998), *The Global Politics of the Environment*, London: Macmillan.** A comprehensive guide to global environmental politics and policies.
- **Homer-Dixon, T. (1999), *Environment, Scarcity, and Violence*, Princeton: Princeton University Press.** Summarizes the author's highly influential work on environmental scarcity and violence.
- **Peluso, N. and Watts, M. (eds.) (2001), *Violent Environments*, Ithaca, NY: Cornell University Press.** A collection of detailed field-based qualitative case studies of environmental disputes.
- **WCED (World Commission on Environment and Development) (1987), *Our Common Future*, Oxford: Oxford University Press.** A foundational report on the environment and common security.

IMPORTANT WEBSITES

- **http://www.wilsoncenter.org/ecsp** The Environmental Change and Security Program at the Woodrow Wilson International Center for Scholars is the pre-eminent centre for environmental security studies in the United States. The site contains a wealth of information including the influential *Environmental Change and Security Project Report*.
- **http://www.gechs.org** The Global Environmental Change and Human Security (GECHS) Project conducts policy-relevant research on environmental change and human security. This site contains some useful publications including policy briefings, and an extensive set of links to related sites.

- **http://www.unep.org** The United Nations Environment Programme provides leadership on environmental issues within the United Nations system. Among other things, this site contains information about global environmental issues, summits, and treaties.

Visit the Online Resource Centre that accompanies this book for lots of interesting additional material: www.oxfordtextbooks.co.uk/orc/collins/

12 Economic Security

CHRISTOPHER M. DENT

Chapter Contents

Reader's Guide

'Economic security' is an increasingly used phrase but also a relatively under-theorized concept in the political economy literature. This chapter examines how recent thinking on economic security has developed and presents a new conceptual approach to it. There are generally two largely separate discourses on economic security: micro-level analyses concentrate on 'localized' agents such as individuals, households and local communities, whereas macro-level economic security tends to focus on nation-states (or other entities capable of conducting a foreign economic policy) and their engagements in the international economic system. It is the latter discourse that this chapter is concerned with, and in this context the definition of economic security advanced here is *safeguarding the structural integrity and prosperity-generating capabilities and interests of a politico-economic entity in the context of various externalized risks and threats that confront it in the international economic system*. More specifically, it is contended that the pursuit of economic security essentially orientates foreign economic policy (FEP) objectives. The new conceptual framework presented here is centred on eight different 'objective typologies' of economic security, the exposition of which forms the main discursive function of this chapter.

Introduction

The increasing attention afforded to economic security can be primarily attributed to the broadening of security conceptualization after the end of Cold War. It hence joins other 'new' sectors that have more substantively extended the usual scope of security concerns beyond the traditional politico-military domain (Buzan 1991a; Romm 1993; Sorenson 1990; Walt 1991). Economic security remains a highly contested concept, not least because scholars have approached it from various disciplinary perspectives. Sociologists and anthropologists tend to adopt a micro-level approach. As I later argue, political scientists still working in the framework of traditional security studies have been more concerned with what I refer to as the economics-security nexus rather than economic security per se. The new conceptual framework offered here is international political economic in perspective, and thus does not claim disciplinary universalism. However, the very multidisciplinary nature of international political economy (IPE) makes it a useful approach to take by its ability to connect and synthesize different disciplinary insights into a holistic framework of analysis.

In general terms economic security analysis may be divided into two narratives, or what can be called a dyadic narrative. On the one hand, *micro-level* economic security concentrates on 'localized' agents such as individuals, households and local communities, and is primarily concerned with safeguarding their livelihoods (Liew 2000; Zalewski 2005). In developing country studies this often concentrates on food security issues. On the other hand, *macro-level* economic security generally deals with FEP powers (e.g. nation-states) and their engagement in the international economic system. Notwithstanding the broadening of the domestic-international interface in an era of globalization, these two discourses have remained largely separate in the academic literature. Yet there are of course overlaps between them, for example when FEP powers persist in agricultural protectionism in order to safeguard the livelihood of their rural communities, e.g. Japan, the EU. Thus, state authorities have economic security duties to fulfil at both the micro and macro levels. Furthermore, multi-level analysis that considers the economic security predicaments of both micro-level and macro-level agents are sometimes, but not frequently, presented (Draguhn and Ash 1999; Liew 2000). However, most economic security analyses can be distinguished as either predominantly domestic (i.e. micro-level) or international (i.e. macro-level) in their point of departure, and it is the latter level of analysis that is the focus of this chapter.

Contemporary thinking on economic security

Post-Cold War ascendancy

The recent growth in interest in macro-level economic security is very much a product of the post-Cold War period. Hence, it derives from the respective shifts from geo-politics to geo-economics, from military superpowers to economic superpowers, and hence from politico-ideological competition to economic competition. As Stremlau (1994) observed in the early 1990s, 'we are entering an era when foreign policy and national security will increasingly revolve around our commercial interests, and when economic diplomacy will be essential to resolving the great issues of our age' (p. 18). Early post-Cold War analyses on the subject considered the emerging (geo)economic foundations of future security systems (Sandholtz et al 1992). During this time, the focus was very much on how the old bipolar geopolitics had given way to a new tripolar world structure of economic superpowers (the US, EU and Japan), and intense debate surrounded which of these 'triadic' powers or regions would emerge pre-eminent in the twenty-first century (Albert 1993, Hart 1992, Thurow 1992). Thus, economic security analysis was then largely fixated on geoeconomic competition, and endeavours to consolidate regional integration (e.g. the Single European Market, NAFTA) were broadly aligned to this. A more co-operative approach between the triadic powers emerged, however, by the mid-1990s, with the US and East Asian states drawing closer together within the Asia-Pacific Economic Co-operation (APEC) forum, the EU and US signing the New Transatlantic Agenda in 1995, and the EU and East Asia initiating the Asia-Europe Meeting (ASEM) dialogue framework in 1996 (Dent 2001).

The policy shift toward a more cogent economic security approach was particularly conspicuous in the US (Shirk and Twomey 1996). Economic security became a key issue in discussions within both the National Security Council (NSC) and Council on Foreign Relations (CFR) from the early 1990s. In January 1993, US President Bill Clinton expanded the NSC's membership to include, among others, the Treasury Secretary and the newly created office of Assistant to the President for Economic Policy, thus acknowledging the greater role of economic issues in the formulation of national security policy. Moreover, shared staffing between the NSC and the newly created National Economic Council was intended to bring greater security policy coherence on these issues. Later on in May 1997, a second term report from the Clinton Administration entitled 'A National Security Strategy for a New Century' placed 'to bolster America's economic prosperity' as one of three core objectives, the others being 'to enhance our security with effective diplomacy and with military forces' and 'to promote democracy abroad'. In these new policy developments, Clinton went beyond previous efforts to operationally integrate US economic policy with national security (DeSouza 2000). Similar shifts to economic security thinking were visible in the perceptions and actions of many other foreign policy elites. The 11 September 2001 terrorist attacks on the US further enhanced comprehensive security thinking amongst security policy circles, incorporating economic security considerations more closely into the strategic calculus. The targets chosen by the terrorists was in itself very significant by intending to cause simultaneous chaos in the US security domain by attacking the Pentagon, and in the economic domain by attacking the World Trade Center, the very totem of American corporate and financial power. The choice of a high profile 'economic' target was important insofar that the al-Qaeda terrorists sought to extend the target spectrum beyond politico-military sites, e.g. embassies, naval vessels.

The economics-security nexus

Social science studies on the connections between economics and politico-military security have been made for some time. According to Mastanduno (1998), these date back to the 1930s and 1940s when Jacob Viner, E.H. Carr, Albert Hirschman and Edward Mead Earle were the first prominent academics to take an interest in the economics-security nexus. However, the subject was surprisingly neglected in the early post-war period despite being a particularly strong feature of US foreign policy (Leitzel 1993, Mastanduno 1998). It took the global shocks of the 1970s and the emergence of IPE as an academic discipline to essentially change this (Knorr and Trager 1977, Friedberg 1991). Yet, the economics-security nexus can be and should be differentiated from that of economic security itself. Technical aspects of the former generally include the:

- *economics of military security (or military security economics)*: these concern allocative, productive, techno-industrial, infrastructural and cost-price aspects of resourcing military security capabilities;

- *subordination of economic policies to security policy interests*: involving the use of FEP measures to support wider foreign policy objectives, or 'low politics' directly serving the needs of 'high politics';
- *subordination of security policies to economic interests*: at a general level, this could relate to making the world safe for the expansion of capitalist activities with this typically attributed to a hegemonic state's duties.

It is admittedly often difficult to establish whether a certain policy action was specifically driven by economic and politico-military security objectives when the intention was to realize both, as recently witnessed in both the US's and EU's generally positive approach to China's WTO accession. Furthermore, the view that both economic policy and traditional security policy measures can be used to affect similar intended outcomes is linked to the fungibility of power argument, which contends that threats on the economic front (e.g. sanctions) can achieve security aims, and vice versa. Such actions establish credible links between action in one domain and a goal in the other (Shirk and Twomey 1996). However, the continued preoccupation with this linkage in the mainstream literature may have been at the expense of developing more cogent ideas about what specifically constitutes the pursuit of economic security in the international system.

This problematical and somewhat unrefined (and even sometimes confused) relationship between the economics-security nexus and economic security dates back some time. Knorr's (1977) contribution to the early economic security debate was indicative of the rather negative terms in which many Cold War period scholars thought about economic security. According to him, the manifestation of economic security policies becomes most apparent when a country 'consciously chooses to accept economic inefficiency to avoid becoming more vulnerable to economic impulses from abroad or when a country stresses national approaches at the expense of international integration' (p. 14). This suggested that high opportunity costs were incurred in making economic security choices: in other words, there were clear trade-offs between pursuing economic security objectives and more 'welfare-rational' economic policy objectives. For example, US Government embargoes on a wide range of US exports to the Soviet Union denied American firms access to this foreign market, thus leading to an under-exploitation of their competitive advantage in a number of industries (e.g. information technology) and the subsequent under-optimization of production and resource efficiencies, leading to net welfare losses. This is because American firms like IBM could have gained greater scale economy cost reductions through expanded export production targeted at the Soviet Union market that generated these efficiencies.

The legacy of this Cold War thinking strongly persists today in that many scholars still equate economic security with aspects of the economic-security nexus, or remain strongly preoccupied with the economic-security nexus rather than advancing theories on economic security itself (Shirk and Twomey 1996; Soeya 1997; Sperling *et al.* 1998). For instance, Harris and Mack (1997) perceived East Asia's 'economic security dilemma' thus: the region's increased wealth has fostered both security-enhancing democratic institutions and interdependence, while also providing the resources to build up military capabilities in potentially destabilizing ways. While such observations on the economics-security nexus may be valid and important, they achieve relatively little in advancing the conceptual analysis of economic security. It is further accepted that the traditional politico-military security sector can impact upon the economic security sector and vice versa, but it is argued here that greater endeavours need to be made to establish the more specific empirical domain of the latter (i.e. area or areas of evidence from the real world from which we may establish the subject study of 'economic security').

Defining the empirical domain and concepts of economic security

Distinguishing the empirical domain of economic security from the economics-security nexus can be problematic, as recognized by a number of scholars. Buzan *et al.* (1998) ask whether the pursuit of economic security merely represents the securitization of economic issues, and furthermore are scholars simply wishing to define it by their attempts to distinguish between politicized economics and security spillovers from the economic sector into others. They conclude that the question of economic security concerns the relationship between the political structure of anarchy and the economic structure of the market, and avoid merging security and economy into a single analytical construct.

At the fundamental level, security relates to guarding or guaranteeing the safety of some entity from extant dangers. Determining the economic security of *what* and of *who* connects with our prior discussion over micro-level and macro-level economic security. In this context, we must consider the relationship between a FEP power's physical economic functions and capacities (e.g. infrastructural, techno-industrial) on the one hand, and the interests of its associated economic agents (which may be extra-territorial, or transnationalized such as multinational enterprises or migrant workforces) on the other. Hence, this raises the old problem of differentiating agent from structure given their mutually constitutive links. For instance, an agent's (e.g. a firm's) corporate interests may form a critical part of the economy's export capacity (a structural aspect), and this agent may represent a substantial proportion of the FEP power's broader economic structure, e.g. Samsung in South Korea's case. Our discussion on micro-level and macro-level economic security has already acknowledged the connections between localized agents and FEP powers pursuing economic security in the international system with the former's interests in mind. It was also previously implied that FEP protagonists (see Key Ideas 12.1 for terms of reference) are charged with identifying and realizing the economic security interests of the economic agents deemed to constitute the FEP power, on both an individual (e.g. a firm lobbying the government on a specific market access issue) and collective basis. In this sense, the economic security of both agent and structure in the international system are combined, as will be illustrated further in the exposition of the new conceptual framework later on. This framework is also founded on the notion that establishing more definitive economic security objectives helps better identify economic security motivations behind foreign (economic) policy actions, thus further defining the empirical domain of economic security.

In pursuing their economic security interests, FEP powers must respond to the changing structural configurations of the international political economy and exploiting the opportunities and minimize the risks or threats these create (Leech 1993). Most economic security scholars have focused on the latter but some have adopted a more multi-dimensional approach: as DeSouza (2000) comments, 'security is not only about preventing certain threatening actions, it is about creating opportunities and a preferred set of circumstances for American interests and mutual gain' (p. 37). In a similar vein, Lubbe (1997) perceived economic security as being determined by two key factors, these being: *economic capability*, concerning the ability of FEP protagonists to execute economic and political tasks that delineate the national interest but also help minimize its vulnerability to external pressures and disruptions; and *external environmental*, where large, powerful states that exercise significant structural power can shape the external environment in which economic security objectives are pursued.

Various approaches to defining economic security have been made. From a hegemon-centric perspective that continues to typify much of the FEP literature, Neu and Wolf (1994) contend that economic security is the 'ability to protect or to advance US economic interests in the face of events, developments, or actions that may threaten or block these interests' (p. xi), and that these may derive from domestic or foreign sources. Some scholars adopt a 'multiple aspect' approach to defining economic security. For example, Cable (1995) first contends that it can refer 'most obviously to those aspects of trade and investment which directly affect a country's ability to defend itself' (p. 306). Second, it can be defined 'in terms of economic policy instruments which are used for purposes of aggression (or defence)' (p. 307), citing sanctions and embargoes as examples. Third, according to Cable, it is based on 'the idea that relative military capacity, or projection of power, may be undermined by relatively poor economic performance and requires an economic policy response' (ibid). These last two definitional approaches suffer from an entwinement with the economics-security nexus, and are therefore not that helpful. In Cable's fourth approach, he contends that there exists 'an even looser concept of economic security which captures the fear of global economic, social and ecological instability' (ibid), thus connecting with the issue of security sector overlap. Sperling and Kirchner's (1997) own multiple aspect approach examines: (1) the concerns of the state to protect the social and economic fabric of society; (2) the ability of the state to act as an effective gatekeeper and to maintain societal integrity; (3) the state's ability in cooperation with others to safeguard the international economic environment from destabilization in order to reinforce military capabilities.

Somewhat generalized and uni-dimensional definitions of economic security are offered by Green (1996)—'the absence of threat of severe deprivation of economic welfare' (p. 22), Wang (1998)— 'the concern about economic security is the state of mind that is constantly worrying about falling under the danger line' (p. 22), and by Thakur (2000)—'the maintenance of given levels of welfare and state power through access to resources, finance, and markets' (p. 230). In general, then, most economic security analyses are premised on the pursuit of 'power and plenty' objectives in a foreign economic policy context, and thus establishes some common ground between neo-liberal and neo-realist views on economic security's empirical domain. As Katzenstein (1976) noted, prosperity (i.e. 'plenty') represents a neo-liberal core concept, while the prime concern of neo-realists is the exercise and interplay of economic power in the international system. Moreover, although radicalist thinkers question the conventional materialist notions of prosperity, they would not necessarily deny the importance of pursuing some alternative interpretation of it, such as sustainable development.

KEY POINTS

- The growing interest in economic security analysis should be understood in a post-Cold War context, centring on the respective shifts from geo-politics to geo-economics, from military superpowers to economic superpowers, and hence from politico-ideological competition to economic competition.
- Linkages between economic policy and traditional or politico-military security policy—the economics-security nexus—have always existed but have become increasingly entwined.
- Despite this closer inter-linkage, the study of the economics-security nexus and economic security are not the same and one often gets confused with the other in the academic literature. Furthermore, many studies of 'economic security' do not explain what is meant by the term.
- In general most economic security analyses are premised on the pursuit of 'power and plenty' and this establishes some common ground between neo-liberal and neo-realist views of economic security.

A new conceptual approach to economic security

Introduction

The pursuit of economic security broadly defines FEP objectives. The conduct of FEP itself can be said to fall into two domains (Dent 2002). The first of these can be referred to as *technical policy realms*, which themselves can be sub-categorized into a *core* element (trade, FDI, international finance, and foreign aid policies) and an *associative* element (e.g. industry policy), whereby the former possesses a more overt and cognitive international focus while the latter is subordinately allied to the former in some functionally supportive, often competitiveness-enhancing manner. The second domain is *economic diplomacy*, which broadly concerns the means and parameters within which trade, investment and other international economic relations are conducted between representative agents of different FEP powers. Economic diplomacy can be generally viewed from different levels of engagement, modalities, exercises of power, and bargaining processes.

Furthermore, our model of FEP analysis incorporates three 'orienting' interactive dimensions: (1) *cognitive-ideological approaches* relate to key ideological 'nodes' of thought (e.g. liberalism, neo-mercantilism), value-system traditions, the accommodation of economic culture and other ideational or value-based factors that shape the thinking behind FEP formation; (2) *contesting 'actor-based' influences* examine how different domestic (e.g. trade unions, industrial associations), international (e.g. foreign governments, international economic organizations) and transnational actors (e.g. TNCs, transnational civil society) seek to affect FEP formation; (3) the third concerns the conceptual framework of *'generic' economic security objectives* itself, which is outlined in the latter half of this article. Thus the pursuit of economic security forms just one (but nevertheless central) aspect of FEP formation. Key terms of reference used in our analysis can be found in Key Ideas 12.1.

KEY IDEAS 12.1

Key terms of reference

Key terms of reference used throughout this analysis are as follows. *FEP formation* is a general term for the structure, conduct and process of foreign economic policy. *FEP protagonists* relate to actors that are responsible for the directing (political or quasi-political leadership) or managing (bureaucratic leadership) of foreign economic policy. These normally relate to central government representatives but can also include those from sub-state units (e.g. local government), supranational or inter-governmental units such as the EU, and even, in some cases, representatives drawn from business or civil society. *FEP powers* refer to the polities that these protagonists represent. These are typically nation-states or some other state-form and can include sub-state units (e.g. states within a federated union such as the US), supranational or inter-governmental units (e.g. the EU), city-states (e.g. Singapore) or quasi-states (e.g. Taiwan). Lastly, *stakeholding FEP constituencies* relate to any groups with a direct interest in, or even leverage over FEP formation. These can include FEP protagonists themselves, as well as representations from business, civil society and institutional communities.

Establishing a definition of economic security

The new conceptual approach to economic security advanced here is founded on a definition that emphasizes a threat-minimizing and opportunity-maximizing take on economic security, the pursuit of which involves *safeguarding the structural integrity and prosperity-generating capabilities and interests of a politico-economic entity in the context of various externalized risks and threats that confront it in the international economic system*. Here, '*politico-economic entity*' broadly equates with an FEP power with respect to its own territorial economy and extra-territorial (e.g. transborder or transnational) economic interests. Hence, FEP protagonists may work to safeguard the transnational commercial interests of its home-based or hosted foreign multinational enterprises (MNEs). Thus, FEP powers are focused on different forms of transnational economic space. This may be relatively localized and comparatively distant, for example where the global connections of 'home-based' firms are extensive. Moreover, FEP powers may work with others to safeguard the security of their transnational economic space through regional and multilateral modes of co-operation, e.g. the EU and WTO.

The '*structural integrity*' aspect of the definition relates essentially to maintaining the internal construction of the economy during its interactions in the global economy, and its ability to meet the basic demands of economic agents located therein. Where meaningfully applied, this can be linked to proximate notions of the economy's survival in the international system and thus the prevention of its structural collapse—a rare event in absolute total terms although this depends on your interpretation of 'structural collapse'. Some appear in a new politico-geographically defined form, e.g. East Germany. Structural integrity is therefore an essential economic security objective. The '*prosperity-generating capabilities and interests*' aspect broadens the conventional boundaries of the economic security concept beyond its usual attention to minimizing direct and immediate economic vulnerabilities. Safeguarding prosperity-generating capabilities and interests works towards this objective anyway through reducing the future scope for economic security risks, vulnerabilities and threats, constituting a sort of 'insurance policy' or 'preventative medicinal' approach. The development and safeguarding of the prosperity-generating capabilities and interests may concern 'technical' (e.g. trade-industry policies) or 'relational' (e.g. economic diplomacy) aspects. Moreover, these can too be linked to welfare maximization—both localized and global—and the externalization of FEP interests, such as championing the interests of home MNEs in their operations abroad.

In comparing these last two aspects of the base definition, safeguarding the 'structural integrity' of the FEP power is more defensive in connotative action, whereas safeguarding 'prosperity-generating capabilities and interests' relates more to promotive or enhancing actions. As such, 'safeguarding' in this latter context involves proactive measures for advancing the FEP power's economic security interests. Instances include foreign economic policies that cultivate certain prosperity-generating functions within the economy, such as the development of strategic export production capabilities, e.g. semiconductors in the IT sector. Strengthening economic diplomacy ties with other FEP powers may also foster trade, foreign investment or finance-related linkages that serve similar economic security objectives.

The objective typologies of economic security

The objective typologies of economic security presented here further develop both the concept and definable pursuits of economic security, as well as the contention that it provides a suitable focal lens for FEP analysis. These typologies may be considered facets of the same analytical lens, which refract in different ways in accordance to various factors such as issue-linkage, interdependence variables, fungibility of power, etc. The objectives of FEP are naturally difficult to compartmentalize, made more so by their differential modalities, e.g. tactical, strategic. However, attempts at classification are viable if a *generic* rather than *specific* approach to classifying different types of FEP objectives are considered. This new framework of economic security analysis is based on eight different typologies.

Supply security

In basic terms, this concerns the securing of key supply chains involving foreign sources. It therefore relates particularly to the various structures of supply through which an FEP power acquires foreign materials, components and technologies, and exercises of economic diplomacy may be necessary to maintain the integrity of these structures. These structures in turn ultimately serve the supply base of the economy, which itself may be thought of in infrastructural terms from the perspective of economic agents (i.e. individuals, firms) who stand to gain external economies of scale and scope from an enhanced supply-base. Thus, supply security can affect the ability of producers to remain or improve their competitiveness, to access key materials and technologies, and help retain the economy's general prosperity-generating capabilities and interests.

In a globalizing world economy, supply diversification (rather than self-dependence) plays an important element of a vulnerability management strategy of economic security, especially in specific circumstances or a general environment marked by closed, costly or unpredictable access. This tends to be the case when foreign FEP powers or firms impose certain supply restrictions, or where oligopolistic-monopolistic concentration exists in the international markets. Both situations can create quantitative and cost uncertainties for 'supplied' FEP powers and producers therein, compromising their ability to respond effectively to changes in international competitive conditions. Foreign economic policy measures—both 'policy-technical' (e.g. trade policy) and economic diplomacy actions—are utilized to address such economic security predicaments. For example, US aid is currently used to develop the oil exporting capacities of ex-Soviet Union republics as a means to diversify America's dependence on Middle East sources.

Market access security

This broadly concerns the FEP power's securing of the best access possible to key foreign markets. This is particularly crucial for export-oriented economies with small domestic markets, although this has become a prime economic diplomacy objective of all FEP powers. Exploiting foreign market potential has long been perceived as a means to generate prosperity for the exporting country, essentially through the foreign 'earnings' procured by export sales. It is also increasingly linked to the 'structural integrity' dimension of economic security by foreign market access helping facilitate domestic techno-industrial restructuring by providing outlets for extra-nationally produced goods from relevant industrial sectors. For example, the development of ascendant sectors, such as biotechnology, often depends on attaining minimum efficiency scale levels of production, and domestic demand alone may be insufficient to help reach this position. Likewise, alleviating the economic and social hardships associated with the structural decline of 'sensitive' industries in western economies, such as steel, may be achieved by improved foreign market demand for these products.

Large economies, like the US and Japan, tend to enjoy the benefit of domestic market self-sufficiency, and therefore one could argue they are not so concerned with market access security. Of course, it is more complicated than that. The US, for instance, is compelled to seek improved market access owing to its persistent trade deficit predicament: exports must help pay for its burgeoning import bill. Japan's aggressive export policies and practices, and its huge trade surpluses, can be primarily attributed to the state's lingering neo-mercantilist ideology and the global market strategies of Japanese MNEs. Furthermore, foreign market competition has intensified for all firms and has thus become a prominent FEP issue. This is largely because globalizing processes have made markets more porous from both the domestic and foreign perspective. Domestic market-oriented firms now face greater competition from foreign rivals, and thus must look to foreign markets themselves to compensate. Similarly, firms now compete more with others outside their respective domestic markets than before. Thus, European and Asian firms compete more vigorously for US market share and across a wider range of product sectors.

Finance-credit security

This entails ensuring insofar as possible the financial solvency of the FEP power in the international system, as well as its maintenance of access to, or influence or control over sources of international credit. In recent times, this has become an acute economic security concern of developing countries in the context of Third World debt and other countries that have lately required significant IMF assistance, e.g. South Korea and Argentina. The pursuit of finance-credit security is perhaps the most problematic of all economic security typologies. Developments in financial globalization have made at least national-level attempts to maintain finance-credit security in the international system an extremely complex and difficult task (Kahler 2004). The risk of exchange rate volatility has increased for many FEP powers over recent years, owing primarily to the ever larger and unpredictable international currency transactions that occur daily in global money markets.

The role of increasingly powerful currency speculators has been at the centre of most financial crises over the last decade or so, most notably during the EU exchange rate mechanism crisis of 1992/93 and the East Asian financial crisis of 1997/98. Indeed, cooperative acts between FEP powers have come to increasingly characterize their pursuit of finance-credit security objectives. Connections here may be made to the complex interdependence of financial globalization, and how therefore deepening connectivity between different national and regional financial systems presents the imperative for greater cooperation on matters of international finance. Thus, finance-credit security interests are closely aligned to those of systemic security and alliance security. Those FEP powers with very large foreign exchange reserves (e.g. Japan, China, Taiwan) have tended, though, to rely on these resources as the basis for pursuing an independent finance-credit security policy. However, there are very few that are conceivably able to attain this position given the financial reserves available to foreign currency speculators, as Hong Kong (the world's sixth largest forex retainer) found out during its efforts to maintain exchange rate stability through market interventions at the time of the East Asian financial crisis (see Case Study 12.1).

Techno-industrial capability security

Developing the ability of the economy to generate prosperity, productivity and other welfare-creating factors through techno-industrial means involves maintaining the economy's position as close as possible to the technological frontier. This may derive from indigenous or foreign sources, and relate to issues of access and acquisition of foreign technology. These capabilities may be deployed to meet specific foreign economic policy objectives (e.g. export competitiveness, attracting high-tech foreign investment, improving the FEP power's relative techno-industrial position in the international economic system, etc.); conversely, certain FEP actions (e.g. trade-industry policy, economic diplomacy) may be used to assist the development of techno-industrial capabilities. Moreover, there is a strong 'strategic' association with the improvement of an FEP power's techno-industrial capabilities. Green (1996) defines a strategic industry as one that 'is essential to the economic and national security interests of the state and one that engages in an activity that affects the national economy with critical forward and backward linkages through the existence of positive externalities' (p. 31). As such, certain forms of strategic industrial activity perform key 'structural integrity' functions through the roles they play via upstream and downstream linkages. This can be seen by the importance of steel production in manufactured products, and information technology as a critical process in service provision. In addition, the underlying technology of strategic industries often provides the foundation for productivity growth, and thus the potential for advancing the FEP power's prosperity-generating capacities and interests. This is particularly found in higher-tech industrial activity by its ability to add value and positively transform both the structural and prosperity-linked prospects of the FEP power.

'Higher-tech' industry itself is, of course, a relative term depending on whereabouts on the techno-industrial ladder FEP powers are generally positioned, but all have an interest in promoting strategic industry development. High-tech industry

CASE STUDY 12.1

The 1997/98 East Asian financial crisis

The 1997/98 financial crisis made a profound impact on East Asia, bringing about significant political and economic change to many countries in the region. The crisis also clearly demonstrated the power and influence of financial speculators in the international economic system, and the general risks associated with 'ungoverned' financial globalization. The 1997/98 crisis caused much soul-searching within the IMF, not least because only in 1996 had it praised Thailand for recent reforms it had made in its financial policies. Attempts at future crisis aversion at the regional level have centred on ASEAN Plus Three (APT) frameworks of cooperation between the Association of Southeast Asian Nations (ASEAN) and the Northeast Asian states of Japan, China and South Korea. Both the Chiang Mai Initiative of bilateral currency swap agreements between APT member states (16 agreements concluded by 2005 totalling $40 billion) and the Asian Bond Market Initiative (devised to foster longer-term regional financial governance development) may be understood as regional economic security endeavours that seek to better manage the growing financial and economic interdependence between East Asian states. In addition, the crisis further revealed how finance-credit security depends not just on financial resources or inter-state cooperation but also on smart approaches to international financial policy. Leading up to the crisis, most if not all of the region's governments had embarked on programmes of financial liberalization from the late 1980s and early 1990s onwards. However, in many instances this was implemented within a weak institutional framework. In other words, financial markets were liberalized but without a proper institutionalization of market order. For example, firms were now free to borrow large sums from foreign banks and other financial institutions but these were not closely monitored or supervised by the government authorities. Consequently, the huge foreign debts run up by firms significantly compromised the finance-credit security interests of these East Asian states. It was no surprise, therefore, that those that had developed smart regulatory and institutional capacities in their international finance policies, such as Taiwan and Singapore, came through the regional crisis contagion relatively unscathed. While, then, financial liberalization may serve the finance-credit security interests of FEP powers by improving access to sources of foreign credit, smart regulatory approaches to international financial policy per se are equally, if not more important.

competition and cooperation between developed FEP powers has been well documented. For developing FEP powers, strategic industry or trade policies may be vindicated in economic welfare terms in that developing countries are promoting the development of infant industries, which eventually intensifies international competition in a positive, global welfare-enhancing manner in the future (Krugman 1986). Furthermore, WTO rules still permit developing countries to subsidize new industries where necessary and to ensure that subsidies are result-oriented through the imposition of performance standards (Amsden and Hikino 2000).

Socio-economic paradigm security

This concerns the 'defence' of a society's preferred socio-economic paradigm (e.g. East Asian developmental statist, European social market, Anglo-Saxon market liberal, and Middle Eastern socio-religious forms of 'economic model') and its welfare goals where defined. It often entails the resistance of foreign pressure to adapt to new international norms that are associated with a counter-paradigm. For those FEP powers with a strong statist tradition, as found in East Asia, this may relate to various levels of resistance (e.g. societal, state bureaucratic) to neo-liberalism. In addition, certain states may deem it a critical objective of their foreign economic policy to defend their socio-economic paradigm against others perceived to directly threatening it. Taiwan's FEP in relation to China may be seen thus, although socio-economic paradigm security should not be equated with the defence of sovereignty rights. This economic security typology also involves maintaining the integrity of the socio-economic paradigm and the prosperity-generating capabilities and interests that may be associated with it. The latter entails issues of prosperity distribution (e.g. growth with equity) and prosperity-generating method (e.g. free markets or guided markets?). In addition, socio-economic paradigms evolve over time in their adaptation to changing domestic and international conditions. However, certain paradigmatic fundamentals (e.g. underlying ideologies and cultural values; embedded institutional and relational frameworks) may remain largely unchanged. For instance, the ideals of liberty and individualism are intrinsic to neo-liberalism, just as the importance of institutionalized state-society relations are to developmental statism.

We may see the concept of 'socio-economic paradigm' as interchangeable with parallel concepts of 'economic system', 'capitalist culture', or 'socio-business order'. The international system is characterized by balances of convergence and competition between the different socio-economic paradigms of FEP powers, or groups of FEP powers. In a generalized example, many currently subscribe to the view that Anglo-Saxon 'market liberal' capitalism has proved itself superior not just to communism but also other capitalist paradigms. They point to evidence from the 1990s, where resurgent US, UK and Australian economies clearly outperformed their continental European and East Asian capitalist counterparts. Their reasoning was premised on the argument that in an era of globalization, those economies that had liberalized and deregulated were best positioned to exploit opportunities arising in an increasingly barrierless world economy and its emergent transnational economic spaces. The extent to which such neo-liberal convergence between different capitalist systems has occurred is highly debatable, and the US's economic troubles in the early 2000s offers scope for revisionist analysis on the above argument.

Transborder community security

This involves the addressing of local regionalized concerns that may either precipitate transborder economic crises or concern localized interdependence issues, e.g. sub-regional economic integration projects. These often centre on transborder spillovers or externalities that require market failure correction policies, and hence the management of a shared transborder economic space. They may thus also focus on issues from other security sectors such as pollution, drug trafficking and economic migration (Kulkarni 1995, Mathews 1989). The development of transborder communities may therefore emerge out of the need to tackle common economic security challenges. The geographic scale of these communities tends to range from sub-national locales (e.g. provinces) contiguous to those from neighbouring countries to wider regional collectives involving a group of nation-states. Moreover, it is generally the case that relatively small FEP powers that are surrounded by a large number of others are more susceptible to transborder community security issues. It will often be the case that the structural integrity and development of participating FEP powers' economies are in some way closely connected, or that potential future changes in one can have a profound impact on another. This may be particularly applicable to those states with larger neighbours (such as Canada and the US, Ireland and the UK, Taiwan and China) and may therefore entail dependency relationships.

Drawing upon an example from East Asia, Singapore's 'growth triangle' relationship with the Malaysian province of Johor to the north and Indonesia's province of Riau to the south and west is essentially driven by the imperatives of the city-state's own techno-industrial restructuring (see Case Study 12.2). Other kinds of sub-regional projects that seek to develop or manage transborder economic spaces are evident around the world, and in contrast may be founded on pre-existing transnational business networks or common natural resource management, e.g. international river zones. Addressing both the interdependence opportunities and threats associated with transborder community security issues are hence linked to safeguarding an FEP power's prosperity-generating capabilities and interests in a number of ways. Issues arising from other new security sectors, such as transborder immigration and pollution, are accepted to have a potentially profound impact upon these capabilities and interests. In the early 1990s, Sweden provided funds to Poland that were designed to minimize the latter's 'export' of acid rain, which was decimating parts of Sweden's agriculture industry as well as incurring substantial clean-up costs. This provides an example of how the pursuit of transborder community security objectives often connects foreign economic policy with 'new sector' foreign policy domains, in this specific case with foreign environmental policy. Mitigating adverse transborder spillover effects may involve different economic diplomacy responses, ranging from defensive unilateral measures (e.g. strict immigration regulations) to acts of cooperative bilateralism, to the development of plurilateral or multilateral frameworks in which comparatively broad transborder community security challenges may be mutually confronted. With respect to the 'interdependence opportunities' dimension, different FEP powers can exploit these through cultivating effective transborder divisions of labour (see Case Study 12.2) or by rational and equitable approaches to sharing common transborder resources. Overall, the more localized nature of transborder community security issues differentiate them from those related to the maintenance of systemic security, which tend to be more global in nature.

Systemic security

This concerns the common interests of FEP powers in upholding the integrity of the international

CASE STUDY 12.2

The Indonesia–Malaysia–Singapore Growth Triangle (IMSGT)

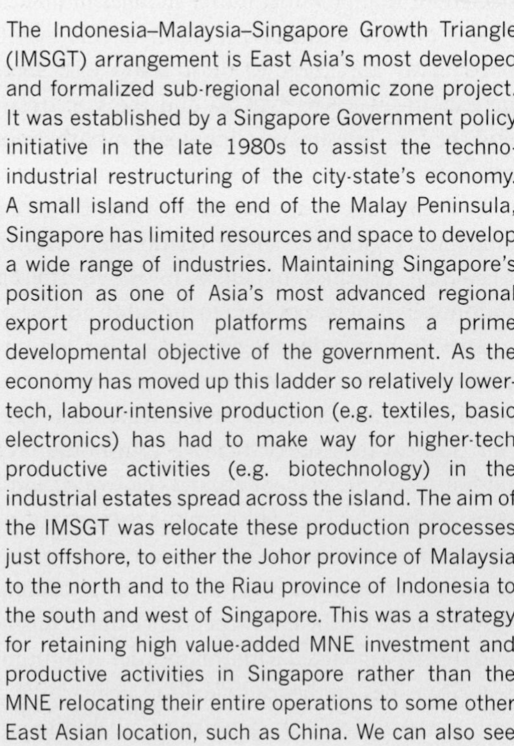

The Indonesia–Malaysia–Singapore Growth Triangle (IMSGT) arrangement is East Asia's most developed and formalized sub-regional economic zone project. It was established by a Singapore Government policy initiative in the late 1980s to assist the techno-industrial restructuring of the city-state's economy. A small island off the end of the Malay Peninsula, Singapore has limited resources and space to develop a wide range of industries. Maintaining Singapore's position as one of Asia's most advanced regional export production platforms remains a prime developmental objective of the government. As the economy has moved up this ladder so relatively lower-tech, labour-intensive production (e.g. textiles, basic electronics) has had to make way for higher-tech productive activities (e.g. biotechnology) in the industrial estates spread across the island. The aim of the IMSGT was relocate these production processes just offshore, to either the Johor province of Malaysia to the north and to the Riau province of Indonesia to the south and west of Singapore. This was a strategy for retaining high value-added MNE investment and productive activities in Singapore rather than the MNE relocating their entire operations to some other East Asian location, such as China. We can also see how supply security and techno-industrial capability security typologies apply here, as well as transborder community security issues. Malaysia and Indonesia also benefit from the IMSGT arrangement in terms of increased flows of the gradually higher-tech investment being displaced in Singapore. Both Johor and Riau's economic development has improved quite significantly as a consequence, thus further developing each province's transborder community security interests with Singapore as the destinies of all three economic zones became increasingly bound together. As part of the IMSGT, industrial estates were jointly established by Singapore's Economic Development Board (EDB) and Indonesian authorities on the Riau Islands of Batam (in 1991) and Bintan (in 1992) to attract 'over-spill' investment from Singapore, especially from Japanese multinationals. Joint infrastructure development projects both here and between Singapore and Johor assisted the parallel development of transnational production and distribution links being forged by MNEs operating in the IMSGT area. Riau and Johor continue to provide a source of low-cost labour and resources, and Singapore continues to act as the core of this transborder sub-regionalized economy.

economic system, entailing cooperative and concessionary acts to uphold multilateral regimes of systemic governance, facilitate inter-state bargains and maintain overall systemic stability. Hence, there is a strong international public goods dimension to this economic security typology, regarding more specifically issues of the provision, distribution and consumption of these 'goods'. Furthermore, systemic security would be emphasized by neo-liberals as being a most important pursuit of economic security generally; although neo-liberals tend to question the viability of pursuing economic security objectives anyway. This argument is based on their view that capitalism (the dominant economic paradigm) by its very nature propagates a state of constant insecurity in the international economic system that derives from the competitive dynamics it creates. As Buzan (1991a) comments, 'capitalism is by definition a competitive system, the whole dynamic of which depends on the interplay of threats, vulnerabilities and opportunities in the market' (p. 235). Thus, neo-liberals generally contend that economic security is a mirage and at best can only be achieved in relative terms, although this is surely a universal predicament that applies to any pursuit of security. Neo-liberals further propose that economic insecurity is not to be feared but embraced insofar as positive responses to foreign competitive threats lead to disciplined improvements in efficiency and productivity. In addition, attempts by losers of this competitive game to 'securitize their plight' merely represents a desperation to change the game's rules (Buzan 1998: 109). More generally, neo-liberals tend to subordinate vulnerability issues in the pursuance of 'plenty', which can only be optimized in a free and open global economy.

However, whether or not economic security is a mirage is not the issue, but rather whether FEP powers *respond positively* to the conditions of economic insecurity that confront them: addressing economic insecurity poses a set of opportunities as well as threats, both of which should not be avoided. Moreover, the maximization of global welfare is contingent upon the security (i.e. stability) of the international economic system: a 'free and open global economy' ultimately depends on the provision of international public goods to ensure both its stability and its positive development. It could therefore be argued that maintaining *systemic security* is the de facto core economic security concern of neo-liberalism, with systemic support being the neo-liberal FEP power's implicit path to pursuing economic security. Furthermore, even ardent neo-liberal FEP powers follow broader economic security aims and strategies (Leech 1993, Mastanduno 1998, Moran 1993, US Council on Competitiveness 1994).[1] We should also consider the neo-liberal institutionalist view regarding complex interdependence and the need for cooperative exercises in international economic security (Keohane and Nye 1977, Axelrod 1984, Oye 1986). The governance architecture of systemic security primarily lies in multilateral economic institutions such as the WTO and IMF, which in turn are key depositories and custodians for the aforementioned international public goods. Regional institutions such as the EU and APEC may also contribute positively towards systemic security where multilateral utility functions have been developed.

From another perspective, Marxists and structuralists stress that economic security concerns arise from significant asymmetries in both global economic development and balances of power within the world capitalist system, from which an accordingly uneven distribution of economic vulnerability occurs amongst FEP powers. Those in the periphery and semi-periphery naturally possess higher vulnerability coefficients, their relative weakness making them more susceptible to economic security risks and exogenous threats. This predicament can be linked to Lee's (1999) argument that the economic security interests of weaker FEP powers are focused on maintaining their structural integrity.

[1] If the tenets of hegemonic stability theory are applied, the hegemonic state is seen as the systemic guarantor or underwriter motivated by the need to enable its competitive producers to expand into a stable and open global market environment.

Alliance security

This economic security typology is essentially subservient in character in that it broadly entails maintaining and developing international economic partnerships with state and non-state actors in pursuance of those economic security objectives already discussed. These partnerships may take various forms, ranging from donor–client alliance relationships to looser cooperative or coordinative arrangements between relatively equal partners. As one would expect, the pursuit of economic alliance security objectives is essentially predicated on cooperative ventures. Indeed, we have previously highlighted how the complex interdependence associated with advancing globalizing processes presents an a priori case for FEP powers to adopt a more cooperative approach to economic security generally.[2] This is certainly what neo-liberal institutionalists would stress, and moreover that non-state actors may play a critical part in this cooperative process. Milner (1992) argues in her examination of cooperative behaviour in international relations that cooperation concerns goal-directed behaviour that produces mutually shared benefits over and above those yielded by non-cooperative behaviour. Different types of this behaviour include: *tacit cooperation*, which occurs without communication or explicit agreement; *negotiated cooperation*, which derives from an explicit bargaining process; *imposed cooperation*, where the stronger party in relationship forces the other(s) to enter into cooperative arrangement, its coercive features making this somewhat anomalous although there are clear links here to hegemonic stability theory.

The problematics associated with this latter category is linked to a broader dilemma emphasised by Lee (1998), who contends that, for an FEP power, it must on the one hand seek to 'preserve its internal autonomy and economic sovereignty from being exploited by external interference', while on the other 'it needs to invite external forces in order to ensure the enhancement of domestic welfare' (p. 21). Neo-realists would certainly concur that economic alliance security interests are subject to the vicissitudes of anarchic inter-state competition, whereby alliances quickly form and then quickly dissolve or are soon re-negotiated in accordance to changing nation-state interests over time. Thus, cooperative frameworks of economic alliance security are essentially transient in nature, and are ultimately dependent upon coincidental alignments of national interests forming in the international economic system.

Inter-relationships between different typologies

When examining what inter-relationships exist between different economic security typologies, we should initially make the point that the first four typologies discussed (supply, market access, finance-credit, techno-industrial capability) can be viewed as more 'technical' policy focused, whereas the second four (socio-economic paradigm, transborder community, systemic, alliance) are generally more relational in nature or economic diplomacy focused. Furthermore, certain relationships between typologies may be co-reinforcing or even conflictual, thus creating in the latter case dialectical tensions between different foreign economic policy goals. To begin with, there are natural overlaps between these different typologies. For example, securing better access to sources of international credit may be deemed either a supply security or finance-credit security objective. Techno-industrial capability security may also be served by supply security where, for example, an infusion of foreign technology through inward FDI or other means enhances the latter. Furthermore, the pursuit of socio-economic paradigm security and market access security interests may be mutually aligned, as we mentioned in connection with the US's exposition of neo-liberal advocacy and free trade and free markets generally. An instance of conflicting economic security interest can arise

[2] As Cable (1995) comments, 'contemporary global conditions often call for a cooperative rather than a confrontational pursuit of an economic security that is a shared condition rather than a goal of individual states' (p. 305).

when FEP powers are fostering certain foreign economic alliances and market access deals (e.g. bilateral free trade agreements) that may run to the pursuit of systemic security interests (e.g. upholding WTO multilateralism). In addition, the hierarchy of typologies in any set of generic FEP objectives will be primarily determined by the interaction of contesting influences from different stakeholding FEP constituencies and cognitive-ideological approaches adopted by FEP protagonists. Moreover, the aforementioned tendency of these typologies to sometimes overlap can make constructing such a hierarchical ordering difficult to establish.

KEY POINTS

- The pursuit of economic security broadly determines how a nation-state or other state-like entity defines their foreign economic policy (FEP) objectives.
- We can define the pursuit of economic security itself as safeguarding the structural integrity and prosperity-generating capabilities and interests of a politico-economic entity (e.g. a nation-state) in the context of various externalized risks and threats that confront it in the international economic system.
- Eight different 'objective typologies' of economic security may be developed from this definition that help us further conceptualize and theorize on economic security analysis, especially with respect to identifying different types of economic security interests.
- These objective typologies are: supply security, market access security, finance-credit security, techno-industrial capability security, socio-economic paradigm security, transborder community security, systemic security, alliance security.
- Understanding the inter-linkages between these different objective typologies is also important, for example how the pursuit of one may be in conflict with another, or work in concert with another.

Conclusion

Economic security is an increasingly discussed but still much under-theorized concept. This chapter has presented a new conceptual framework of economic security analysis as an attempt to advance its theoretical development. In setting its context, we have examined the key theoretical and methodological issues pertaining to economic security analysis. Important distinctions have been made between the dyadic pursuits of micro-level and macro-level economic security, as well as between economic security generally and the economics-security nexus. Regarding the latter, it has been argued that it is particularly important to distinguish between their respective empirical domains whilst acknowledging inter-sectoral connections between the politico-military security and economic security. This was examined at various fundamental levels that in turn provided the discursive platform for the base definition of the new conceptual framework presented here, which posited that the pursuit of economic security entailed *safeguarding the structural integrity and prosperity-generating capabilities and interests of a politico-economic entity in the context of various externalized risks and threats that confront it in the international economic system*. Moreover, it was this pursuit in its multifarious forms that broadly oriented the foreign economic policy (FEP) objectives of states and state-like powers (e.g. the EU, local provincial governments). From this definition, a series of eight different 'objective typologies' of economic security were developed. These form the substantive structure of the new conceptual framework, and hence provide the analytical lens through which we can understand the definable generic nature of FEP objectives. It is therefore hoped that this chapter has also made a valuable contribution to the linked discourses of economic security and foreign economic policy analysis.

QUESTIONS

Why is it important to distinguish between micro-level and macro-level studies of economic security?

How did the end of the Cold War impact upon economic security analysis?

Why is it important to distinguish between economic security analysis and the economics- security nexus?

Why is it that in the international economic system it is not just nation-states that we need to consider the economic security interests of?

Under what objective typology or typologies of economic security would you assign to this situation: Managing a fresh water resource shared by two neighbouring countries? Explain your reasoning.

Under what objective typology or typologies of economic security would you assign to this situation: Region-level endeavours to address international worker migration issues? Explain your reasoning.

Under what objective typology or typologies of economic security would you assign to this situation: Averting the collapse of multilateral trade negotiations at the WTO? Explain your reasoning.

Under what objective typology or typologies of economic security would you assign to this situation: Policies aimed at attracting high-tech inward foreign direct investment? Explain your reasoning.

Under what objective typology or typologies of economic security would you assign to this situation: Singapore's signing of a free trade agreement with the United States? Explain your reasoning.

Under what objective typology or typologies of economic security would you assign to this situation: Japan conferring a new multi-billion dollar foreign aid programme to Southeast Asia? Explain your reasoning.

FURTHER READING

- **Buzan, B., Wæver, O., and de Wilde, J. (1998), *Security: A New Framework of Analysis*, Boulder, Co: Lynne Rienner.** There is a chapter on economic security that views the concept from the author's groundbreaking work on 'securitization'. The whole book is very thought-provoking.

- **Dent, C.M. (2002), *The Foreign Economic Policies of Singapore, South Korea and Taiwan*, Cheltenham: Edward Elgar.** The theorization on economic security presented in this chapter primarily derives from this work. Here, I place the pursuit of economic security as the main determining factor of foreign economic policy objectives generally.

■ **Kahler, M. (2004), 'Economic Security in an Era of Globalisation: Definition and Provision', *Pacific Review*, Vol. 17(4), 485–502.** This article critically examines economic security in today's globalizing world economy. Amongst other things, it questions whether economic security issues can be identified as being specifically national in an era of globalization, and moreover cautions against thinking that globalization just brings greater economic insecurity for nation-states and regions.

■ **Lee, C. (1999), 'On Economic Security', in G. Wilson-Roberts (ed.), *An Asia-Pacific Security Crisis?: New Challenges to Regional Stability*, Wellington, NZ: Centre for Strategic Studies.** This paper makes a very good review of other key works and offers some useful ideas also on the economic security conceptualization.

IMPORTANT WEBSITES

- **http://www.whitehouse.gov/nsc/** US National Security Council is the President's principal forum for considering national security and foreign policy matters with his senior national security advisors and cabinet officials.
- **http://www.whitehouse.gov/ecom/** This provides details of the US White House's economic security policy.
- **http://www.security-policy.org/papers/1992/92-T140.html** Centre for Security Policy paper on putting security into the 'Economic Security Council' (ESC), which is in the White House and reports directly to the President.
- **http://www.globalpolicy.org/socecon/un/reformindex.htm** Global Policy Forum paper on the Economic and Social Council (ECOSOC); the principal UN body coordinating the economic and social work of the organization.

Visit the Online Resource Centre that accompanies this book for lots of interesting additional material: www.oxfordtextbooks.co.uk/orc/collins/

PART 3

Traditional and Non-Traditional Security

13 Coercive Diplomacy

PETER VIGGO JAKOBSEN

Chapter Contents

Reader's Guide

Coercive diplomacy involves the use of threats and/or limited force in order to convince an actor to stop or undo actions already undertaken. The use of threats/limited force may, but need not, be accompanied by offers of inducements in order to enhance the adversary's incentive to comply with the coercer's demand. Coercive diplomacy has become part and parcel of Western conflict management since the end of the Cold War, but the Western states have been bad at translating their overwhelming military superiority into coercive diplomacy successes. In addition to explaining this failure, this chapter will relate coercive diplomacy to other threat-based strategies such as deterrence and compellence. It will explain the increasing resort to coercive diplomacy since the Cold War, indicate when the strategy is likely to be employed by Western-led coalitions, explain why coercive diplomacy succeeds and fails, identify the limitations of the strategy, and assess the prospects for its successful use in the future.

Introduction

The principal strategic challenge facing the Western states and the international community as a whole during the Cold War was the avoidance of great power war. The risk that a local armed conflict could escalate into nuclear war between the two superpower blocs naturally put a premium on policies and instruments that sought to prevent this worst case scenario. The principal mission performed by Western military forces during this period was thus to deter the Soviet Union from attacking their homelands. This mission disappeared with the collapse of the Soviet Union and was replaced by the more challenging one of managing the disorder emanating from civil or ethnic wars within weak or failing states, mass violations of human rights committed within the borders of sovereign states, and efforts by a small number of states and non-state actors to acquire or develop weapons of mass destruction (WMD). Instead of preventing Western adversaries from acting, the principal post-Cold War challenge has been to persuade, coerce and, on occasion, force them to change their behaviour.

This shift has had a profound effect on strategic thinking and the way in which force is threatened, used and legitimized. Whereas Western threats and use of force primarily had been justified with reference to national security and the need to avoid war and counter the spread of Communism, the need to protect human rights, promote democracy and prevent the spread of WMD took centre stage in the course of the 1990s. The overriding concern was no longer to avoid great power war and escalation. Instead, Western policy makers became convinced that international peace and stability were better served by the spread of human rights, democracy and market economy.

The Clinton Administration played a key role in this development as it replaced the American Cold War strategy of containment with a strategy dedicated to 'enlarge the community of democratic nations'. Inspired by the democratic peace theory which holds that democracies do not go to war against each other, the Clinton Administration argued that it served 'all of America's strategic interest—from promoting prosperity at home to checking global threats abroad' (Gowa 1999: 3). Most Western states and international organizations followed suit, and sustainable peace defined in terms of peace building and the establishment of democracy became the objective of the increasing number of military interventions launched by the international community.

The favourable geopolitical environment characterized by an overwhelming Western military superiority and a low risk of hostile great power intervention generated pressures on as well as incentives for Western policy makers to use threats and force in order to promote their new policy agenda and manage the armed conflicts emanating from the weak and failing states in the international system. It is therefore not surprising that they began to use coercive diplomacy and force more often than had been the case during the Cold War. Coercive diplomacy was employed against Iraq in the run-up to the 1991 Gulf War and subsequently in the various crises created by the Iraqi unwillingness to cooperate with the United Nations (UN) inspectors seeking to determine whether Iraq had terminated its WMD programmes; it was employed by the Western powers in the Balkans in their attempts to manage the armed conflicts in Bosnia and in Kosovo; and the United States employed it against the military leadership in Haiti to reverse the overthrow of the first democratically elected president.

The September 11 attacks on the World Trade Center and the Pentagon in 2001 reinforced this trend by increasing the American willingness to threaten and use force to counter the threats emanating from mass casualty terrorism, WMD proliferation and failing states (The White House 2002). Since September 11 coercive diplomacy has been employed in attempts to coerce Iran, Iraq, Libya, and North Korea to stop their development of nuclear weapons; and in attempts to coerce the Taliban in Afghanistan to stop supporting al-Qaida. Finally, it has also been employed in the so-called war against terror to coerce states, terrorist groups and non-state actors from cooperating with al-Qaida and affiliated groups.

Success does not explain the increased resort to coercive diplomacy. Coercive diplomacy failed to coerce Iraq to comply fully with UN and US demands between 1990 and 2003; it failed to coerce the Taliban to stop supporting al-Qaida; success came at a high cost in Bosnia and Kosovo where thousands were killed before the North Atlantic Treaty Organization (NATO) in the end had to bomb the Serbs to the negotiating table; and its effectiveness with respect to coercing non-state actors and terrorist groups to stop their support and cooperation with al-Qaida and its associates is unclear. To date, the strategy's potential for peaceful conflict resolution has only been realized three times: in 1994 when Haiti's generals were coerced to step down; in 2001 when Pakistan was coerced to stop supporting the Taliban; and in 2003 when Libya was coerced to terminate its support for terrorism and its nuclear programme. In spite hereof the strategy is likely to remain central to Western conflict management because of the continuing need to stop or undo hostile and destabilizing actions.

The difficulty of translating Western military superiority into coercive diplomacy success came as a surprise to Western governments in both Bosnia and Kosovo. This difficulty is less surprising from a theoretical perspective as the existing theories regard coercive diplomacy as a high-risk, hard-to-use strategy. But the theoretical understanding of the coercive diplomacy remains wanting in several respects. A better understanding of the strategy and its requirements for success is therefore required to enhance the strategy's potential for resolving conflicts short of war.

KEY POINTS

- The end of the Cold War rivalry made it easier for Western states to threaten and use force because the risk of uncontrollable escalation vanished.
- Coercive diplomacy has become an integral part of Western crisis and conflict management.
- Western military superiority should make coercive diplomacy easier to conduct successfully.
- It has proved difficult to use coercive diplomacy to stop or reverse acts of aggression, end (support for) terrorism and end WMD programmes.
- Coercive diplomacy will continue to play a central role in Western conflict management in the foreseeable future because the need to stop or undo undesirable actions remains a key challenge.
- Understanding the conditions under which coercive diplomacy succeeds or fails represents a major challenge for theory and practice.

What is coercive diplomacy?

Coercive diplomacy seeks to resolve crises and armed conflicts without resorting to full-scale war. It relies on threats and the limited use of force to influence an adversary to stop or undo the consequences of actions already undertaken. The use of threats and limited force (sticks) may be coupled with the use of inducements (carrots) to enhance the adversary's incentive to comply with the coercer's demand, but the stick has to instil fear in the mind of the adversary for the strategy to qualify as coercive diplomacy.

If compliance is not caused, partly at least, by fear of the coercer's threat, then coercion has not taken place. A strategy that stops aggression or a WMD programme by buying off the opponent constitutes appeasement, not coercive diplomacy.

Compellence is another term for coercive diplomacy, but it covers a broader set of phenomena. Whereas coercive diplomacy only covers reactive threats employed in response to actions taken by an adversary, compellence also involves threats aimed at initiating adversary action. A threat to coerce a state to give up part of its territory would thus count as compellence but not as coercive diplomacy because the latter only covers situations where the adversary has made the first move.

It is also the reactive nature that distinguishes coercive diplomacy from its sister strategy of deterrence, which involves the use of threats to influence adversaries not to undertake undesired actions in the first place. Deterrence is used before the adversary has acted whereas coercive diplomacy is employed once the adversary has taken the first step. Deterrence was the cornerstone of the Western strategy employed against the Soviet Union during the Cold War. The Western states threatened to respond to a Soviet attack by using nuclear weapons in the hope that it would convince the Soviet leadership that an attack on the Western states would be too costly. If a deterrent threat fails to prevent an attack, the coercer then has to consider whether to respond by threatening to use force to influence the enemy to stop the attack and withdraw, to use limited force to influence the enemy to do so, or to use full-scale or brute force to force it to stop and withdraw.

Whereas the use of threats and limited force count as coercive diplomacy, the use of brute force to defeat the attacker does not. Coercive diplomacy is employed in order to avoid or limit the use of force. It is an influence strategy that is intended to obtain compliance from the adversary without defeating it first. It leaves an element of choice with the target; it has to make a decision whether to comply or fight on. Full-scale or brute force, on the other hand, aims at defeating the adversary. It does not seek to influence but to control by imposing compliance upon the adversary by depriving it of any say in the issue at hand. The 2001–02 Afghanistan War illustrates this difference. The United States initially threatened to attack the Taliban regime unless Osama bin Laden and other key al-Qaida leaders were handed over and their training camps closed. Non-compliance then led to American air strikes on key military installations coupled with threats of escalation. In the first phase of the war, the United States refrained from attacking the Taliban frontlines and from providing direct military support to the Northern Alliance, the Afghan groups that were fighting the Taliban. It also, somewhat unconvincingly, offered to leave the Taliban regime in place if it complied with US demands. When the United States became convinced that compliance was not forthcoming, it escalated its use of force to defeat the Taliban. At that stage the American strategy changed from influence to control.

The distinction between limited force and full-scale/brute force is crucial because resort to brute force means that coercive diplomacy has failed. It is important to understand that this distinction is not based on the amount of force used. It is not a question of the number of bombs dropped on the adversary. The distinction rests on the purpose that the use of force seeks to accomplish and the element of choice left to the adversary. Coercive diplomacy uses limited force as a bargaining tool. It is used to increase the costs of non-compliance and to threaten with more of the same unless compliance is forthcoming. It always leaves room for the adversary to decide whether to comply or not. Brute force does not leave such a choice; its purpose is to defeat the adversary. The resort to brute force means that diplomacy has been abandoned and that the coercer has lost faith in negotiation and decided to impose its will by force.

The distinction can be difficult to make in practice, but a useful rule of thumb is that use of air and sea power usually will be limited in nature as it leaves the decision whether to comply or suffer more attacks to the adversary. The air campaigns in the 1991 Gulf War and the 1999 Kosovo War provide examples of the use of limited force as part of coercive diplomacy strategies. The ground war that followed the air campaign in the Gulf War signified a shift from coercive diplomacy to brute force. Once the land campaign began, force was no longer used to 'persuade' Iraq to withdraw its forces from Kuwait, but to physically throw them out. As a consequence, the initiation of the land war also meant that coercive diplomacy had failed.

Note that this definition of 'limited' force allows for major use of force. The strategic air campaigns waged against Germany and Japan during the Second World War thus constitute limited force according to this definition even though the number of bombs dropped and the damage inflicted were enormous. For this reason limited force is typically defined as 'demonstrative' or 'symbolic' use, meaning 'just enough force of an appropriate kind to demonstrate resolution and to give credibility to the threat that greater force will be used if necessary' (George 1993: 10; see also Art 2003: 9). This definition is vague and hard to employ in practice, which is why this chapter defines limited in terms of how force is used rather than in terms of how much. The practical implication is that the scope for coercive diplomacy success is broadened. NATO's air campaign in the Kosovo conflict is thus counted as a coercive diplomacy success in this chapter, whereas the more conventional definition employed by Art, George and others will result in the coding of this case as a failure.

The distinction between coercive diplomacy and full-scale use of force cannot be made solely on the basis of how force is used, however. When coercive diplomacy is used as part of an escalation sequence which culminates in brute force, as was the case in the 1991 Gulf War, the 2001–02 Afghanistan War, and the 2003 Iraq War, it has to be determined whether the coercer was pursuing a peaceful solution or merely using threats and limited force in order to legitimize the resort to brute force that followed. One way to do this is to consider whether the coercer deliberately made demands that it knew that the adversary could not meet, and whether the adversary was denied sufficient time to comply. If that is the case, the conclusion must be that the coercer preferred war to adversary compliance. It has been debated in the wake of the 2003 Iraq War whether the Bush Administration preferred regime change to compliance in order to get rid of Saddam Hussein once and for all. If that were the case, the American use of threats in the run-up to the war would not qualify as coercive diplomacy.

KEY POINTS

- Coercive diplomacy seeks to resolve crises and armed conflicts short of full-scale war.
- It is a reactive strategy relying on threats, limited force and inducements to influence an adversary to stop or undo the consequences of actions already undertaken.
- Coercive diplomacy is an influence strategy that leaves the choice between compliance and defiance to the adversary.
- Full-scale or brute force is a control strategy that deprives the adversary of any choice by forcing compliance upon it.
- Escalation from limited to brute force means that coercive diplomacy has failed.
- Use of threats and limited force only constitute coercive diplomacy if the coercer prefers compliance to full-scale war.

Theories and requirements for success

Whereas the study of deterrence, which enjoyed a dominant position in the field of strategic studies during the Cold War, has produced books and articles enough to fill an entire library, the works on coercive diplomacy and compellence do not fill more than a bookshelf. Whereas an internet search for deterrence produces 7.81 million hits, coercive diplomacy and compellence only produce 94,700 and 17,500 hits respectively.

Although the practice of coercive diplomacy, as it has been defined here, has always been an integral part of crisis and conflict management, theorizing about it has not been a popular pastime. Only two major theoretical works exist: Thomas C. Schelling's *Arms and Influence* (1966), which coined the term compellence, and Alexander L. George et al.'s *Limits to Coercive Diplomacy* (1971), which pioneered the study of coercive diplomacy. These classic works continue to shape the study of coercive diplomacy today. Schelling, inspired by game theory, deductively identified five conditions that he considered necessary for compellence success. Since Schelling was primarily interested in discerning the general conditions influencing the use of compellence, he did not try to formulate specific policy prescriptions or confront his conditions with empirical evidence.

In contrast, George and his associates employed an inductive research strategy with the objective of developing a policy-relevant theory. They used a set of questions confronting policy makers wanting to use coercive diplomacy as their point of departure and relied on Case Study analysis to identify a total of 14 factors influencing the outcome of coercive diplomacy attempts. George and his associates distinguish between contextual variables and conditions favouring success, and the idea is that they should be used by decision makers at different stages of the policy making process. The contextual variables should be used initially to decide whether coercive diplomacy is a viable strategy in a given crisis. The success variables only enter the decision-making process in the second stage if analysis of the contextual variables suggests that a coercive diplomacy strategy may work. The success variables are then supposed to help policy makers in the task of conceiving an effective strategy.

The main strength of Schelling's theory is its coherent and parsimonious nature. But parsimony is also its greatest weakness as its highly abstract nature makes it difficult to use in practice. Schelling offers no help to policy makers wanting to know how to devise a potent threat, to make a threat credible in the mind of the opponent or assure the adversary that compliance will not lead to new demands. Schelling himself gave up when asked by the Johnson Administration to use his theory to devise an air campaign against North Vietnam in 1964. The administration then had a go itself but the result—Operation Rolling Thunder—failed to coerce the North Vietnamese to comply with US demands (Kaplan 1983: 330–6).

The problem is exactly the opposite with the George and Simons' checklist as the high number of factors makes it hard to use and coercive diplomacy outcomes difficult to explain. It is hard to know which of the many factors actually cause success or failure in a given case. According to George and Simons, success is unlikely unless all their nine success conditions are present but logically the

KEY IDEAS 13.1

Schelling's necessary conditions for compellence success

1. The threat conveyed must be sufficiently potent to convince the adversary that the costs of non-compliance will be unbearable.
2. The threat must be credible in the mind of the adversary; he must be convinced that the coercer has the will and the capability to execute it in case of non-compliance.
3. The adversary must be given time to comply with the demand.
4. The coercer must assure the adversary that compliance will not lead to more demands in the future.
5. The conflict must not be perceived as zero-sum. A degree of common interest in avoiding full-scale war must exist. Each side must be persuaded that it can gain more by bargaining than by trying unilaterally to take what it wants by force.

(Adapted from Schelling 1966: 1, 3–4, 69–76, 89)

KEY IDEAS 13.2

George and Simons' checklist of factors influencing the use of coercive diplomacy

Contextual variables

1. Global strategic environment
2. Type of provocation
3. Image of war
4. Unilateral or coalitional coercive diplomacy
5. The isolation of the adversary

Conditions favouring success

1. Clarity of objective
2. Strength of motivation
3. *Asymmetry of motivation*
4. *Sense of urgency*
5. Strong leadership
6. Domestic support
7. International support
8. *Opponent's fear of unacceptable escalation*
9. *Clarity concerning the precise terms of settlement of the crisis*

Italicized factors are deemed 'particularly significant' for success.

(George and Simons 1994: 271–74, 287–88, 292)

presence of their four 'particularly significant' conditions should suffice. One would expect the opponent to comply if it fears unacceptable escalation, perceives the balance of interest as unfavourable, feels the need to comply as urgent, and regards the terms of settlement as clear. Even more problematic is the failure to operationalize several of the factors in a way that makes it possible to measure whether they apply or not in a given crisis. The three of the four conditions deemed 'particularly significant', asymmetry of motivation, opponent's fear of unacceptable escalation and urgency for compliance, can only be measured after the fact. This significantly reduces the analytic value of their checklist.

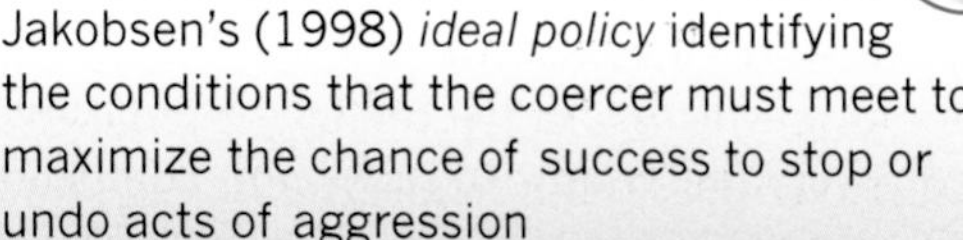

KEY IDEAS 13.3

Jakobsen's (1998) *ideal policy* identifying the conditions that the coercer must meet to maximize the chance of success to stop or undo acts of aggression

1. A threat of force to defeat the opponent or deny him his objectives quickly with little cost.
2. A deadline for compliance.
3. An assurance to the adversary against future demands.
4. An offer of inducements for compliance.

Jakobsen's *ideal policy* attempts to overcome the weaknesses in Schelling's and George's work. The *ideal policy* was developed with two objectives in mind. The first was to reduce the number of success conditions to a more manageable number. For this reason it is narrower in scope and developed to apply to attempts to counter aggression only, but its logic should hold for attempts to counter terrorism and WMD acquisition as well. The second was to operationalize the success conditions to make it possible to determine whether they apply or not in specific crises. To minimize the risk of excluding important factors, the *ideal policy* incorporates Schelling's necessary conditions for success and the conditions that George and Simons deem particularly significant.

The first success condition in the *ideal policy* is designed to make the threat so potent that non-compliance will be too costly for actors that have resorted to force. Opponents who have resorted to force have signalled a willingness to accept high costs to achieve their goals, making it reasonable to assume that threats of force will be required to make non-compliance too costly in most cases. The poor record that economic sanctions have with respect to stopping or reversing military aggression supports this assumption (Jakobsen 1998: 27). That sanctions usually take a long time to work is another reason why they are ill suited for stopping military aggression, which in most cases will require swift action.

It is not enough merely to issue a threat of force, however. The nature of the military action threatened is very important. To make non-compliance too costly, the coercer must threaten to defeat the adversary or deny him his objectives quickly with little cost in terms of blood and treasure. The threat has to be designed in this way to accomplish two things. The first is to create the fear of unacceptable escalation in the mind of the opponent, which George and Simons emphasize as particularly significant for success. A threat to deny the opponent what it so desperately wants is the most direct way to do this. The second is to make the threat credible in the eyes of the opponent: threats of quick, low-cost defeats are essential to this end. In light of the difficulties that Western democracies have with respect to sustaining domestic support and suffering casualties in conflicts not threatening their vital interests, opponents will regard Western threats involving a commitment to fight a protracted war in such conflicts as bluff. A threat to fight a prolonged war will only be credible in the eyes of the opponent if the coercer's vital interests are directly threatened. In practice this means that the coercer not only needs to enjoy a significant military superiority, it must also be capable of denying the opponent the ability to retaliate and impose costs on the opponent. The coercer must in the words of Byman *et al.* (1999) enjoy 'escalation-dominance'. The lack of escalation dominance and the perception that vital interests were not at stake explain the failure of the Western powers to coerce the Bosnian Serbs between 1992 and 1995. Western coercion was invariably countered by a variety of Bosnian Serb responses aimed at undermining Western resolve. Typical were empty promises to comply with Western demands, threats aimed at deterring the Western powers from executing their threats and acts of escalation such as hostage-taking. The Bosnian Serbs used hostage-taking of UN personnel to neutralize NATO air strikes with great success between April 1994 and July 1995, when the Western powers took effective measures to reduce the vulnerability of their troops in Yugoslavia to retaliation (Jakobsen 1998: 107).

To maximize credibility, a threat of quick defeat backed by the required capability is not sufficient, however. A deadline for compliance must accompany it. The literature on misperception and deterrence failure shows that decision makers finding themselves in no-win situations are likely to interpret the actions and signals made by their opponent in a manner consistent with their own expectations and desires (Jervis 1976). An actor being asked to stop or undo an act of aggression or terminate a costly WMD programme can hence be expected to be prone to wishful thinking. It follows that failure to set a deadline for compliance is likely to be interpreted as evidence that the coercer lacks the will to implement the threat. Opponents will simply not perceive a threat of force as credible unless it is accompanied by a deadline for compliance. A deadline for compliance hence constitutes the second condition in the *ideal policy*. Apart from reducing the risk of misperception and miscalculation, a deadline also serves to reduce the scope for delaying tactics and counter-coercion.

Assurance against new demands must also be included in the *ideal policy* to enhance the prospects of success. As pointed out by Schelling, the opponent's incentive to comply will be significantly reduced if he fears that compliance will merely result in new demands. George and Simons make the same point when they stress clear terms of settlement as a 'particularly significant' condition for success. The Finnish refusal to hand over a few small islands to the Soviet Union in 1939 illustrates the importance of providing assurances. Fear that compliance would result in more demands played an important role in their refusal, which triggered the Winter War (Jakobson 1961: 139).

Use of inducements is the fourth and last ingredient in the *ideal policy*. Inducements should be used as sweeteners or face-savers to help an opponent fearing the coercer's threat to comply with a minimum of humiliation. By increasing the opponent's incentive to comply inducements help to prevent zero-sum situations (Schelling's fifth condition), and they also serve to give assurances against future demands more credibility. The cases summarized below clearly demonstrate that the use of inducements enhance the prospects of success. Inducements are involved in most of the successes and absent in most of the failures. The findings are not so strong as to suggest that inducements are necessary for success, but strong enough to suggest that inducements are important facilitators that may make the difference between success and failure.

The *ideal policy* improves upon Schelling's and George's lists of success conditions in at least three ways. First, it can explain the outcome of attempts to use coercive diplomacy to stop/undo military aggression just as accurately with fewer conditions. Second, all the conditions in the *ideal policy* framework are operationalized so that it becomes easier to determine whether they are present or not in a given case. Third, it is an analytical tool that requires little knowledge about the opponent. It rests on the claim that one can explain and predict outcomes of coercive diplomacy attempts against aggressors by focusing on the policy pursued by the coercer and black-boxing the opponent. If the coercer lacks the capability and the will to meet the requirements of the *ideal policy*, coercive diplomacy can be expected to fail. While it goes without saying that a coercer needs a good understanding of the adversary and actionable intelligence to devise the most effective mix of threats and inducements in a real world crisis, the *ideal policy* remains useful because it highlights what the coercer at a minimum must do to succeed.

This said, implementation of the *ideal policy* does not guarantee success. Whereas non-implementation of the *ideal policy* is a recipe for failure, its implementation only maximizes the probability of success. A coercive diplomacy attempt meeting the requirements of the *ideal policy* may fail due to factors outside the coercer's control, such as misperception or miscalculation by the opponent, or because the opponent prefers to fight and lose to preserve honour rather than complying with the coercer's demand.

It cannot, and is not intended to, say anything about the contextual factors influencing the use of coercive diplomacy. For example, it cannot explain why a government decided (not) to implement the *ideal policy*. A complete theory should also specify the conditions under which Western governments will be willing to meet the requirements for success. These conditions are discussed further in the conclusion.

KEY POINTS

- Coercive diplomacy is an understudied strategy.
- Schelling and George laid the foundations for the study of coercive diplomacy.
- Jakobsen's *ideal policy* framework focuses on the use of coercive diplomacy to counter aggression.
- The *ideal policy* framework explains and predicts coercive diplomacy outcomes with a minimum of success conditions on the basis of the coercer's actions only.
- A complete theory should also specify when the success conditions are likely to be met.

The challenge of defining success

Defining coercive diplomacy success is easy in theory. Coercive diplomacy succeeds when the communication of a threat or the use of limited force produces adversary compliance with the coercer's demands. Similarly, failure occurs if the threat or limited use of force does not result in compliance with the coercer's demand. In practice several factors complicate the task of measuring success. First, most studies of coercive diplomacy define success in binary terms: coercive diplomacy either fails or succeeds. The problem with this approach is that success in most cases is a question of degree. Coercers may settle for partial compliance or reduce their demands in the negotiation process that coercive diplomacy by definition involves. To give an example, Serbia only complied with NATO's demands regarding Kosovo in 1999 after NATO had lowered its demands. This has led some to claim that Serbia was not coerced by NATO, and that Serbian compliance resulted from NATO's concessions and the loss of Russian support.

This example also illustrates a related second problem: that it will often be difficult to isolate the effect that the threat of force or the use of limited force has had in a specific case. As discussed earlier, compliance must partly be caused by fear for coercion to have taken place. This was undoubtedly the case in Kosovo, as Serbian compliance (and Serbia's loss of Russian support) would not have been forthcoming in the absence of NATO's air campaign. The stick does not have to be sufficient for success, however, since it would certainly be wrong to regard a case where both inducements and sticks proved necessary for compliance as a coercive diplomacy failure. The question to ask is consequently not whether the stick employed as part of coercive diplomacy strategy was sufficient for success, but whether it was a necessary contributing factor.

Third, success should be regarded as a function of the amount of coercion required for compliance. Ideally, coercion should not be required at all to solve disputes. But if the threshold from persuasion to coercion is crossed, the degree of successfulness is negatively correlated to the amount of coercion (and inducement) required for compliance. When the threshold between limited and brute force is crossed, coercive diplomacy fails. The challenge, in short, is to obtain compliance without having to use force. As the Chinese military thinker Sun Tzu has observed, winning without fighting 'is the true pinnacle of excellence'.

Finally, it is important to distinguish between tactical/temporary and strategic/lasting success. Western use of coercion has generally been protracted affairs involving a series of inconclusive coercive diplomacy exchanges that resulted in tactical/temporary successes followed by new acts of non-compliance. Western use of coercion in Bosnia from 1992–95 is a case in point. It involved seven major coercive diplomacy exchanges each involving (1) acts of aggression committed by the Bosnian Serbs, (2) a response from the Western powers in the form of a demand coupled with a threat of force and (3) the response to this threat from the Bosnian Serbs. Three of these exchanges can be considered tactical/temporary successes because Western threats coerced the Serbs to back down and comply with Western demands. From a strategic perspective, they cannot be considered successes, however, because compliance did not last for long.

These considerations lead to the operationalization of success depicted in Table 13.1. Coercive diplomacy successes resulting from the use of threats and sanctions (inducements may, but need not be employed) are classified as cheap successes, whereas successes resulting from the use of limited force count as costly ones. Escalation to brute force means that coercive diplomacy has failed.

KEY POINTS

- Coercive diplomacy succeeds when a threat or limited use of force is necessary for compliance.
- Escalation from limited to brute force represents failure.
- Coercive diplomacy success is a question of degree.
- Success is negatively correlated with the amount of coercion (and inducements) required to obtain compliance.
- It is important to distinguish between temporary and lasting successes.
- To be genuine, coercive diplomacy success has to be lasting.

Table 13.1 Success is a function of the amount of coercion required for compliance

Strategies	Diplomacy	Coercive diplomacy (CD)		War
Instruments	Persuasion and inducements	Threats, sanctions (and inducements)	Limited force (and inducements)	Full-scale/brute force
Degree of success	CD not needed for success	Cheap CD success	Costly CD success	CD failure

Western use of coercive diplomacy 1990–2005

Western use of coercive diplomacy involving threats and use of limited force has sought to end and undo acts of aggression, acts of terrorism and attempts to acquire WMD in the post-Cold War era. To qualify as a case of coercive diplomacy, explicit threats, sanctions or limited force have to be employed by a Western coercer. Cases involving implicit threats and shows of force such as the crises between the United States and China over Taiwan have consequently been excluded from the list below. The cases have been identified in the studies listed in the guide to further reading at the end of the chapter and the coding is based on the information provided in these studies.

The literature shows that coercive diplomacy primarily has been employed to stop and undo acts of aggression. A total of 21 coercive diplomacy exchanges have taken place between Western states and various agressors in eight different conflicts. Twelve exchanges ended in failure, five resulted in temporary successes followed by new acts of non-compliance, three resulted in costly lasting successes requiring limited use of force, and only one resulted in cheap success in which compliance was obtained without a shot. The *ideal policy* identifying the minimum requirements for success was only implemented to the letter in six exchanges, all of which resulted in temporary or lasting successes.

Western governments have sought to stop four WMD programmes during the period. Nine coercive diplomacy exchanges ended in four temporary successes followed by subsequent non-compliance, two failures, one cheap success and two exchanges were ongoing at the time of writing. In none of the cases was the *ideal policy* implemented, as it proved impossible to use force to deny the adversary's objectives quickly with little cost. Threats of force were not employed explicitly during the negotiations, which led to Libya's decisions to terminate its WMD programmes and its support for terrorist activities in 2003. On the contrary, assurance against regime change was crucial for success.

Finally, Western states used coercive diplomacy against state sponsors of terrorism and al-Qaida on eight occasions. It is difficult to tell whether it had any effect against Iraq and Sudan, it failed against al-Qaida and the Taliban on three occasions and two cheap successes were obtained against Libya and Pakistan. The *ideal policy* was only employed to the letter against Pakistan.

KEY POINTS

- The Western states only obtained six lasting successes in 36 coercive diplomacy exchanges and five of them were preceded by failures in earlier exchanges.
- Coercive diplomacy only scored three cheap successes in 36 attempts.
- Use of the *ideal policy* resulted in success but it was only implemented in seven exchanges.
- The Western states are most likely to use coercive diplomacy to counter acts of aggression.
- Threats and limited use of force are very difficult to employ successfully to stop terrorism and WMD.

Why coercive diplomacy is hard

Several factors complicate the use of coercive diplomacy and some of them are inherent in the nature of the strategy and in attempts to use it to counter aggression, terrorism and WMD acquisition. The difficulties are further compounded by practical challenges related to the design of effective strategies meeting the requirements for success.

Inherent difficulties

Coercive diplomacy is tough because the requirements for success are contradictory. To succeed, the coercer must frighten and reassure the adversary at the same time. It must create fear of uncontrollable escalation and a sense of urgency in the mind of the adversary and convince it that compliance will not lead to further demands in the future. It is no easy task to use threats or limited force without hardening the adversary's motivation to resist, and equally hard to offer inducements and assurances to prevent this without appearing weak.

That success ultimately rests on perceptual, psychological and emotional factors adds to the difficulty. Since success hinges on cooperation from the adversary, there is always a risk that misperception or miscalculation will defeat even a well-executed strategy meeting all the requirements for success. Adversaries finding themselves in what they may perceive as no-win situations will be prone to wishful thinking. That this was the principal reason why coercive diplomacy failed to persuade Saddam Hussein to withdraw his forces from Kuwait prior to the start of the fighting in 1991 cannot be ruled out.

The likelihood that this might happen is enhanced by the fact that compliance requires a visible change in behaviour, for instance withdrawal of military forces or termination of a nuclear programme. As a consequence, compliance is not only likely to be perceived as humiliating, it may also be positively dangerous for the adversary's leaders since their surrender may be perceived as a betrayal and trigger attempts to overthrow them by democratic or military means. Standing up to the coercer may also make the leadership more popular since the use of coercion may produce a rally-around-the-flag effect. History shows that populations and groups tend to unite behind their leaders in times of crisis or war; even unpopular leaders may benefit from this effect.

In addition to these complications that apply to the use of coercive diplomacy in general, its use to counter aggression, terrorism and WMD pose special problems of their own. Such cases are especially hard, because actors engaging in such behaviour are fully aware that force might be used to stop them. Most actors fearing hostile military responses will be deterred from resorting to force or terrorism or embarking on a high-cost, high-risk gamble to acquire WMD. Actors engaging in such behaviour

CASE STUDY 13.1

Failure in Afghanistan

Pre-9/11 context

At the time of the September 11 attacks, the United States was already engaged in a coercive diplomacy campaign against the Taliban regime. Cruise missiles had been employed in an attack on al-Qaida targets in 1998 and the following year sanctions were imposed in an attempt to coerce the Taliban to extradite Osama bin Laden. The Taliban flatly refused to force him out or hand him over to an 'infidel nation', however (Crenshaw 2003: 328).

US response to the 9/11 attacks

On 20 September 2001 the United States issued a public ultimatum to the Taliban demanding that the Taliban immediately hand over the al-Qaida leadership and close the terrorist camps in Afghanistan. These demands were accompanied by threats of force and an offer to leave the Taliban regime in place. While the credibility of the threats was enhanced by military preparations, strong international support and successful coercion that cut the Taliban off from Pakistani support, the Taliban had good reason to question the American offer to leave the regime in place. The Taliban response was defiant. It engaged in counter-coercion and refused to hand over Osama bin Laden and associates. The United States then began to bomb military airfields and the few high-value targets that Afghanistan presented to US air power: command centres, air defence systems and leadership residences. The United States also began to provide military materiel and financial support to the Northern Alliance, the Afghan groups that were fighting the Taliban.

Escalation to brute force and failure

On 11 October the United States offered to end its use of force in return for compliance with the American demands. Now regime change had been added to the list of demands. The Taliban regime now had to go but prospects of participation in a future Afghan government were held open for moderate members of the existing regime. The Taliban responded with defiance and the United States then began to bomb Taliban frontline positions and offer direct military support to the Northern Alliance. The Taliban had no response and their regime quickly collapsed.

Was the Taliban impossible to coerce?

The Taliban had no reason to doubt American resolve and threat credibility could not be higher. Their failure to comply may consequently stem from belief that the US would seek their overthrow whether they complied or not, religious/ideological beliefs ruling out compliance, an inability to comply or a combination of the three. If the Taliban effectively depended upon financial and military support from al-Qaida for regime survival as the Central Intelligence Agency (CIA) concluded (Woodward 2001), then it may simply not have been able to comply with US demands.

are likely to perceive their vital interests as threatened and regard the issues at stake in zero-sum terms. As a consequence, the room for compromise that coercive diplomacy requires for success may simply not exist. This will almost certainly be the case if the coercer is demanding regime or leadership change, as was the case in Haiti, Afghanistan and in the crisis preceding the 2003 Iraq War. Leaders fearing for their hold on power or their lives have little incentive to comply unless they are faced with certain defeat and offered very juicy inducements such as golden exiles. The American ability to do this paved the way for coercive success in Haiti in 1994, but it is unlikely to be possible very often. Similarly, threats and limited use of force will not impress terrorists willing to die for their cause.

Finally, the political scope for offering inducements to such adversaries may be very limited. This problem was underlined by the argument made by the British and American governments during the 1990–91 Gulf conflict that Saddam Hussein did not deserve any inducements, because he should never have attacked Kuwait in the first place. A similar logic applies to state sponsors of terrorism, terrorists and actors pursuing WMD. Offers of inducements to convince North Korea and Iran to stop their nuclear programmes have thus been criticized along the same lines.

Practical problems

In addition to the inherent difficulties, practitioners trying to put a strategy together face a set of practical problems, of which five stand out as particularly hard to overcome. To devise an effective mix of threats and inducements the coercer needs a good understanding of the adversary's mindset, motivations, interests, behavioural style, and decision-making process. In addition, actionable intelligence is required to target the adversary's forces, bases and WMD installations. A poor understanding of the adversary and lack of intelligence has been a major obstacle limiting the effectiveness of Western coercion in the post-Cold War era. The widespread tendency in the West to label adversaries as rogue, irrational, fanatical, fundamentalist, crazy and uncivilized is quite indicative of this problem, and it has been compounded by the inability to penetrate their societies and organizations to obtain the intelligence required to threaten with effective military action. The problem has been particularly acute with respect to terrorist groups and the Iranian, Iraqi and North Korean nuclear programmes.

It is not only the different nature of the adversaries that complicates the use of Western coercion. Their tendency to rely on irregular or asymmetric military strategies such as guerrilla warfare or terrorism also complicates the use of coercive diplomacy by making it hard to threaten and, if need be, defeat the opponent's military strategy quickly with little cost. Actors, be they states or non-state actors, adopting such strategies offer few high-value targets to destroy or hold at risk and deny Western forces the ability to rely on air power to win quickly with little cost. As a consequence threats and use of force either have little utility or require high-risk operations involving ground troops over an extended period of time. The Serbian success with respect to neutralizing the effectiveness of NATO air power forced NATO to contemplate a high-risk invasion with ground forces, and the effectiveness of guerrilla strategy with respect to neutralizing Western military superiority is also illustrated by the success of the insurgents in Iraq in 2003–2005. The cases summarized above demonstrate that the ability to deny Western forces quick low-cost victories have a strong deterrent effect upon Western decision makers in crises and conflicts that do not threaten their vital interests directly.

A related problem is the difficulty of verifying compliance with respect to terrorism and WMD. While it is easy to verify whether an aggressor withdraws or not, it is very hard to verify whether a state stops covert support for terrorist activities, whether terrorist groups cease from engaging in terrorist activities or whether states or non-state actors stop clandestine efforts to acquire WMD. This has been a problem in all the WMD and terrorist cases listed above.

A fourth practical problem is the need to coerce several opponents with conflicting interests at the same time. This will often be the case when coercive diplomacy is being used to manage internal conflicts where several parties are fighting each other. Western decision makers faced this problem in Bosnia and Kosovo where the parties fighting the Serbs on several occasions resisted Western attempts to find a diplomatic solution and sought to persuade Western states to help them defeat the Serbs instead. The Kosovo Liberation Army (KLA) was highly successful in this respect as its policy of attacking Serbian civilians to provoke Serbian forces to retaliate against Kosovo Albanian civilians in the end convinced NATO leaders of the need to use force against the Serbs and deploy a large peacekeeping force in Kosovo. Thus the KLA effectively got NATO to evict Serbian forces from Kosovo, something it could never have done by itself.

A fifth problem stems from the need to engage in coalitional coercion. Western coercion is usually coalitional and conducted with a mandate from an international organization such as the UN or NATO. While coalitional coercive diplomacy holds a number of advantages in terms of burden sharing, enhanced legitimacy and increased isolation of the adversary, these advantages may be offset by the difficulty of creating consensus on the need to threaten and use force. Since coercive diplomacy is a high-risk and potentially high-cost strategy, states tend to free ride and be unwilling to put their troops in harm's way in conflicts that pose no direct threat to their own security. As a consequence, coalitional consensus on the need to threaten and use force usually requires the presence of one or more great

CASE STUDY 13.2

Costly success in Kosovo

The context

Kosovo had long been regarded as a powder keg when violence finally broke out in spring 1998. The Serbian security forces responded to the armed bid for independence launched by the KLA with excessive use of force, which immediately drew international condemnation and mediation aimed at ending the violence.

Half-hearted coercion

NATO governments threatened to undertake air strikes in June 1998 unless the fighting ended and the Serbian forces were withdrawn from Kosovo. Threat credibility was undermined by Russian opposition and visible opposition to the use of force within NATO, however, and the situation was further complicated by KLA insistence on independence and their unwillingness to meet with American negotiators. Western governments consequently settled for a symbolic deployment of 50 observers and turned a blind eye as the Serbs launched a major offensive to defeat the KLA.

Temporary success

In October implementation of a coercive strategy meeting the requirements of the *ideal policy* paved the way for a deployment of 2,000 unarmed observers in Kosovo. To obtain Serbian compliance NATO postponed its deadline twice and allowed more than 20,000 Serbian personnel to remain in Kosovo. The underlying sources of conflict were not addressed and since the KLA was not party to the agreement and vowed to fight on, few believed that the agreement would serve to end the violence.

Escalation to limited use of force

Continued fighting resulted in peace negotiations, the failure of which resulted in a NATO ultimatum demanding that Serbs sign the proposed peace agreement or face air strikes. The proposed agreement gave NATO unimpeded access to all of Serbia, involved a deployment of a large NATO force in Kosovo and a referendum on the future status of Kosovo that could only lead to independence. The Serbs were not offered any inducements or assurances to facilitate their compliance, and the context was not conducive to coercive diplomacy success: China and Russia opposed the use of force forcing NATO to attack without a UN mandate, several NATO members had questioned the wisdom of resorting to force and the United States had publicly ruled out the use of ground forces. Against this background it is hardly surprising that Milosevic decided to fight and hold out for a better agreement rather than comply. By ruling out the use of ground forces NATO guaranteed Milosevic that Kosovo would not be taken from him unless he agreed to hand it over, and this left him with considerable leverage.

Explaining Serbian compliance after 78 days of bombing

Milosevic exploited this leverage to obtain a better agreement than the one he had been offered before the bombing. The final agreement made no mention of a referendum on Kosovo's future, affirmed Serbia's sovereignty and territorial integrity, NATO was not granted access to Serbia proper, and the NATO force deployed in Kosovo had a UN mandate and Russian participation. In addition to these inducements and assurances, three other factors account for Milosevic's decision to comply. The first was NATO's ability to maintain its unity and escalate its bombing campaign, the second was a credible threat of a ground invasion if the bombing failed, and the third was the loss of Russian support. Taken together these new factors meant that the requirements of the *ideal policy* had been met.

powers that are willing to take the lead and bear most of the costs in blood and treasure that the use of force involve (Jakobsen 1998: 138–9).

Even with effective great power leadership coalitional coercive diplomacy may still lack the necessary credibility in the eyes of the adversary, however. Disagreements within the coalition may convince the adversary that the coalition will either fall apart once the battle has been joined or fail to escalate the use of force sufficiently to make non-compliance too costly. Belief that they would be able to undermine coalition unity by engaging in counter-coercion and propaganda campaigns probably provides an important part of the explanation why Saddam Hussein refused to withdraw from Kuwait without a fight in 1991 and why it took a 78-day bombing campaign to persuade Serbian President Milosevic to do so from Kosovo in 1999.

KEY POINTS

- It is difficult to frighten and reassure the adversary at the same time.
- Compliance hinges on psychological, perceptual and emotional factors outside the coercer's control.
- Coercive diplomacy against aggressors, terrorists and actors seeking WMD is especially hard because such opponents are likely to perceive the issues at stake in zero-sum terms.
- It has proven difficult to obtain the knowledge and intelligence required to devise effective coercive strategies.
- Actors relying on terrorism or guerrilla strategies are hard to target and coerce militarily.
- It is extremely difficult to verify whether opponents have stopped terrorist activities or WMD programmes.
- Coalitional coercive diplomacy requires great power leadership to be effective.

Table 13.2 Western use of coercive diplomacy to stop/undo acts of aggression 1990–2005

Location	Demand	Adversary	Coercive strategy*	Outcome
Iraq				
Round 1 1990–1991	Withdraw from Kuwait	Iraq	Sanctions Threats of force Deadline	Failure; escalation to limited force
Round 2 January–February 1991	Withdraw from Kuwait and leave heavy weapons behind	Iraq	Sanctions Limited use of force Deadline	Failure; escalation to brute force
Slovenia				
1991	End aggression	Serbia (Yugoslavia)	Sanctions Deadlines Inducements Assurances	Failure; compliance not caused by coercion
Croatia				
1991–92	End aggression	Serbia	Sanctions Deadlines Inducements Assurances	Failure; compliance not caused by coercion
Bosnia				
Round 1 June 1992	End shelling of Sarajevo airport and interference with relief operation	Serbia and Bosnian Serb Army (BSA)	Weak military threat Sanctions Deadline Inducements Assurances	Temporary success
Round 2 August–November 1992	End aggression and interference with relief efforts	Serbia and the BSA	Weak military threats No-fly zone Tighter sanctions Inducements Assurances	Failure

Table 13.2 *(Cont.)*

Location	Demand	Adversary	Coercive strategy*	Outcome
Round 3 April 1993	End aggression and sign peace plan	Serbia and the BSA	Weak military threats Threat to arm Bosnian forces Tighter sanctions	Failure
Round 4 August 1993	Withdraw forces from positions overlooking Sarajevo	Serbia and the BSA	Weak military threats Deadline Inducements Assurances	Failure; appeasement not coercion
Round 5 February 1994	Withdraw heavy weapons from Sarajevo	Serbia and the BSA	*Credible military threats* *Deadline* *Inducements* *Assurances*	Temporary success
Round 6 April 1994	Stop offensive; withdraw from Gorazde	Serbia and the BSA	Limited use of force Threats of escalation Deadline Assurances	Temporary success
Round 7 August–September 1995	Stop attacks and cease military activities, withdraw heavy weapons	Serbia and the BSA	*Limited use of force* *Deadline* *Inducements* *Assurances*	Costly success
Haiti				
Round 1 1991–92	Step down and restore president to power	Haitian military	Ineffective sanctions	Failure
Round 2 1993 to April 1994	Step down and restore president to power	Haitian military	More sanctions Deadline	Failure
Round 3 May–September 1994	Step down and restore president to power	Haitian military	*Credible military threat* *Deadline* *Inducements* *Assurances*	Cheap success
Somalia				
Round 1 1992 to May 1993	End fighting and interference with relief operation; hide weapons	Several Somali clans	*Threats and limited use of force* *Deadlines* *Inducements* *Assurances*	Temporary success

Table 13.2 *(Cont.)*

Location	Demand	Adversary	Coercive strategy*	Outcome
Round 2 June–October 1993	End fighting, disarm and hand over power to representative councils	Several Somali clans	Threats and limited use of force	Failure; escalation to brute force
Iraq 1996	Withdraw from Iraqi Kurdistan	Iraq	Attack with 44 cruise missiles** Expansion of no-fly zone	Costly success
Kosovo Round 1 June 1998	End violence, start negotiations, withdraw forces	Serbia	Sanctions Weak military threats Deadline Inducements Assurances	Failure
Round 2 September–October 1998	End violence, withdraw some forces, accept deployment of observer force	Serbia	*Sanctions* *Credible military threats* *Deadline* *Inducements* *Assurances*	Temporary success
Round 3 February–March 1999	Give NATO access throughout Serbia; withdraw from Kosovo, accept referendum on independence	Serbia	Sanctions Credible military threats Deadline	Failure
Round 4 March–June 1999	End violence, withdraw from Kosovo, accept peace plan	Serbia	*Sanctions* *Limited use of force* *Deadline* *Inducements* *Assurances*	Costly success

* Italic indicates implementation of the *ideal policy*.
** Unilateral US attack. All other cases are coalitional.

Table 13.3 Western use of coercive diplomacy to suspend or end WMD programmes 1990–2005

Location	Demand	Adversary	Coercive strategy	Outcome
Iraq				
Round 1 1992–93	Stop violating the no-fly zones and obstructing UN inspections	Iraq	Sanctions Limited use of force	Temporary success
Round 2 December 1997–February 1998	Stop obstructing UN inspections	Iraq	Sanctions Credible military threats Deadline	Temporary success
Round 3 November 1998	Stop obstructing UN inspections	Iraq	Sanctions Credible military threats Inducements	Temporary success
Round 4 2002–2003	Declare all WMD programmes, plants and materials; cooperate with UN inspectors	Iraq	Economic sanctions Air strikes Credible military threats Threats of regime change Deadlines	Failure; partial Iraqi compliance triggers US-led escalation to brute force
Libya				
Round 1 1992–1997	End WMD programmes; cease terrorist activities; hand over terrorist suspects; provide compensation	Libya	Sanctions Weak threats of force Threats of regime change	Failure
Round 2 1997–2003	End WMD programmes; cease terrorist activities; hand over terrorist suspects; provide compensation	Libya	Sanctions Implicit threats of force Carrots Assurances	Cheap success
North Korea				
Round 1 1993–1994	Freeze nuclear programme	North Korea	US sanction Threats of UN sanctions and force Inducements Assurances	Temporary success
Round 2 2002–	End nuclear programme	North Korea	US sanctions Indirect threats of force Inducements Assurances	?; ongoing negotiations
Iran				
2002–	End nuclear programme	Iran	Weak threats of sanctions and force Deadlines Inducements	?; ongoing negotiations

Table 13.4 Western use of coercive diplomacy to stop support for or use of terrorism 1990–2005

Location	Demand	Adversary	Coercive strategy*	Outcome
Libya				
Round 1 1992–1997	End WMD programmes; cease terrorist activities; hand over terrorist suspects; provide compensation	Libya	Sanctions Weak threats of force Threats of regime change	Failure
Round 2 1997–2003	End WMD programmes; cease terrorist activities; hand over terrorist suspects; provide compensation	Libya	Sanctions Implicit threats of force Carrots Assurances	Cheap success
Iraq				
1993	Stop targeting the US	Iraq	Attack with 23 cruise missiles**	?
Sudan				
1998	Stop support and use of terrorism	Sudan and al-Qaida	UN and US sanctions Attack with 6–7 cruise missiles**	Sudan?; al-Qaida failure
Afghanistan				
Round 1 1998–2001	Stop support and use of terrorism; hand over Osama bin Laden	Taliban and al-Qaida	Attack with 60–70 cruise missiles** Sanctions	Failure
Round 2 September–October 2001	Stop support and use of terrorism; hand over al-Qaida leadership	Taliban and al-Qaida	Sanctions Credible threats of force Deadline Inducements	Failure; escalation to limited force
Round 3 October 2001	Stop support and use of terrorism; hand over al-Qaida leadership; accept power sharing arrangement	Taliban and al-Qaida	Sanctions Use of limited force and threats of escalation Deadline Inducements	Failure; escalation to brute force
Pakistan				
2001	End support for Taliban; support US war against Afghanistan	Pakistan	*Threats of sanctions and force*** *Deadline* *Inducements* *Assurances*	Cheap success

* Italic indicate implementation of the *ideal policy*.
** Unilateral American use of coercive diplomacy. All other cases are coalitional.

Conclusion

Coercive diplomacy is an attractive strategy because it can be used to stop and/or reverse acts of military aggression, terrorism and attempts to acquire WMD with limited or, at the best of times, no use of force. While coercive diplomacy is a low-cost strategy when it succeeds, failure may be very costly as the coercer then faces the grim choice of backing down or executing his threat. This is a choice that Western policy makers have been faced with time and again since the end of the Cold War. The strategy's potential for peaceful conflict resolution has only been realized in three of the 36 coercive diplomacy exchanges listed in this chapter. A total of six lasting successes in 36 attempts is hardly an encouraging success rate, and it serves to underline the principal conclusion drawn in the literature: that it is a high-risk, hard-to-use strategy.

The conditions for success are clear in the abstract and coercive diplomacy generally succeed when the Western states meet the requirements of the *ideal policy* framework: (1) make credible threats of force and/or use limited force to defeat the adversary's gains quickly with little cost; (2) issue deadlines for compliance; (3) offer inducements; and (4) reassure opponents that compliance will not trigger new demands. The problem is that Western governments rarely devise coercive strategies that meet these requirements. As a consequence, the main problem is not misperception, miscalculation or irrationality on the part of Western adversaries, as it is often claimed (see e.g. Tarzi 2005). The main problem is that the Western states either lack the will to threaten and use force in the manner prescribed by the *ideal policy* framework, or conversely, when the willingness to do so exists, they fail to couple the stick with adequate inducements and credible assurances.

It is a paradoxical feature of coercive diplomacy that the prospects of cheap success are highest when the coercer is willing to go all the way and escalate to brute force if need be. Unfortunately for Western decision makers it was all too apparent that they lacked the willingness to do so in most of the coercive diplomacy exchanges they were involved in during the 1990s. Western policy makers were very reluctant to put their troops in harm's way in Somalia, the Balkans and in Haiti. After the traumatic withdrawal from Somalia, the Western and especially the American preoccupation with force protection undermined the initial attempts to coerce the military leadership in Haiti and the Serbs in Bosnia and Kosovo, and it also played a major role in deterring Western governments from launching a timely intervention to stop the genocide in Rwanda in 1994.

This problem did not go away after September 11; it continues to apply to most contemporary conflicts that are unrelated to the war on terrorism. Western governments remain extremely reluctant to threaten and use force credibly to end armed conflicts on the African continent, for example, preferring to leave the management of these conflicts to the UN and Africa's regional organizations. As was the case in the 1990s, coercive diplomacy will only be employed effectively to counter aggression in conflicts that pose no direct threat to Western security, provided that the prospects of military success are high and the risk of casualties low. Very few contemporary conflicts fit this description.

The problem is the opposite when Western states use coercive diplomacy to counter terrorism and WMD acquisition. In these conflicts September 11 has made a huge difference. After the fall of the Taliban and Saddam Hussein, few actors engaged in terrorist and WMD activities are likely to doubt Western resolve with respect to threatening with and using force. In these conflicts the principal problem from a coercive diplomacy perspective is that Western decision makers tend to see these confrontations in zero-sum terms and make demands that give the adversaries little incentive to comply. American demands for regime change are likely to crowd out the prospects of coercive diplomacy success in most cases, as it gives the opponents no incentive to cooperate. American demands for regime change made coercive diplomacy success next to impossible to obtain in the confrontations with the Taliban and Saddam Hussein, and credible assurances that regime change would not be pursued were key in the successful negotiations that coerced Libya to terminate its support for terrorism and its nuclear programme. Similarly, it is hard to see the regimes in North Korea and Iran giving up their nuclear programmes as long as they have good reason to believe that the United States is seeking their overthrow.

While the Libyan case suggests that coercion coupled with skilful use of assurances and inducements can coerce states to end WMD programmes, the prospects of success look considerably less bright with apocalyptical terrorist groups like al-Qaida. The principal problem here is not unwillingness to use inducements and assurances, but lack of feasibility. Such groups are hard to locate and target militarily, engaged in a zero-sum struggle and willing to die for their cause. Against these actors it is only possible to use coercive diplomacy indirectly to coerce state sponsors and less radical terrorist groups to stop their cooperation with al-Qaida and affiliated groups.

It is in short unlikely that coercive diplomacy will have a higher rate of success in the foreseeable future than it has enjoyed since the end of the Cold War. Western governments will simply not be able to meet the requirements for success very often. Western policy makers would therefore be well advised to strive harder to prevent the need for coercive diplomacy from arising in the first place.

? QUESTIONS

Why has the Western use of coercive diplomacy increased since the end of the Cold War?

What distinguishes coercive diplomacy from brute force?

Consider the pros and cons of the definition of limited force employed in this chapter.

How do you determine whether the coercer wants to avoid the use of force or is using coercive diplomacy to legitimize it?

List the advantages and limitations of the *ideal policy* framework.

Why is it difficult to define coercive diplomacy success?

Does the implementation of the *ideal policy* yield the predicted results?

List the factors complicating the use of coercive diplomacy.

Why is coercive diplomacy unlikely to become more successful in the foreseeable future?

How could Western governments reduce their need for coercive diplomacy and force to counter aggression, terrorism and WMD?

FURTHER READING

■ **Art, Robert J. and Cronin, P.M. (eds.) (2003), *The United States and Coercive Diplomacy*, Washington D.C.: United States Institute of Peace.** Applies refined version of George's theory to sixteen new cases. Useful for its case studies but analytic value reduced by inconsistent coding of cases and outcomes as well as vague definitions of key concepts.

- **Bratton, P.C. (2005), 'When Is Coercion Successful? And Why Can't We Agree on It?', *Naval War College Review*, 58/3: 99–120**. Good review of the various definitions of success employed in the coercion literature.

- **Byman, D. and Waxman, M. (2000), *Confronting Iraq: U.S. Policy and the Use of Force Since the Gulf War*, Santa Monica, CA: RAND, MR-1146-OSD**. Analyses use of coercive diplomacy against Iraq 1991–1998.

- **Freedman, L. (ed.) (1998), *Strategic Coercion: Concepts and Cases*, Oxford: Oxford University Press**. Discusses strategic coercion, coercive diplomacy and compellence and contains eight case studies.

- **George, A.L., Hall, D., and Simons, W.E. (1971), *The Limits of Coercive Diplomacy: Laos, Cuba, Vietnam*, Boston, MA: Little, Brown**. The initial formulation of George's theory applied to three cases.

- **George, A.L. and Simons, W.E. (eds.) (1994), *The Limits of Coercive Diplomacy*, Boulder, CO: Westview, 2nd revised edn.** Refined version of theory presented in 1971 volume applied to seven cases.

- **Jakobsen, P.V. (1998), *Western Use of Coercive Diplomacy after the Cold War: A Challenge for Theory and Practice*, London: Macmillan**. Develops and tests the *ideal policy* concept in three cases and identifies the conditions under which Western governments are most likely to threaten and use force.

- **Jentleson, B.W. and Whytock, C.A. (2005–06), 'Who "Won" Libya? The Force–Diplomacy Debate and Its Implications for Theory and Policy', *International Security*, 30/3 (Winter): 47–86**. Refinement of George's theory applied to Libya.

- **Pape, R.A. (1996), *Bombing to Win: Air Power and Coercion in War*, Ithaca, NY: Cornell University Press**. Very influential work introducing the distinction between punishment and denial to the study of coercion. Contains five case studies.

- **Schelling, T.C. (1966), *Arms and Influence*, New Haven, CT: Yale University Press**. The theory of compellence is presented and the concept is distinguished from deterrence and brute force.

IMPORTANT WEBSITES

- **http://www.crisisgroup.org** The International Crisis Group's website contains high-quality analysis of ongoing and potential armed conflicts.

- **http://www.globalsecurity.org** GlobalSecurity.org contains useful background information on armed conflicts past and present as well as developing news stories in the fields of defence and security.

- **http://www.rand.org** The Rand Corporation's website contains excellent studies of coercion and air power available in full text.

Visit the Online Resource Centre that accompanies this book for lots of interesting additional material: www.oxfordtextbooks.co.uk/orc/collins/

14 The Role of Intelligence in National Security

STAN A. TAYLOR

Chapter Contents

- Introduction
- Definitions and theory of intelligence
- Intelligence services of different nations
- Intelligence collection disciplines
- The intelligence process
- Intelligence and security since the Second World War
- Legal and ethical issues involving intelligence
- Covert action
- Terrorism, Iraq, and the contemporary security condition
- Conclusion

Reader's Guide

This chapter explores the tenuous and increasingly complex and critical relationship between security and intelligence. Following some basic introductory remarks, including definitions and a theoretical framework, it then presents an overview of some of the more significant intelligence services in major nations, it describes the variety of intelligence disciplines (the ways intelligence is collected) followed by a discussion of what is called the intelligence process—the way information needs are defined by decision makers and what happens between then and the time they receive that information. After giving examples of intelligence successes and failures in modern history, the chapter concludes with a discussion of some of the ethical issues involved in intelligence and a brief discussion of the contemporary security/intelligence environment.

Introduction

Security is a fundamental goal of all states in contemporary world affairs. To support that search for security, all states collect intelligence—some merely devote more resources to the process than others. The significance of intelligence has been recognized for centuries. In one of the earliest recorded uses of spies, Moses ordered spies into Canaan to 'spy out the land' to see whether or not the Israelites could occupy it. The Chinese general Sun Tzu (ca. 500 BC) devoted the last chapter in his still widely read book, *The Art of War*, to the role of spies. Sun Tzu, like most early users of intelligence, sought information about the military capabilities and plans of potential enemies. Roman armies under Caesar scouted the movements and capabilities of enemy troops. In most cases the information was useful, but not always critical to the battle outcome.

Although the desire and need for intelligence has been constant for centuries, the information available, the technology of communications, the means of collection, and the speed and accuracy of turning raw information into finished intelligence for decision makers have all changed dramatically. These changes have become the critical and defining characteristics of what is now called the Information Age. Both the information sought and the means by it which was sought were one thing in, for example, the industrial age. But they are completely different in a post-industrial, post-service economy information age where governments, businesses, and common social intercourse are all driven by the need for and availability of information, as well as by the need, at times, to keep information secret from others.

KEY QUOTES 14.1

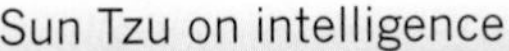

Sun Tzu on intelligence

Thus, what enables the wise sovereign and the good general to strike and conquer, and achieve things beyond the reach of ordinary men, is foreknowledge. Now this foreknowledge cannot be elicited from spirits; it cannot be obtained inductively from experience, nor by any deductive calculation. Knowledge of the enemy's dispositions can only be obtained from other men. Therefore, enlightened rulers and good generals who are able to obtain intelligent agents as spies are certain for great achievements.

If you know the enemy and know yourself, you need not fear a hundred battles. If you know yourself and not the enemy, for every victory you will suffer a defeat. If you know neither yourself nor the enemy, you are a fool and will meet defeat in every battle.

(From Chapter 13, 'On Spies' by Sun Tzu, *The Art of War*, translated by Lionel Giles; 13:006 in the Shonsi system.)

KEY POINTS

- The collection, analysis, and use of intelligence are ubiquitous—all states do this to one degree or another.
- Intelligence has been used by rulers and generals from earliest times to the present.
- The information available, as well as the means to collect and analyse it, has changed dramatically in the Information Age.

Definitions and theory of intelligence

The term *intelligence*, as used in this chapter, refers to the collection, analysis, production, and utilization of information about potentially hostile states, groups, individuals, or activities. It differs from other sources of information in that it is often, but not always, collected clandestinely and that states attempt to keep other states from obtaining it. It may also include special activities meant to influence the foreign or domestic policy choices of other states without revealing the source of the influence. *Intelligence* also refers to the government entities that collect and analyse information as well as to the process by which this function is performed.

A general theory of intelligence can be drawn from cybernetics, a discipline developed in 1947 by mathematician Norbert Weiner and others. The word *cybernetics* comes from a Greek work meaning helmsman or governor—one who steers a ship. A helmsman must use skill, intuition, and constant feedback from the environment to permit accurate steerage of the vessel. Cybernetics is a complex science drawn from biology, neural modelling, psychology, mathematics, electrical engineering, as well as other disciplines. It is the science of feedback—the study of how information can maintain or alter any biological, social, mechanical, or artificial system. Cybernetics has contributed to the development of General Systems Theory, Artificial Intelligence, and Robotics.

Cybernetics is a perfect metaphor for the role of intelligence applied to statecraft. Decision makers are the helmsmen, the governors, who must use skill, intuition, and a constant flow of information or intelligence to optimize efficiency (defined as the most security at the least cost) for the state. Cybernetics is the iterative flow of information that allows thermostats to maintain temperature in a building, but it is also much more than that. It is about goal-oriented behaviour at all levels of living systems. It allows these systems to reach defined goals based on information flows. It is a unifying theory that runs through all levels of human interaction. Though not frequently acknowledged, it played a role in the development of constructivism, particularly social constructivism—the notion that social institutions adapt through the constant processing of stimuli (information) from the environment.

Intelligence, whether defined as process, product, or people, involves collecting and analysing billions of stimuli from the international environment. The resulting information is used by decision makers as they act as helmsmen in steering the ship of state through the hazardous waters of international politics.

KEY POINTS

- Intelligence refers to the process of defining needs, collecting and analysing information, and providing information needed by decision makers to make sound decisions about a state's policies.
- Intelligence also refers to the process by which this is done, to the people and institutions that do it, and to the occasional use of secret activities to influence a foreign state's policies.
- The theory of cybernetics assumes that the intelligence process is but part of the flow of information that then acts as feedback to maximize a state's efficiency in achieving its foreign policy goals.

Intelligence services of different nations

As mentioned above, every nation collects, analyses, and uses intelligence—some merely devote more resources to it than others. This section outlines a general organizational sketch for most nations and examines in greater detail the specific organizations of some selected countries. As Phillip Knightley (1986: 5) has said, 'spies have been around for centuries, but intelligence services are new'. They began in most countries as military intelligence units supplying information to commanders and were usually cut back or eliminated when hostilities ended.

The early national intelligence services that appeared in the last three decades of the nineteenth century were generally small, poorly funded, and somewhat obscure. It was not until around the turn of that century that truly national intelligence services appeared in European states. Sometime between 1900 and 1920 nearly every European power had a permanent national intelligence organization with worldwide interests. America was the only exception. In spite of fairly active and effective military intelligence units, the United States did not create a permanent civilian intelligence organization with global interests until 1947.

In general, most large and globally active nations have some or all of the following types of intelligence agencies. The nature of each agency will vary according to the different political cultures, legal systems, and bureaucratic styles of each country.

1. An overall supervisory office or group of offices charged with coordinating the several different agencies that make up a country's intelligence community (IC).
2. An agency responsible for collecting, analysing, and producing intelligence drawn from foreign countries and other external sources.
3. An agency responsible for collecting, analysing, and producing intelligence about domestic threats to security.
4. An agency responsible for the collection and distribution of signals intelligence (sigint).
5. An agency that works under the direction of the military department or departments of a government to provide intelligence required by military forces.
6. Depending on size and global involvement, nations may have agencies specifically charged with anti-terrorism; the development, operation, and exploitation of satellite and overhead imagery; counterintelligence; border protection; and other special functions.

Table 14.1 shows the essential structure of the intelligence communities of the United States, the United Kingdom, Russia, Germany, and France. The overall outlines of each nation are quite similar; however, the services of each country vary greatly. The greatest differences do not show in Table 14.1. They appear in the size, scope, nature of the supervisory structures, and in the extensiveness of public accountability through legislative oversight.

Historically, intelligence organizations and operations were shrouded in secrecy. Quite often the organizations were created and controlled by a very small number of government officials. In some nations it was not uncommon for intelligence operations to be directed against citizens or other branches of their own governments. The intelligence services in the Soviet Union were clearly above the law and their efforts were directed as much, or more, against Soviet citizens as they were against foreign intelligence targets. The same was true in Nazi Germany where the intelligence services were virtually unrestrained in their domestic operations.

Table 14.1 Intelligence communities of five major nations

Country	United Kingdom	United States	Russia	France	Germany
Supervisory Structure	1. Prime Minister 2. Foreign Minister (for SIS and GCHQ) 3. Home Secretary (for M15) 4. Special Cabinet Committees 5. Joint Intelligence Committee (JIC)	1. President 2. National Security Council (NSC) 3. Director of National Intelligence (DNI) 4. Secretary of Defense for DIA,NSA,GIA, and Uniformed Services Intelligence	1. President 2. Russian National Security Council 3. Permanent Interbranch Commissions of the Russian National Security Council 4. Ministry of Defence (for the GRU)	1. Prime Minister 2. General Secretary for National Defence 3. Inter-departmental Intelligence Committee 4. Domestic Security Council 5. Ministry of Defence	1. Chancellor 2. Parliamentary Control Commission (PKK) 3. German Federal Armed Forces (for MAD) 4. Federal Ministry of the Interior (for BfV)
Foreign Intelligence	Secret Intelligence Service (MI6)	Central Intelligence Agency (CIA)	Foreign Intelligence Service (SVR)	General Directorate for External Security (DGSE)	Federal Intelligence Service (BND)
Domestic Intelligence	Security Service (MI5)	Federal Bureau of Investigation (FBI)	Federal Security Service (FSB)	General Intelligence (RG)	Federal Office for the Protection of the Constitution (BfV)
Signals Intelligence	Government Communications Headquarters (GCHQ)	National Security Agency (NSA)	Federal Agency for Government Communications and Information (FAPSI)	Intelligence and Electronic Warfare Brigade (BRGE)	Office for Radio Monitoring of the Federal Armed Forces (AFMBw)
Military Intelligence	1. Defence Intelligence Staff (DIS) 2. Various Military Service Intelligence Groups	1. Defense Intelligence Agency 2. Various Military Service Intelligence Groups	Main Intelligence Administration (GRU)	1. Directorate of Military Intelligence (DRM) 2. Directorate for Defence Protection and Security (DPSD)	1. Office of Intelligence of the Federal Armed Forces (ANBw) 2. Military Security Service (MAD)
Other	1. Defence Geographic and Imagery Intelligence Agency (DGIA) 2. National Criminal Intelligence Service (NCIS) 3. Metropolitan Police (Scotland Yard)	1. Department of Homeland Security (DHS) 2. National Reconnaissance Office (NRO) 3. National Geospatial-Intelligence Agency (NGA)	1. Federal Protective Service (FSO) 2. Ministry of Internal Affairs (MVD) 3. Federal Border Service (FPS)	1. Central Information Systems Security Division (DCSSI) 2. Directorate of Territorial Security (DST)	1. State Offices for the Protection of the Constitution (LfV) 2. Federal office for Information Technology Security (BSI)

In the contemporary world, only the US, UK, and Russian services can claim to have truly global intelligence coverage and activities. The US intelligence community is by far the largest and best funded, but the British services are taken seriously partially because of their history and relationship to the US. Russian intelligence is still very extensive and continues to be directed against Russian citizens and groups, though less so than during the Soviet period. Germany and France are the only other Western nations with extensive intelligence services, but both are hampered by fragmentation and by chequered pasts.

In 1976, the US became the first nation to place its IC under permanent legislative oversight. Since that time, most democratic nations have followed suit to one degree or another. Australia and Canada moved in this direction in 1979 and 1984, respectively, with most other European nations following suit through the 1980s and 1990s (Born, Johnson, and Leigh 2005: 4). European nations did this partially in response to changing interpretations of certain provisions of the European Declaration of Human Rights. The degree of oversight varies from nation to nation with the US being the most extensive and Russia being the least. Although there is growing sentiment for legislative oversight of intelligence services and operations, particularly in democratic nations, certain branches of some intelligence services still operate under executive supervision only.

KEY POINTS

- The intelligence communities of most large nations contain agencies that perform foreign and domestic intelligence collection and analysis, an agency that collects various kinds of electronic communications, and agencies that support military activities.
- Although intelligence functions have been performed by nations for centuries, the agencies that performed them were unknown to the public and were supervised only by heads of state and their close associates.
- Although all states have used spies to support military efforts for centuries, national civilian intelligence organizations with global operations did not appear until early in the twentieth century in Europe and in 1947 in America.
- Only in the late twentieth century did intelligence services begin to have statutory authorizations and fall under some degree of legislative supervision.
- Only American, British, and Russian intelligence services can be described as truly global in operations and structure in today's world—most others have regional interests and more limited operations.

Intelligence collection disciplines

Each different method of collecting intelligence is referred to as an intelligence discipline. These disciplines are usually divided into two general types—human intelligence collection (or humint in intelligence jargon) and technical intelligence collection (techint). (See Table 14.2.)

Humint

The use of spies (humint) is the oldest such discipline. It may not be, as it is often called, the second oldest profession, but for as long as tribes, clans, nations, or empires have been fighting one another,

Table 14.2 Intelligence collection disciplines

HUMINT	Human intelligence: information collected by intelligence officers usually stationed in foreign nations.
TECHINT	Technical intelligence: originally referred to information about weapons systems but now used to refer to intelligence collected from the interception of a variety of electronic signals by the use of sophisticated technical means.
SIGINT	Signals intelligence: all kinds of information collected through various electronic devices, including the following sub-disciplines.
IMINT	Imagery intelligence: any photographic or digital images collected by orbiting (satellite) or ground-based (airplanes or unmanned aerial vehicles) systems.
PHOTINT	Photographic intelligence: an earlier term for IMINT. Used widely to describe both film and digital photographs taken from satellites.
COMINT	Communications intelligence: the interception of communications between two or more parties.
TELINT	Telemetry intelligence: the interception of data transmitted during the testing of various kinds of weapons systems.
ELINT	Electronic intelligence: the interception of electronic emissions emanating from weapons and tracking systems.
MASINT	Measures and signatures intelligence: a more recent form of SIGINT using more sophisticated devices that can sense material used in various types of modern weapons.
RADINT	Information derived from the use of radar signals emanating from overhead satellites, aircraft, or from ground-based sources.
OSINT	Open source intelligence: the collection of intelligence information from a wide variety of publicly available sources (media, government information, scholarly publications, etc.).

Adapted from Lowenthal (2003), Ch. 5

there have been spies. The methods used by these spies have changed over the centuries but the goal has always been the same—to gain some advantage over an opponent by accessing his secrets, usually through stealthy observation or by intercepting written messages carried by couriers.

This kind of work has always required men and women who know the language and culture of the country to which they are assigned and who are comfortable living a double life. Today's intelligence officers operate quite differently from the way they are portrayed in literature or cinema. They are seldom armed and are usually putative employees of a nation's diplomatic service working in a foreign country. While there, they attempt to recruit locals who have access to classified information and who, for whatever reason, may wish to reveal that information to them. An intelligence officer's primary responsibility is to develop secure ways to exchange information in a manner that will not compromise the person providing it.

Techint

Until the Second World War, technical intelligence (techint) referred to intelligence regarding an enemy's weapons systems. Today the term is used to describe virtually all intelligence collected through technical means. Techint developed in response to scientific advances in electronic communications.

Three advances are particularly noteworthy: first, the development of wire-based electronic communications; second, the development of wireless electronic communications; and third, the development of the aeroplane.

In the late 1830s, states began to communicate with their diplomatic and military personnel abroad over fixed, land-based telegraphic wires. This also meant, however, that other states could tap into these wires and intercept communications.

By the early 1900s, following Marconi's development of wireless communications, governments could send messages to their representatives abroad literally through the air. This made it even easier to intercept electronic signals since, once an electronic signal is sent into the air, it becomes a free good and intelligence agencies around the world soon learned to intercept such transmissions and even to decode or decipher them when they were sent in secret codes and ciphers. All other means of techint have descended from these twentieth century developments.

A third widely used techint collection discipline became possible with the development of the aeroplane in 1903. The Wright brothers correctly believed their invention would be of critical use to military services. They were not disappointed. Long before aeroplanes were used as fighting weapons, however, they were used for aerial reconnaissance. In France, developments in photography made it possible to take pictures of troop locations from aircraft. Photographic intelligence (photint) was born when the first aerial photographs in a battle zone were taken by Italian aviators in the **Italian-Turkish War** in October 1911. By the latter half of the twentieth century, the major powers were conducting surveillance by the use of aircraft, satellites, and (in the twenty-first century) by unmanned aerial vehicles (UAVs).

KEY POINTS

- Different ways of collecting intelligence are called intelligence disciplines.
- The earliest form of intelligence collection was humint.
- The development of electronic means of communication led to commensurate means of intercepting electronic communications through the latter half of the twentieth century. These techniques are called sigint or techint.
- Sigint capabilities can be divided into sigint, masint, comint, radint, and elint, each with related sub-disciplines.
- The invention of manned flight led to the development of photographic intelligence (photint).

The intelligence process

The intelligence process, also called the intelligence cycle, begins with national security and foreign policy officials needing to know something about other states or other global actors involved in world affairs whose actions might impinge on the security of their state. That need-to-know, along with literally hundreds of others, will be prioritized and eventually assigned to one or more entities that make up a state's intelligence community. This prioritization stage also involves decisions about which intelligence disciplines will be used to collect the information. The requested information may be about empirical and observable developments (missile characteristics, WMD, types of weapons, foreign commitments, etc.) or it may be about intentions (what a state or group plans to do with its weapons, etc.). But above all, the information is usually something that the target state or group does not want other states to obtain.

Next is the collection stage. Various intelligence agencies and sub-agencies will begin to collect information through humint, techint, osint, or, usually, a combination of all disciplines, particularly if the topic is prioritized at a high level. In the buildup to the 2003 Iraqi war, for example, nearly every intelligence entity in several major states was focused on Iraq. Satellite photography, airborne listening devices, and other highly sophisticated instruments were focused on Iraqi developments, while sigint agencies were intercepting public and private communications. At the same time, some intelligence officers were interviewing defectors, émigrés, as well as official and non-official visitors to Iraq while other officers were trying to develop sources of information within the Iraqi government itself.

Following the collection stage, and often contemporaneous with it, some processing occurs. Material in foreign languages needs to be translated, photographs must be interpreted, and coded communications need to be decoded. Because of sheer volume, translating intercepted communications may take many months and deciphering coded communications may take several years.

Analysis is the next stage in the intelligence process. All collected and processed information is eventually fed to analysts who must place it into historical contexts and try to separate the valid information from the disinformation put out by the intelligence target to confuse any collecting state. Many consider analysis the most important and the most difficult stage in the intelligence process. Information sent to analysts is called raw or unfinished intelligence; it is often conflicting, ambiguous, contradictory, or even occasionally accurate. When information leaves the analysts it is called finished intelligence.

Production follows analysis. Obviously, critical and time-sensitive information will be delivered immediately to decision makers. But most analysis is put into some finished form before being sent to decision makers as an intelligence product. The product can take a variety of forms. It may be daily or occasional briefs to decision makers or it may be what are called intelligence estimates—periodic printed assessments of important developments.

The final stage in the intelligence process closes the cycle. It involves the dissemination or delivery of the information to those who requested it in the first place. Obviously, throughout the cycle additional related information gets added to the specific information gathered in response to the original questions, but it is at this stage that intelligence theoretically adds value to the decision making process. Senior government officials, armed with the intelligence product, are able to pursue policies and practise statecraft in a more informed manner and, theoretically, better able to enhance either state or alliance security.

The word *theoretically* must be emphasized. The intelligence cycle is logical and sound as described. It is also misleading. Unfortunately, many problems that can lead to intelligence failures enter into the process at virtually every stage (see Think Point 14.1). Decision makers often do not know which questions to ask. Few decision makers before the mid-1990s, for example, were asking about bin Laden and al-Qaeda. Other problems

THINK POINT 14.1

Intelligence failure or policy failure?

The phrase 'intelligence failure' is widely used but minimally understood. One of the frustrating facts of life faced by intelligence agencies in any country is that they are, in one sense, always in a 'lose-lose' situation. The phrase 'policy failure' is seldom heard, while the phrase 'intelligence failure' is heard with increasing frequency. If a government initiative works, it will always be touted as a 'policy success' but seldom as an 'intelligence success'. If a government policy is not successful, accusations of 'intelligence failure' fill the media but 'policy failure' is seldom seen or heard.

occur at the prioritization stage. A question, or set of questions, may not be given a high priority. For example, prior to 9/11, both bin Laden and al-Qaeda were on the priority lists of several nations, but they were not very high on those lists. The Bush administration came into office in 2001, in fact, with WMD in rogue states as its highest priority. Only after 9/11 did bin Laden rise to the top of every list (Taylor and Goldman 2004: 425).

Processing and collecting failures also occur. Communications may not be translated, spy planes may be shot down, intelligence officers or their agents may be caught, or codes may not be broken. Although American cryptographers were intercepting vast amounts of Soviet coded messages in the 1940s, they could not decipher them. It was not until 1948 that the US and Britain began to break the Soviet communications code. Starting in late 1942 and then with gradually increasing success into the late 1950s, what was called the VENONA Project revealed vast Soviet penetrations into the American, British, West German, French, and Australian governments. But often the decrypted messages were being worked on two to five years after they were intercepted. VENONA confirmed the treason of Kim Philby and the other Cambridge spies, Julius and Ethyl Rosenberg (the American atomic spies), Klaus Fuchs (the British atomic spy), Alger Hiss (an advisor to President Franklin D. Roosevelt) as well as Soviet spies in highly placed positions in virtually all Western governments, including the US and Britain. But the decryptions either came too late to be useful or could not be used in legal trials out of fear that their use would reveal to the Soviets that the West had broken their codes. Being able to read Soviet codes was deemed of higher value than the prosecution of traitors.

Another weakness in the cycle occurs during the analysis stage. Most intelligence failures occur during this stage. Analysts may be overwhelmed by too much intelligence or kept in the dark because of insufficient intelligence; they may have prejudices that cause them to emphasize unimportant clues or to ignore important ones. They may fall victim to groupthink or they may want to cook their analysis to fit a decision maker's recipe. Or they may be overly cautious so that they do not become embarrassed for being wrong and thus lose bureaucratic influence. A proliferation of analytical agencies within a nation's intelligence community contributes to this problem.

Finally, at any stage in the cycle, 'stovepiping' may occur. Either collectors or analysts may take what they deem to be pleasing information directly to the decision maker and thus circumvent the critical analytical process. For example, at one point in the prelude to the Iraq invasion, two American Defense Department officials took information directly to their superiors rather than submit it to intelligence community analysts. The information proved misleading and would have been seen in better perspective had it gone through the normal analytical process.

KEY POINTS

- With only slight variations, every national government has an intelligence cycle or process that identifies critical intelligence questions, assigns tasks to various collecting agencies, processes and analyses information, and delivers it to decision makers. In theory this process improves and informs the decision making process and enhances national security.
- Breakdowns, often resulting from a failure to correlate and coordinate between agencies and sub-agencies, occur at virtually every stage of the process.
- Without detracting from the importance and difficulty of developing contacts inside hostile governments or terrorist groups, analysis is probably the most difficult and important stage in the process. Most intelligence failures arise in this stage.

Intelligence and security since the Second World War

The Cold War

A full understanding of the contributions of intelligence to security in modern times includes many developments during the first fifty years of the twentieth century. The role of British intelligence in getting America into the First World War (the Zimmerman Telegraph affair), the intelligence failure that got America into the Second World War (Pearl Harbor), the dramatic impact of cryptography during the Second World War (the Enigma development), and the amazing success of British counterintelligence in using Hitler's spies for their own purposes (the Doublecross operation) are all interesting and important. But for the purposes of this book we will begin with the Cold War.

Four Second World War intelligence developments set the stage for intelligence during the Cold War. First, in reaction to the Pearl Harbor attack in 1941, the US created its first civilian intelligence agency—the Office of Strategic Services (OSS). By the end of the war, the OSS had become a fairly large and sophisticated intelligence operation with experience in nearly all phases of intelligence—collection, analysis, special operations, and psychological warfare. However, shortly after the war ended, American President Harry S. Truman disbanded the OSS. Parts of it were transferred to other departments and Truman immediately initiated planning for a new civilian agency. The National Security Act of 1947 created, among other things, the Central Intelligence Agency (CIA) and America now joined other major world powers with a peacetime civilian intelligence agency.

Second, the extensive sigint cooperation established between Great Britain and the United States led to the world's first intelligence treaty between nations. The BRUSA agreement of May 1943 followed a series of both formal and informal exchanges of personnel and information between Britain and the US. Five years, and scores of negotiations later, this turned into the UK–USA Agreement (UKUSA). The treaty bound the UK, US, Canada, Australia, and New Zealand to cooperate fully in the collection and sharing of sigint information. It even divided geographical collection responsibilities between those nations. UKUSA has weathered some difficult times—concern about Soviet penetration of British intelligence, the Suez crisis, and a small episode when New Zealand banned nuclear armed and powered vessels from its harbours in 1985—but it still exists today.

Third, aerial overhead imagery, first begun during the First World War, became much more sophisticated during the Second World War. As that war ended and the Cold War began, Western nations believed it even more important to be able to obtain information about Soviet weapons developments through overhead imagery. Both American and British aircraft gathered sigint and imint intelligence by flying over international waters but as close to the Soviet territorial borders as possible. Then, in 1956, after the Soviets rejected US President Eisenhower's Open Skies Proposal, the Americans put into service the U-2 spy plane—an aircraft that could fly directly over Soviet territory 70,000 feet in the sky and, it was believed, 20,000 feet beyond the range of Soviet planes and missiles, yet take photographs and other images that revealed a great deal about Soviet weapons systems. Within two years, virtually all Western hard intelligence about Soviet weapons developments came from U-2 overflights. That source ended on 1 May 1960 when the Soviets shot down a U-2 plane and captured its pilot, Gary Powers, alive.

Spy planes played a critical role in the discovery and documentation of Soviet missiles in Cuba in 1962 as well as in the discovery of Iraqi missile sites in 1991. But they were no longer used in flights over Soviet territory after the 1 May 1960 incident. Instead, the US developed satellites that could take a variety of images from hundreds of miles in space while either orbiting the planet or geosynchronous above Soviet territory. The first American satellite to cross Soviet territory was Discoverer 13 in August 1960. Discoverer 14, the next in the series, was responsible for more photographs of the Soviet Union than came from all U-2 overflights. The Soviets soon developed their own photographic satellites and the era of 'eyes in the sky' began. This gave both sides in the Cold War the ability to monitor weapons developments and to verify compliance with the arms control agreements that began in the 1970s. Contrary to what some believed at the time, intelligence gained from satellite reconnaissance actually added to international stability and even played a role in the eventual ending of the Cold War. In fact, it may be said that in the absence of this intelligence source, arms control agreements would have been unlikely.

The fourth Second World War development that both set the stage for, and carried into, the Cold War, was the intense human espionage conducted on both sides is of the Iron Curtain. Before the war ended, the Soviet Union had more spies working against its allies than its enemies. In the early post-war years, a remarkably large number of British, American, and West German citizens were working for Soviet intelligence. Senior British intelligence and Foreign Office personnel became traitors and several well-placed US and West German bureaucrats and government officials betrayed their countries.

The so-called 'Cambridge Five' compromised many British and American military and political secrets. At least three of them had access to strategic plans during the UN-approved, but US-led, Korean War. Early efforts to keep several Eastern European countries from falling into the Communist Bloc were frustrated by other compromises and, as a result, scores of Western intelligence officers and local resistance fighters were betrayed and killed. Soviet intelligence officers in Britain and the US recruited scientists and others working on the secret efforts to develop atomic weapons. When Klaus Fuchs, a German émigré scientist working on the British atomic project, and later assigned to be part of the British team working on the US atomic project, fell under suspicion and was interrogated, the ring of 'Atomic Spies' began to unravel. Several critical scientific and engineering secrets were nevertheless betrayed to Soviet intelligence. As a result, the Soviet atomic bomb came five to seven years earlier than it otherwise would have come.

Soviet defectors who stayed in their positions yet reported to Western intelligence (Oleg Penkovsky, Adolf Tolkachev, and Oleg Gordievsky, for example) added to the intrigue of the latter half of the twentieth century and large-scale and expensive intelligence agencies became a fact of life in most globally active states.

KEY POINTS

- The sigint capabilities of major powers came to play an increasingly significant role in international security matters.
- The Cold War saw the development of the first US peacetime civilian intelligence agency (the CIA), the formalization of intelligence cooperation through the UKUSA Agreement, the growth of spy-counterspy efforts on both sides of the **Iron Curtain**, and the heavy reliance on high tech 'eyes in the sky' surveillance.
- Overhead satellite reconnaissance, first instituted to assist in preventing future surprise wars, later came to be a valuable aid in stabilizing and reducing the tension of the Cold War.

Legal and ethical issues involving intelligence

The twenty-first century has seen an increase in the need for and use of intelligence and an increase in the ways it can be collected. But these developments have also raised even more questions about the legality and ethics of intelligence operations. Much has been written on this topic, but it is not as complicated as some think. First, the domestic laws of the collecting nation always permit (either expressly in statutes which create intelligence agencies or tacitly through the existence of such agencies) the sending of their own personnel abroad for such purposes. The nation recruits these people; it trains them, pays them, and provides for their retirement.

Second, positive international law (bilateral and multilateral treaty obligations between states) is generally silent or permissive on the subject of espionage. Some interpret the presence of verification clauses in a variety of arms control, disarmament, non-proliferation, and other international treaties as legitimizing that aspect of intelligence collection. Most of these treaties contain a clause to the effect that no state that is a party to the agreement will interfere with national technical means (NTM) of verification. NTM normally refers to overhead surveillance or other electronic collection techniques. Customary international law (traditional and accepted patterns of international interaction) is ambiguous on the subject—most authors view the ubiquity of spying as evidence of some legitimacy while a few view spying as illegal under virtually any circumstances.

Third, the laws of all nations prohibit their own citizens from revealing state secrets to other nations. In short, it is legal under the laws of one's own nation to be sent abroad to persuade citizens of other nations to do what their own laws prohibit and international law largely ignores.

Discussions of the ethics of intelligence collection usually treat two aspects. The first aspect is the relationship of means to ends. As long as the purpose of the espionage is to protect and enhance a nation's security, and as long as the means chosen are the least intrusive available, many deem intelligence collection as ethical.

The second aspect refers to the overall international environment in which the collection occurs. In an anarchic international environment with minimal or no international sources of security beyond the individual nation, the 'others do it' theory is often used as an ethical justification of collection. That is, as long as other nations are spying on us and, in effect, are compromising our security, it is ethical for us to spy on them if it enhances our security.

KEY POINTS

- The growing importance of intelligence to national security has raised many questions about legal and ethical issues in both the collection and use of intelligence.
- The ubiquity of intelligence activities throughout the world suggests that nations do not consider it to be in violation of their own domestic law to support such activities.
- International law is largely silent on the legality of intelligence, although intelligence activities that violate the sovereignty of other nations require careful thought and more sophisticated justification.
- Many treaties and agreements between nations tacitly acknowledge the use of NTM for treaty verification. In fact, many arms control, disarmament, non-proliferation, and drug control agreements are based on the assumption of intelligence collection techniques for verification purposes and would not exist were such intelligence activities not possible.

Covert action

Covert action (CA), sometimes called special activities, refers to activities carried out by one state to alter political or economic developments in another state while disguising the source of that influence. Thus, the 1986 surprise American bombing of Libya was a secret military action but was not covert action since no attempt was made to disguise the source of the attack. However, CIA attempts to assassination Cuban leader Fidel Castro in the mid-1960s, although they failed, were meant to remain secret forever.

Some of these activities are relatively benign and minimally intrusive; others clearly violate the UN requirement not to interfere with the political independence or territorial integrity of other states. At the least intrusive end of the continuum are such activities as financial or political support to friendly political parties, labour groups, popular movements, media, etc. in foreign nations where the democratic process is generally intact but under siege from anti-democratic forces. Some scholars feel that no sovereignty is abridged in such cases while others believe that any secret attempt to influence developments in another state violates that state's sovereignty.

At the other end of the continuum are CA operations to support favourable groups or factions involved in civil conflicts, secretly provide weapons or military personnel in such conflicts, engineer coups to remove unfriendly political leaders or even attempt assassinations. (See Case Study 14.1.)

While CA gets huge press attention, it actually involves a relatively small percentage of the time and money of all intelligence agencies. The American CIA, the agency widely thought to conduct CA all over the globe, probably has less than 5% of its personnel involved in CA and spends well over 90% of its budget on normal collection and analysis efforts (Gates 1988: 216). Getting accurate information about CA is very difficult. More is usually known about operations that fail than those that succeed. Failed operations become public and are frequently written about by journalists and

CASE STUDY 14.1

Assassinations

Few intelligence topics attract more interest than that of assassinations. Most are surprised to find that spy novels and cinema romanticize a topic that does not deserve to be romanticized. Political officials and military officers are killed during war and civil unrest. But those deaths are usually corollary to the military actions—they are normally not killed by intelligence officers. Most covert action assassinations in the twentieth century have been carried out only by Soviet and Israeli intelligence agencies. British, French, and American agencies have talked about assassinations, but even in these cases, only one was actually attempted and it failed.

The CIA has been accused of ordering the assassinations of several foreign political leaders. However, thorough examinations by a committee of the US Senate found that while the CIA may have talked about getting rid of five foreign political officials, they actually only attempted to do so in one case. In the case of Fidel Castro, long time ruler of Cuba, the CIA ran several unsuccessful assassination attempts and, in one of the most bizarre developments in American history, actually sub-contracted the job to the criminal Mafia on one occasion. All attempts failed.

Soviet intelligence agencies were quite successful in eliminating political émigrés. From the ice-axe used to kill Leon Trotsky in Mexico to the poisoned pellets delivered on the end of an umbrella in the London Underground, Soviet agents, in many cases by their own admission, carried out many assassination plots before and during the Cold War.

Israeli intelligence agents methodically tracked and killed most of the PLO group that attacked Israeli athletes in the 1972 Olympics in Munich. Unfortunately they also killed an innocent person in Norway in 1974.

scholars. Successful operations, however, remain covert or secret for many years.

The use of covert activities to alter developments in other nations is a singularly dangerous foreign policy tool which must be used very sparingly. In fact, in the absence of similar activities by other nations, it would be easy to argue that, at least in peacetime, nations should refrain completely from any covert actions. Given the anarchic nature of the international environment, as long as some nations engage in CA, other nations use that fact to justify their own CA.

Can covert action be justified?

Those who attempt to justify CA argue that it fills a gap between diplomacy and war. This is called, 'the gap theory of Covert Action'. That is, after a state has pursued policies, beginning with the least intrusive and continuing up to the most serious diplomatic action, and war still appears to be inevitable, some argue that some variations of CA might be better than war and may actually prevent war.

One effort to make CA more ethically acceptable is to apply some of the principles drawn from the famous Just War Theory to CA. For example, one could argue a nation must consider six criteria before initiating CA.

1. Essentiality. The desired goal of the CA must be essential to national security. CA to accomplish ends short of this should not be undertaken. CA should never be considered routine. It should be deemed essential by both executive and parliamentary institutions.
2. Feasibility. The proposed CA must be feasible. That is, it must involve resources that are available and that will not be jeopardized by routine domestic political changes.
3. Last resort. Covert action must be the best, if not the only, means to accomplish the desired goal. All too often policymakers have turned to covert action, not because it was the best way to accomplish a task, but because it was seen as secret, and therefore, the easiest option. It should never be initiated merely because it is secret, because it will not remain secret for long.
4. Legitimacy. Approval procedures for CA must be spelled out clearly and must require the written approval of senior officials. Covert action is the most intrusive and potentially dangerous of all government foreign policy tools and should not be authorized by word of mouth, by low-level officials nor, even worse, by operators in the field.
5. Commensurability. The degree of force, intrusiveness, and deception must be commensurate with the nature of the threat. In democratic nations, the public will usually support CA if such is the case. They will not support it if massive clandestine efforts appear to be in response to minor irritants or embarrassments and pursued merely because they are covert.
6. Popular Support. All CA, even those few carried out in complete secrecy, must be able to stand the light of public awareness eventually. When knowledge of CA eventually seeps out, governments must not be embarrassed by that knowledge.

KEY POINTS

- Covert actions are secret activities by one state to influence political and economic developments in another state without the source of the influence being known.
- The overwhelming majority of covert actions are fairly benign but some clearly violate the sovereignty of the target state.
- Assassination attempts by intelligence agencies are quite rare except in the case of the former Soviet Union and Israeli intelligence. The US actually tried, unsuccessfully, to assassinate Fidel Castro while other states have considered contingency plans for assassinations.
- Covert actions are a very small part of the operations of most intelligence agencies.
- Some believe that 'the Gap Theory' does justify covert actions; others believe that the Just War Theory can be adapted to evaluate the ethicality of covert actions.

Terrorism, Iraq, and the contemporary security condition

Few events have heightened the relationship between security and intelligence more than the al-Qaeda sponsored terrorist attacks that began in Somalia in 1993 and have continued up to the present day. Chapter 16 will discuss terrorism in more detail but this chapter will highlight some of the ways these attacks have altered the security and intelligence environment.

First, the amount of public funds devoted to intelligence services and operations has increased markedly. While the budgets of intelligence agencies are usually secret, in a variety of very public ways it is clear that money is flowing into them at ever-increasing rates. In some cases, it is more money than the agencies themselves have requested; but for obvious political reasons, legislative bodies have not wanted to seem cheap on this issue (Taylor and Goldman 2004: 421).

Second, an increasing percentage of intelligence spending is being targeted against terrorism. This is not surprising, but it is leaving other traditional intelligence targets (non-proliferation, transnational drugs and crime, and even WMD, for example) under-funded and ripe for surprise.

Third, the most immediate result of 9/11 was the 2001 invasion of Afghanistan, an Islamist government providing safe haven for Osama bin Laden and his al-Qaeda base. But as that war progressed, some nations, particularly the US and the UK, believed that Iraq was also supporting Islamist terrorism and was developing WMD that, in the hands of future terrorists, could be more damaging than hijacked airplanes.

Western intelligence organizations had been monitoring Iraqi developments for many years, at least since the first war against Iraq brought on by an Iraqi invasion of Kuwait in 1990. But the desire to attack terrorists anywhere they might be and to change regimes that might be harbouring terrorists triggered increased intelligence efforts about Iraq following the widely supported 1991 war. Virtually every Western intelligence organization significantly increased collection efforts against Iraq, especially after UN inspectors were forced out of Iraq in 1998. And by 9/11, every Western intelligence organization (UK, US, German, French, and Israeli) believed that Iraq was continuing WMD development in violation of UN sanctions, that it had missiles with ranges beyond the proscribed by the UN, and that within five to seven years, it could arm these missiles with nuclear weapons.

Failing to get UN approval for an invasion, the UK and the US (with help from Australia, Poland, and, to a lesser extent, other states) launched an attack against Iraq in 2003. The war was over quickly but the challenges of occupation and pacification proved to be much more than anticipated. Even more importantly, virtually no evidence was found to support the conclusions of the various intelligence reports on which the decision to go to war had been based. Some have called this one of the worst intelligence failures of all time (see Key Ideas 14.1).

Fourth, allegations of intelligence failure have brought about reform efforts in several Western nations. Since 9/11 the intelligence services of several major countries have been studied and investigated more than at any previous time in history. Two parliamentary inquiries and two additional commissions studied aspects of British intelligence. The Butler Commission made several recommendations about intelligence procedures that the Blair government accepted. In the US, three congressional reports and scores of think tank and other independent commissions made recommendations for reform. The most significant intelligence reform

KEY IDEAS 14.1

What went wrong about Iraq: four theories

The following are summaries of theories that explain why British and American intelligence agencies were wrong about WMD prior to the 2003 invasion of Iraq. In fact, virtually all Western intelligence agencies, including Russia and Israel, were—to one degree or another—wrong about this. Each theory is followed by a brief evaluation.

1. Intelligence Conspiracy Theory: British and American intelligence agencies were so anxious to get into a war with Iraq that they fed government decision makers patently false information about the extent of WMD in Iraq.

Fact: no investigation of intelligence agencies in Britain or America has turned up any evidence to support this theory. In fact, some agencies in both countries argued that no evidence of an advanced nuclear programme existed.

2. Defence Intelligence Conspiracy Theory: defence-related intelligence agencies in both countries falsified evidence so they could get their military forces into Iraq.

Fact: again, no investigation has provided any evidence to support this theory. However, at least within the American defence-related intelligence agencies, evidence supports the notion that some intelligence officials, anxious to please their superiors and to meet their strenuous and repeated requests for intelligence to support the invasion, relied on Iraqi defectors and other questionable sources of information that was not put through the normal intelligence cycle. This is referred to as 'cherry picking', providing unanalysed information to decision makers.

3. Groupthink Theory: this theory asserts that as intelligence analysts working on the issue of WMD in Iraq evaluated and discussed available evidence, they gradually came to accept prevailing interpretations of ambiguous evidence because of a desire to conform to group beliefs.

Fact: no investigations have revealed the slightest hint that would justify this interpretation. Senior analysts in both Britain and America have ridiculed this interpretation in confidential interviews with the author.

4. Bureaucratic Pressure Theory: this theory, often called 'cooking the intelligence to fit the decision maker's recipe', argues that recurring appeals from senior decision makers to find intelligence support for an Iraqi invasion caused analysts to interpret ambiguous evidence in a way most friendly to their supervisors who had to deal frequently with the senior decision makers.

Fact: this theory, with some modifications, is probably the best explanation of what happened in Iraq. It is true that very senior decision makers, close to the head of state in each country, met frequently with senior IC managers and asked for intelligence about WMD in Iraq prior to the invasion. No evidence exists that these decision makers ordered intelligence to be fabricated. But they did repeatedly encourage the analysts to 're-evaluate' and 'keep looking' and this created within the analytical branches a sense of pressure to phrase the evidence in certain ways. It also led to the 'cherry picking' discussed above. This phenomenon was enhanced in a climate of multiple analytical centres across a nation's IC, each trying to gain bureaucratic advantages and favour. It is possible in some analytical centers that 'groupthink' became a factor at a certain point in the process.

since the creation of the CIA in 1947 came about in 2005 with the creation of a National Intelligence Director (NID) along with a large support office. The bulk of these institutional and/or procedural reforms are meant to increase intelligence coordination within each nation and greater intelligence cooperation between nations.

Two ironies ought to be noted, however. First, throughout the modern history of intelligence, nearly every intelligence failure has been abetted, if not caused, by national intelligence communities grown so large and cumbersome that internal cooperation and external collaboration became scarce and difficult. At the same time, the political response to accusations of intelligence failure has usually been the creation of more agencies and sub-agencies, more money, and more personnel—thus feeding the very condition that contributed to the intelligence failure in the first place (Taylor and Goldman 2004: 421). Second, one effect of the global response to modern terrorism has been to diminish, in various ways and degrees in diverse countries, the very democratic conditions that people in democracies deem worthy of defence.

KEY POINTS

- Two approaches to combating contemporary Jihadist terrorism have been to create new intelligence agencies and sub-agencies and to devote ever larger sums to counterterrorism. These very responses increase the cumbersome nature of intelligence agencies and diminish coordination and correlation—the very source of intelligence failures.
- The tendency to assume that the next terrorist attack will be like the last one takes intelligence assets away from the developments that may lead to the next, and different, attack.
- The 2003 Iraqi War (in ways merely part of the War on Terrorism) was initiated on the basis of faulty intelligence brought about by decision makers so hungry for supporting evidence that they could shop around for analytical products that supported their predilections and could use raw, unprocessed, intelligence if it supported their views.
- The question of whether the decision to invade Iraq was an intelligence failure or a policy failure is still open to debate, although sufficient blame exists to taint both decision makers as well as the practices of some intelligence agencies.

Conclusion

From time immemorial, tribes, clans, empires, and nations have collected information about other groups in order to make more informed decisions when dealing with them. This information is called intelligence and its collection may well be the 'second oldest profession' in the world. As from the beginning, modern nations believe that the collection, analysis, and use of good intelligence will enhance their security in an anarchic world.

Nineteenth-century intelligence was generally minimal and focused on potential enemies. But by the beginning of the twentieth century, most global powers, with the exception of the US, had both military and civilian intelligence agencies operating in times of peace as well as war. The first two wars of this century saw the growth and institutionalization of these agencies which, at times, made significant contributions to the war effort. The Japanese surprise attack on Pearl Harbor in December 1941 convinced the Americans that they needed to have a civilian intelligence agency. More than any other war before it, the Second World War was an intelligence war. The famous British military historian, John Keegan (2004: 28), argues that intelligence does not win wars—that it takes the courage and skills of fighting men and women to do that. But through the Second World War, intelligence made significant contributions to the war effort in many different ways—the war in the Pacific was turned around by intelligence, the war in the Atlantic profited from intelligence, counterintelligence efforts in Britain and the US virtually eliminated German

CASE STUDY 14.2

Operations Ryan and Able/Archer: the 'security dilemma ' at work

The 'security dilemma' describes a condition in which insignificant, or even benign, actions on the part of one state can be interpreted as threatening to another state, particularly during times of crisis such as the Cold War. The second state then takes what it deems are defensive actions which are in turn interpreted by the first state as a confirmation of intended hostilities. This action and reaction may continue until actual hostilities break out. A set of Soviet and Western intelligence and political actions in the early 1980s illustrate this model.

In May 1981, Soviet Premier Leonid Brezhnev told a KGB conference that American President Reagan was preparing for a nuclear attack on the USSR. KGB head Yuri Andropov then announced Operation RYAN (Raketno Yadernoye Napdenie—Russian for nuclear missile attack), a combined KGB/GRU intelligence initiative that by 1983 involved nearly all Soviet Bloc intelligence services. Even though KGB American experts were sceptical of this interpretation of American intentions, Operation RYAN launched an enormous increase, both sigint and humint, in the monitoring of Western military planning.

Of course, Western intelligence collectors picked up this increased Soviet monitoring and tensions increased even more. By 1983, conservative American President Ronald Reagan was in his third year in the White House and conservative British Prime Minister Margaret Thatcher was in her second term at 10 Downing Street. Western rhetoric (Reagan labeled the Soviet Union an 'evil empire' in March 1983 and announced his Strategic Defense Initiative in the same month) as well as Cold War policies (the December 1979 Soviet invasion of Afghanistan, Western and Islamic states' boycott of the Moscow 1980 Olympics, the American refusal to ratify the SALT II agreement, and Reagan's unilateral invasion of Grenada in October 1983, among others) had increased Cold War tensions to even greater heights.

In August 1983 the Soviets tested their first missile with multiple warheads—the SS-X-24. On the night of that test, Western intelligence put their entire missile test monitoring collectors in place. Next, Soviet radar that was monitoring the flight paths of American sensor aircraft began tracking the flight of a civilian Korean passenger airliner (KAL 007) and early in the morning of 1 September shot it down with a loss of 269 lives. Owing to pilot error, the jet had strayed off course and was over Soviet-controlled Sakhalin Island.

Western leaders denounced what they called 'uncivilized' behaviour and the Soviet's Operation RYAN was seen as an even more threatening portent of Soviet intentions. President Reagan called for greater vigilance and called for a major diplomatic effort to keep attention focused on Soviet behaviour. On the other hand, Operation RYAN now seemed more important to Soviet leaders who denounced NATO's placement of Pershing missiles into Western Germany on 23 November.

In the mean time, NATO, in reaction to Operation RYAN and the KAL 007 shootdown, launched a command exercise called Operation ABLE ARCHER in order to test communications and decision making equipment and procedures in case it was necessary to invade the Soviet Union. This was essentially a command and control exercise and did not involve the movement of any military forces. But, as Richelson (1995: 386) states, 'While the Soviets and their allies monitored ABLE ARCHER, the United States and its allies used their SIGINT to monitor the monitors'. A senior KGB defector, Oleg Gordievsky, pointed out the dangers of such intelligence collection and military exercises when he said, 'The world did not quite reach the edge of the nuclear abyss during [these operations], [b]ut . . . it had come close—certainly closer than at any time since the Cuban missile crisis of 1962' (Andrew and Gordievsky (1991: 605).

In mid-1984 tensions eventually resumed normal levels as it became clear that neither side was actually planning a nuclear attack. But Operations RYAN and ABLE ARCHER are still reminders of one of the potential hazards of intelligence-collecting activities.

spies, and the intelligence-devised deception associated with the **D-Day Invasion** was critical.

Intelligence during the Cold War had two major characteristics. First, techint became extremely sophisticated. Spy planes, satellite surveillance, computer-assisted cryptography, and remote-controlled listening and imaging devices changed the way much intelligence was collected. Second, humint became pervasive. State secrets of every major power were betrayed to other states. In the early days of the Cold War, most traitors were ideologically motivated. Westerners sympathetic to communism penetrated their own military, intelligence, and government structures. And Russians sympathetic to democratic ideals betrayed Soviet secrets to Western intelligence. But as idealism faded, most traitors went into the business for money.

Keegan's pessimism about the role of intelligence might be more correct for the Cold War than for the shooting wars. One wonders, for example, about the net effect of all of the spy–counterspy interactions. To what degree were largely defensive intelligence activities on one side seen as provocative by the other? (See Case Study 14.2.) Perhaps the best that could be said for Cold War intelligence is that the sophisticated verification and monitoring abilities of the protagonists eventually reduced tensions, provided some stability, and may have prevented benign activities from being perceived as threatening and thus triggering violent responses. Moreover, a major source for political reform in the Soviet Union came from intelligence officers who had travelled and lived in Western nations more freely than other Soviet citizens were allowed. They could see the disadvantages of a command economy combined with a dictatorial political system and began to lead efforts for reform.

In the 1990s, just when people in many nations were thinking intelligence agencies could be eliminated or, at least, reduced, international terrorism provoked cries for increased intelligence. Terrorism was not new. It had been around literally for centuries. But the dramatic rise of terrorism sponsored by extremist Islamist groups raised the stakes to unprecedented heights. The **al-Qaeda** attacks beginning in the early 1990s challenged the security of many states as well as global stability. They, along with issues of weapons proliferation and international drug and criminal activities, have brought about the greatest expansion of intelligence agencies and the greatest infusion of money in history.

At the same time, the failures of intelligence agencies to predict **al-Qaeda** attacks and the faulty intelligence about WMD in Iraq have brought about unprecedented scrutiny and transparency of intelligence agencies. Heads of intelligence agencies are now public figures. Their operations have become so public that some believe the phrase 'secret intelligence' has become an oxymoron. Moreover, to prevent terrorists from organizing cells in a country, intelligence agencies, with parliamentary and legislative authority, have become more pervasive and their very actions seem to some to threaten the civil liberties that characterize Western civilization. The modern security environment (terrorism, nuclear proliferation, cross-national drugs and crimes—all occurring during unprecedented globalization) has brought about calls for stronger intelligence activities while at the same time it has created concerns about the unintended consequences of intelligence activities.

When the intelligence process works well—when decision makers ask penetrating questions, when collectors are creative and successful, when analysts paint accurate pictures, and when political pressures on intelligence agencies are at a minimum—when these conditions exist, intelligence can and has made valuable contributions to national security in every state. When the process does not work well, national security may be diminished and the foreign reactions intelligence activities generate may complicate diplomacy and increase international tensions.

QUESTIONS

The word *intelligence* has many meanings. What is the meaning used in this chapter?

If the gathering of intelligence is ancient, what has changed about it in the post-service economy information age?

How does the theory of cybernetics explain the function of intelligence?

While the intelligence community of every nation is somewhat unique, what functions are quite common between them?

In what ways has intelligence contributed to various arms control treaties and agreements?

What developments have changed technical intelligence (techint) collection techniques?

How does the actual intelligence cycle or process differ from the theoretical one?

Do you think that intelligence collection violates international law? Why?

What significant techint development began in 1956 after the Soviets rejected the American Open Skies proposal?

Do you agree or disagree with the author's attempt to apply the Just War Theory to covert actions? Why?

Which do you think occurs more frequently, 'policy failures' or 'intelligence failures'?

What effect has contemporary jihadism had on intelligence activities in most Western nations?

Discuss how aggressive intelligence collection might actually increase international tension.

FURTHER READING

■ **Andrew, Christopher (1987), *Her Majesty's Secret Service: The Making of the British Intelligence Community,* New York: Penguin**. A thorough history of the origins of British intelligence. Andrew has also written the best histories of both American and Soviet intelligence in *For the President's Eyes Only: Secret Intelligence and the American Presidency from Washington to Bush* (New York: Harper Collins, 1995) and, with Oleg Gordievsky, *KGB: The Inside Story* (New York: Harper Collins, 1990).

■ **Richelson, Jeffrey T. (1995), A *Century of Spies: Intelligence in the Twentieth Century,* Oxford: Oxford University Press**. One of the better books with a multinational approach to modern intelligence history.

■ **Haufler, Hervie (2003), *Codebreakers' Victory: How the Allied Cryptographers Won World War II,* New York: New American Library and Keegan, John (2003), *Intelligence in War: Knowledge of the Enemy from Napoleon to Al-Qaeda,* London:Hutchinson.** These take somewhat contradictory sides on the relationship between intelligence and military victory. Both are very readable.

■ **Kahn, David (1996), *The Code-Breakers: The Comprehensive History of Secret Communication from Ancient Times to the Internet,* rev. ed., New York: Scribner.** Pretty much what it claims to be—an excellent, definitive, and lengthy history of cryptography.

■ **Lowenthal, Mark M. (2006), *Intelligence: From Secrets to Policy,* Washington D.C.: CQ Press**. Takes a US-centric approach but may be the best short introduction to the intelligence process. It includes one chapter on the intelligence services of other major nations.

- **Johnson, Loch K. and Wirtz, James J. (eds.) (2004), *Strategic Intelligence: Windows into a Secret World*, Los Angeles: Roxbury Press**. The best, nearly the only, intelligence anthology. Its contributors represent the best scholarship in the rapidly growing field of intelligence scholarship.

- **Born, Hans, Johnson, Loch K., and Leigh, Ian (eds.) (2005), *Who's Watching the Spies: Establishing Intelligence Service Accountability*, Dulles, VA: Potomac Books**. The best introduction to the issues of democratic accountability and government oversight of intelligence from a global perspective.

- **Herman, Michael (1996), *Intelligence power in Peace and War*, Cambridge: Cambridge University Press**. One of the only general works on intelligence that takes a somewhat theoretical and global perspective.

Intelligence and National Security and the ***International Journal of Intelligence and CounterIntelligence*** are the two best academic journals on this topic. They address a wide range of intelligence topics and both are now published by Routledge of the Taylor & Francis Group.

IMPORTANT WEBSITES

Official websites of national intelligence agencies or communities:

- **http://www.csis-scrs.gc.ca** Canadian Security Intelligence Service.
- **http://www.intelligence.gov** Official access point for all US intelligence agencies.
- **http://www.mi5.gov.uk** UK domestic intelligence service—MI5.
- **http://gchq.gov.uk** UK signals intelligence agency.

Think tanks or research centres working on intelligence:

- **http://fas.org** Homepage of the Federation of American Scientists whose intelligence links and data are one of the best available about intelligence in all major nations.
- **http://exastriscientia.fateback.com/intelligenceagencies.htm** Unofficial, quirky, but authoritative description of the intelligence structures and agencies of thirty-three nations based on official government sources.
- **http://intellit.muskingum.edu** Best web-based bibliography.
- **http://www.gwu.edu/~nsarchiv/** Quite critical, but still best documentary source about US intelligence.
- **http://www.loyola.edu/dept/politics/intel.html** Best university intelligence web page with links to every available national intelligence service home page.

Visit the Online Resource Centre that accompanies this book for lots of interesting additional material: www.oxfordtextbooks.co.uk/orc/collins/

15 Weapons of Mass Destruction

JAMES WIRTZ

Chapter Contents

Reader's Guide

Today, policy makers everywhere are deeply concerned about the possibility that weapons of mass destruction—chemical, biological, nuclear and radiological weapons—are not only becoming fixtures in the arsenals of states, but might fall into the hands of terrorists. This chapter explains how these weapons work and the effects they might have if used on the battlefield or against civilian targets. It describes how they have been used in war and how they have shaped the practice of international politics.

Introduction

Although many observers hoped that the danger posed by weapons of mass destruction (WMD)—chemical, biological, nuclear and radiological weapons—would fade with the end of the Cold War, these armaments continue to pose a worldwide threat. Some progress has been made in terms of rolling back WMD proliferation. Iraq no longer menaces its neighbours with its chemical arsenal and its efforts to acquire nuclear and biological weapons have been thwarted. Libya has also abandoned its nuclear weapons programme. The international community has bolstered the non-proliferation regime by undertaking a series of diplomatic efforts, for example the Chemical Weapons Convention, the Biological Weapons Convention, the Proliferation Security Initiative and the 2002 Moscow Treaty. Despite these concerted efforts, however, several state and non-state actors find WMD to be an attractive part of their arsenals. Black-market trade in nuclear materials, technology and know how is increasing. In 2004, revelations that the Pakistani scientist A.Q. Khan might have provided information about gas-centrifuges (used to produce weapons-grade uranium) and nuclear bomb designs to North Korea, Iraq, Iran, Libya and Syria sent a shock wave through the non-proliferation community (Clary 2004; Albright and Hinderstein 2005). Indigenous nuclear programmes also are making existing proliferation safeguards obsolete (Braun and Chyba 2004). For some states, WMD provide a way to offset their inferiority in conventional armaments compared to stronger regional rivals or the United States and its allies. Leaders of these regimes probably hope that the threat of chemical, biological or nuclear warfare might deter stronger opponents contemplating attack, defeat those opponents once battle is joined or even threaten domestic opponents (Lavoy, Sagan and Wirtz 2000). Weapons of mass destruction also serve as status symbols that highlight the 'success' of otherwise dubious regimes.

If the threat posed by WMD proliferation to state actors is of increasing concern, then the possibility that these weapons could fall into the hands of terrorists is alarming. A chemical weapons attack against a major sporting venue could kill thousands of people, while a successful anthrax attack might place hundreds of thousands at risk. A 'dirty bomb', a device that uses high explosives to spread radioactive contamination, could poison scores of city blocks. It would be extraordinarily difficult for even a well-funded terrorist organization to construct a primitive gun-type nuclear weapon, but international terrorist networks, domestic terrorist organizations, or even individuals have the resources and materials to construct and use chemical, biological and radiological weapons. Weapons of mass destruction have been used in terrorist attacks, albeit with relatively limited effects. In 1995, for instance, Chechen rebels planted radiological source (caesium-137) in Moscow's Izmailovsky Park, probably to show Russian authorities that they had the capability to make a 'dirty bomb'. The Aum Shinrikyo (Aum Supreme Truth) cult experimented with several toxic substances before launching their Sarin attack against the Tokyo subway in 1995 that injured thousands of people. In the wake of the 11 September 2001 terrorist attacks against the World Trade Center and Pentagon, some person or group in 2001 used the US postal system to mail letters contaminated with anthrax, which was probably derived from materials supplied to US weapons laboratories.

Weapons of mass destruction vary greatly in terms of their availability, lethality, destructive potential, and the ease with which they can be manufactured and employed. High-yield, lightweight nuclear weapons are some of the most sophisticated machines ever manufactured by humans, while some chemical and biological weapons have been available for centuries. What separates WMD from conventional weapons, created from chemical-based explosives, however, is their potential to generate truly catastrophic levels of death and destruction. A small nuclear weapon can devastate a city: the fission device that destroyed Hiroshima produced an explosive blast (yield) that was equivalent to about 20 kilotons (kt) of trinitrotoluene (TNT). A smallpox attack against an unprotected (unvaccinated) population could kill 30% of its victims and leave survivors horribly scarred for life. Because of their ability to strike terror worldwide, these weapons are attractive as political instruments.

The remainder of this chapter will first describe the technology that underlies nuclear, chemical and biological weapons, and explain how they are constructed. What is reassuring about this overview is the fact that while these weapons can be extraordinarily destructive, state and non-state actors would have to overcome significant technical hurdles before they could maximize their destructive power. The chapter will also describe their destructive effects, the systems used to deliver them, and the history of their use in war. It will then outline the impact these weapons have on national defence policy and international security.

Nuclear weapons

The design and development of nuclear weapons were based on advances in theoretical and experimental physics that began at the start of the last century. By the late 1930s, Leo Szilard, a physicist who escaped Nazi persecution by fleeing to the United States, realized that it might be possible to construct an 'atomic bomb'. Unlike conventional (chemical) explosions, which are produced by a rapid rearrangement of the hydrogen, oxygen, carbon and nitrogen atoms that are components of TNT, for example, Szilard suggested that a nuclear explosion could be created by a change in atomic nuclei themselves. If an atom of **uranium-235**, for instance, is fragmented into two relatively equal parts, the remaining mass of the two new atoms would have less mass than the original atom. The lost mass would be instantaneously converted into energy. Nuclear weapons are so powerful because, as Albert Einstein predicted, under certain conditions mass and energy are interchangeable ($E = MC^2$). The difficult aspect of setting off this interchange would be to create a device that would sustain a nuclear reaction for a fraction of a second before it is destroyed in the resulting nuclear explosion.

Szilard's opinion was not widely shared among American scientists or government officials, so he enlisted the aid of his friend, Albert Einstein, to bring the issue to the attention of President Franklin D. Roosevelt. In a letter dated 2 August 1939, Einstein informed Roosevelt that it was theoretically possible to construct an atomic bomb and that the Nazis might be hard at work constructing such a device. It took the US entry into the Second World War to launch a full-scale project to construct a nuclear weapon, the British-American **Manhattan Project** that began in September 1942. The first nuclear (fission) device was ready for testing at Alamagordo New Mexico on 6 July 1945. It was quickly followed by the detonation of 'Little Boy' over Hiroshima on 6 August 1945 and 'Fat Man' over Nagasaki on 9 August 1945.

Fission weapons all share similar components: fissile material (e.g., U-235 or Plutonium); chemical explosives; non-fissile materials to reflect neutrons and tamp the explosion; and some sort of neutron generator to help initiate the nuclear reaction. Weapons also need triggers, a mechanical safety, arming and firing mechanisms. There are two basic types of fission weapons. 'Little Boy' was a gun-type fission device. This is the simplest and least efficient nuclear weapon design (the design requires a relatively large amount of fissile material to produce a relatively small blast). In a gun-design, two sub-critical masses of U-235 are fired down a barrel, striking each other at extremely high velocities producing a fission reaction. Gun-type devices, however, are rugged and have a relatively high probability of 'going critical', i.e., producing a nuclear detonation. The second design, an implosion-type device, uses high-explosive lenses to compress the fissile material— 'Fat Man' utilized plutonium—until it reaches criticality. Implosion devices are relatively difficult to manufacture and assemble because the shaped charges that compress the fissile material need to be manufactured to critical tolerances and detonated with more than split-second timing. The physics and engineering behind the design and manufacture of nuclear weapons are widely available. What is far more difficult to acquire are highly enriched uranium (U-235) and plutonium. These materials are under safeguards and their production and storage are monitored by the **International Atomic Energy Agency (IAEA)** and the declared and undeclared nuclear weapons states themselves.

Table 15.1 Nuclear weapons states

Country	Fission Device	Fusion Device
United States	1945	1952
Soviet Union	1949	1953
Great Britain	1952	1957
France	1960	1966
PRC	1964	1967
Israel	1967?	1973?
India	1974	1998?
Pakistan	1998	1998?
North Korea	2002?	

A fusion weapon is a three-stage bomb that uses an implosion device to trigger a fission reaction, which in turn detonates a fusion reaction (a process whereby one heavier nucleus is produced from two lighter nuclei). When the nuclei of light elements are combined, the resulting heaver element has less mass than the two original nuclei, and the difference in mass is instantaneously translated into energy. Often referred to as a thermo-nuclear weapon, or a hydrogen bomb, fusion weapons can be relatively small, light-weight, and pack virtually unlimited destructive force. During the Cold War, large nuclear weapons had yields in the millions of tons—megatons (mgt)—of TNT. On 31 October 1952, for example, the United Stated tested its first fusion device (Test Mike) at Eniwetok atoll in the Pacific Ocean. It produced a yield of about 10 mgt, which is equivalent to 10,000 kt. The most powerful nuclear weapon ever detonated was the Tsar Bomba (King of Bombs), which was a reduced-yield test of a 100-mgt bomb design. A product of Soviet science, the device was detonated with a 50-mgt yield on 30 October 1961 at the Mityushikha Bay Test range, Novayua Zemlya Island, producing a flash so bright that it was visible 1,000 km away. Bombs in the multi-megaton range generally have limited military utility since their destructive radius often exceeds the size of potential urban or military targets.

Nuclear weapons effects

Compared to the devices we encounter in our everyday lives, nuclear weapons operate at the extremes of time, pressure, and temperature. The entire explosive process of a hydrogen bomb, for example, occurs over the period of a few thousand nanoseconds (a nanosecond is 1/100,000,000 of a second). Pressure within a fusion bomb core can reach up to 8,000,000,000 tons per square inch and temperatures exceeding those found on the surface of the sun (6,000°C). Nuclear weapons introduce galactic scale forces into a terrestrial environment, producing devastating consequences.

Nuclear weapons effects are shaped by a variety of factors including the weapon's explosive yield, its height of detonation, weather conditions and terrain features. For example, an airburst occurs when the nuclear fireball does not touch the ground. Airbursts distribute the explosive blast and the radiation burst produced at detonation over a relatively wide area. Raising the height of burst lowers the pressure generated immediately below the detonation, but covers a larger area with somewhat lower overpressure. A ground burst maximizes the overpressure against a specific target—a missile silo or a command and control complex. A ground burst produces a great deal of fallout because the fireball irradiates and lofts dirt and debris high into the atmosphere. Nuclear weapons also can be driven deep beneath the earth's surface in an effort to more efficiently couple their explosive power to the ground to destroy deeply buried and hardened targets.

All nuclear weapons produce similar effects, although the balance between these effects can be somewhat altered by design. An average nuclear weapon (about 100 kt) detonated in the atmosphere will deliver 50% of its energy as blast, 35% as thermal radiation and about 15% into gamma and residual radiation. A so-called neutron bomb, for instance, shifts some of the energy involved in a nuclear detonation from blast into radiation effects. Not all nuclear effects, however, are known or well understood. In the aftermath of a US high-altitude test of a 1.4 mgt weapon in 1962, for example, scientists were surprised to learn that the resulting electro-magnetic pulse (EMP) burned out street lights, fuses and opened circuit breakers 800 miles away in Oahu (Hansen 1988). In the 1980s, scientists and analysts also debated whether a full-scale nuclear exchange would plunge the world into nuclear winter (Turco et al 1990). By contrast, nuclear blast and thermal effects can be predicted with great precision; the US military generally relies on blast effects to estimate the damage that will be produced by a nuclear detonation.

The best-known and most important nuclear weapons effects are EMP, a thermal-light pulse, blast, and fallout. EMP and the thermal-light pulse are produced at the instant of detonation. Electromagnetic pulse occurs when gamma radiation interacts with matter (e.g., the atmosphere)—a process known as the Compton effect. EMP produces a high-voltage electrical charge, which is harmless to humans, but can destroy electronic systems that are not specifically shielded against its effects. EMP effects are maximized by detonating weapons at relatively high altitudes (100,000 ft). In theory, a single high-altitude nuclear detonation could temporarily knock out most electronic systems in a medium-sized country. Thermal-light pulse, which lasts about two seconds, can cause flash blindness and fire. A 1-mgt airburst could produce flash blindness in individuals fifty-three miles away on a clear night and thirteen miles away on a clear day. At closer ranges, retinal burn (permanent blindness) might occur if an individual was looking directly at the thermal-light pulse. This airburst would cause first-degree burns on unprotected skin seven miles away, second-degree burns at about 6 miles away and third-degree burns at about five miles away. Third degree burns over 25% of the body will cause the victim to go into shock quickly, a condition that requires immediate medical attention.

A shockwave (a sudden rise in atmosphere pressure) and dynamic overpressure (wind) follows a few seconds behind the thermal light pulse. At about one mile away, a 1-mgt airburst will produce 20 pounds per square inch (psi) overpressure and 470 mph winds, pressure sufficient to level steel-reinforced concrete structures. At three miles away, overpressure reaches 10 psi, producing winds of about 290 mph, sufficient to destroy most commercial structures and private residences. At five miles away, winds reach about 160 mph and overpressure reaches 5 psi, enough to damage most structures and subject people caught in the open to lethal collisions with flying debris. Blast effects were generally used by military planners to calculate casualty rates in a nuclear attack: it was estimated that about 50% of the people living within five miles of a 1-mgt airburst would either be killed or wounded by blast effects.

Individuals can be exposed to the fourth nuclear effect, radiation, either in the initial nuclear detonation or from fallout, which is irradiated debris picked up by the nuclear fireball and lofted into the atmosphere. A REM (roentgen-equivalent-man) is a measure of radiation energy absorbed by living creatures. 600 REM is likely to produce lethal radiation sickness in an exposed population, while a dose of 300 REM would produce lethal radiation sickness in about 10% of an exposed population. Exposure to about 250 REM, however, impedes the body's ability to heal from burns and kinetic injury, making non-lethal injuries deadly. Exposure to about 50 REM increases the incidence of cancer across an entire population by about 2% (United States Congress 1979).

A dirty bomb uses chemical high-explosive to disperse radioactive material. It primarily relies on radiation to produce a lethal effect. A dirty bomb's lethality thus would be governed by how far radioactive materials might be lofted by the conventional chemical explosive and the radioactivity of the material used in the bomb. Many observers believe that the explosive blast produced by a dirty bomb, not the radioactive material it disperses, would cause the greatest amount of actual damage. Panic set off by even a limited dispersion of radioactive material, however, might be more costly in terms of the disruption it causes than the actual casualties or damage to property produced by the detonation of a dirty bomb.

Methods of delivery

Nuclear weapons have taken a variety of forms over the years. Early weapons were relatively large and heavy; only four-engine bombers were capable of lifting them. With the advent of thermonuclear (fusion) weapons, the size and weight of weapons began to decrease as their yields increased. Nuclear 'warheads' were soon mounted on cruise missiles, medium range ballistic missiles and eventually intercontinental ballistic missiles (ICBMs) and submarine-launched ballistic missiles that were launched beneath the surface of the ocean from nuclear-powered submarines. By the 1970s, multiple independently targetable reentry vehicles were being installed aboard US and Soviet ICBMs, giving both superpowers the ability to strike up to a dozen targets with one missile. Nuclear warheads were soon available for air-to-air missiles that were to be fired by aircraft to knock down incoming bombers, artillery shells, and even man-portable demolition charges. Neutron warheads were created to arm interceptor missiles that were part of the Safeguard Anti-Ballistic Missile System, which was developed by the United States in the 1970s. Safeguard interceptor warheads were intended to detonate in close proximity to incoming warheads, bathing them in EMP and turning them into duds. Both superpowers also investigated the possibility of deploying Fractional Orbital Bombardment Systems (FOBS), i.e., parking nuclear weapons in orbit so that they could be armed and targeted following an alert from ground control stations. Mercifully, officials on both sides of the Cold War divide thought better of living literally with a sword of Damocles over their heads and in the 1967 Outer Space Treaty, they banned placement of nuclear weapons in space.

Today, officials are worried about the possibility that terrorists might somehow manufacture or acquire a nuclear weapon or a radiological device. Although a missile or airborne attack is possible, there is much concern that a weapon might be smuggled into a country in one of the thousands of marine shipping containers that travel the world's oceans everyday. There is also a possibility that a weapon's components could be shipped separately and assembled on site. Local police forces and national intelligence agencies also closely monitor efforts to sell radioactive materials on the black market. In 1998, for instance, Mamdough Mamud Salim, an al-Qaeda operative, was arrested after attempting to buy 'enriched uranium' in Western Europe (Boureston 2002). Nuclear or radiological weapons manufactured by terrorists would probably be relatively crude, suggesting that they would be relatively large and difficult to transport. Small, man-portable nuclear devices (e.g., atomic demolitions) were manufactured by the superpowers during the Cold War, which has raised concerns that these weapons might find their way onto the black market. In September 1997, for instance, the CBS news program *Sixty Minutes* reported that former Russian National Security Advisor Aleksander Lebed claimed that the Russian military had lost track of 100 'suit-case bombs', each with a yield of about 10 kt. Russian officials confirmed that such devices were constructed, but it remains unclear if they have been secured or destroyed.

Impact on international politics

Despite the fact that nuclear weapons emerged on the world scene over sixty years ago and have played a dominant role in the Cold War standoff between the North Atlantic Treaty Organisation (NATO) and the Warsaw Pact, debate continues about their impact on world politics (Paul, Harknett and Wirtz 1998). Disarmament advocates bemoan the failure of the existing nuclear powers to reduce their reliance on nuclear weapons, the failure of the US Senate to ratify the Comprehensive Test Ban Treaty, and the decision of the George W. Bush administration' to withdraw from the 1972 Anti-Ballistic Missile Treaty, which in their mind threatens a new round in the arms race. They also are concerned that the non-proliferation regime is slowly losing ground as several states continue to press ahead with covert and overt programmes to develop nuclear weapons. Others see the cup as half full. The United States and Russia have greatly decreased the size of their deployed nuclear forces—the 2002 Moscow Treaty cuts Russian and American nuclear forces to about 20% of the level they reached during the Cold War. The Bush administration's 2002 Nuclear Posture Review also declared an end to the nuclear deterrence relationship that dominated Soviet (Russian)–American relations for nearly sixty years. The chance that nuclear Armageddon will occur, a fear that preoccupied people for decades, is lower now that it ever was during the Cold War.

Scholars are divided about the impact of nuclear weapons on world politics (Sagan and Waltz 2002). Some believe that a nuclear arsenal helps to deter attack by other states armed with conventional and nuclear weapons. The ability to retaliate with nuclear weapons after suffering an attack—known as a secure second-strike capability—is especially desirable because it can effectively eliminate an opponent's potential gain produced by using nuclear weapons first, a situation known as crisis stability. Because even a few nuclear weapons can cause catastrophic destruction and it is virtually impossible to defend against the effects of nuclear weapons, these scholars believe that they are truly revolutionary weapons that force militaries to concentrate on preventing, not fighting wars (Brodie 1946). Some, focusing on Soviet-American relations during the Cold War, suggest that peace is the logical outcome, especially if potential enemies obtain secure-second strike capabilities: it is not logical for officials to engage in conflicts if they know in advance that a nuclear exchange will devastate, if not completely destroy, their country (Jervis 1989).

By contrast, proliferation pessimists worry that the superpower Cold War experience was at best an anomaly, and at worse, a situation that often teetered on the brink of disaster. They worry that human frailty, communication failures and misperception, bureaucratic snafus or psychological or technological breakdowns in a crisis can cause failures of deterrence, leading to inadvertent or accidental nuclear war. Others point to normal accidents—the inability to anticipate all human-machine interaction in complex systems—as a potential path to accidental nuclear war, especially because nuclear warning and command and control systems interact intensively during a crisis. Proliferation pessimists also point out that there is no guarantee that all militaries and governments will be good stewards of their nuclear arsenals. Those who possess nuclear weapons might take risks that expose their arsenals to sabotage, loss through theft, or accidental or inadvertent use.

Some governments might not use their newly found weapons for deterrence purposes, but instead for purposes of intimidation or aggression. They might gravitate toward nuclear warfighting strategies that seek to introduce nuclear weapons quickly and massively on the battlefield in an attempt either to pre-empt an adversary's use of nuclear weapons or to end a conflict with a quick knock-out blow.

Although the debate between optimists and pessimists continues, all agree that the spread of nuclear or radiological weapons to non-state actors or even individuals would be a global disaster. Existing deterrent strategies and capabilities do not address terrorist use of nuclear weapons. The threat that these nuclear weapons could fall into the hands of non-state actors will force states to heighten domestic surveillance and security efforts.

KEY POINTS

- A gun-type fission device is a relatively simple, reliable and rugged nuclear-weapon design that would be attractive to terrorist organizations or states developing a nuclear programme.
- Fusion weapons are highly complex devices that can produce enormous destructive energy from relatively small, light-weight packages.
- Primary nuclear effects are electromagnetic pulse, thermal-light energy, blast and radiation.
- Although the risk of nuclear Armageddon has receded since the end of the Cold War, concerns are increasing that terrorists might acquire and detonate a dirty bomb or a gun-type device.
- Scholars continue to debate if nuclear weapons are a source of peace in world politics or an unjustified risk to international security.

Chemical weapons

Although poisons and chemicals have been used in war since ancient times, chemical weapons emerged in the late 1800s as part of the modern chemical industry. Scholars debate whether chemical weapons should be considered a weapon of mass destruction because large quantities of chemical weapons often have to be used on the battlefield to have a significant effect against a prepared opponent and these weapons have to be expertly employed to produce massive casualties. On 20 March 1995, for instance, the Aum Shinrikyo cult launched a sarin attack against the Tokyo subway system that resulted in twelve deaths. By contrast, the al-Qaeda attack against the Madrid train system on 11 March 2004 used conventional explosives and killed nearly two hundred innocent civilians. What worries analysts, however, is that any state with a chemical industry could quickly convert production processes from civilian use to weapons manufacturing and that even readily available household products can be mixed to create relatively dangerous concoctions. Weapons can be created from commonly available chemicals using well-understood technologies. Household insecticides, for example, are simply 'watered-down' nerve agents.

The first significant employment of chemical weapons occurred in the First World War as both sides sought a way to break through the stalemate of trench warfare. On 22 April 1915, German units unleashed a cloud of chlorine gas (an asphyxiating agent) against allied lines at Ypres, Belgium, but failed to exploit the gap created in the French lines. Petrified by the sight of corpses that exhibited no obvious causes of death, attacking German soldiers refused to advance. The Germans introduced mustard gas (a blistering agent) on the battlefield on 12 July 1917. The Allies also developed their own blister agent, Lewisite, but it was just reaching the battlefield as the First World War came to an end. Although chemical weapons only caused about 4% of the casualties suffered by all sides during the First World War, the use of gas on the battlefield affected societies everywhere as veterans related stories of helpless soldiers struggling to put on gas masks as they chocked to death or were blinded by blister agents. This imagery, best exemplified by the painting of a field dressing station in Arras, France, made by the American artist John Singer Sargent, highlighted the horror and cruelty of gas warfare.

Photo 15.1 John Singer Sargent (1918) 'Gassed'

Source: Reproduced with permission from the Art Archive/Imperial War Museum.

Although the Italians employed mustard agent against Ethopia in 1935 and the Japanese attacked Chinese troops with chemical weapons in the 1930s, chemical weapons were not used extensively on Second World War battlefields. Many speculate that Adolf Hitler, a mustard gas casualty in the First World War, was personally reluctant to be the first to introduce these weapons in Europe (although this apparent aversion did not stop the Nazis from using Zyclon-B, a prussic acid based substance used as a pesticide and disinfectant, to kill thousands of victims in gas chambers). In fact, only one major chemical weapons incident occurred during the war. On 2 December 1943, a Nazi air raid on the harbour in Bari, Italy, damaged a merchant ship carrying 2,000 100 lb M 47A1 bombs filled with mustard agent. The accidental release of agent affected thousands of allied soldiers and civilians. It was not until the Iran–Iraq war, however, that chemical weapons were again employed on the battlefield. In 1982, Iraqi units, hard pressed by far more numerous Iranian forces, dispensed mass concentrations of the riot control agent CS to break up opposing formations. By 1983, Iraq was using mustard agents on the battlefield and continued experimenting with more lethal agents and concoctions. In a February 1986 strike against al-Faw, the Iraqis employed a mixture of mustard and tabun (a nerve agent) against the Iranians, which resulted in thousands of casualties. Saddam Hussein's murderous regime also attacked its own citizens with chemical weapons. On 16 March 1988 Iraq forces sprayed a mixture of mustard and nerve agents over the Kurdish village of Halabja, killing more than 10,000 civilians.

Chemical weapons effects

Chemical weapons vary in terms of their lethality, their complexity, and the way they cause injury and death. They also vary in terms of their persistence: some disperse quickly allowing attacking troops to move through an area while 'area denial agents', which might be used to attack an airfield to reduce the tempo of flight operations, might persist for a long time. Traditionally, chemical weapons have been characterized as blood agents, choking agents, blister agents, nerve agents and incapacitants.

Blood agents, which are generally based on hydrocyanic acid (HCN), interfere with the body's ability to transport oxygen in the blood. Because cyanide has been used as a poison throughout history, several countries experimented with using this agent as a weapon. Owing to its high volatility—it evaporates quickly, making it hard to create a lethal concentration over a battlefield—most states long ago abandoned it as a toxic agent for military use.

Choking agents—phosgene and chlorine—get their name from the fact that their victims literally drown in the fluids produced when the tissues lining the lungs interact with the agent. Choking agents produce hydrochloric acid when they are inhaled, causing blood and fluid to infiltrate the lungs. Phosgene, which reacts with water in the body to produce hydrochloric acid, is a common industrial chemical which is more toxic than chlorine. Most of the deaths caused in the First World War by chemical weapons were caused by phosgene.

Blister agents are primarily intended to generate serious causalities in an opposing force, thereby placing enormous demands on supporting medical services. Before the development of more lethal nerve agents, sulphur mustard, was considered to be the chemical weapon of choice. It exists as a thick liquid at room temperature, but can be suspended in air (i.e., turned into an aerosol that can be inhaled) by using a conventional explosive. It can also be used to contaminate people, terrain or equipment. Although the exact reason why mustard agent is an extreme irritant is not well understood, it causes severe blistering on exposed skin and mucous membranes. It also can cause temporary blindness. Long-term effects from a single moderate exposure to mustard agent are not usually lethal. The effects of mustard can sometimes take several hours to develop; Lewisite, another blister agent, works more rapidly than mustard.

Nerve agents are by far the most lethal chemical weapons. Invented during the 1930s as insecticides, they entered Nazi and Allied military inventories in the Second World War but were not used in combat. The name 'nerve agent' reflects the fact that these chemicals interfere with the body's neurological system by irreversibly inactivating acetyl cholinesterase (AChE), which 'deactivates' the neurotransmitter acetylcholine. Nerve agents bind to the active site of AchE, making it incapable of deactivating acetylcholine. Without an ability to deactivate acetylcholine, muscles fire continuously, glandular hypersecretion occurs (e.g., excess saliva) leading to paralysis and suffocation. Second generation nerve agents, G (German) series agents (GA) Tabun, (GB) Sarin, (GD) Soman, (GF) Cyclosarin, are considered to be non-persistent agents. G series agents are all water and fat soluble, and can enter the skin and cause lethal effects. Third generation V Series—VX, VE, VG, VM—nerve agents, a product of British science, are persistent agents that are about ten times more lethal than Sarin. Less is publicly known about fourth generation A-series agents (also known as 'Novichok' agents), a product of Soviet science. Exposure to high aerosol concentrations of nerve agents causes prompt collapse and death.

Incapacitants are used for riot control (CS or tear gas) or for personal protection (CN or mace). They are less toxic than other chemical weapons and usually do not produce lethal effects when used in the open at a proper concentration. Vomiting agents (adamsite) have been developed for use in combat. Both Soviet and US scientists also experimented with psychochemicals (i.e., lysergic acid diethylamide [LSD] and BZ) in an effort to cause altered states of situational awareness. BZ was weaponized by the United States, but it was dropped from its arsenal because its effects were unpredictable. In October 2002, Russian security forces used an opiod form of fentanyl in an attempt to incapacitate Chechin separatists who were holding 800 hostages in a Moscow theatre. Owing to either a lack of prompt medical attention or an overdose of fentanyl, 126 people died from this 'incapacitant'.

Methods of delivery

Chemical weapons are delivered either from a line or a point source. Bombs, artillery shells, missile warheads or parcels, for instance, are all point sources because they deliver chemical weapons to a specific location. A line source, which is generated by a series of dispensing devices, a crop duster or even a moving crop sprayer, creates a cloud or 'line' of gas that drifts towards the target. Wind, temperature, and terrain can effect the lethality and persistence of an agent. For example, a gallon of VX is sufficient to kill thousands of people, but only if individuals are brought into contact with the correct amount of agent to cause casualties. Agents can be blown off target, diluted by rain or even solidify if the temperature drops too low.

Because proper dispersal is key to employing chemical weapons, analysts are most concerned about their use in closed venues such as sporting arenas or large buildings with ventilation systems that could be subject to tampering. Aum Shinryko targeted the Tokyo subway because of the large numbers of people who travel daily through its contained spaces and choke points. The cult experimented with a suitcase mechanism to deliver sarin aerosol in the subway: two small electric fans were used to disperse chemical agent after it was released from vials stored inside the suitcase. To conduct the actual attack, however, the cult relied on a far simpler method: they punched holes in plastic bags containing sarin and simply allowed the agent to evaporate in the subway cars.

Impact on international politics

By the 1970s, NATO militaries began to view chemical weapons as a deterrent, not as a weapon they preferred to use on the battlefield. Chemical weapons pose obvious difficulties in terms of transportation and handling, and most military observers agree there are safer and more efficient ways to hold targets at risk. Thus the preferences of military professionals helped to foster a taboo against the use of chemical weapons in war, restraint codified in the 1925 *Geneva Protocol for the Prohibition of the Use in War of Asphyxiating, Poisonous, or Other Gases, and of Bacteriological Methods of Warfare*. Although the Geneva Protocol banned first use of chemical weapons, it did not prevent states from stockpiling chemical munitions. The Chemical Weapons Convention (CWC), which entered into force on 29 April 1997, makes it illegal for signatories to possess or employ chemical weapons, with the exception of small samples used to test protective equipment. States party to the CWC are required to declare their existing stocks of chemical weapons, to identify facilities that once were involved in chemical weapons production, and to announce when their existing stocks will be completely destroyed. The Organization for the Prohibition of Chemical Weapons (OPCW) is authorized to verify compliance with the CWC and can undertake challenge inspections when demanded by states parties (Larsen 2002).

While 148 nations have ratified the CWC, about twenty countries, some of which maintain a large chemical arsenal (e.g., North Korea and Syria) have not signed the treaty. Most military analysts believe that these large arsenals would have only a modest effect on well-equipped and trained troops on the battlefield. In their view, a chemical arsenal is the 'poor man's' weapon of mass destruction because it is based on old, relatively simple, and inexpensive technologies that have limited military utility. Nevertheless, if employed deliberately against relatively defenseless civilian populations, these weapons could wreak havoc. Analysts are most concerned that terrorist organizations or even individuals might gain access to poisonous chemicals that are part of industrial processes and attack urban targets. Iraqi use of chemical weapons in war is considered an anomaly; the fear is that Aum Shinrikyo's sarin attack might be a harbinger of things to come.

KEY POINTS

- There are five types of chemical weapons: blood agents, choking agents, blister agents, nerve agents and incapacitants.
- Chemical agents can be persistent or non-persistent and can be delivered from a point or a line source.
- State and non-state actors with access to even a rudimentary chemical industry can acquire chemical weapons.
- The nearly universal Chemical Weapons Convention bans the manufacture or use of chemical weapons and only allows signatories to possess small amounts of agents for research into defensive equipment and prophylaxis.

Biological weapons

Biological weapons (BW) make use of living organisms or toxins to sicken or kill humans, animals and plants. These organisms and toxins all occur in nature, which makes it difficult to differentiate natural disease outbreaks from a BW attack. BW is probably the most potentially destructive weapon known to humans in the sense that a single organism or infected individual can affect millions of human beings, although scientists debate the degree of difficulty any state or non-state actor might encounter in infecting large numbers of people quickly. Although extremely contagious diseases are generally not lethal, some, smallpox, for example, are easily transmitted and produce high morbidity. Sometimes, diseases that are considered relatively mundane can be extremely lethal: the 1918–1919 'Spanish Flu' killed upwards of 40 million people, striking hardest among healthy adults between the ages of 20 and 40.

Disease has been a part of war throughout history. Until recently, most people died in war from illness, not from wounds suffered in combat. Deliberate use of disease as a weapon of war, however, has been sporadic, producing mixed results. In 1346, Mongol invaders hurled the corpses of soldiers who had died from bubonic plague into the besieged city of Kaffa in an effort to deliberately spread disease. The Mongols did not know, however, that the causative bacteria of plague *Yersinia pestis* is spread by fleas that only feed on live hosts. At the end of the Seven Years War (1756–1763), British forces apparently provided American Indians with smallpox-infected blankets, although it is difficult to determine whether or not they succeeded in infecting anyone because smallpox was already endemic in the Americas and had decimated Indian populations about two hundred years earlier. During the First World War, German saboteurs apparently succeeded in infecting horses used by the allies with glanders. During the Second World War, the Japanese filled glass bombs with plague-infected fleas to spread disease and Japanese scientists working in the infamous Unit 731 conducted biological warfare experiments on prisoners of war.

Although the United States, Britain and Canada conducted research into the weaponization of Anthrax, Tularemia, Q-fever, Venezuelan equine encephalitis and anti-agricultural agents, biological weapons were generally viewed in the West as lacking military utility. By contrast, Soviet researchers concentrated on perfecting a variety of biological agents during the Cold War and exploited the emerging science of genetic engineering to better weaponize naturally occurring diseases. According to Ken Alibek, who was a leading figure in Biopreperat, the Soviet Union's complex of biological weapons facilities, Soviet science worked with a variety of bacteria (e.g., an antibiotic-resistant strain of anthrax), viruses (e.g., smallpox) and even haemorrhagic fevers, e.g., Ebola (Alibek 2000). Although the 'Soviet' biological weapons programme apparently ended in Russia in the early 1990s, experts still debate what motivated the Soviets to undertake such an extensive BW programme. The Soviets probably saw their BW program as a counter to the precision, global-strike complex that was emerging in NATO in the 1970s or as a way to retard Western recovery following an all-out nuclear exchange. The Soviets apparently loaded several SS-18 intercontinental ballistic missiles with plague in an attempt to provide Western survivors of a nuclear war with an additional reason to envy the dead.

Biological weapons effects

Although naturally occurring diseases have been a scourge of humankind, not every disease provides the basis for an effective biological weapon. An agent's storage, delivery, mode of transmission, and its very resilience (i.e., how long can it survive in the environment) can shape its effects on a target population. Military professionals believe that most biological weapons are simply too unpredictable in their effects to be a reliable weapon. Because they are easy to manufacture and can be potentially highly lethal in small quantities—any basic medical laboratory has the capability to cultivate a biological agent—biological agents might be attractive and available to terrorists. Relatively large industrial facilities are needed to produce militarily significant quantities of chemical weapons, but relatively small fermenters used to make legitimate vaccines, for instance, could be quickly converted to produce biological agents.

There are three varieties of biological agents: bacteria, viruses, and toxins. As an area attack agent, anthrax is probably the best-known bacterial agent. Its spores are extremely hardy (they can live for literally hundreds of years) and it can be spread quickly across large areas. Anthrax is not contagious, so its effects can be relatively contained and focused on specific targets. It also can be genetically engineered to be resistant to most antibiotics and it can be formulated with inert matter to better form an aerosol. These qualities make anthrax the

Table 15.2 Likely biological warfare agents—bacterial and rickettsial agents

Agent/Disease	Organism	Lethality	Onset	Symptoms	Target
Anthrax	*Bacillus anthracis*	80% lethality, non-contagious	1–5 days	Pulmonary form: chest cold symptoms, respiratory distress, fever, shock death	Area attack
Brucellosis	Brucella	3–20% lethality, non-contagious	5–60 days	Fever, headaches, pain in joints and mussels fatigue	Area attack
Plague	*Yersinia pesstis*	80% lethality, contagious	2–3 days	High fever, headache, extreme weakness, haemorrhages in skin and mucous membranes	Area attack
Tularemia	*Francisella tularensis*	50% lethality contagious	2–10 days	Chills, fever, headache, loss of body fluids	Area attack
Q Fever	Coxiella burnettii	2% lethality non-contagious	10–40 days	Fever, headache, cough, muscle and joint pain	Area attack

agent of choice for many biological weapons programmes. The cutaneous form of anthrax occurs in the animal industry and can be treated relatively easily; by contrast, the inhalation form of the disease is extremely dangerous. By the time the victim begins to show symptoms of inhalation anthrax, a near-lethal dose of toxins produced by the anthrax bacteria has already built up in the body. The Aum Shinrikyo cult attempted to disperse anthrax in Tokyo in 1996; they failed because they used a non-toxic vaccine strain of the virus. The terrorist who sent anthrax through the US mail in autumn 2001, however, used a deadly 'Ames' strain which US weapons laboratories employ to test defensive equipment and prophylaxis (Stern 2000).

Although haemorrhagic fevers—Marburg, Lassa fever, or Ebola—are viral agents that could serve as potent weapons, policy makers are most worried about the threat posed by smallpox. As smallpox was eradicated as a naturally occurring disease, global vaccination programmes were terminated, leaving entire generations unprotected against the disease for the first time in hundreds of years. Smallpox is an airborne virus that is about as contagious as the flu, but it has a lethality of about 30% in its ordinary form (rarer malignant and haemorrhagic forms of smallpox are 100% lethal). It also leaves survivors horribly scarred by its effects. Smallpox vaccination can stop the disease, even if administered a few days after exposure, but to prevent a pandemic, potentially millions of doses of vaccine need to be made quickly available. Reintroduction of general inoculation programmes, however, have not been advocated by

Table 15.3 Likely biological warfare agents—viral agents

Agent/Disease	Organism	Lethality	Onset	Symptoms	Target
Smallpox	Variola virus	2–49% lethality, contagious	7–17 days	Severe fever, small blisters on skin, bleeding on skin and mucous	Area attack
Viral encephalitis	Eastern Equine Encephalitis (EEE) virus	80% lethality, non-contagious	1–14 days	Headache, general aches and pains, photophobia	Area attack
Viral haemorrhagic fevers	Ebola	80% lethality, contagious	4–21 days	Subcutaneous haemorrhage, bleeding from body orifices, headache, fever, stupor, convulsion	Area attack

Table 15.4 Likely biological warfare agents—toxins

Agent/Disease	Organism	Lethality	Onset	Symptoms	Target
Botulinum Toxin	*Clostridium botulinum*	80% lethality, non-contagious	1–5 days	Blurred vision, photophobia, paralysis	Proximity attack
SEB Toxin	*Staphylococcus aureus*	2% lethality, non-contagious	1–6 hours	Headache, sudden fever, nausea, vomiting	Proximity attack

public health authorities because the smallpox vaccine itself leads to about 50 instances of side effects per one million people vaccinated. The impact of a smallpox outbreak, however, cannot be underestimated. The 'Dark Winter' exercise run by the US Federal Emergency Management Agency in June 2001 was based on a smallpox outbreak in the American Midwest. Within 30 days, over 300,000 people in 25 states and 10 foreign countries had already contracted the disease. Smallpox truly has the capability of creating a global catastrophe.

Although toxins are not living organisms and are in fact a by-product of metabolic activity, they are generally discussed as a biological weapon. Toxins are probably best thought of as a poison, which is often used to attack specific individuals. Like chemical weapons, individuals have to be brought into direct contact with the toxin to suffer from its effects. Toxins, however, can be extremely lethal. Ricin, which is made from castor bean, kills by inhibiting protein synthesis within cells. Used as an assassination weapon—the Bulgarian dissident Georgy Markov was killed by a ricin injection in 1978—it can kill within three days. Because it can be made easily from readily available materials, many analysts believe that terrorists will seek to use ricin. In 2003, for instance, British officials arrested a terrorist who was plotting to smear ricin on the door handles of cars and buildings in London. In 2004, Victor Yushchenko was badly disfigured from a toxin attack (see Think Point 15.1).

Methods of delivery

Biological agents are generally delivered in the form of an infectious aerosol. Precise preparation of the aerosol is crucial because the agent has to be the proper size to infect a host by lodging in the small alveoli of the lungs. Vectors—lice, fleas, mosquitoes—transmit disease in nature, but it would be difficult to use this mode of transmission as a military weapon because it is inherently difficult to control. Terrorists might attempt to infect individuals surreptitiously with a disease such as smallpox, but the disease is difficult to grow in vitro and the terrorists themselves would have to be vaccinated to work with the virus. Because smallpox vaccine is not readily available, seeking vaccine might allow public health officials to detect some nefarious scheme. The difficulty of controlling infectious diseases also should give terrorists pause. Unleashing highly contagious diseases can backfire because a pandemic does not respect religious, political, or cultural boundaries, although public health services in rich countries are far more likely to cope with an outbreak of infectious disease than poorer countries whose health care system is already stretched to the breaking point.

Impact on international politics

Following revelations in the early 1990s about the Soviet biological weapons programme and renewed concerns about biological warfare following the 1991 Gulf War, policy makers devoted renewed attention to strengthening the 1972 Biological and Toxin Weapons Convention (BWC) by devising an inspection protocol similar to the verification mechanism embedded in the CWC. By late 2001, however, negotiations over an inspection protocol for the BWC reached an impasse. Officials concluded that it was too difficult to devise an inspection regime that could provide any significant insight into what was being manufactured in the tens of thousands of medical laboratories around the planet and that regardless of the efforts of inspection teams, it was simply too easy to conceal work on biological agents. Efforts instead shifted from the diplomatic realm to strengthening domestic criminal laws against the manufacture or possession of biological weapons or agents and improving international health monitoring to spot the outbreak of infectious diseases.

THINK POINT 15.1

Who poisoned Yushchenko?

Although toxins could be employed against troops in the field or against large groups of individuals in sporting arenas or transportation systems, history suggests that they often serve as an exotic weapon for assassination. In the latest example of attempted 'toxin assassination', Austrian doctors reported in December 2004 that Ukrainian presidential candidate Victor Yushchenko was suffering from dioxin poisoning. Yushchenko apparently developed symptoms—fatigue, pain and disfiguring chloracne—quickly after he had apparently ingested TCDD dioxin in his food. The concentration of dioxin in Yushchenko's body, the second highest ever recorded, was as least 1,000 times more than is found in most people. Some observes speculate that dioxin was used because it would disfigure and sicken Yushchenko, literally making him an unattractive candidate to the Ukrainian electorate. Compaigning in extreme pain, and badly disfigured by dioxin, Yushchenko went on to ride the 'Orange Revolution' in Ukraine that followed the electoral fraud in the November 2004 presidential elections. He took office as the Ukraine's President on 23 January 2005.

Photo 15.2 Who poisoned Yushchenko?

Combination image shows the changing face of Ukraine's opposition leader Viktor Yushchenko in file photos taken on 4 July 2004 (left) and 1 November 2004 (right).

Source: Reproduced with permission from Reuters/Gleb Garanich and Vasily Fedosenko.

KEY POINTS

- Biological weapons are derived from naturally occurring diseases and can be manufactured in medical laboratories.
- Biological weapons vary in terms of their lethality and whether or not they are contagious.
- Anthrax is a biological agent of great concern because it is a hardy, non-contagious agent that can be used to contaminate large areas. It can potentially directly infect many people quickly.
- The revolution in genetic engineering has been used to weaponize naturally occurring diseases.

Conclusion: the future of WMD

In some respects, the WMD threat has greatly receded since the end of the Cold War. The number of deployed Soviet (Russian) and American strategic nuclear warheads has been reduced by 80% over the last decade, and US tactical nuclear weapons have largely been withdrawn from service. The threat of Armageddon produced by a massive nuclear exchange is now only a remote possibility. The International Non-proliferation Regime has survived the 1998 Indian and Pakistani nuclear tests and a de facto nuclear test ban remains in place, despite the fact that the US Senate failed to ratify the Comprehensive Test Ban Treaty. The CWC and BWC not only provide a basis in international law to stop the spread of these deadly chemical and biological agents, but they also serve as a useful diplomatic framework for devising new ways to stop the spread and use of these weapons. The Proliferation Security Initiative (PSI), for instance, is a new international undertaking to stop illicit trade in materials related to chemical, biological and nuclear weapons. The PSI also reflects a shift towards counterproliferation in the international effort to stop the spread of chemical, biological and nuclear weapons. In the wake of revelations about A.Q. Khan's clandestine nuclear supply network and the interception of a shipment of North Korean SCUD missiles that were bound for Yemen, officials are taking more active steps to stop trade in illicit materials, weapons and delivery systems.

Although Iranian efforts to develop a nuclear weapon or the fact that North Korea has a nascent nuclear arsenal dominates headlines, officials today are most concerned by the prospect that WMD is escaping the control of state actors. Because terrorists rely on shock to hold their audience, many observers believe that they might be attracted to WMD because it is the next rung in the escalation ladder and it is bound to gain worldwide attention. This would not be an unprecedented development. Non-state actors already have employed chemical, biological and radiological weapons. WMD terrorism, however, poses a threat that is not easily met by today's policy or military establishments. Officials everywhere are scrambling to develop effective responses to this potential threat.

Since the First World War, the use of WMD in war has been episodic. Nation-states have mostly abandoned their chemical and biological arsenals. Terrorists' efforts to use chemical, biological or radiological weapons have been largely ineffective. Nuclear weapons, the centrepiece of the Soviet–American Cold War competition, have only been used on the battlefield twice. Lingering questions remain. Is there a taboo against the use of weapons of mass destruction? Have we all just been incredibly lucky?

QUESTIONS

Why might nuclear weapons be a source of stability in international relations?

Why do you think that the use of weapons of mass destruction in war is relatively rare?

Why would terrorists be attracted to chemical, biological, radiological or nuclear weapons?

What effect would another use of nuclear weapons have on world politics?

Toxins are often used against what type of target?

Which variety of WMD is most destructive? Which is most easily manufactured?

What steps should governments take to prevent WMD terrorism?

Is direct action or international negotiation the best way to counter the spread of WMD?

Do you think Aum Shinrikyo's experience with sarin will be emulated by other groups or individuals?

Do you think that weapons of mass destruction serve as status symbols in world politics?

FURTHER READING

■ **Freedman, Lawrence (2003), *The Evolution of Nuclear Strategy*, 3rd edn, New York: Palgrave Macmillan**. This is the best single volume on the history of nuclear arsenals and the strategic thinking that guided nuclear strategy.

■ ***The Effects of Nuclear War* (1979), Washington, DC**: Office of Technology Assessment. This volume provides a fine overview of nuclear weapons effects.

■ **Schell, Jonathan (1982), *The Fate of the Earth*, New York: Knopf**. This is probably the best description of the existential threat posed by the widespread use of nuclear weapons.

■ **Sagan, Scott D. and Waltz, Kenneth (2002), *The Spread of Nuclear Weapons: A Debate Renewed*, 2nd edn, New York: W.W. Norton & Co**. Provides an engaging debate between proliferation optimists and pessimists.

■ **Croddy, Eric A. and Wirtz, James J. (eds.) (2005), *Weapons of Mass Destruction: An Encyclopedia of Worldwide Policy, Technology, and History* 2 vols., Santa Barbara, CA: ABC-Clio**. A handy reference on WMD.

IMPORTANT WEBSITES

● **http://ww.cdc.gov/** Center for Disease Control and Prevention provides information on diseases.

● **http://www.ucsusa.org/** Union of Concerned Scientists. Established in 1969, this is an independent non-profit alliance of more than 100,000 citizens and scientists concerned by the misuse of science and technology in society.

● **www.ccc.nps.navy.mil** Center for Contemporary Conflict. Launched in 2001, the CCC conducts research on current and emerging security issues and conveys its findings to US and Allied policy-makers and military forces.

- **http://nuclearweaponarchive.org/** Nuclear Weapons Archive. The purpose of this archive is to illuminate the reader regarding the effects of these destructive devices, and to warn against their use.
- **http://cns.miis.edu/** Center for Nonproliferation Studies, Monterey Institute of International Studies. The Center strives to combat the spread of weapons of mass destruction (WMD) by training the next generation of nonproliferation specialists and disseminating timely information and analysis.
- **http://www.fas.org/main/home.jsp** Federation of American Scientists. Formed in 1945 by atomic scientists from the Manhattan Project, the FAS conducts research and provides education on nuclear arms control and global security; conventional arms transfers; proliferation of weapons of mass destruction; information technology for human health; and government information policy.

Visit the Online Resource Centre that accompanies this book for lots of interesting additional material: www.oxfordtextbooks.co.uk/orc/collins/

16

Terrorism

BRENDA LUTZ AND JAMES LUTZ

Chapter Contents

Reader's Guide

This chapter analyses the threat that **terrorism** poses for countries and the world. Efforts to deal with terrorism can be considered within the framework of terrorism as warfare, terrorism as crime, and terrorism as disease. Which of these views is adopted determines what kinds of countermeasures countries will use in their effort to deal with terrorism. Terrorism is a technique of action available to all groups; security measures that work with one group may not be effective with others. Dealing with terrorism in today's world can be a very complex process indeed.

Introduction

Terrorism has become an important phenomenon, as well as a major security issue for many countries. The attacks on 11 September 2001 on the World Trade Center in New York City and the Pentagon near Washington DC highlighted the great damage that such attacks could cause. Since that time, large-scale attacks on tourist facilities on Bali in 2002 and again in 2005, on commuter trains in Madrid in 2004, on a Russian middle school in Beslan in 2004, and the suicide bombings in London in 2005 all demonstrate the continuing threat that terrorism can pose. Further, the continuing terrorist campaigns that persist over time have claimed many victims; it is not only the spectacular attacks that constitute a threat. The cumulative effects of such campaigns are important. Multiple attacks by a variety of dissident groups in Turkey between 1975 and 1980 left more than 5,000 dead and 15,000 injured (Bal and Laciner 2001: 106), a toll heavier than the casualties inflicted on 9/11. Casualty lists have demonstrated the continuing vulnerability of people everywhere to terrorism, and more recently concern has grown that terrorists might use weapons of mass destruction (biological, chemical, or nuclear).

While terrorism is a technique that has been around for millennia and used by different groups, the more pressing concern for governments today is the groups currently operating. Groups have adapted to changing circumstances. During the Cold War, terrorist groups often gained the support of the Soviet Union or the United States or their respective allies. Today, there are no competing superpowers, and overt support for terrorist groups can generate a massive military response as the Taliban regime in Afghanistan discovered. In response terrorist organizations have developed networks that provide mutual assistance. Groups like al-Qaeda in some respects now have structures that resemble multinational criminal networks (see Case Study 16.1). Terrorist groups have also developed linkages with criminal organizations, especially those involved in drug trafficking. Both the terrorists and the drug cartels benefit from weak governments that find it difficult to interfere with their activities. These loosely connected international networks can be more difficult to attack and defeat.

While terrorism and terrorists have been analysed from a variety of theoretical perspectives, one of the most useful has been proposed by Peter Sederberg (2003), who suggests that terrorism can be viewed from three perspectives. The first perspective is to think of terrorism in the context of an enemy to be defeated in war. The war analogy presumes that the use of military methods can be successful and that it is possible to achieve victory. A second perspective for dealing with terrorists is to rely on normal police techniques. The criminal analogy has two quite important implications. First, it suggests that terrorism, like crime, will not disappear; it can only be contained. Second, this approach is a reactive one—criminals are normally caught after they commit their crimes. The third perspective is to consider terrorism as a disease, emphasizing both symptoms and underlying causes. It assumes that there is a need for long-term strategies even if there can be successes along the way in treating symptoms. The three perspectives, of course, are not mutually exclusive, but they can represent dominant ways in which terrorism is viewed. They are important for analysing the phenomenon and for government officials who make choices in terms of how to deal with terrorist activity. Which perspective is adopted will suggest mechanisms for dealing with terrorism. Before 11 September 2001, authorities in the United States largely dealt with acts of terrorism from the criminal perspective. Terrorists were caught (eventually in some cases) and brought to trial (although not always convicted). Normal police techniques, including the use of informers and the infiltration of agents into potentially dangerous groups (like the Ku Klux Klan in the 1960s) drew upon conventional practices. After 9/11, however, the war analogy became dominant for the administration of President Bush, and references to the global war on terrorism appeared regularly.

CASE STUDY 16.1

Al-Qaeda and decentralized structures

Al-Qaeda (the Base) provides the most prominent example of a network form of terrorist organization that has always maintained links with distinct groups operating in different countries, especially groups favouring the creation of more Islamic government. It has provided assistance and cooperated with groups in Algeria, Egypt, the Philippines, and Indonesia among other countries. There is a fear that there are many 'sleeper cells' of al-Qaeda activists or those in agreement with its goals scattered around the world ready to strike when mobilized. The organization itself is relatively small, and provides technical and financial leadership and support to these groups. The coordination permits individuals to use existing local contacts for their operations, and provides channels for obtaining arms and for laundering money. Al-Qaeda was willing to fund projects presented to it by terrorist groups if the leaders were convinced that the project held promise of success (Nedoroscik 2002). The flexibility and willingness of the organization to use these local groups effectively extended the reach of the group. The loose, decentralized structure provided protection from infiltration or disruption by security forces. This structure and contacts with local Muslim extremist groups helps to explain how the organization was able to direct and support the attacks on commuter trains in Madrid in 2004 and the transit system in London in 2005 while its leaders and many of its other personnel were being actively sought by security forces around the world. (Also, see Table 16.7)

KEY POINTS

- Terrorism was a problem long before the 11 September attacks.
- Terrorism can be viewed as a problem to be resolved by military means (war on terrorism), by normal police techniques (terrorism as crime), or as a medical problem with underlying causes and symptoms (terrorism as disease).
- How terrorism is viewed will help to determine which policies governments will adopt to deal with terrorism.

Concepts and definitions

There are a number of key concepts that are essential to any discussion of terrorism. The first is selecting a workable definition. A second concern involves targets and techniques, including the increasing concern about the danger that weapons of mass destruction present. A third key issue involves the prevalence of terrorism and the distinction between domestic and international terrorism, a distinction becoming more blurred with the passage of time. Finally, it is useful to distinguish among some basic types of terrorist groups, including ethnic, religious, and ideological.

Definition of terrorism

There has been a multitude of definitions used for terrorism, partially because of disagreements among commentators or analysts and partially because some definers seek to exclude groups that they support or to include groups that they wish to denounce. Courts and police agencies require definitions that permit prosecution and incarceration; political leaders may have different needs and agendas. A working definition that is relatively neutral recognizes the basic fact that terrorism is a tactic used by many different kinds of groups. It includes six major elements. Terrorism involves (1) the use of violence or threat of violence (2) by an organized group (3) to achieve political objectives. The violence (4) is directed against a target audience that extends beyond the immediate victims, who are often innocent civilians. Further, (5) while a government can either be the perpetrator of violence or the target, it is only considered an act of terrorism if the other actor is not a government. Finally, (6) terrorism is a weapon of the weak (Lutz and Lutz 2005: 7).

This definition excludes kidnappings for financial gain and excludes acts by individuals, even those with political objectives. Organization is essential for a successful campaign to bring about the political goals that are being sought. While the exact political objectives vary, they can include changes in government policies or practices, changes in government leaders or structures, demands for regional autonomy or independence, or a mix of such political issues. While organization is necessary for any chance of a successful campaign, individuals may operate in loose affiliation with a group. The individual dissidents may receive suggestions from leaders who maintain their distance from the operatives in the field in an organizational form that has come to be known as **leaderless resistance**. The individuals providing 'guidance' in this context are careful to avoid giving direct orders or encouraging violence against specific individuals to avoid any criminal or civil charges (Jenkins 2001). This type of activity has been used by animal rights groups to coordinate actions in defence of animals (Monaghan 2000). More recently al-Qaeda has drawn upon some of the same methods. Terrorist violence is a form of psychological warfare that undermines opposition to their goals (Chalk 1996: 13). They generate fear in a target audience by attacking individuals who are representative of the larger group. This group can be members of the elite, supporters of the governments, members of a particular ethnic or religious community, or the general public. Civilians are often chosen as targets because they are more vulnerable than members of the security forces; furthermore, their deaths or injuries heighten the level of insecurity in the larger audience. It is often suggested that terrorist targets are chosen at random, but in fact terrorists usually pick their targets very carefully in order to influence an audience. The media often becomes important for this aspect of terrorism since media coverage is very important for spreading fear, or at least in reaching the target audience more quickly, although target populations will usually became aware of attacks even when media attention is limited. Finally, terrorism is also a weapon utilized by the weak. Groups that can win elections or seize control of the government will do so; groups that cannot hope to win their objectives in other ways, however, may resort to terrorism.

While terrorism can involve governments as targets or perpetrators, it does not include cases during cold and hot wars where governments use terror tactics against each other. These government to government attacks are a different security issue and are not included in definitions of terrorism even if they involve massacres, atrocities, or war crimes. Governments, however, are often the targets of dissident terrorists. While governments usually oppose terrorist attacking their citizens, at times political leaders may tolerate terrorist attacks by private groups against enemies, potential dissidents, or unpopular minorities (ethnic, religious, cultural, or ideological). The government may fail to investigate or prosecute the perpetrators of the violence. In other cases governments may provide active support and in extreme cases even form death squads to attack its enemies while maintaining at least an illusion of deniability. While this governmental involvement in terrorism is quite important, it will not be the focus of the present chapter since the violence does not begin as a security concern (although violent groups that are tolerated may later challenge the government, as occurred with the **Fascists** in Italy). The use of private groups or death squads does correspond with the idea that terrorism is a weapon of the weak. Governments that are strong enough to deal with dissidents or to protect dissidents from private violence do not need to tolerate or use such forms of control.

Techniques and targets

The range of techniques available to terrorists is varied, but most activities are variations of standard practices—bombings, kidnappings, assaults including assassinations, and takeovers of buildings or planes or ships, invariably with hostages. Bombs can be used to just damage property or in efforts to inflict casualties, sometimes in large numbers. Car bombs have increasingly become a favourite device for terrorist groups because of the damage that they can do. Kidnapping frequently provides a publicity bonanza for terrorist groups. In some cases ransoms from kidnappings have provided an important source of funding for terrorist groups, and in other cases terrorists have been able to gain some concessions from governments in turn for the release of the victims. Assaults are usually directed at individuals who represent a particular group (politicians, police, military personnel, journalists, etc.). Sometimes the intent is to wound while in other cases the goal is the assassination of the individual or individuals. No one assassination is likely to bring about the changes the terrorists desire, but a campaign of such assassinations generates greater fear. Hostage situations in airline hijackings or the capture of buildings (the Japanese embassy in Peru in December 1996) demonstrate the vulnerability of society and generate publicity for the terrorist cause. Even when governments refuse to make major concessions, they often will publicize a list of demands by the terrorists or publish other kinds of communiqués.

Weapons of mass destruction (WMD) have become a special security concern for governments. There is a great fear that some terrorist groups will use biological, chemical, nuclear, or radiological (dirty) weapons to cause more casualties. To some extent terrorist groups have already gained a psychological edge simply because of the fear of use. There have only been few such attacks to date. **Aum Shinriyko**, the Japanese cult, attempted to use nerve gas in the Tokyo subway system to cause mass casualties but failed. This attempt did demonstrate what might happen. The anthrax attacks in the United States after 11 September generated great fear, but there were only a few deaths. A single bomb might have killed more, but the form of the anthrax attacks made them more terrifying. Such weapons have not been used very often because they require major resources to develop and trained personnel. Further, most terrorist groups still prefer to stick to the tried-and-true techniques, at least until the utility of a new technique, such as car bombs, has been demonstrated.

One deadly technique that has been used by terrorists involves suicide attacks. Such attacks with bombs can be more deadly since the detonation can occur at the last minute or when casualties will be maximized. Suicide attacks are not an especially new technique. The **Assassins** active from the eleventh through the thirteenth centuries expected to die, as did the anarchists who undertook assassinations in the late nineteenth century. Recent attacks have been more devastating, as with the airliners on 9/11 and bombers in Israel. The single most important source of suicide attacks in terms of numbers has been neither Middle Eastern nor Islamic. The Liberation Tigers of Tamil Eelam (LTTE) in Sri Lanka, more commonly know as the **Tamil Tigers**, were responsible for more suicide attacks than all other groups put together between 1980 and 2000 (Radu 2002). Many of these attacks have inflicted large numbers of casualties while others were directed against important political figures. Perhaps the greatest danger in the future is that a suicide attack might be combined with the use of biological, chemical, or radiological weapons. If the persons involved in the use of these weapons are willing to die in the effort, many of the problems involved in using WMD will have been reduced.

Terrorists have great flexibility in choosing their targets, and if one target is too carefully protected, they can simply shift to another. Some other individual, building, or large gathering of people will serve to send the message that everyone in the target audience is vulnerable. The ability to find vulnerable targets may be greater in democratic states since government security is likely to be weaker than in equivalent authoritarian societies. There are limitations on how much a democratic state can monitor its citizens and visitors. Democracies also provide greater publicity for the cause since the media face few, if any, restraints. Further, even if the terrorists are caught, they will be tried in some type of impartial judicial setting where proof of guilt must be established. Of course, it is not only democratic countries that are vulnerable. Security forces may be weak in a variety of non-democratic political systems providing terrorist groups with similar opportunities to operate relatively freely.

Prevalence of terrorism

Although terrorism has occurred widely in the world, it is only recently that we have anything approaching decent statistics on its extent. Table 16.1 contains totals for international terrorist incidents from 1991 to 2003. Tables 16.2 and 16.3 indicate the extent of international terrorist incidents

Table 16.1 Casualties in International terrorist incidents 1991–2002

Year	Incidents	Dead	Injured	Total	Dead/ Incident	Injured/ Incident	Total/ Incident
1991	565	—	—	317	—	—	0.56
1992	363	—	—	729	—	—	2.01
1993	431	—	—	1,510	—	—	3.50
1994	322	314	674	988	0.98	2.09	3.07
1995	440	165	6,291	6,454	0.38	14.30	14.68
1996	296	311	2,654	2,965	1.05	8.97	10.02
1997	304	221	693	914	0.73	2.28	3.01
1998	273	741	6,313	7,054	2.71	23.12	25.84
1999	392	233	706	939	0.59	1.80	2.40
2000	423	405	791	1,196	0.96	1.87	2.82
2001	355	2,689	1,776	4,465	7.57	5.00	12.57
2002	199	725	2,013	2,738	3.64	10.12	13.76
2003	208	—	—	4,886	—	—	23.49

Source: US Department of State, *Patterns of Terrorism*, various years, online at http://www.state.gov/s/ct/rls/pgtrpt

Table 16.2 Number of international terrorist incidents by region

YEAR	REGION							
	Africa	Asia	Eurasia*	Latin America	Europe	Middle East	North America	Total
1991	3	48	6	199	229	78	2	565
1992	10	13	3	113	143	79	2	363
1993	6	37	5	185	97	100	1	431
1994	25	24	11	88	58	116	0	322
1995	10	16	5	272	92	45	0	440
1996	11	11	24	121	84	45	0	296
1997	11	21	42	128	52	37	13	304
1998	21	49	14	110	48	31	0	273
1999	52	72	35	121	85	25	2	392
2000	55	98	31	193	30	16	0	423
2001	33	68	3	201	17	29	4	355
2002	5	99	7	50	9	29	0	199

*Former Communist countries of Eastern Europe and successor states of the Soviet Union.

Source: US Department of State (various years) *Patterns of Terrorism*, online at http://www.state.gov./s/ct/rls/pgtrpt.

by region and the casualties (dead and injured). International terrorist incidents are considered to be actions where indigenous terrorists attack a foreign target (kidnapping foreign tourists), where terrorists launch an attack against a target in another country (the 11 September attacks), or when a foreign country is used because it is convenient (IRA attacks against British soldiers in Germany). The compilation of statistics for these kinds of incidents is usually more complete than records for domestic attacks since such incidents attract more attention. The tables indicate that international actions have been widespread. North America has been the scene of very few attacks, but the 1993 attack on the World Trade Center resulted in many injuries, while the 2001 attacks resulted in many deaths (and undercounts on the number of injuries). Latin America typically has had large numbers of incidents. Heavy casualties have occurred in different regions for different years, reflecting singularly deadly attacks such as the East Africa embassy attacks in 1998, the World Trade Center disaster in 2001, and the heavy toll in Bali in 2002.

The distinction between domestic and international attacks has become increasingly blurred, especially when international terrorist networks are included. British citizens apparently undertook the attacks in London in 2005, but this fact did not make them domestic attacks given the international nature of the probable goals of the suicide attackers. Assassination of a domestic leader on foreign soil qualifies as international terrorism but the choice of the foreign country could simply be one of convenience. Domestic terrorism does not generate the

Table 16.3 Number of casualties due to international terrorist incidents by region

YEAR	REGION							
	Africa	Asia	Eurasia*	Latin America	Europe	Middle East	North America	Total
1991	3	150	7	68	56	33	0	317
1992	28	25	0	374	65	236	1	729
1993	7	135	1	66	117	178	1,006	1,510
1994	55	71	151	329	126	256	0	988
1995	8	5,639	29	46	287	445	0	6,454
1996	80	1,507	20	18	503	837	0	2,965
1997	28	344	27	11	17	480	7	914
1998	5,379	635	12	195	405	68	0	7,054
1999	185	690	8	9	16	31	0	939
2000	102	898	103	20	4	69	0	1,196
2001	150	651	0	6	20	513	4,091	5,341
2002	12	1,281	615	52	6	772	0	2,718
2003	14	1,427	615	79	928	1,823	0	4,886

*Former Communist countries of Eastern Europe and successor states of the Soviet Union.

Source: US Department of State (various years) *Patterns of Terrorism*, online at http://www.state.gov./s/ct/rls/pgtrpt.

media attention that international incidents have, but it is by far the most prevalent form of terrorism. There is more complete data for terrorist acts between 1998 and 2004, with data on incidents, injuries, and fatalities for international and domestic terrorism. Tables 16.4, 16.5, and 16. 6 contain statistics by region for these years. Domestic incidents are more prevalent than international incidents. There are probably missing incidents that did not cause casualties, but the numbers would indicate that domestic incidents can be ten times as high with correspondingly higher figures for injuries and deaths. North America experienced very few attacks (although some were major of course); West Europe was more likely to be the scene of terrorist violence. For the seven years in question, it was South Asia that had the largest number of recorded fatalities overall, reflecting relatively high death tolls every year. The relative importance of domestic incidents is most obvious in the fact that the number of incidents in 2002, 2003, and 2004 was higher than in 2001 and that the totals for injuries and deaths in 2004 were higher than the totals for 2001, which included the attacks on New York and Washington DC. Terrorist violence has obviously been increasing in the twenty-first century and is becoming more dangerous as well. Whether terrorism is addressed within the context of war, crime, or disease, it is not likely to be eliminated as a security concern in the immediate future.

Table 16.4 Incidents of domestic and international terrorism by region: 1998–2004

Region	Year						
	1998	1999	2000	2001	2002	2003	2004
North America	6	8	9	39	16	18	6
West Europe	284	433	372	550	342	372	271
East Europe	313	86	27	104	215	125	167
East and Central Asia	20	—	—	23	12	13	15
South Asia	126	88	96	197	836	613	626
Southeast Asia and Oceania	27	28	72	122	96	30	49
Middle East	205	350	309	508	627	496	1,291
Africa	107	53	28	27	29	29	36
Latin America	186	113	225	163	477	199	167
Totals	1,274	1,159	1,138	1,833	2,650	1,895	2,461

No information reported for East and Central Asia in 1999 and 2000. Information is either lacking or the numbers are included in other regions.

Source: National Memorial Institute for the Prevention of Terrorism, www.tkb.org/Home.jsp

Table 16.5 Injuries of domestic and international terrorism by region: 1998–2004

Region	Year						
	1998	1999	2000	2001	2002	2003	2004
North America	2	14	0	11	3	0	0
West Europe	145	34	153	213	1914	114	653
East Europe	260	775	234	259	1,236	689	1,232
East and Central Asia	20	—	—	23	3	1	43
South Asia	1,193	675	1,043	1,171	2,158	1,326	2,929
Southeast Asia and Oceania	94	104	601	494	975	394	406
Middle East	413	334	190	1,267	1,914	3,205	4,921
Africa	5,858	372	139	239	183	51	402
Latin America	120	25	176	306	757	473	1,232
Totals	8,166	2,333	2,397	3,983	7,333	6,253	10,586

No information reported for East and Central Asia in 1999 and 2000. Information is either lacking or the numbers are included in other regions. Figures for North America for 2001 obviously do not include the uncertain number of injuries on 11 September.

Source: National Memorial Institute for the Prevention of Terrorism, www.tkb.org/Home.jsp

Table 16.6 Fatalities from domestic and international terrorism by region: 1998–2004

Region	1998	1999	2000	2001	2002	2003	2004
North America	1	3	0	2,987	3	0	0
West Europe	52	6	33	31	15	6	194
East Europe	133	350	65	70	375	266	543
East and Central Asia	71	—	—	13	3	21	26
South Asia	585	201	297	440	1,017	803	883
Southeast Asia and Oceania	9	16	87	161	351	72	202
Middle East	168	113	60	257	564	907	2,598
Africa	1,078	93	37	289	129	109	388
Latin America	142	67	198	307	297	185	543
Totals	2,239	849	777	4,555	2,754	2,369	4,834

No information reported for East and Central Asia in 1999 and 2000. Information is either lacking or the numbers are included in other regions.

Source: National Memorial Institute for the Prevention of Terrorism, www.tkb.org/Home.jsp

KEY POINTS

- Statistics indicate that terrorism is actually increasing.
- Domestic terrorism is often not as newsworthy as international actions, but it accounts for a large majority of terrorist attacks.
- Terrorist groups can be very flexible in their choice of targets.
- Terrorist groups often find that democratic states or weaker authoritarian political systems are more inviting targets.
- Some groups may be willing to use weapons of mass destruction, but most terrorist organizations continue to rely on conventional weapons for their attacks.

Types and causes of terrorism

Terrorism has been widespread, and there is no single cause that explains outbreaks of this kind of violence. It is a complex phenomenon with many facets. Linked with the causes of terrorism are the motivations of the various organizations involved in the violence, motivations that provide clues as to the underlying causes. These motivations can be used to categorize groups in terms of their objectives. The basic types are religious, ethnic or nationalist, and ideological. Additionally, there are a few groups that are more difficult to place into any particular category given the complexity of their motivations.

Categories

Religious groups obviously come to mind in the twenty-first century given their prevalence in recent years. Al-Qaeda is the most prominent example today with the global nature of its attacks (see Table 16.7), but it is not the only such group in operation. There are other Islamic groups, some with linkages to al-Qaeda, that have been active in Indonesia, India, Egypt, Israel and the Occupied Territories,

Table 16.7 Major al-Qaeda attacks

Date	Place	Target	Method	Fatalities
25 June 1996	Dhahran, Saudi Arabia	Khobar Towers housing US military	Truck bomb	19
7 August 1998	Nairobi, Kenya	US Embassy	Truck bomb	247
7 August 1998	Dar-es-Salaam, Tanzania	US Embassy	Truck bomb	10
11 September 2001	New York Washington DC	World Trade Center Pentagon	Aircraft flown into buildings	2,973
12 October 2001	Aden, Yemen	*USS Cole*, US destroyer	Explosives on boat	17
22 December 2001	Paris–Miami flight	Airliner	Attempted suicide attack with shoe bomb	0
11 April 2002	Djerba, Tunisia	Synagogue and tourists	Truck bomb	19
14 June 2002	Karachi, Pakistan	US consulate	Suicide car bomb	19
6 October 2002	Mina al-Dabah, Yemen	French tanker	Boat bomb	1
12 October 2002	Bali, Indonesia	Nightclub area and Western tourists	Car bomb	202
28 November 2002	Mombasa, Kenya	Israeli-owned hotel	Suicide car bomb	16
12 May 2003	Riyadh, Saudi Arabia	Three compounds for Westerners	Car bombs	25
16 May 2003	Casablanca, Morocco	Five sites	Suicide bombs	42
5 August 2003	Jakarta, Indonesia	Marriott Hotel	Car bomb	10
11 March 2004	Madrid, Spain	Commuter trains	Bombs	191
7 July 2005	London, England	Underground trains and bus	Suicide bombs	56

Source: *Washington Post* database.

Algeria, the Philippines, and other countries. Religious terrorism, however, has not been limited to Islamic organizations; extremist groups in other religious traditions have also used the technique. The violent anti-abortion activities in the United States are based in Christian viewpoints. Christian beliefs were used to justify ethnic cleansing activities against Muslims in Bosnia. There was a guerrilla struggle in the Indian **Punjab** in the 1980s and 1990s that pitted **Sikhs** against Hindus. The Sikh uprising was in part a reaction to extremist Hindu groups in India that sought to reclaim the subcontinent for their religion. Jewish extremists justifying their actions by their religious beliefs have used terrorist tactics against Palestinians. Aum Shinrikyo was willing to attack Japanese society given the cult's belief in the future and the need for a cleansing of the impure. Many religious groups are too weak to impose their views in other fashions, and terrorism becomes the weapon of choice.

Groups defined by their ethnic or linguistic identifications are another broad category (see Case Study 16.2). The Basque **Euzkadi ta Askatasuna** (ETA—Basque for Homeland and Freedom) has been seeking independence for the Basque region of Spain for more than 25 years. The Tamil Tigers continue to seek independence (or at least autonomy) for those areas of Sri Lanka where Tamils are a majority. Turkey has faced significant terrorist attacks from **Kurdish** separatist groups. The **Aceh Sumatra Liberation Front** has used both guerrilla warfare and terrorism in its efforts to gain independence from Indonesia. A large number of anti-colonial groups in the past were ethnically based and used terrorism as one tactic in their efforts to gain independence. Algerians mounted a major urban terrorism campaign against the French in the late 1950s to supplement guerrilla activities. Greek Cypriots also used urban terrorism and guerrilla attacks against the British in the same period. In Palestine, Jewish settler groups (who qualify as nationalist in this context since most of the settlers were quite secular) relied only on terrorism in their successful efforts to force the British to leave the territory.

Other terrorist groups have drawn their ideas from ideologies. There was a wave of terrorist violence in Europe in the 1970s and 1980s rooted

CASE STUDY 16.2

Palestinian Liberation Organization (PLO)

The struggle between the Israelis and the Palestinians is often seen as a religious conflict, but most of the initial Jewish settlers were largely secular and the original Palestinian resistance movements were overwhelmingly secular as well. Only in the early 1990s did the Palestinian opposition take on overtly religious objectives such as the creation of an Islamic Palestinian state in all of the Occupied Territories and Israel. The PLO always focused on Palestinian nationalism and stressed secular themes so that it could appeal to both Muslim and Christian Palestinians. It was an umbrella organization that included many different Palestinian nationalist groups, but it never included avowedly Islamic groups. **Fatah,** the organization led by Yasser Arafat, was one of the most important but others like the **Popular Front for the Liberation of Palestine (PFLP)** and its later splinters combined leftist ideology with Palestinian nationalism. For them the Palestinians were an oppressed Third World people battling against the evils of global capitalism and its Israeli representatives in the Middle East. The PLO initially used guerrilla raids against Israel, but after the defeat of the Arab armies in the 1967 war, it shifted to terrorism as the remaining hope for creating a Palestinian homeland. At various times groups, such as the PFLP and others, left the PLO because of disputes with Arafat over the course of action to be followed—for example, when the PLO limited terrorist attacks. Departures occurred after the peace initiatives that eventually led to the creation of the Palestinian Authority. In these and other cases, some organizations were later permitted to rejoin the PLO.

in various leftist and Marxist ideologies. The **Red Brigades** in Italy, the **Red Army Faction** in Germany, and other groups in Europe were joined by Japanese groups, the **Weathermen** in the United States, and organizations in Latin America. This leftist wave was on the wane by the last part of the 1980s when the collapse of communism in East Europe and the Soviet Union weakened the surviving groups even further. Terrorist groups based in right-wing ideologies have also been present. Such groups were relatively weak in the years after the Second World War, but a great number of them appeared in the 1990s in Western Europe. These groups have often been opposed to foreign influences, a large state, or leftist ideas. They have often targeted migrants and foreign workers, especially those from the Middle East, South Asia, or sub-Saharan Africa where cultural, ethnic, and religious differences often reinforced each other. These groups have their counterparts in the United States with *xenophobic* and anti-black groups. The Ku Klux Klan was once one of the largest of such groups (see Case Study 16.3). It was severely weakened in the 1960s and 1970s, but its place has been taken by a larger number of smaller groups espousing some of the same racist and anti-foreign ideas. When groups from the left and right have battled each other, more conservative governments tolerated the violent right-wing groups that targeted members of the left. At times governments have used death squads against leftist dissidents.

Some groups are more difficult to categorize. A number of right-wing groups in the United States incorporate Christianity into their ideologies (sometimes in unusual ways). The IRA in Northern Ireland has mobilized support on the basis of Irish versus British nationalities, but the role of religion in the struggles in the province cannot be denied. Ideology has also appeared in this struggle since the **Irish National Liberation Army** (INLA) shared the ethnic Irish basis of the IRA but also included a Marxist-Leninist ideological component. In Colombia there were some straightforwardly Marxist-Leninist terrorist groups that operated in the country, but others such as the **Revolutionary Armed Forces of Colombia** (FARC) joined forces with the drug cartels. In Peru in the 1980s and 1990s dissident organizations using terror combined leftist ideology with an ethnic appeal to the Indian communities that have been ignored by the Europeanized elite of the country. These Peruvian

CASE STUDY 16.3

The Ku Klux Klan (KKK)

The KKK is the classic American terrorist group that propounded racist and right-wing views in the 1950s and 1960s. It tried to terrorize Black Americans and their white supporters during the civil rights struggle of those years. Lynchings, murders, and bombs were used in the failed attempt to dissuade people from agitating for equal rights. This period, violent though it was, resulted in hundreds of deaths. The most active period for the KKK was in the 1920s. In this period the KKK combined its racist orientation with opposition to the presence of Catholics, Jews, and Orientals. It also was opposed to the arrival of new immigrants (many of whom were Catholic or Jewish). In these years the KKK had noticeable strength outside the Southern states; in fact, Indiana at one time had the largest membership of any state branches. The overall level of violence by the KKK was much greater in this period with lynchings and murders totalling in the thousands (Sinclair 2003: 231). Many of the dead were Black Americans, but members of other groups were also victims. Whites were at times the main targets because they were considered more dangerous than the Black Americans since they were often contaminated by foreign ideas (Tucker 1991: 5). The KKK eventually declined, partially as a consequence of a major scandal that involved the leader of the Indiana chapter (Bennett 1988: 199–237).

groups also developed links with the weaker drug cartels in that country.

Causes

The causes of terrorism in many ways are similar to the causes of most other forms of political violence (such as riots, rebellions, coups, and civil wars). Individuals in a society become so discontented or frustrated with their inability to bring about what they see as necessary changes that they resort to violence. The dissidents have a perception that society and the political system discriminate or are unfair. What is ultimately important are the perceptions of the dissidents, although greater levels of exploitation may drive larger numbers to attempt violent change.

There are some specific factors, however, that can contribute to outbreaks of terrorism. Democracies with their limitations on the security forces provide opportunities for terrorists. Limited political participation and repression by government forces can also breed the necessary popular discontent for violence, but states with strong security forces and firm control of their societies usually can prevent terrorists from operating. Dissidents and potential dissidents can be jailed, suspects can be tortured, families can be held hostage, and convictions can be guaranteed in the courts (if trials occur). When the Soviet Union was a strong centralized system, terrorism was virtually unknown. The successor states are weaker, and some like Russia have faced significant terrorist problems. It is the inability of the government of Colombia to function effectively in many parts of the country that has provided significant opportunities for guerrillas and terrorists, as well as the drug cartels, to survive and prosper. Similarly, the weak state structure present in Lebanon for the last part of the twentieth century permitted terrorist groups to form and operate. Lebanon not only saw terrorism used in the struggles to control the country, but Lebanon became a base for terrorist groups operating elsewhere.

The processes involved with globalization have also contributed to outbreaks of terrorism. With faster communications and transportation outside forces—usually Western—intrude into local societies. Economies are disrupted, and even if winners outnumber losers, there are still losers. Further, local cultures including religious components are threatened by globalization, especially when it has been accompanied by secularization. Terrorism in many cases can be seen as a reaction to globalization. Leftist groups around the world have opposed the spread of capitalism and all its evils. Secular globalization also leads to religious and ethnic fragmentation (Ramakrishna and Tan 2003: 3–4). Many religious groups (Christian, Jewish, Muslim, Hindu) are opposed to the secularism that comes with modernity (Pillar 2001: 65). Right wing, ethnocentric groups have opposed the dilution of their cultures by the outside ideas that accompany migrants, guest workers, and refugees. It is perhaps ironic that Muslims in the Middle East feel threatened by the intrusion of European or Western values at the same time that groups in Europe feel threatened by individuals from Middle Eastern cultures and with Islamic ideas. Terrorism rooted in ethnic differences can also reflect the intrusion of outside forces as groups like the Irish and the Basques fear the submergence of their language and culture into a larger ethnic identity (Dingley and Kirk-Smith 2002). There is another potential connection between democracy and nationalism that has come with globalization or been a response to it. Walter Laqueur (2001: 11) has suggested that the overlap between democracy and nationalism provides more opportunities for terrorism. Nationalism provides a spark that can exacerbate ethnic differences, and democracy allows for the expression of opposing nationalist views. If Laqueur's analysis is correct, the wave of democratization that occurred at the end of the twentieth century may have increased the chances of new outbreaks of terrorism, although increasing democratization in stable countries may eventually remove many of the conditions that contribute to terrorism.

KEY POINTS

- There is no one cause of terrorism.
- Terrorism is a technique that is available to different kinds of groups pursuing different types of objectives.
- Terrorism is not unique to Islam or to the Middle East.

Security measures

Leaders and governments facing terrorist attacks have to defend against the danger of these attacks. Since there is no one overwhelming cause or source of terrorism, partially because it is a technique that can be used by different groups for different causes, countermeasures become more difficult. Sederberg's threefold typology is relevant as a point of reference because some security or counterterrorism measures are more in keeping with viewing terrorism as war, others fit terrorism as crime, and yet others are more relevant for the disease analogy. Counterterrorism measures can also be considered within the scope of prevention, response to attacks, international collaboration, and the effects of security measures on civil liberties.

Prevention

Prevention is normally associated with the concept of terrorism as war or crime. All governments will practise prevention—repression from the terrorist perspective—by seeking to arrest or eliminate those actively involved in the violence. Security forces attack the terrorists before they strike (war) or they are arrested after the attack (crime). Clearly, which concept of battling terrorism is chosen helps to determine security policy. The war conceptualization, for example, permits a stronger pre-emptive response. In actual fact, however, the military and police functions do not have a precise dividing line. Police forces dealing with dangerous criminals (terrorist or otherwise) may shoot first and ask questions later. In both the warfare and criminal models, there may be a desire to capture terrorists to elicit further intelligence, sometimes by offering shorter sentences to captured terrorists in exchange for information. Informers, whether members who have turned or agents, inside the terrorist groups can be key assets for the security forces for gathering intelligence. Such intelligence gathering is hard for small groups; they are usually too cohesive for effective infiltration. Larger organizations are easier to penetrate and gain information, but it is unlikely that all the operations of larger groups can be stopped except with the passage of time. Similarly, loose network groups like al-Qaeda and right-wing extremist groups in the United States and Europe are unlikely to be dismantled due to any single intelligence coup, although actions based on successful intelligence gathering can weaken them.

Greater physical security measures are another preventive option that has merit whether one views terrorism as war, crime, or disease. Not every possible target can be protected, but key installations, including potential sources of materials for weapons of mass destruction, however, need to be secured. In other cases security can be enhanced for many potential targets even if all attacks cannot be prevented. Some terrorist activities might be foiled, and in other cases some members of the dissident

THINK POINT 16.1

Security and the law of unintended consequences

Sometimes improved security can have unintended, and negative, consequences. In the 1960s and 1970s the United States and other countries suffered through a wave of airline hijackings. Individuals from a variety of groups (and loners with no cause but a desire for publicity) skyjacked airliners, issuing communiqués justifying their actions. Many of the aircraft were flown to Cuba or Algeria where the hijackers received asylum in return for releasing the planes and passengers. In response to the hijackings airport security was improved so that hijackings virtually ceased. Groups could no longer use this tactic to publicize their cause; therefore, some organizations shifted to planting bombs on the airliners to raise public consciousness of their objectives. The terrorists even developed sophisticated bombs that would only begin a countdown to detonation when a certain altitude was reached. Eventually, baggage security at airports improved so that only an occasional bomb could be successfully placed on planes, but not before a number of airliners had been destroyed in mid-flight. In some ways the use of airliners as bombs on 11 September was a response to the difficulties of placing bombs on aircraft. These examples demonstrate that while defensive security precautions can be important, committed terrorists can find new techniques that can also be more deadly than the ones that they replace.

groups may be captured or killed as a consequence of improved security. These preventive measures will not stop determined terrorists who will seek other, more vulnerable targets (see Think Point 16.1). Increased security, of course, will mean increased costs, and the money spent on physical security and target hardening is not available elsewhere in the economy.

Responses

Responses to terrorist attacks vary, either explicitly or implicitly, if terrorism is seen as warfare, crime, or disease. If the war analogy holds, retaliation and punishment become the norms. Pre-emptive strikes against training facilities, at headquarters, or even assassinations of key individuals in the terrorist organizations are potential responses. The United States and its allies have attempted to follow this strategy against al-Qaeda. In their confrontations before the **Oslo Accords**, Israel and the **PLO** basically viewed their struggle in terms of covert warfare. Even though Israel regarded the PLO and other Palestinian groups as terrorists—and definitely not as soldiers, the context of the struggle was one of warfare. Today, Israel has adopted the same approach to dealing with **Hamas** and **Islamic Jihad**.

Arrest, capture, trial (fair or otherwise), and incarceration reflect the crime perspective. The ultimate goal of police forces is to deter action by demonstrating that criminals will be caught and punished. The same goal is present with terrorists; capture and punishment are inevitable. While the warfare analogy also presumes deterrence at times, deterrence is more central to a justice system. Pre-emptive strikes and assassinations are not normally part of the arsenal of crime fighting unless a government unleashes death squads as a form of state violence or permits groups allied with the government to attack in this fashion. In these circumstances governments have shifted from the crime perspective to one closer to the warfare analogy. The extent of pre-emption available in a normal criminal context is detention of suspects, sometimes for lengthy periods (but not indefinite ones), and perhaps judicial harassment. Hostage situations are one area where terrorism as crime is most frequently the response. It is normally police forces that are better equipped and trained to deal with these kinds of situations. Even rescue attempts are not foreign to typical police practice. The war response might consider the hostages as potential casualties of the conflict rather than considering their safety as the prime objective of dealing with terrorists.

If terrorism is viewed as a disease, the range of responses will change. Since diseases have both symptoms and causes, this perspective requires that some of the responses related to the war and crime views be applied. Terrorist violence, as a symptom, will need to be dealt with by arrest or prevention. The disease perspective also leads to efforts to deal with the underlying causes. Reform packages may become part of the government response in an effort to reduce the appeal of the terrorist groups within the population. If ethnic or religious discrimination is present, laws forbidding discrimination may be passed. If poverty is perceived to be fuelling support for the terrorists, then governmental programmes to reduce poverty in a region or group may be instituted (at least if the funds are available). If the terrorists are operating in a colonial situation, then the ultimate reform that is possible is for the colonial power to grant independence. Of course, it has been argued that reforms will simply encourage the terrorists to continue the violence because they are being rewarded. As one leader of a terrorist group argued, more was won by a few months of violence than by years of peaceful politics (Ash 2003: 63). Under these circumstances reforms may become concessions that fuel the violence rather than a mechanism for ending it.

It is clear for other reasons that reforms will not always eliminate the presence of terrorism. Demands by the terrorist dissidents for the establishment of a religious state, a leftist government, the repression of a minority, or removal of all foreigners or foreign elements may not be acceptable to the majority. The leftists in the 1970s and 1980s in Europe wanted to do away with the international capitalist system, yet most Europeans wanted to continue to receive the benefits of capitalism. Most of the inhabitants of Puerto Rico do not want independence, but groups with this objective have used terror attacks against the United States. The United States cannot prevent the spread of globalization or the intrusion of outside values and new cultures into the Middle East. In other cases, extremist groups in the same country may have mutually incompatible goals. Extreme Jewish settler groups in Israel want complete control of the West Bank and all Palestinians to leave; Hamas wants to create an Islamic state in the whole of Israel, the West Bank, and the Gaza Strip. No Israeli government can meet the demands of both groups. In the 1970s dissident terrorists from the left and the right attacked the Turkish government. There was no programme available that could meet the demands of both groups. Given situations such as the ones noted above, even a government or political leaders inclined to reforms will frequently have to rely on other options.

International measures

International cooperation among countries is another important counter-terrorist technique. Intelligence agencies operate best on their own soil or in their own region; national intelligence is not equally effective everywhere. Collaboration among intelligence agencies, therefore, will contribute to the prevention of terrorism. International cooperation can also provide the necessary support for reforms that reduce the severity of terrorism. Sanctions against countries aiding terrorists will be more effective if there is international support. The cumulative effect of economic sanctions (and declining oil prices) led Libya to reduce its support for foreign terrorist groups (Crenshaw 2003: 165). Extreme military sanctions (an invasion) ended the support that the Taliban regime was providing to al-Qaeda, and this military action had widespread international support (unlike the later military action against Iraq). While cooperative international sanctions do not always work, it is important to note that they do not always fail.

A great deal of international diplomacy has involved attempts to define terrorism so that all countries could then take steps to eliminate terrorist groups. These efforts have faltered because countries often support or sympathize with dissidents who use violence against repressive governments. Governments in the developing world have wanted to avoid situations where anti-colonial struggles are labelled as terrorism. Most countries have sought to avoid too strict a definition since they want the flexibility to avoid extradition or punishment of some political dissidents. It is hard to envision the United States accepting a terrorist label in 2003 for anti-Saddam Hussein dissidents who attacked members of his regime. There have been some successes in the international sphere. Certain types of actions, such as air piracy, have been outlawed and most members of the United Nations have signed these treaties and conventions (Pillar 2001: 77–79). These partial agreements are a positive step in the process of containing terrorism by defining certain terrorist acts as crime. When global agreements are not possible, diplomacy can achieve agreements among smaller groups of countries, providing for greater cooperation and bilateral arrangements to automatically avoid asylum for individuals associated with certain groups. The United States and the United Kingdom, for example, eventually signed a bilateral agreement making the extradition of suspected IRA members from the United States easier.

Civil liberties in peril

A final concern that has appeared with counterterrorism efforts in many countries is the potential threat that such measures can have for civil liberties. While authoritarian states do not worry about this issue, there are limits on intelligence gathering and pre-emptive actions in democracies. Increased security measures can lead to infringements on the rights of citizens or of foreign residents. In the United States, the Patriot Act has permitted more intrusive searches and wiretaps, while persons captured overseas have been placed in indefinite detention at the Guantanamo Naval Base in Cuba. There has also been consideration of establishing special tribunals to try suspected terrorists that would be expected to operate in ways to convict suspects. In Northern Ireland IRA intimidation of jurors led to the use of courts without juries, and preventative detention was also introduced. Special terrorism laws were passed in the United Kingdom in the wake of IRA attacks. The danger of wrongful convictions is possible even without special legislation; judges and juries may be quick to assume the guilt of suspected terrorists. Germany, France, and Australia—like the United Kingdom and the United States—passed

CASE STUDY 16.4

Miscarriages of justice with Irish defendants

In 1974 IRA attack teams set off bombs in Woolwich in London and Guildford in Surrey that killed off duty service personnel (and others). A month later two pubs in Birmingham were bombed. These bombings led to the passage of the **Prevention of Terrorism Acts** (Temporary Provisions)—since periodically renewed—which provided for longer detention of IRA suspects for questioning and other changes that facilitated intelligence gathering. Four suspects (the Guildford Four) were arrested, convicted, and imprisoned on shaky evidence and coerced confessions. Their arrests also led to the arrest and conviction on weak forensic evidence of seven more suspects (the Maguire Seven). The bombings in Birmingham resulted in the conviction of six individuals (the Birmingham Six) with weak evidence and coerced confessions. Sixteen of the seventeen individuals were Irish and the seventeenth was the English girlfriend of one of the suspects. The special interrogation procedures available to the authorities permitted overzealous police to coerce confessions and manipulate evidence to convict those that the police thought were guilty. Juries were clearly inclined to believe the police and doubtful of the Irish suspects. While there is no evidence that the police, the courts, or the government had a concerted policy to manufacture convictions, the climate of fear and the desire to convict someone for the crimes contributed to these miscarriages of justice (Lutz, Lutz, and Ulmschneider 2002).

new legislation after the events of 11 September giving government security forces greater powers to detain and interrogate those suspected of terrorism (Haubrick 2003; Hocking 2003). In such circumstances there is always the danger of convicting innocent people (see Case Study 16.4). Civil liberties are in the least danger if terrorism is viewed as a disease where the root causes need to be treated. The crime model provides for some threat to civil liberties, but defenders of civil liberties are used to dealing with the police and criminal justice system. The greatest danger comes when governments regard the battle against terrorism as warfare because most democratic countries permit greater restrictions on the rights of individuals during wartime. As a consequence, viewing the struggle with terrorism as war tends to bring with it the idea that temporary personal sacrifices of liberties may be necessary in the interest of victory.

KEY POINTS

- Detection and prevention of terrorist attacks will not always be possible.
- Dealing with terrorism within the context of warfare is more likely to result in pre-emptive actions.
- Considering terrorism within the disease perspective places greater emphasis on reforms than either the crime or war perspective.
- International cooperation for dealing with terrorism would appear to have natural limits, and any global agreements on a meaningful definition of terrorism are unlikely.
- The greatest threat to civil liberties in democracies comes in those contexts where the battle against terrorism is seen as being equivalent to war.

Conclusion

It is clear that terrorism will remain a major security threat for years to come. The ethnic, religious, and ideological disputes that have fuelled terrorism have not disappeared. While ideological terrorism has declined since the end of communism, it has not disappeared, and ethnic and religiously inspired terrorism remains very important. Groups that cannot attain their goals through the electoral process or government takeovers will often adopt terrorism as a technique. Globalization will continue to disrupt economic, political, social, religious, and cultural systems. Weak states will be inviting targets for attacks or provide terrorists with convenient bases. Government repression will generate opposition. Connections between terrorists and drug operations could increase the relative threat even more.

Providing security against terrorism will not be easy. There are too many targets for total protection, and terrorists have the advantage of being able to choose the targets that are not defended. No one countermeasure will defeat terrorism. It has multifaceted causes, especially since terrorism is a technique that is available to many different groups. Counterterrorist successes against one group will not automatically guarantee victory against groups elsewhere. Groups come from different backgrounds, have different kinds of support, and seek different objectives. Under these circumstances it would be amazing if there was one countermeasure that would always work. In some cases, normal police methods will be successful. Treating terrorism as crime, for example, is quite appropriate when terrorists have linked up with drug cartels. Curtailing drug operations will help to deprive the terrorist organizations of an important source of funding. Considering terrorism as war is relevant in cases where the dissident groups combine terrorism with guerrilla activities, as has been the case with the Tamil Tigers in Sri Lanka. In other circumstances, and even in Sri Lanka, there may be some value in the government considering reforms as one means of weakening support for the dissidents or as a compromise to end the violence. Looking at terrorism from the perspective of war, crime, or disease is useful for analysis and for pinpointing problems that can occur when one or the other of these particular views is taken, but many terrorist groups and situations do not fit neatly into one or the other of these three situations. The necessary response will often be a mixture of elements involved with all three, and determining the appropriate mix of security programmes and responses to terrorism will never be easy. Security measures for dealing with terrorist threats is likely to require flexibility and government security forces will have to change techniques as circumstances change.

? QUESTIONS

Which type of terrorism is currently the most prevalent in the Middle East, Asia, Europe, and the United States and why?

Which areas of the world are most vulnerable to terrorism and why?

What other categories might be added to religious, ideological, and ethnic terrorism?

What role does the media play in international terrorism and domestic terrorism?

Is terrorism more widespread in the twenty-first century than it was in the last half of the twentieth century?

What techniques might be most effective in dealing with different kinds of terrorism? Why?

Is terrorism best dealt with as war, crime, or disease in your own country?

What counter-terrorism measures would be most effective in dealing with terrorism in your country?

What changes (if any) will occur in the next decade in how terrorist groups operate? How will ways of providing security against terrorism change?

Are efforts to defeat or contain terrorism a great threat to civil liberties?

FURTHER READING

- **Bjorgo, Tore (ed.) (1995), *Terror from the Extreme Right*, London: Frank Cass**. This compilation provides examples of right wing terrorist groups that are operating in a variety of countries, indicating the extent of such activities.

- **Campbell, Bruce D. and Brenner, Arthur D. (eds.) (2000), *Death Squads in a Global Perspective: Murder with Deniability*, New York: St. Martin's**. This book is a compilation of case studies of the use of death squads in all parts of the world and an excellent introduction for this form of government-supported terrorism.

- **Crenshaw, Martha and Pimlot, John (eds.) (1997), *Encyclopedia of World Terrorism,* Armonk, NY: M.E. Sharpe**. This three-volume work provides brief but comprehensive coverage of terrorist groups around the world and deals with basic types of terrorism and government responses.

- **Hoffman, Bruce (1998), *Inside Terrorism,* New York: Columbia University Press**. This volume is an excellent work outlining some of the classic types of terrorism and movements.

- **Juergensmeyer, Mark (2000), *Terror in the Mind of God: The Global Rise of Religious Violence,* Berkeley: University of California Press**. Juergensmeyer provides a needed global perspective on the rise of religious groups willing to use terrorist violence.

- **Kegley, Charles W. Jr. (ed.) (2003), *The New Global Terrorism: Characteristics, Causes, Controls,* Upper Saddle River, NJ: Prentice Hall**. This collection is undoubtedly the best recent compilation of short works in the field, covering basic issues from a variety of perspectives.

- **Laqueur, Walter (2001), *A History of Terrorism,* Brunswick, NJ: Transaction Publishers**. This book is in part an update of earlier works. It contains a broad overview of terrorism over time and details the difficulties of viewing terrorism from one or a limited number of perspectives.

- **Lutz, James M. and Lutz, Brenda J. (2004), *Global Terrorism,* London: Routledge**. This textbook uses case studies to provide historical and geographical depth to the discussion of terrorism. While it covers both Islamic terrorism and the Middle Eastern events, it clearly avoids concentrating on either one to the exclusion of other groups.

- **Tucker, Jonathan B. (ed.) (2000), *Toxic Terror: Assessing Terrorist Use of Chemical and Biological Weapons,* Cambridge, MA: MIT Press**. This volume documents various attempts to use chemical and biological weapons by terrorist or potential terrorist groups. It indicates that most of the attempted uses have ended in failure, although the efforts of Aum Shinrikyo in Japan are an obvious exception.

- **Wilkinson, Paul (2000), *Terrorism versus Democracy: The Liberal State Response,* London: Frank Cass**. Wilkinson provides an extensive overview of terrorism and terrorist groups and discusses the effects that terrorism has had on Western democracies.

IMPORTANT WEBSITES

- **www.tkb.org/Home.jsp** National Memorial Institute for the Prevention of Terrorism (MIPT). This website contains invaluable statistics on terrorists actions by country or group. The material can also be organized by year. The data begin in 1968, and only include international terrorist incidents from 1968 to 1997. From 1998 onward they include both international and domestic attacks.

- **www.comw.org/rma/fulltest/terrorism.html** Project on Defense Alternatives, Revolution on Military Affairs (RMA)—maintained by Commonwealth Institute, Cambridge, MA. This website provides access to papers and other works dealing with terrorism, including some papers (from conferences or as working papers) that are not readily available elsewhere.

- **www.state.gov/s/ct/rls/pgfrpt** United State Department of State, *Patterns of Terrorism* series on line. This series is a compilation on international terrorist incidents around the world. The series began in 1991. The data are not restricted to attacks involving the United States and against US interests or American citizens abroad. The data from 1991 to 2003 are comprehensive and considered reliable. Questions were raised about the 2004 data, which were then withdrawn for possible correction and later release.

Visit the Online Resource Centre that accompanies this book for lots of interesting additional material: www.oxfordtextbooks.co.uk/orc/collins/

17 The Defence Trade

JOANNA SPEAR AND NEIL COOPER

Chapter Contents

Reader's Guide

This chapter aims to provide the reader with an understanding of key aspects of the contemporary defence trade. It begins by examining the main theoretical approaches that have been developed to explain why states acquire defence equipment. This section includes an analysis of the action-reaction, domestic factor and technological imperative models as well as a brief discussion of the military-industrial complex thesis. The first section concludes by considering the various ways in which the symbolic meaning attached to military technology may influence decisions on both the acquisition and sale of defence equipment.

The chapter then examines trends in both defence expenditure and defence exports. With respect to the former, it highlights, in particular, the way in which the US war on terror has legitimized a return to Cold War levels of defence expenditure and how the vast amounts expended on defence by the US is creating a growing technology gap between it and other producers. With respect to the latter, the chapter draws on the notion of 'tiers' in the defence market to analyse trends in the defence export trade, focusing on the policies of specific states that can be viewed as exemplars of each tier. This section also includes a brief discussion of the role played by non-state actors in the supply of defence material as well as an examination of demand factors in the market. The final section of the chapter outlines the changes in the content of the contemporary defence trade, in particular the shift away from the supply of complete major weapons systems to the provision of upgrades, dual-use technologies, communications equipment, spare parts and training.

The authors would like to extend sincere thanks to Mandy Turner for her research work for this project and to Saket Vemprala for preparing all the tables and charts.

Introduction

This chapter aims to outline both the dynamics underpinning the acquisition of defence technology and the various features of the contemporary export market in defence goods. The first section briefly outlines the main schools of thought that have been developed to explain why states acquire arms. We then go on to outline the key trends in defence expenditure both globally and for key states as well as examining current trends in the defence export market and the way the market itself is changing. We use the term 'defence trade' throughout this chapter when discussing the export market to indicate that the contemporary market involves much more than the supply of arms.

Explaining the arms dynamic

This section will examine the various attempts to conceptualize the factors that drive actors to acquire weapons and defence technology.

Perhaps the first point to note is that academic analyses of the motivations underpinning the acquisition of arms more commonly refer to the **arms dynamic** which can be understood as 'the entire set of pressures that make actors (usually states) both acquire armed forces and change the quantity and quality of the armed forces they already possess' (Buzan and Herring 1998: 790). The arms dynamic can be distinguished in two important ways. First, one can make a distinction between arms dynamics that have different levels of intensity e.g. build-down, maintenance, competition/build-up and arms racing (ibid: 75–81). Second, one can also distinguish between the notion of a **primary arms dynamic**, which describes the set of pressures to acquire armed forces that are experienced by major arms producers and a **secondary arms dynamic**, which describes the set of pressures experienced by part-producers or non-producers who are far more reliant on defence imports and who may therefore be open to a different mix of pressures.

There have been various attempts to theorize the processes that drive the arms dynamic but they are commonly differentiated according to whether they emphasize either **action-reaction factors**, **domestic factors** or what is termed **the technological imperative**. We also discuss the symbolic meaning attached to weapons as a factor influencing the acquisition of defence equipment. These are not necessarily mutually exclusive models, however. Indeed, most commentators on the arms dynamic would probably take the view that for most, if not all societies with significant military forces, some combination of these models is likely to be in operation. Rather, the key question concerns the extent to which one or the other factor predominates.

Action-reaction

The action-reaction model assumes that actors increase either the quantity or quality of their military forces in response to increases on the part of potential adversaries. The pressure for states to act in this way is rooted in the conditions of the **security dilemma**, under which any attempt by states to provide for their own defence are, regardless of intent, viewed by others as potentially threatening (Herz 1950; Snyder 1984; Wheeler and Booth

1992). Not least, because a self-help international system creates pressures for states to make worst-case analyses of the actions of others.

The action-reaction model is at the heart of the notion that particularly intense rivalries can give rise to arms races. However, there remain significant debates both about exactly what characteristics distinguish arms races from the regular operation of the arms dynamic (Hammond 1993), whether arms races make conflict more likely or less, and indeed, over whether the concept has any explanatory value at all (Gray 1986). Similarly, critics point to a number of key problems in the action-reaction model. These include questions over the timing of reaction and whether the concept needs to (and can) incorporate anticipatory reactions based on assumptions about what potential enemies might do in the future. These issues are particularly salient given the long lead times involved in the development of major weapons systems, which means that by the time a weapon actually rolls off the production line the threat it was originally designed to respond to may well have changed or disappeared altogether—the example of the Typhoon noted in Case Study 17.1 being a case in point. Other issues concern the scale of the activity required before one can identify a reaction, the form in which a reaction occurs (quantitative, qualitative, like for like, like for unlike) and the extent to which broader factors such as strategic culture and economic constraints limiting the ability of governments to react need to be taken into account, or whether doing so essentially undermines the model itself.

Moreover, specific studies of the weapons acquisition process tend to highlight the fact that strategic necessity may often be of marginal significance in the decision to procure specific weapons. For instance, Farrell has contrasted the concern over micro-wastage in US weapons procurement (e.g. political controversies over the excessive cost of basic equipment such as hammers or toilet seats) with the macro-wastage that arises from spending on billion dollar weapons systems that are not actually needed (Farrell 1997).

Domestic factor explanations

In these explanations emphasis is placed on the idea of a domestic arms dynamic that, to varying degrees, is self-generating and not strongly linked to the external actions of other states. Domestic factor explanations can be broadly sub-divided into four types: bureaucratic/organizational explanations, political explanations, economic explanations and Military-Industrial Complex perspectives. Bureaucratic or organizational explanations emphasize the idea that defence procurement decisions can be understood either as the outcome of bureaucratic politics—bargaining between different sets of policy actors—or as a reflection of particular organizational cultures such as the traditions and military doctrines of the armed services (Allison 1971; Farrell 1996, 1997).

Political explanations focus on the role that domestic political considerations may play in both defence budgeting and weapons acquisition. These can include a concern with the way public opinion influences defence spending (Hartley and Russet 1992) or alternatively with the way in which politicians may use increases in defence spending to garner political support (Nincic 1982: 32–3; Mayer 1991: 203–7). A common feature of political explanations focused on the US emphasizes the way in which electoral funding from defence contractors has the potential to shape the attitudes of legislators towards budgeting and procurement decisions and/or the way electoral considerations lead members of Congress to promote weapons and defence contracts that will benefit their constituents irrespective of their merit (Stiles 1995: 74–6). This latter phenomenon is known as 'pork barrel' politics, although there is evidence to suggest the phenomenon may be more apparent than real (Mayer 1991; Lindsay 1991).

Economic explanations can take a number of forms. First, some analyses emphasize the way in which increases in defence spending are sometimes used by governments to provide a boost to the economy in times of economic downturn or to protect jobs in particular regions or industrial sectors (Cooper 1997: 9–12). Second, it is argued that the need to maintain a viable defence industrial base can create a 'follow-on imperative' under which governments place orders simply to keep companies and skilled workers in being rather than as a function of any immediate military necessity. At its worst, according to Kaldor (1982), the follow-on imperative can combine with the innate conservatism of the military to produce successive incremental changes to existing major defence systems that result in 'baroque weapons'. Such weapons are hugely expensive, overly sophisticated to the point that their effectiveness in combat is debatable, frequently break down and are ill-suited to the real military needs of the armed forces. Third, Marxist analyses have argued that military expenditure and war production is intimately linked to the needs and nature of capitalism, either because it is necessary for the maintenance of capitalism as an economic system, because it produces specifically capitalist forms of weaponry, or because it is linked to capitalist imperialism (Baran and Sweezy 1966; Shaw 1984; Stavrianakis 2005).

Elements of the various domestic factor explanations: bureaucratic, political, economic, have often been combined in approaches that explain arms acquisition as a function of the Military Industrial Complex. Although the term was coined by President Eisenhower in his 1961 farewell speech, some of the key ideas underpinning the term had already been elaborated by C. Wright Mills in his book *The Power Elite*. For Mills there was a coincidence of interest that existed between economic, political and military actors which had led to the creation of a permanent war economy in the US and 'a nation whose elite and whose underlying population have accepted what can only be called a military definition of reality' (1956: 198). The notion of a military industrial complex or iron triangle (Adams 1982) was particularly popular in accounts of US arms policy in the 1960s, 1970s and early 1980s. However, whilst there is a significant body of work that utilizes the term with respect to both the US (Melman 1970; Lens 1970; Stiles 1995) and other states (Andersson 1992; Conca 1997) there is little consensus on what groups form part of the complex, how powerful it is in relation to other groups in society and how much cohesion it really has.

Nevertheless the concept has experienced something of a resurgence of late. For example, James Der Derian (2001) has produced a variant of it in his concept of a military-industrial-media-entertainment network whilst others have attempted to re-work it to take account of new mechanisms by which defence industrial interests are promoted. In the UK, for instance, Mayhew has highlighted the disproportionate influence of the defence industry on the numerous, and often unaccountable, task forces, policy review and advisory groups established by the Blair government to advise on aspects of defence policy (Mayhew 2005). Similarly, the influence of the defence industry in policy task forces established by the European Commission has been taken as evidence of an emerging EU Military-Industrial Complex (Slijper 2005). It is also worth noting that a series of transnational mergers and other linkages amongst defence companies has led to debates about the globalization of the defence industry (Bitzinger 2003). For some, this may presage an era of global private arsenals—relatively few defence-industrial giants possessing near monopoly control over 'world weapons' sourced from a variety of countries (Markusen 1999).

Technological imperative (TI) explanations

TI explanations can take a number of forms. One approach places particular emphasis on the way the predominance of military research and development activity—both at the domestic and the global level—creates an autonomous push for the continued development of weapons technology that is distinct from broader action-reaction and domestic factor processes (Thee 1986). This also raises questions about the extent to which military research distorts the direction of the civilian economy (Buzan and Sen 1990). Other studies, however, are more sceptical about the extent to which technology or the influence of technologists is an independent force in the arms dynamic highlighting the way social forces, military culture, the direction of resources and strategic goals have a significant influence in determining what technologies are taken up and in what ways (Mackenzie 1990).

A second and more contemporary way of understanding the idea of a technological imperative is to view military modernization as a process that is both fuelled and shaped by an underlying process of permanent technological change in the civil sector. This has become a particularly popular conception given the way in which civil advances in electronics, computing and IT are feeding into contemporary military technology producing what some see as a revolution in military affairs (RMA) (see below). Whereas during the Cold War it was common to talk of 'spin offs' from military technology to the civil sector, it is now more usual to see 'spin ons' from civil technologies to the military sector.

It is also argued that the spread of specific Western military technologies (e.g. the weapons system) underpinned by military aid, commercial sales and military training programmes provided to allies has produced a global military culture which has established the possession of capital-intensive high-tech weapons supported by professional armies as the norm. Not only does this underpin broader relations of dependency between developed world suppliers and developing world recipients but it results in the acquisition of weapons that are inordinately expensive and which may actually be unsuitable for recipients (Wendt and Barnett 1993).

To the extent that states then attempt to establish the domestic production of defence goods in this context, it is also possible to describe a global military order or hierarchy of states (Krause 1992; Held et al 1999: 87–148) of the sort that we outline below, where different states have attained different levels of production capability but where all are geared around essentially the same models (if not sophistication) of technology.

A related aspect of this debate is the idea that the current model of defence technology based around high-tech weapons systems and perpetual advances in capability produces inexorable real terms rises in weapons costs. For some this is producing a form of **military Malthusianism**—in which there is a growing mismatch between the cost of weapons and the ability of national defence budgets to afford them. In this view, states are thus likely to be faced with either purchasing fewer weapons, cheaper versions of existing models or opting out of the current global military culture (Scheetz 2004).

The symbolic meaning of weapons

The notion of a global military culture also highlights the way in which motivations for the acquisition of defence technology may have less to do with objective threats and the military application of technology and more to do with the meanings attached to such technology. Indeed, given the limits on most national defence budgets and the high cost of modern weaponry it can be argued that, for most states in the international system, the conventional idea that arms, and even armed forces, are acquired to enable actors to fight independent wars is far from the reality. Thus, weapons and armed forces may more often be acquired for reasons of national prestige, as symbols of statehood, as both agents and symbols of modernization, as vehicles to cement alliances, or simply to act as trip-wires that signal a state of emergency to which others may be expected to respond.

Postmodernists take such ideas even further, arguing that the practice of foreign policy is not about responding to objective threats but about manufacturing an 'other' against which an imagined political identity can be forged. In this context, the acquisition of armies and arms are both an outcome of this manufacturing of the other and part of a series of performative acts by which borders, identities and difference are inscribed (Campbell 1998a).

Similarly, the decision to provide or prohibit the supply of weapons may be a function of the specific meaning attached to them. Thus, from this perspective what is interesting about the ban on the production and trade in landmines is not so much the arguments about how odious they may or may not be as weapons but how, within a few short years, a particular meaning came to be attached to them as odious weapons where no such meaning had previously existed. Similarly, Mutimer has highlighted how the language used to describe the transfer of conventional weapons ('defence trade', 'arms trade' etc.) invokes a commercial metaphor that is implicitly legitimizing even when it is deployed by critics decrying the activities of the 'merchants of death' (Mutimer 2000).

KEY POINTS

- The notion of an 'arms dynamic' refers to the set of pressures that make actors acquire armed forces and adjust their quantity and quality.
- Action-reaction explanations of the arms dynamic explain arms acquisition as a response to the external actions of potential adversaries.
- Domestic factor explanations emphasize the idea that the arms dynamic is primarily self-generating and is a function of bureaucratic, economic or domestic political factors.
- Technological imperative explanations understand the arms dynamic either as a function of the disproportionate influence of military R&D (Research and Development) or as fuelled by perpetual modernization in the civil sector.
- Symbolic explanations suggest that both the acquisition and prohibition of defence technology may be more a function of the meanings invested in weapons rather than strategic necessity or any inherent qualities they may have.

Trends in defence expenditure

In the next section of the chapter we first highlight key differences between the high-technology defence trade and that in low-technology equipment. We then outline the trends in defence expenditure, highlighting some of the major players and other states who illustrate key trends.

Within the defence market there is a clear distinction between the high-technology defence trade and the low-technology defence trade. The distinction is in terms of the suppliers, the recipients, the money involved, the attention paid to the deals and the degree to which the trade is seen as political.

Somewhat counter-intuitively the high-tech defence trade is increasingly depoliticized and seen primarily in terms of economics, whereas the supply of second-hand and low-tech weapons is often highly politicized as these are the weapons that are being used in conflicts. This disparity is highlighted by the two examples of defence sales outlined in Case Studies 17.1 and 17.2.

One thing that both of the deals show, however, is that there is over-supply in the defence trade and this means that at the low-tech end weapons are cheap and plentiful and at the high-tech end, competition to make sales is intense. This leads analysts to characterize the market as a buyer's market.

Defence expenditure includes not only weapons and equipment but wages, training, pensions, etc. Defence expenditure on equipment can either be through **domestic procurement** (i.e. buying from a defence firm in your state) or international purchase.

The high-point in global defence expenditures came in the mid-1980s during the Cold War, when significant percentages of gross domestic product (GDP) were channelled into defence spending.

CASE STUDY 17.1

A high-technology sale

Some of the key aspects of the high-tech defence trade can be illustrated by examining one big defence sale: the December 2005 announcement by BAE Systems and the British Government of a deal to supply Saudi Arabia with the Eurofighter *Typhoon*. From this we can see that:

- Defence sales are now primarily discussed in terms of economic and employment issues. There has been no discussion of the impact of the sale on the military balance in the region, nor of the threat that these aircraft will guard against. This may be because the *Typhoon* is seen by some critics as unsuited to Saudi Arabia's defence needs.
- So keen were the British to secure the deal that they have pledged that the first 24 aircraft will be drawn from the British Royal Air Force's production run of 89 Tranche 2 fighters. Thus, the Royal Saudi Air Force will get some of the fighters before the British do (Hoyle 2005).
- The deal has been valued at anything between £8 and £20 billion, depending on how many aircraft and what equipment the Saudis acquire (Hope 2005). It has also been touted as securing 14,000 British jobs for the next ten years and will secure defence industry jobs throughout Europe.
- Upon news of the deal BAE Systems shares increased 6% in value (Smith 2005).
- Rather than paying for the aircraft in cash, following past precedents, the Saudi government is expected to pay in a mix of cash and oil.
- In order to secure the deal both Prime Minister Blair and Defence Minister Reid visited Saudi Arabia and agreed a crucial memorandum of understanding promising to 'establish a greater partnership in modernising the Saudi Arabian Armed Forces and developing close service-to-service contacts especially through joint training and exercises' (cited in *Guardian* 2005). Thus the British government's commitment was crucial to making the deal.
- Although this has been touted as a British deal, in actual fact the *Typhoon* is made by a consortium of BAE Systems, the European aerospace group EADS and Italian Alenia Aerospazio.
- BAE Systems will also be involved in a number of **offset** deals, whereby the cost of the purchase is offset by investment in the Saudi economy. Saudi Arabia routinely asks for 30% offsets into commercially viable businesses on all defence sales. This deal includes defence technology transfers and establishing defence facilities in the country (Hoyle 2005). Past offset deals between BAE Systems' predecessor British Aerospace and the Saudi Arabian government included education and training, joint ventures such as that to establish the pharmaceutical firm Glaxo Saudi Arabia (*Gulf Industry Magazine* 2004), and one to produce polymers for the paint and adhesives market, establishing a sugar refinery, a propylene manufacturing plant, an aluminium smelter, and a project to convert petroleum gas into benzene and xylene (British Offset). All of these initiatives are designed to diversify the Saudi economy but the track record is of significant underperformance.

Things have changed somewhat over time as Table 17.1 below shows. The main trends that can be discerned here are as follows.

The United States is back at the peak military expenditure levels of the Cold War as it prosecutes the Global War on Terror (GWOT) and faces regional challenges. It is predicted that in 2006 US military spending will surpass that of the rest of the world combined (Anderson 2005). US involvement in Afghanistan and Iraq is increasingly costly and has led to defence cuts in other areas (for example, the National Defense University in Washington DC has experienced an across-the-board cut of 20%) and a diversion of funds to the

CASE STUDY 17.2

A low-technology sale

In 1994 war was raging in the former Yugoslavia and the position of the Muslim-led government of Bosnia-Herzegovina looked particularly dire. The United Nations had imposed an arms embargo on the region in the hope of stopping the fighting but it had the counter-productive effect of giving an advantage to Serb forces that had access to the defence industries of the former Yugoslavia.

There was some pressure from the US Congress to lift the embargo, but British Foreign Secretary Douglas Hurd said he did not want to 'level the killing field' (Sims 2001) and the US government was concerned about the precedent that unilaterally breaching the embargo would have on their attempts to keep United Nations' sanctions on Iraq. President Clinton therefore publicly declined to act.

However, the Croatian government (which had recently made peace with Bosnia) secretly approached the Clinton Administration and asked if the US would object if it created an arms pipeline to Bosnia (*Newshour* 1996). The Clinton Administration replied that they neither approved nor objected to what they were doing; tacitly giving Croatia the go-ahead.

- The weapons came from Iran—via Turkey and Croatia—to Bosnia and involved cooperation from sub-state Islamist groups such as the Afghan Mojahedin and pro-Iran Hizbullah (Wiebes 2003).
- The weapons were small arms, anti-tank weapons, surface-to-surface missiles, and mortars. Many tons of the weapons were transferred at relatively low cost, as the weapons were cheap and particularly plentiful since the end of the Cold War had resulted in many states putting their arsenals on the market.
- Part of the reason for the large shipments was that Croatia imposed a high 'transit tax' on all the weapons, creaming off between 20 and 50% of every shipment (Aldrich 2002).
- The deal was financed by Saudi Arabia.
- The weapons deals were seen as providing a political entrée into Bosnia for Iran. Subsequently the Clinton Administration was heavily criticized by its Republican opponents for tacitly approving the deal as it allowed Islamists to establish a foothold in Bosnia where they trained and fought beside the Bosnian Muslims (Cox 1996).
- Whilst the US was involved in arming the Bosnians, Ukraine, Greece and Israel were arming the Bosnian Serbs.

This then was a highly political arms transfer, with minimal economic significance, but which was justified on the grounds that it helped ensure the survival of the Bosnian Government and led the way to the Dayton Peace Accord of 1995.

two conflicts. The Congressional Research Service has calculated that for Fiscal Years 2001 to 2006 Defense Department funding for Iraq and Afghanistan amounts to at least $318.6 billion (Belasco 2005: 2). There is also an expectation that the President will ask Congress for extra money for the two conflicts in 2006.

The USSR/Russia has seen a significant decline in defence expenditure. With the end of the Cold War and domestic economic and social needs more pressing, defence expenditures were dramatically decreased, at great cost to the traditionally cosseted defence industrial complex. There were unsuccessful attempts at defence 'conversion' (Zisk 1997). Subsequently Russia has been trying to raise more money to spend on national defence by selling more weapons abroad. They have run into stiff competition from former Soviet States such as Ukraine and Belarus, who retained sections of the USSR's military industrial complex and have sold the weapons they produce at rock-bottom prices.

China's military expenditures might be understated in Table 17.1 for a number of reasons. The first is the current under-valuation of the Chinese

Table 17.1 Military expenditures for selected countries 1984–2004

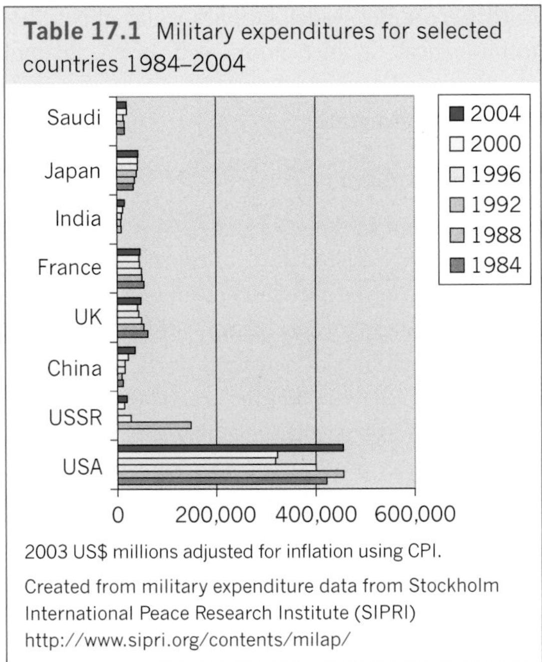

2003 US$ millions adjusted for inflation using CPI.

Created from military expenditure data from Stockholm International Peace Research Institute (SIPRI) http://www.sipri.org/contents/milap/

currency, the renminbi. Second is that the cost of living is cheap in China (though rising) so pensions, wages, etc. are relatively low. Third is that the People's Liberation Army is a major entrepreneur within the economy and earns money that goes into defence spending as well as being engaged in arms production that is not covered in national defence expenditure statistics. Despite the clear disparity between Chinese and US defence spending levels, the US Department of Defense has recently raised the alarm over China's military progress. Defense Secretary Rumsfeld declared that China now has the world's third-largest military budget, behind the United States and Russia (CNN 2005).

Britain and France still invest major resources in their militaries. Despite significant pressure to shift spending into social programmes, both regard themselves as significant military players and have sought efficiency savings and economies of scale through joint purchases rather than contemplating large cuts in defence spending. British defence spending has been rising due to operations such as Sierra Leone, Afghanistan (where it assumed control of the ISAF (International Security Assistance Force) in 2006) and Iraq. There is increasing discussion of British military 'overstretch', primarily in terms of personnel.

A panel reported to the French Defence Minister in 2005 that all European Union spending on military hardware is equal to a third of the US's equipment budget, while research and development spending across the whole EU is around one fifth of US expenditure, suggesting an ever-widening technology gap between the US and Europe with implications for alliance operations and the future of European defence sales (Anderson 2005a).

Japan has surprisingly significant and steady levels of defence spending, despite a constitution that limits her military forces to a self-defence role. Japan's military spending did not diminish with the end of the Cold War in large part because her major concern is China, whose spending has been creeping up.

India's military expenditure has risen since the end of the Cold War when she lost the support of her traditional ally USSR/Russia (including subsidized defence sales) and had to prepare to protect herself alone. India perceives major (conventional and nuclear) threats from China and Pakistan and is fighting an insurgency against Pakistani-supported militants in Kashmir.

Saudi Arabia is an apparent conundrum as it has relatively high levels of military expenditure but to date does not have a well-regarded defence capability. The answer to this riddle is that Saudi Arabia uses its military expenditure to buy allies and mutual defence agreements; it needs a less able force of its own if it knows that the US, France and Britain (its major defence suppliers) will come to its aid if it is threatened.

A number of the countries we have considered here are also significant arms producers and exporters. Every unit that they sell abroad gives them a lower unit price on military equipment that they buy from their defence industries. This makes competition for all sales significant and for big defence contracts very intense. Indeed, the variety of subsidies, offset and financing deals now offered by exporters to secure deals has led critics to suggest that, despite the huge sums involved, the economic benefits of defence sales to the economies of major exporters may actually be negligible or even non-existent (Ingram and Davis 2001; Hartung 1998).

Suppliers and recipients in the defence market

In order to categorize suppliers we use the notion of 'tiers' in the defence trade taken from the work of Keith Krause (Krause 1992). The first tier is composed of suppliers who are at the highest levels of technological sophistication across the entire range of defence production. At the second tier of the trade, suppliers have some research and development capabilities and exhibit some areas of technological sophistication, but the majority of their defence products are below the cutting edge. At the third tier of the trade, supplier states show little technological sophistication and often do not progress much beyond slightly modifying products made under licence.

Figure 17.1 Major exporters 2001

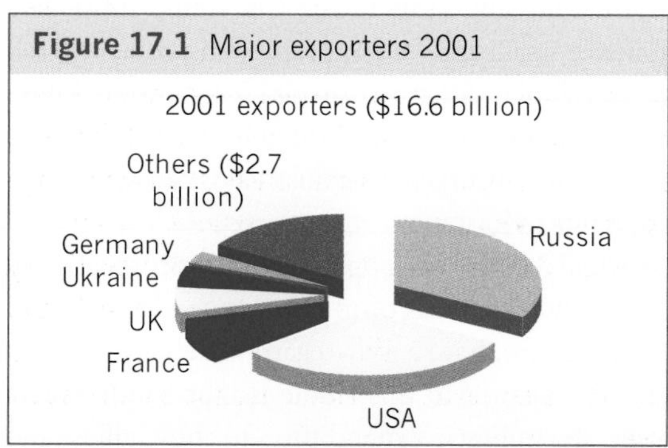

First-tier suppliers

(A) The United States

Since the early 1990s, the United States has stood unchallenged as the pre-eminent supplier. According to trend-indicator data from SIPRI shown in Table 17.2 the US made deliveries worth $12.8 billion in 1989 (all currency figures are 1990 dollars). In 1997 Ethan Kapstein concluded that '. . . the market is now America's to lose . . .' (Kapstein 1997: 77). Although delivery levels rose in the years 1991–1999 (Table 17.3), there has been a significant drop in weapons exports (globally and for the US) since 2000.

One factor in US primacy is that the battlefield performance of US weaponry in conflicts in the Persian Gulf in 1991 and 2003 and Afghanistan in 2001–02 increased the desire of many states to obtain US high-technology weaponry—in particular because US weapons performed so much better than the Russian equipment used by their opponents.

It has been pointed out (bitterly, by other would-be suppliers) that there is no 'level playing field' for defence industries, as the geo-strategic position and interests of the US significantly advantages

Table 17.2 Selected weapons exporters 1989

Country	Exports $ value
USSR	13,902
USA	12,832
France	3,259
UK	1,932
F R Germany	930
Israel	272

(All figures in 1990 $ millions)

Table 17.3 Selected weapons exporters 2001

Country	Export $ value
Russia	5,516
USA	5,079
France	1,111
UK	1,081
Germany	529
Israel	226

(All figures in 1990 $ millions)

American firms. This is illustrated by a joke, which was told to us by a representative of a European defence firm:

> “A Middle Eastern country is interested in acquiring fighter aircraft and is considering various bids from defence firms. The head of state gets a call from the US President who says that he is very keen that a US firm secures the contract as their fighter is obviously the best in the world, but that if the state failed to buy American, he would be forced to pull the US Sixth Fleet out of the Gulf region, with negative security consequences for this Middle East state. The following day the head of the Middle Eastern state gets a telephone call from the President of France who is anxious to ensure that the French fighter wins the competition. He tells the head of state that the French plane is obviously the best on the market, but that if the state failed to buy it, he would be forced to withdraw the French soccer team from the region . . . ”
>
> **(Transparency International 2001)**

Although a joke, this is quite telling as to the balance of power between the US and other suppliers. Nevertheless, representatives of American defence firms have made it clear that *they* feel disadvantaged in the defence market by the close ties that some European states have with their ex-colonies.

Although Table 17.3 suggests Russia is managing to maintain parity with the US in the defence export market, the reality is really one of US primacy. All other supplier states are essentially engaged in a Darwinian struggle to maintain their shares of the contracted defence market. Rather than trying to move up to the next technology tier, suppliers are fighting to avoid sinking into the tiers below.

(B) Russia

In the immediate aftermath of the Cold War, Russian defence deliveries dropped precipitously, from $12.2 billion in 1989 to $763 million in 1994. Although recovering, Russian defence transfers remain nowhere near Cold War levels. The more recent improvement in trade levels is due to a combination of bargain prices and a willingness to transfer technologies and even production facilities. Russia has also shown increasing creativity in the ways that it finances deals; e.g., using defence transfers to pay off the massive debts of the Soviet regime.

John Dowdy has noted that Russian technologies lag behind those of the West as a consequence of the old business practices retained from the Soviet era (Dowdy 1997: 93). Russia is currently trading on its heritage as a superpower first-tier supplier and is not making the necessary investments in research and development. Whether it will be able to maintain a foothold in the first-tier for much longer is, therefore, in severe doubt.

Second-tier suppliers

(A) West European states

West European supplier states have traditionally occupied the second tier of the trade, exhibiting some areas of technological primacy, but not across the board (Krause 1992: 127–52). As second-tier suppliers, they have increasingly seen their positions in the market threatened both by the US—which has been sweeping into new areas of the market (such as Eastern Europe) with high-technology weaponry—and by third-tier suppliers willing to provide plentiful amounts of more basic weaponry at bargain prices. This trend is clear from the data in Tables 17.2 and 17.3 showing French, German and British defence deliveries in decline in the years 1989–2001.

Although losing ground to the US in high-technology sales, one of the ways in which European suppliers have shored up defence sales levels has been through clever financing and **offset** deals. The European share of the defence trade has been shored up to an extent because some recipient states fear over-dependence on the US, and have therefore continued to make purchases from these second-tier suppliers, for example, the United Arab Emirates (UAE).

One of the strategies increasingly being exploited by European supplier states is to work on creating market ‘niches’, in such areas as air-to-surface missiles, frigates and corvettes.

Third-tier suppliers

Third-tier suppliers are those with limited innovative capacity. They primarily copy and reproduce existing technologies, and often aim to develop their own defence industries, intending to enhance their status as regional military powers, with a secondary interest in becoming suppliers (often for economic reasons). Most of the states in the third tier have been unable to move beyond fairly basic weapons production (Krause: 158–81). They have been badly affected by the post-Gulf War 'flight to quality', that is, to Western technologies.

(A) Israel

From its inception the Israeli state has sought to build up a defence industrial base (DIB). By the 1980s Israel had earned a reputation as a serious competitor in the international defence market (Kleinman 1985: ix). Over the last decade of fiscal austerity, Israel has moved towards using its comparative advantage in key areas to become a 'niche supplier', specializing in upgrading aircraft, systems integration and UAV (Unmanned Aerial Vehicle) technology. It is a major player in the latter sector and has been at the forefront of their development, although this is an increasingly competitive sector of the market.

Israel has benefited from the end of the Cold War and the US-sponsored peace process, both of which opened up new markets for her (Bruce 1994; Reuters 1999). Nonetheless, the 1989–2001 period witnessed fluctuating weapons sales, and Israel's weapons export earnings have not significantly improved, as the data in Tables 17.2 and 17.3 indicate.

(B) South Korea

Seoul has ambitions to a 'full service' defence industry, fed by 'spin-ons' (as opposed to 'spin-offs') from civilian industries (Seok-jae 1995). Overall, the aim is to reduce South Korean military industrial dependence on allies. With American help, South Korea's defence industrial base seemed to be flourishing by the early 1990s. However, although it has proved adept at assembling platform technologies and producing goods under licence, it has not been successful in the sphere of development.

The Asian economic crisis of the late 1990s had a profound effect on defence production in South Korea, with the privately owned *chaebols* experiencing severe economic problems that made them unable to continue to subsidize (thus far uneconomic) indigenous defence production.

Given the primacy of developing a DIB over being a defence trade exporter in South Korean planning, Seoul's supplier role in the defence market is unlikely to significantly expand as its energies will be increasingly directed inwards.

(C) China

Although only a third-tier player in terms of technological advancement, China is nevertheless the only remaining developing world 'full-service' supplier, offering major land, sea and air systems to recipients (Bitzinger 1992: 84). According to Arthur Ding, China has a couple of 'pockets of excellence' in indigenous production, particularly surface-to-surface missiles and sea-based anti-warship cruise missiles (Ding 2000: 62).

China has technologies that are desired by those states at even lower levels of technological sophistication. For example, Pakistan and China have organized a joint venture to produce the *Al-Khalid* tank, with Pakistan expected to produce up to 50% of the main battle tank in the initial stages (Farooq 1999: 15). This is illustrative of the ways in which a third-tier supplier can institute relationships that may affect balances of power in a conflict zone.

(D) Eastern Europe

The position of many of the East European supplier states is precarious, as many of them manufacture out-of-date Soviet-derived technologies. This brings them into competition with the states of the FSU (including Russia) and other licensed producers such as India and China. Competition is stiff and the East European states have been losing ground.

Despite having benefited from offset agreements, questions remain whether these states will be able to maintain a position in the competitive defence market of the twenty-first century. The manipulation of direct offsets to help modernize

Table 17.4 South American weapons exporters

Country	1989	2002
Brazil	218	31
Chile	—	2

(All figures in 1990 $ millions)

their defence industries will keep them in the market for longer, although possibly more as components manufacturers than suppliers of finished weapons systems.

(E) Latin America

As Table 17.4 shows, third-tier suppliers such as Chile and Brazil are struggling to maintain their market shares. Some firms in the third tier are seeking creative ways to re-orient their defence industries. For example, Brazil's Embraer nearly went bankrupt in 1994 when the firm was under the control of the Brazilian Air Force. However, since its privatization in 1994 and its reorientation towards the civilian market, it has recovered to become the fourth-largest civil aircraft manufacturer and Brazil's largest exporter (Barham and Owen 1999).

Chile's defence industry has always pursued a market orientation, with the industry built around private firms associated with branches of the armed forces. One of the methods employed by Chile has been to align with other third-tier suppliers. In the 1990s it formed defence industrial partnerships with China, Malaysia, Paraguay, South Korea, Brazil and improved its relationship with Russia.

All third-tier suppliers in the twenty-first century market are clearly fighting for survival. Most third-tier suppliers are receiving technical assistance via offset agreements and technology transfers from second-tier suppliers eager to maintain their role in the market, even at the cost of their long-term positions. For their part, several third-tier suppliers have begun trading with states that have less advanced DIBs. However, this strategy is unlikely to work for much longer and one can predict further market exits from the third tier.

Market entrants

Despite the obvious competition, a number of states are trying to enter the defence market at present. Motives for this vary, but can include a sense of threat driving the development of an indigenous defence industrial base, the desire to profit from the one functioning manufacturing sector bequeathed to them, or a desire to assert sovereignty and gain prestige through defence independence (Pengelly 1997: 19–21; McCarthy 2000: 16). We consider two suppliers who had an established DIB from the Cold War period, and after an initial downturn are now beginning to have an impact on the market: Ukraine and Croatia.

(A) Ukraine

States such as Ukraine, Belarus and Kazakhstan are attempting to capitalize on the ex-Soviet defence industries within their territories (Vasilevitch and Belosludtsev 2001: 8–20). This means that they are directly competing with Russia, and undercutting Moscow by offering newly manufactured Soviet-era weaponry at bargain prices (*Arms Trade News* 1997: 3). Areas of the market where Ukraine has potential advantage are ballistic missile technologies, space technologies and launch services.

(B) Croatia

Croatia is attempting to carve out for itself a number of niches in the international defence trade, specifically on two fronts:

> “One consists of highly specialized, 'exotic' weapons, such as those usually associated with the special forces, while the other revolves around 'hybrid' weapons systems. These systems combine different technologies, along the East-West axis, which have been indigenously assimilated, modified, applied and eventually upgraded”
>
> **(Simunovic 1998: 140–1)**

The experience of war allows the Croatians to market their weaponry as 'battle tested', seen as a distinct advantage in an overcrowded market. To date, Croatia's impact on the defence trade has been limited, with only one significant delivery year, 2000. Nevertheless, its marketing efforts are having a psychological impact, which Croatia hopes will be turned into future sales.

Another class of emerging players should also be briefly considered: non-state suppliers. The end of the Cold War and the subsequent release of vast amounts of second-hand, relatively low-technology weapons into the market place has provided much greater opportunities for brokers and middle-men than existed before. Moreover, increasingly independent defence firms and enterprises (particularly those struggling to survive) are sometimes willing to deal not only with state recipients, but with brokers. They are actors that cannot be ignored in any serious analysis of the operation of the defence trade in the twenty-first century (Wood and Peleman 1999). Markusen has drawn attention to the potential change in the balance of power in state–firm relations:

> ". . . the dramatic decline in the number of major weapons manufacturers and their increasing international orientation will shift the balance of power in the arms market away from governments and towards business"
>
> **(Markusen 1999: 47)**

The black arms trade, controlled mainly by crime syndicates and arms dealers, is composed of sales that are clearly illegal, either because of the type of transfer involved, the source of supply or the recipient, or because the transaction breaks an international embargo (Guy 1989). The imposition of an arms embargo is a sales opportunity for an entrepreneurial supplier state or broker. Karp argues that black markets primarily serve crime syndicates and drugs cartels because insurgent groups cannot afford black market prices. Hence, the market is best suited to providing select high-value items (Karp 1994: 175–89).

Figure 17.2 Major recipients 2001

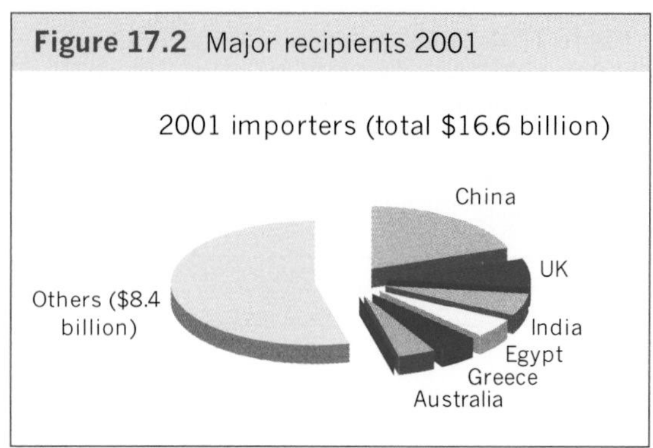

To briefly consider recipients, there have been important structural changes that are affecting the demand for major weapons, with old Cold War protagonists for the most part significantly scaling back high-technology procurement (exceptions being areas of lingering tension such as the Korean Peninsula). The reality is that there are fewer major recipients in the market than there are suppliers. In this buyer's market recipients are able to play suppliers off against each other to extract the best possible deals.

The most important regional defence markets are East Asia and the Middle East. The rise in importance of non-state recipients should also be considered. Sales opportunities previously thought too risky because of the legal and ethical difficulties involved are now being considered and even actively pursued by some suppliers. Moreover, the use of middle-men and brokers has allowed some states to benefit from making transfers to non-state actors such as terrorist groups, without having to pay any direct political price.

KEY POINTS

- There is a distinction between the high-technology defence trade and the low-technology defence trade with the former increasingly depoliticized and the latter often highly politicized.
- The US has returned to the military expenditure levels of the Cold War with defence expenditure in 2006 predicted to exceed that of the rest of the world combined.
- A useful way of categorizing producers in the defence trade is by reference to their position in the various 'tiers' of the market. The first tier consists of suppliers who produce an extensive range of defence equipment to a high level of technological sophistication. The second tier consists of suppliers that retain significant capacity for independent production and possess some areas of technological sophistication. The third tier of suppliers are those that generally possess more limited capacity for independent production, whose products exhibit little technological sophistication and who may specialize in the provision of goods or services for particular niches of the defence market.
- The end of the Cold War and the release of large amounts of second-hand weaponry has provided a market opportunity for a variety of non-state actors to act as suppliers, particularly to customers in the black market.

The content of the contemporary defence trade

The twenty-first century is witnessing changes in the substance of the defence trade with moves away from the supply of complete major weapons platforms (aircraft, ships, etc.). For example, in 1998 the premier defence supplier, the US, transferred 180 aircraft around the world. By 2004 the number was down to 51. The trade is moving towards the purchase of upgrades, dual-use technologies, communications equipment and spare parts. Indeed, a lot of what counts as the high-tech defence trade does not look anything like a weapon—hence our abandonment of the term 'arms trade'. Amongst the key trends in the trade are the following.

Modernization of platforms and upgrades: in an era of constrained procurement budgets, the emphasis is on various forms of **force multipliers** to be incorporated into existing platforms (e.g. new engines, weapons pods), as opposed to new purchases. Indigenous modernization is also occurring, as recipient states apply their ingenuity to improving weapons they bought. Upgrades offer the opportunity to hybridize weapons systems: marrying western technologies to eastern platforms—or vice versa. For example, Israeli and Russian cooperation to upgrade MiG fighters offers the opportunity to install advanced Western avionics (some of which were developed for the Lavi fighter) into the solid platforms of the Soviet era (Sher 1995: 40).

Retro-fitting: the increasing trade in upgrades involves the retro-fitting of sophisticated new technologies to existing systems. The move to modular weapons systems mean that retro-fitting and upgrading are increasingly practised and can extend the life of a basic platform significantly. In terms of threat assessment it means that you can no longer look at a particular weapons platform and know what its capabilities are.

Re-transfers: there is an increasing trade in re-transfers (second-hand sales). Weapons and weapons platforms that are surplus to requirements are sold on rather than stored or scrapped (Tusa 1994, *Flight International* 1994). They are a challenge to new sales as they tend to be cut-price and are often fairly sophisticated technologies.

Dual use technologies: a major trend in the international market is towards the supply of technologies, whose spread is more difficult to control. Part of this greater trade is accounted for in **dual use technologies**; those with both legitimate civil and military applications. For example, computers and software which can coordinate air traffic control can also coordinate battlefield operations or missile attacks. There is increased pressure within states to loosen the controls over dual-use exports—on the grounds that in the aftermath of the Cold War, the security risks attached to such sales are much lower.

The trade in dual-use goods brings into the market a whole stratum of new firms and (possibly) states. In addition to the deliberate marketing of goods as militarily useful, there is an increasing range of goods not marketed with military intent, but having latent military applicability. One of the more extreme examples of latent military applicability was the Sony PlayStation2. According to Japanese trade officials these video game consoles contain a graphics processing facility fast enough to help guide some types of missile towards their target (McCurry 2000).

Systems Integration: with the hybridization of weapons systems comes the birth of a new type of defence sale: systems integration to make the different systems work together. The work requires highly skilled personnel. Israel has made good inroads into this area of the market. Occasionally though, systems just do not combine well. For example, in 2006 the US Defense Department abandoned an attempt to procure a combined regional jet produced by Embraer SA of Brazil with a multi-intelligence sensor system from Lockheed Martin Corporation, designed to detect enemy signals and troop movements from 37,000 feet. Essentially the US Army wanted too much crammed into a small platform and the technical problems were too expensive to fix (Merle 2006: A8).

Training: Countries like India and Israel are marketing their ability to train fighter pilots—in India's case, in response to the perceived inadequacy of Russian support services. Israel trained fifteen Ugandan pilots to fly the three MiG-21 fighters the state acquired in 1998. Israel Aircraft Industries upgraded the fighters and the pilots spent a year in Tel Aviv undergoing training (*Xinuha*, 2000). Corporate giants such as SAIC, BDM, and its subsidiary Vinnell Corporation, are primarily high-technology suppliers but have diversified into military training. They are contracted by the Saudi Arabian government to upgrade and train its armed forces in the use of mainly US weaponry (Shearer 1999: 84).

People: the transfers of personnel are taken to higher levels in the Middle East, where several countries employ foreign military specialists not just to maintain and repair equipment, but to actually use it. For example, Saudi Arabia has for many years employed foreign nationals such as Pakistanis (on leave from their national armed forces) to fly their fighter planes. This enables the Pakistanis to maintain a large, well-trained reserve force without incurring massive costs (Lock 1998). For Saudi Arabia, this helps to fill a skills and employment gap.

Software and Software Source Codes: modern weapons increasingly rely on sophisticated software. Of fundamental importance are the software source codes. Simply put:

> “These codes provide a blueprint of how a specific system's software works and are at the heart of nearly all modern weaponry. The codes are the keys to understanding everything about a weapon, including its avionics, communications and guidance system. If an enemy gains access to such codes, they can clone the weapon, pinpoint its weak points and build counter-technology”
>
> **(Defense News 1999: 56)**

In some instances these valuable commodities are 'black boxed' by a supplier to ensure that although the systems work, the technology is protected and cannot be reverse-engineered. However, in a buyer's defence market, the would-be recipients often demand access to software source codes as the price for securing the deal.

Leasing: states do not always purchase weapons nowadays; there are also attractive leasing deals on offer. For example, in 2001 Hungary struck a deal to lease 14 *Gripen* fighters from the Swedish Air Force and in 2004 the Czech Republic struck a similar leasing deal (Air Force Technology 2006).

Revolution in Military Affairs (RMA): this is the term given to a basket of military technologies and approaches to warfare that has the potential to 'transform' the nature of military operations. The introduction of precision guided munitions and 'smart' weapons has resulted in conventional weapons achieving previously unimaginable levels of lethality and accuracy. There have also been improvements in materials, aircraft design and military avionics, which led to the emergence of a new generation of 'stealthy' aircraft and ships. The advantage—and the problem—of stealth is that it re-introduces the possibility of surprise attack. Equally important have been technological improvements in stand-off missiles; that is, missiles launched from weapons platforms miles outside the theatre of operation which are then guided to a distant target.

Developments on the non-weapons side of the equation include electronic warfare technologies, sensors, radars and night vision equipment. These technologies act as **force multipliers** through permitting the real-time relay of vital information to the battlefield and by allowing all-weather and night use of military hardware.

One interesting aspect of the RMA is the increased use of unmanned aircraft. These unmanned aerial vehicles (UAVs) were initially thought of in terms of reconnaissance missions, but are now being deployed in a variety of lethal missions, including US remote attacks on terrorists in Yemen, Afghanistan and elsewhere. The UAV has a number of advantages, including removing the danger of losing valuable pilots over hostile territory.

Taken together, these technological trends have the potential to revolutionize the battlefield. To date the only country able to reap the technological advantage has been the United States. The US technological edge—amply demonstrated by the Gulf Wars of 1991 and 2003—has, however, not proved so useful in the counterinsurgency campaigns in Iraq and Afghanistan, though there is increasing adaptation of some of these technologies for urban guerrilla warfare.

Small Arms and Light Weapons (SALW): a more instantly recognized form of defence trade is in SALW, where business has been facilitated by an abundance of supplies from excess post-Cold War stocks, lower transport costs as a consequence of globalization, sustained demand from a number of internal conflicts that have raged in the last fifteen years and the reality of porous borders. With respect to the latter for instance, one study has identified 21 known arms trafficking routes into Colombia from Venezuela, 26 from Ecuador, 37 from Panama and 14 from Brazil (Cragin and Hoffman 2003). One feature of the small arms trade that has come under particular scrutiny in the post-Cold War era is the way the trade in 'conflict goods' or 'conflict commodities' (e.g. diamonds, timber, coltan) from conflict zones have been used to fund the acquisition of arms by combatants (Le Billon 2005). Concern about this relationship has even led the UN to impose commodity embargoes on some actors such as UNITA in Angola (diamonds) and the regime of Charles Taylor in Liberia (diamonds and timber).

KEY POINTS

- The post-Cold War defence export market has been characterized by a move away from the supply of complete weapons systems to the provision of upgrades, dual-use technologies, communications equipment and spare parts.
- The term 'revolution in military affairs' is often used to describe the way in which simultaneous advances in a number of technologies are deemed to be radically transforming, or have the potential to transform, the way military operations are conducted.

Conclusion

Like all issues in international relations, the main focus of academic engagement with the defence trade has shifted in response to changes in the nature of global politics. Thus, in the Cold War, the concern was to investigate the ways in which defence expenditure, weapons acquisition and defence sales were either determined by superpower rivalry via the logic of action-reaction or, alternatively, how they determined superpower rivalry via the institutionalization of the military-industrial complex or the mechanisms of military aid. The end of the Cold War, however, saw a relative decline in the study of such factors and a turn to research on those aspects of the arms trade that seemed more germane to the political concerns of the day—at the higher end of the defence trade this has been reflected in a concern with the mechanisms of nuclear proliferation, whilst at the lower end of the trade, research and policy activity has focused on the role played by the trade in small arms in sustaining the 'new wars' of the post-Cold War. As we have already noted, this both reflected and reinforced the fact that the conventional trade in major weapons has become profoundly de-politicized.

Interestingly however, the war on terror and its various corollaries—e.g. the huge increase in US defence expenditure and (at least in some cases) a renewed emphasis on the politics as well as the economics of defence sales and military aid—appears to be producing something of a renewed concern with issues such as the relationship between an apparent threat (now understood as global terrorism) and defence spending, or with the existence, role and nature of a putative military-industrial (media-entertainment) complex. Nevertheless, this has yet to translate into solid academic work on these issues.

In addition some areas of study that were only beginning to emerge towards the end of the Cold War have become far more consolidated—in particular the challenge of fighting a stateless and globally networked enemy, combined with the opportunities presented by an apparent RMA has spurred academic and policy engagement with the idea of network-centric warfare and the implications this is having, and will have, for our way of doing war. These are interesting and important issues for a new generation of security analysts to explore.

? QUESTIONS

Which model of the arms dynamic is more convincing and why?

Does the notion of a military-industrial complex still have relevance given the globalization of the defence industry and the growing emphasis on dual-use technologies?

To what extent does the symbolic meaning attached to defence technology determine both supply and demand in the defence trade?

'Arms embargoes simply create new market opportunities for illicit weapons dealers'. Discuss.

To what extent has the content of the defence trade changed and what does this imply for attempts at regulation?

Is it accurate for commentators to refer to a revolution in military affairs, and if so, what are its likely consequences?

To what extent has the transfer of major conventional weapons been depoliticized in the post-Cold War era?

How does the trade in 'conflict goods' contribute to the trade in small arms?

What are the differences between the licit and illicit trade in small arms?

Defence exports are often justified on the basis of the economic benefits they provide to the economies of suppliers. What is the evidence to support this contention?

FURTHER READING

- **Bitzinger, Richard A. (2003), *Towards a Brave New Arms Industry?* Adelphi Paper 356, London: International Institute for Strategic Studies**. An excellent survey of what Bitzinger describes as the 'hub and spoke model' of arms industry globalization.

- **Buzan, Barry and Herring, Eric (1998), *The Arms Dynamic in World Politics*, London: Lynne Rienner**. A revised (and improved) follow-up to Buzan's *Introduction to Strategic Studies*, this is essential reading for students wishing to understand the various debates on the arms trade and the methods for controlling it.

- **Der Derian, James (2001), *Virtuous War: Mapping the Military-Industrial-Media-Entertainment Network*, Boulder, Co: Westview**. At its worst, this book lapses into self-indulgent travelogue, but it nevertheless manages to reinvent the notion of the military industrial complex for the post-Cold War era and contains important insights into the relationship between modern military technology, the media and the nature of modern warfare.

- **Farrell, Theo (1997), *Weapons Without A Cause: The Politics of Weapons Acquisition in the United States*, London: Macmillan**. Although somewhat dated now, this nevertheless remains an excellent account of the factors that influence procurement decisions, particularly in the USA.

- **Hammond, Grant T. (1993), *Plowshares into Swords: Arms Races in International Politics, 1840–1991*, Colombia: University of South Carolina Press**. An impressive attempt to refine the concept of arms racing based on a number of case studies dating back to the nineteenth century.

- **Krause, Keith (1992), *Arms and the State: Patterns of Military Production and Trade*, Cambridge: Cambridge University Press**. This book provides a thorough analysis of the history and structure of the arms trade.

- **Le Billon, Philippe (2005), 'Fuelling War: Natural Resources and Armed Conflict', *Adelphi Paper*, Vol. 45, No. 373**. There is a growing literature on the relationship between the trade in 'conflict goods' and conflict but this provides an excellent survey of the key issues as well as a detailed discussion of the various regulatory initiatives that have emerged to address the connection between natural resources and conflict.

- **Markusen, Ann (1999), 'The Rise of World Weapons', *Foreign Policy*, 114 (Spring): 40–51**. This is a provocative analysis of the challenges implied by the globalization of the defence industry.

- **Mutimer, David (2000), *The Weapons State: Proliferation and the Framing of Security*, Boulder, CO: Lynne Rienner**. This is the definitive postmodern take on both nuclear proliferation and the defence trade more generally.

There are two very good yearbooks on aspects of the defence trade:

- **The Stockholm International Peace Research Institute (SIPRI) publishes *The SIPRI Yearbook: Armaments, Disarmament and International Security* (Oxford: Oxford University Press).** This contains extensive quantitative data on military expenditure and the defence trade. It also has excellent analytical essays on features of the trade such as the activities of key defence firms.

- **The Small Arms Survey publishes an annual *Small Arms Survey* (Oxford: Oxford University Press)** and is a major attempt to get over the problem of lack of information about the trade in SALW.

There are a number of defence magazines that provide good coverage of the trade.

- *Defense News* is published in the US and comes out weekly. *Jane's Defence Weekly* is published in the UK. Both have excellent coverage of the market.

IMPORTANT WEBSITES

- An excellent source for information on global military expenditures is the SIPRI website **http://www.sipri.org**

- The Small Arms Survey is an excellent source on SALW issues **http://www.smallarmssurvey.org**

- The Federation of American Scientists provides excellent coverage of all aspects of the defence trade as well as web links to relevant reports. It also publishes an annual newsletter, *Arms Sales Monitor* **http://www.fas.org/main/home.jsp**

- The British American Security Information Council engages with a wide range of defence-related issues from nuclear weapons to the small arms trade **http://www.basic.org**

- The Centre for Defense Information covers a wide range of defence-related topics including the arms trade and small arms **http://www.cdi.org/index.cfm**

- The Arms Trade Resource Centre of the World Policy Institute is a particularly useful resource for information on the US defence trade **http://www.worldpolicy.org/projects/arms/index.html**

Visit the Online Resource Centre that accompanies this book for lots of interesting additional material: www.oxfordtextbooks.co.uk/orc/collins/

18 HIV/AIDS and Security

STEFAN ELBE

Chapter Contents

Reader's Guide

This chapter shows how the AIDS pandemic is no longer just a global health and development issue, but also has important security implications. Following an initial overview of the scope of the global AIDS pandemic, the chapter begins to explore both the direct and indirect effects of HIV/AIDS on human security. The chapter then goes on to highlight how in some of the worst-affected countries the AIDS pandemic also has national security implications because of its eroding effects on the armed forces and state capacity. HIV/AIDS even has implications for international security, as the chapter subsequently illustrates by highlighting the role of HIV/AIDS in international peacekeeping operations. Awareness of these security implications is vital for understanding the seriousness of the global challenge posed by HIV/AIDS, and because the security sector can make an important contribution to wider international efforts to reduce the transmission of HIV/AIDS.

Introduction

On 10 January 2000 the United Nations Security Council held a historic meeting. Not only was this the first session of the Council in the twenty-first century and in the new millennium; it was also the first time in its history that it declared a health issue—HIV/AIDS—as a threat to international peace and security. In his position as President of the World Bank, James Wolfensohn (2000) argued unequivocally before the Council that '[m]any of us used to think of AIDS as a health issue. We were wrong. . . . Nothing we have seen is a greater challenge to the peace and stability of African societies than the epidemic of AIDS. . . . We face a major development crisis, and more than that, a security crisis.' The scope of the global AIDS **pandemic** is clearly immense. Throughout the world an estimated 40 million people are living with HIV, while in some southern African countries national HIV prevalence rates are currently thought to be well in excess of one-third of the adult population. It is similarly clear that in the worst-affected countries, the effects of HIV/AIDS will not be confined to the individual human tragedies suffered by those persons living with the virus and by their respective families; the pandemic will have a plethora of wider economic, political, demographic, and social implications that will need to be carefully considered and addressed. But in what ways are these cumulative effects serious enough to merit the designation of the pandemic as a *security* issue? This is the question addressed in greater detail below.

After commencing with an overview of the current scope of the global AIDS pandemic, the chapter begins to unfold how HIV/AIDS touches upon three different conceptions of security: human security, national security, and international security. HIV/AIDS has important direct implications for human security because it is a lethal illness claiming the lives of millions on an annual basis, and because it also has a host of more indirect but no less debilitating social consequences that adversely affect human security. In some of the worst-affected countries, HIV/AIDS also has further national security implications because it undermines the armed forces that are experiencing high HIV/AIDS **prevalence rates**, and because the high **morbidity** and mortality generated by the epidemic has negative social, economic, and political consequences that undermine state capacity. HIV/AIDS even has implications for international security because international peacekeeping operations are also affected by the issue of HIV/AIDS. Awareness of these security implications is crucial for recognizing the seriousness of the challenge posed by the global AIDS pandemic, and because the security sector can make a modest but important contribution to international efforts to reduce the transmission of HIV/AIDS.

The global HIV/AIDS pandemic

How many people are affected worldwide by HIV/AIDS? Even though the magnitude of the pandemic is clearly immense, determining its precise extent is fraught with complex difficulties. To date the most comprehensive data on the pandemic has been jointly compiled by the World Health Organization (WHO) and the Joint United Nations Program on HIV/AIDS (UNAIDS). Even the figures provided by the WHO and UNAIDS are only estimates, however, and should not be taken as exact representations. They are subject to considerable political pressures and logistical difficulties, several of which remain beyond the control of UNAIDS. In many countries, systematic HIV/AIDS surveillance remains mostly inadequate, making it hard to obtain reliable data and to detect hidden **epidemics** not captured by existing surveillance mechanisms. Nonetheless, the figures compiled by UNAIDS illustrate the global scope of HIV/AIDS very clearly. As of December 2004, UNAIDS estimates that around 39.4 million people are living with HIV or have AIDS. This number exceeds the entire population of a country like Spain or Argentina. Of these 39.4 million people, 37.2 million are thought to be adults (aged 15–49), and 2.2 million are children (under the age of 15). In terms of mortality, it is estimated that in 2004 alone 3.1 million people died of AIDS-related illnesses, and roughly 4.9 million persons became newly infected with HIV (UNAIDS 2004). This means that on average almost three times as many persons continue to die from AIDS-related illnesses *every day*, than died during the terrorist attacks on 11 September 2001. UNAIDS also believes that cumulatively around 25 million people have died from AIDS-related illnesses throughout the world to date.

Contrary to widespread belief, HIV/AIDS is not at all confined to sub-Saharan Africa. Every region of the world currently has a significant number of people living with HIV/AIDS. Epidemiological indicators show that HIV is spreading quickly in Asia, the Indian subcontinent, the Caribbean, Russia, and in Eastern Europe. Table 18.1 shows the current UNAIDS (2004) estimates for the regional distribution of persons living with HIV at the end of 2004.

Putting these figures into historical perspective reveals the AIDS pandemic to be, at least in numerical terms, amongst the worst pandemics to have confronted mankind. In the first decade of the twenty-first century alone it may well claim more victims than the Spanish influenza epidemic of 1918–19, which is thought to have caused between 25 and 40 million deaths worldwide. It will, in all likelihood, also exceed the number of victims of the bubonic plague in Europe given that UNAIDS

Table 18.1 People living with HIV/AIDS at the end of 2004

Region	Adults and children living with HIV	Adults and children newly infected with HIV	Adult and child deaths due to AIDS
Sub-Saharan Africa	25.4 million	3.1 million	2.3 million
North Africa and Middle East	540,000	92,000	28,000
South and Southeast Asia	7.1 million	890,000	490,000
East Asia	1.1 million	290,000	51,000
Oceania	35,000	5,000	700
Latin America	1.7 million	240,000	95,000
Caribbean	440,000	53,000	36,000
Eastern Europe and Central Asia	1.4 million	210,000	60,000
Western and Central Europe	610,000	21,000	6,500
North America	1 million	44,000	16,000
World Total	**39.4 million**	**5 million**	**3.1 million**

estimates an additional 45 million persons will become infected with HIV by 2010 unless stronger and successful efforts are made to curb transmission rates. It is also precisely this immense and unanticipated scale of the AIDS pandemic that raises important questions as to whether it might have implications that go beyond the health sector and extend into the security sector as well.

KEY POINTS

- An estimated 40 million people are living with HIV/AIDS around the world.
- AIDS is one of the worst pandemics in modern human history.
- HIV/AIDS is not just an African issue but is spreading in many regions outside of Africa.

HIV/AIDS and human security

One way in which HIV/AIDS is already having important security ramifications, and will continue to do so for many years to come, is within the broader framework of 'human security'. This notion, advanced by the UN Development Program in its 1994 *Human Development Report*, seeks to redress the perceived imbalance in security thinking that has predominated over past decades, and wishes to refocus its attention on the needs and welfare of individuals, rather than just that of states and territories. Within its sphere of legitimate security concerns human security includes a variety of non-military threats to the survival and welfare of individuals and societies, including disease. For more on human security see Chapter 6.

Although this particular way of thinking about security has provoked considerable debate in post-Cold War security studies, especially regarding its breadth as an analytical concept, it is important to bear in mind that such thinking about the notion of security is not as novel as it might initially appear in the context of the contemporary debate. Many of these ideas have evident Enlightenment roots that can be traced back at least to the eighteenth and nineteenth century, if not earlier. From this perspective, the narrowing of security thinking in the course of the twentieth century represents an historical anomaly—one linked, perhaps, to the extraordinarily violent nature the twentieth century. In either case, the idea of human security has not only been partially embraced by the United Nations Security Council, it has also attracted a wide coalition of national governments, including Canada, Norway, and Japan.

Implications of HIV/AIDS for human security

If the human security approach is intimately concerned with securing not only the survival of the state, but also the survival of individual human beings, then HIV/AIDS clearly amounts to a paramount security issue within this framework. In quantitative terms, HIV/AIDS is already amongst the five most frequent causes of death worldwide. In Africa the illness even vies for the unenviable position of posing the greatest human security threat. There, HIV/AIDS is not only the leading cause of death; it is also estimated to cause more than ten times as many deaths as armed conflict. AIDS thus already poses a numerically greater risk to the survival of many Africans than armed conflict. Qualitatively, moreover, HIV/AIDS also directly and indirectly affects most of the components of human security identified by the United Nations Development Program. At the most basic level, HIV/AIDS is a lethal illness that threatens the life of those who develop AIDS and who do not enjoy access to life-saving medicines. As a result, the average life expectancy in some African countries is likely to drop by as much as twenty to thirty years over the next decades. By 2010 the life expectancy in many countries could even be lower than at the beginning of the twentieth century, to no small extent due to the impact of HIV/AIDS.

Beyond these individual tragedies, HIV/AIDS also has a plethora of direct and indirect human security ramifications for those families and communities affected by the illness. Unlike many other illnesses associated with old age, AIDS-related illnesses affect persons at a much younger and more productive age. Consequently there is an important relationship, for example, between high HIV prevalence rates and levels of food security. As persons become too ill they may become unable to provide or acquire nourishment for their families, or be unable to tend to the fields in order to secure adequate levels of food. They may even have to sell off their possessions and/or livestock in order to compensate for this lack of income. The same holds true more generally for their ability to generate income. As individuals become too ill to maintain steady employment, and families face additional medical and funeral costs due to the illness, their economic security too becomes adversely affected.

High rates of HIV/AIDS also have human security implications in terms of the level of education individuals may benefit from. If one or both parents become ill, children may be kept away from school in order to help in the domestic household, or to generate income themselves. Eventually, many of these children will also become orphans. To this must be added the immense impact of HIV/AIDS on the education sector as a whole, as scores of teachers succumb to the illness. It is thought that in some regions in southern Africa around a fifth of secondary school teachers are currently HIV-positive, with the result that some schools are already being forced to close. In 1999 it was estimated that 860,000 primary school children in Sub-Saharan Africa had lost teachers due to AIDS-related illnesses.

The human security of individuals may also be affected more intangibly, through social stigma and exclusion, which can manifest itself in violent attacks on persons known to be living with HIV. One particularly tragic case occurred in South Africa where Gugu Dlamini died at the age of 36 as the result of a beating she received by her neighbours in the outskirts of Durban in December of 1998 after she revealed—on World AIDS Day—that she was HIV-positive. Even when the virus itself does not kill immediately, the stigma surrounding the illness can. When viewed from the perspective of human security, therefore, HIV/AIDS is undoubtedly a security issue of overwhelming proportions, and this represents one of the most important ways in which HIV/AIDS is already evolving a significant security dimension. Indeed, the immense individual and social impact of HIV/AIDS is precisely the kind of issue that human security advocates would like to draw attention to.

KEY POINTS

- Over the past decade many international organizations, governments, scholars, non-governmental organizations, and activists have been exploring a new 'human security' approach that focuses on the threats to the daily lives of ordinary individuals, rather than just ensuring the survival of states.
- AIDS is a *direct* threat to human security because it kills an estimated three million people every year.
- AIDS is also an *indirect* human security threat because it adversely affects many of the components of the human security agenda, such as economic security, food security, health security, personal security, etc.

HIV/AIDS and national security

The security dimensions of HIV/AIDS are not, however, restricted to the field of human security alone. In countries currently experiencing very high HIV prevalence rates, HIV/AIDS is also beginning to have implications for the more traditional and conventional framework of national security. Within a state-centric security perspective the impact of HIV/AIDS on the armed forces and on the political stability of the worst-affected countries are particular causes for concern. Crucially, the armed forces are not a marginal group within the global AIDS pandemic, but occupy a central position within it. Prevalence rates of sexually transmitted diseases among military populations in peacetime are in many cases believed to exceed those of the comparative civilian population. Although data currently remains inadequate and patchy, intelligence assessments indicate that in many African militaries this also holds true in the case of HIV (UNAIDS 1998: 2). There are several factors that can expose military populations to higher levels of HIV prevalence, including that soldiers are of a sexually active age, that they are mobile and stationed away from home for long periods of time, that they often valorize violent and risky behaviour, that they have opportunities for casual sexual relations, that they seek to relieve themselves from the stress of combat, and because other sexually transmitted diseases increase the chance of HIV transmission during unprotected sexual intercourse.

As a result of these factors several defence ministries in sub-Saharan Africa are now documenting HIV prevalence rates among the armed forces of between 10% and 20%. This is only the average figure, however, with some countries where the AIDS virus has been present for more than ten years reaching rates as high as 50% to 60%. The National Intelligence Council (2000) in the United States believes HIV prevalence in selected military populations in sub-Saharan Africa to be: Angola 40–60%, Congo-Brazzaville 10–25%, Côte d'Ivoire 10–20%, Democratic Republic of Congo 40–60%, Eritrea 10%, Nigeria 10–20%, and Tanzania 15–30%. Although it is impossible to verify these figures generated by classified means, they are compatible with a defence intelligence assessment carried out by South Africa (Heinecken 2001), which provided the following figures: Angola 50%, Botswana 33%, Democratic Republic of Congo 50%, Lesotho 40%, Malawi 50%, Namibia 16%, South Africa 15–20%, Swaziland 48%, Zambia 60%, and Zimbabwe 55%.

Impact of HIV/AIDS on the armed forces

High prevalence rates in the military are having an impact in at least four areas that are important to the efficient operation of the armed forces. First, they are generating a need for additional resources to train and recruit new soldiers to replace sick ones, ones who have died, or ones who are expected to die in the near future. More resources will also be needed for looking after those members of the armed forces who are ill or in the process of dying. Second, these high prevalence rates are also affecting staffing issues in the armed forces. High HIV rates eventually lead to a decrease in the available civilian conscription pool to draw upon for new recruits, lead to deaths among the more senior and experienced officers at higher levels of the chain of command, and can lead to a loss of highly specialized and technically trained staff that can be replaced neither easily nor quickly. Third, although persons living with HIV can usually carry out normal duties, AIDS has implications for the ability of daily military tasks to be carried out efficiently by leading to an increased absenteeism and to lower levels of morale as healthy soldiers have to deal with increased work loads until sick ones are replaced, and have to watch fellow soldiers die a painful death. Fears of attending to injured soldiers in light of the possibility of becoming infected with the lethal illness, and the question of how to secure the blood supply during military operations, are similarly becoming concerns for the efficient execution of deployments. Finally, HIV/AIDS generates new political and legal challenges for civil-military relations in terms of how to deal with the issue of HIV/AIDS in the ranks and how to treat persons living with HIV. The Namibian armed forces, for example, lost a lengthy court case as to whether its decision to exclude HIV-positive persons from joining the armed forces is constitutional.

Beyond this direct impact on the armed forces of countries in which prevalence rates are highest, the growing AIDS pandemic also has security implications in terms of political stability within these states. This link is more difficult to assess, but there are already four countries in sub-Saharan Africa where HIV prevalence is estimated to exceed 30% of the adult population: Botswana (38.8%),

CASE STUDY 18.1

The South African National Defence Force (SANDF)

Information about the impact of HIV/AIDS on Africa's armed forces is extremely difficult to obtain due to its sensitive nature. Even in those militaries that test soldiers for HIV/AIDS, officials are extremely reluctant to make such information public as it may well point to potential weaknesses in the armed forces. Over the past years some information has nevertheless begun to emerge about the ways in which HIV/AIDS has begun to affect the South African National Defence Force (SANDF).

South Africa is already home to the largest number of persons living with HIV/AIDS in Africa. The adult (aged 15–49) HIV prevalence rate among the civilian population is estimated by UNAIDS to be 21.5%, and according to the South African Department of Health more than 6 million people have now been infected with HIV in the country. The South African National Defence Force (SANDF) claims that HIV prevalence in the armed forces is around 23%, which is slightly higher than the civilian population and which amounts to roughly 16,000 soldiers. Many analysts believe that in reality this figure may be much higher, perhaps as high as 40%, which would put the number closer to 28,000. Even the official figure is high enough, however, to prompt the United States and SANDF to set up a programme aimed at establishing the rate of HIV infection in the armed forces more conclusively and evaluating the effects of anti-retroviral treatments on SANDF. Because of human rights considerations, SANDF cannot force their soldiers to be tested, but SANDF has now set up a programme where soldiers can come forward voluntarily to be tested. To date, 1,089 soldiers have come forward of whom 947 (89%) tested positive. The average age of those who tested positive was 34 years, and 60% of them were married. Although this figure is not representative of SANDF as a whole (most of those who came forward to be tested probably suspected that they were HIV-positive already), it leaves no doubt that the issue of HIV/AIDS is rapidly becoming very serious for many armed forces in Africa.

In light of these figures, senior officials in SANDF have expressed serious concern about the impact of HIV/AIDS on the military's combat readiness because of the high levels of absenteeism the illness induces. They estimate that a soldier in the early stages of illness will be absent on average 20 days a year, which rises to 45 days for soldiers displaying symptoms. Soldiers who have developed full-blown AIDS are estimated to be absent on average for a minimum of 120 days per year. SANDF believes that it will lose between 338,000 and 560,000 working days annually due to the illness. SANDF is also concerned with the fact that many of those most affected by HIV/AIDS in SANDF are in the age group of 23–32, which is the age group from which most of the operationally deployable soldiers, officers, non-commissioned officers and highly skilled members of the armed forces are drawn. HIV/AIDS may thus hollow out this middle rank, creating gaps and shortfalls within the armed forces. This impact is all the more difficult because of South Africa's leadership role on the African continent and because the country wishes to play an expanding role in African peacekeeping operations, which it can only do with a healthy military.

Lesotho (31%), Swaziland (33.4%) and Zimbabwe (33.7%)—raising important questions about the longer term impact of such prevalence rates on their political stability. When states become unstable or fail, it is often because the central monopoly on the use of armed force is disputed, and because the government's popular legitimacy has been severely eroded. State collapse, moreover, is usually a multi-faceted phenomenon involving at least three inter-related processes: the transformation or destruction of the economy; the weakening or dissolution of political institutions at local and national levels; and the damaging of a wide array of social institutions such as the family, the education system, and the health care sector. Although HIV/AIDS is unlikely to generate state collapse independently of other factors, high rates of HIV/AIDS nevertheless contribute to all three of these processes, thus giving rise to significant concern about the long-term impact of HIV/AIDS on the worst-affected states if life-prolonging medicines are not made widely available.

Economic impact

HIV/AIDS contributes to the first trajectory involved in processes of state collapse in that it exacerbates the resource burden faced by countries and can thus contribute to an intensification of resource competition between different social groups. The armed forces, for example, are likely to attempt to secure a greater share of public expenditure in order to offset some of their emerging resource demands. The civilian sector will simultaneously be facing a similar increase in demand for resources, thus fuelling resource competition between these two groups. In Malawi, the public health system is already inundated by the pandemic with up to 70% of hospital bed occupancy taken up by patients suffering from AIDS-related illnesses.

Such competition over scarce resources between the military and civilian sector will be exacerbated further because even though the most severe impact is probably going to occur at the level of individual households and particular industries, AIDS is predicted to have a long-term macroeconomic impact in those states worst affected by the illness. Although the extent of this impact is still a matter of considerable debate amongst economists, a report by the World Health Organization (2001: 31) conservatively estimates that AIDS will account for 17% of the lost earning potential of sub-Saharan Africa's total 1999 gross domestic product. While these kinds of losses could be absorbed for a year or two, they pose larger problems when they become cumulative, occurring year after year as they are likely to do. Given that HIV/AIDS affects the economically most productive demographic group, that HIV/AIDS undermines the belief in the long-term sustainability of the economy, that it could discourage private as well as foreign investment, and given that AIDS affects the middle management of many companies as well as their highly trained workers that are in shorter supply, these figures could well be indicative of broad trends. In future, both military and civilian sectors will thus have to compete with each other in order to try to secure a higher proportion of public resources to meet their higher costs.

Political impact

HIV/AIDS also contributes to the second trajectory usually involved in processes of state collapse by generating additional challenges to the political sphere in countries where prevalence rates are very high. HIV/AIDS could further undermine the ability of state officials to govern effectively in the long run. Crucial resources are already being reportedly diverted from running state services to treating people with HIV/AIDS. Basic government services will thus become more difficult to deliver as mortality rates amongst those working for the state increase. In many countries with high prevalence rates the effectiveness of the police forces, too, is coming under increasing pressure from the illness. The police forces of the fourteen member states of the Southern African Development Community

(SADC) are now taking HIV/AIDS very seriously, and are trying to find ways to cope with the reduction in personnel as well as bracing themselves for things to become much worse in the years to come. The judicial system, too, is affected, with staff serving in justice institutions, such as judges, prosecutors, court clerks and lawyers facing similar levels of mortality as other sectors of society. All other things held equal, this means that in future it will become more difficult to fight crime and fewer arrests can be made. It will also become more difficult to handle internal rebels or domestic challenges to power.

HIV/AIDS could also facilitate political tensions over decisions about who will have access to life-saving medicines. Diseases have ravaged many countries for decades without necessarily fuelling political instability. Yet, unlike other diseases that are strongly linked with poverty, HIV/AIDS additionally afflicts the educated and moderately wealthy middle classes. Given the current availability of anti-retroviral treatments for HIV/AIDS, many elites with access to resources will be able to substantially relieve their predicament by purchasing expensive medicines. The plight of other social groups, however, is less certain. If the elites are not seen to be working in their interests and securing the availability of medications for them as well, some analysts have argued, this could contribute to further social polarization. Indeed, those living with HIV might become increasingly susceptible to populist leaders promising radical solutions, rather than relying on more democratic ones.

HIV/AIDS also contributes to the third trajectory frequently involved in processes of state collapse, namely the undermining of a wide array of social institutions such as the family, the education system, and the health care sector. These dimensions were already outlined when considering the human security implications of HIV/AIDS, and include not only the decrease in average life expectancy, but also the potential generation of up to 40 million orphans in the years to come. Many of these children will be exposed to the stigma of the illness and will be more vulnerable to malnutrition, illness, abuse and sexual exploitation. Often children are also left to exchange sexual services in return for other vital goods, such as shelter, food, physical protection and money. This development is not only of concern for human security theorists. One South African analyst (Schönteich 1999) has already linked this rise in the number of orphans due to HIV/AIDS with an exponentially increasing crime rate for the next five to twenty years. He argues that these orphans will be susceptible to exploitation and radicalization, and might well turn towards crime and militias in order to maintain their existence as they receive inadequate support from their families and communities. Alas, such bands and militias not only promise to address the material needs of youths; they can also perform important psychological functions such as providing them with surrogate father figures and role models.

In these ways HIV/AIDS can potentially exacerbate a variety of economic, political, and social tensions within the worst affected countries. In so doing HIV/AIDS also contributes to all three trajectories usually associated with processes of political instability and state failure. This diminishing impact on state stability, in conjunction with the aforementioned effect on the armed forces, generates additional national security concerns for those countries in sub-Saharan Africa seriously affected by the pandemic, as well as for those with interests in these regions. Unless effective measures are taken to address these effects, the significance of this dimension is likely to grow considerably in the years to come as mortality rates increase further. If, moreover, such high prevalence rates also emerge in strategically significant countries such as China, India, and Russia in the years ahead, this could have national security implications beyond the African continent. All of these countries are important international security actors who have yet to respond adequately to the challenge posed by HIV/AIDS.

KEY POINTS

- HIV/AIDS is not just a human security issue, but is becoming an important national security issue as well.
- The impact of HIV/AIDS on the armed forces is raising concern about HIV/AIDS amongst the security sector.
- In countries where prevalence rates are high, HIV/AIDS also has a diminishing impact on the core institutions of the state, such as the economy, political institutions, etc.

HIV/AIDS and international security

Many armed forces with high HIV prevalence rates regularly contribute to international peacekeeping operations aimed at mitigating and containing the outbreak of armed conflicts—giving the pandemic an important international security dimension as well. HIV/AIDS has already begun to pose additional logistical and political problems for such peacekeeping operations as it becomes increasingly well known that peacekeepers are at a special risk both of contracting and spreading HIV when and where they are deployed. There are three important ways in which HIV/AIDS has begun to affect peacekeeping operations in recent years.

Peacekeepers as a vector of HIV/AIDS

First, it has become increasingly well-known that deployed peacekeepers can contribute to the spread of HIV. In Sierra Leone, for example, the civil war seems to have escalated the number of infections partially due to peacekeepers who were, amongst other places, from Zambia, Kenya and Nigeria—all countries with high prevalence rates in the military. The recognition that peacekeepers can be sources of HIV transmission has begun to create political problems for international peacekeeping operations, as countries cite this problem as a ground for refusing to host such missions. In eastern Africa, Eritrean officials initially demanded a guarantee that no HIV-positive soldiers would be deployed there. They wrote to the Security Council in March of 2001 explicitly requesting that countries contributing troops should screen them for HIV. This political problem was further exacerbated by the subsequent emergence of accusations of sexual abuse against one peacekeeper. The Eritrean government has demanded that the peacekeeper accused of sexually abusing an under-age girl be brought to justice and used the opportunity to add its concern that it had asked peacekeepers to be tested for HIV/AIDS, but that this had not yet been properly implemented. In April 2005, the United Nations Mission in Ethiopia and Eritrea (UNMEE) finally decided to launch a formal investigation into the allegations of sexual abuse made by several Eritrean women.

In Asia, political problems have also been emerging over the past decade regarding the transition authority in Cambodia. As the United Nations arrived in Cambodia between the spring of 1992 and September 1993 in order to implement the peace agreement and in order to organize democratic elections, the HIV rate appears to have increased dramatically. By the end of 1999 there were an estimated 220,000 people living with HIV. Although there are insufficient data to discern what proportion of this increase was due to the presence of international peacekeepers, some officials in Phnom Penh place considerable blame for the

CASE STUDY 18.2

United Nations peacekeeping in Sierra Leone

On 17 July 2000 the United Nations Security Council passed Resolution 1308 in order to begin addressing the issue of HIV/AIDS in peacekeeping operations. The resolution expressed concern at the potentially damaging impact of HIV/AIDS on the health of international peacekeeping personnel, and demanded that the United Nations make HIV/AIDS training a central component of pre-deployment and ongoing training for peacekeepers. The United Nations Department of Peacekeeping Operations together with the Joint United Nations Program on HIV/AIDS (UNAIDS) subsequently began to look at the links between HIV/AIDS and peacekeeping operations in greater detail. The detailed analysis (Bazergan 2002) of the role that HIV/AIDS played during the United Nations Mission in Sierra Leone (UNAMSIL) was an important step forward in this regard and revealed some of the problems and complexities associated with the issue of HIV/AIDS in peacekeeping operations.

The United Nations Security Council authorized this mission in the west-African state of Sierra Leone on 22 October 1999 under the powers granted to it by Chapter VII of the United Nations Charter. The aim of the mission was to cooperate with the government and the other parties in implementing the Lomé Peace Agreement and to assist in the implementation of the disarmament, demobilization and reintegration plan. To this end the Council approved a deployment of up to 17,500 troops to the country, including 260 military observers and up to 170 civilian police personnel. In total, some 38 countries contributed peacekeepers, military observers, or civilian police to the mission. There was consequently concern that, as with other recent peacekeeping operations in Africa, such a deployment might facilitate the spread of HIV/AIDS in Sierra Leone.

Under current policy, the United Nations Department of Peacekeeping Operations (UNDPKO) cannot ensure that only HIV-negative peacekeepers are deployed. Indeed, UNDPKO does not preclude HIV positive soldiers who do not show clinical manifestations of AIDS from peacekeeping operations on human rights grounds. Nevertheless, it *recommends* that persons living with HIV not be selected by troop-contributing countries, because (i) medical treatment in peacekeeping missions may not be adequate to meet the medical needs of these persons; (ii) because exposure to endemic infections and exhaustive immunization requirements may be detrimental to their health; and (iii) because of the risk of transmitting HIV to medical personnel, fellow peacekeepers and sex workers in the mission. This is only a recommendation, however, and UNDPKO has no strict enforcement mechanism. Indeed, the UN does not test these troops and does not request such information from troop-contributing countries.

The case of UNAMSIL showed that ultimately relying on the troop-contributing countries to fulfil these recommendations is problematic. Although most countries that contributed to the mission in Sierra Leone officially claimed to be engaged in pre-deployment testing, at least four UNAMSIL peacekeepers died between November 1999 and March 2002, while another ten soldiers were sent back to their country of origin because they were symptomatic of AIDS, pointing to considerable weaknesses in many countries' pre-deployment testing. As long as this remains the case, the United Nations cannot effectively preclude the possibility that in some instances UN peacekeepers may spread the virus where and when they are deployed. In order to further address this problem, the United Nations now also deploys AIDS advisors with peacekeeping missions and has developed a plastic AIDS awareness card which was piloted in Sierra Leone. The card includes basic facts about the transmission and nature of the disease, a 'pocket' to hold a condom, and it reiterates the peace-keeper's code of conduct. The card is now produced in several languages and is routinely deployed to peacekeepers around the world. Its effectiveness has yet to be properly evaluated, however.

spread of the epidemic in Cambodia on the United Nations Transition Authority in Cambodia (UNTAC). The UNTAC mission was unique at the time and brought more than 20,000 foreign people into Cambodia. This influx of people, many of whom were civilian officials and not just peacekeepers, also infused a fair amount of money into a country otherwise struggling with poverty for many years. On average, sex workers (coming in some cases from as far away as Eastern Europe) reportedly doubled the number of their clients per night from five to ten during the time of the UN mission. Subsequent testing on UNTAC soldiers from the United States and from Uruguay shows that they were infected with the HIV subtype E, which had previously only been found in Southeast Asia and in Central Africa. Realizing the potential problem with the Cambodia mission, the Indonesian military decided to screen 3,627 soldiers who participated in UNTAC. Twelve of these tested HIV-positive, at least seven infections of which are likely to have been acquired whilst in Cambodia. This figure exceeded the only other two deaths amongst Indonesian peacekeepers that resulted from non-AIDS-related causes. Nor is this a problem confined to Asia and Africa. During the Balkans conflict, Zagreb officials, too, made a vocal attempt to ensure that African peacekeepers do not serve in Croatia in light of the risk of HIV transmission. HIV/AIDS is thus already being politicized within the context of hosting peacekeeping operations.

A second way in which the impact of HIV/AIDS on armed forces could pose a future challenge for international peacekeeping operations is that it may also make such missions increasingly unpopular amongst those countries that contribute peacekeepers to them. After all, many of the factors that render national military populations a high-risk group in terms of HIV/AIDS apply just as well to international peacekeepers. Peacekeepers, too, can be posted away from home for long periods of time. In one case, Nigerian peacekeepers were on field duty, without rotation, for up to three years. In this particular case the incidence rate was actually correlated to the duration of the deployment, increasing of 7% in the first year, to 10% after two years, and even 15% after three. Peacekeeping missions additionally tend to attract large numbers of sex workers, thus linking two high-risk groups. Countries may consequently become reluctant to contribute to peacekeeping operations if they realize that some of those who are deployed will return HIV-positive. Of the 10,000 troops that Nigeria sent to Sierra Leone in 1997, 11% of the returning ones tested HIV-positive. The Nigerian government admitted in December 1999 that there was an extremely high prevalence rate amongst its troops participating in the ECOWAS Monitoring Group (ECOMOG) peacekeeping operations in neighbouring West African states. Such losses are not only regrettable from the point of view of the individual soldiers and the armed forces, but also for peacekeeping operations in general as soldiers with valuable prior experience die prematurely from AIDS-related illnesses.

Third, the high rate of HIV in the African armed forces also makes it more difficult to staff international peacekeeping operations if the latter are now to be manned by HIV-negative soldiers only. Depending on the mission involved, peacekeeping operations can be notoriously difficult to staff and it is not always easy for the United Nations to find sufficient peacekeepers to meet its operational demands. This problem is further exacerbated by HIV/AIDS, which could lead to a decrease in the personnel that states can contribute to such operations. During the SADC Blue Crane peacekeeping exercise, which was held in South Africa in April 1999, nearly 50% of the 4,500 participating troops reportedly turned out to be HIV-positive. Moreover, 30% of the South African contingent was not medically fit for deployment, raising particular questions about the ability of South Africa to contribute to international peacekeeping operations in the years ahead, and more general questions regarding the Western strategy of devolving peacekeeping operations to the sub-regional level in Africa. In future, HIV/AIDS could thus also add to the increasing strain on the number of soldiers that armies can contribute for peacekeeping operations.

The Security Council has taken this issue seriously enough to address it formally through Resolution 1308, which urges member states to screen their soldiers voluntarily. It also calls upon the Secretary-General to provide pre-deployment orientation on the prevention of the spread of HIV for peacekeepers. The United Nations Department of Peacekeeping Operations has since begun to look at the issue of HIV/AIDS more closely, and has developed an AIDS-awareness card to distribute to peacekeepers, which contains information about the illness and how it is transmitted. Despite these important efforts, the impact of HIV/AIDS on the peacekeeping operations adds an important international security dimension to the pandemic as well, especially as it will prove very difficult in practical terms for the United Nations to deploy only HIV-negative soldiers in light of the important human rights considerations involved, and the need to rely on certain armed forces to meet their operational requirements.

KEY POINTS

- Even for those states who do not have high HIV prevalence rates, HIV/AIDS is becoming an important international security issue.
- The impact of HIV/AIDS on peacekeeping operations is a matter of particular concern.
- HIV/AIDS is complicating the task of staffing and deploying peacekeeping operations.

Conclusion

This chapter has highlighted the important human, national, and international security dimensions of the global AIDS pandemic. It is important to acknowledge these dimensions and study them in greater detail for several reasons. First, awareness of these security dimensions of HIV/AIDS is necessary for arriving at a more comprehensive understanding of the nature and extent of the contemporary pandemic. While the economic and social implications are now being considered more widely and seriously by scholars and policy-makers on a country-by-country basis, this is not yet occurring with reference to the security dimensions of HIV/AIDS. Second, it is necessary to acknowledge these emerging security dimensions in order for the level of the international response to become commensurate with the extent of the global challenge posed by the AIDS pandemic. International efforts will have to be intensified and more resources made available in order to address these emerging security dimensions, as well as the immense humanitarian catastrophe this pandemic signifies. Finally, these security dimensions must also be taken seriously because the armed forces, as a high-risk group and vector of the virus, must also make a responsible contribution to international efforts to reduce the transmission of HIV.

Indeed, armed forces around the world should be encouraged to implement responsible HIV/AIDS education programmes that discuss the illness in an open and serious manner, and that simultaneously work to reduce the stigma attached to the illness. Armed forces should thus strive to make voluntary and fully confidential testing available on a widespread basis, including counselling both before and after the test, and should re-evaluate what military practices expose soldiers to particularly high risk with regard to HIV transmission, making amendments where possible. Crucially, however, the armed forces will have to address the issue of HIV/AIDS with due consideration of the important human rights issues involved. Human beings living with the virus are not the enemy in the quest to address the illness, but the most important source for making viable improvements in future. Consequently, they must also be included rather than excluded from these processes. Finally, those armed forces possessing advanced medical infrastructure should continue research for a viable and affordable AIDS vaccine as it would be in the evident self-interest of Western militaries to engage in research on those strands that predominate in the various regions of Africa to which they might be deployed at some point in the future.

In addition to these very specific measures that international agencies and the armed forces can adopt in addressing the global AIDS pandemic, an effective strategy for the security sector with regard to HIV/AIDS would also incorporate, secondly, a greater appreciation and support for the wider efforts currently being made to combat the pandemic, such as making cheaper drugs available internationally and contributing to the Global Fund to Fight AIDS, **tuberculosis** and **malaria**. Such wider efforts are necessary because the root causes of the AIDS pandemic are located in a much broader set of economic, political, and structural conditions that will have to be re-evaluated and alleviated if any attempt to turn back the spread of the pandemic is to be successful in the future. The security sector would do well to recognize the convergence of interest with regards to addressing the global AIDS pandemic and to broadly support this wider endeavour. All the new security challenges that HIV/AIDS is presently giving rise to are likely to lessen if there is a significant decrease in the AIDS pandemic. Such wider international efforts to reduce the transmission of HIV, in turn, will only be successful in the long run if they also take into account the multiple security dimensions of the AIDS pandemic outlined above.

? QUESTIONS

What kinds of human insecurities does HIV/AIDS generate?

What are the implications of HIV/AIDS for national security?

To what extent is the global AIDS pandemic a threat to international security?

What can the armed forces do to reduce the spread of HIV/AIDS?

What is gained by calling HIV/AIDS a security issue, rather than a health or development issue?

What lessons can be learned from the securitization of HIV/AIDS for securitization theory?

Is it appropriate for the Security Council to get involved in health issues?

Should HIV/AIDS be singled out from other diseases as a threat to international security?

How does HIV/AIDS affect international peacekeeping operations?

Do other infectious diseases have security implications as well?

FURTHER READING

■ **Elbe, Stefan (2003), *The Strategic Dimensions of HIV/AIDS*, International Institute for Strategic Studies, Oxford: Oxford University Press**. A detailed overview of the impact of HIV/AIDS on the armed forces, on peacekeeping operations, and on state stability.

■ **Garrett, Laurie (2005), *HIV and National Security: Where are the Links?* New York: Council on Foreign Relations http://www.cfr.org/pub8248/laurie_garrett/hiv_and_national_security_where_are_the_links.php**. An influential report published by the Council on Foreign Relations and authored by one of the most well-known writers on global public health. Offers a concise summary of the linkages between HIV/AIDS and security.

■ **ICG (2001), *HIV/AIDS as a Security Issue*, Washington DC and Brussels: International Crisis Group**. An early report by the International Crisis Group tracing the implications of HIV/AIDS for several different conceptions of security.

■ **McNeill, William (1998), *Plagues and People*, New York: Anchor Books**. A classic study of how diseases have altered and shaped the course of world history at several crucial junctures.

- **National Intelligence Council (2000),** ***The Global Infectious Disease Threat and Its Implications for the US*****, Washington DC http://www.cia.gov/cia/reports/nie/report/nie99–17d.html** A declassified report by the US National Intelligence Council outlining the long-term implications of infectious diseases for the national security of the United States.

- **Ostergard, Robert L. Jr. (ed.) (2006),** ***HIV, AIDS and the Threat to National and International Security*****. London: Palgrave**. A collection of essays by the leading scholars in the field covering the various the linkages between HIV/AIDS and security.

- **Price-Smith, Andrew (2001),** ***The Health of Nations: Infectious Disease, Environmental Change, and Their Effects on National Security and Development*****. Cambridge, MA: MIT Press**. A ground-breaking study of the impact of infectious diseases on national security and development that advances a model for measuring this impact.

- **UNAIDS (1998),** ***AIDS and the Military*****, Geneva**. A study into the impact of HIV/AIDS on the armed forces carried out by the Joint United Nations Program on HIV/AIDS.

- **Watts, Sheldon (1997),** ***Epidemics and History: Disease, Power, and Imperialism*****, New Haven: Yale University Press**. A detailed study of the historical importance of several diseases, including plague, cholera, yellow fever, leprosy and smallpox.

IMPORTANT WEBSITES

- **http://www.unaids.org/Unaids/EN/In+focus/HIV_AIDS_security+and+humanitarian+response/HIV_AIDS+and+security.asp** The UNAIDS website for the security implications of HIV/AIDS.

- **http://www.globalhealth.org** Website of the Global Health Council. Has information on global health issues and recent developments in global health.

- **http://www.ukglobalhealth.org** Website of the UK Partnership for Global Health. Has information on the relationship between Health and Foreign Policy, as well as Health and Governance.

Visit the Online Resource Centre that accompanies this book for lots of interesting additional material: www.oxfordtextbooks.co.uk/orc/collins/

19 Transnational Crime

JEANNE GIRALDO AND HAROLD TRINKUNAS

Chapter Contents

Reader's Guide

This chapter explains why many governments have increasingly come to consider transnational crime a threat to national security. It explores both the reasons for and the nature of the increase in transnational crime in the 1990s. It also considers what we know about how transnational crime is organized and finds that our understanding is quite limited. Three competing models of the nature of organized crime—based on hierarchies, networks, and markets—are often used to make sense of the fragmentary evidence available on transnational crime. Each has different implications for how seriously the threat should be taken and the policy measures that should be employed against it. The chapter also explores debates over the strength and nature of the 'nexus' between transnational crime and terrorism. It concludes by discussing how the government response to transnational crime has evolved over time.

Introduction

During the 1990s, the popular media, academic journal articles, and 'threat assessments' produced by think tanks and the military and intelligence communities trumpeted the dangers posed by transnational crime. A 1994 conference organized by a leading Washington think tank, the Center for Strategic and International Studies, labelled transnational crime the 'new empire of evil'. A 1996 UN report asserted that transnational crime had become the 'new form of geopolitics'. The US National Security Strategy released in 1996 presented this phenomenon as a major national security threat. Governments no longer looked at transnational crime as a threat just to individuals or society, but to the very state itself. Looking back, has transnational crime lived up to its billing? Does it represent a major international security threat today?

The growth of transnational crime during the last quarter century is indisputable, but its impact varies considerably across the globe. While organized crime has always been with us, new trends in the international system, particularly globalization, are making it increasingly possible for criminal enterprises to cross borders. As the rate of globalization of trade, finances, and travel accelerates, we should expect organized crime to become even more transnational in the future and increasingly to adopt efficient network forms of organization. This means that more countries will be exposed to the effect of transnational crime on individual security, societies, and the rule of law at a time when the phenomenon is becoming more difficult to address and contain. The persistence of poorly governed or essentially ungoverned countries around the globe, which provide fertile home bases for transnational crime, means that even states with strong law enforcement are vulnerable to spillover effects.

Thinking about transnational crime is difficult from a traditional international security perspective, which typically focuses on questions of war and peace, conflict and cooperation, often from a state-centric perspective. The threat posed by transnational crime has both international and sub-national dimensions and, as we will see in this chapter, it has implications for national security, public safety, and even the stability of regimes. Its ability to transcend borders and commit crimes far from its origins, its covert nature, and its ability to corrupt and subvert government agents makes it challenging for states to anticipate threats and prepare their defences. It is even more difficult for governments to know about whether this type of threat can be countered effectively with traditional security instruments, although there have been controversial calls for a greater use of military and intelligence assets to counter transnational crime. For this reason, the theoretical lenses used in this chapter to understand the problem have less to do with our traditional interpretations of international relations and draw more heavily on theories about organizational forms and domestic politics.

This chapter examines the emergence of transnational crime as an international security threat. We provide an overview of how transnational crime changed during the 1990s and why. We discuss the debates over how transnational crime is organized, which range from those who view it as highly hierarchical to those who argue it is closer to a decentralized market, and the implications of each model for our understanding of the severity of the threat and how to counter it. This includes an assessment of the latest arguments concerning the potential links that may develop between transnational crime and terrorism. We conclude by analysing government responses to transnational crime.

KEY POINTS

- Transnational crime is increasingly perceived as a major international security threat by governments and scholars, but traditional theories of international relations are less useful for understanding the threat.
- International trends such as globalization may have the unintended consequence of opening new spaces for the development of transnational crime.
- The threat posed by transnational crime is growing in scope and severity, and it affects even states with strong law enforcement agencies.
- Using theories about organizational forms and domestic politics provides us with insights about the nature of the threat and how to address it.

Is transnational crime a threat to national security?

Transnational criminal groups cause harm to individuals and societies with the profit-driven crimes they carry out. For example, drug trafficking contributes to levels of substance abuse, petty crime, and the spread of HIV/AIDS by intravenous drug users. Coca production in South America has led to the deforestation of increasing areas of the Amazon forest and to the pollution of land and waterways with the chemicals used for growing and processing coca. The trafficking in women for prostitution by organized crime, typically from developing countries to the West, violates individual civil and human rights, and endangers the health and welfare of the women, their families, and their home and host communities. In coordinating their response to transnational crime, governments need to use more than law enforcement agencies, bringing to bear the public health sector, environmental protection, and social welfare agencies to address broad threats to individual security and public safety.

When can the harm caused by transnational crime be characterized as a national security threat, requiring a quantitatively and qualitatively different response from government? Some decry the damage done to national security when the *level* of harm caused by transnational crime reaches epidemic proportions—for example, the increase in the HIV infection rate unleashed by drug use in Russia. Most often, however, the *perpetrators* of transnational crime—rather than the crimes themselves—are seen as the real threats to national security. According to this view, increasingly wealthy and powerful criminals undermine the state, democracy, and the economy through the use of corruption, violence, and reinvestment of their profits in the licit economy. By the 1990s, this meant that many governments believed that traditional law enforcement approaches designed to provide security for individuals or public safety for communities were no longer deemed adequate (Williams and Savona 1996).

On a very basic level, the ability of transnational crime enterprises to evade state border controls and provide new avenues for the illicit transportation of goods and persons challenges the state's ability to exercise its core functions as guarantor of national sovereignty, the holder of the monopoly on force, and provider of the common good. In the course of their activities, transnational criminal enterprises corrupt and undermine numerous state agencies, providing mechanisms by which transnational criminal enterprises can affect the very nature of government and state policy in the host countries.

At the extremes, transnational criminal enterprises become so powerful as to challenge and replace the state's monopoly on the use of force, as has occurred in some remote areas of the drug-producing regions of Colombia, Peru and Bolivia. As we will see in the discussion of the terrorism-transnational crime nexus, some analysts have raised the possibility that the same illicit channels used for transnational smuggling and trafficking could be used by terrorist organizations.

Second, governments view transnational crime as a security threat to the extent that it undermines democratic stability. The third wave of democracy which began with the Portuguese revolution of 1974 has produced an unprecedented expansion in human liberty, yet in many states, transnational criminal enterprises have taken advantage of the instability that has accompanied these transitions to become entrenched, using corruption to extend their influence into the upper reaches of the state and thus shield themselves from law enforcement. The corruption of public institutions and the perceived fecklessness of law enforcement in new democracies contribute to undermining public confidence and loyalty to the new regime. In the extreme, popular reaction can lead to the replacement of governments or regimes, sometimes producing a restoration of democracy as occurred during the Orange Revolution in Ukraine in 2004, but at other times leading to a nostalgia for more authoritarian forms of government, as has arguably occurred in Russia during the Putin administration.

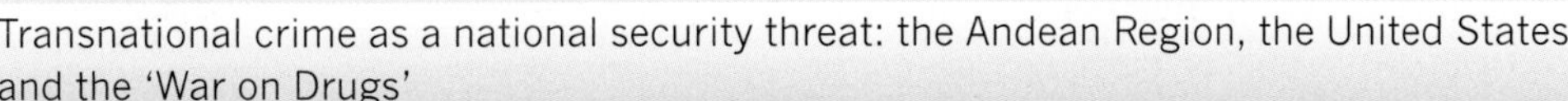

Transnational crime as a national security threat: the Andean Region, the United States and the 'War on Drugs'

Ongoing large-scale drug trafficking from countries in the Andean Ridge of Latin America (Bolivia, Colombia, Peru) to the United States exemplifies the multiple levels at which organized crime poses a threat to public safety, the social fabric, and national security. At a very fundamental level, the drug trade poses a threat to public safety, both through the illegal use of violence by traffickers themselves to enforce their authority over production and distribution networks and through the activities of addicts who engage in petty crime to support their habits. In some countries, such as Colombia, right-wing paramilitary forces and left-wing insurgents extract protection money from drug trafficking organizations or engage directly in the drug trade to support their own violent anti-government activities. Here, drug money fuels violence directed against the state and civilians disrupting the social fabric by producing mass internal refugee movements.

Drug trafficking produces serious economic distortions as well. Money-laundered proceeds from drugs are often reinvested in businesses in the United States and Andean Ridge countries. This relatively 'cheap' source of capital provides drug-associated enterprises with an unfair advantage against legitimate businesses that depend on more expensive legitimate sources of capital such as banks and stock markets.

Drug-related corruption also threatens the integrity of law enforcement and judiciaries in both the Andes and the United States. To the extent that organized crime is able to penetrate politics, social organizations and business communities, governments become less and less able to resist the influence of organized crime. Unchecked, this means that organized crime can eventually undermine the ability of the state to preserve its national security.

Transnational cooperation to counter narcotics trafficking in the region has had unintended consequences for regional security in the Andes. Successful efforts by the United States in the mid-1990s to support anti-narcotics programmes in Peru and Bolivia reduced production in those countries. However, transnational crime organizations were able to adapt to US-supported efforts by shifting production to Colombia, where it fuelled a major resurgence of insurgent activity. As the United States and Colombia work to address the effects of narcotics trafficking today, there is concern that success there may push drug trafficking back towards its former havens in Peru and Bolivia.

This aspect of the threat posed by transnational crime is of concern to major powers, such as the United States and the European Union, which have a vested interest in promoting democracy.

Third, transnational crime is seen as a threat to economic development (and therefore national security). During the 1990s, international financial institutions, international private banks, and transnational non-governmental organizations (NGOs) such as Transparency International increasingly focused on good government as a prerequisite for economic growth and have been promoting efforts to reduce corruption and improve judicial systems. International investors, who provide the capital critical for promoting economic growth in the developing world, also focus on transparency in government, the rule of law, and the reduction of corruption because it improves the likelihood that their investments will succeed and remain secure from either government or criminal interference. Organized crime is perceived as a threat to development insofar as it undermines the rule of law and deters foreign investment by increasing the level of violence and insecurity in host communities. In addition, criminals often reinvest their proceeds in the legal economy as part of its money laundering efforts, and these criminally affiliated businesses often have an unfair competitive advantage through their access to cheap capital and their ability to intimidate commercial adversaries. In societies with high levels of transnational crime, legitimate investors are often reluctant to commit resources.

KEY POINTS

- The crimes committed by transnational criminal groups often harm individuals and societies, but these are usually addressed by law enforcement and relevant social service agencies.
- Transnational crime often comes to be seen as a national security threat because of the added danger posed by the *modus operandi* of the perpetrators of transnational crime.
- Wealthy and powerful criminal groups engage in corruption and violence and reinvest their illicit profits in ways that undermine the basic functions of the state, democracy, and the economy.
- Unchecked, organized crime can penetrate the political and social elites of countries, at which point it is very difficult to defeat.

Definitions and key concepts

Transnational crime

Traditionally, transnational crime has referred to criminal activities extending into and violating the laws of two or more countries. Recently, the United Nations in its Convention Against Transnational Organized Crime has defined transnational crime a bit more broadly, to include any criminal activity that is conducted in more than one state, planned in one state but perpetrated in another, or committed in one state where there are spillover effects into neighbouring jurisdictions (United Nations Convention against Transnational Organized Crime 2000). Efforts to typify the nature of the activities labelled as transnational crime are similarly encompassing, as is suggested in Background 19.1.

There is widespread agreement that increasing globalization of economic activity has provided a wider range of activities and opportunities for truly transnational criminal enterprises to emerge. Just as businesses in the licit economy do, transnational criminals seek to match supply and demand and to take advantage of differences in profits, regulations, and risk levels between markets. These differences

BACKGROUND 19.1

Categories of transnational crime

1. Money laundering
2. Illicit drug trafficking
3. Corruption of public officials
4. Infiltration of legal businesses
5. Fraudulent bankruptcy
6. Insurance fraud
7. Computer crime
8. Theft of intellectual property
9. Illicit traffic in arms
10. Terrorism
11. Aircraft hijacking
12. Piracy
13. Hijacking on land
14. Trafficking in persons
15. Trade in human body parts
16. Theft of art and cultural objects
17. Environmental crime
18. Other illicit smuggling

***Source*: Gerhard O. W. Mueller (2001: 14); Fourth United Nations Survey of Crime Trends and Operations of Criminal Justice Systems (1994).**

may emerge from the availability of supply in certain regions that can be matched to demand in others, such as the flow of narcotics from Afghanistan and South America into Europe and the United States. In other cases, criminals may exploit differences in the regulation of activities, as is often the case in **money laundering** transactions that exploit variations in banking secrecy between off-shore financial havens and conventional banks. Variations in risk in performing activities may also shape the geographical presence of transnational crime, with criminal enterprises developing their **home bases** in low-risk, poorly governed states, such as Nigeria. Criminal activities are likely to take place in **host nations** where higher risks are compensated for by the lure of higher profits. Other countries are less important as markets (or hosts) for transnational crime groups, but contribute to the illicit economy as transshipment states, through which illicit goods pass, or as **service states** (as in the case of money laundering havens).

Although the terms 'transnational crime' and 'organized crime' are sometimes used interchangeably, not all transnational crime is committed by organized crime groups nor do all organized crime groups engage in transnational crime. Despite this distinction, most discussions of transnational crime *do* focus narrowly on crimes committed by organizations that exist specifically for the pursuit of profit through illicit activity. So-called 'occasional criminals'—individuals or businesses otherwise engaged in legitimate commercial activities who may commit transnational crimes—are excluded from consideration. Following this approach, the recent United Nations Convention addressing the threat from transnational crime focuses on transnational *organized* crime. This raises a number of questions. What is organized crime? Why should we focus on the organized groups that commit transnational crime rather than on the criminal activities themselves?

Organized crime

While there are few disagreements on what makes crime transnational, the meaning of organized crime has been hotly debated for decades. These debates have largely centred on the question of how organized crime is structured and what sets organized crime apart from other forms of crime (such as 'ordinary' street crimes or white-collar crime). (For a more detailed discussion of these debates, see the section on 'The organization of transnational crime: competing visions' below.)

Despite these ongoing disagreements, most observers agree that criminal groups differ widely in structure, strength, size and the range and diversity of activities that they undertake. This rather catholic view of the 'organized' in 'organized crime' is reflected in the most recent international definition of the term, which casts its net broadly in order to encompass a diversity of groups, as we can see in Background 19.2. According to article 2 of the UN Convention Against Transnational Organized Crime signed in December 2000, organized crime is defined as any 'structured group of three or more persons existing for a period of time and acting in concert with the aim of committing one or more serious crimes or offenses [. . .] in order to obtain, directly, or indirectly, a financial or other material benefit . . . '. A structured group is one that is 'not randomly formed for the immediate commission of an offence and that does not need to have formally defined roles for its members, continuity of its membership or a developed structure'.

The UN Convention's focus on *profit-driven* crime, which distinguishes organized crime from 'ordinary' crimes like rape or murder, also echoes prevailing definitions of organized crime. These profit-driven crimes can be grouped into three categories: predatory crimes for profit, which involve involuntary transfers (e.g., fraud); market-based exchanges in which illegal goods or services are sold for profit (e.g., drug trafficking); and commercial exchanges which involve the illegal production or distribution of otherwise legal goods or services (e.g., smuggling of cigarettes) (Naylor 2003).

Finally, the drafters of the UN Convention seem to share the view of analysts who have often highlighted three other characteristic features of organized crime: (1) the tendency to employ systematic corruption and violence; (2) the receipt of abnormally high rates of return relative to other

BACKGROUND 19.2

Sample of prominent transnational criminal groups

Italian Mafia: In Italy, this is a generic term applied to the Sicilian Mafia, Neapolitan Camorra, Calabrian 'Ndrangheta and the Apulian Sacra Corona Unita. Known for its connections to other organized crime elements such as the Colombian drug trafficking cartels.

Russian organized crime: based on legacy organized crime groupings that exploited the inefficiency of the Soviet centrally planned economy, now able to operate more freely in the lax post-Communist Russian state. These groups include persons from all the former Soviet states, including prominently Russians, Ukrainians, Chechens, Georgians and Azeris. They are known to have connections to organized crime in the United States and Western Europe.

Chinese Triads: Working predominantly from Hong Kong and Taiwan rather than the Chinese mainland, this is a highly fluid group that is based on ethnic affiliation. Involved with drug trafficking, prostitution, gambling, extortion and human trafficking. Have developed a presence throughout the Chinese international diaspora.

Japanese Yakuza (Boryokudan): Japan-based gangs that engage in some transnational crime, mainly drug trafficking and human smuggling for prostitution. Their activities are concentrated in Japan, South East Asia and the United States.

Colombian and other Latin American drug cartels: These groups are highly specialized and organized around the various stages of production and transportation of cocaine, heroin and marijuana from Bolivia, Peru and Colombia into the United States through Central America, Mexico and the Caribbean. Insurgent groups in Colombia and Peru have become involved in this type of organized crime as have transnational criminal groupings based in Mexico and in Central America.

Nigerian organized crime: These transnational organizations take advantage of weak rule of law in their home country and the Nigerian diaspora throughout the world to engage in organized drug trafficking, computer and mail fraud, and various forms of financial fraud.

***Source*: Williams and Savona (1998).**

criminal organizations; and (3) the subversion and infiltration of the legal economy through the reinvestment of illicit profits. These three characteristics are used to justify singling out organized crime as a subject of special concern. The modes of operation of organized crime groups and their resulting wealth and power are seen as posing a special harm to society, the economy, and the polity (though corruption, violence, and participation in the licit economy) that goes beyond the harm created by the profit-driven crimes (e.g., drug trafficking, fraud) they commit. This explains the long-standing law enforcement emphasis on dismantling criminal organizations and 'follow-the-money' methods which target criminal assets. A similar understanding is reflected in the articles of the recent UN Convention on Transnational Organized Crime which outlaw membership in an organized crime group, criminalize corruption, and target the profits of organized crime groups through anti-money laundering and asset forfeiture provisions.

KEY POINTS

- Transnational crime involves profit-driven criminal activity that crosses national boundaries.
- Not all organized crime is transnational, but there are growing incentives for criminal enterprises to operate across national borders due to differences in the supply and demand for illegal goods and services among countries.
- Organized crime is thought to be distinguished from other kinds of criminal activity not only by its structure but through its reliance on corruption and systematic violence to attain high profit levels which are often laundered through reinvestment in the legal economy.

The increase in transnational crime

Transnational crime is not a new phenomenon. Organized crime groups have operated transnationally for decades, if not centuries—consider, for example, the relations between the Italian and American Mafias since the 1950s, the smuggling operations of the Chinese triads, and cocaine trafficking by the Colombian Cali and Medellin drug 'cartels'. How then can we account for the widespread alarm over transnational crime in the 1990s?

Many observers argue that much of the concern was generated by the military, intelligence, and broader national security communities, which needed a new justification for their relevance (and budgets) in the post Cold War era (e.g., Beare 2003). Although there is some truth to this, there is also a consensus that a very real increase in the scale and scope of transnational crime occurred in the 1980s and 1990s. Transnational crime has become global in scale and is no longer exclusive to certain geographical areas or ethnic groups. There has been a marked increase in the number and size of illegal markets, the number of groups involved, the number of countries affected, and the overall amount of illicit trade (although it is not clear that the ratio of illicit to licit trade has increased). Whereas illegal markets were small and isolated in the past, today illicit markets tend to be interrelated and mutually supporting and to be more embedded in the legal economy than ever.

The increased scale and scope of transnational crime can be explained in large part by two developments. First, the increased transnational flow of people, goods, and money in the second half of the twentieth century (a process often referred to as 'globalization') has contributed to the growth of both licit and illicit economies which operate across national boundaries. Second, a wave of 'dual transitions' (away from closed economies and authoritarian political regimes) and an increase in civil unrest with the end of the Cold War have undermined state authority in a number of countries, providing a home base for crime groups or otherwise facilitating the operation of transnational criminal networks.

Globalization

Globalization refers to the increased transnational flow of people, goods, and money that has occurred during the second half of the twentieth century. This mobility has been greatly facilitated by advances in communications and transportation technologies, such as the advent of passenger air travel, the personal computer, the internet, and cellular communications. Contrary to what many argue, the importance of these technological changes for international mobility *can* be overstated; after all, they arguably do not represent as great a leap forward as the invention of the telegraph or the steamship—inventions which did not lead to an explosion in transnational crime (Levi 2002). However, the process of globalization, properly understood, is not just a matter of technological innovation but is even more fundamentally linked to the economic and political reforms that reduced the restrictions on the international movement of goods, people, and money in the 1980s and 1990s. A wave of market-oriented reforms in the developing and developed world beginning in the 1970s reduced barriers to trade and promoted the development of export-based economies. In addition, a wave of transitions toward democracy, beginning in 1974 in Southern Europe and moving to Latin America in the 1980s and on to Africa, Eastern Europe and the former Soviet Union following the fall of the Berlin Wall, increased transnational flows. Borders that had been closed shut under authoritarian rule now spilled open.

This largely positive process of economic and political liberalization had a 'dark side'. In an increasingly global marketplace, illicit actors, like their licit counterparts, take advantage of business opportunities wherever they occur. The growth of global trade and global financial networks provided an infrastructure and cover that illicit actors could exploit. For example, as a result of the creation of the North American Free Trade Area, trade between the United States and Mexico grew from $81 billion in 1993 to $243 billion in 2000 (Zoellick 2001). This land border is also one of the main routes for the smuggling of illegal goods and aliens into the United States. Burgeoning cross-border traffic increases the opportunities for criminals to hide their activities within the flow of legal commerce, while law enforcement reports ever greater difficulty in monitoring this traffic. Only 5% of bulk shipping containers entering the United States by sea undergo physical inspection (Robinson, Lake and Seghetti 2005: 14). The globalization of financial markets has accelerated dramatically since the 1990s, making it easier for criminals to quickly and secretly move and store their profits (IMF WEO 2005: 109–10). The challenge to governments is to find the criminal 'signal' within the 'noise' generated by the large and growing amounts of international trade and finance produced by globalization.

In addition to enabling movement of people across borders, globalization has made it easier for migrants to remain in contact with their homelands long after they have resettled elsewhere. The end of the Cold War created new opportunities for economic migrants from the former Soviet states, as did the continuing economic disparities between the developing and developed world. The sharp increase in civil conflicts around the globe also created a new generation of refugees. These diasporas have provided some of the avenues by which individuals in different states can achieve the level of mutual trust required to sustain a transnational criminal enterprise. Groups such as the Chinese triads operating in Hong Kong, the United States, and Western Europe or Kosovar drug smuggling networks in Western Europe depend on the links maintained between individuals of similar cultural backgrounds across borders. Unassimilated ethnic minority populations are often vulnerable to exploitation by criminals yet also fearful of cooperation with law enforcement. In addition, there is evidence that globalization has also allowed the creation of new forms of cooperation among transnational criminal organizations that do not depend on ethnic ties to maintain trust, as suggested in recent studies by both the European Union (2003) and the United Nations (2002).

The undermining of state authority

As noted above, dual transitions toward free-market economies and democracy in the 1980s and 1990s contributed greatly to the increased mobility of people, goods, and money that provided increased opportunities for transnational crime. In many countries these dual transitions have contributed to the spread of transnational crime in another way as well. This section refers to transitions that have gone awry, leaving behind a state that is often unable to assert the rule of law (so-called 'grey' areas) or even exert control over its territory (creating 'ungoverned spaces'). These grey and ungoverned areas have provided the home base for a wide range of groups engaged in transnational criminal activities: from organized criminals to warlords to insurgents.

A paradigmatic case of the emergence of organized crime in the wake of dual transitions can be found in post-Soviet Russia. Here, economic 'fixers' who had greased the wheels of the pre-1991 command economy and small organized crime groups that survived the Soviet period joined with some discharged elements of the Soviet intelligence and security apparatus and emerging entrepreneurs to take advantage of the poorly regulated transitional economy. Combining inside knowledge of state enterprises and resources, access to intelligence and surveillance files, experience and contacts in the West, and expertise in violence and intimidation, these new organized crime elements were well positioned to exploit the weaknesses of the emerging Russian state to great personal advantage (Fickenauer and Voronin 2001: 6–9). The efforts of these emerging organized crime groups did much to undermine investor confidence in the Russian economy, driving up the cost of doing business and aggravating a scarcity of legal capital for legitimate business development. They also delegitimized the new Russian democratic regime by calling into question its ability to maintain the rule of law and provide for public safety.

The ethnic and civil conflicts that re-emerged in the wake of the Cold War also provided an exceptionally conducive environment for the development of complex transnational criminal enterprises. The collapse in governability in areas such as Somalia after 1990 led to warlordism, in which the military power of tribal and clan militias was sustained by illegal activities, particularly the Qat narcotics trade. Here, armed groups did not always cross borders regionally to engage in criminal activities, but often worked with a network of middlemen to traffic narcotics to customers outside the Horn of Africa (Piombo 2006).

Similarly, the internecine warfare of the Balkans created particularly complex networks that included organized crime, paramilitaries, intelligence officials, military forces and law enforcement agencies within the former Yugoslavia. The embargo against the warring states created new asymmetries that could be exploited by organized crime through the trafficking of commodities, gasoline, and arms. With the connivance of local authorities, organized crime groups trafficked women into Western Europe and, in some instances, to the peacekeeping forces attempting to reduce the level of conflict. These groups included the highest levels of society within the former Yugoslavia, including the leadership of Serbia, which used these networks to enrich themselves and provide the supplies necessary for their forces to continue the war. Similarly, Kosovar drug traffickers in Western Europe generated funding necessary to support the insurgency of the Kosovo Liberation Army in their home territory. In the wake of the war, these organized crime elements proved to be particularly difficult to control, at one point even participating in the assassination of the Serbian Prime Minister, Zoran Dindic, in 2003. The inclusion of law enforcement, intelligence and military officials in these transnational crime networks explains their ability to endure beyond the end of the Balkan wars and the advent of democracy in the region (Saponja-Hadzic 2003).

KEY POINTS

- Transnational crime increased in scale and scope by the 1990s, with a jump in the number of groups involved, range of countries affected, and the number and density of illicit markets.
- The increased globalization of trade, finances, and travel has produced an environment conducive to transnational crime by making it easier for criminals to move illicit profits and illegal goods, provide service, and smuggle persons across state borders.
- The wave of political transitions to democracy and economic transitions to free markets since the 1980s, often simultaneously in the same country, have occasionally gone awry, undermining state capacity to enforce the rule of law and creating new opportunities for organized crime to penetrate societies in transition.
- The multiplication of ethnically and religiously based civil wars since the end of the Cold War have produced the breakdown of the rule of law in many parts of the globe and created new opportunities for organized crime to profit from smuggling weapons, supplies, and people, often under the protection of the warring parties.

The organization of transnational crime: competing visions

Key features of the organization of TNC

In the 1990s 'network' forms of organization became increasingly important for both legal and illegal enterprises. Hierarchical organizations no longer had to recruit personnel with the full range of specialized skill sets necessary for various illicit operations. Instead, fluid and readily adaptable networks of individuals and organizations could group together and disband as required by the needs of particular criminal ventures. Operations like money laundering or the manufacturing of false identities could be outsourced to independent specialized contractors, who might very well be part of multiple criminal networks. Networks (defined simply as a relationship between 'nodes') coexist with, and increase the efficiency of, hierarchies and markets.

A series of changes, all apparent by the 1990s, can explain the increasing importance of networks. Innovations in technology greatly facilitated communication among and between individuals and groups, enhancing their ability to form and disband networks as circumstances warranted. These innovations and the proliferation of illicit markets had the effect of 'democratizing' the criminal underworld, making it easier for individuals to participate in crime without the need for large, hierarchical organizations to provide the infrastructure and necessary social contacts. In addition, the increasing incidence of the network form can be seen as a by-product of law enforcement's success in targeting large organized crime groups. Some stress how clever criminals, engaging in a process of strategic risk minimization, have chosen networks as the optimal form of organization to elude capture. Others simply note that the network form was what was left behind after law enforcement dismantled the upper leadership of key groups such as the Medellin and Cali cartels in Colombia.

As a result, transnational organized crime groups in the 1990s vary greatly in their size, structure, and activities. The entry of new criminal groups into illicit markets in the 1990s and the ability to group and disband with ease permits a wider variety of groups than ever before to participate effectively in transnational crime. Significantly, the groups vary in the extent to which they use corruption and political influence to facilitate their crimes and in the degree to which they penetrate the legal economy—all features typically thought to be characteristic of organized crime (UN 2002).

Finally, transnational crime groups often compete with one another, but they also engage in a great deal of collaboration in order to gain access to markets or product and benefit from economies of scale. Although organized crime was widely thought to be organized along ethnic lines in the past, it is now clear that opportunism, as much as shared social characteristics, drives collaboration (European Union 2003). An earlier harbinger of this trend was the widely noted alliance between Colombian cartels and the Sicilian mafia in the late 1980s to facilitate the entry of cocaine into Europe. This and other alliances (particularly involving Russian crime groups in the 1990s) suggested to some observers that transnational partnerships provided organized crime with a greater reach than ever.

Despite agreeing on these organizational features of transnational organized crime, analysts tend to divide into three different camps when assessing their significance. Each camp focuses on one of the diverse organizational forms which coexist—hierarchy, networks, or markets—as the most important for understanding the 'true' nature of transnational crime, with implications for how harmful we consider organized crime groups and how the threat should be addressed. (See Think Point 19.1 for an illustration.)

THINK POINT 19.1

Competing visions of the Cali and Medellin drug trafficking cartels

Critics of the hierarchical view of organized crime note that the Italian Cosa Nostra in the United States, the Sicilian mafia, and the Cali and Medellin drug trafficking cartels in Colombia were *not* organized as monopolistic business corporations which 'cornered' the criminal market. Despite their label, the Colombian drug trafficking organizations were not cartels that controlled the levels of production of cocaine or its distribution. While the groups were structured hierarchically to provide *governance* of the illicit marketplace (e.g., the use of violence to enforce contracts), they did not exercise close control over the operation of profit-making activities by their members, which often depended on the independent initiative of subordinates in the hierarchy who kept much of the profits for themselves. In spite of this, law enforcement officials and many analysts argued that the large and hierarchical nature of these organizations posed a significant threat to political stability in Colombia. For example, Pablo Escobar, head of the Medellin cartel, orchestrated the assassination of police officers and politicians as part of his campaign to avoid extradition to the United States. The Cali cartel, in contrast, worked quietly behind the scenes to undermine democracy, offering bribes to politicians (including an alleged $6 million contribution to the successful presidential campaign of Ernesto Samper). According to the hierarchical perspective, the government's defeat of the cartels in the early to mid 1990s removed an important threat to the Colombian state, even though it had little impact on the overall drug trade. Advocates of the network perspective view the same set of events somewhat differently. They emphasize the network forms of organization that coexisted with the hierarchical cartels, and the ability of these networks to continue drug production and trafficking largely uninterrupted after the jailing of the cartels' top leadership. They also stress how these smaller groups may be even more dangerous than the cartels they replaced. As decentralized groups, they are presumably more efficient and their lower profile and the lack of government intelligence on their operations allows them to work more surreptitiously than the cartels had. Finally, the market advocates place somewhat less importance on the organizational forms that drug trafficking takes, pointing instead to the profits to be earned from the drug trade as a guarantee of its continued existence.

Hierarchical visions of transnational organized crime

The term 'organized crime' was originally used to refer to hierarchical crime groups which were believed to monopolize the criminal market in a given area and which systematically deployed violence and corruption in pursuit of their ends. This view lent itself to notions of a centrally orchestrated conspiracy by leaders of organized crime groups to carve up the world into their own individual fiefdoms. While almost all analysts dismiss notions of monopolistic control today, many still believe that hierarchically organized groups play a strategic role in transnational crime today and are more powerful, wealthy, and dangerous than other organized criminals (UN 2002).

Two key sets of widely adopted policy recommendations flow from this analysis, which focuses on the extra level of harm posed by organized crime groups above and beyond the damage caused by the profit-driven crimes they commit. First is the need to target the leadership of criminal organizations, with the expectation that the downfall of these groups that are responsible for a large share of criminal activity in a given market would lead to a decrease in crime levels. Second is the targeting of the proceeds of criminal groups as a way of reducing the power of these groups, particularly the extent to which they could undermine the legitimate economy.

Network visions of transnational organized crime

This school of thought identifies the network form of organization as the defining characteristic of transnational crime since the 1990s, highlighting the entrepreneurial flair, scale, sophistication, flexibility, and resilience of this form of organization. Like the hierarchical approach, this school believes criminal organizations themselves pose a threat to society that goes far beyond the harm posed by the profit-driven crimes they commit. Criminal organizations use violence and corruption, accumulate wealth and power, and engage in strategic collaboration with other groups, increasing both their effectiveness and the danger they present. While there is no formal centralized group or confederation of leaders that directs this collaboration, networks permit a level of cooperation that is ultimately more threatening, because it is much less vulnerable to law enforcement. Individual organizations display a level of sophistication and resilience that is beyond the capability of most law enforcement agencies to address.

As with the hierarchical approach, the policy response is to target the criminal organizations and their proceeds, but the networked nature of criminal groups demands certain innovations. Rather than targeting the leadership of organizations, the 'nodes' crucial to the operation of the network must be identified and disabled. In addition to changing tactics, governments must fundamentally change their way of being to combat criminal networks. Government bureaucracies—inflexible hierarchies largely incapable of cooperating fluidly across jurisdictions or agency lines—must 'form networks to fight networks' (Williams 2001).

Market visions of transnational organized crime

Finally, a key group of scholars argues that it is more important to think of transnational crime as a marketplace rather than a network of groups (Beare, Naylor 2002). The need to minimize risk (i.e., avoid law enforcement) and other limits imposed by the illicit marketplace means criminal organizations will tend to be small, vulnerable and competitive—a far cry from the monopolies or collusive oligarchies stressed in the hierarchical vision of organized crime. While network theorists point to the adaptability and sophistication of criminal networks as a key source of their resilience in the face of law enforcement efforts, the market scholars note that the 'great majority of crime is the province of small-time losers' (Naylor 2002: 10). From this perspective, the resilience of transnational crime can be attributed to the inexorable logic of the marketplace—supply rising to meet demand—rather than the sophistication or entrepreneurial flair of individual organizations.

For market theorists, collaboration among criminals is neither an innovation of the illicit marketplace of the 1990s nor is it a particularly fearsome development. 'Tactical alliances' among criminal groups have a long history—for example, the long-standing agreement between French-Corsican mafia groups and Turkish heroin producers to smuggle heroin into the United States in the 1960s and 1970s. Market analysts, citing numerous instances of grossly over-inflated official estimates of criminal profits, doubt that criminal alliances create organizations with the level of wealth and power that government rhetoric commonly attributes to them. If the wealth of these groups is not as great as is widely believed, their threat to the licit economy is reduced. In fact, market analysts believe that white-collar and corporate crimes contribute much more to undermining the licit economy. Similarly, this camp argues that organized crime groups are no more prone than ordinary street criminals and corporate criminals to use violence and corruption, respectively.

From this perspective, an emphasis on transnational *organized* crime, like that embodied in the recent UN Convention, is misplaced. Instead, transnational crime writ large should be of concern to the international community; collaborators of organized crime groups in the licit sector should be targeted with as much, if not more, vigour as the career criminals themselves; and policy makers should conduct market-by-market analyses of different illicit activities to yield strategies that are more useful than generic, tactical advice to target criminal groups.

KEY POINTS

- Most observers agree that transnational crime groups vary greatly in their size, organization, and modes of operation; that in the 1990s network forms of organization became more important; and that there is a high level of cooperation between groups.
- Analysts disagree over whether the dominant organizational form of transnational crime is hierarchical, networked or market based. This matters because different organizational forms imply different levels of threat to societies and therefore justify different levels and types of government response.
- Proponents of a hierarchical view of organized crime view these groups as wealthy, powerful, violent, and under the control of a small number of individuals.
- Networks have been used to describe more recent forms of criminal organization in which hierarchy is less important and activities are decentralized. Analysts argue that networks represent the best compromise between profit maximizing and risk minimizing organizational forms.
- Critics of the hierarchy and the network perspectives argue that organized crime is in fact highly disorganized, and resembles more a market for illicit goods and services than an organization. Proponents of this view minimize the threat posed by organized criminals to states and societies.

Transnational crime and terrorism

At the height of the US 'war on drugs' in the 1980s analysts and policy makers, noting a growing guerrilla involvement in the drug trade in Colombia and Peru, first began to express real concern over a crime-terror 'nexus'. Was this nexus a 'strategic alliance' or a mere 'marriage of convenience'? Advocates of the former perspective believed that guerrillas and drug traffickers would work hand in glove in pursuit of their shared interests in money-making and destabilizing the state; the multiplier effect of such cooperation would be potentially devastating. Critics of this view stressed the different motives possessed by the two groups (ideology versus profit) and argued that criminal groups would most likely eschew collaboration with terrorists so as to stay off law enforcement's radar screen. Cooperation would be tactical and short term, and thus of little significance. In addition, criminals would jealously guard their control over illicit enterprises, thus creating barriers to entry for terrorists interested in engaging in criminal activities.

As attention to the drug war waned in the United States in the 1990s, so too did interest in the possible connections between transnational crime and terrorism. The terrorist attacks of 11 September 2001 in the United States changed all this and gave rise to a new wave of studies on the topic. Most observers believe that the 1990s witnessed a growing direct participation of 'terrorist' groups in transnational crime, as state sponsorship for terrorism declined as a result of the end of the Cold War and as religiously motivated terrorism (which generally did not receive direct state sponsorship) increased in importance. Members or supporters of Hezbollah engaged in various criminal schemes in the United States, such as cigarette smuggling and coupon fraud, and in smuggling and counterfeiting in the largely lawless 'Tri-border' frontier area of Argentina, Brazil and Paraguay. Al-Qaeda cells in Western Europe engaged in credit card fraud. Notably, for neither of these groups was criminal activity amongst their most important source of funds, nor is it clear whether the crimes rose to the level of 'transnational' until the illicit gains were transferred abroad. To the extent that the Marxist-Leninist terrorist groups of the 1970s and 1980s engaged primarily in domestic crimes—bank robbery, extortion, or kidnapping in the country where they operated—the 1990s represented a change.

If 'terrorist' is used broadly to refer to all non-state actors that employ terrorism as a tactic—including insurgents whose goal is to overthrow a given government and 'warlords' with claims to political power at a subnational level—then we might more safely say that there has been an increase in terrorist reliance on transnational crime. Since the end of the Cold War, these groups have proliferated in 'ungoverned' areas and can exploit natural resources under their control or profit from trafficking routes that pass through their territory. Warlords in Africa have benefited from illicit trade in diamonds; Iraqi insurgents resale hijacked petroleum and traffic in drugs; and guerrillas and paramilitary groups in Colombia have greatly increased their participation in the cocaine trade in the 1990s with the demise of the Medellin and Cali cartels. As the latter example suggests, the decentralization of transnational crime groups that was evident by the 1990s has contributed to the ability of 'terrorists' to increase their involvement in crime. Illicit markets are characterized less by large criminal groups protecting their turf from incursion and more by smaller groups seeking to network with terrorists.

There is less agreement on whether there is a 'strategic alliance' between terrorists and criminal groups (and what the significance of such an alliance might be). The US State Department emphasizes that the two groups share 'methods but not motives'. Terrorists may rely on criminal activities to raise money and carry out their operations (e.g., forfeiting documents, illegally crossing borders), but their goal remains ideological rather than the sole pursuit of profit. A growing number of analysts, however, have begun to stress the 'blurring of lines' between criminals and terrorists (Shelley 2005). It has become commonplace to indiscriminately label all insurgent groups engaged heavily in crime as a means of fund raising as 'fighters turned felons'—a label that ignores the ongoing ideological motivations of these groups. (For a critical evaluation of the link between criminals and terrorists, see Prefontaine and Dandurand.)

A potentially important phenomenon which has received much less attention is the case of what might be called 'felons turned zealots'. There is some evidence that criminals and terrorists who share jail cells also develop shared interests in joint criminal and terrorist ventures upon their release. This has been documented not only in South Asia, but also in the Madrid bombings, in which a radicalized drug dealing organization played an instrumental role.

Analysts who raise the spectre of a 'strategic alliance' believe that such a partnership will increase the danger posed by terrorist groups, which will no longer have to divert resources to engage in crime themselves, will have access to greater financial resources, and will be able to apply criminal expertise to their terrorist operations. Sceptics believe that the alliance between criminals and terrorists is, at best, exaggerated and, at worst, manufactured by governments to criminalize and repress legitimate insurgent groups (Naylor 2002).

KEY POINTS

- Terrorist groups often rely on crime to fund and carry out their operations.
- There is increasing concern over the convergence of terrorism and transnational crime, but there is no consensus about whether this phenomenon is a long-term strategic alliance or episodic 'marriages of convenience'.
- There is growing evidence that terrorists and organized crime groups may converge in their motives because of the radicalization of criminals by terrorists during periods when they are in close proximity, such as when they share prisons.

Government responses

Prior to the end of the Cold War, organized crime was seen primarily as a domestic problem and the transnational dimensions were often handled in an ad hoc and bilateral manner. The only institutionalized international venues for information sharing were the UN Crime Prevention and Criminal Justice Division and Interpol. In particular, Interpol was primarily seen as a vehicle for addressing the problem posed by criminals crossing state boundaries to evade capture. However, since then, state responses to transnational crime have evolved in parallel with the growing perception that this phenomenon represents a national security threat.

The US 'war on drugs' in the 1970s and especially the 1980s, rather than a concern with transnational crime per se, led to an increased emphasis on both bilateral and multilateral cooperation on law enforcement. In particular, the United States used financial carrots and sticks on a bilateral basis to induce host states to increase regulation and enforcement against transnational crime. In the case of cocaine trafficking from the Andean region, the United States both provided the carrot of increased assistance and training to countries where the drug cartels operated, and also used the threat of decertification (which provided for the suspension of US assistance) to increase the costs of not cooperating with the United States. During the 1970s and 1980s, US drug enforcement agencies also cooperated with European law enforcement to export more aggressive investigative and intelligence-based approaches to countering narcotics trafficking. They were not always successful, particularly because there was some resistance from Europeans to techniques based on undercover work, such as entrapment of drug consumers and the 'flipping' of traffickers to develop informants. In addition, some countries resisted criminalization of drugs and advocated a public health approach, most notably the Netherlands (Nadelmann 1999).

US and European efforts to control narcotics trafficking also led to the emergence of the first international norms and conventions explicitly addressing transnational crime. These included the UN Convention against Illicit Traffic in Narcotic Drugs and Pyschotropic Substances (1988) and the establishment of the Financial Action Task Force (1990) under G8 auspices to tackle money laundering.

With the extension of transnational crime to new areas of the globe in the 1990s, increasing numbers of nations began to see transnational crime as a serious problem and were willing to take measures to reduce the asymmetries between countries though harmonization of legislation and increasing police capacity. The United States, for example, in the 1996 US National Security strategy took a renewed interest in fostering international mechanisms for tackling transnational crime (see Background 19.3). The European Union also responded by building more robust regional responses, such as the European Police Office, EUROPOL, which began limited operations in 1994 and reached full operational status in 1999 in response to a rising tide of organized criminal enterprises emanating from the former Soviet states and the conflict-ridden Balkans (see Case Study 19.2). In addition, international financial institutions, which were major promoters of the internationalization of trade and finance, began to fund programmes to address the unintended increase in crime that accompanied the process of globalization. The World Bank was particularly at the forefront of emphasizing building up the capacity of judicial systems as a mechanism to ensure good government and the rule of law.

International diplomacy under the auspices of the United Nations also played an important role in creating uniform legislation addressing transnational crime. The UN Convention on Transnational Organized Crime finally came into effect in September 2003, and signatory states were bound to put its provisions into effect by changing their national legislation and procedures. This measure, together with the Convention against Corruption which came into effect in December 2005, was accompanied by major efforts to draft model legislation and develop other supporting measures that would allow signatory states to implement uniform legislation.

BACKGROUND 19.3

1996 US National Security Strategy on the threat of transnational crime

International organized crime jeopardizes the global trend toward peace and freedom, undermines fragile new democracies, saps the strength from developing countries and threatens our efforts to build a safer, more prosperous world. The rise of organized crime in the new independent states of the former Soviet Union and Central Europe weakens new democracies and poses a direct threat to US interests, particularly in light of the potential for the theft and smuggling by organized criminals of nuclear materials left within some of these nations.

. . .

Because the threat of organized crime comes from abroad as well as at home, we will work with other nations to keep our citizens safe. The President's invitation at the United Nations to all countries to join the United States in fighting international organized crime by measures of their own and by negotiating and endorsing an international declaration on citizens' safety—a declaration which would include a 'no-sanctuary for organized criminals' pledge—is an effort to enhance our international cooperative efforts to protect our people.

***Source*: The White House, *A National Security Strategy of Enlargement and Engagement*, February 1996.**

CASE STUDY 19.2

EUROPOL

The European Police Organization (EUROPOL) was first conceived as part of the Maastricht Treaty negotiations by European Union member states in 1992. The convention formally creating the organization was ratified by the EU members in 1998 and began operations in 1999. Based in The Hague in the Netherlands, it initially focused on fighting drug trafficking, but later expanded to target a broader array of transnational crimes, including trafficking in human beings, smuggling, terrorism, financial crimes and money laundering. EUROPOL assists member states with criminal intelligence and information sharing, providing technical support for investigations, sharing best investigative practices among members, and providing strategic threat assessments for the European Union.

***Source*: www.europol.eu.int**

In addition, as transnational crime became increasingly perceived as a national security threat, governments turned to more drastic responses. Many government devoted additional resources to law enforcement and introduced more draconian legal measures, some of which arguably endangered civil liberties, such as the forfeiture of all assets held by persons participating in organized crime schemes, not just those related to the crime itself. In addition, governments considered how emerging technologies, often derived from military programmes, could be put to use in improving the ability of government to gather information on transnational crime and, in some cases, how the military could be used to attack this threat. The arguments that emerged after the 9/11 attacks on the United States around an alleged terrorism-organized crime nexus also seem to be leading governments down the path to the militarization of law enforcement once again.

However, an intermediate approach to transnational crime is emerging, one which acknowledges the national security dimensions of the threat, but calls for using all elements of national power to address it. These include a focus on targeting the illicit markets that facilitate the operation of transnational criminal enterprises and the underlying conditions that facilitate such markets, such as state failure or corruption. It also calls for better use of national strategic intelligence assets to support law enforcement efforts on transnational crime, rather than the militarization of the response. The private sector and non-governmental organizations can be incorporated into the solution, both by setting industry-wide standards designed to combat organized crime, as has been done by the international banking industry, and through civic education designed to help citizens resist the influence of these groups in their lives. NGOs can also play an important role in linking transnational crime and a wide range of other important issues on the international agenda such as responses to conflict situations, peacekeeping, promotion of the rule of law, and protection of human rights (Godson and Williams 1998). This brings a new set of groups and agencies to bear on the problem, checks the penetration of government and the private sector by transnational crime, and provides new avenues by which citizens can hold states accountable for this problem.

KEY POINTS

- The US war on drugs largely drove initial state and international responses to transnational crime in the 1980s.
- As transnational crime spread in the 1990s, more and more nations became interested in coordinating regional and international responses to the issue.
- Governments have increasingly come to perceive transnational crime as a national security threat, leading to the temptation to use intelligence assets and the military to supplement law enforcement.
- At the same time, the concern of international financial institutions and non-governmental organizations with corruption and state failure—two issues closely related to transnational crime—holds the promise of more comprehensive national responses to supplement law enforcement.

Conclusion

Transnational crime has expanded aggressively in the last quarter century, particularly since the end of the Cold War has opened up new possibilities for criminal enterprises. Globalization has particularly facilitated not only the development of new criminal markets but also new forms of organization. The available evidence suggests that organized crime is becoming more difficult to fight because it has become more adaptable and resistant to available law enforcement strategies. Even if organized crime networks turn out to be more vulnerable than many analysts believe, the ability for organized crime to form tactical or strategic alliances more easily today should give governments cause for concern.

Ironically, the global trends most welcomed by leaders in developed countries, globalization, democratization and economic liberalization, also have a dark side: the capacity to create new spaces for the spread of transnational crime. Just as these trends promote greater political, economic and personal freedom, they also facilitate the ability of criminals to transcend national jurisdictions. Even if countries were to decide that the costs of globalization outweighed the benefits, these are trends that are largely beyond the control of any single government. The question becomes one of how to contain this phenomenon and reduce the harm it causes.

This is particularly true if we consider that organized crime not only targets individuals but undermines societies, particularly those in transition to democracy and free markets. The threat that transnational crime poses to whole regions, be it the Horn of Africa or the Balkans, means that even governments with relatively robust law enforcement capabilities and well established rule of law are faced with the spillover effects of transnational crime based in poorly governed areas of the globe.

Does this rise to the level of a national security threat, justifying the use of intelligence and military assets, and perhaps even a certain level of expediency in the pursuit of justice? Not all governments or societies will concur. Those countries where law enforcement and judiciaries are highly capable and adapt sufficiently quickly to contain transnational crime are unlikely to face such a choice. However, in countries where voters believe that the rule of law and personal safety is disappearing, pressure will develop for politicians to seek more draconian solutions. This is particularly true where a link is established, correctly or not, between transnational crime and terrorism. In extreme cases, it can lead to support for more authoritarian forms of government and restrictions on free markets, as is arguably occurring today in Russia.

The question is therefore what can governments, the private sector and civil society do to reduce the harm caused by transnational crime before they are driven to extreme measures? Clearly, there is some room for solutions short of militarization. One approach suggests greater cooperation between law enforcement and national intelligence assets to address threats that cross borders. Others have suggested greater attention to preventive measures, particularly by those developed states with the greatest stake in the success of the emerging international system. To the extent that the United States, Western Europe, Australia and Japan value democracy and free markets, then it makes sense for them to engage in capacity building processes designed to strengthen the rule of law and law enforcement agencies, particularly in countries that are experiencing so-called dual transitions. Given what we also know about the consequences of civil war for the proliferation of transnational crime, this also suggests another arena for anticipatory measures.

? QUESTIONS

What factors enabled the expansion of transnational crime during the 1990s?

What is new about transnational crime in the 1990s?

Does it matter if transnational crime is organized as hierarchies, as networks, or as markets?

Is transnational organized crime a greater threat than other forms of illicit activity?

In what ways has the process of globalization affected the levels and nature of transnational crime?

What factors affect the extent to which terrorist groups and transnational criminal groups cooperate?

What factors make countries attractive as home bases for transnational crime? As host nations or service states?

What indicators should we consider in deciding whether transnational crime has become a national security threat?

According to the competing visions on the organization of transnational crime, are efforts by the United Nations to develop an international convention against transnational crime well conceived and effective?

What factors affect the willingness of governments to cooperate across borders to fight transnational crimes?

FURTHER READING

- **Beare, Margaret E. (ed.) (2003),** ***Critical Reflections on Transnational Organized Crime, Money Laundering, and Corruption*****, Toronto: University of Toronto Press**. A critical review of mainstream understandings of transnational organized crime and the costs and unanticipated consequences of law enforcement strategies to deal with the problem.

- **Berdal, M. and Serrano, M. (eds.) (2002),** ***Transnational Organized Crime and International Security: Business as Usual?*** **Boulder, CO: Lynne Rienner Publishers**. An edited volume that surveys the relationship between globalization, economic reform, and transnational organized crime; the response of international organizations to the threat; and regional trends in transnational organized crime.

- **Nadelmann, Ethan A. (1999),** ***Cops Across Borders: The Internationalization of U.S. Criminal Law Enforcement*****, University Park, PA: Penn State Press**. A seminal examination of the spread of U.S. law enforcement practices and techniques to other law enforcement establishments across the world.

- **Naylor, R.T. (2002),** ***Wages of Crime: Black Markets, Illegal Finances, and the Wages of Crime*****, Cornell, NY: Cornell University Press**. This book presents a critique of both the views of organized crime as a powerful hierarchical organization and a threat to national security.

- **Prefontaine, D.C. and Dandurand, Yvon (2004), 'Terrorism and Organized Crime: Reflections on an Illusive Link and its Implications for Criminal Law Reform', paper prepared for the annual meeting of the International Society for Criminal Law Reform, Montreal, August accessed at http://www.icclr.law.ubc.ca/Publications/Reports/International%20Society%20Paper%20of%20Terrorism.pdf** provides a comprehensive and critical review of the argument that terrorism and transnational criminal organizations are converging and may begin to cooperate to a greater extent.

- **United Nations Office on Drugs and Crime, Global Programme Against Transnational Organized Crime (2002),** ***Results of a Pilot Survey of Forty Selected Organized Criminal Groups in Sixteen Countries*****, September**. Reports the findings from a 1999 survey of law enforcement and academic experts on organized crime that attempts to gather systematic information on trends in transnational crime and the organizational forms that transnational crime groups take.

- **Williams, Phil (2001), 'Transnational Criminal Networks' in J. Arquilla and D. Ronfeldt (eds.),** ***Networks and Netwars: The Future of Terror, Crime and Militancy*****. Santa Monica, CA: RAND Corporation 61–97**. This RAND study uses network theory to explain the organization of transnational crime and argues that networked criminal organizations are more flexible and robust than the governments that target them.

- **Williams, Phil and Vlassos, Dimitri (eds.) (2001),** ***Combating Transnational Crime: Concepts, Activities and Responses*****, London: Frank Cass Publishers**. Comprehensive survey of the state of transnational crime and the attempts by governments to respond to this threat.

IMPORTANT WEBSITES

- **www.unodc.org** United Nations Office on Drugs and Crime (UNODC): The UNODC is one of the leading international agencies focused on assisting states in developing international efforts to fight drug trafficking, terrorism, and organized crime. This website is a good source of information on international conventions dealing with transnational crime.
- **www.interpol.int** Interpol—International Criminal Police Organization: Interpol is the leading international police organization with 184 member states. This website provides information on how member states cooperate on transnational crime issues.
- **www.american.edu/tracc/** Transnational Crime and Corruption Center—American University: This centre brings together a large collection of academic and policy research on transnational crime, as well as providing a comprehensive set of links to other online resources on this subject.
- **www.ojp.usdoj.gov/nij/international/welcome.html** US National Institute of Justice—International Programmes: This website provides a gateway to information on US policies and programmes targeting transnational crime. It also provides access to government-sponsored academic research and numerous links to other organizations focusing on transnational crime issues.
- **www.europol.eu.int** EUROPOL—European Police Office: This website provides a good overview of European Union efforts to combat transnational crime.

Visit the Online Resource Centre that accompanies this book for lots of interesting additional material: www.oxfordtextbooks.co.uk/orc/collins/

20 Children and War

HELEN BROCKLEHURST

Chapter Contents

Reader's Guide

This chapter introduces the reader to the agency of children in international relations and their presence in practices of security. It begins with an outline of children in the international political system and then moves on to consider the implications of thinking about children in the context of security. It uncovers many of their roles in a range of wars and then focuses on child soldiers. It is argued that children's smaller bodies and less developed minds contribute to practices of war. In addition, constructs of childhood and innocence are at work in our everyday conceptions of what matters in security. Issues of reintegration of children after war are illustrated, and finally a reconsideration of children in our concepts of what is political is explored.

Introduction: children in global politics

Since wars have been recorded children have been involved in their prosecution; many successfully or famously so, such as Alexander the Great, Joan of Arc, the mythic children's crusaders and captains of 'nursery' ships under Napoleon. Many children today are also participating in wars and conflicts but arguably in a greater variety of roles than they experienced in the past, particularly as 'underage', illegal or hidden child soldiers, and as soft targets and victims. It is a reflection of the importance of children and scale of their involvement in war that they have now become part of the agenda in 'high politics' or recognized in the subject of security. In 1999, for the first time, the UN Security Council passed a resolution on 'Children and Armed Conflict'; since then it has produced another three. In December 2003 the European Union's Political and Security Committee also agreed to its own guidelines on 'Children and Armed Conflict'. In February 2005 the United Nations Security Council again began considering the recruitment or use of child soldiers, their abuse in war and their reintegration and rehabilitation.

However, children have long had political capital and agency within the international political system more generally, not only or most significantly as child combatants; it is mostly our recognition, not children's presence that is new. From the Cold War to civil wars, and from total war to totalitarianism, there are many recorded and often parallel uses of children as political currency in some way—as threats, models, investments, instruments, resources, symbols and icons. Through institutions of the home, school and military, propaganda and through policies of health and welfare, children have often been at the centre of security-driven practices and participated significantly in intra-state and interstate practices of security and insecurity (Brocklehurst 2006). Children's bodies, minds, and adults' vulnerability towards particular ideas about children can function to make children effective weapons. The construction or the image of a child is also important here, invoked in the minds of those fighting for their 'women and children' or evidenced in the Latin American protest movement *The Mothers of the Plaza de Mayo* whose grown-up children 'disappeared' during Argentine military rule.

Which children—whose security?

There is no single agreed definition of a child which is in use worldwide for any purpose. Neither is there agreement on the related question of how long childhood is, or for example at what point we become adults, or what it is that makes childhood unique, special or a time of 'innocence'. Such definitions and contexts are, however, important and determine or help explain how we treat children. You may have been surprised to see a chapter on children in a book about security. You may also expect it to be about particular kinds of children who are soldiers or made victims. In this way you too assist in making children the social, cultural and political constructs they are, rather than simply biological facts.

An internationally accepted definition of children, codified in the UN Convention on the Rights of the Child for example, is that children are all persons under the age of 18. In the eyes of the law a young person under 18 years may be variously termed a child, a juvenile, a minor, and not yet a citizen. Such a person may, however, also be a worker, a patriot, a fighter, a carer, a mother or father, a husband or wife. Perhaps surprisingly, the most common duration of childhood in practice is far shorter than in the West, and ends from about eight years old to twelve years old; before puberty, marriage or developed labour capacity. Beyond that period 'children' in many parts of the world may be indistinguishable from most adults in many key respects. They may work or have apprenticeships, hold rights and responsibilities, and be entrusted with the care of other children. As Boyden and Levison note (2000: 28) 'because they raise children's social and economic status and constitute public affirmation of community membership, such transitions far outweigh the universal age-based threshold in their significance for children'.

Children's experiences are shaped not only by their *underdevelopment* as persons, but by these conceptions of them, which are earned and bestowed, constructed and determined by the many individuals and groups who set and hold expectations of children, individually, collectively, simultaneously, arbitrarily and even contradictorily. Birth, infancy, early childhood, childhood and adolescence are all stages in what we may often think of as simply 'childhood'. Within each stage, 'children' may be discriminated against or contribute to practices of security in unique ways. Childhood is also a concept which can in important ways vary with the priorities of society especially during war. Children's status can be deliberately altered. Through Military Orders imposed by Israel for example, Palestinians have been exclusively reclassified as adults from the age of sixteen (Cook et al 2004: 135). They thus can experience 'adult' treatment and incarceration and do not have the same rights as their Israeli counterparts of the same age a few streets away.

Children, or some children, are arguably vulnerable in different and disproportionate ways compared to adults, and may experience physical, mental and emotional harm differently from adults and may be specifically maltreated with this intention. It is precisely the qualities that make children vulnerable that also make them valuable. Such preciousness or weakness is a double edged sword. We may seek to protect, be weakened ourselves by this role, and also be vulnerable to extreme pain at the loss of a child. Targeting children indirectly targets parents/guardians and children have been killed precisely to damage adults. However, as Nordstrom reminds us, 'it is both dangerous and unrealistic to look at the abuse of children, in war, in another country, in another context as if that were somehow different and more barbaric than the patterns of abuse that characterize our own everyday cultures, in peace and war'. Citing examples of child abuse in the USA she says 'we should be asking instead what it is that makes such behaviors possible where they are found' (1999: 26).

It is not difficult to damage children, especially in early childhood. Young children in particular, below the age of five, are essentially different from *all* other adults and dependants in that they are still developing in terms of vital organs, immunity and personality, making them uniquely weak and liable to permanent damage and change in both these respects. There is clearly a sliding scale of vulnerability here, which accounts for their high prevalence of victims. If we perceive security, more widely in terms of right to appropriate nutrition and survival, the picture looks very different for infants than it does for older children and adults (Kent 2005) and far worse again for female children.

Though childhood remains a hugely variant construction worldwide, it is arguably ubiquitous (Western) constructs of an ideal 'developed' child that anchor and fix many current assumptions about children. The current paradigm shift underway in childhood studies also suggests that we are late in recognizing the multiple ways in which children have agency and power. The latest research on children as moral and ethical reasoners for example suggests that they can engage morally from the ages of four or five and reach adult levels from the ages of twelve. What is lacking is efforts to have equal partnerships with children to facilitate their development. We may therefore at present be largely hindering child development within many arguably developed societies.

KEY POINTS

- Definitions of childhood vary considerably worldwide.
- Childhood is much shorter (or adulthood starts earlier) outside the West.
- Childhood is a very complex issue, especially its ending and legality.
- We may need to think more about stages of childhood instead of one category of children.
- Children are capable of being social, moral and political actors.
- We do not commonly regard the child as a political actor, *least of all* as an *actor* in the international system.
- Very few features distinguish children from other social groups: children are younger than adults, typically symbolize innocence (especially girls) and in early childhood (below six years) have developing, in addition to maturing, bodies.

Children as security?

Children have throughout history been a constituent part of nation-building, and the means employed to counter fear about declining birthrate and with this a decline of the security and influence of states. In Britain, many agencies 'exported' children to Australia and New Zealand from 1850 until as recently as 1967. *Barnardo's* alone exported 33,000 children between 1882 and 1965, a move that it now recognizes as misguided. Within Australia, children of Aboriginal and Torres Strait islander peoples were forcibly removed from their parents and fostered and assimilated into white society. This practice also remained legal until 1967 (Frean 1998). Children were conceptualized as embodiments or potential vessels of national security or strength and also a conveniently mobile collective body that could be moved at will. A more contemporary example is the mass baby-lift organized by the Americans when they left Vietnam in 1975. Vietnamese 'orphans' were taken from villages to prevent them from being further exposed to the Communist threat and given new adoptive parents in the United States. In all these cases children's lesser size, strength and cognition may have allowed them to be subject to this attention and manipulated by the 'surrogate' state.

Infanticide and population wars

Children may also feature prominently in discourses of population policy, though it is the mother, as container of the future child, who is used and targeted in practice. French **pronatalist** policies during the Third Republic and Fascist Italy's 'battle for births' both evidence the perception of children's increased numbers as an emblem and guarantor of state health. In 1919, the Italian government created 'Children's Colonies'—free summer holidays for thousands of children in order to preserve their health and Mussolini's closest advisors suggested annulling childless marriages and criminalizing celibacy (Quine 1996: 42). As Kennedy-Pipe notes in Chapter 5, the policy of encouraging births is again returning to France nearly a century later.

From the 1990s the world's population has been deliberately and systematically imbalanced where there is pressure to reduce the number of children. Despite a legal basis from which to protect girls, discrimination against girl children is pervasive with millions of families resorting to **infanticide** of girls to make sure their one child is a boy. In China's 2000 census there were an estimated 19 million more boys than girls and a sex ratio of 100 girls to

120 boys, achieved through sex-selective abortion and a nutrition rights and care bias against girls. The perceived difference between a boy and a girl in cultural terms is often then a matter of life or death. States may not even declare this gendered information in their census return. As Yuval Davis points out, however, it was concern for 'political security in the Third World which in turn would create security problems to the US' that in part provoked and funded these measures in the South and invoked the necessary gendered and cultural frames of reference which helped to make it happen (1997: 34).

War rape and war babies

In war, however, the idea of the 'national identity' of children may also become of paramount importance and pronatalist practices may be pursued with more urgency as an additional means of securing the political body of the state. Pronatalist practices may also serve as a dual strategy of violence and renationalization against the enemy, for example, in the mass rape of women; the mother conquered and appropriated as if yielding national territory. Women may be viewed primarily in relation to their (future) children: indeed women can be seen to *reproduce* nations, biologically, culturally and symbolically (Yuval Davies and Anthias 1989; Pettman 1996; Yuval Davies 1997).

In the Serbian occupied territories of Bosnia Hercegovina and Croatia for example, Serbians combined ethnic cleansing and population policy by committing mass rape and serial rape to populate and maintain the greater Serbian state. Croatian and Bosnian men have also been attacked, specifically to make them sterile, to prevent them from fathering Croatian children. Women already pregnant prior to assaults had their fetuses removed (Nenadic 1996: 458) and women and girls interned in various types of Serbian concentration and rape/death camps were kept for at least twenty-one to twenty-eight days to ensure pregnancy. The rapists verbally emphasized that the women would give birth to their children. Though these children would be born of 'enemy' mothers they were forcibly conceived as part of the (re)nationalization of territory of which women's bodies formed a part. The enemy was thus able to create a future national asset and a prize of war. Such 'war babies', their experiences and their generational impact is a growing issue. In Rwanda, for example, as many as 10,000 babies were born as a result of the rape campaigns of 1994 according to the Rwandan government.

KEY POINTS

- Children are clearly identified as a form of security and insecurity.
- Before children's rights and mass media became established, unaccompanied children were often forcibly relocated to serve the needs of the state.
- The issue of war rape and war babies has only recently begun to be addressed.

Children at war: vulnerable and valuable

Children do not often choose wars. But war makers do often seek out children. Terrorism, civil war and total war are dependent to varying degrees on the manipulation of children and appropriation of the child or civic familial sphere as the following brief examples show. In Mozambique and South Africa both countries' education systems harboured critical practices of nationalization and militarization of mobilization. The family unit functioned as a totem of nationalist strategies for Afrikaners and in Mozambique, families were targeted as a means of dual *de*stabilization of family and state. Nazi Germany also yields extensive examples of nationalization and militarization directed at children. There is evidence of children featuring in Nazi propaganda, policy, speeches and images, anti-natalist and pro-natalist practices of racial and military security, and an incremental correlation between the ages of children targeted and the progress of the Nazi regime. A totalitarian regime, driving towards world war, its explicit use of children, amongst many other horrific acts, mirrors the intensity, scale and urgency of its objectives. Political socialization was employed in the school, children's leisure time and their 'youth' movements were appropriated for military means, and the family unit and family values were recoursed to amidst gross inhumanity to man.

Children may also perform a role in conflict by virtue of their presence. Three widely different examples can illustrate this. When the Serbs laid siege to Srebrenica in April 1993, children and their mothers were not evacuated out of the city. Moslem leaders believed instead that their particular presence strengthened Moslem claims to territory. In effect, children remained hostages in their own homes to their own fathers. Their bodies were kept in place as a physical claim to territory and a symbol of nationalism. The presence of children may also be used to temporarily halt conflict and begin negotiations. The idea of children as 'zones of peace' emerged in Norway in the 1980s and the most successful example of this practice, pioneered by UNICEF, occurred in Sudan. The Executive General of UNICEF met with the leaders of the Sudan People's Liberation Army and the Government to negotiate a temporary ceasefire in order for humanitarian aid workers to reach children. In 'Operation Lifeline Sudan', eight corridors of relief were created allowing food to reach up to 90,000 children. Aid agencies were able to negotiate peace zones for children, by reference to children's innocence in war and their need to be protected. In El Salvador from 1985 to the end of the war in 1991, three-day tranquility spaces allowed 20,000 health workers to immunize 250,000 children against polio. Similar zones were organized in Uganda in 1986 and in Lebanon in 1989.

In other conflicts, however, such recognition of children's vulnerability has given rise to the reverse, their targeting by the enemy group. Children's status as precious or valued within a family gives purpose to their systematic killing; an act which might normally be explained as simply aggressive. In the Rwandan civil war male Tutsi children were deliberately targeted as a means of eradicating the Tutsi Army of the Future (Hamilton 1995: 46). Children were thus killed strategically. As one political commentator broadcast to Rwanda before the violence erupted, '[t]o kill the big rats you have to kill the little rats' (Bellamy 1995: 14).

Thus, children have different political instrumentalities. Bosnian Moslem children were kept in place as indicators of nationalist resolve, Sudanese children were presented as embodiments of innocence and thus constituted a peace tactics and Tutsi children became a targeted presence. Children, like adults, may adopt many roles and identities simultaneously; as guardians and parents, targets and soldiers, stakeholders and slaves, peacemakers and labourers. Within each role gender also plays a part in determining the nature and cost of their participation.

KEY POINTS

Children's roles in war include:

- child soldiers/child parents (including combatants)
- girl soldiers and sex slaves
- children as targets, killed or maimed or captured
- children as minesweepers
- children born of war rape
- children as stakeholders in war
- children as morally and politically developed by war
- children as peacemakers.

Young soldiers

If, in Clausewitzian terms, war is the extension of politics, can we speak of politics being extended through the arms of an eleven-year-old? The question isn't rhetorical. What, exactly, does this say about the nature of power? Of force? And of political participation? No state code in the world today recognizes a child as an adult political actor. So what politics are forged in the conveyance of war through non-political actors, through underage soldiers? (Nordstrom 2004: 76).

In spite of the international legal norm that a child is a person under the age of eighteen, the international age limit for soldiers' voluntary recruitment and use is currently set at sixteen and many are much younger than this. *The Optional Protocol to the 1989 UN Convention on the Rights of the Child on the Involvement of Children in Armed Conflict* (OP-CRC-CAC, or OP-CRC) was adopted by the UN General Assembly in May 2000 and entered into force in February 2002. In effect it allows for voluntary recruitment of children from sixteen but demonstrates a powerful renegotiation of an international norm which was previously set at fifteen. Child soldiers remain the subject of much contention in international law and human rights law. Here, NGOs significantly inform IGOs such as the UN, and over three thousand NGOs were invited to inform the General Assembly session on children in 2001. The UN Security Council also sought the views of NGOs, even though it is 'relatively rare for the Security Council to solicit the views of NGOs. Moreover this move signaled a willingness to open up international security discourse to include human rights issues like the use of child soldiers' (Geske and Ensalaco 2005: 115).

There is, however, no simple profile of a child soldier, though the images we are presented with in the media are invariably of teenage boys—fearless, defiant and positioned as if separated from adults. However, there is simply not yet the will or capacity to find out how many children are caught up in war and in what age-specific or even gendered roles. Over forty-five states are estimated to use approximately 300,000 child soldiers (Høiskar 2001: 342). Their lives are highly expendable and, as such, the total figure must run far higher. The majority are active in government armed forces and the youngest are often to be found in armed groups (Harvey 2003). Up to 50% of soldiers may be girls. As the UN Security Council also acknowledged, there is still a need for a monitoring and reporting mechanism to track the recruitment of child soldiers and other children's rights violations.

Children may constitute 10% of current armed combatants (Singer 2001). The changing character of warfare in the latter half of the twentieth century has significantly altered the range of tasks open to children. Light weaponry may weigh as little as six kilos and be easily acquired, assembled and used (Cohn and Goodwin-Gill 1997). Many 'child soldiers' like their adult counterparts do not have to be armed or ready to fire to be effective or dangerous. The **Cape Town Principles**, agreed in 1977, also indicate this. 'Child soldier' refers here to:

> “any person under 18 years of age who is part of any kind of regular or irregular armed force or armed group in any capacity, including but not limited to cooks, porters, messengers, and those accompanying such groups, other than purely as family members. It includes girls recruited for sexual purposes and forced marriage. It does not, therefore, only refer to a child who is carrying or has carried arms.”

Boys and girls perform such soldiering 'roles' in war from six upwards. Figure 20.1 (which is not exhaustive) contains typical roles adopted or assumed by children and currently recognized and addressed by advocates of children's rights. Child soldiers may be participating in any of the combinations of roles and circumstances. The top box illustrates the potential difficulty in recognizing a child soldier, who may be unarmed, without a uniform and forcibly participating in a militia group, for example as a female cook, messenger or sex slave. Her male counterpart may be armed, uniformed, and technically a volunteer with the same group. Both are soldiers. Only one may be assisted adequately after war. No prizes if you guessed it was the male soldier.

In practice we cannot assume that a child's status as even a child or a soldier or involved in the combinations noted above, is shared or agreed by all parties concerned. Child soldiers may act with other children, under the direction of adults, or even under the command of older children. We do not always know how to respond to them. Children's roles as soldiers may overlap with those of adults and some children may clearly relish taking control. We cannot necessarily recognize them when we choose to, especially in the fog of war. Because children may be soldiers from the age of 15, all those who may look this age are also vulnerable to identification as soldiers. Conversely, child status may cause an almost operational paralysis by troops unwilling to open fire on them. As P.W. Singer notes, the prospect of ambush by children is increasing, as evidenced in British Operation 'Barras', carried out by the Special Air Service (SAS) against the West Side Boys militia in Sierra Leone in 2000, which had taken a squad of British troops hostage (2005). The spectrum of autonomy that childhood yields, further complicates the picture of victim and perpetrator, as does the extra-ordinary moral question of war.

In today's conflicts the distinction between voluntary and enforced recruitment is also often blurred, given the fact that militias may offer far more to children than just a life of combat. Up to 30% of the soldiers in Charles Taylor's National Patriotic Front of Liberia, for example, were estimated to be under seventeen. It had a separate unit for boys (Kaldor 1999: 94). The army later set up in Sierra Leone also benefited from recruiting children from the streets. In Uganda, the Lord's Resistance Army led by Joseph Kony has been abducting children since the 1990s. There are, however, many children who are not physically forced to join armed groups but choose to. A recent International Labour Organization study found that volunteers accounted for two thirds of child soldiers interviewed in four Central African countries (Brett and Specht 2004: 1). Children may be motivated to enlist to ward off poverty and insecurity, attracted

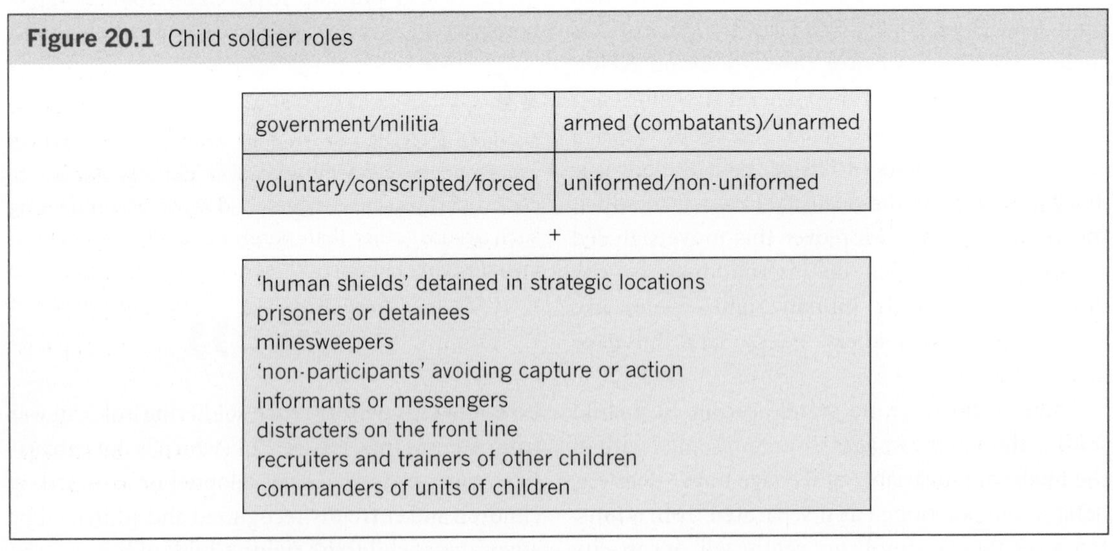

Figure 20.1 Child soldier roles

by the familial-style environment, food and clothing. There is a cyclical impact of war here, as orphaned and traumatized children may be drawn into the combat they escaped from and 'simply' receive food or treats in return for 'using' guns. Their role may allow survival in the face of other threats: starvation, isolation, or abduction, or physical abuse and exploitation at home, to name but a few. Children may therefore join to *live*— not to kill or be killed.

Child soldiering may also be experienced as development and apprenticeship. It is after all a job, and additionally a moral standpoint. Jo Boyden has shown how children may develop morally through war and maintain the right to act in defence of their values and family. The more unstable a country is, the more the military may even resemble a safe harbour in some senses. Groups such as the Tamil Tigers of Sri Lanka have been known to provide education integrated with military experience, tutoring boys from the age of nine in the importance of discipline, honesty and respect for the rights of ordinary citizens. Here, some child soldiers may imitate adults in combat but only in specific positions that do not exceed their strengths or place them at risk of physical harm; they are in effect 'apprentices' behind the frontline. They are also 'free' to leave.

Games of war

There are, however, also changing and increasingly complex experiences in warfare which are creating new opportunities for children's agency especially as soldiers. Roles may be specially designed for them based on assumptions about their physical and mental underdevelopment and opportunities found within. Colombian child soldiers are nicknamed 'little bells' by the military, which uses them as expendable sentries, and 'little bees' by the guerrillas, because they 'sting' their enemies before they know they are under attack.

Lighter weaponry coupled with extreme poverty, Western training techniques and educational indoctrination for example, have considerably advanced the capacity of the child soldiers and young resistance fighters from the age of six, and with this also created new opportunities for children's abuse. Pete Singer has documented this trait of so-called new wars (2005). A significant change in child soldiering is the deliberate use of children as combatants because of their perceived limitations or weaknesses. Children can be encouraged to 'play at war', take drugs or fire indiscriminately in close familial environments. Mozambican children, abducted by the resistance army RENAMO (formed by Portuguese special forces) were forced to return to their villages and attack them. It was hoped that this often barbaric and shameful action would prevent them from ever returning home and thus guarantee allegiance to their unit. Children can be forced do what their adult counterparts do not want to do or think that children can do better. They have thus become deadlier, most feared, and most likely to die. Such child soldiers, increasing in number, create potential dilemmas in combat for their adversaries and leave post-conflict challenges of personal and societal restoration in their wake.

A 'just war' is supposed to be fought in a way that distinguishes combatants from non-combatants. For child soldiers this distinction is presently complicated. Current different standards in international law provide contradictory interpretations of children's legal status as combatants. Soldiers of sixteen or seventeen years, for example, may be treated as victims in international law and yet also be permitted to become child soldiers under international humanitarian law. All participants in war, including the armed forces engaging with illegal child soldiers, shape perceptions of children's appropriate roles and responses to conflict. In practice some if not all child soldiers can be engaged with in non-lethal ways which also assist in their surrender, escape and later safe refuge. But, as Singer notes, there is yet no doctrine for engagement with child soldiers used by mission planners or deployed units (2001).

THINK POINT 20.1

Child soldier examples

- In 1998 it was estimated that up to 300,000 children were actively involved in armed conflict in government armed forces, government militias and in a range of armed opposition groups. This number is believed to have remained relatively constant although exact figures are impossible to determine.
- The problem is most critical in Africa, where up to 100,000 children, some as young as nine, were estimated to be involved in armed conflict in mid 2004. Children are also used as soldiers in various Asian countries and in parts of Latin America, Europe and the Middle East.
- The majority of the world's child soldiers are involved in a variety of armed political groups. These include government-backed paramilitary groups, militias and self-defence units operating in many conflict zones. Others include armed groups opposed to central government rule, groups composed of ethnic religious and other minorities and clan-based or factional groups fighting governments and each other to defend territory and resources.
- Most child soldiers are aged between 14 and 18. While many enlist 'voluntarily' research shows that such adolescents see few alternatives to involvement in armed conflict. Some enlist as a means of survival in war-torn regions after family, social and economic structures collapse or after seeing family members tortured or killed by government forces or armed groups. Others join up because of poverty and lack of work or educational opportunities. Many girls have reported enlisting to escape domestic servitude, violence and sexual abuse.
- Forcible abductions, sometimes of large numbers of children, continue to occur in some countries. Children as young as nine have been abducted and used in combat.
- Demobilization, disarmament and reintegration (DDR) programmes specifically aimed at child soldiers have been established in many countries, both during and after armed conflict, and have assisted former child soldiers to acquire new skills and return to their communities. However, the programmes lack funds and adequate resources. Sustained long-term investment is needed if they are to be effective.
- Despite growing recognition of girls' involvement in armed conflict, girls are often deliberately or inadvertently excluded from DDR programmes. Girl soldiers are frequently subjected to rape and other forms of sexual violence as well as being involved in combat and other roles. In some cases they are stigmatized by their home communities when they return. DDR programmes should be sensitively constructed and designed to respond to the needs of girl soldiers.

(*Coalition to Stop the Use of Child Soldiers*, September 2005).

KEY POINTS

- There is yet no official guidance or rules of engagement with child soldiers.
- Children can be used as armed child soldiers from the age of six.
- The term combatant is used to distinguish an armed soldier from an unarmed soldier.
- Children can be useful in war, performing roles that adults cannot.
- Girl soldiers are increasing in number yet their roles are underrepresented.

Post conflict—post children?

Children are acknowledged as one of the 'new' factors challenging the principles and practices of humanitarian intervention. Perhaps correspondingly, children and war have become a policy area in government organizations. Whilst many organizations have been formed to raise the profile of children in armed conflicts it was only the very recent ending of the Cold War that released the political will, or perhaps the incentives, for an international agenda for children's rights to be formed. War, the bloodiest testing ground of children's rights, now yields higher numbers of child casualties in ever more complex and damaging ways. However, such interest in children and war secedes almost complete deference to children's roles in warfare and their broader multi-faceted political capital. Mainstream texts on war and security issues, and on ethical considerations, are exclusively about adults and for adults. Children, it may be noted, are frequently missing from them; typically they receive only scant attention at best, despite what should now be clearly seen as the interconnectedness of the child's world and adult's world.

Children's political presence often illustrates a continuum between preparation for war and acts of war. Despite this, we and they are typically unprepared for the reality of their political and military enfranchisement. Children may make moral decisions because of war, or develop morally through the impact of war (Boyden 2003). Children who have been active in political violence have often become newly aware of a political rather than personal concept of security yet typically their 'rehabilitation' seeks effectively to depoliticize them (Cairns 1996: 186; Dodge and Raundalen 1991). In apartheid South Africa, children and youth have acted as social and political agents and defenders of communities, yet in their subsequent portrayal their enemies exaggerated their ages, or switched to the term 'youth', and used criminal descriptors such as 'rioters' as if also to render them politically impotent. After the struggle their political contribution has had little recognition. Their new-found political agency became wasted. Ironically, if recalled or repeated, it redefined them as 'problematic elements' and isolated them from the very community they helped to bring about (Marks 2001). The word 'youth' might potentially be used for both sexes but is nearly always assumed by western commentators to describe a male collective. It is also imbued with overtones of strength, violence and potentially political violence. It is consequently a pejorative description that may incite fear.

In the multitude of ways that war is harmful, it is typically more so for young children and may make them first in the queue for protection. Young children's physical survival may be encoded in the psychologically reassuring proximity of older primary carers. Should we for example also secure (young) children's immediate guardians in order to best secure them? Even after conflict, young women and girls, many of whom are also caring for children, experience a continuation of violence and exploitation and rightfully question the boundaries of war implicit in current post-war reconstruction policy (Meintjes, Pillay and Turshen 2002: 3–4). Girl soldiers in particular may have been subject to sexual assaults which prevent them from entering into accepted roles in society. Child soldiers pose a further significant problem as their often illegal use by state and militia cannot be immediately acknowledged for fear of reprisals or raising post-war tensions further, with implications for their rehabilitation and their society.

The conceptual separation of political experiences and childhood accentuates the need for an acknowledgement of what they have experienced, integrated with restoration of their childhood through appropriate reparation, rehabilitation, and reconstruction. Further, children who perceive themselves to be *neither* victims nor combatants, are significant in number yet rarely traced or consulted in post-conflict reconciliation and integration programmes (Peters et al 2003). Their agency remains unknown and potentially untapped.

KEY POINTS

- In practice child soldiers can be engaged with in non-lethal ways which also assist in their escape and later safe refuge. This rarely occurs.
- Children who have participated in war require complex and difficult reintegration. They may still behave and feel like children.
- Many children are unhelpfully regarded as criminals or 'lost' children after war. We talk of children losing their childhood or innocence without really saying what this means.
- Many children's roles and experiences in war have not been documented or addressed. This is especially true of gendered roles and war crimes such as rape.

Infant power and soft tactics

Whilst much of this chapter has drawn attention to children's presence in war and marginalization of their agency, it is ironic that war children are very often seen, if not often heard. Focusing on the plight of the child is a technique frequently employed in the reporting of international news and foreign conflicts. Crises in far away places intrude on our consciousness through the work of the media. The children whose faces and terror are zoomed in on, are part of what Erica Burman describes as the iconography of emergencies, or disaster pornography (1992). The beautiful, infant child rendered as an iconographic image of vulnerability is often used in war propaganda, polarizing the threat to the child, indicating the need for protectors, the gravitas of the situation, and also the urgency of a patriotic and protectionist response. Propagandists retain infantile qualities in older bodies, by making use of particular physical qualities. In Nazi and Soviet propaganda of the Second World War, for example, children were likely to be blonde, aesthetic, wide-eyed and pleading to receive attention and or be cared for; small, pre-adolescent, silent and still, and isolated from a familial context.

One of the greatest propaganda stories of this decade—manufactured by the American PR firm 'Hill and Knowlton' and paid for by the Kuwaiti Royal family—told of Kuwaiti babies forcibly removed from their incubators by Iraqi soldiers. The story succeeded in generating enormous Western support for military intervention. Male politicians regularly kiss babies in public during their campaigns. In Bosnia, Ratko Mladic's troops handed out chocolates to Moslem children and patted their heads for the benefit of television, whilst removing and killing their fathers (Swain 1995). Politicians under threat commit family hug scenes for the cameramen as a way of showing that they are still wanted, hanging on, secure in at least one sense. In these scenes children become the visual equivalent of 'last words' in each case. Reference to children is used to indicate a sincerity of purpose that defies immediate rebuke.

The traditional cry 'womenandchildren' is typical graphic shorthand for non-combatants, suggesting by default victims, casualties, refugees, and displaced, and the weak and feminine. During the Gulf War 'womenandchildren' rolled easily off network tongues (Enloe 1993: 166) and as Enloe points out, the running together of these two words by broadcasters and writers to mean victimhood renders both as child-like. During the Vietnam war American troops were kicked into action by descriptions of their enemy as just a bunch of 'women and children' (Enloe and Zalewski 1995: 10–11) and in South Africa, Afrikaner white youth were militarized in the school and in youth movements against the threat of otherwise becoming 'mommy's boys' (Cock 1979: 70–1). Terrorists may aim specifically at those with wives and children, the 'soft targets'. Conversely, 'naturally', 'unpolitical' qualities assigned to women and children, have also enabled their use as paramilitary actors, above suspicion and below questioning.

Embodying particular and universal qualities of weakness, it is infants who are most typically used in pleas to the national conscience. The term *infant power* describes such strategic harnessing of very young and/or feminine images of children for political ends. Put simply, infant power thus describes practices of **infantilization**, particularly in a military context. During the Cold War, propaganda used by both the United States and the Soviet Union featured sinister representations of Armageddon counterpoised with images of blonde, beautiful children (Stephens 1997). In the American 'Cold War Consensus' of the 1950s and early 1960s the nuclear threat was personified as an iconographic image of vulnerable Western childhood. Sharon Stephens explains that:

> [c]hildren were widely depicted in the Cold War era as innocent beings at the heart of the contained domestic world, as objects of strictly gender-divided parental care and protection, and as the vulnerable core of American society, whose protection from foreign enemies required the construction of a vast and powerful nuclear defense system . . . dominant Cold War images of abstract, generic children (invariably presented as white and middle class) [were counterposed with] the actual children most vulnerable to risks associated with nuclear weapons production and testing, and with government-sponsored radiation experiments. In various ways, these were all seen as 'deviant' children, whose lives could legitimately be put at risk in the interests of safeguarding 'normal' children at the heart of Cold War visions of American society.

One cannot also escape the phenomenon of feminine innocence that is chosen as the face of fear in so many cases. Aesthetics are tied up here with innocence. Our attention on them may, in Robert J. Lifton's words, create a 'domesticisation of the unthinkable' (Brown 1988: 84). Lifton uses the term 'dissociated language' to describe how ideas function within language to counteract genocidal imagery. For example, nuclear weapons, described in terms of little boys and babies, explosions likened to births, and nuclear capability associated with creative capacity, despite its destructive potential (Lifton and Markusen 1990: 214–5, Cohn 1987). This is perhaps a classic example of the construct of the child to create 'dissociation' at the highest level of strategic or nuclear culture.

This *containment* is to an extent recognizable in the studies of children which have informed debates, particularly at the beginning of the twenty-first century. As Wyness et al (2004: 81) state:

> Children are seen as 'presocial', unable to articulate a set of coherent political views (Sears and Valentino 1997). The social science community has thus treated children's political participation as a contradiction in terms. A political community has an exclusive adult membership with children unable to provide qualifications for entry. . . . these research assumptions connect with broader social forces of convention. For many the very essence of childhood, at least in contemporary western terms, prohibits political participation such that the 'political child' is seen as the 'unchild', a counter-stereotypical image of children that does not fit with the way we commonly view childhood
>
> **(Stainton-Rogers and Stainton-Rogers 1992: 32–3).**

New research suggests that children's agency and particularly their level of moral reasoning and inclusive moral engagement is more advanced than we have mostly given them credit for. Children are now suspected of being able to reason morally during the period of middle childhood, from seven upwards, and in a comparable way to adults from about the age of twelve. The possibilities for children's participation in citizenship and implications for child soldiers and indeed all children who think about (child) soldiers are profound. Whole generations may be able to contribute to ideas about security and indeed may be found to have already done so. During the Cold War era, schooling included preparation for nuclear war and drills for civil defence. American school children were thus taught 'to equate emotional maturity with an attitude of calm acceptance toward nuclear war', (Brown 1988: 90). Crying was out. In turn, gimmicks and everyday routines incorporated aspects of the nuclear threat to help children 'get used' to the idea. Did war thus also begin in the minds of children when millions of free, plastic atomic-bomb 'toys' spilled out of breakfast cereal packets across America? In the context of such deliberate practices of 'dissociation'—was ethical debate with these children really not possible? This may have been the first time that children might have been better advised to skip the first meal of the day.

KEY POINTS

- We are especially motivated by images of young children.
- New research on children suggests that they are capable of thinking about moral and political issues far earlier than we expect.
- 'Child agency' means that children contribute to processes that they have some understanding of.
- We have rarely attempted to establish children's understanding of many moral concepts associated with war, death and security throughout history.

Conclusion

Conflict, periods of military intensification, secession or disintegration give rise to intensified practices of nationalization and militarization. The case studies show that practices of nationalization and militarization which involve appropriation of the child and familial sphere are often in place and active prior to the actual outbreak of conflict. The incorporation of children and the family into militarized practices, and the logical corollary of this, the targeting of the (enemy) civilian sphere, dispel the myth that children are simply the protected or only victims. Children and their guardians are a form of security in themselves (whether alive or dead) and are clearly treated as such. Terrorism, civil war and total war are dependent to varying degrees on the manipulation of children, and share similar rationales. Battles which use children's bodies and minds as effective weapons have so far taken place without being recorded in the pages of security textbooks and have remained outside the knowledge of those who accept the typically presented parameters and ontology of security. As Peterson notes, 'the dichotomies of protector–protected, direct–indirect violence, and war–peace are inter-woven; denying them as oppositional dichotomies means recognizing the complexity of (inter)dependence, the interrelationship of oppressions, and the uncertainty of security' (1992: 56).

Women and children are seemingly still fought for as if they are 'safely inside' and away from the politics that will be acted out for them. To notice anything different would be to shatter this illusion. It is not that children are not thought about at all, it is that they are represented in such a way as to also serve political purposes.

Children, as we have seen, are like adults in that they may instrumentalize roles and identities simultaneously; as guardians and parents, targets, stakeholders, peacemakers, soldiers, educators, friends, and labourers. Our responses to them do not accommodate this multiple instrumentality. Those (sensationalized, posed, isolated) children that we do see clearly in a political context, typically child soldiers or disaster victims, foster the illusion that children were not prior members of the political sphere but were *exceptionally* and *temporarily* drawn in to it. That child soldiers and child victims are sensationalized yet also described as having *lost their childhood* in many cases leads to difficulties in their reintegration into society and our recognition of their capacity. War exposes the roles, practices, manipulation, exploitation, uses and expectations of childhood that exist in global politics. Yet, such children's politicization is enabled because it is also underrepresented and underplayed. This book is one of the ways in which this narrow representation is challenged. However, if we are only just beginning to understand children's agency then perhaps we can only just begin to know the extent to which responsibility for them and responsibilities also held by them are being met. For many, however, it is already too late.

QUESTIONS

Why have child soldiers only recently reached agendas in high politics?

Given that children form nearly half the population, and experience the world differently, should we afford them more attention?

Should children be first in the queue for protection in war?

How can we explain the hidden nature of war for girls?

Why has it been possible to evacuate children from war?

Can we justify intervention in order to protect young children?

Should we consult all children over their involvement in war?

Does war merely accentuate the way our political systems already fail children?

Why do politicians kiss babies? Which babies?

Why are books about security not written for children?

FURTHER READING

■ **Singer, Pete W. (2005), *Children at war*, Pantheon.** From Afghanistan, Thailand and Lebanon to Sudan, Kosovo and Sierra Leone, Singer examines how children are recruited and indoctrinated into warfare. He says Western forces should prepare themselves for facing children in battle.

■ **Brocklehurst, Helen (2006), *Who's afraid of children? Children, Conflict and International Relations*, Aldershot: Ashgate.** My own book presents in expanded form some of the arguments presented in this chapter. It provides historical and comparative evidence of children's roles in global politics and seeks to integrate an understanding of the role of children in international conflict into the larger body of critical IR theory.

■ **McEvoy-Levy, Siobhán (2006), *Troublemakers or Peacemakers? Youth and Post-Accord Peace Building*, Notre Dame, IN: University of Notre Dame Press.** In contemporary armed conflicts, youth are often on the frontlines of combat and, after peace accords are signed, they are both potential threats to peace and significant peace-building resources. *Troublemakers or Peacemakers?* explores youth actions, perceptions, and needs as central components of the challenge of post-war peace building. The contributors develop theory and policy recommendations based on field research in Sierra Leone, Rwanda, Guatemala, Colombia, Angola, Northern Ireland, Bosnia, and Israel-Palestine.

IMPORTANT WEBSITES

- Since 1997 the Secretary-General of the United Nations has appointed a *Special Representative for Children and Armed Conflict*. They are tasked to build awareness of the needs of war-affected children, propose ideas and approaches to enhance their protection, bring key actors within and outside the UN to promote adequate responses, and to undertake humanitarian and diplomatic initiatives **http://www.un.org/special-rep/children-armed-conflict/**

- *Save the Children* fights for children's rights. The founder drafted the first declaration on children's rights, which later formed the basis for the United Nations Convention on the Rights of the Child. Today 27 organizations make up the *International Save the Children Alliance*, the world's largest independent movement for children, making improvements for children in over 110 countries. **http://www.savethechildren.net/alliance/**

- *The Coalition to Stop the Use of Child Soldiers* works to prevent the recruitment and use of children as soldiers, to secure their demobilization and to ensure their rehabilitation and reintegration into society. **http://www.child-soldiers.org/**

- *The Children and Armed Conflict Unit* is a joint project of the Children's Legal Centre and the Human Rights Centre at the University of Essex, UK. It works around the world to improve the situation for civilian children caught up in armed conflict and civil unrest through measures to restore civil society and children's rights. Like the websites listed above, this website provides extensive links to material on children and war. **http://www.essex.ac.uk/armedcon/**

Visit the Online Resource Centre that accompanies this book for lots of interesting additional material: www.oxfordtextbooks.co.uk/orc/collins/

21

After the Return to Theory: The Past, Present, and Future of Security Studies

OLE WÆVER AND BARRY BUZAN

Chapter Contents

- Introduction
- The origins and institutional structure of security studies
- Security studies' 'Golden Age'
- Institutionalization and stagnation
- Disciplinary questioning and theoretical re-launch
- Conclusion: the powers of theory and the challenges of the future

Reader's guide

This chapter presents an interpretation of the past and present of security studies with an emphasis on the changing periods of theory production and practical problem solving. The field started out as a distinct US speciality much shaped by the new conditions of the 1940s set by nuclear weapons and a long-term mobilization against the Soviet Union, two factors that created a need for a new kind of civilian experts in defence and strategy. From an American, think tank based, interdisciplinary field, security studies became institutionalized as a part of one discipline, International Relations (IR), increasingly international and with theory anchored in the universities. Since the 1990s, the field has been in a new period of high theory productivity, but largely in two separate clusters with the US and Europe as centres of each. This analysis is used as a basis for raising some central questions and predictions about the future of the field.

Introduction

The fact that a book like the present one can be made, indeed had to be made, to present an existing field to even more people who might be entering it, testifies to major change in security studies. Had a similar book been produced in previous decades, it would have looked very different. A 1950s version would have been very short. In the 1960s, it would have been structured with chapters on different kinds of policy questions—strategy, economy of defence, decision making—and in some of these (notably the chapter on strategy) there would have been a lot of theory, but the theories would not have competed for dealing with the same questions, a division of labour would have kept them in different chapters. The 1970s edition would probably have been thinner on theory and more comprehensive in the thematic chapters—and it would have come with a companion volume (in German) denouncing the whole field as part of the repressive, militarized, Cold War system. The 1980s text book would have been a reader of texts arguing for and against the continued relevance of the field, its possible widening or even dissolution and merger into wider fields. With developments in the 1990s, the field has come to take a shape as reflected in the structure of this volume: the wideners have succeeded enough for chapters on different sectors of security to be necessary, and a number of theories now compete for tackling the whole field of security. In the first decade of the twenty-first century, this reshaped discipline seems to gain increased attention, generate more undergraduate courses and not least more—often theoretically inclined—Ph.D. projects. This augmented attraction is supported by both the prominence of 'security' in the era of the 'global war on terror', and by the availability of this family of theories that sprang up during the 1990s.

Our focus in this chapter is on *security theory*, which we define as theory that aims at the understanding and/or management of security issues. Such theory can at different points in time resemble developments within general IR theory, while at other points there can be less contact. For instance, some major developments in IR theory like 1970s interdependence and regime theory had

KEY IDEAS 21.1

Terminology

The names 'strategic studies' and 'security studies' (or 'international security studies') are by some authors used interchangeably, while others use them systematically on different objects. It is possible to give distinct definitions, typically with security studies being broader, and strategic studies the narrower sub-set oriented towards military issues (e.g. Buzan 1991; Betts 1997). However, in a historical overview like the present, it would be anachronistic to use such terminology for the whole period. 'Strategic studies' was the established term from the 1940s into the 1980s, and we use it accordingly, retaining the construction of the time with most often military affairs as the self-evident core of the field and circles around this drawn more or less narrowly. From the 1980s and onwards, this field was in most contexts relabelled as security studies, and only in some places but far from all was the hard-core military part of this field assigned the specific name 'strategic studies'. Therefore, we do not use here a systematic distinction between the two terms, but let them cover the whole area and use mostly strategic studies in the early period and security studies in the later. Today, the name 'strategic studies' seems mostly to linger on because it is institutionalized in outfits like the 'International Institute for Strategic Studies', 'Journal of Strategic Studies' and 'Journal of Military and Strategic Studies'. The dominance of the term 'strategic studies' during the Cold War was in any case more pervasive in the UK than in the US.

minimal impact on security studies (at the time, at least), and some security theories were (originally) specific to security studies like deterrence theory or the **Copenhagen School**, not general theories of IR. Other cases of security theory are simultaneously IR and security theory like **constructivism**, feminism or democratic peace. While distinct from IR theory, security theory is different also from security studies at large, because much work in security studies does not deal explicitly with theory. Thus, security theory is a specific sub-set of security studies and one whose development has gone through distinctive phases.

One peculiarity of this field is that it is divided more strongly than comparable fields into sub-sets without mutual recognition, often without even mutual awareness. Especially in European journals, conferences, departments and research centres, one finds a lively discussion of a number of recent approaches: critical security studies, feminism, the Copenhagen school, the **Paris school** and the merits of all these compared to 'the traditional approach'. Go to most departments in the US or the leading journals, like *International Security* and *Security Studies*, and most scholars would say 'who?' and 'what?' to most of the authors intensely discussed by scholars mostly located in Europe and parts of the third world (Wæver 2004a). In turn, the mostly American main scene has had debates centred on offensive versus defensive realism, the relative importance of ideational variables and the role of power and institutions in orders/empires. These debates did not structure the universe for most scholars in the rest of the world.

Therefore, when this concluding chapter attempts an assessment of where we are, where we came from, and not least where we might be going, it needs to follow an asymmetrical structure, where the first part treats the field as homogeneous—a kind of unified centre-periphery structure with the US definition of security studies unrivalled—while the later part splits into two parallel tracks. The chapter is structured chronologically. The first section looks at the origins and institutional structure of security studies—what and where is it? The second covers the so-called 'Golden Age', the formative period of strategic studies when most notably deterrence theory was developed and game theory applied to it (and in turn given much original impetus at the level of abstract theory), to assist in the handling of novel challenges from nuclear weapons. The third section is about the immediate post-Golden Age when strategic studies was most consolidated as an integral part of the security establishment, and theory often lost out to 'hectic empiricism' (Buzan 1981, 2000), which might in turn have contributed to the decline of strategic studies as a field. A fourth section deals with the soul-searching debates on widening and (sub)disciplinary identity during the 1980s and 1990s culminating in various theoretical innovations. The final section looks from the current situation of theoretical wealth into a future where these theories might change their mutual relationships while also becoming involved with the main issues on the policy agenda.

The first and second sections overwhelmingly deal with the US, because this is where modern strategic studies emerged and found its characteristic shape. When modern-style strategic studies grew elsewhere, even where independent traditions existed, this happened to such a large extent by attempts to copy or import the American experience, that the formative period and events of American strategic studies became referent points for the field everywhere. A systematic comparison of American and European strategic studies is therefore presented towards the end of the second section (referring to the status in the early 1970s), and only in the latest phases do distinct trajectories become self-reliant enough that a story of two parallel tracks can explain the above mentioned peculiarity of debates unrecognizable to each other.

The origins and institutional structure of security studies

War and peace, threats and strategy, as well as welfare and epidemics: issues like these have been on the agenda of thinkers and writers for centuries. However, anything resembling security studies as we now know it did not become a distinct field of study until around the end of the Second World War. As always, *when* a field is established, it is easy to see predecessors and preparatory work done in previous phases, and thus security studies can be projected back into the interwar period with reference to work done on the causes and prevention of wars (Baldwin 1995).

The novelty in the 1940s, however, was the emergence of a distinct category of work at the intersection of military expertise and university-based social science aimed at delivering policy-relevant knowledge supported by a broad, interdisciplinary academic knowledge base. In large part because of the unprecedented implications of nuclear weapons for war fighting, but also because of the broad-spectrum challenge to the US posed by the Soviet Union (ideological and economic, as well as military) and the general prestige gained during the Second World War by both natural scientists (new weapons, code breaking) and social scientists (e.g. in advising on strategic bombing priorities), civilian experts would now also specialize in military issues under the heading of security.

This institutional innovation happened at the same time as the concept of security moved to the centre becoming the guiding idea over previously supreme aims like defence and national interest (Yergin 1977; Wæver 2006).

General enabling conditions in the US were: optimism about the usefulness of science, the possibility of rational solutions to societal problems, novel security issues that seemed not only urgent and primary but very much so (nuclear weapons and the Soviet, communist threat), generous funding for research, and exponential expansion of higher education.

The main key to the emergence of strategic studies around the time of the end of the Second World War and the beginning of the Cold War was the need for civilian experts to balance the military leadership, a need driven certainly by technological developments (nuclear weapons and the rapid rise of war avoidance as the key strategic imperative), but probably also by broader political considerations about the potential political implications of long-term mobilization.

The military driver is straightforward: gradually, it became clear how radically nuclear weapons would transform the security equations, and the kind of expertise needed differed from the classical military one. At some risk of oversimplification (actual planning was a bit more mixed), the problem was that wars should no longer be fought but avoided, and ways should be found so that the possibility/impossibility of war generated by nuclear deployments could be manipulated for political gain. The centre of gravity shifted from the tactical and operational level to true long-term strategy, and from the deployment of a given technology to the targeted development of fast changing technologies for the future. Although at first it seemed that even the games of deterrence could be seen as controlled by the bottom line of what would happen in an actual fight, it gradually became necessary to treat nuclear strategy as a partly independent universe to be analysed in its own right. This demanded a completely different form of knowledge from the one delivered by military experts. As succinctly put by Richard Betts (1997: 13), 'Nuclear war spurred theorizing because it was inherently more theoretical than empirical: none had ever occurred'. Or in the words of Richard Smoke (1975: 275), the first precondition for the emergence of security studies was a 'complexity dissectible by abstract analysis'.

While this is probably a relatively uncontroversial interpretation of the emergence of security studies, it should also be noticed that the combination of nuclear weapons and the Cold War meant a need to coordinate more closely military and non-military considerations. Already the wartime experience had shown, especially in the US, how challenging it was to coordinate economic, political and military planning (Etzold 1978: 1–2; Hogan 1998: 25). As it began to be clear that the Cold War could become a drawn-out, all-encompassing and existential struggle, the idea took hold that one needed a form of integrated understanding, where these different forms of knowledge could become combined, and this was a major part of the reasoning behind the National Security Act of 1947 (in addition to closer coordination of the services plus intelligence reform).

The specific challenge of the US with its 'no standing armies' tradition having to organize for long-term mobilization, shaped the emerging civil–military interface in strategic studies. It was a deep-seated argument within American political thought that a permanent military institution would be a threat to democracy because it could be misused by 'a tyrant', an anti-democratic executive (Bailyn 1992; Publius 1787–8; Deudney 1995). Also, it was only during the Second World War that 'the uniformed heads of the US armed services assumed a pivotal and unprecedented role in the formulation of the nation's foreign policies' (Stoler 2000: ix). Therefore, when the US moved towards institutionalizing an unprecedented level of military mobilization, this could not be done purely in terms of 'war' or 'defence'. This is a central part of the explanation for the rise of the term 'security' to cover the mobilization in more inclusive and 'civilian' terms (Wæver 2004b, 2006). And it conditioned a particular space for civilian expertise in a military-centred universe. The Cold War mobilization inevitably entailed a tension between American liberalism and military professionalism, and the field of strategic studies emerged as part of the institutional responses to this tension (Huntington 1957; Lasswell 1950).

KEY POINTS

- Security studies as a distinct field of study was born in the 1940s in the US.
- Nuclear weapons created a strategic challenge not covered by traditional military expertise.
- Long-term, broad-based mobilization collided with an American wariness of 'standing armies'. Where the US had traditionally kept war and peace more distinct than other states, the new situation called for a new cover term (security) and new experts (security studies) in order not to end up in permanent war and at the mercy of the military—or the enemy.

Security studies' 'Golden Age'

The period of the 1950s and 1960s is widely celebrated as one where the field was simultaneously productive, influential, and relatively coherent. Although the field contained a wide variety of other kinds of work (to which we return shortly), the central and defining area was game theory and nuclear strategy. We pay particular attention to this period for two reasons. First, it was the formative period of the new discipline, and therefore developments in the so-called Golden Age are not just episodes equal to many others, they defined how security studies was perceived; for good and bad these developments were the quintessential work of security studies. Second, this marked a (first) high point of *theorization*, and we want to point to the pattern of flow, ebb and flow of theory making within security studies.

The work on game theory and deterrence theory was a rare instance of an intellectual development that scores high in terms of theoretical creativity and sophistication, and simultaneously policy relevance. Very often this is seen as a trade-off—policy relevance/utility versus theoretical abstraction/sophistication (cf. Lepgold and Nincic 2001; Hill 1994)—but when nuclear weapons created a novel challenge of understanding a situation that was hypothetical and speculative through-and-through and open to swift and dramatic developments, a very sophisticated theoretical boom gained centrality politically. At the same time, this development became highly influential within the academic world, because the nature of the object allowed for a high degree of abstraction and formalization which scored well on the criteria of the day for a new, more 'scientific' form of International Relations. Under a Cold War situation with a booming US economy, a mood of technological optimism and a willingness to support social science as part of the solution to social challenges (including not only the Cold War struggle but social problems of all kinds), the reward was high for new approaches that seemed to move IR in the direction of the use of scientific methods and tools, ranging from coding of events data allowing for computerized data processing, through cybernetic models and experimental psychology to game theory. Deterrence theory became a success story in this context for two reasons. On the one hand, it produced a seemingly productive ('progressive') research programme where theoretical work produced ever new and more complex problems which could in turn be dealt with by new theoretical moves. On the other hand, all this seemed highly useful because the theories actually produced their own reality of abstractions, the world of 'secure second strike capability', 'extended deterrence' and 'escalation dominance'.

This was reflected in the critique from Peace Research and Critical Theory that the whole 'Golden Age' idea is a self-glorifying construction of academics whose real accomplishment was to make morally corrupt government policies (MAD, Vietnam) look respectable and/or inevitable.

Some critics said that this whole literature produced validating smokescreens for what the politicians and the military wanted to do anyway: build up a huge nuclear force and promote military Keynesianism (Green 1966, 1968; Senghaas 1969). Although undoubtedly true that these theories legitimized deterrence and nuclear weapons as such, it is not fair to conclude that their 'influence' on policy was illusory. Theories of deterrence shaped the whole way of making sense of nuclear weapons, and thereby influenced the shape if not necessarily the size of investments. The relative merits and roles of bombers, missiles, submarines, the uses and non-uses of tactical nuclear weapons and how to avoid vulnerability of systems (the famous basing study by Wohlstetter et al in 1954)—for all such policies, there was a clear link from theorists to policymakers. But in relation to targeting, there was a major slippage where Strategic Air Command largely continued with their own roughly 'first strike' oriented policy (Rosenberg 1983). If one counterfactually imagined that the civilian experts had not existed at all, it seems much more probable that the whole nuclear build-up would have been shaped by an old-fashioned military logic of maximizing 'fire power' without much concern for overall stability and the political possibilities for signalling and manoeuvring. Nuclear *quantity* was probably a product of semi-independent dynamics having to do with the military industrial complex and the overall politics of sizing the defence budget, but it should be beyond doubt that Golden Age theorizing produced a different mix of nuclear weapons with different qualities and locations, and a different role in policy, from what would otherwise have happened. For better or worse, this story of the golden age and deterrence theory became the heart of the discipline—its founding myth somewhat similar to the way the first great debate operates in IR theory.

What is most unique about this particular episode is, however, the degree to which policy-oriented work made significant contributions to general theory. This was not just application of work done elsewhere to policy questions or transfer of knowledge to the political world, as we have come to expect it of think tanks. Neither was it, as with the most recent think tanks, primarily about lobbying for specific policies, although the work of RAND clearly served the general interests of the air force and had built-in biases towards a distrustful policy vis-à-vis the Soviet Union (Green 1968). This did not prevent lasting contributions to game theory. Even a mathematician prefacing the sixtieth anniversary edition of von Neumann and Morgenstern's foundational 'Theory of Games and Economic Behavior' (Kuhn 2004: x) posits that 'many observers agree' that RAND was one of two centres in which game theory flourished in the first post-war decade (see also Diamond and Diamond 1996: 142–3). One need just mention the 1950 invention at RAND of the prisoner's dilemma (Poundstone 1992: 103) and the late 1950s bargaining twist given to game theory by Thomas Schelling (1960b). It is quite easy to see how these developments grew out of specific challenges relating especially to the nuclear situation. Noticeably, these were also major contributions to basic science at the same time.

The second biggest example from the 'Golden Age' of policy-relevant work that simultaneously constituted general theory was systems analysis, a method for solving problems of force structure and resource allocation that drew on economic theory as well as operations research developed by natural scientists, engineers and economists during the Second World War (Stern 1967; Smoke 1975: 290–3). Several pioneering RAND studies were implemented into policy, notably the famous 'air bases' study by Wohlstetter et al (1954). Several of the leading representatives entered the Kennedy administration (McNamara's 'whiz kids'; Kaplan 1983; Brodie 1965). From there, this method and related RAND techniques like the 'Planning-Programming-Budgeting-System' 'spread through most of the federal government' (Smoke 1975: 292). It is generally underestimated today how much of early strategic studies was not only inspired by the *discipline* of economics (Hitch 1960; Schelling 1960a) but actually *about* economics. A typical early course or 1960s–1970s textbook in strategic studies had strategy and deterrence as the biggest sub-field, but the second biggest would usually be 'the economics of defence'. Not so puzzling given the size of the American defence budget! (See Knorr and Trager 1977 for a broader treatment of 'economic issues and national security'.) Often it is the image today that Cold War strategic studies was obsessed with military questions, and this is partly true—it was mostly the economics of *defence* planning—but strategy was closely followed by economics as a concern.

Many other things happened in strategic studies around this nexus, but the identity and nature of the field was shaped by the Golden Age episode. Beyond nuclear strategy, important areas within strategic studies were systems analysis (planning, organization), arms control, alliance politics, counter-insurgency and organization of government institutions and decision making (Smoke 1975). In the late 1960s and early 1970s were added area studies and internal developments (bureaucratic politics; decision making). Later in the 1970s came perceptions, arms race theory, proliferation of nuclear weapons, proliferation of advanced military technology, utility of force, strategic intelligence, conventional strategy and self-reflections of the field (Bull 1968; Gray 1977; Howard 1979).

Many of the new developments (notably perceptions and decision making) were reactions to the difficulties that the classical form of security studies ran into. Especially the Vietnam War became a turning point towards the next phase. The US entered the war with all the instruments of strategic studies in high esteem. The Kennedy administration and McNamara's time as Secretary of Defence marked a high point in the belief in the social scientific vision of security knowledge (Morgenthau 1962). But in the words of Colin Gray (1982: 90), the strategists knew 'next to nothing' about 'peasant nationalism in Southeast Asia or about the mechanics of a counterrevolutionary war'.

KEY POINTS

- The defining moment—or founding myth—for security studies was the development of deterrence theory, which both spurred general theory of a 'basic science' nature (game theory) and simultaneously fed directly into policy.
- The economics of defence was the second biggest field in early security studies.

Institutionalization and stagnation

The crisis for security studies—or what Baldwin (1995) dubs the move into a phase of 'decline'—was, however, not only about external challenges to an otherwise perfect theoretical construction. The previous period had already witnessed some 'internal weakening' of the mainstream strategy scholarship. Even in the core area of nuclear (and other forms of military) strategy, the highly theoretical and academic scholarship of the earlier period had succumbed to 'hectic empiricism' (Buzan 2000). The task of security scholarship was to keep up with fast changing technologies and the twists and turns of political developments. Increasing amounts of effort therefore went into ever more detailed work on technical specificities and narrow perfection of isolated bits of knowledge.

The corrupting influence of policy was, however, not the only explanation. During the 1970s and 1980s, the very abstraction of deterrence logic more or less broke down under the weight of its own complexity (ex post/ex ante, limited nuclear war, rationality debates), causing an exhausted drift towards general or existential deterrence (Morgan 1983; Freedman 1988). The Golden Age lost its lustre also because the internal logic of its key contribution broke down.

A further complication of the policy–academe interaction has to do with an aspect that is very often ignored in the debates these days, especially within the more critical and/or European forms of security studies: in the post-Golden Age period, the field was marked by a gradual IR'ification of security studies. It moved from inter-disciplinarity into becoming one of IR's two pillars, paralleling IPE (International Political Economy). Not only did this mean that IR became almost formalized as consisting of these two components (in the US symbolized by two lead journals, *International Security* and *International Organization*), more importantly in the present context—seen from the angle of security studies itself—it meant that IR became the main disciplinary context for security studies theorizing, in striking contrast to the early Golden Age situation. Then, the leading scholars came from a variety of backgrounds—sociology, mathematics, psychology, natural sciences, political science and quite a lot of economists. Increasingly, one discipline came to dominate: political science.

Since the late 1960s, 'strategic studies' became the subject for specific courses as part of general IR/political science departments (Smoke 1975: 292; Gray 1982: 86) and not least in specific, specialized institutes, often with government support like SAIS at Johns Hopkins, the Saltzman Institute at Columbia, and Harvard's 'John M. Olin Institute'. The military academies and (especially in the US) 'war schools' of each service became another arena for systematic teaching of courses in security studies. Particularly in the US, scholars—with military or civilian background— in these latter institutions have been natural participants in the 'International security studies'/'international security and arms control' sections of ISA and APSA that were set up in the 1980s. 'Security *theory*' almost only develops within the civilian, university-based part—no longer in the think tanks. This is important as background for understanding the current situation regarding security theory, because the field is now closely intertwined with the (sub)discipline of IR in universities.

The potential problem for policy in this academicized development has been compensated by a gradual modification of the role of think tanks in the US. In the early period, the leading think tanks—notably the pioneering RAND Corporation—housed (within their social science sections) heavy theory work and large innovative projects. Today theory has moved to the universities, and think tanks have come under strong competitive pressure for delivering fast, usable policy guidance. Some think tanks have been politicized and operate not only from a political angle but as a key element in political strategies for (neo-) conservatives or liberals, others are still loosely tied to the services, but follow the policy agenda closely (Rich 2004). It has become much rarer to find theory even explicitly discussed in think tank work, but it is clearly drawn upon. The result is a chain construct, where academe, think tanks and policy makers are distinct and each purify their role. Persons might travel between the categories—move from think tank to university or to policy, or vice versa—but as institutions, they are distinct. This is, as we will return to in the next section, much less clearly the case outside the US (probably due to weaker competitive pressures on the intellectual market).

Structural observation about the different kinds of intellectual institutions in strategic studies is also the ideal context for characterizing the difference between the US and Western Europe during the early decades, a comparison which should be introduced here because the contrast will carry increasing weight as our story unfolds. In Europe, even the UK, think tanks from the beginning had mostly the roles that they are today associated with: to influence policy in a specific direction, to mobilize the public behind policy, and at best to digest, popularize and apply academic work done elsewhere into a more useful format for policy-makers (Parmar 2004; Haas 2002; Abelson 2002). In the area of foreign and security affairs, most policy-oriented work took place in 'foreign policy institutes', which rarely engaged in more theoretical efforts. One partial exception was the early decades of IISS, the International Institute for Strategic Studies, in London, where especially the series of *Adelphi Papers* included serious research often by scholars from around the world who were resident at the Institute for a period. But generally, during the Cold War Europeans characteristically conducted their political arguments over political and military strategy—often against the US—on the basis of theories made in the US.

The most important non-American contributions to strategic studies were probably Hedley Bull's foundational work on arms control (1961) and the continuous interaction of American social science scholarship with a tradition of British work steeped in classical military strategy (Basil Liddell Hart, Michael Howard, Lawrence Freedman and P.M.S. Blackett). The US–European contrast is clearly expressed in the way France's leading IR scholar, Raymond Aron, wrote repeatedly about Clausewitz, and France's main entries in the history of post-war strategic thought are two generals involved with the argument behind France's independent nuclear force. This in contrast to the centrality in the US of a kind of strategy rooted in modern social science and relatively independent of classical military strategy. In hindsight, it can be seen that Pierre Hassner (1997) throughout the Cold War and after produced a unique series of analyses of the political dimension of security anchored in political theory, but this did not take off as a style or approach establishing itself as a distinct presence in security studies, and most of his work during the Cold War appeared in policy-oriented anthologies on current challenges as 'the French chapter', rarely recognized for the theory work they constituted (Gloannec and Smolar 2003).

The distinct phenomenon of strategic studies emerged in Europe clearly as an imported American speciality. A most revealing testimony to the asymmetrical relationship is the incredibly condescending tone in Wohlstetter and Wohlstetter's 1963 report on the state of strategic studies in Europe. They give marks to the different national research communities (good to Sweden, not so good England, hope for Germany, etc.). Security studies was not born simultaneously in two places, and developments cannot be compared as independent phenomena. It emerged in the US and was exported to Europe. Since European security studies mostly took shape in the late 1960s and early 1970s, it became the post-Golden, institutionalized, theory-has-already-been-done kind of work that struggled to keep up with the newest technological developments to assess optimal Western military policy vis-à-vis the Soviet Union.

Strategic studies beyond the NATO area (Japan, third world, Israel, etc.), has been almost solely of the kind resembling political argumentation with a bit of factual, technical expertise—never 'basic conceptual analysis' (Wohlstetter and Wohlstetter 1966). An interesting parallel to the US case was the Soviet one, where Think Tank-like 'Institutes' gained a distinct niche, where they developed research with a different theoretical orientation than the (Marxist-Leninist) one in the dominant academic institutions. It is far beyond the remit of this chapter to include a detailed and nuanced coverage of this development but in striking parallel to the US, real world challenges formed the basis for innovative work in an institutional setting that combined a relationship and distance to high academe and the same duality to policy itself. Similar developments were not found to the same extent in Europe.

Nowhere beyond the US occurred, within an independent field of strategic studies, something similar to 'RAND's ability to produce systematic, long-range, "creative" research rather than to engage in mere short-range tinkering with other peoples' ideas' (Green 1968: 304). If one chooses anachronistically to project the history of security studies back into the inter-war period, it can be noted that the think tanks of the day (the first such) produced policy-oriented work that simultaneously was theoretically innovative and entered the annals of IR theory history. This happened in think tanks like 'Institute for Government Research' (Later Brookings), Carnegie, Council on Foreign Relations, and Hoover Institution plus Chatham House in Britain. They contributed to the formulation of plans for the international order in the inter-war period, and much of the thinking recorded in IR theory's history as 'idealism' was produced in connection to these.

Thus, the simultaneity of policy and theory work in universities and especially in separate institutions characterized both the inter-war and the first post-war periods in the US, but this changed towards the end of the 1960s. 'Having played a central role in the development of deterrence theory, economists were by [the 1970s] found hardly anywhere in the academic study of military affairs. RAND had also evolved into a bureaucratized contract research organization as much as a think tank and was no longer the hothouse of theoretical ferment it had been in the 1950s' (Betts 1997: 16).

A final element to cover regarding this phase is the parallel track constituted by peace research in relation to security studies. These two tracks meet only in a later period and peace research was certainly not seen as security/strategic studies at the time—quite the contrary. By the 1970s, the two had formed in clear contrast to each other. Early peace research ironically emerged in forms reminiscent of strategic studies—as a scientific alternative to mainstream IR. Much inter-war IR had been programmatically constructed as aiming for the production of peace, and thus the history of peace research can quite easily be anchored in inter-war (and immediate post-war) classics like Quincy Wright's *A Study of War* (1942) and Lewis Fry Richardson's books *Generalized Foreign Politics* (1939), *Arms and Insecurity* (1949), and *Statistics of Deadly Quarrels* (1950). After 1945, the UNESCO-sponsored attempt to form a social science based study of war was dismissed by the emerging discipline of International Relations (Aron 1957; Waltz 1959), and consequently peace research formed with roots mostly in the 'softer' or more humanistic social sciences like sociology and psychology, with pioneers like Herbert Kelman and Johan Galtung. The irony of this is that the same impulse towards 'scientific' approaches spurred the development of strategic studies mostly anchored in game theory and thus economics. Especially in Europe, peace research went through a radicalization in the late 1960s and early 1970s and so-called 'critical peace research' with strongholds in Germany, the Netherlands and Scandinavia, came to see strategic studies as part of the problem.

Especially in analyses like Dieter Senghaas's critique of deterrence theory (Senghaas 1969) and Johan Galtung's work on violence (Galtung 1969), mainstream theories were understood as part of the balance of terror, bipolar, Cold War system of militarization, superpower dominance and exploitation of the third world. Critical peace research was usually not seen as part of strategic studies or even security studies, either by the main stream or by the critics themselves. The critics did not write in the name of security, but more often in the name of *peace* depicting 'security' as a destructive pursuit (Jahn et al 1987; Wæver 2004b). Peace and security were symbols of the opposing sides during the Cold War (Buzan 1984; Wæver 2004b).

The period 1965–1980 has been seen by many observers as less successful, and by Baldwin (1995) even labelled 'decline'. Already in the 1970s, however, some new developments had begun that came into clearer focus in the 1980s. Critics of the traditional approach had started to make the case for inclusion of security challenges in e.g. the economic and environmental sectors (Brandt et al 1980; Palme et al 1982; Buzan 1983; Ullmann 1983; Nye and Lynne-Jones 1988; Mathews 1989).

KEY POINTS

- 1965–1980 marked a period of both stagnation for security studies in terms of theory development, and institutionalization in text books, courses and organizations.
- Security studies went from being inter-disciplinary to being mostly understood as political science, often as one of International Relations' two pillars (IPE being the other).
- Security studies, invented in the USA, was copied—often with direct American assistance—in Western Europe and in the rest of the world, especially among allies.
- The think tanks gradually stopped being innovative, inter-disciplinary places for thinking and became increasingly routinized producers of more narrow, technical problem-solving.
- Peace research developed on a parallel but so far separate track, and especially its most distinct, critical branch was seen neither by its representatives nor by security studies as part of the latter.

Disciplinary questioning and theoretical re-launch

There is no need here to rehash the familiar story of the wide/narrow debate of the 1970s and especially 1980s. The debate as such is covered well elsewhere—within and beyond the present volume— but for the present purpose of this article, it is necessary to understand the way the field developed theoretically in the 1980s and 1990s, not so much the debate as such, but the theoretical approaches that emerged out of this debate.

Of particular interest is the parallel turn to increasingly abstract and ambitious theorizing on both sides of the Atlantic, at the same time these theories developed on separate tracks. The US mainstream of security studies focused on debates over offensive and defensive realism, some discussion of constructivism, democratic peace and an emerging debate on power vs. institutions in empire/order building—all shaped by a quest for empirically validated generalizations about cause–effect relationships. A specific form of knowledge is hegemonic: cause–effect statements backed up by either statistical data or more often historical case studies (Walt 1999; Wæver 2004a). In Europe, a debate emerged between a number of more or less critical theories: CSS, feminism, Copenhagen school, Paris school and post-structuralism.

The different form of knowledge relates to a conflicting conception of the relationship to policy; less inclined to search for cause–effect generalizations to assist policy makers in calculating policy, more partaking in political reflections, i.e. more the role of public 'intellectual' than 'expert'. It is striking, however, that parallel to both these theoretical clusters, lots of specific 'technical expertise' developed on both sides and they were often less different than the theories: knowledge about AIDS as security problem, health security or missile defence. On top of this practical, empirical knowledge, two *different* clusters of theorization have developed. This general split partly reflects a more 'problem-solving' tradition in US social science, vs. a more critical one in Europe, but recent developments are more extreme than the usual pattern, and security studies was largely coherent across the Atlantic during the Cold War, with the deep split developing only during the 1980s and especially after the end of the Cold War.

While it would probably be wrong to *explain* this difference by policy needs (i.e. externalist sociology of science), the pattern is clearly reinforced by the pattern of world power at the beginning of the twenty-first century. In a world that might be described as consisting of one superpower and four great powers ('1+4' according to Buzan and Wæver 2003; Buzan 2004) or uni-multipolar (Huntington 1999) with the US seeing and handling it as unipolar and the other great powers acting according to multipolar logic, the different angles of watching the world point to different *forms* of knowledge (Wæver 2004a): US decision-makers and academics see the US as the actor that shapes the world and accordingly they need knowledge about cause–effect relationships in order to understand how to work the material they act upon (the world).

From a European perspective, in contrast, it is more common to see the main voice of security as an external factor to deal with (the US) and therefore to be in a tension-ridden relationship to security as such. Calls for action in the name of security can be seen as part of the US attempts to organize the world (currently especially under the slogan of a global war on terror; Buzan and Wæver 2003: 297, 300, 303; Wæver 2005; Buzan forthcoming), and therefore 'Europe' takes a position vis-à-vis security where it is possible to problematize pronouncements about what is a security issue as such (i.e. de-securitize) and insist on a wider concept of security e.g. an interpretation of terror and terror-fighting that emphasizes economic and political mechanisms. Therefore, the whole question of what should and should not count as security issues and how to conceptualize security is much closer to the European policy agenda than to the US one.

The difference also expresses a general meta-theoretical divide—with the US the more rationalist, Europe the more reflectivist—but this is far from the whole story. At least two other elements need to be taken into account (Wæver 2004a): one is the different relationship to the *concept of security*. In Europe, the debate on this has stayed part of the field. It is seen as part of the on-going practice of being a security analyst, to reflect on and problematize the concept—in order to understand and unveil the practices by practitioners in the name of security, but also as the politico-ethical self-reflection of a scholar who inevitably 'does security' when working in the name of security. In the US, the question of

THINK POINT 21.1

Places, persons, and paradigms

When we talk in broad terms about 'European' and 'US' theories, this should not be taken as statements generalizing about scholars in Europe and the US respectively, but refer to distinct arenas of theoretical discussions. Some scholars located in the US draw from and contribute to debates that mostly take place in Europe and—more clearly—many scholars in Europe work from theories made in the US and aim their publications at American colleagues. In the discipline of International Relations, there is a US-centred, global discipline that overlaps and intersects with weaker independent traditions like the English school, French IR and non-Western contributions. We do not want to deny the importance of 'American style' work done by Europeans and vice versa, but we want to point out how disconnected different sets of theoretical debate are, and these tend to have their main institutional anchorage (journals, research institutions, organizations) in different continents.

the concept of security is seen as at most a necessary 'define your terms' operation in order to delineate what is counted in and out. When done with, one knows what is security or not, and the concept is not interesting in itself any more.

The other element is the exact form of knowledge that is valued. In contrast to the situation in general IR, where the US is defined by rational choice, the US security studies field is absolutely *not* hard core rational choice. The leading security theory journals, *International Security* and *Security Studies*, publish rather little formalized rational choice, and even soft rational choice that draws on economic theory or organizational theory is far from valued the way it is in journals like *International Organization* or *International Studies Quarterly* (Wæver 1998; Brown et al 2000). The typical article in *International Security* uses historical case studies—maybe one in-depth historical case study—to examine a hypothesis framed as cause–effect relationships and very often tied into general debates that are on the one hand of sweeping magnitude, on the other hand boiled down to the measurement of one or a few variables, such as offensive versus defensive motivations (do states maximise power or security), the importance of ideational variables, or whether international order builds on pure power or also on institutions and legitimacy. Although each of these debates could easily be phrased as broad philosophical issues (as predecessors of each were in previous decades) or as ethical dilemmas, the American security literature constructs these questions as part of a tight, deductive logic in the spirit of Waltz, where a single, crucial question of how the logic unfolds is to be settled by empirical knowledge.

The most focused and sustained debate is probably offensive versus defensive realism, where a number of monographs (some major ones reviewed in Rose 1998) tried to use historical case studies to settle big, causal questions (see also Mearsheimer 2001). Similarly, the challenge from constructivism that in Europe turned into major self-reflective debates on the conditions and responsibility of scholarship became in US security studies mostly a question of testing the influence of ideational variables in the big causal picture (Desch 1998; Tannenwald and Wohlforth 2005).

The top level policy debate on American grand strategy under presumed unipolarity was academically addressed mainly in terms of the proper expectations regarding the balancing behaviour of others (Brooks and Wohlforth 2005), which again hinges mostly on the general questions from the offensive/defensive realism debate, and second on the power of institutions. The latter question generated a very focused debate easily stylized (and taught) as Ikenberry versus Wohlforth (Ikenberry 2002). Realism traditionally took unipolarity to be impossible, and the strictest of neo-realists—Waltz himself—actually predicted that it *would* not last long. Those who wanted to argue that some kind of preponderance could endure faced the challenge of *explaining* its relative stability. The major competing explanations emphasized on the one hand the US's uniquely reassuring liberal form of hegemony partly derived from attributes of the US state, partly built into US policy of institution-building and self-binding, and on the other hand the purely power-based stability of a situation where the US is *so* superior that balancing becomes impossible. (The debate is collected in Ikenberry 2002; see also Mearsheimer 2001; Bush 2002; Buzan and Wæver 2003; Buzan 2004; Brooks and Wohlforth 2005; Deudney 2006). The debate clearly has immediate implications for optimizing American grand strategy. But it is conducted less in terms of a future-oriented, purposive, and partly ethical debate about what future to aim for, and almost solely as (if it was) a theoretical-empirical debate over what theory can explain the past record. During the presidency of Bill Clinton, the debate on democratic peace had much the same status: the seemingly most relevant knowledge for security studies to supply to policy makers is whether there is or isn't a reliable causal connection between democracy and peace (Lepgold and Nincic 2001: ch. 5).

The common denominator tying together these differences is diverging understandings of the *role* of security studies, their function vis-à-vis policy. In the US, this is most clearly understood as theory uncovering causal laws about the workings of world politics which enables policy makers to make the right choices when facing situations where these relationships are relevant. This in turn reflects a situation of an *acting* power, one that has to decide about how to shape world affairs, and it reflects a clear division of labour between politics, policy advice and academic research.

In circles more clearly anchored on the European side, the trend was towards critical theories of various kinds that reflected on the practices of policy and problematized the nature of security making. This goes for Aberystwyth-style critical security studies, the Bourdieu-inspired work around Didier Bigo as well as the Copenhagen School, feminists and radical post-modernists like Dillon, Constantinou and Der Derian. Here, the concept of security has stayed part of the on-going debate, and the form of knowledge differs from the one in the American mainstream, and closer to that of a critical intellectual reflecting openly about one's own political responsibility—who argues about one's analytical and theoretical choices in terms of their political implications (Booth 1997; Jones 1999; Bigo 2002a, b; Huysmans 2002, 2006; Buzan et al 1998).

A part of this story is the role of peace research and its change during the 1980s. With the new peace movement, peace research suddenly gained a new practical relevance. What Håkan Wiberg (1988) has called 'the peace research movement' had to fulfil its function as the natural intellectual adviser (more or less asked for) to the peace movement (Jahn 1984). This led in much of North European peace research to a new 'realism'. Peace research became pro-security and pro-Europe (where previously it had been anti-security in the name of peace and anti-Europe in the name of the third world). Even defence was re-appropriated as alternative defence (non-offensive defence) (Møller 1991).

Security became during this period a meeting ground for strategic studies which had until then operated more with *power* as the guiding concept and peace research having obviously *peace* as the key concept. In the 1980s, *security* emerged as a more constructive analytical concept (Buzan 1984; Jahn et al 1987). Power thinking is a national concern and sees anarchy as inescapable and the end of the story—peace is cosmopolitan and claims that anarchy has to go before anything good can be achieved. In contrast, security is a relational concept (i.e. in-between national and cosmopolitan), and sees anarchy as a spectrum, where conditions can be improved in the direction of a mature anarchy (Buzan 1984). In this sense, security became the middle ground and increasingly explicit as the basis for much IR work from the 1980s and onwards.

Peace research institutes especially in the 1980s were often in a position somewhat parallel to that of think tanks during Golden Age strategic studies. The link to policy was very different— not official advisors to policy makers—but European security studies gained political relevance (in a broader sense) due to the politicization of security issues during the period defined by the peace movement, Reagan, and Gorbachev. The setting was—as in the 1950s—simultaneously inter-disciplinary and connected to current developments in theory in the different disciplines. Peace research in contrast to university IR was under pressure to deal with relevant issues, but there was no expectation of immediate delivery of policy answers. At RAND in the 1950s, the theorists were given extraordinary leeway to pursue highly abstract, idiosyncratic theoretical tracks, which clearly couldn't be justified in terms of guaranteed pay-off vis-à-vis products to be delivered to policy makers (Stern 1967). Exactly, therefore, publications often ended up being innovative solutions to policy questions. Similarly peace research was inter-disciplinary, politically oriented, but with a distance both to immediate policy responsibility and to the major powers of the academic system. It is less clear whether there were policy effects, but our main point here is the impact of political involvement on theory. As rightly noted by Betts in relation to traditional strategic studies, 'Ironically, in the past quarter century, policy experience has enriched academic research more than the reverse' (1997: 32). The same might be said about the 1980s and the birth of critical, European theories. A volatile political situation, a sense of importance and relevance, and engagement in heated political debates clearly contributed to the birth of these theories, and in a few cases, theorists probably had some role as intellectuals of or for social movements like the peace movements and Pugwash as well as some, mostly oppositional, political parties, but in general the effect of practice on theory was probably larger than vice versa.

Several observers (and observer participants) have noted that the debates among the new critical schools of security studies—to some extent seen as a 'European' development—have become surprisingly productive and generated theory of broader relevance and inspiration to the field of IR in general (Huysmans 1998; Eriksson 1999; Williams 2003). Security studies in the US largely works with theories that are developed within IR and then tested and refined within security studies on security cases—neo-realism, soft constructivism, etc. (Wæver 2004a). The most monumental illustration of this is the nature of constructivism in American security studies. The main work here is the big Katzenstein volume on *The Culture of National Security* (Katzenstein 1996). This was mainly manned by scholars who did not have a long-term involvement with security affairs. They were IR scholars who had taken part in the theory wars on the constructivist side, and it seemed the right move at the time to prove constructivism on the home ground of materialist approaches: security. Quite visibly this is a foray by general IR theorists into security studies for the sake of making a point within IR theory debates. The new 'European' schools, in contrast, did not develop deductively from the guiding symbolic positions within the theory debates (and therefore they are often hard to pin down—is the Copenhagen school constructivist, neo-realist or post-modernist?)—they emerged as part of the engagements on a distinct security scene, and the theoretical innovations *have become* part of the theory landscape in IR theory. For instance, one can find discussions of securitization theory in general IR journals (Williams 2003; Balzacq 2005) in ways that constitute the main investigations of the potential for IR of drawing on speech act theory in general. Similarly, debates within the discipline (at least in Europe) of the political role of researchers have been conducted with security theory as the platform (Huysmans 2002; Eriksson 1999). The fate of Frankfurt style 'Critical Theory' in IR has also been decisively influenced by security studies. The attempts in the 'fourth debate' in the 1980s to launch Critical Theory were largely abortive, and post-modern approaches came to structure the meta-theoretical scene to a much larger extent, but gradually Critical Theory gained a position in the general IR landscape to a large extent due to the success of Ken Booth and others in showing its value within the area of security (Jones 1999).

One might ask now, whether these lively debates in and among the new schools still qualify as 'security studies'. Have they simply become IR and lost the in-between position that defines security studies? Where the first generation representatives of the different schools—Booth, Bigo, Buzan, Wæver—had developed their arguments in engagements with policy questions and in direct interaction with policy makers and think tanks, the next generation would be more clearly academically defined and develop these arguments in a more isolated academic setting. However, the set-up continues to be one where security theory is located between the IR discipline as such and technical experts and practitioners, only with the arrows somewhat different from the North American ones (see Fig. 21.1).

The place of security experts here underlines the point that much work in European and North American research institutes is quite similar: detailed technical work on AIDS as an epidemic, on the proliferation of missile technology, on the efficiency of various counter-terrorist strategies. Most of what goes on in foreign policy institutes as well as the IISS in Europe and in American think tanks is of this nature, delivering on the demand of politicians for factual knowledge here-and-now on a question that came up yesterday and needs an answer tomorrow (maybe with the main difference, that in the US this is often structured more as a partisan advocacy for a specific policy, and in

Figure 21.1 The position of security theory in North America and Europe

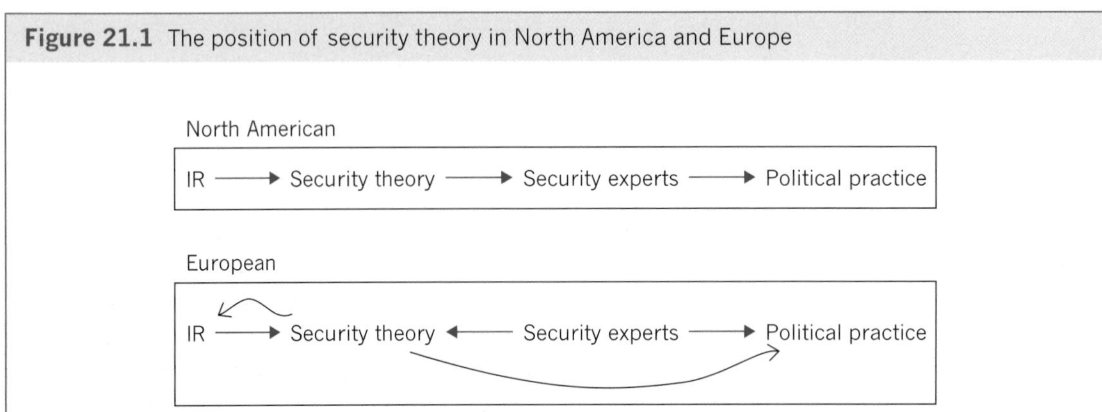

Europe as seemingly neutral, technical background knowledge). The point here is that as soon as this is reflected on in terms of theory—when an interaction emerges between on the one hand technical experts in say European foreign policy institutes or Washington think tanks, and on the other, university circles, for instance through Ph.D. students who do work that is simultaneously part of their university-based Ph.D. and part of the research institute, the theoretical context differs. In the US, this will usually be the discussions reflected in *International Security*, whereas in parts of Europe, the young scholars will relate to and draw inspiration from these new theories that emerged in European research institutes and now mainly thrive in European universities.

On both sides, it is essential to the particular nature of security theory that there is a distinct category of 'policy knowledge' that functions as expertise supporting policy—a form of knowledge that security theory in the US wants to assist while security theory in Europe (to draw the contrast sharply) treats it as a main empirical source for critical analysis. Critics of current policy in the US will aim to obtain a policy change by presenting theoretical generalizations based on empirical data that give scientific credentials to a different policy as more likely to achieve the aims aspired to. Critics working with the theories here associated with European security studies are more likely to criticize politically and ethically the current policy for its aims and effects and to expose the involved 'policy knowledge' as a part of policy making, structurally complicit and produced from the policy maker's perspective, rather than criticizing it for being scientifically wrong and up for revision.

KEY POINTS

- After the debates in the 1980s over wide vs. narrow concepts of security and the continuation or not of security studies, the 1990s saw a new turn to ambitious theorizing.
- The Europe-anchored debates continued the reflection on the concept of security and the role and self-understanding of security experts, generally with the politics of security as the over-arching theme.
- The US kind of security studies worked on general IR theories to produce empirically validated cause–effect understandings of the relationships most important to contemporary security.
- The contrast corresponds both to differences in the policy perspective from the only superpower and a region of great powers respectively, to different meta-theoretical traditions, and to contrasting conceptions of the role of a security expert.

Conclusion: the powers of theory and the challenges of the future

Security studies at present is in a strong position. It has been through a second decade of theoretical productivity. Strangely, this has happened to roughly parallel degrees in Europe and the US despite the very minimal connections between these two sets of theoretical developments. Now it is well equipped with a battery of theories and the field is simultaneously seen as generally important, so it attracts bright students, and increasingly, funding. What kind of development will this lead to?

It is quite plausible that the new 'European' security studies does not remain structured by separate 'schools' (Wæver 2004a). There is a tendency in the fast growing and very active trans-European community of Ph.D. students to move among and across these schools. Thereby they become treated more as *theories*, where one has to understand their distinct character—they do not blend into one synthesized European security theory—but they can be drawn upon in individual projects as inspiration and instruments. While it is still possible to find contributions (e.g. Booth 2005a) that try to cultivate a situation of competition and theory construction through caricaturing others, it is clearly more common among the emerging generation of scholars to see the combined field of 'New European Security Theories' (NEST) as a joint debate where the different theories are developed and applied through their interaction (Büger and Stritzel 2005).

The future of security theory in the US should be assessed in a different manner, because the theories there are less free-standing than the European theories and more closely integrated into the main constellation of IR theories. The future of these security theories is therefore inseparable from the general prospects for IR theory. As often noticed (e.g. Goldmann 1988), US theory debates in IR tend to be about general theories—frameworks potentially explaining everything or at least a major part of every important question. The main theories in the security field are expressed in such general terms that, if valid, they would be overarching frameworks for our general understanding of international relations. Therefore, their fate as security theories hinges on their ability to prevail in the general debates in the discipline of IR, and these are at the moment quite inconclusive and somewhat unfocused (Wæver 2006). The only strong candidate for a kind of hegemony is rational choice as meta-theory, and this is exactly the theory that is comparatively weak within security studies even in the US. Therefore, it is unlikely that the internal dynamics of the theory debate will be decided by a general prevalence of one of the current candidates.

More important for the future development of each theory in both Europe and the US is probably how it handles some of the current issues on the political agenda. The two sets of theories will be working on partly overlapping sets of questions, as indicated in many chapters of this book. Probably, it will mostly be the European theories that try to make sense out of environmental security, health security, identity issues and gender, while the US theories will be most active in areas like proliferation of weapons of mass destruction and global military stability. Both will work on terror and its counterpart, the US-centred international order, and where the first waves after 9/11 mainly came from the US, it has become a main object of analysis to European scholars, not only think tanks and the terrorism experts, but also from the theory-inclined academics. Conversely, both will work on migration and the tension between security and liberty including the logic of exceptionalism, although at least at present the theoretical side of this is far more developed in the debate among the European schools, where in the US this is mostly policy work disconnected from the main theories but with some notable exceptions (like Andreas and Biersteker 2003). Both will be working on the role and nature of technology, globalization, risk society and international economic order. This quick picture shows that there will actually be a lot of points of contact between the currently disconnected fields of theory. A major question is, therefore: will they merge again—not in agreement but in debate? Will there be more exchange between the different research environments? Some signs in this direction can be found in the acceptance of a somewhat widened security agenda in American text books, while—as always—all major American theories are read in Europe.

What will happen when they meet on issues of common concern? Will they try to learn from contrasting insights from different kinds of theories? The most likely key issue will be *terror and order*, the one that will probably top the American agenda and still be high enough on the European one for contributions to come from here too. It is potentially broad enough to become a prism through which the importance of other issues like environment and gender can be seen.

What can here be envisaged is not a 'new great debate' between clusters of security theories—rather a new encounter between different debates.

With or without such a meeting, this will be a time when theory is central to security studies. The theories of the 1990s will have to prove themselves in a dual challenge. The first question is do they have the inner vitality to become a dynamic research programme that continues to evolve? This depends largely on the constellation of key concepts—is this at once tight enough to be operational and open enough to generate puzzles and research problems? So far the signs here are quite promising. The second challenge is to be able to take up in interesting ways the political challenges of the day. In that regard, and particularly in relation to how it deals with terrorism and state responses to it, security studies will continue to grapple with the problem long ago noted by Waltz (1979: 112): 'States, like people, are insecure in proportion to the extent of their freedom. If freedom is wanted, insecurity must be accepted'.

KEY POINTS

- Security studies is in the advantageous position of housing much theoretical productivity and issues high on the public agenda, attracting therefore both funding and talent. Whether this opportunity will be used to produce better theories is yet to be seen.
- The different new 'schools' in Europe increasingly intersect and form a field with opportunities for a new generation to combine and innovate across the theories.
- In the US, the development of security theory is tied up with the general trends of the IR discipline.
- Both families of theories as well as their interaction will be much influenced by their ability to engage in relevant ways with the main issues on the policy agenda.

? QUESTIONS

Why was it primarily in the US that strategic studies formed as a separate field?

Why did the Vietnam War not become the generator of new waves of theorization to deliver on this new policy challenge?

On the basis of the previous chapters in this book as well as this chapter, to what extent does 'security studies' appear to be one integrated field, or is it more appropriately seen as two or more arenas sharing a name but separated by either geographical or meta-theoretical distance?

Would you explain the increasing distance between security theorizing in Europe and the US mainly by differences in foreign policy, general philosophical orientations, institutional differences within the academic world, or other factors?

Why does constructivism lead to such different kinds of work in the US and Europe?

What is different between the form of knowledge in US and European work?

What institutional reforms regarding universities, think tanks, policy institutes or policy making would be most conducive to better security theory and better security policy?

What are the most important questions on the policy agenda to get a better understanding of, and why do these not become the most active areas of research?

Do the current policy challenges point to a need for new inter-disciplinary relations?

Is a close connection between theory and policy conducive or disruptive for good theory?

FURTHER READING

■ **Schelling, Thomas C. (1960), *The Strategy of Conflict*, Cambridge: Harvard University Press.** One of the most original works from the (first) Golden Age, produced at RAND, eventually earning the author a 2005 Nobel Prize in economy (or in security studies, if one reads closely the justification from The Royal Swedish Academy of Sciences). Even fun to read.

■ **Gray, Colin (1982), *Strategic Studies and Public Policy: The American Experience*, Lexington: University Press of Kentucky.** A critical history of early strategic studies, which combines observations about institutions, politics and theory.

■ **Jervis, Robert (1976), *Perception and Misperception in International Politics*, Princeton: Princeton University Press.** One of the main books (together with Allison's *Essence of Decision*) to open up the psychological and decision-making approaches to strategic thinking in opposition to rational actor models.

■ **Buzan, Barry (1983), *People, States and Fear: The National Security Problem in International Relations*, Brighton: Wheatsheaf (2nd edn subtitled *An Agenda for International Security Studies in the Post Cold War Era*, Boulder CO: Lynne Rienner 2001; re-issued with new introduction as ECPR classic 2007).** A defining work from the second productive period, which both summarizes the preceding reflections on the concept of security and puts forward an original synthesis that made one of the first coherent cases for widening.

■ **Krause, Keith and Williams, Michael C. (eds.) (1997), *Critical Security Studies*: Concepts and cases, Minneapolis: University of Minnesota Press.** The defining work from 'Critical Security Studies' which includes sufficient diversity to represent much of the new work in general, not only one narrowly defined school, but paradoxically thereby producing the ideal manifesto for CSS.

■ **Buzan, Barry, Wæver, Ole, and de Wilde, Jaap (1998), *Security: A New Framework for Analysis*, Boulder, CO: Lynne Rienner (Chinese translation 2004; follow-on edition in 2007 entitled *The Politics of Security*).** The main theoretical statement from the Copenhagen School. While its world analysis is more fully elaborated in a later book, the defining categories of the theory are put forward here: securitization and sectors.

■ **Croft, Stuart and Terriff, Terry (eds.) (2000), *Critical Reflections on Security and Change*, London: Frank Cass.** Combines reflections on more traditional security studies—realism, liberalism, etc.—with the new debates.

■ **Brown, Michael E. (ed.) (2000), *Rational Choice and Security Studies: Stephen Walt and His Critics*, Cambridge, MA: MIT Press**. Stephen Walt's attack on rational choice approaches to security is both interesting as an exploration of the pros and cons of this approach, and as a clarification of how security studies, *International Security* style, defines itself methodologically and meta-theoretically.

■ **Ikenberry, John G. (ed.) (2002), *American Unrivaled: The Future of the Balance of Power*, Ithaca, NY: Cornell**. Includes a number of powerful contributions that represent the main American debates over both offensive/defensive realism and international orders built on power/institutions.

■ **Guzzini, Stefano and Jung, Dietrich (eds.) (2004), *Contemporary Security Analysis and Copenhagen Peace Research*, London: Routledge**. Explores the role of peace research (especially in Northern Europe) in furthering the emergence of the new European security theories.

IMPORTANT WEBSITES

- **http://www.isn.ethz.ch/** International Relations and Security Network, Center for Security Studies, ETH, Zürich, Switzerland. A good collection of links to both current security issues and centres of research. From here one can get to the institutes, journals and organizations, of which there are too many to list individually here.
- **http://critical.libertysecurity.org/** Open Working Group on Critical Approaches to Security In Europe: a good road especially to the younger generation of scholars working with the new European approaches.
- **http://www.intlsecurity.org/** Joint webpage for the International Security Studies Section (ISSS) of International Studies Association (ISA) and the International Security and Arms Control (ISAC) section of the American Political Science Association (APSA).
- **http://www.mitpressjournals.org/loi/isec** *International Security*, the leading mainstream journal.
- **http://www.tandf.co.uk/journals/titles/09636412.asp** *Security Studies*, another high-ranking journal mostly publishing American mainstream research, but often more open to deep theoretical debate than *International Security*.
- **http://ejt.sagepub.com/** *European Journal of International Relations*. Much of the debate over the new European theories has taken place in general IR journals like *EJIR*, *Review of International Studies* and *Millennium*.
- **http://sdi. sagepub.com/** *Security Dialogue* has recently developed into one of the leading places for discussion on both 'human security', 'gender and security' and the new European theories, while also strong on policy articles.

Visit the Online Resource Centre that accompanies this book for lots of interesting additional material: www.oxfordtextbooks.co.uk/orc/collins/

Bibliography

Abelson, Donald E. (2002), *Do Think Tanks Matter? Assessing the Impact of Public Policy Institutes*, McGill-Queen's University Press.

Adams, Gordon (1982), *The Politics of Defense Contracting: the Iron Triangle*, New Brunswick, NJ: Transaction Books.

Adler, E. and Burnett, M. (1998), *Security Communities*, Cambridge: Cambridge University Press.

Air Force Technology (2006), 'Gripen Multirole Fighter Aircraft, Sweden', *airforce-technology.com*. http://www.airforce-technology. com/projects/gripen/

Albert, M. (1993), *Capitalism Against Capitalism*, London: Whurr.

Albright, D. and Hinderstein, C. (2005), 'Unraveling the A.Q. Khan and Future Proliferation Networks', *The Washington Quarterly* 28/2: 111–28.

Aldrich, Richard J. (2002), 'America Used Islamists to Arm the Bosnian Muslims', *The Guardian*, 22 April. http://www.guardian.co.uk/print/0,3858,4398721-103677,00.html

Alibek, K. (2000), *Biohazard*, New York: Random House.

Alison, Graham (1971), *Essence of Decision: Explaining the Cuban Missile Crisis*, Boston: Little, Brown and Co.

Al-Jazeera (2005), 'Ahmadinejad: wipe Israel off map', *Al-Jazeera.net*, 26 Oct.

Alkiri, S. (2004), 'A Vital Core that Must be Treated with the Same Gravitas as Traditional Security Threats'. *Security Dialogue*, 35/3: 359–60.

Allan, J. (2002), *The Middle East Water Question: Hydropolitics and the Global Economy*, London: I.B. Taurus Publishers.

Alonso Harriet Hyman (1993), *Peace as a Woman's Issue: History of the US Movement for World Peace and Women's Rights*, Syracuse University Press.

Amsden, A. and Hikino, T. (2000), 'The Bark is Worse than the Bite: New WTO Law and Late Industrialisation', *Annals of American Political and Social Science*, Vol. 570 (July), 104–14.

Anderson, Guy (2005a) 'US Defense Budget Will Equal ROW Combined within 12 Months', *Jane's Defence Industry*, 4 May. http://www.janes.com/defence/news/jdi/jdi050504_1_n.shtml

—— (2005b), 'Discrepancy Between US and ROW Spending is Highlighted Again', *Jane's Defence Industry*, 7 June. http://www.janes.com/defence/news/jdi/jdi050607_1_n.shtml

Andreas, Peter and Biersteker, Thomas J. (2003), *The Rebordering of North America: Integration and Exclusion in a New Security Context*, Routledge.

Andrew, C. and Gordievsky, O. (1991), *KGB: The Inside Story*, New York: HarperCollins Publishers.

Andrew, C. (1987), *Her Majesty's Secret Service: The Making of the British Intelligence Community*, London: Penguin Books.

Anthony, M., Emmers, R., and Acharya, A. (eds.) (2006), *Non-Traditional Security in Asia: Dilemmas in Securitization*, London: Ashgate Publishing.

Arms Trade News (1997) 'Ukraine Underselling Russian Arms', July, 3.

Aron, Raymond (1957), 'Conflict and war from the viewpoint of historical sociology' in *The Nature of Conflict*, UNESCO, 177–203.

Art, R.J. (2003), 'Introduction', in R.J. Art and P.M. Cronin (eds.), *The United States and Coercive Diplomacy*, Washington, DC: United States Institute of Peace, 3–20.

Ash, Timothy Garton (2003), 'Is There a Good Terrorist?' in Charles W. Kegley, Jr. (ed.), *The New Global Terrorism: Characteristics, Causes, Controls*, Upper Saddle River, NJ: Prentice Hall, 60–70.

Axelrod, R. (1984), *The Evolution of Co-operation*, New York: Basic Books.

Aydelott, Denise (1993), 'Mass Rape During War: Prosecuting Bosnian Rapists Under International Law', *Emory Law Review* Vol. 7. Fall. No. 2. 585–631.

Ayoob, M. (1995), *The Third World Security Predicament: State Making, Regional Conflict, and the International System*, Boulder, CO: Lynne Rienner.

—— (1997), 'Defining Security: A subaltern realist perspective' in Krause, Keith and Michael C. Williams (eds.), *Critical Security Studies: Concepts and Cases*, Minneapolis: University of Minnesota Press, 121–46.

Baechler, G. (1999), *Violence Through Environmental Discrimination: Causes, Rwanda Arena, and Conflict Model*, Dordrecht: Kluwer.

Bailyn, Bernard (1992), *The Ideological Origins of the American Revolution*, Cambridge, MA, and London: The Belknap Press and Harvard University Press.

Bal, Ihsan, and Laciner, Sedat (2001), 'The Challenge of Revolutionary Terrorism to Turkish Democracy', *Terrorism and Political Violence*, Vol. 14, No. 4, 90–115.

Baldwin, David (1995), 'Security Studies and the End of the Cold War', *World Politics*, Vol. 48, 117–41.

Balzacq, Thierry (2005), 'The Three Faces of Securitization: Political Agency, Audience and Context', *European Journal of International Relations*, Vol. 11: 171–201.

Baran, Paul A. and Sweezy, Paul M. (1966), *Monopoly Capital*, New York: Monthly Review Press.

Barham, John and Owen, David (1999), 'Embraer: French Buy $200m Stake in Brazilian Jetmaker', *Financial Times*, 26 October.

Barkawi, Tarak (2005), *War and Globalization*, London: Rowman & Littlefield.

—— (ed.) (2001), *Democracy, Liberalism and War: Rethinking the Democratic Peace Debates*, Boulder, CO: Lynne Rienner Publishers.

—— and Laffey, Mark (1999), 'The Imperial Peace: Democracy, Force and Globalization', *European Journal of International Relations*, 5/4, 403–34.

Barnett, J. (2001), *The Meaning of Environmental Security: Ecological Politics and Policy in the New Security Era*, London: Zed Books.

—— and Adger, N. (2003), 'Climate Dangers and Atoll Countries', *Climatic Change*, 61/3: 321–37.

Bazergan, Roxanne (2002), *HIV/AIDS & Peacekeeping: A field study of the policies of the United Nations Mission in Sierra Leone*, London: International Policy Institute, September 2002.

BBC News (2003), 'Thais swear to stay Drug-Free', 1 April 2003.

Beare, Margaret E. (ed.) (2003), *Critical Reflections on Transnational Organized Crime, Money Laundering, and Corruption*, Toronto: University of Toronto Press.

Beevor, Antony (2002), *Berlin: The Downfall 1945*, London: Penguin.

Beier, Marshall (2001), 'Postcards from the Outskirts of Security: Defence Professionals, Semiotics, and the NMD Initiative', *Canadian Foreign Policy* 8/2.

Belasco, Amy (2005), 'The Costs of Iraq, Afghanistan and Enhanced Base Security Since 9/11', *CRS Report for Congress*, Congressional Research Service, 7 October. These reports are routinely classified but are often made available by workers interested in governmental transparency and put up on the Federation of American Scientists website. http://www.fas.org/sgp/crs/natsec/RL33110.pdf

Bennett, David H. (1988), *The Party of Fear: From Nativist Movements to the New Right in American History*, Chapel Hill: University of North Carolina Press.

Berlin, Isaiah (1981), *Against the Current: Essays in the History of Ideas*, Oxford: Oxford University Press.

Betts, Richard (1997), 'Should Strategic Studies Survive', *World Politics*, Vol. 50: 1, October, 7–33.

Bigo, Didier (2002a), 'To Reassure and Protect, After September 11' on web-page by the Social Science Research Council 'after September 11' http://www.ssrc.org/sept11/essays/bigo.htm

—— (2002b) 'Security and Immigration: Toward a Critique of the Governmentality of Unease', *Alternatives*, Vol. 27: supplement, Feb. 2002, 63–92.

Bitzinger, Richard A. (Fall 1992), 'Arms to Go: Chinese Arms Sales to the Third World', *International Security*, Vol. 17, No. 2, 84–111.

—— (2003), *Towards a Brave New Arms Industry?* Adelphi Paper 356, London: International Institute for Strategic Studies.

Böge, V. (1999), 'Mining, Environmental Degradation and War: The Bougainville Case', in M. Suliman (ed.), *Ecology, Politics and Violent Conflict*, London: Zed Books, 211–27.

Booth, K. (1991), 'Security and Emancipation', *Review of International Studies*, 17/4: 313–26.

—— (1997), 'Security and Self: Reflections of a fallen realist' in Krause, Keith and Michael C. Williams, *Critical Security Studies: Concepts and Cases*, Minneapolis: University of Minnesota Press, 83–119.

—— (2005b), 'Beyond Critical Security Studies' in Booth, Ken (ed.), *Critical Security Studies and World Politics*, Boulder, CO: Lynne Rienner, 259–78.

—— (ed.) (2005a), *Critical Security Studies and World Politics*, Boulder, CO: Lynne Rienner.

Born, H., Johnson, L., and Leigh, I. (2005), *Who's Watching the Spies: Establishing Intelligence Service Accountability*, Dulles, VA: Potomac Books.

Boureston, J. (2002), 'Assessing Al Qaeda's WMD Capabilities', 2 September http://www.ccc.nps.navy.mil/rsepResources/si/sept02/ wmd.asp

Boyden, J. (2003), 'The moral development of child soldiers: what do adults have to fear?' *Peace and Conflict*, 9(4), 343–62.

—— and Levison, D. (2000), *Children as Economic and Social Actors in the Development Process*, Working paper 2000: 1, EGDI: Expert Group on Development Issues, Ministry for Foreign Affairs, Stockholm, Sweden.

Boyden, S., Dovers, S., and Shirlow, M. (1990), *Our Biosphere Under Threat: Ecological Realities and Australia's Opportunities*, Melbourne: Oxford University Press.

Brandt, W. (1980), *North-South: A Programme for Survival: Report of the Independent Commission on International Development Issues*, Cambridge, MA: MIT Press.

Braun, C. and Chyba, C.F. (2004), 'Proliferation Rings: New Challenges to the Nuclear Nonproliferation Regime', *International Security*, 29/2: 5–49.

Brett, R. and Specht, I. (2004), *Young soldiers: why they choose to fight*, Boulder, CO: Lynne Rienner.

British Offset, Opportunities through Economic Cooperation in Saudi Arabia http://www.britishoffset.com/pages/content/index.asp?PageID=10 accessed 14 January 2006.

Brocklehurst, H. (2003), 'Kids r Us? Children as Political Bodies', *International Journal of Politics and Ethics.*, Vol. 3, 1, 79–92. Reproduced in Mark Evans (2004) (ed.) *Ethical Theory in the Study of International Politics*, York: Nova Science 91–104.

—— (2005), 'Just children? Just war' in M. Evans (ed.) *Just War theory: A Reappraisal*, Edinburgh: Edinburgh University Press.

—— (2006), *Who's Afraid of Children? Children, Conflict and International Relations*, Aldershot: Ashgate.

Brodie, B. (ed.) (1946), *The Absolute Weapon: Atomic Power and World Order*, New York: Harcourt, Brace & Co.

—— (1965), 'The McNamara Phenomenon', *World Politics*, Vol 17 (July), 672–86.

Brooks, Edwin (1974), 'The Implications of Ecological Limits to Development in Terms of Expectations and Aspirations in Developed and Less Developed Countries', in Anthony Vann and Paul Rogers (eds.) *Human Ecology and World Development*, London and New York: Plenum Press.

Brooks, Stephen G. and Wohlforth, William C. (2005), 'Hard Times for Soft Balancing', *International Security*, Vol. 30: 1, 72–108.

Brown, JoAnne (1988), ' "A Is for Atom, B Is for Bomb": Civil Defense in American Public Education, 1948–1963', *Journal of American History*, Vol. 75, no. 1, 68–90.

Brown, L. (1977), 'Redefining National Security', Worldwatch Paper No. 14, Washington: Worldwatch Institute.

Brown, Michael E. (ed.) (2000), *Rational Choice and Security Studies: Stephen Walt and his Critics*, MIT Press.

Brownmiller, Susan (1975), *Against our Will: Men, Women and Rape*, New York: Simon and Schuster.

Bruce, James (1994), 'Peace Widens Israel's Markets', *Jane's Defence Weekly*, 19 November, 23;

Buckley, Mary (1989), *Women and Ideology in the Soviet Union*, London: Harvester Wheatsheaf.

Büger, Christian and Stritzel, Holget (2005), 'Tagungsbericht: Critical Approaches to Security in Europe, Rencontres doctorales Européennes sur le thème de la Sécurité, Paris 2004', in Zeitschrift für Internationale Beziehungen, Vol. XXX.

Bull, Hedley (1961), *The Control of the Arms Race: Disarmament and Arms Control in the Missile Age*, New York: Praeger (2nd edn 1965).

Bull, Hedley (1968), 'Strategic Studies and Its Critics', *World Politics* 20 (July), 599–600.

Burman, Erica (1992), 'Innocents abroad: western fantasies of childhood and the iconography of emergencies', *Disasters*, Vol. 18, no. 3, 238–53.

Buzan, B. (1981), 'Change and Insecurity: A Critique of Security Studies' in Barry Buzan and R.J. Barry Jones (eds.), *Change and the Study of International Relations: The Evaded Dimension*, London: Pinter, 155–72.

—— (1983), *People, States and Fear: The National Security Problem in International Relations*, Brighton: Wheatsheaf Books.

—— (1984), 'Peace, Power, and Security: Contending Concepts in the Study of International Relations', *Journal of Peace Research*, 21(2), 109–25.

—— (1991a), *People, States and Fear: An Agenda for International Security Studies in the Post-Cold War* Era, London: Harvester Wheatsheaf, 2nd edn.

—— (1991b), 'Is International Security Possible?', in K. Booth, *New Thinking About Strategy and International Security*, London: Harper Collins, 31–55.

—— (1993), 'Societal Security, State Security, and Internationalisation', in Ole Wæver, B. Buzan, M. Kelstrup and P. Lemaitre (eds.) *Identity, Migration and the New Security Agenda in Europe*, London: Pinter, 41–58.

—— (2000), ' "Change and Insecurity" Reconsidered' in Stuart Croft and Terry Terriff (eds.), *Critical Reflections on Security and Change*, London: Frank Cass, 1–17.

—— (2004), *United States and the Great Powers*, Cambridge: Polity.

—— (forthcoming), 'The "War on Terrorism" as the new "macro-securitisation"?'

—— and Gautam, Sen (1990), 'The impact of military research and development priorities on the evolution of the civil economy in capitalist states', *Review of International Studies*, 16/4: 321–39.

—— and Herring, Eric (1998), *The Arms Dynamic in World Politics*, London: Lynne Rienner.

—— Jones, C., and Little, R. (1993), *The Logic of Anarchy: Neorealism to Structural Realism*, New York: Columbia University Press.

—— and Wæver, O. (1997), 'Slippery? Contradictory? Sociologically Untenable? The Copenhagen School Replies', *Review of International Studies*, 23/2: 241–50.

—— and Wæver, O. (2003), *Regions and Power: The Structure of International Society*, Cambridge: Cambridge University Press.

—— Wæver O., and De Wilde J. (1998), *Security: A New Framework for Analysis*, Boulder, CO: Lynne Rienner.

Byman, D. Waxman, M., and Larson, E. (1999), *Air Power as a Coercive Instrument*, Santa Monica, CA: RAND, MR-1061-AF.

Cable, V. (1995), 'What is International Economic Security?', *International Affairs*, Vol. 71(2), 305–24.

Cairns, Ed (1996), *Children and Political Violence*, Oxford: Blackwell Publishers.

Campbell, David (1993), *Politics Without Principle. Sovereignty, Ethics and the Narratives of the Gulf War*, Boulder, CO: Lynne Rienner Publishers.

—— (1998a), *Writing Security: United States foreign policy and the politics of identity*, Revised Edition, Minneapolis: University of Minnesota Press.

—— (1998b), *National Deconstruction: Violence, identity, and justice in Bosnia*, Minneapolis: University of Minnesota Press.

Carson, R. (1962), *Silent Spring*, Boston, MA: Houghton Mifflin.

Chalk, Peter (1996), *West European Terrorism and Counter-Terrorism: The Evolving Dynamic*, Houndsmill, Basingstoke: Macmillan.

Clary, C. (2004), 'A.Q. Khan and the Limits of the Non-proliferation Regime', *Disarmament Forum*, 4: 33–42.

CNN, 'Rumsfeld Warns on China Military', *CNN.com*, 4 June 2005 http://www.cnn.com/2005/WORLD/asiapcf/06/04/rumsfeld.asia.ap/

Coalition to Stop the Use of Child Soldiers, http://www.child-soldiers.org/childsoldiers/some-facts/ accessed 18 September 2005.

Cochrane, J. (2003), 'Blood in Bangkok Streets', *Newsweek*, 10 March 2003.

Cock, Jacklyn (1979), *Women and War in South Africa*, London: Gollancz.

Cohn, Carol, 'Sex and Death in the Rational World of Defence Intellectuals', *Signs*, Vol. 12 (1987), 687–718.

Cohn, Ilene and Goodwin-Gill, Guy S. (1997), *Child Soldiers: The Role of Children in Armed Conflict*, Oxford: Claredon Press.

Coker, C. (2002), *Globalisation and Insecurity in the Twenty-first Century: NATO and the Management of Risk*, Adelphi Paper no. 345, Oxford: Oxford University Press.

Collier, P. (2000), *Economic Causes of Civil Conflict and Their Implications for Policy*, Washington: The World Bank.

Collins, A. (2003), *Security and Southeast Asia: Domestic, Regional and Global Issues,* Boulder, CO: Lynne Rienner.

—— (2005), 'Securitization, Frankenstein's Monster and Malaysian Education', *Pacific Review*, 18/4: 565–86.

Conca, K. (2002), 'The case for environmental peacemaking', in Conka and Dabelko (eds), *Environmental Peacemaking*, Baltimore: John Hopkins University Press.

—— (1997), *Manufacturing Insecurity: The Rise and Fall of Brazil's Military-Industrial Complex*, London: Lynne Rienner.

—— and Dabelko, G. (2002) (eds.), *Environmental Peacemaking*, Baltimore: John Hopkins University Press.

Cook, Catherine, Hanieh, Adam, and Adah, Kay (2004), *Stolen Youth: The Politics of. Israeli Detention of Palestinian Children*, Pluto Press.

Cox, Christopher (1996), Chairman, 'Iran-Bosnia Credibility Gap', House Republican Policy Committee *Policy Perspective* 26 http://www.fas.org/irp/news/1996/hrpc_irancred. htm

Crandall, Russell (2002), *Driven By Drugs: U.S. Policy Toward Colombia*, Boulder, CO: Lynne Rienner Publishers.

Crenshaw, M. (2003), 'Coercive Diplomacy and the Response to Terrorism', in R.J. Art and P.M. Cronin (eds.), *The United States and Coercive Diplomacy*, Washington, DC: United States Institute of Peace, 305–57.

Dalby, S. (1992), 'Ecopolitical Discourse: "Environmental Security" and Political Geography', *Progress in Human Geography*, 16/4: 503–22.

Dauvergne, P. (1998), 'Weak States, Strong States: A State-in-Society Perspective', in P. Dauvergne (ed.), *Weak and Strong States in Asia-Pacific Societies*, Australia: Allen and Unwin.

Davie, Maurice R. (1929, reprint 2003), *The Evolution of War: A Study of Its Role in Early Societies*, Dover Publications.

Dawson, Doyne (1996), *The Origins of Western Warfare*, Boulder, CO: Westview.

de Soysa, I. (2000), 'The Resource Curse: Are Civil Wars Driven By Rapacity Or Paucity?', in M. Berdal and D. Malone (eds.), *Greed and Grievance: Economic Agendas and Civil Wars*, Boulder, CO: Lynne Rienner, 113–36.

Dent, C.M. (2001), 'The Eurasian Economic Axis: Its Significance for East Asia' (2001) *Journal of Asian Studies*, Vol. 60(3), 731–59.

—— (2002), *The Foreign Economic Policies of Singapore, South Korea and Taiwan*, Cheltenham: Edward Elgar.

Der Derian, James (1995), 'The Value of Security: Hobbes, Marx, Nietzsche, and Baudrillard' in Ronnie D. Lipschutz (ed.) *On Security*, New York: Columbia University Press, 24–45.

—— (2001), *Virtuous War: Mapping the Military-Industrial-Media-Entertainment Network*, Boulder, CO: Westview.

Desch, Michael C. (1998), 'Culture Clash: Assessing the Importance of Ideas in Security Studies'. *International Security*, 23, No. 1 (Summer), 141–70.

DeSouza, P.J. (2000), 'Introduction and Overview', in P.J. DeSouza (ed.) *Economic Strategy and National Security*, Boulder, CO: Westview Press.

Deudney, D. (1990), 'The Case Against Linking Environmental Degradation and National Security', *Millennium: Journal of International Studies*, 19/3: 461–76.

—— (1995) 'The Philadelphia System: Sovereignty, Arms Control, and Balance of Power in the American States-Union, Circa 1787–1861', *International Organization*, Vol. 49: 2, 191–228.

—— (2006), *Bounding Power: Republican Security Theory from the Polis to the Global Village*, Princeton: Princeton University Press.

Dillon, Michael (1996), *Politics of Security. Towards a Political Philosophy of Continental Thought*, London: Routledge.

—— (2006), *Governing Terror*, London: Palgrave/Macmillan.

Ding, Arthur S. (2000), 'Is China A Threat? A Defense Industry Analysis', *Issues & Studies*, Vol. 36, No. 1 (January/February), 49–75.

Dingley, James and Kirk-Smith, Michael (2002), 'Symbolism and Sacrifice in Terrorism', *Small Wars and Insurgencies*, Vol. 13, No. 1, 102–28.

Dixon, Norman (1976), *On the Psychology of Military Incompetence*, London: Basic Books.

Dodge, Cole, P. and Raundalen, Magne (1991), *Reaching Children in War: Sudan, Uganda and Mozambique*, Bergen, Norway: Sigma Forlag.

Dowdy, John J. (1997), 'Winners and Losers in the Arms Industry Downturn', *Foreign Policy*, Issue 107 (Summer), 88–101.

Draguhn, W. and Ash, R. (eds.) (1999), *China's Economic Security*, London: Carton Press.

Dycus, S. (1996), *National Defense and the Environment*, Hanover, NH: University Press of New England.

Editorial, 'Project Source Codes', *Defense News*, 18 October 1999, 56.

Edwards, Ruth Dudley (1999), *The Faithful Tribe*, London: Harper Collins.

Elbe, Stefan (2003), *The Strategic Dimensions of HIV/AIDS*. Adelphi Paper 357, International Institute for Strategic Studies, Oxford: Oxford University Press.

Elshtain, Jean Bethke (1987), *Women and War*, New York: Basic Books.

—— and Tobias, Sheila (eds.) (1990), *Women, Militarism and War*, Savage, MD: Rowman and Littlefield.

Emmers, R. (2004), *Non-Traditional Security in the Asia-Pacific: The Dynamics of Securitisation*, Singapore: Eastern Universities Press.

Enloe, Cynthia (1998), *Does Khaki Become You? The Militarisation of Women's Lives*, London: Pandora.

—— (1993), *The Morning After: Sexual Politics at the End of the Cold War*, London: University of California Press.

—— and Zalewski, Marysia (1995), 'Questions about Identity in International Relations' in Smith and Booth (eds.), *International Relations Theory Today*, Oxford: Polity Press.

Eriksson, Johan (1999), 'Observers or Advocates? On the political role of security analysts', *Cooperation and Conflict* 34/3: 311–30.

Esty, D., Goldstone, J., Gurr, T., Harff, B., Levy, M., Dabelko, G., Surko, P., and Unger, A. (1999), 'State Failure Task Force Report: Phase II Findings', *Environmental Change and Security Project Report*, 5: 49–72.

Etzold, Thomas H. (1978), 'American Organization for National Security 1945–50' in Thomas H. Etzold and John Lewis Gaddis (eds.), *Containment: Documents on American Policy and Strategy, 1945–50*, New York: Columbia University Press, 1–23.

EUROPOL, *European Union 2003 Organised Crime Situation Report*, Luxembourg: Office for Official Publications of the European Communities, 2003. Accessed at http://www.europol.eu.int/publications/EUOrganisedCrimeSitRep/2003/EUOrganisedCrimeSitRep2003.pdf

Falk, R. (1971), *This Endangered Planet: Prospects and Proposals for Human Survival*, New York: Random House.

Farooq, Umer (1999), 'Production Under Way on Pakistan's Al-Khalid MBT', *Jane's Defence Weekly*, Vol. 32, No. 13, 29 September 1999, 15.

Farrell, Theo (1996), 'Figuring out Fighting Organisations: The New Organisational Analysis in Strategic Studies', *Journal of Strategic Studies*, 19/1: 128–42.

—— (1997), *Weapons Without A Cause: The Politics of Weapons Acquisition in the United States*, London: Macmillan.

Fearon, James D. and Laitin, David D. (2000), 'Violence and the Social Construction of Identity', *International Organization*, 54/4, 845–77.

—— and —— (2003), 'Ethnicity, Insurgency, and Civil War', *American Political Science Review*, 97/1: 75–90.

Fickenaeur, James O. and Voronin, Yuri A. 'The Threat of Russian Organized Crime', National Institute of Justice, NCJ 187085, June 2001.

Flight International (1994) 'UK C-130 Hercules For Sale', 4 October.

Frean, Alexandra (1998), 'Empire's forgotten children strike back', *The Times*, 18 May, 7.

Freedman, Lawrence (1998), 'International Security: Changing Targets', *Foreign Policy*, Spring, 48–63.

Friedberg, A.L. (1991), 'The Changing Relationship Between Economics and National Security', *Political Science Quarterly*, Vol. 106(2), 265–76.

Galtung, J (1969), 'Violence, peace and peace research', *Journal of Peace Research*, 3, 169–92.

Garrett, Laurie (2005), *HIV and National Security: Where are the Links?* New York: Council on Foreign Relations, http://www.cfr.org/pub8248/laurie_garrett/hiv_and_national_security_where_are_the_links.php

Gates, R. (1987/88), 'The CIA and Foreign Policy', *Foreign Affairs*, 66: 215–30.

George, A.L. (1994), 'Diplomacy: Definition and Characteristics', in A.L. George and W.E. Simons, *The Limits of Coercive Diplomacy*, Boulder, CO: Westview, 2nd revised edn, 7–11.

—— and Hall, D., and Simons, W.E. (1971), *The Limits of Coercive Diplomacy: Laos, Cuba, Vietnam*, Boston, MA: Little, Brown.

Geske, Mary, B. with Ensalaco, M. (2005), 'Three prints in the Dirt: Child Soldiers and Human Rights', in Ensalaco, M. and Majka, Linda C. (eds.), *Children's Human Rights: Progress and Challenges for Children Worldwide*, Oxford: Rowman and Littlefield.

Gilpin, Robert (1981), *War and Change in World Politics*, New York: Cambridge University Press.

Gleik, P. (1991), 'Environment and Security: The Clear Connections', *The Bulletin of the Atomic Scientists*, 47/3: 17–21.

Gloannec, Anne-Marie Le and Aleksander, Smolar (eds.) (2003), *Entre Kant et Kosovo: Études offertes à Pierre Hassner*, Paris: Presses de Sciences Po.

Godson, Roy and Williams, Phil, 'Strengthening Cooperation against Transnational Crime', *Survival*, Vol. 40, No. 3, Autumn 1998.

Goldmann, Kjell (1988), *Change and Stability in Foreign Policy: The Problems and Possibilities of Detente*, Princeton, NJ: Princeton University Press.

Gowa, J.A. (1999), *Ballots and Bullets: The Elusive Democratic Peace*, Princeton, NJ: Princeton University Press.

Graham, D.T. (2000), 'The People Paradox: Human Movements and Human Security in a Globalising World', in D.T. Graham and N.K. Poku (eds.), *Migration, Globalisation and Human Security*, London: Routledge, 192–9.

Gray, Colin (1971), 'What RAND Hath Wrought', *Foreign Policy*, vol. 4, 111–29.

Gray, Colin (1982), *Strategic Studies and Public Policy: The American Experience*, Lexington: University Press of Kentucky.

—— (1996), 'Arms Races and Other Pathetic Fallacies: A case for Deconstruction', *Review of International Studies*, 22/3: 323–35.

Grayson, K. (2003), 'Securitization and the Boomerang Debate: A Rejoinder to Liotta and Smith-Windsor', *Security Dialogue*, 34/3.

Green, E.M. (1996), *Economic Security and High Technology Competition in an Age of Transition*, Praeger, Westport.

Green, Philip (1966), *Deadly Logic: The Theory of Nuclear Deterrence*, Columbus.

—— (1968), 'Science, Government, and the Case of RAND: A Singular Pluralism', *World Politics*, vol. 20: 2, January, 301–26.

Green, W. John (2005). 'Guerillas, Soldiers, Paramilitaries, Assassins, Narcos, and Gringos: The Unhappy Prospects for Peace and Democracy in Colombia', *Latin American Research Review*, 40/2, 37–149.

Guardian, 'Eurofighter Sale to Saudi Arabia Agreed', *Guardian Unlimited*, 21 December 2005 http://politics.guardian.co.uk/ foreignaffairs/story/0,11538,1672166,00.html

Gulf Industry, 'Glaxo SA to Enlarge Product Range: Reader Inquiry No. 23', *Gulf Industry Online Edition*, Vol. 13, No. 5 (Sept–Oct 2004) http://www.gulfindustryworldwide.com/

Gurr, T. (2000), *People Versus States: Minorities at Risk in the New Century*, Washington DC: United States Institute of Peace Press.

Gusterson, Hugh (1998), *Nuclear Rites: A weapons laboratory at the end of the Cold War*, Berkeley: University of California Press.

Guy, Jess (1989), 'Illegal Trafficking of Arms by Small Time Operators', in Peter Unsinger (ed.), *The International Legal and Illegal Trafficking of Arms*, Springfield: C.C. Thomas.

Haas, Richard N. (2002), Think Tanks and U.S. Foreign Policy: A Policy-Maker's Perspective' in U.S. Foreign Policy Agenda, Vol. 7: 3, November usinfo.state.gov/journals/itps/1101/ijpe/pj73toc.htm

Hamilton, Carolyn (1995), 'Children in armed conflict—New moves for an old problem', *Journal of Child Law*, Vol. 7, No. 1.

Hammes, Thomas X. (2004). *The Sling and the Stone: On War in the 21st Century*, St. Paul, MN: Zenith.

Hammond, Grant T. (1993), *Plowshares into Swords: Arms Races in International Politics, 1840–1991*, Colombia: University of South Carolina Press.

Hansen, C. (1988), *US Nuclear Weapons: The Secret History*, New York: Orion Books, 87.

Hansen, Lene (2000), 'The Little Mermaid's Silent Security Dilemma and the Absence of Gender in the Copenhagen School' *Millennium* 29/2: 285–306.

Harris, S. and Mack, A. (1997), 'Security and Economics in East Asia', in S. Harris and A. Mack (eds.), *Asia-Pacific Security: The Economics-Politics Nexus*, Allen & Unwin, Pymble.

Hart, J. (1992), *Rival Capitalists*, Cornell University Press, Ithaca.

Hartley, Thomas, and Russet, Bruce (1992), 'Public Opinion and the Common Defense: Who Governs Military Spending in the United States', *American Political Science Review*, 86(4): 905–15.

Harvey, Rachel (2003), *Children and Armed conflict: A guide to international and humanitarian human rights law*, The Children and Armed Conflict Unit, Essex University and the International Bureau of Children's Rights.

Hassner, Pierre (1997) *Violence and Peace: From the Atomic Bomb to Ethnic Cleansing*, Budapest: Central European University Press.

Haubrich, Dirk (2003), 'September 11, Anti-Terror Laws and Civil Liberties: Britain, France and Germany Compared', *Government and Opposition*, Vol. 38, No. 1, 3–28.

Hayden, R. (1996), 'Imagined Communities and Real Victims: Self-Determination and Ethnic Cleansing in Yugoslavia', *American Ethnologist*, 23/4: 273–96.

Heinecken, Lindy (2001), Living in Terror: The Looming Security Threat to Southern Africa. *African Security Review* 10(4): 7–17.

Heininen, L. (1994), 'The Military and the Environment: An Arctic Case', in J. Kakonen (ed.), *Green Security or Militarized Environment*, Aldershot: Dartmouth, 155–67.

Held, David et al (1999), *Global Transformations: Politics, Economics and Culture*, Cambridge: Polity Press.

Henderson, Errol A. (2002), *Democracy and War: The End of an Illusion?* Boulder, CO: Lynne Rienner Publishers.

Herd, G.P. and Lofgren, J. (2001), ' "Societal Security" in the Baltic States and EU Integration', *Cooperation and Conflict*, 36/3: 273–96.

Herring, Eric and Rangwala, Glen (2006), *Iraq in Fragments: The Occupation and its Legacy*, London: Hurst and Cornell University Press.

Herz, John H. (1950), 'Idealist Internationalism and the Security Dilemma', *World Politics*, 2: 157–80.

Hicks Stiehm, Judith (ed.) (1983), *Women and Men's Wars*, Oxford: Pergamon Press.

—— (1989), *Arms and the Enlisted Woman*, Philadelphia: Temple.

Hitch, Charles J. (1960), The Uses of Economics, P-2179-RC, Santa Monica: The Rand Corporation.

Hobbes, T. (1914), *Leviathan*. London: J.M. Dent & Sons Ltd.

Hocking, Jenny (2003), 'Counter-Terrorism and the Criminalisation of Politics: Australia's New Security Powers of Detention, Proscription and Control', *Australian Journal of Politics and History*, Vol. 49, No. 3, 355–71.

Hogan, Michael J. (1998), *A Cross of Iron: Harry S. Truman and the Origins of the National Security State, 1945–1954*, Cambridge: Cambridge University Press.

Høiskar, Astri Halsan (2001), 'Underage and Under Fire: An Inquiry into the Use of Child Soldiers 1994–8', *Childhood* 8(3): 340–60.

Hollingdale, R.J. (1977), trans. *A Nietzsche Reader*, London: Penguin.

Holsti, K. (1996), *The State, War, and the State of War*, Cambridge: Cambridge University Press.

Homer-Dixon, T. (1991), 'On the Threshold: Environmental Changes as Causes of Acute Conflict', *International Security*, 16/2: 76–116.

—— (1999), *Environment, Scarcity, and Violence*, Princeton: Princeton University Press.

Hooks, Bell (1995), 'Feminism and Militarism; a comment', *Woman's Studies Quarterly*, Nos 3 & 4.

Hope, Christopher (2005), '£20bn Jets Deal Will Secure 14,000 Jobs', *Daily Telegraph*, 22 December 2005. http://portal.telegraph.co.uk/news/main.jhtml?xml = /news/2005/12/22/nbae22.xml&sSheet=/portal/2005/12/22/ixportal.html

Hoyle, Craig (2005), 'Saudi Arabia Commits to Eurofighter Typhoon Deal', *Flight International*, 21 December. http://www.flightinternational.com/Articles/2005/12/21/Navigation/177/203773/Saudi+Arabia+commits+to+Eurofighter+Typhoon+deal.html

Hubert, D. (2004), 'An Idea that Works in Practice'. *Security Dialogue*, 35/3: 351–2.

Human Rights Watch (1999), World Report, Violence Against Women. http://www.hrw.org/hrw/world report 99.

Human Security Centre (2005), *Human Security News* on-line www. hsc.list@ubc.ca

Huntington, Samuel P. (1957), *The Soldier and the State: The Theory and Politics of Civil-Military Relations*, Cambridge, MA: Harvard University Press.

—— (1999), 'The Lonely Superpower', *Foreign Affairs*, Vol. 78(2): 35–49.

Hutchinson, J. (1994), 'Cultural Nationalism and Moral Regeneration', in J. Hutchinson and A.D. Smith (eds.), *Nationalism*, Oxford: Oxford University Press, 122–31.

Huysmans, J. (1995), 'Migrants as a Security Issue: The Dangers of "Securitizing" Societal Issues', in R. Miles and D. Thranhardt (eds.), *Migration and European Security: The Dynamics of Inclusion and Exclusion*, London: Pinter, 53–72.

—— (1998), 'Revisiting Copenhagen: Or, On the Creative Development of a Security Studies Agenda in Europe', *European Journal of International Relations*, 4 (4): 479–506.

—— (2002), 'The Normative Dilemma of Writing Security', *Alternatives*, 27/Special Issue: 41–62.

—— (2006), *The Politics of Insecurity: Security, Migration and Asylum in the EU*, London: Routledge.

ICG (2001), *HIV/AIDS as a Security Issue*. Washington D.C. and Brussels, Belgium: International Crisis Group.

Ignatieff, Michael (1997), *Blood and Belonging. Journeys into the New Nationalism*, London: Vintage.

Ikenberry, John G. (ed.) (2002), *American Unrivaled: The Future of the Balance of Power*, Ithaca, NY: Cornell University Press.

International Commission on Intervention and State Sovereignty (2001), *The Responsibility to Protect*. Report of the International Commission on Intervention and State Sovereignty, Ottawa: International Development Centre.

International Monetary Fund (2005), *World Economic Outlook 2005: Building Institutions*, Washington D.C.: The International Monetary Fund, Publication Services (September), accessed at http://www.imf.org/external/pubs/ft/weo/2005/02

Isaksson Eva (ed.) (1988), *Women and the Military System*, Basingstoke: Palgrave Macmillan.

Jackson, R. (1990), *Quasi-States: Sovereignty, International Relations, and the Third World*, New York: Cambridge University Press.

Jahn, Egbert (1984), 'Zum Verhältnis von Friedensforschung, Friedenspolitik und Friedensbewegung', in dialog, Vol. 1, No. 1, 21–31.

—— and Lemaitre, Pierre and Wæver, Ole (1997), *European Security: Problems of Research on Non-Military Aspects*, Copenhagen: Copenhagen Papers 1, Copenhagen Peace Research Institute.

Jakobsen, P.V. (1998), *Western Use of Coercive Diplomacy after the Cold War: A Challenge for Theory and Practice*, London: Macmillan Press Ltd.

Jakobson, M. (1961), *The Diplomacy of the Winter War: An Account of the Russo-Finnish Conflict, 1939–1940*, Cambridge, MA: Harvard University Press.

Jenkins, Brian M. (2001), 'Terrorism and Beyond: A 21st Century Perspective', *Studies in Conflict and Terrorism*, Vol. 24, No. 5, 321–27.

Jervis, R. (1976), *Perception and Misperception in International Politics*, Princeton, NJ: Princeton University Press.

—— (1989), *The Meaning of the Nuclear Revolution*, Ithaca: Cornell University Press.

Job, B.A. (ed.) (1992), *The Insecurity Dilemma: National Security of Third World States*, Boulder, CO: Lynne Rienner.

Jones, Richard Wyn (1999), *Security, Strategy, and Critical Theory*, Boulder, CO: Lynne Rienner.

Jones, S.G., Wilson, J.M. Rathmell, A. and Riley, K.J. (2005), *Establishing Law and Order After Conflict*, Santa Monica, California: RAND Corporation.

Jung, D., and Schlichte, K. (1999), 'From Inter-state War to Warlordism: Changing Forms of Collective Violence in the International System', in H. Wiberg and C. Scherrer (eds.), *Ethnicity and Intra-State Conflict: Types, Causes and Peace Strategies*, Aldershot: Ashgate.

Kahler, M. (2004), 'Economic Security in an Era of Globalisation: Definition and Provision', *Pacific Review*, Vol. 17(4), 485–502.

Kaldor, Mary (1982), *The Baroque Arsenal*, London: Andre Deutsch.

—— (1999), *New and Old Wars: Organised Violence in a Global Era*, Cambridge: Polity Press.

Kaplan, F. (1983), *Wizards of Armageddon*, Stanford, CA: Stanford University Press.

—— (1991), *The Wizards of Armageddon*, Stanford, CA: Stanford University Press.

Kapstein, Ethan B. (1997), 'Advanced Industrialized Countries', in Andrew J. Pierre (ed.), *Cascade of Arms: Managing Conventional Weapons Proliferation* Cambridge, MA: World Peace Foundation and The Brookings Institution Press, 75–88.

Karp, Aaron (1994), 'The Rise of Black and Gray Markets', *The Annals of the American Academy of Political and Social Science*, Vol. 535 (September): 175–89.

Katzenstein, P.J. (1976), 'International Relations and Domestic Structures: Foreign Economic Policies of Advanced Industrial States', *International Organisation*, Vol 30 (1), 1–45.

—— (ed.) (1996), *The Culture of National Security. Norms and Identity in World Politics*, New York: Columbia University Press.

Kaufman, Chaim (1996), 'Possible and Impossible Solutions to Ethnic Civil Wars', *International Security*, 20/4, 136–75.

Keegan, John (1998), *War and Our World*, London: Pimlico.

—— (2003), *Intelligence in War: Knowledge of the Enemy from Napoleon to Al-Qaeda*, London: Hutchinson.

Kennedy-Pipe, Caroline (2004) 'Whose Security? State-Building and the "Emancipation" of Women in Central Asia, *International Relations*, Vol. 18 No. 1, March.

—— and Welch, Stephen (2001), 'Women in the Military: Future Prospects and Ways Ahead', in Alex Alexandrou, Richard Bartle and Richard Holmes (eds), *New People Strategies for the British Armed Forces*, London: Frank Cass.

Kent, George (2005), *Freedom from Want: The Human Right to Adequate Food*, Georgetown University Press.

Keohane, R.O. and Nye, J.S. (1977), *Power and Interdependence*, Boston: Little, Brown.

Keohane, Robert (1988), 'International Institutions: Two Approaches', *International Studies Quarterly* 32/4: 379–96.

Kerr, P. (2003), 'The Evolving Dialectic Between State-Centric and Human-Centric Security', Working Paper 2003/4, Canberra: Department of International Relations, The Australian National University, 1–34.

—— and Tow, W.T., and Hanson, M. (2003), 'The Utility of the Human Security Agenda for Policy-makers', *Asian Journal of Political Science*, 11/2: 89–114.

Klein, Bradley (1994), *Strategic Studies and World Order*, Cambridge: Cambridge University Press.

Klieman, Aaron S. (1985), *Israel's Global Reach: Arms Sales as Diplomacy*, Oxford: Pergamon-Brasseys.

Knightley, P. (1986), *The Second Oldest Profession: Spies and Spying in the Twentieth Century*, London: Penguin Books.

Knorr, K. (1977), 'Economic Interdependence and National Security', in K. Knorr and F.N. Trager (eds.), *Economic Issues and National Security*, Lawrence, KS: Regents Press.

—— and Truger, Frank N. (1977), *Economic Issues and National Security*, Lawrence, KS: Regents Press.

Kratochwil, Friedrich (1991), *Rules, Norms, and Decisions: On the Conditions of Practical and Legal Reasoning in International Relations and Domestic Affairs*, Cambridge: Cambridge University Press.

Krause, Keith (1992), *Arms and the State: Patterns of Military Production and Trade*, Cambridge: Cambridge University Press.

—— (1998), 'Critical Theory and Security Studies: The Research Programme of "Critical Security Studies" ', *Cooperation and Conflict* 33/3: 298–333.

—— and Williams, Michael C. (1997a), *Critical Security Studies: Concepts and Cases*, Minneapolis: University of Minnesota Press.

—— and —— (1997b), 'From Strategy to Security: Foundations of Critical Security Studies', in *Critical Security Studies: Concepts and Cases*, Minneapolis: University of Minnesota Press, 33–59.

Krugman, P. (1986), *Strategic Trade Policy and the New International Economics*, Cambridge, MA: MIT Press.

Kuhn, Harold W. (2004), 'Introduction' in John von Neumann and Oskar Morgenstern, *Theory of Games and Economic Behavior*, Sixtieth-Anniversary Edition, Princeton: Princeton University Press, vii–xiv.

Laqueur, Walter (2001), *A History of Terrorism*, New Brunswick, NJ: Transaction Publishers.

Larsen, J. (ed.) (2002), *Arms Control: Cooperative Security in a Changing Environment*, Boulder, CO: Lynne Rienner Publishers.

Lasswell, Harold D. (1950), *National Security and Individual Freedom*, New York, Toronto, London: McGraw-Hill.

Laville, Helen (1997), 'The Committee of Correspondence: CIA Funding of Women's Groups 1952–1967' in Rhodri Jeffreys-Jones and Christopher Andrew, *Eternal Vigilance? 50 Years of the CIA*, London: Frank Cass.

Lavoy, P.R., Sagan, S.D., and Wirtz, J.J. (eds.) (2000), *Planning the Unthinkable: How New Powers will use Nuclear, Chemical and Biological Weapons*, Ithaca, NY: Cornell University Press.

Lee, C. (1999), 'On Economic Security', in G. Wilson-Roberts (ed.) *An Asia-Pacific Security Crisis?: New Challenges to Regional Stability*, Wellington, NZ: Centre for Strategic Studies.

Leech, D.P. (1993), 'Conversion, Integration, and Foreign Dependency: Prelude to a New US Economic Security Strategy, *Geojournal*, Vol. 31(2), 193–206.

Leitzel, J. (ed.) (1993), *Economics and National Security*, Boulder, CO: Westview Press.

Lens, Sidney, (1970), *The Military Industrial Complex*, Philadelphia, PA: Pilgrim Press.

Lepgold, Joseph and Nincic, Miroslav (2001), *Beyond the Ivory Tower: International Relations Theory and the Issue of Policy Relevance*, New York: Columbia UP.

Levi, Michael, 'Breaking the Economic Power of Organised Crime Groups', Paper prepared for CIROC Seminar, Amsterdam, 2002, accessed at http://tkfy.asp4all.nl/ciroc/nl/html/Seminars/levivermogen.pdf

Libiszewski, S. (1997), 'Integrating Political and Technical Approaches: Lessons from the Israeli-Jordanian Water Negotiations', in N. Gleditsch (ed.), *Conflict and the Environment*, Dordrecht: Kluwer, 385–402.

Lieblich, Amia (1997), The POW wife—Another Perspective on Heroism', *Women's Studies International Forum*, September–December, Vol. 20, 621–30.

Liew, L. (2000), 'Human Security and Economic Security: Is There a Nexus?', in W. Tow, R. Thakur and I.T. Hyun (eds.) *Asia's Emerging Regional Order: Reconciling Traditional and Human Security*, New York: United Nations University Press.

Lifton, Robert Jay and Markusen, Eric (1990), *The Genocidal Mentality: Nazi Holocaust and Nuclear Threat*, London: Macmillan.

Lindsay, James M. (1991), *Congress and Nuclear Weapons*, Baltimore: John Hopkins University Press.

Lock, Peter (1998), 'Military Downsizing and Growth in the Security Industry in Sub-Saharan Africa', *Strategic Analysis*, Vol. 22, No. 9, Dec., 1393–1426.

Lodgaard, S. (2000), 'Human Security: Concept and Operationisation', paper presented at the Expert Seminar on Human Rights, Palaise Wilson, Geneva, 8–9 December 2000, 1–25, http://www.hsph.harvard.edu/hpcr/events/hswokshop/ lodgaarrd.pdf

Lonergan, S. (1997), 'Water Resources and Conflict: Examples from the Middle East', in N. Gleditsch (ed.), *Conflict and the Environment*, Dordrecht: Kluwer, 375–84.

Lowenthal, M. (2003), *Intelligence: From Secrets to Policy*, 2nd edn, Washington, D.C.: CQ Press.

Lubbe, A. (1997), 'National Economic Security', *Polish Quarterly of International Affairs*, Vol. 6(4), 59–76.

Lucas, M.R. (1991), 'The Decline of Export Security Controls in the 1980s and Several Options for Policy Reform', in E.A. Stubbs (ed.) *Soviet Foreign Economic Policy and International Security*, Armonk, NY: M.E. Sharpe.

Luttwak, Edward N. (1995), 'Toward Post Heroic Warfare', *Foreign Affairs*, May–June, 109–122.

Lutz, Brenda J., Lutz, James M., and Ulmschneider, Georgia Wralstrad (2002), 'British Trials of Irish Nationalist Defendants: The Quality of Justice Strained', *Studies in Conflict and Terrorism*, Vol. 25, No. 4, 227–44.

Lutz, James M. and Lutz, Brenda J. (2005), *Terrorism: Origins and Evolution*, New York: Palgrave.

Mack, A. (2004), 'A Signifier of Shared Values', *Security Dialogue*, 35/3: 366–67.

Mackenzie, Donald (1990), *Inventing Accuracy: A Historical Sociology of Nuclear Missile Guidance*, Cambridge, MA: MIT Press.

Mann, James (2004), *Rise of the Vulcans: The History of Bush's War Cabinet*, London: Penguin.

Maoz, Zeev and Russett, Bruce (1993), 'Normative and Structural Causes of Democratic Peace', *American Political Science Review*, 87/3, 624–38.

Markusen, Ann (1999), 'The Rise of World Weapons', *Foreign Policy*, 114 (Spring): 40–51.

Mastanduno, M. (1998), 'Economics and Security in Statescraft and Scholarship', *International Organisation*, Vol. 52(4), 825–54.

Mathews, J. (1989), Redefining Security, *Foreign Affairs*, 68/2: 162–77.

Mayer, Kenneth R. (1991), *The Political Economy of Defense Contracting*, New Haven: Yale University Press.

McCarth, Rory (2000), 'Pakistan Enters Arms Market', *The Guardian*, 7 November, 16.

McCurry, Justin (2000), 'Games Machine "Poses Military Threat"', *The Guardian*, 17 April, 10.

McNeill, William (1998), *Plagues and People*, New York: Anchor Books.

McSweeny, Bill (1996), 'Identity and security: Buzan and the Copenhagen School', *Review of International Studies* 22/1: 81–93.

Mearsheimer, John (2001), *The Tragedy of Great Power Politics*, New York: Norton.

Meintjes, S., Pillay, A., and Turshen, M. (eds.) (2002), *The Aftermath: Women in Post Conflict Transformation*, London: Zed books.

Melman, Seymour (1970), *Pentagon Capitalism*, New York: McGraw-Hill.

Merle, Renae (2006), 'Army Ends Lockheed Contract for New Spy Plane', *Washington Post*, 13 January, A8.

Migdal, J. (1988), *Strong Societies and Weak States: State-Society Relations and State Capabilities in the Third World*, Princeton, NJ: Princeton University Press.

Mills, C. Wright (1956), *The Power Elite*, Oxford: Oxford University Press.

Milner, H. (1992), 'International Theories of Co-operation Among Nations: Strengths and Weaknesses', *World Politics*, Vol. 44 (April), 466–96.

Monaghan, Rachel (2000), 'Terrorism in the Name of Animal Rights', in Max Taylor and John Horgan (eds.), *The Future of Terrorism*, London: Frank Cass, 159–69.

Moran, T. (1993), 'An Economic Agenda for Neo-Realists', *International Security*, Vol. 18(2), 211–5.

Morgenthau, Hans J. (1962), 'The Trouble with Kennedy', *Commentary*, Vol. 33: 1, 51–5.

Mueller, John (2000), 'The Banality of "Ethnic War"', *International Security*, 25/1, 42–70.

Muggah, R. and Gainsbury, S. (2003), 'Holding up Development: The Effects of Small Arms and Light Weapons in Developing Countries', *id21 media*, http://www.id21.org/id21-media/arms.html, accessed 18 September 2005.

Mutimer, David (2000), *The Weapons State: Proliferation and the Framing of Security*, Boulder, CO: Lynne Rienner.

Myers, N. (1986), 'The Environmental Dimension to Security Issues', *The Environmentalist*, 6/4: 251–7.

—— (1987), 'Population, Environment, and Conflict', *Environmental Conservation*, 14/1: 15–22.

Nadelmann, Ethan A. (1999), *Cops Across Borders: The Internationalization of U.S. Criminal Law Enforcement*, University Park, PA: Penn State Press.

Naff, T. (1992), 'Water Scarcity, Resource Management, and Conflict in the Middle East', in E. Kirk (ed.), *Environmental Dimensions of Security: Proceedings from a AAAS Annual Meeting Symposium*, Washington: American Association for the Advancement of Science, 25–30.

Nagl, John (2002), *Counterinsurgency Lessons from Malaya and Vietnam: Learning to Eat Soup with a Knife*, Westport, CT: Praeger.

Nantais, Cynthia and F. Lee, Martha (1999). 'Women in the United States Military: Protectors or Protected? The Case of Prisoner of War, Melissa Rathburn-Nealy', *Journal of Gender Studies*, Vol. 8 No. 2, 181–90.

National Intelligence Council (2000), *The Global Infectious Disease Threat and Its Implications for the US*. Washington D.C. http://www.cia.gov/cia/reports/nie/report/nie99-17d.html

Naylor, R.T. (2002), *Wages of Crime: Black Markets, Illegal Finances, and the Wages of Crime*. Ithaca, NY: Cornell University Press.

—— (2003), 'Predators, Parasites, or Free-Market Pioneers: Reflections on the Nature and Analysis of Profit-Driven Crime', in Margaret E. Beare (ed.), *Critical Reflections on Transnational Organized Crime, Money Laundering, and Corruption*, Toronto: University of Toronto Press.

Nenadic, Natalie (1996), 'Femicide: A framework for understanding Genocide', in Diane Bell and Renate Kline, *Radically Speaking: Feminism Reclaimed*, London: Zed Books.

Neu, C.R. and Wolf, C. (1994), *The Economic Dimensions of National Security*, Santa Monica, CA: Rand Corporation.

Newshour (1996), 'Gun Running', Public Broadcasting Service transcript, *Online Newshour* 24 April http://www.pbs.org/newshour/bb/bosnia/iran_4-24.html

Nicarchos, Catherine (1995), 'Women, War and Rape: Challenges Facing the International Tribunal for the Former Yugoslavia', *Human Rights*, Vol. 17, 668–71.

Nincic, Miroslav (1982), *The Arms Race: The Political Economy of Military Growth*, New York: Prager.

Nordstrom, C. (1999), 'Visible Wars and Invisible Girls, Shadow Industries, and the Politics of Not-Knowing', *International Feminist Journal of Politics*, Vol. 1, No. 1, 14–33.

Nye, Joseph and Lynn-Jones, Sean (1988), 'International Security Studies: A Report of a Conference on the State of the Field', *International Security*, Vol. 12: 4, 5–27.

—— (1990), *Bound to Lead: The Changing Nature of American Power*, New York: Basic Books.

O'Tuathail, G. (1996), *Critical Geopolitics*, London: Routledge.

Onuf, Nicholas (1989), *World of Our Making: Rules and Rule in Social Theory and International Relations*, Columbia SC: University of South Carolina Press.

Ostergard, Robert L. Jr. (ed.) (2005), *HIV AIDS and the Threat to National and International Security*, London: Palgrave.

Owen, Wilfred (1995), *The Collected War Poems*, New York: Norton.

Oye, K.A. (1986), *Co-operation Under Anarchy*, Princeton, NJ: Princeton University Press.

Palme, O. (1982), *Common Security: A Blueprint for Survival: Report of the Independent Commission on Disarmament and Security Issues*, New York: Simon and Schuster.

Paris, R. (1997), 'Peacebuilding and the Limits of Liberal Internationalism', *International Security* 22/2: 54–89.

—— (2004), 'Still an Inscrutable Concept'. *Security Dialogue*, 35(3): 370–1.

Parmar, Inderjeet (2004), 'Institutes of International Affairs. Their roles in foreign policy-making, opinion mobilization and unofficial diplomacy', in Diane Stone and Andrew Denham (eds.), *Think Tank Traditions: Policy research and the politics of ideas*, Manchester: Manchester University Press, 19–33.

Parry, Albert (1976), *Terrorism: From Robespierre to Arafat*, New York: Vanguard Press.

Paul, T.V., Harknett, R.J., and Wirtz, J.J. (eds.) (1998), *The Absolute Weapon Revisited: Nuclear Arms and the Emerging International Order*, Ann Arbor, MI: University of Michigan Press.

Peluso, N. and Harwell, E. (2001), 'Territory, Custom, and the Cultural Politics of Ethnic War in West Kalimantan, Indonesia', in N. Peluso and M. Watts (eds.), *Violent Environments*, Ithaca, NY: Cornell University Press, 83–116.

Pengelley, Rupert (1997), 'Jordan: Looking to an Arms Industry of Their Own', *Jane's Defence Weekly*, 15 January: 19–21.

Peters, Krijn, Richards, Paul, and Vlassenroot, Koen (2003), '*What Happens to Youth During and After Wars? A Preliminary Review of Literature on Africa and an Assessment of the Debate*'. The Netherlands Development Assistance Research Council (RAWOO) Working Paper, 1–48.

Peterson, V. Spike (1992), 'Security and Sovereign States: What is at Stake in Taking Feminism Seriously' in V. Spike Peterson (ed.), *Gendered States: Feminist Revisions of International Relations Theory*, Boulder, CO: Lynne Rienner.

Pettman, Jan Jindy (1996), *Worlding Women*, London: Routledge.

Pick, Daniel (1993), *War Machine. The Rationalisation of Slaughter in the Modern Age*, New Haven and London: Yale University Press.

Pillar, Paul R. (2001), *Terrorism and U.S. Foreign Policy*, Washington D.C.: Brookings Institution.

Piombo, Jessica (2006), 'Terrorism Financing and Government Response in East Africa' in Jeanne K. Giraldo and Harold A. Trinkunas (eds.), in *Terrorism Financing and State Responses*, Stanford, CA: Stanford University Press.

Poundstone, William (1992), *Prisoner's Dilemma*, New York: Doubleday.

Prefontaine, D. C. and Dandurand, Yvon (2004), '*Terrorism and Organized Crime: Reflections on an Illusive Link and its Implications for Criminal Law Reform*'. Paper prepared for the annual meeting of the International Society for Criminal Law Reform, Montreal, August 2004, accessed at http://www.icclr.law.ubc.ca/Publications/Reports/International%20Society%20Paper%20of%20Terrorism.pdf

Price-Smith, Andrew (2001), *The Health of Nations: Infectious Disease, Environmental Change, and Their Effects on National Security and Development*, Cambridge, MA: MIT Press.

Prins, G. (ed.) (1993), *Threats Without Enemies: Facing Environmental Insecurity*, London: Earthscan.

Publius (Alexander Hamilton, James Madison, and John Jay) (1787–8), The Federalist, http://www.constitution.org/fed/federa00.htm

Quine, Maria Sophia (1996), *Population Politics in Twentieth Century Europe*, London: Routledge.

Radu, Michael (2002), 'Terrorism after the Cold War', *Orbis*, Vol. 46, No. 2, 363–79.

Ramakrishna, Kumar, and Tan, Andrew (2002), 'The New Terrorism: Diagnosis and Prescriptions', in Andrew Tan and Kumar Ramakrishna (eds.), *The New Terrorism: Anatomy, Trends and Counter-Strategies*, Singapore: Eastern Universities Press, 3–9.

Ramsbotham, Oliver, Woodhouse, Tom and Miall, Hugh (2005), *Contemporary Conflict Resolution*, Cambridge and Malden: Polity Press.

Rengger, Nicholas (1999), *International Relations, Political Theory and the Problem of Order. Beyond International Relations Theory?* London: Routledge.

Renner, M. (1991), 'Assessing the Military's War on the Environment', in L. Brown (ed.), *State of the World 1991*, New York: W.W. Norton, 132–52.

Reuters (1999), 'Israeli Firm Gets Go-Ahead to Sell Arms to Jordan', 18 October.

Rich, Andrew (2004), *Think Tanks, Public Policy, and the Politics of Expertise*, Cambridge: Cambridge University Press.

Richardson, L.F. (1960), *Statistics of Deadly Quarrels*, Pittsburg, PA: Boxwood Press.

Richelson, J. (1995), *A Century of Spies: Intelligence in the Twentieth Century*, New York: Oxford University Press.

Robinson, William, Lake, Jennifer E., and Seghetti, Lisa M. 'Border Transportation Security: Possible New Policy Options and Directions', Congressional Research Service, Library of Congress, 29 March 2005.

Roe, P. (2002), 'Misperception and Ethnic Conflict: Transylvania's Societal Security Dilemma', *Review of International Studies*, 28/1: 57–74.

Rogers, K. (1997), 'Ecological Security and Multinational Corporations', *Environmental Change and Security Project Report*, 3: 29–36.

Rogers, Paul (2002), *Losing Control: Global Security in the 21st Century*, London: Pluto Press.

—— and Ramsbotham, Oliver (1999), 'Then and Now: Peace Research—Past and Future', *Political Studies*, XLVII, 740–54.

Romm, J.J. (1993), *Defining National Security: The Nonmilitary Aspects*, New York: Council of Foreign Relations Press.

Rose, Gideon (1998), 'Neoclassical realism and theories of foreign policy' *World Politics*, Vol. 51: 1, October, 144–72.

Rosenberg, David Alan (1983), 'The Origins of Overkill', *International Security*, 7 (Spring), 3–71.

Russett, Bruce and O'Neal, John (2001), *Triangulating Peace: Democracy, Interdependence and International Organizations*, New York: W.W. Norton.

Sagan, S. and Waltz, Kenneth (2003), *The Spread of Nuclear Weapons: A Debate Renewed*, 2nd edn, New York: Norton.

Sagan, Scott D. (1996/97), 'Why Do States Build Nuclear Weapons? Three Models in Search of a Bomb', *International Security*, 21/3, 54–86.

Sandholtz, W., Borrus, M., Zysman, J., Conca, K., Stowsky, J., Vogel, S., and Weber, S. (1992), *The Highest Stakes: The Economic Foundations of the Next Security System*, Oxford: Oxford University Press.

Saponja-Hadzic, Milanka (2003), 'Serbia after Djindjic: The maelstrom of its own crimes, *World Press Review*. 50.6 June: 32.

Scheetz, Thomas (2004), 'The Argentine Defense Industry: An Evaluation', in Jurgen Brauer and J. Paul Dunne, *Arms Trade and Economic Development: Theory, Policy and Cases in Arms Trade Offsets*, London: Routledge, 205–16.

Schelling, T.C. (1960a), The Role of Theory in the Study of Conflict, RAND Research Memorandum 2515 (abridged version published in *Midwest Journal of Political Science*, May 1960 and as ch. 1 of Schelling 1960b).

—— (1960b), *The Strategy of Conflict*, Cambridge: Harvard University Press.

—— (1966), *Arms and Influence*, New Haven, CT: Yale University Press.

Schmid, H. (1968), 'Peace research and politics', *Journal of Peace Research*, 5/3, 217–32.

Schönteich, Martin (1999), 'Age and AIDS: South Africa's crime time bomb?' *African Security Review* 8(4): 34–44.

Seager, J. (1993), *Earth Follies*, New York: Routledge.

Sears, D. and Valentino, N. (1997), 'Politics Matters: Political Events as Catalysts for Pre-Adolescent Socialisation', *American Political Science Review* 91(1): 45–65.

Sederburg, Peter C. (2003), 'Global Terrorism: Problems of Challenge and Response', in Charles W. Kegley, Jr. (ed.), *The New Global Terrorism: Characteristics, Causes, Controls*, Upper Saddle River, NJ: Prentice Hall, 267–84.

Sen, A. (1999), *Development as Freedom*, New York: Anchor Books.

Senghaas, Dieter (1969), *Abschreckung und Frieden: Studien zur Kritik organisierter Friedlosigkeit*, Frankfurt/M.: Suhrkamp.

Seok-jae, Kang (1995), 'Korea to Rank First in Global Shipbuilding by 2005', *Newsreview*, 2 December, 15, 19, 21.

Shaw, Martin (ed.) (1984), *War, State and Society*, London: Macmillan Press.

—— (2005), *The New Western Way of War*, Cambridge: Polity.

Shearer, David (1999), 'Private Military Force and Challenges for the Future', *Cambridge Review of International Affairs*, Vol. 8, No. 1 (Autumn–Winter), 80–94.

Sheehan, Michael (2005), *International Security: An Analytical Survey*, Boulder, CO: Lynne Rienner.

Shelley, Louise (2005), 'Unraveling the New Criminal Nexus', *Georgetown Journal of International Affairs* 6: 1 (Winter): 5–12.

Sher, Hanan (1995), 'Flying With the Russians', *The Jerusalem Report*, 27 July, 40.

Sherry, Michael S. (1995), *In the Shadow of War. The United States since the 1930s*, New Haven, CT: Yale University Press.

Shirk, S.L. and Twomey, C.P. (eds) (1996), *Power and Prosperity: Economics and Security Linkages in the Asia-Pacific*, London: Transaction Publishers.

Sims, Brendan (2001), *Unfinest Hour: Britain and the Destruction of Bosnia*, London: Alan Lane.

Simunovic, Pjer (1998), 'Croatian Arms For Sale: Evolution, Structure and Export Potential of Croatia's Defence Industry', *Contemporary Security Policy*, Vol. 19, No. 3 (December): 128–51.

Sinclair, Andrew (2003), *An Anatomy of Terror: A History of Terrorism*, London: Macmillan.

Singer, P.W. (2005a), 'Western militaries confront child soldiers threat', *Jane's Intelligence Review*, January.

—— (2005b), *Children at war*, Pantheon.

Slijper, Frank (2005), *The Emerging EU Military-Industrial Complex: Arms Industry Lobbying in Brussels*, Amsterdam: Transnational Institute.

Small, M. and Singer, D. (1982), *Resort to Arms: International and Civil Wars, 1816–1980*, Beverly Hills, CA: Sage.

Smith, A.D. (1993), 'The Ethnic Sources of Nationalism', *Survival*, 35/1: 48–62.

Smith, Michael (2005), 'Iraq battle stress worse than WWII', *The Sunday Times*, 7 November.

Smith, Rich (2005), 'Typhoon in Saudi Arabia: BAE Systems Wins a Huge Arms Sale', *Motley Fool*, 22 December, http://msnbc.msn.com/id/10573979/

Smith, Steve (2005), 'The Contested Concept of Security' in Booth, Ken (ed.), *Critical Security Studies and World Politics*, Boulder, CO: Lynne Rienner, 27–62.

Smoke, Richard (1975), 'National Security Affairs' in Fred Greenstein and Nelson W. Polsby (eds.), *Handbook of Political Science*, Vol. 8, Reading, MA: Addison-Wesley, 247–361.

Snyder, Glenn H. (1984), 'The Security Dilemma in Alliance Politics', *World Politics*, 36: 4, 461–95.

Soeya, Y. (1997), 'Japan's Economic Security', in S. Harris and A. Mack (eds.), *Asia-Pacific Security: The Economics-Politics Nexus*, St Leonards, Australia: Allen & Unwin.

Solingen, Etel (1994), 'The Political Economy of Nuclear Restraint', *International Security*, 19/2, 126–69.

—— (1998), *Regional Orders at Century's Dawn*, Princeton, NJ: Princeton University Press.

Sorenson, Brigitte Refslund (1999), 'Recovering from Conflict, Does Gender Make a Difference?', *UN Chronicle*, No. 2. 26–27.

Sorenson, T.C. (1990), 'Rethinking National Security', *Foreign Affairs*, Vol. 69(3), 1–18.

Sorokin, P. (1937), *Social and Cultural Dynamics*, New York: American Books.

Soroos, M. (1994), 'Global Change, Environmental Security, and the Prisoner's Dilemma', *Journal of Peace Research*, 39/3: 317–32.

—— (1997), *The Endangered Atmosphere: Preserving a Global Commons*, Columbia: University of South Carolina Press.

Sperling, J. and Kirchner, E. (1997), *Recasting the European Order: Security Architectures and Economic Co-operation*, Manchester: Manchester University Press.

—— and Malik, Y., and Louscher, D. (eds.) (1998), *Zones of Amity, Zones of Enmity: The Prospects for Economic and Military Security in Asia*, Leiden: Brill.

Sprout, H. and Sprout, M. (1971), *Toward a Politics of Planet Earth*, New York: Von Norstrand Reinhold.

Stainton-Rogers, W. and Stainton-Rogers, R. (1992), *Stories of Childhood*, London: Harvester Wheatsheaf.

Stavrianakis, Anna (2005), 'UK Arms exports and Military Globalisation', Paper presented at the British International Studies Association Conference, St Andrews.

Steans, Jill (1998), *Gender and International Relations. An Introduction*, London: Polity.

Stephens, Sharon (1997), 'Nationalism, nuclear policy, and children in Cold War America', *Childhood*, Vol. 4, No. 1, 103–23.

Stern, J. (2000), *The Ultimate Terrorists*, Cambridge, MA: Harvard University Press.

Stern, Sol (1967), 'Who thinks in a think tank' *New York Times Magazine*, 16 April.

Stiglmayer, Alexandra (ed.) (1994), *The War Against Women in Bosnia-Herzegovina*, London: University of Nebraska.

Stiles, Kendall W. (1995), *Case Histories in International Politics*, New York: HarperCollins.

Stokes, Crandall correspondence (2002), 'Debating Plan Colombia', *Survival*, 44/2, 183–8.

Stokes, Doug (2004), *America's Other War: Terrorizing Colombia*, London: Zed.

Stoler, Mark A. (2000), *Allies and Adversaries: The Joint Chiefs of Staff, the Grand Alliance, and U.S. Strategy in World War II*, Chapel Hill, NC: University of North Carolina Press.

Stremlau, J. (1994), 'Clinton's Dollar Diplomacy', *Foreign Policy*, No. 97, 18–35.

Suhrke, A. (2004), 'A Stalled Initiative', *Security Dialogue*, 35/3: 365.

Swain, Jon (1995), 'Bosnia endures more atrocities', *Sunday Times*, 23 July, 1 and 13.

Sylvester, Christine (1996), 'The Contributions of Feminist Theory to International Relations' in Steve Smith, Ken Booth, Maryisa Zalewski (eds.) *International Theory: Positivism and Beyond*, Cambridge: Cambridge University Press.

Tannenwald, Nina and Wohlforth, William Curti (eds.) (2005), Special issue on 'The Role of Ideas and the End of the Cold War', *Journal of Cold War Studies*, Vol. 7: 2, Spring.

Tarzi, S.M. (2005), 'Coercive Diplomacy and an "Irrational" Regime. Understanding the American Confrontation with the Taliban', *International Studies*, 42/1: 21–41.

Taylor, S. and Goldman, D. (2004), 'Intelligence Reform: Will More Agencies, Money, and Personnel Help?', *Intelligence and National Security*, 19/3: 416–35.

Thakur, R. (2000), 'Human Security Regimes', in W. Tow, R. Thakur and I.T. Hyun (eds.), *Asia's Emerging Regional Order: Reconciling Traditional and Human Security*, New York: United Nations University Press.

—— (2004), 'A Political Worldview', *Security Dialogue*, 35/3: 347.

The White House (2002), *The National Security Strategy of the United States of America* (Washington D.C.), http://www.whitehouse.gov/nsc/nss.html

Thee, Marek (1986), *Military Technology, Military Strategy and the Arms Race*, London: Croom Helm.

Theiler, T. (2003), 'Societal Security and Social Psychology', *Review of International Studies*, 29/2: 249–68.

Thomas, C. (1987), *In Search of Security: The Third World in International Relations*, Boulder, CO: Lynne Rienner.

Thurow, L. (1992), *Head to Head: The Coming Economic Battle Among Japan, Europe and America*, London: Nicholas Brealey.

Tickner J. Ann (1992), *Gender in International Relations. Feminist Perspectives on Achieving Global Security*, New York: Columbia.

—— (1995), 'Revisioning Security' in Ken Booth and Steve Smith, *International Relations Theory Today*, London: Polity.

Tilly, Charles (1989), *Big Structures, Large Processes, Huge Comparisons*, Russell Sage Foundation.

—— (1990), *Coercion, Capital and European States, AD 990–1990*, Cambridge, MA: Basil Blackwell.

—— (2003), *The Politics of Collective Violence*, Cambridge: Cambridge University Press.

Tow, W.T. (2001), 'Alternative Security Models: Implications for ASEAN', in A. Tan and K. Boutin (eds.), *Non-Traditional Security Issues in Southeast Asia*, Singapore: Institute of Defence and Strategic Studies, 257–85.

Transparency International (2001), paraphrased unattributable joke told at the '*Corruption in the Official Arms Trade*' conference convened by Transparency International, University of Cambridge, April.

Tuchman Mathews, J. (1989), 'Redefining Security', *Foreign Affairs*, 68/2: 162–77.

Tucker, Richard K. (1991), *The Dragon and the Cross: The Rise and Fall of the Ku Klux Klan in Middle America*, Hamden, CT: Archon Books.

Turco, R.P., Toon, O.B., Ackerman, T.P., Pollack, J.B., and Sagan, C. (1990), 'Climate and Smoke: An Appraisal of Nuclear Winter', *Science* 247: 166–76.

Tusa, Francis (1994), 'Old But Fit: Bargains Galore in the Secondhand Ship Market', *Armed Forces Journal International*, November: 30–1.

Ullman, R. (1983), 'Redefining Security', *International Security*, 8/1: 129–53.

UNAIDS (Joint United Nations Programme on HIV/AIDS) (1998), *AIDS and the Military*, Geneva.

—— (2004), *AIDS Epidemic Update: December 2004*, Geneva.

UNDP (United Nations Development Program) (1994), *Human Development Report 1994*, New York: Oxford University Press.

—— (1998), *Human Development Report 1998*, New York: Oxford University Press.

—— (2005), *Human Development Report 2005*, Oxford: Oxford University Press.

UNEP (United Nations Environment Program) (2003), *Global Environmental Outlook 3*, London: Earthscan.

—— (2005), *One Planet, Many People: Atlas of Our Changing Environment*, Nairobi: UNEP.

United Nations (2004), *A More Secure World: Our Shared Responsibility*, Report of the Secretary General's High-level Panel on Threats, Challenges and Change. New York: United Nations, http://www.un.org/secureworld/

—— (2005a), *Draft Outcome Document*, 2005 World Summit, 13 September 2005, http://www.un.org/apps/news/story.asp?NewsID=15853&Cr=world&Cr1=summit

—— (2005b), *In Larger Freedom*, Report of the Secretary-General of the United Nations for Decision by Heads of State and Government in September 2005, New York: United Nations, http://www.un.org/largerfreedom/

United Nations Convention against Transnational Crime (2000), accessed at http://www.unodc.org/unodc/en/crime_cicp_convention.html

United Nations Office on Drugs and Crime (2002), Global Programme Against Transnational Organized Crime, *Results of a Pilot Survey of Forty Selected Organized Criminal Groups in Sixteen Countries*, September.

United States Congress (1979), *The Effects of Nuclear War*, Washington, Congress of the U.S., Office of Technology Assessment: Supt of Docs., U.S. Gov. Printing Office.

US Council on Competitiveness (1994), *Economic Security: The Dollars and Sense of US Foreign Policy*, Washington D.C: US Council on Competitiveness.

Van Niekerk, P. (2002), 'Making a Killing: The Business of War', The Center for Public Integrity, http://www.icij.org/bow/default.aspx accessed 18 September 2005.

Vasilevitch, Alexander and Belosludtsev, Oleg (2001), 'Ukraine and Belarus: In Search of a Niche on the Arms Market', *Eksport Vooruzheniy*, No. 1, Centre for Analysis of Strategies and Technologies: 8–20.

Wæver, O. (1993), 'Societal Security: The Concept', in Ole Wæver, B. Buzan, M. Kelstrup and P. Lemaitre (eds.), *Identity, Migration and the New Security Agenda in Europe*, London: Pinter: 17–40.

—— (1994), 'Insecurity and Identity Unlimited', Working Paper No. XIV, Copenhagen: Copenhagen Peace Research Institute.

—— (1995), 'Securitization and Desecuritization', in R.D. Lipschutz (eds.), *On Security*, New York: Columbia University Press, 46–86.

—— (1998) 'The Sociology of a Not So International Discipline: American and European Developments in International Relations', *International Organization*, Vol. 52: 4 (October), 687–727.

—— (1999), 'Securitizing Sectors: Reply to Eriksson', *Cooperation and Conflict*, 34/3: 334–40.

—— (2004a), 'Aberystwyth, Paris, Copenhagen: New "Schools" in Security Theory and their Origins between Core and Periphery', paper for ISA in Montreal, March 2004, http://zope.polforsk1.dk/securitytheory/waevermontreal/

—— (2004b), 'Peace and Security: two concepts and their relationship' in Stefano Guzzini and Dietrich Jung (eds.), *Contemporary Security Analysis and Copenhagen Peace Research*, London: Routledge, 53–65.

—— (2005), 'The constellation of securities in Europe', in Ersel Aydinli and James N. Rosenau (eds.), *Globalization, security, and the nation-state: paradigms in transition*, New York: State University of New York Press, 151–74.

—— (2006), 'Security: A Conceptual History for International Relations', manuscript in preparation—March 2006 version posted on www.libertysecurity.org

Walker R.B.J. (1993), *Inside/Outside*, Cambridge: Cambridge University Press.

—— (1997), 'The Subject of Security', in Krause, Keith and Michael C. Williams, *Critical Security Studies: Concepts and Cases*, Minneapolis: University of Minnesota Press, 61–81.

Walt, S. (1987), *The Origins of Alliances*, Ithaca, NY: Cornell University Press.

—— (1991), 'The Renaissance of Security Studies', *International Studies Quarterly*, Vol. 35(2), 211–39.

—— (1996), *Revolution and War*, Ithaca, NY: Cornell University Press.

—— (1999), 'Rigor or Rigor Mortis? Rational Choice and Security Studies' *International Security*, Vol. 23: 4 (Spring).

Waltz, Kenneth N. (1959), *Man, the State, and War*, New York: Columbia University Press.

—— (1979), *Theory of International Politics*, New York: McGraw-Hill.

Walzer, Michael (2005), *Arguing About War*, New Haven, CT: Yale University Press.

Wang, H.H. (1998), *Technology, Economic Security, State, and the Political Economy of Economic Networks*, Lanham, NY: University Press of America.

Watts, M. (2001), 'Petro-Violence: Community, Extraction, and Political Ecology of a Mythic Commodity', in N. Peluso and M. Watts (eds.), *Violent Environments*, Ithaca, NY: Cornell University Press, 189–212.

Watts, Sheldon (1997), *Epidemics and History: Disease, Power, and Imperialism*, New Haven, CT: Yale University Press.

WCED (World Commission on Environment and Development) (1987), *Our Common Future*, Oxford: Oxford University Press.

Weldes, Jutta (1999), *Constructing National Interests: The United States and the Cuban Missile Crisis*, London: University of Minnesota Press.

—— Mark Laffey, Gusterson, Hugh and Duvall, Raymond (eds.) (1999), *Cultures of Insecurity. States, Communities and the Production of Danger*, London: University of Minneapolis Press.

Wendt, Alexander (1999), *Social Theory of International Politics*, Cambridge: Cambridge University Press.

—— Barnett, Michael (1993), 'Dependent State Formation and Third World Militarization', *Review of International Studies*, Vol. 19, No. 4: 321–47.

Westing, A. (1986), 'An Expanded Concept of International Security', in A. Westing (ed.), *Global Resources and International Conflict: Environmental Factors in Strategic Policy and Action*, Oxford: Oxford University Press, 183–200.

Wheeler, Nicholas J. and Booth, Ken (1992), 'The Security Dilemma', in John Baylis and Nicholas J. Rengger (eds.), *Dilemmas of World Politics: International Issues in a Changing World*, Oxford: Oxford University Press, 29–60.

Wiberg, Hakan (1988), 'The peace research movement', in Peter Wallensteen (ed.) *Peace Research: Achievements and Challenges*, Boulder/London: Westview Press, 30–53.

Wiebe, Cees (2003), *Intelligence and the War in Bosnia, 1992–1995*, Transaction Publishers.

Williams, M.C. (1998), 'Modernity, Identity and Security: A Comment on the "Copenhagen Controversy" ', *Review of International Studies*, 24/3: 435–9.

—— (2003), 'Words, Images, Enemies: Securitization and International Politics', *International Studies Quarterly*, 47/4: 511–31.

Williams, Michael C. and Krause, Keith (1997), 'Preface: Toward Critical Security Studies' in *Critical Security Studies: Concepts and Cases,* Minneapolis: University of Minnesota Press, vii–xxi.

Williams, P.D. and Bellamy, Alex J. (2005), 'The Responsibility to Protect and the Crisis in Darfur', *Security Dialogue*, 36/1: 27–47.

Williams, Phil (2001), 'Transnational Criminal Networks', in J. Arquilla and D. Ronfeldt (eds.), *Networks and Netwars: The Future of Terror, Crime and Militancy*, Santa Monica, CA: RAND Corporation, 61–97 available at http://www.rand.org/publications/MR/MR1382/MR1382.ch3.pdf.

—— and Vlassos, Dimitri (eds.) (2001), *Combating Transnational Crime: Concepts, Activities and Responses*, London: Frank Cass Publishers.

—— and Savona, Ernesto U. (eds.) (1996), *The United Nations and Transnational Organized Crime*, London: Frank Cass Publishers.

Wohlstetter, A.J., Hoffman, F.S., Lutz, R.J., and Rowen, H.S. (1954), Selection and Use of Strategic Air Bases, R-266, Santa Monica, CA: the RAND Corporation.

—— and Wohlstetter, Roberta (1963), *The state of strategic studies in Europe*, report prepared for the Ford Foundation.

—— and Wohlstetter, Roberta (1966), *The state of strategic studies in Japan, India, Israel*, report prepared for the Carnegie Endowment for International Peace.

Wolf, A. (1999), 'Water Wars and Water Reality: Conflict and Cooperation Along International Waterways', in S. Lonergan (ed.), *Environmental Change, Adaptation, and Security*, Dordrecht: Kluwer, 251–65.

Wolfensohn, James (2000), 10 January, speech delivered to the UN Security Council, New York.

Woodward, B. (2001), 'Bin Laden Said to "Own" The Taliban. Bush Is Told He Gave Regime $100 Million', *The Washington Post*, 11 October, A01.

World Health Organization (2001), *Macroeconomics and Health: Investing in Health for Economic Development*, report of the Commission on Macroeconomics and Health, Geneva.

Wright, Q. (1942), *A Study of War*, Chicago, University of Chicago Press.

Wyness, M., Harrison, L., and Buchanan, I. (2004), 'Childhood, Politics and Ambiguity: Towards an Agenda for Children's Political Inclusion', *Sociology*, Vol. 38(1): 81–99.

Xinuha News Agency (2000), 16 November.

Yergin, Daniel (1977), *Shattered Peace: The Origins of the Cold War and the National Security State*, Boston: Houghton Mifflin Company.

Zalewski, D.A. (2005), 'Economic Security and the Myth of the Efficiency/Equity Trade-Off', *Journal of Economic Issues*, Vol. 39(2), 383–90.

Zeldin, Theodore (1998), *An Intimate History of Humanity*, London: Vintage.

Zisk, Kimberly Marten (1997), *Weapons, Culture, and Self-Interest: Soviet Defense Managers in the New Russia*, New York: Columbia University Press.

Glossary

There is no single correct or agreed-upon definition of any of these terms, as you will no doubt have noticed already. This can be unsettling if you are used to the idea that there is a 'right answer' or the 'right definition'. The definitions offered below indicate how they have been used in this book. The important thing is for you to be clear about how your sources use these terms and be clear about how you are using them yourself.

1925 Geneva Protocol for the Prohibition of the Use in War of Asphyxiating, Poisonous, or Other Gases, and of Bacteriological Methods of Warfare Outlawed the use in war of asphyxiating, poisonous gases and liquids in war.

1972 Anti-Ballistic Missile Treaty The treaty banned the United States and the Soviet Union from constructing national missile defences. After giving the six-months' notice called for by the Treaty, the United States withdrew from the agreement in June 2002, citing the Treaty's fundamental obsolescence. Critics decried the move, but the deployment of extremely modest US missile defences have failed to generate an appreciable international response.

1972 Biological and Toxin Weapons Convention (BWC) Opened for signature on April 1972. Parties agreed not to acquire stockpile biological weapons and toxins. In 1996, the fourth review conference failed to reach an agreement on verification procedures to strengthen the 1972 agreement. Although signatories continue to abide by the agreement, the treaty has not entered into force.

2002 Moscow Treaty Agreement between the United States and Russia to cut deployed offensive strategic nuclear warheads to between 1,700 and 2,200 by 31 December 2012. Unlike previous arms control treaties between the Superpowers, this treaty leaves it up to the parties to determine the pace of reductions and exact composition of its forces on New Year's Eve, 2012.

9/11 A widely accepted shorthand way of referring to the 11 September 2001 al-Qaeda attack on the two towers of the World Trade Center in New York City, the Pentagon in Washington D.C., and the failed attempt to crash a fourth aircraft into the White House.

Aceh Sumatra Liberation Front A group in the northern part of Sumatra that has used terrorism and guerrilla warfare in an effort to win independence from Indonesia.

Action-reaction model of the arms dynamic The idea that actors increase the quantity or quality of their military forces in response to increases on the part of a potential adversary.

Agenda for Peace A report to the UN Secretary General in January 1992 advocating peacekeeping, peace-making and conflict prevention as priorities for avoiding military confrontations.

AIDS Acquired Immunodeficiency Syndrome or Acquired Immune Deficiency Syndrome; it refers to a host of symptoms and illnesses caused by the weakening of human immune system due to infection with the human immunodeficiency virus.

AIDS-related illnesses Illnesses such as pneumocystis pneumonia (a lung infection) and Kaposi's sarcoma (a skin cancer) that accompany the onset of AIDS; strictly speaking people do not die of AIDS, but of AIDS-related illnesses.

Al-Qaeda/Al Qa'ida (The Base) A network of extremist Muslim groups, initially organized by Osama bin Laden, which seeks to drive Western ideas and influence out of Muslim countries.

Anarchy In the field of international politics, a term for the absence of any ultimate power and authority over states. In short, the absence of a world or regional government, or binding international law, that is superior to states.

Anthrax Disease caused by the *Bacillus anthracis* bacterium that forms in spores. The infection in humans can occur in the skin, lungs and digestive tract and is often contracted from infected animals (e.g., sheep). It is not contagious, but because humans can be infected by coming into contact with anthrax spores, it is considered to be a good candidate for weaponization.

Anti-natalist Preventing birth.

Arlington Cemetery Home to the Women in Military Service for America Memorial, this was dedicated on 18 October 1997.

Arms dynamic Is best understood as the various factors that lead actors such as states or other significant political entities to acquire armed forces and change the quantity and/or quality of those forces they already maintain.

Assassins An unorthodox sect of Shia Muslims who used assassination to protect themselves from the surrounding rulers who adhered to the Sunni majority views.

Asset forfeiture Often draconian technique used by law enforcement organizations and judicial systems to compel participants in organized crime networks to give up their property. Proceeds from asset forfeiture is sometimes used to finance further law enforcement investigations and prosecutions, leading some critics to suggest that there may be a conflict of interest for the participating agencies.

Audience It consists of a group (public opinion, politicians, military officers or other elites) who needs to be convinced that a referent object is existentially threatened.

Aum Shinriyko A Japanese religious cult that released sarin gas in the Tokyo subway system in an effort to kill thousands.

Autonomy Being free from any higher power or authority, or, inside a state, being free within a specified geographical area or sphere of activity from such authority. In international politics states claim autonomy on a scale unmatched by, accorded to, or exercised by any other political actor.

Balance of power In international politics, a term used primarily in three ways. First, to refer to an existing distribution of power among members of an international system. Second, to refer to a distribution of power in which—among the major members—power is distributed so the members balance each other's power and therefore constrain each other. Third, to label a strategy for state security that is preoccupied with creating or maintaining a distribution of power in the system that is considered beneficial in terms of maintaining security and stability.

Bandwagon When the response by a government to the rise of an increasingly powerful state is to associate or ally itself with it. This is in contrast to a strategy of opposing or balancing—trying to offset the power of—such a powerful state.

Baruch and Gromyko Plans Competing US and Soviet proposals in 1946 to bring nuclear weapons under the control of the international community. Each was unacceptable to the other.

Berlin Air Lift A crisis between June 1948 and May 1949 when the Soviet Union blocked the ground routes to Berlin, and the US, UK and other Western states responded with a massive airlift of supplies to the city.

Biopolitics In his later writings, Michel Foucault turned to the analysis of contemporary political life, and argued that since the middle of the nineteenth century the state has been basing claims to legitimacy on its capacity to make populations live. That is, the state has increasingly come into the business of providing for the health, education and well-being of its people, which has in turn underpinned the state's claim to the right to continue. This notion of the biopolitical states is in contrast to the traditional sovereign state, which based its legitimacy on the basis of its ability to kill.

Bipolar The label for a power distribution in an international system in which two states are roughly equal in power and are each much more powerful than any of the other members. As a result, the power of each balances that of the other, and each has a number of states associated or allied with it. The relations between the two giants and between the two blocs dominate the politics of the system.

Brute/full-scale force Use of force to impose compliance on the adversary or settle the dispute at hand.

Cambridge Five The popular name for a ring of British citizens recruited by Soviet intelligence before and during the Second World War. It consisted of Guy Burgess, Donald Maclean, Harold (Kim) Philby, Anthony Blunt, and John Cairncross. As more information has been released during the 1990s, it appears that several others were also involved.

Cape Town Principles Cape Town principles and best practice on the prevention of recruitment of children into the armed forces and demobilization and social reintegration of child soldiers in Africa. Adopted by the participants in the Symposium on the Prevention of Recruitment of Children into the Armed Forces and Demobilization and Social Reintegration of Child

Soldiers in Africa, organized by UNICEF in cooperation with the NGO Sub-group of the NGO Working Group on the Convention on the Rights of the Child, Cape Town, 30 April 1997.

Chemical Weapons Convention An agreement by which State Parties agree to never under any circumstances acquire, stockpile or transfer chemical weapons, to use chemical weapons, to prepare to use chemical weapons or to induce others to engage in activity prohibited by the Convention. The Convention entered into force on 29 April 1997. The Organization for the Prohibition of Chemical Weapons in The Hague, Netherlands is responsible for implementing the Chemical Weapons Convention.

Civil society (1) The totality of all individuals and groups in a society who are not acting as participants in any government institutions, or (2) all individuals and groups who are neither participants in government nor acting in the interests of commercial companies. The two meanings are incompatible and contested. There is a third meaning: the network of social institutions and practices (economic relationships, family and kinship groups, religious, and other social affiliations) which underlie strictly political institutions.

Coercive diplomacy Use of threats and limited force to influence the adversary to stop or undo something it has already embarked upon.

Cold War The global competition from 1945 to 1989 (when the wall dividing West and East Germany came down) between capitalist and Communist states in which the United States and Soviet Union did not fight each other directly but backed local rivals in armed conflicts. At its peak in the early 1980s, the two alliances (NATO and the Warsaw Pact) deployed over 60,000 nuclear weapons and spent $1,000 billion a year (2006 prices) on the military.

Common security Joint action by a number of states to address shared problems that cannot be solved by the actions of any single state.

Compellence Use of threats and limited force to influence the adversary to do something.

Comprehensive Test Ban Treaty A disarmament measure, the treaty bans nuclear testing, thereby disrupting the development of human capital and technology needed to create and maintain a nuclear arsenal. Over 148 countries have signed the CTBT. The United States Senate failed to ratify the treaty in December 1999. The United States and the rest of the world, however, have maintained a nuclear test moratorium so far this century.

Conflict management Concerns the amelioration of conflict between one or more parties.

Constructivism General 'school' within IR theory which rose during the late 1980s-early 1990s to become the leading alternative to the dominant rationalist theories of neo-realism and neo-liberalism. Constructivists emphasize the importance of ideational factors such as culture, beliefs, norms, ideas and identity. Constructivism covers a wide spectrum from the borderland to post-structuralism/post-modernism to 'soft constructivists' who share the postivism and state-centrism of mainstream approaches.

Containment The creation of strategic alliances in order to check the expansion of a hostile power or force it to negotiate peacefully.

Copenhagen School It emerged at the Conflict and Peace Research Institute (COPRI) of Copenhagen and is represented by the writings of Barry Buzan, Ole Wæver, Jaap de Wilde, and others. It is partly about widening the threats and referent objects, especially societal/identity, partly about paying more attention to the regional level, but mainly about focusing on securitization—the social processes by which groups of people construct something as a threat—thus offering a constructivist counterpoint to the materialist threat analysis of traditional Strategic Studies.

Critical security studies Partly based on a critique of the state-centric paradigm and partly on the prescription for emancipatory action. See Chapter 4 in this volume.

Cuba Missile Crisis One of the most dangerous crises of the Cold War in October 1962 when the United States blocked Soviet installation of medium-range nuclear-armed missiles in Cuba.

Cultural autonomy The granting of rights in relation to the means of cultural reproduction, such as autonomy over educational and religious institutions.

Cultural cleansing The deliberate destruction of symbols, signs, and institutions, such as schools, museums, and places of worship of one ethnic group by another.

Cultural nationalism A movement/project designed to generate strong feelings of self-identification, emphasizing various commonalities such as language, religion, and history.

Defence offsets Generally refers to the legitimate provision of some form of compensation to purchasers of defence equipment for the high levels of expenditure they incur on such goods. Such compensation usually manifests itself in the provision of some kind of compensatory economic benefit to the purchaser but it may also include the provision of non-economic benefits such as the promotion of cultural exchanges or the visit of a national football team. Offsets come in two forms: (a) direct offsets, under which the purchaser receives work or technology directly related to the defence sale in question, for instance, an agreement to source specific components from the purchasing country or an agreement to establish the licensed production of the equipment in the buying country itself; (b) indirect offsets, under which the purchaser receives some form of benefit that is unrelated to the particular defence sale in question. This might include acceptance of payment in kind (examples include payment in oil, palm oil or chickens), a commitment to promote investment in the country, to promote the exports of a particular industrial sector or to transfer civil technology.

Defence sale This is a broad term that can refer to the sale of either a complete weapons system such as a tank or a fighter plane but can also include the sale of components, training, spares and other defence services. The term can also encapsulate commercial arrangements such as the leasing of defence equipment. Payment for such sales can either be made in cash or in kind (e.g. through the provision of other goods such as oil) or through some combination of the two. Defence sales, it should be noted, are rarely perfect examples of free market competition with factors such as price and quality often taking second place to considerations such as prestige or security of supply as well as the effectiveness of suppliers in lobbying decision makers, a process that may well extend to the provision of bribes.

Democratic peace theory A theory claiming that democratic states do not go to war with each other, with variants of the theory differing as to what it is about democracies—as democracies—that produces this behaviour.

Desecuritization Refers to a process that re-introduces a securitized matter into the standard political domain.

Deterrence Use of threats and specific actions to discourage the adversary from doing something in the first place.

Development Extensive enhancement of a society's basic capabilities and resources. This is of great interest to many governments because they can tap the additional capabilities and resources for their own purposes and can cite them to build political popularity and legitimacy with citizens.

Dien Bien Phu A French military garrison in North Vietnam, the loss of which to Viet Minh insurgents in May 1954 led to the end of the Indo-China War.

Discourse In its most loose usage of the term by adherents of objectivism, a discourse is simply a way of describing or labeling a real phenomenon. In contrast, for constructivists, discourses are practices (words and other actions) which play an active role by giving phenomena meaning, by being inherently normative (that is, having inbuilt ideas of right and wrong) and by silencing (that is, making it more difficult to understand the phenomenon in other ways).

Domestic factor models of the arms dynamic The idea that domestic military expenditure and weapons procurement decisions are not strongly linked to the external actions of other states. Instead, emphasis is placed on a variety of *domestic* bureaucratic, political or economic explanations. For example, it is sometimes argued that the need to maintain a defence industrial base creates a 'follow-on' imperative under which governments place orders simply to keep companies and skilled workers rather than as a function of any immediate military necessity.

Domestic procurement This is the term used to describe the acquisition of defence goods from a firm within the country of a purchasing government.

Doublecross system An elaborate deception operation began in 1939 when a Welsh electrical engineer who had been reported to British intelligence about his business trips to pre-war Germany decided to spy instead for Germany. He later changed his mind and became a double agent for the British, sending deceptive information back to Germany. This led to a large ring of German agents being rounded up in Britain and given the choice of being executed or being used to send additional false information back to Germany. It was called the Doublecross system because, as a pun, the British intelligence committee that ran the system was called the Twenty (XX) Committee.

Dual use technology Refers to equipment or technology that has both military and civilian applications.

Economic security Safeguarding the structural integrity and prosperity-generating capabilities and interests of a politico-economic entity in the context of various externalized risks and threats that confront it in the international economic system.

Economics-security nexus The linkages between economic policy and traditional or politico-military security policy.

ECOWAS monitoring group (ECOMOG) A multinational armed force that was established in West Africa by the Economic Community of West African States (ECOWAS); it is not a standing army, but rather an agreement for cooperation between several militaries in the region to work together when necessary.

Elite accommodation The process of managing or accommodating the threat by powerful elites, including strongmen, to the security of the regime, usually through various forms of power-sharing, patronage or graft.

Emancipation Emancipation refers to the freeing of people from the structures of oppression or domination in which they find themselves. Various forms of critical theory are driven by a political commitment to emancipation from different structures of oppression and domination. Generally, post-Marxist Critical Theory will speak of emancipation in the singular, emphasizing its belief that the political economy is the root of all oppression; post-structural critical theories are more likely to speak of emancipations in the plural, emphasizing the multiple forms of domination, or the multiple means of subjection.

Empirical Relating to facts as opposed to abstractions such as theories or values.

Enigma A German electrical enciphering machine use by Germany during the Second World War. With help from French intelligence and some Polish mathematicians, British code-breakers at Bletchley Park, using a prototype computer, deciphered the code. The intelligence gained from this feat was critical for victory in the war.

Environment That part of the Earth's surface which includes living organisms, the remains of living organisms and the physical and chemical components of the total system necessary for, or involved in the process of life (Boyden et al 1990: 314).

Environmental change Short and long term changes in biological, physical and chemical components and systems resulting from both human activities and natural processes.

Environmental security The assurance that individuals and groups have that they can avoid or adapt to environmental change without critical adverse effects.

Epidemic An usually large or rapid outbreak of a contagious disease that exceeds the normal level in a particular population at a given time.

Epistemology Epistemology is the *study* of the way we know. Within a theory or approach, the epistemology refers to the set of assumptions about how knowledge is generated that inform that theory or approach. All forms of scholarship must make assumptions about knowledge, therefore they must have an epistemology.

Ethnic cleansing The deliberate killing, use of violence, or deportation of members of one ethnic group by another.

Euzkadi ta Askatasuna (ETA) The Basque dissident group that has used terrorism for over twenty-five years in an effort to achieve independence.

Existential threat Threats to the continued existence of a referent object. Individuals face an existential threat when they are threatened with death; states face an existential threat when, among other things, they are threatened with external invasion and conquest. Existential threats are the most serious threats a referent object can face, and thus are seen to justify the most extensive measures to secure against them.

Extraordinary measures Such measures go beyond rules ordinarily abided by and are thus located outside the bounds of political procedures and practices. Their adoption involves the identification and classification of some issue as an existential threat.

Fascists (Italy) The right-wing party that used violence and terrorism to help Benito Mussolini take power in Italy in 1922.

Feminism The advocacy of women's rights based upon ideas of equality between men and women. Note, though, that there are many variations of feminism. These include liberal, radical and Marxist categories.

Force multipliers The term refers to factors, usually understood as technological development, that significantly increase the combat effectiveness of militaries.

Foreign direct investment (FDI) Investment carried out with the aim of acquiring a lasting interest in an enterprise operating in an economy other than that of the investor, the investor's purpose being to have an effective voice in the management of the enterprise.

Foreign economic policy (FEP) power Typically nation-states or some other state-form and can include sub-state units (e.g. states within a federated union such as the US), supranational or inter-governmental units (e.g. the EU), city-states (e.g. Singapore) or quasi-states (e.g. Taiwan).

Foreign economic policy (FEP) May be broadly thought of as having two main dimensions. The 'policy-technical' dimension comprises the technical operation of trade policy, international finance policy, foreign direct investment policy, overseas development assistance policy, and so on. The second 'economic diplomacy' dimension concerns how FEP powers (e.g. nation-states) manage their economic relations with other powers and agencies within the international system.

Free ride Obtaining something valuable by relying on the efforts of others to supply it while doing little oneself to obtain it. For example, a country in a strategically vital location may remain safe while doing little to protect itself if it has a powerful ally (a good example is Japan).

Fylingdales Situated on the North York Moors, this is a long-range radar system which forms part of the ballistic missile early warning system and space surveillance network. It is the subject of two agreements between the American and British Governments made in 1960 and 1979.

Gamma radiation Also known as penetrating radiation because dense shielding is needed to protect individuals from its effects. Gamma radiation is high-energy ionizing radiation, which is one of the first effects produced by a nuclear detonation. Because it can penetrate the body, it is usually the primary cause of radiation sickness.

Gender Refers not just to the biological differences between men and women but to a set of culturally shaped and defined characteristics, which underpin the notion of what it is to be a man or a woman.

Geneva Conventions There are four Geneva Conventions, signed 12 August 1949, and the two additional Protocols of 8 June 1977. In addition, there are many other international treaties which govern the conduct of war or establish human rights standards.

Global War on Terror A general term used by President George W Bush of the United States to cover the vigorous US response to the 9/11 attacks in New York and Washington.

Greenham Common Site of a US airbase. From 1981 through until 1999 tens of thousands of women either lived at or visited the Greenham Common airbase in the UK. The women protested against the decision made by NATO to site cruise missiles at the base. It was the site of a number of high-profile protests. In December 1982, for example, 30,000 women joined hands to 'embrace the base'. In March 1991 the United States removed the cruise missiles under the terms of the 1987 INF (Intermediate Nuclear Forces) agreement.

Group of 77 The unofficial term for the bloc of southern states attempting to negotiate trade reform in their relations with northern industrial states, especially in the 1960s and 1970s.

Guantanamo Naval Base US naval base in Cuba that has served as a prison for suspected terrorists.

Guerrilla Someone fighting for primarily political purposes, usually against a state, as part of a group which is not as rigidly hierarchically organized as a regular army. Literally someone fighting a small war.

Hamas (acronym in Arabic for Islamic Resistance Movement) Islamic group in the Gaza Strip and West Bank that seeks to create an Islamic Palestinian state encompassing both the Occupied Territories and Israel and which has relied on suicide attacks.

Hegemon A state or coalition much more powerful than any other state or likely coalition and thus able to dominate an international system.

Hegemonic stability theory The theoretical claim that a hegemonic state may provide favourable circumstances for the emergence of an extended period of stability in an international system. This is because the hegemon is strong enough to deter any challenges by force to the status quo, to prevent disruptions to the system, and to encourage considerable management of the system. Within these conditions rivalries among other states can relax and cooperation can increase.

Historical materialist/materialism The broadly Marxist view that human history, politics and ideology is driven primarily by economic factors and associated relations between classes.

HIV The human immunodeficiency virus that causes AIDS. It is transmitted through sexual contact with an infected person, by sharing needles with someone who is infected, from mother to child during or after birth, and through transfusions with infected blood.

Home bases Used to designate countries where organized crime groups originate, often because the rule of law is weak and law enforcement is ineffective.

Horizontal competition Where groups must change their ways because of the overriding linguistic and cultural influences of others.

Host nations Term used to designate countries that are the main targets of transnational crime organizations.

Human security Emphasises the safety and well being of individuals, groups, and communities as opposed to prioritizing the state and its interests.

Humanitarian intervention Article 24(1) Chapter VII of the UN Charter gives the Security Council the power to 'restore international peace and stability' if a threat, including a humanitarian disaster, is imminent and if there is consensus in the Council. The intervention in the Kosovo crisis, however, was undertaken without the Security Council's approval.

Independent and dependent variable Controversial terms used in the social sciences usually to describe the relationship between two entities: the dependent variable is the entity under observation or the effect and the independent variable is the entity that affects it or is the cause.

Indo-China War Fought between the French and Viet Minh insurgents, 1946–54, ending in defeat for the French.

Infanticide The killing of infants.

Infantilization To reduce to an infantile status or condition. To associate with infantile qualities.

Insecurity dilemma The unique situation in which a state's primary threats originate from the internal rather than external sphere, and where efforts by the ruling elite to increase regime security creates further insecurity for the regime, the state and society.

Insecurity The risk of something bad happening to a thing that is valued.

Insurgent A guerrilla seeking to overthrow a state. This term has fewer connotations of legitimacy than guerrilla, and even fewer than the term 'resistance' member.

International Atomic Energy Agency (IAEA) An agency of the United Nations, the IAEA was created as part of the Eisenhower administration's 'Atoms for Peace' initiative to allow the civilian application of nuclear power to generate electricity. The IAEA is charged with monitoring the civilian application of nuclear technology to guarantee that nuclear materials and know-how is not diverted into clandestine programmes to develop nuclear weapons.

International civil society The label for the efforts of myriads of non-governmental organizations active in international politics in pressuring and lobbying governments, in calling attention to issues, problems and developments, and in taking direct action to deal with them. These efforts are seen by some analysts as evidence of, and a major contribution to, the development of a global community.

International Criminal Court The first ever permanent, treaty-based, international criminal court established to promote the rule of law and ensure that the gravest international crimes do not go unpunished. The Court is complementary to national criminal jurisdictions. The jurisdiction and functioning of the Court are governed by the provisions of the Rome Statute. The Rome Statute of the International Criminal Court was established on 17 July 1998 and entered into force on 1 July 2002.

International regimes Clusters of norms and patterns of behaviour, sometimes codified in international agreements and managed through international organizations, that have been developed to manage the interactions among states and other entities in specific areas of activity. Examples include the regimes on the conduct and treatment of diplomatic personnel, on nuclear non-proliferation, and on proper reactions to the outbreak of highly contagious and lethal diseases.

International relations An interdisciplinary area of study, also called international politics, which at its core examines interactions between states but with the inclusion of world politics now canvasses a broader array of interactions, issues and actors.

Intrastate war The primary form of international conflict today, in which organized and sustained political violence takes place between armed groups representing the state and one or more non-state groups. It takes place primarily within the borders of a single state, but usually has significant international dimensions and a tendency to spill over into bordering states.

IRA (Irish Republican Army) Group that has used terrorism and violence in its efforts to achieve the union of Northern Ireland with the Republic of Ireland.

Irish National Liberation Army (INLA) Dissident group in Northern Ireland that has combined nationalist with a Marxist-Leninist leftist ideology to justify its attacks.

Iron Curtain A term made famous by Winston Churchill in a speech in Fulton, Missouri in 1946. It was used to describe the barrier to the exchange of ideas and goods created by Soviet policies of secrecy and repression.

Islamic Jihad Small group in the Gaza Strip and West Bank that has sought to create an Islamic Palestinian state and which has relied on suicide attacks.

Italian-Turkish War A war in 1911 and 1912 in which Italy seized some territories (the Dodecanese and Tripoli) from the Ottoman Empire.

Just War Theory An ancient notion drawn principally from the Christian tradition but with some contribution from Islamic thought that assumes that states occasionally need to go to war with one another but attempts to minimize war's dire consequences by spelling out both the conditions that must exist before the war is initiated (*jus ad bellum*) and what states can and cannot do during the conflict (*jus in bello*).

Korean War One of the worst East–West confrontations of the Cold War era, the Korean War (1950–53) initially involved a North Korean invasion of South Korea in June 1953 but was fought principally between the Chinese and a UN force headed by the United States.

Ku Klux Klan (KKK) American racist and right-wing group that first appeared after the Civil War and which was active in the 1920s and 1960s and 1970s.

Kurds Ethnic group in Turkey (and Iraq and Iran) that has been involved in terrorist campaigns directed towards creating an independent state.

Leaderless resistance Term used to describe loose organizations where the leadership suggests courses of action or identifies possible targets but avoids issuing direct orders to avoid arrest or prosecution.

Liberal/liberalism A school of thought in the study of international politics emphasizing the existence of an international society with common habits and practices that enable growing cooperation and collective management of international politics. Liberals tend to believe that world politics is basically evolving towards tolerance and peace because these cooperative developments lead to reducing conflict, insecurity, and warfare without sacrificing national sovereignty.

Macro-level economic security Concerned with FEP powers (e.g. nation-states) and their engagement in the international economic system (see 'economic security' above).

Malaria A life-threatening parasitic disease transmitted by mosquitoes; it is characterized by fever and influenza-like symptoms, including chills, headache, and malaise.

Manhattan Project Codename given to the British-American effort to build a fission bomb during the Second World War.

Q-Fever Caused by the bacterium *Coxiella burneti*, only about half of the people infected by the bacteria show symptoms. Because the bacterium is resistant to heat and drying, it would make a suitable agent for aerosol delivery. Lethal in only about 2% of cases,

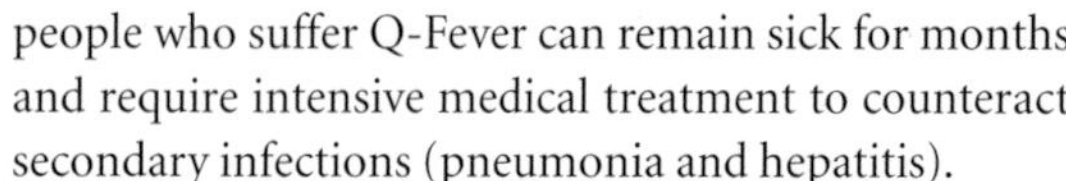

people who suffer Q-Fever can remain sick for months and require intensive medical treatment to counteract secondary infections (pneumonia and hepatitis).

Marxism An influential school of thought in international politics derived from the ideas of Karl Marx, Lenin and others. It stresses the role of dominant classes and the dynamics of international capitalism in shaping the behaviour of governments, and of dominant states and societies in maintaining a very unequal, and exploitative, international system.

Masculinity Those qualities which are considered appropriate to a man, usually associated with strength and bravery.

Micro-level economic security Concerns the economic security of 'localized' agents such as individuals, households and local communities, and is primarily concerned with safeguarding their livelihoods.

Migration The movement of people from one place to settle in another, especially a foreign country. The host society, through a shift in the composition of the population, might be changed by the influx of those from outside.

Militarism The prevalence of military sentiments amongst people and the idea that military efficiency or military preparedness is the highest duty of the state.

Military Malthusianism This is a term used to describe the idea that the defence budgets of states are unable to keep up with constant real terms increase in the cost of defence equipment thereby creating a situation in which states are faced with purchasing fewer or lower quality weapons.

Misogyny A dislike, perhaps even a deep-seated dislike, for women or characteristics traditionally associated with women.

Money laundering Process by which money derived from illegal activities is made to appear as if proceeding from legitimate business enterprises.

Morbidity The number of people in a given population afflicted with a disease.

Multinational enterprise (MNE) A company that controls and operates assets over two or more countries.

Multipolar A power distribution in an international system in which three or more major states are much more powerful than any others and roughly equivalent in power among themselves. Shifting patterns of collusion and rivalry among these states, reflecting their preoccupation with the distribution of power among them, dominates the politics of the system.

National Organization for Women (NOW) A charitable organization designed to secure equality and fair treatment for women in all aspects of American life. Currently opposing much of the Bush agenda in both domestic and foreign policy.

Necessary but not sufficient The best way to explain this concept is to use an analogy—sunlight is necessary for a flower to grow but it is not sufficient because the flower also requires water and probably good soil. Together, sunlight, water and soil are the necessary and sufficient conditions for flowers to grow. In the same way, when conceptualizing security, it can be argued that the realist state-centric argument is a necessary but not sufficient argument and likewise human security.

Neorealism—Structural Realism A variant of the realist theoretical perspective which emphasizes anarchy and the distribution of power among the major states (the system structure) as the key factors shaping the behaviour of governments, as opposed to the domestic characteristics of states—leadership, nature of political system, national culture, etc. This was the dominant approach in the field in the 1970s and 1980s.

Networks A series of nodes that are connected.

Nodes The elements that make up a network. These may be individuals or organizations. Law enforcement attempts to identify the nodes which are most critical to the functioning of the network and strike at these.

Non-politicized issue An issue is said to be non-politicized when it is not a matter for state action and is not included in public debate.

Non-Proliferation Treaty One of the key arms control treaties of the Cold War era, the NPT was open for signature in 1968 and allows countries to develop civil nuclear power under international inspection, but not nuclear weapons. By 2006, 187 countries had signed.

Non-state actor A term widely used to mean any actor that is not a government. Ambiguity is best avoided by referring separately to categories, transnational actors and international organizations.

Non-traditional security This category of security studies focuses on non-military challenges to security. It incorporates the state but also includes other referent objects.

Norms Concern the moral and ethical dimensions of international affairs, such as rules, beliefs, and ideas.

Objectivism The view that we can know what is real and what has been distorted by misrepresentation in ideology, propaganda or, in its loosest sense, discourse.

Ontology Ontology is the *study* of being. Within a theory or approach, the ontology refers to the set of assumptions about the nature of being in the world that inform that theory or approach. All forms of social investigation must make assumptions about the nature of the world they investigate (what kinds of thing populate that world, what sorts of relationship exist among those things), therefore they must have an ontology.

Open Skies Proposal A proposal made by American President Eisenhower to Soviet First Secretary Nikita Khrushchev during their 1955 Geneva Summit. The proposal called for both nations to allow aerial surveillance of their territory in order to allow verification of the existence of weapons systems and to reduce international tensions. Khrushchev vetoed the proposal and, in response, Eisenhower initiated clandestine overflights of the Soviet Union using the then secret American spy plane, the U-2.

Organized crime Profit-driven crime committed by any 'structured group of three or more persons existing for a period of time and acting in concert'.

Oslo Accords Agreement in 1993 between Israel and the PLO that provided for increasing degrees of self-governance for the Palestinians in parts of the West Bank and the Gaza Strip but which collapsed in the face of attacks by extremists on both sides.

Ottawa Treaty A convention on the prohibition of the use, stockpiling and transfer of anti-personnel mines and their destruction which became international law on 1 March 1999.

Pandemic The outbreak of infectious disease across a geographically extensive area; a regional or global epidemic.

Paramilitary Someone fighting for primarily political purposes, usually on behalf of a state, as part of a group which is not as rigidly hierarchically organized as a regular army.

Paris School Draws especially on the theories of Pierre Bourdieu and Michel Foucault to establish an approach which studies the discursive and non-discursive practices through which especially bureaucratic agencies construct insecurity and unease in their competition for tasks and control. Technologies of surveillance and control are much emphasized, especially in the study of issues such as migration and terrorism.

Patriot Act (United States) Legislation passed after 11 September 2001 providing the government with greater surveillance opportunities and greater freedom to deal with suspected terrorists.

Peace building Actions which support political, economic, social, and military measures and structures, aiming to strengthen and solidify political settlements in order to redress the causes of conflict.

PLO (Palestinian Liberation Organization) Umbrella liberation organization representing a variety of secular and nationalist Palestinian groups.

Policy community All the actors that inform and participate in the process of formulating policy, which can include politicians, members of the judiciary, public servants, academics, members of the private sector, think-tanks, civil society groups, and policy analysts.

Political (ethnic) autonomy As with cultural nationalism, the granting of rights in relation to the means of cultural reproduction, but where this involves territorially defined self-government along a wider range of issues, such as autonomous policing and finance.

Political (ethnic) nationalism As with cultural nationalism, a movement/project designed to generate feelings of self-identification, but where this carries with it an explicit territorial element.

Politicized issue An issue becomes politicized when it is part of public policy and managed within the standard political system.

Popular Front for the Liberation of Palestine (PFLP) Palestinian group that combined nationalism with Marxist-Leninist views and which was frequently at odds with the PLO leadership.

Post-positivism Post-positivism is a generic term to refer to those theories and approaches that reject positivism as an adequate epistemology for the investigation of social life. Most forms of critical social theory are post-positivist in their epistemologies.

Post-structuralist/structuralism This is the most thoroughgoing version of constructivism and places even more emphasis on the analysis of discourse.

Prevalence rate An epidemiological term referring to the proportion of those suffering from a disease in a particular population; it is usually cited in percentages.

Prevention of Terrorism Acts (United Kingdom) Series of acts giving the British government increased powers and discretion to deal first with suspected IRA terrorists and then with terrorists in general.

Primary arms dynamic Refers to the set of pressures to acquire armed forces experienced by those states that possess the capacity to independently produce all or most of their defence equipment.

Prisoners of War (POWS) Prisoners of War are combatants captured by the opposing side in war. They are imprisoned, usually until the end of conflict, but may be traded. Historically, few rules have governed the treatment of POWs until the Geneva and Hague Conference and the conventions of 1864, 1899 and 1907, which declared that POWs should be treated humanely.

Pronatalist Promoting birth.

Pugwash The Pugwash Conferences on Science and World Affairs is an international organization facilitating international dialogue among scholars and political practitioners to handle global security threats. A manifesto by Bertrand Russell and Albert Einstein in 1955 called for scientists to face the dangers of nuclear weapons, and a conference was held in Pugwash, Nova Scotia in 1957. During the Cold War, the organization was often an important back-channel between US and Soviet experts and intellectuals. Pugwash and its co-founder Joseph Rotblat received the Nobel Peace Prize in 1995 for their work for nuclear disarmament.

Punjab Indian province where Sikh dissidents used guerrilla warfare and terrorism in an effort to gain autonomy or independence for their religious group.

RAND RAND Corporation was set up in 1946 by the US Air Force under contract to the Douglas Aircraft Company. In 1948 it became an independent non-profit organization and during the 1950s it formed the model for the modern think tank, famous enough to make it into the film *Dr. Strangelove* as 'the BLAND Corporation'. In addition to research in engineering, health policy and many other fields, inter-disciplinary work between especially mathematics, economics and political science pioneered game theory and deterrence theory.

Rape/genocidal rape The forcing of women to have sex without their consent. Genocidal rape refers to the use of sex as an instrument of war used to deliberately humiliate women of a certain ethnicity or identity.

Rational choice Theories that focus on strategic, instrumental calculation and draw on economics in establishing models, where actors and their incentives are given, while often sophisticated calculations drawn from game theory explain behaviour, outcomes, and the effects of institutions and other conditions.

Rationalism One side of the main theoretical debate in IR theory during the 1980s and 1990s—the position, which adopts from rational choice theory the general premise that theory should start from actors with given identities and interests, is that and on the basis of a specified rationality assumption explains behaviour (without necessarily including the more technical instruments of rational choice theory). Neo-realism and neo-liberal institutionalism have been the main representatives of rationalist IR theory. (The terminology of rationalism vs. reflectionism was introduced by Robert Keohane in 1988.)

Realist/realism The view that world politics is anarchic (in the sense of there being no overall authority, not chaos), the key actors are states, the key element of power is military power, and the moral duty of the decision-maker is to serve the national interest. Realists assert that they see world politics as it really is, that world politics changes but does not progress and it is the inherent sense of state insecurity that is critical in understanding the dynamics of international politics.

Realpolitik Politics based on practical rather than moral or ideological considerations.

Red Army Faction (also often referred to as the Baader-Meinhof Gang) Small group of West German terrorists that mounted attacks against the state, and capitalism in general, in the 1970s and 1980s.

Red Brigades Large Italian leftist group that launched a major terrorist campaign which at times disrupted the Italian state and which took years for the state to defeat.

Referent object (of security) Common to most notions of security is the *protection* of some thing from a threat of some kind. The thing to be protected is the referent object. In conventional security studies, the referent object is generally considered to be the state. Other approaches to security consider other referent objects: for example, individuals, societies, economies, or the environment.

Reflectivism The counter-position to rationalism, where constructivists, feminists, post-structuralists, critical theorists, and moral theorists, among others, argue that state identities and interests are not given or stable but produced and reproduced continously. Norms and identity shape policy as much as material interests. Often reflectivist theories will posit understanding rather than science-like explanation as the aim of research. (The terminology of rationalism vs. reflectionism was introduced by Robert Keohane in 1988.)

Regime security A condition where the governing elite are secure from the threat of forced removal from office and can generally rule without major challenges to their authority.

Revolutionary Armed Forces of Colombia (FARC) Leftist group that has joined with Colombian drug cartels to prevent government control of significant areas of the country and has threatened the stability of the government.

Rule Effective control over a specified territory and the people who reside there by exercising the powers of a government.

Safety One of the main components of security for states and their societies. Most emphasis is normally placed on being safe from deliberate efforts by outsiders, or disaffected insiders, to inflict harm. But under various circumstances this can extend to seeking to ensure safety from a number of other kinds of harm as well.

Sarin A chemical weapon, originally developed in Germany as a pesticide in the 1930s, Sarin is a colourless, odourless and tasteless liquid at room temperature. It interferes with the nervous system by impeding the proper function of the neurotransmitter acetylcholine. Exposure to Sarin causes neurons to be continuously stimulated by acetylcholine, leading to convulsions, coma and suffocation.

Secondary arms dynamic Refers to the set of pressures to acquire armed forces experienced by those states that have limited or no capacity for independent production of defence equipment and which are therefore reliant on the import of defence technology.

Securitize A so-called speech act which elevates an issue with the objective of making it critically important.

Securitization Refers to the accepted classification of certain and not other phenomena, persons or entities as existential threats requiring emergency measures. Through an act of securitization, a concern is framed as a security issue and moved from the politicized to the securitized.

Securitized issue An issue is securitized when it requires emergency actions beyond the state's standard political procedures.

Securitizing actor Refers to an actor who initiates a move of securitization through a speech act. Securitizing actors can be policymakers or bureaucracies but also transnational actors and individuals.

Security dilemma The situation that arises when one state, in seeking to be more secure, expands its military capabilities but, in doing so, increases fears in other states about their security so that they also build up their military capabilities. The dilemma is that states end up no more secure, perhaps even less, in spite of and because of their individual efforts to make themselves safe.

Security The assurance people have that they will continue to enjoy those things that are most important to their survival and well-being.

Service states Used to designate countries where transnational criminal organizations can easily access services designed to provide cover for their activities, such as false identities, or launder the proceeds of their activities.

Sikhs Religious group in India that included extremists who attempted to achieve autonomy or independence to maintain itself vis-à-vis the majority Hindu population.

Social scientific This approach assumes that fact and value can be separated sufficiently to generate theoretically grounded hypotheses which can be tested against evidence. In other words, description (what is), explanation (why it is) and prescription (what should be) are treated as separable.

Societal identity The self-identification by members of the community as constituting 'us'; that is to say, a shared sense of belonging to the same collectivity, most often ethno-national and religious groups.

Societal security dilemma Where the actions of one society, in trying to increase its security (strengthen its identity), causes a reaction in a second, which, in the end, causes a decrease in its own security (weakens its identity).

Soft power In contrast to the power to physically coerce, this is the power to influence and persuade flowing from such elements as prestige, status, moral authority, leadership in shaping international endeavours, and so on.

Soft security Emphasizes mechanisms other than military ones which enhance the safety and well being of states or other actors.

Southern African Development Community (SADC) An international organization promoting regional cooperation in economic development in southern Africa.

Sovereignty The legal status of having effective control over a specified territory and the people who reside there, and recognized by other sovereign states as having such control and being entitled to be regarded as sovereign. Being sovereign entitles a state, and its government, to be free, under most circumstances, of responsibility to any higher authority and of interference from outside in its internal affairs.

Speech act Consists of a discursive representation of a certain issue as an existential threat to security.

Speech-act theory Speech is commonly considered to refer to objects and actions outside itself; speech-act theory examines those instances in which actions are performed *by virtue* of their being spoken. Naming, marrying and promising are notable examples of speech acts. Securitization treats security as a speech-act.

Stand-off missiles These are missiles capable of being launched outside a theatre of operation and then guided to a distant target.

State collapse A condition where the main state institutions and governing processes completely fail and cease to function in any meaningful sense, either through internal processes of mismanagement or overwhelming challenges to state authority. The most visible signal of state collapse is the total breakdown of law and order. State collapse creates a power vacuum which is then filled by alternative forms of power and governance.

State security A condition where the institutions, processes and structures of the state are able to continue functioning without the threat of collapse or significant opposition, despite threats to the current regime or changes to the make-up of the ruling elite.

State-centric A term which is used loosely, often to describe the realist paradigm which is said to give priority to protection of the state above all else. See Chapter 2.

Strongmen A term used to describe individuals or groups who possess a degree of coercive power in their own right and who pose a challenge to weak state rulers. Typically, they include local politicians or tribal leaders with private armies, warlords and criminal gangs, well-armed and organized ethnic or religious groups and various private militia.

Taliban Extreme Islamic government formerly in power in Afghanistan that provided support to Osama bin Laden and al-Qaeda until overthrown by domestic groups and foreign troops after 9/11.

Tamil Tigers (Liberation Front of Tamil Eelam) Group in Sri Lanka that has used guerrilla warfare and terrorist attacks (including many suicide attacks) in an effort to achieve an independent Tamil state on the island.

Technological imperative explanations of the arms dynamic The constant modernization of defence equipment as a function of an imperative to update equipment that is created as a consequence either of the institutionalization of military R&D or as a by-product of a process of permanent technological change in the civil sector.

Terrorism The use of force or the threat of force by organized groups too weak to use other methods in an effort to achieve political goals with attacks directed towards a target audience that involves non-governmental actors.

Think tank A research institute or other organization providing advice and ideas for policy makers or business leaders. Around 1960 the term came to be used primarily to describe RAND and other institutions assisting the armed forces and defence planners. The number and partisan affiliation of think tanks in the US accelerated during the 1980s and 1990s, leading to a decline in their status as independent advisers and an increase in their role as producers of ideological munition. Foreign policy institutes and to some extent peace research institutes have fulfilled parallel functions in Europe and elsewhere, where, however, American-style think tanks have begun to expand as well.

Traditional security Security is defined in geo-political terms, encompassing aspects such as deterrence, power balancing, and military strategy. The state, and especially its defence from external military attacks, is the exclusive focus of study.

Transnational crime Criminal activity that is conducted in more than one state, planned in one state but perpetrated in another, or committed in one state where there are spillover effects into neighbouring jurisdictions. The phrase is often used more specifically to refer to transnational *organized* crime—crimes that cross national borders, are profit-driven, and are committed by a group organized for that purpose.

Tuberculosis A bacterial disease that usually attacks the lungs, but can also affect the kidney, spine or brain. Like the common cold, it is contagious and spreads through the air from person to person. If left untreated, tuberculosis is fatal. More recently, some strains of tuberculosis resistant to all medicines have also emerged.

Tularemia Disease caused by bacterium *Francisella tularensis* often found in animals (e.g., rodents). The vector (means of transmission) to humans in naturally occurring disease is the flea. As a weapon, the bacterium is highly infectious and would probably be distributed as an aerosol that would produce a severe respiratory illness.

UAV A remote-controlled unmanned aerial vehicle used for both intelligence collection (imagery) and, more recently, for the delivery of missiles.

UN Conference on the Human Environment (UNCHE) Also known as the Stockholm Environment Conference, this was held in May 1972 and was the first major international meeting on global environmental issues.

UN Conference on Trade and Development (UNCTAD) A UN agency set up specifically to improve the trading position of third world states. It met for the first time in Geneva in 1964.

Unipolar The term for the structure of an international system that has a hegemon—the one dominant state provides a single pole of concentrated power, and this structure dominates the politics of the system.

United Nations Charter The Charter is the legal regime that created the United Nations as the world's only 'supranational' organization. It is the key legal document limiting the use of force to instances of self-defence and collective peace enforcement endorsed by the United Nations Security Council.

Universal Declaration of Human Rights Established on 10 December 1948 by the General Assembly of the United Nations. It recognizes the inherent dignity and equal and inalienable rights of all members of the human family as the foundation of freedom, justice and peace in the world.

Uranium-235 A key ingredient of a nuclear weapon. It is called a 'fissile' material because an atom of uranium-235 can be split into roughly two equal-mass pieces when struck by a neutron. If a large enough mass of uranium-235 is brought together, a self-sustaining chain reaction results after the first fission occurs. If large amounts of U-235 are brought together quickly, a supercritical reaction occurs, which is the basis of both fission and fusion nuclear weapons.

Venezuelan equine encephalitis This disease a mosquito-borne viral illness that causes flu-like symptoms, which can progress to encephalitis in a relatively small number of cases. Because it is a virus, observers fear that it could be subject to genetic manipulation to infect and incapacitate thousands of people quickly.

VENONA A code word used to characterize the intelligence gathered by the US and the UK (code named BRIDE in the UK) from intercepted Soviet classified communications during the last two years of the Second World War. Though the enciphered texts were not decoded until late 1948, the intelligence derived from them revealed massive Soviet penetration into the highest decision bodies in the US, the UK, and other countries.

Vertical competition Where groups are pushed towards either narrower or wider societal identities because of integration or disintegration.

Veteran A term used to describe people who have served in national armed forces. This term is usually associated with those who have served in the US military.

Viet Minh The North Vietnamese insurgent force that defeated the French in 1954 and resulted in the independence of four countries in Indo-China—North Vietnam, South Vietnam, Laos and Cambodia.

Vietnam War Fought between the Viet Cong guerrillas and the North Vietnamese Army on the one hand, and the South Vietnam Army and the United States on the other. US involvement was principally between 1965 and its final withdrawal in 1973. North and South Vietnam were ultimately unified under the control of the North.

Warlord A military leader who exercises civil power in a region, such as collecting taxes, providing a semblance of law and order and engaging in commerce, either in alliance with or in defiance of, the central state. The warlord commands the personal loyalty of a private army and rules by virtue of his war-making ability.

Weak states States possessing one or more of the following characteristics: infrastructural incapacity, evidenced by weak institutions and the inability to penetrate and control society effectively or enforce state policies; lack of coercive power and a failure to achieve or maintain a monopoly on the instruments of violence; and the lack of national identity and social and political consensus on the idea of the state.

Weathermen Radical leftist group in the United States that used terrorist tactics in their opposition to the government and the war in Vietnam but never achieved the notoriety or gained the support that some West European leftist groups did.

Wilsonian internationalism A powerful component of American thinking and preferences in foreign policy since early in the twentieth century, which received its initial elaboration in President Woodrow Wilson's efforts after the First World War to use American leadership to reorder the international system along liberalist lines so as to eliminate major wars.

Xenophobic Term used to describe those who are violently opposed to foreigners or foreign ideas and cultures.

Zimmerman Telegraph A 16 January 1917 diplomatic message from the German Foreign Minister (Arthur Zimmerman) to the German ambassador in Mexico offering Mexico support in reclaiming 'lost' territory in Texas, New Mexico, and Arizona in return for Mexican support if the United States should enter the war against Germany. British naval intelligence intercepted and decoded the note and provided it to US President Woodrow Wilson to help bring America into the war on the British side. It worked, as it was actually more important than the sinking of the Lusitania or unrestricted U-boat warfare in getting America into the war.

Index

A

B

C

D

E

F

G

H

I

J

K

L

M

N

O

R

S

T

U

V

W

X

Y

Z